BOUNDLESS
HORIZONS

BOUNDLESS HORIZONS

The Autobiography of

Chris Bonington

Originally published in three volumes:

I CHOSE TO CLIMB

THE NEXT HORIZON

THE EVEREST YEARS

Weidenfeld & Nicolson

LONDON

I Chose To Climb first published in Great Britain in 1966
by Victor Gollancz
© Chris Bonington 1966

The Next Horizon first published in Great Britain in 1973
by Victor Gollancz
© Chris Bonington 1973

The Everest Years first published in Great Britain in 1986
by Hodder & Stoughton
© Chris Bonington 1986

This edition first published in Great Britain in 2000 by Weidenfeld & Nicolson

A CIP catalogue record for this book
is available from the British Library.

ISBN 0 297 64635 4

Typeset by Selwood Systems, Midsomer Norton

Set in Minion

Printed in Great Britain by
Butler & Tanner Ltd, Frome and London

Weidenfeld & Nicolson

The Orion Publishing Group Ltd
Orion House
5 Upper Saint Martin's Lane
London, WC2H 9EA

Contents

Illustrations

THE NEXT HORIZON

Maps and Diagrams (maps by Wendy Bonington)

I CHOSE
TO CLIMB

With a Foreword by
Eric Shipton

To
my Mother
and Wendy

CONTENTS

AUTHOR'S NOTE

I am most grateful to those of my friends who have kindly allowed me the use of their photographs in this book. Acknowledgment is made individually beneath each reproduction. All other photographs are my own.

I am also grateful to my wife for drawing the diagrams.

C. B.

Foreword
by Eric Shipton

There is today a wide gulf between the 'classical' mountaineer and the expert in modern climbing techniques; and there are many famous climbers still in their prime who would be quite incapable of tackling the more difficult routes in the Alps, or even of using modern methods and equipment effectively. This curious anomaly is due to the fact that until comparatively recently the development of these techniques was virtually confined to the Alps, while those who made their reputations in other ranges, where competition was far less keen and where the new methods were often still not applicable, had no need to employ them to break new ground.

The revolutionary development of modern mountaineering began in the twenties and was a direct result of the greatly increased popularity of the sport. Hitherto, mountain climbing had been largely confined to the comparatively affluent; but with the practice of guideless climbing, which became general after the First World War, it was found to be one of the least expensive of pastimes, available to a vast number of young people who lived within easy reach of the Alps. Increased popularity led inevitably to keener competition for the dwindling supply of possible new routes, and this to the evolution of bold new techniques, novel equipment and, it must be said, to the acceptance of narrower margins of safety. The inter-war years saw in the Alps a spectacular advance in standards of achievement, which at that time was matched nowhere else in the world.

The British, who can be said with some justice to have started the sport of mountaineering and who had the field almost to themselves during the Golden Age of the mid-nineteenth century, played almost no part in the developments of this great era in the Alps. Certainly they were not inactive in the more distant ranges, and our rock climbers achieved great forward strides in the perfection of their art. But the latter were largely content to remain in their home environment, and British crag climbing seemed to have become a separate sport, almost divorced from the field of greater mountaineering.

In the last two decades, however, there has been an astonishing reversal of this trend. Shortly after the War, Tom Bourdillon (who was fired by an almost missionary zeal to put British Alpine achievement back on the map), Arthur Dolphin and others began to climb some of the great new routes of the thirties, on which British climbers had never ventured before, and even to pioneer new lines of their own. Their lead was followed by scores of young men trained on British rock, who quickly adapted themselves to the Alpine environment, the ice and snow and rotten rock (the old bugbears of the pure cragsman), the enormously greater scale of the climbs; they soon mastered the techniques of 'artificial' climbing and learnt the art of survival in bivouacs in the most rigorous and terrifying situations, which are unavoidable on the great modern routes. They have made a truly remarkable breakthrough into this world of achievement; and their performance has often astonished their continental colleagues as, for example, when Joe Brown and Don Whillans made the fourth ascent (in record time) of the West Face of the Dru, a climb which a short time before had been hailed as opening a new chapter in the history of mountaineering.

Since the War, the advance in Alpine standards has been fully maintained; but a more significant development has been the increasing application of modern Alpine techniques in the Himalaya, the Karakoram, the Andes and elsewhere. Thus in these great ranges, too, the limits of possibility are being thrust further and further back to open a boundless horizon of fresh endeavour.

By his ability and his dedication, Chris Bonington has won a prominent place among climbers of the younger generation. Written with frankness and perception, his book illustrates well the relentless spirit which inspires some of his contemporaries and is a fine record of his own achievements.

E. S.

CHAPTER ONE

The Choice

'We have considered your letter and regret that we cannot accede to your suggestion that we should release you to join this mountaineering expedition ... That you should be very anxious to go on this expedition is understandable enough but you should see the problem exactly for what it is. If you were to regard mountaineering as a holiday pastime, that would be one thing; but if you still want to pursue it to the point of long-term expeditions in distant parts of the world, then you must see mountineering not as something which can be combined with your business career but as something which is incompatible with it. Put as plainly as possible, the time has come for you to make up your mind whether you leave mountaineering or Van den Berghs.

'It was very much in our minds when you joined us after returning from an expedition to the Himalaya that it was your intention to settle down uninterruptedly to a business career, particularly as you were a few years older than most people who join us as Management Trainees. I also think that from a business point of view an interruption of some six months in your training would not be advantageous to yourself or the Company.'

I read the letter a second time. It went straight to the root of my problem, the question I had been struggling to solve for the previous few weeks – this conflict between my love of climbing and the need to find a worthwhile career.

And then I looked up and glanced round our furnished room, at the big double bed in one corner, at the half-opened door that led into the cupboard-like kitchenette, at the washing in front of the gas fire. My wife, Wendy, was crouched over the table, at work illustrating a children's book, her paints and papers overflowing on to the floor. We were cramped, overwhelmed by the narrow limits of our room whose every drawer and cupboard seemed to bulge with our possessions. Our landlady, an elderly and fragile Russian, who none the less possessed an iron will, passed our french window (we were on the ground floor), and glanced into the room with a disapproving glare. A few seconds later, as she stormed up the stairs outside the room, we could hear her mutter, 'They do not care. They make my room untidy. They live like animals.' She was used to young bachelors and unmarried girls who were out at work all day, had the bare minimum of possessions and kept their rooms at a barrack-room standard of tidiness.

I picked up the other letter that lay on my desk. It was an invitation to climb the Towers of Paine in South Patagonia. The leader was taking his wife with him, so, presumably, I could do so as well. There were some photographs showing three spectacular, almost improbable rock spires that looked more like huge, windowless skyscrapers than natural mountains. They seemed to jut straight up from the rolling Pampas and there was an impression of boundless space, of exciting, unknown land. But it was not just a question of whether to go on another expedition or not – the letter from Van den Berghs made that quite clear. I now had to choose between a career with an assured future, or a life based on mountaineering. Up till then, I had effected an uneasy compromise between my work and climbing. Now I should have to make a choice one way or the other.

My background and early years gave little hint of my erratic future as a mountaineer. I was born in London in 1934. Neither of my parents had the slightest interest in the mountains though my father had had the wanderlust. After my parents' marriage broke up, he passed the years before the war drifting about the Far East and Australia. He had plenty of physical courage and joined the Special Air Service during the war, but was captured on his first operational mission and spent the rest of the war as a prisoner. As a result I saw him only a few times in my first fifteen years and he had no influence on my upbringing. In my early years I was brought up by my grandmother, while my mother went out to earn a living.

Looking back, it is only too easy to see signs of future behaviour in childhood escapades, but I did seem to have inherited my father's wandering nature. I had a passion for running away that dated from the age of three, when I took flight with a girl-friend on to Hampstead Heath. We were caught only three hours later by a policeman and taken to the police-station. They were heartily glad to return us to our parents, for by that time we had emptied the Inspector's bottle of milk over his desk and torn up the contents of his filing cabinet.

During the war I was evacuated to a boarding-school in Westmoreland. I was still an enthusiastic escaper and twice ran away from school, not to go home, but just for the sake of it.

I saw mountains for the first time during this period, but I was too young for them to make a real impression. Nevertheless, I scrambled around the hills near Grasmere in the Lake District with immense enthusiasm, my patient and very devoted grandmother plodding behind me.

Towards the end of the war, when I was eight, I was brought back to the

South of England, first to a boarding-school near Letchworth where I was desperately unhappy and then, after only half a term, home to London, where my mother now looked after me. After a year at a small private school I was sent to the junior branch of University College School – a public day school. Both there, and at the Senior School, I was neither wildly happy nor unhappy – I made a few friends but was never particularly popular. I was shy and very unsure of myself. Games, at first, were sheer purgatory. I detested cricket, was frightened of the hard ball and was thoroughly bored by the game, surreptitiously reading a book when on the field. I was slightly better at playing rugger and even came to enjoy it, eventually reaching the giddy heights of the Third Fifteen, where I made up for a complete lack of ball sense with a great deal of enthusiasm and a certain amount of brute force. In school work I was average to bright, though tended to be lazy, working only at the things that interested me. I had a passion for military history, read a great deal about it and fought imaginary battles in my head.

I was sixteen when I went to stay with my grandfather who lived near Dublin. The line to Holyhead skirts the Welsh coast, and the hills thrust it on to the very shore. I gazed out of the carriage window, enthralled. There was something strangely exciting about the way the deep-cut, utterly desolate valleys wound their ways into the mountains. There were no crags, just big rounded hills that gave a feeling of emptiness, of the unknown.

When I reached Dublin, I found that my grandfather's house was on the very doorstep of the Wicklow Hills. These had not got quite the atmosphere of the mountains I had seen from the train but they were still exciting. I wanted to explore them to find out more about them, but at the same time I was frightened by their size and my own lack of experience. I stayed with my grandfather for two weeks. He was nearly eighty, very short, shrivelled by years in the tropics, though you could still see how tough he had been in his prime: his shoulders were still very broad, his chest deep, and you could feel the power of his personality. He had led a fascinating life. He was born in Denmark in the late 1860s; his family had a shipyard, building sailing ships, but he was unhappy at home, and ran away to sea in his early teens. He spent the next few years before the mast on a variety of sailing ships and had any number of adventures. He rounded the Horn, jumped ship in Nova Scotia and served for a time in the U.S. Marines; deserted and joined another sailing ship, which finally was wrecked off Cape Hatteras in a storm, but he managed to swim ashore.

Eventually he ended up in Bombay and secured a commission in the Royal Indian Marine. He was serving on the troopship *Warren Hastings* when it was wrecked off Mauritius, and distinguished himself by going down below as the ship sank to secure the water-tight doors; in doing this he had very little chance of survival. For his courage he was awarded a permanent billet in the dockyard at Bombay.

He was then offered a position in the Andaman penal settlement, in the Indian Ocean, to establish a shipyard; he spent the rest of his working life there, for he loved the islands and became particularly interested in the pygmy inhabitants. He transferred to the Forestry Service and became officer-in-charge of aborigines. He did a great deal to help these fierce and very primitive people and probably saved them from being wiped out altogether by various punitive expeditions. He also made a complete survey of both the Andaman Islands and the Nicobars, which must have been a monumental task for the archipelago comprises literally hundreds of densely forested islands.

His home was filled with relics of his work in the Andamans and pre-sentations from the many people he had helped. Even in his eighties he managed a large greenhouse and was known and respected by all his neighbours.

On my way back from Ireland at the tail-end of the summer holiday I stayed with an aunt in the flat surburbia of Wallasey in the Wirral Peninsula. One night we called on some of her friends. While they talked, I idly picked up a book of photographs of Scotland and suddenly my imagination was jolted in a way I had never previously experienced. The book was full of photographs of mountains: the Cairngorms, huge and rounded; the Cuil-lins of Skye, all jagged rock and sinuous ridges; but what impressed me most of all was a picture taken from the summit of Bidean nam Bian in Glencoe, with the serried folds of the hills and valleys merging into a blur on the horizon. To me it was wild, virgin country, and yet it was just within my reach: I could imagine exploring these hills for myself. A book of Alpine or Himalayan peaks could never have had the same effect, for they would have been unattainable. I spent the rest of the holiday examining every picture; I no longer planned battles but worked out expeditions through the mountains instead.

Once back at school, I started to put my dreams into practice; the first thing was to find someone to share my enthusiasm. Shortly before Christmas I persuaded one of my form-mates to join me in an expedition to Wales. We set out just after Christmas and hitch-hiked up to Snowdonia. Anton had only his shoes to walk in, while I had bought a pair of ex-army boots that had a few studs in the soles. We had no windproofs, but relied on our school burberries.

We had chosen one of the hardest winters of recent years for our intro-duction to the hills. There was barely any traffic on the road and we spent the entire day getting from Llangollen, near the Welsh border, to Capel Curig in the heart of Snowdonia, but this did not matter, it was all so new and exciting; even the walks between lifts were enjoyable, as the country got progressively more bleak and wild and the hills got higher. Just as it grew dark we reached Capel Curig. There are few views to beat that of Snowdon from Capel, especially when the mountains are covered with snow. The three peaks of the Snowdon Horse Shoe stood isolated a good seven miles away, but in the crisp, clear air it seemed even farther. They had all the grandeur of Himalayan giants yet were within our grasp.

That night, in the Youth Hostel, Anton and I made our plans. We had not the faintest idea of what mountaineering would entail, and looking round the common-room at all the confident, experienced climbers, I felt very green. We sat huddled in a corner, very conscious of our complete ignorance and the fact that we did not look the part, that we had none of the right clothes. I longed for a pair of proper climbing boots with plenty of nails in the soles, or real climbing breeches and a well darned sweater.

The conversation for the most part was in a climbing jargon that was difficult to understand, every one talking at the top of his voice about the day's exploits, and, as far as one could see, no one really listening. A big, bearded man with a hole in the seat of his camouflaged ex-army windproofs was sitting immediately behind us and was describing, with a wealth of gestures, a narrow escape that day.

'The ice was at least eighty degrees with an inch of powder snow on top. I'd run out sixty feet without a runner and Roy only had an axe belay. Near the top it got even steeper and turned to black ice. There was only an inch of it and you hit rock. It was all I could do to get up it.'

I couldn't really understand what he was talking about though it sounded most impressive. I was much too shy to talk to anyone, but just sat in a corner and listened. I looked ridiculously young for my age anyway; though I was nearly six foot tall and of average build, I had a fresh complexion and smooth skin that made me look little more than fourteen. I was always intensely aware of this, and this as much as anything made me shy and tongue-tied at first in the company of strangers.

We had a map, and there was a path marked all the way up Snowdon from Pen y Pass, so we decided to follow it the next day. We did not like consulting anyone about our plans, but if we had done, I am sure we should have been warned off Snowdon, for in severe winter conditions even the easiest way up can be dangerous and has claimed many lives. The next morning, happily ignorant, we hitch-hiked to Pen y Pass, just below Crib Goch. The path, marked on our maps, ran along the side of the ridge above the deeply glaciated cwm of Glas Llyn, but standing by the roadside it did not seem to be much help. The weather had changed overnight; the cloud was down and it was beginning to snow. From the road, the white of the snow, broken only by black gashes of exposed rocks, merged imperceptibly with the cloud. There were a few tracks in the snow but whether these were the paths marked on the map, who could tell?

We were about to turn back when a group of three climbers, who looked very professional with their ice-axes and windproofs, strode past and plunged into the snow. We followed them; soon we had not the faintest idea where we were as the snow swirled around us, and we floundered up to our waists in it. My feet quickly lost all sense of feeling, it was so cold. Anton was in an even worse state without proper boots, and continually slipping. The figures in front were vague blurs in the rushing snow; above us loomed black cliffs, below, the steeply dropping white slope merged into the cloud and only occasionally could we see the dull black surface of Glas Llyn through a momentary break. We ended up in a minor avalanche when we must have been quite high on the slopes of Crib Goch. Suddenly, everything around us was moving and we rolled and slid in a steadily moving chute of snow down the slope. We had no real comprehension of danger, and arrived at the bottom laughing. If there had been a cliff on the way down we could have been seriously injured. The people we had followed had not had any more sense than us and had floundered about in the soft snow just as incompetently. I returned to the Hostel that night soaked to the skin, exhausted but completely happy – it was the most exciting and enjoyable day I had ever had. Anton did not share my enthusiasm; he returned to London the next day and never came back to the hills. I stayed on by myself for a few more days. For the most part I kept to the roads and walked from one Youth Hostel to the next, but I could never pluck up courage to talk to anyone in the evenings until my last night. The Youth Hostel at Capel Curig was full, and so I found a little bed-and-breakfast place to spend the night in. Two climbers arrived just as it got dark and we spent the evening together. It was easy to talk to them, to find out something about real rock climbing, and what they told me confirmed my ambition to be a climber.

Back at school I dreamt of the mountains and of rock climbing. I read every book I could lay my hands on. But the real problem was to find someone to climb with. In Wales I had seen the danger of solitary wandering, and anyway wanted to climb properly with a rope. Today, even in the last twelve years, climbing has expanded out of all recognition: in London there are many local clubs all of which encourage beginners and welcome new members; there are organisations such as the Mountaineering Association and the Central Council of Physical Recreation, that organise training courses, so that it is not too difficult to learn how to climb. In 1951, however, there were few local clubs anywhere and none in London. No one at school was interested in the mountains and there seemed no way of finding anyone to teach me to climb.

Finally, I ran down a friend of the family who had done some climbing. He agreed to take me down to Harrison's Rocks, an outcrop in Kent only forty miles south of London. It seemed incredible that there could be crags so close to the city in Southern England. I had always associated climbing with the bleak hills of Scotland and Wales, certainly not with the hop fields of Kent. I met Cliff one Sunday morning at the end of March on Victoria Station. I had an irrational feeling of superiority over all the thousands of other travellers who were merely going down to the coast for a day by the sea and was intensely conscious of the length of old hemp rope in my rucksack; I longed to take it out and sling it round my shoulder but felt too self-conscious to do so. We were not the only mountaineers travelling down to Tunbridge Wells – you could tell them from the patches in their trousers and the battered anoraks. We all piled out of the train at Groombridge and walked up an ordinary country road. There was still no sign of any rocks, even when we went through a wood of young trees; and then, suddenly, we came to the top of a sandstone cliff. It was only thirty feet high; the trees growing at its base towered above its crest; a railway ran along the bed of the valley through fields of hops and past an oast house. I could not help being disappointed: it was all so peaceful and rustic. We scrambled to the foot of the cliff and walked along a path, looking up at the rocks as we went. There was nearly a mile of them – all very steep, seamed with cracks, weathered by wind and rain, sometimes completely hidden by the trees or covered with an uninviting black slime, but where the trees had receded there were stretches of clean grey-brown rock. As we walked along the foot, Cliff sounded like a guide in a stately home showing off the prized possessions to his visitors.

'That's Dick's Diversion up there,' pointing to a seemingly holdless, vertical wall. 'It's one of the hardest routes here; I've never done it.' I wondered how anyone could, except perhaps a human spider – and then a bit farther on, he said, 'There's Slim Finger Crack – you can see why it's called that.' I could. The wall was overhanging at the bottom, and the crack that split it seemed barely wide enough to take one's fingers. It was difficult to believe that practically every square foot of rock had been climbed and had then been mapped and recorded, given a name and a standard of difficulty.

People were beginning to climb; for the most part they looped their climbing rope round a tree at the top of the rocks, tied on to one end, while a friend pulled it in at the bottom, so that they could not possibly hurt themselves if they slipped. This precaution was particularly advisable since the sandstone holds were often frail and could easily break off. We stopped to watch one of the climbers perform; there was already a good audience gathered at the foot of the cliff. The climb, called Long Layback, ran up a steep crack of about thirty-five feet. He started off in fine form, his feet pressing against the rock at the side of the crack, his body almost parallel to the ground, leaning back on his arms. But then as he got higher he began to tire; his body sagged back on to the rope, and then the audience came to life, several climbers shouting different directions all at the tops of their voices.

'Cock your right foot up on to the scrape by your shoulder and layback on the little pock.'

While another yelled, 'That's no good, Jack, jam your left foot in the crack to your left and reach up for the jug . . . come on, reach, man, reach . . . you're nearly there.'

Jack, panting hard – 'Tight rope . . . tighter, for God's sake' – gasps and grunts, and forces his unwilling body an inch higher, and the man holding the rope heaves and pulls at the bottom. But it's no good, he slumps back on the rope. Yells and ironic cheers from the audience.

'Let me down,' groans Jack.

'Come on, Jack. Have another go. You were nearly there,' shout the supporters' club.

'I can't. I've no bloody strength left in my arms and the rope's cutting me in two. Come on, let me down for Christ's sake.'

But his tormentors are now enjoying themselves.

'Go on, Jack. Fight it. You'll never make a mountaineer if you give in that easily.'

At this stage Jack is hanging unashamedly on the rope, having lost all contact with the rock, and is lowered to the ground. The next man quickly takes his place and starts up the crack, but because he has done the route many times before, climbs it quickly and easily. At Harrison's Rocks climbing becomes almost a spectator sport. People living in the area go there for their Sunday afternoon walk with the dog, and some of the climbers themselves rarely leave the ground, but prefer to drift from audience to audience, to watch their friends and to talk about climbing.

Cliff soon had me on the end of a rope and I had my first taste of climbing. When he had gone up the narrow little chimney he had chosen for my first climb, it had looked easy, almost effortless – he had seemed to coax his way up the rock, stepping and pulling with a controlled precision; but when I followed I started to fight it and soon exhausted myself to no real effect, for I could make no further upward progress and all my struggles seemed to jam me even more firmly in the crack.

'Try to relax, Chris, you can't hurt yourself, you'll only come on to the rope,' Cliff said quietly.

I began to think, to look around me, to try and find somewhere to put my feet, something to pull on, and suddenly it was no longer a struggle, but an absorbing exercise.

I reached the top of that first climb and we went on to more, sometimes using the rope and on the shorter routes doing without it. There were plenty of climbs I could not get up, plenty of times when I began to fight, only to end by hanging on the end of the rope, to be lowered to the ground. By the end of the day my fingers were like strips of limp rubber and opened out the moment I pulled up on them; every limb ached with weariness. But what a day! I felt a sympathy with the rock; I found that my body somehow slipped into balance naturally, without any conscious thought on my part. There was not much height to worry about, for the crag was only thirty feet, but what there was did not worry me; if anything, I found it stimulating. I knew that I had found a pursuit that I loved, that my body and my temperament seemed designed for it, and that I was happy.

Up to that time I had found no complete release in physical expression. Although I enjoyed rugger, I was always aware of my limitations, my instinctive fear of the ball, the slowness of my reactions. Even in the gymnasium, I was limited. I lacked the speed of reaction to control my limbs with quick precision and, perhaps as a result, I always experienced a quick jab of fear as I launched myself into a vault or handspring. This acted as a kind of brake, and I therefore often landed badly or ended the exercise in an uncontrolled tangle of arms and legs. But even on that first visit to the rocks, I experienced none of these limitations; I was conscious only of feelings of confidence and intense enjoyment that I had never experienced before.

On the way back to London, I asked Cliff once again, 'Wouldn't you like to go climbing in Wales this Easter, just for a few days?'

He replied, 'I wish I could, but I've got too much work to catch up on. I shall have a word with Tom Blackburn, though – I've done most of my climbing with him – he might take you.'

Cliff took me round to see Tom Blackburn that same week – I felt like an applicant for an important job, I was so anxious to make a good impression – and be invited to go climbing. Tom was a schoolmaster so he had a good holiday at Easter, but he was married and had three children. Nevertheless, he promised to spend a few days in Wales with me immediately after Easter, and at least to give me a grounding in climbing. I was delighted – it seemed almost too good to be true – that he, a complete stranger, should be prepared to saddle himself with a schoolboy and complete novice to climbing, especially after a term of teaching boys like myself.

I did very little work at school for the rest of that term, but spent my entire time dreaming of the hills. I had a few pounds saved up and went into Black's, a climbing shop in London, to buy my first pair of boots – a magnificent pair bristling with clinker nails and a good two sizes too big. Cliff had given me an old hemp rope that was so worn that it looked as if it had been used by the Victorian pioneers, and my final item of equipment was an old school waterproof that I had cut down to look like an anorak.

At last it was time to set out on my first real climbing holiday. I was to meet Tom Blackburn at a climber's hut in the Llanberis Valley of North Wales. I hitched up to Chester, and then along the coast to Caernarvon, ending with a long walk from Llanberis up the valley. As I walked up, I gazed around me excitedly and wondered which of the myriad of crags that bristled on either side of the road I should climb in the next three days, or whether they were climbable at all. The tops were all covered with snow, and this seemed to increase the scale of everything. I had asked the way to Ynys Etws, the climbing hut, in Nant Peris, and had been told that it was the last house up the valley. It was a long, low building of local stone, with just a few small windows. As I walked along the track towards it I felt shy, rather like a boy going to a new school. I wondered how many people I should find there, and what they would be like; I felt terribly conscious of my complete inexperience and hoped with all my heart that Tom Blackburn would already be there. But there was no sign of him – only a telegram with the brief message – 'Children mumps hope arrive Thursday.'

The only other occupant of the hut was a man in his mid-twenties. He was sitting in the big kitchen-living-room in front of a roaring fire. He was obviously a full-blooded climber, having a look of quiet ownership in the hut as if he were permanently installed, and in his talk showed that he had an intimate knowledge of the area, which indeed he did, for Tony Moulam was one of the leading rock climbers of that period. I don't imagine he was particularly pleased to find himself suddenly landed with a young lad, who had never been climbing before, but he was very patient with me, especially in answering all my questions, most of which were very naïve.

I spent the next few days wandering the hills on my own. The weather was consistently bad and Moulam, in spite of my broad hints, preferred to sit in front of the fire rather than take a young novice out on to the crags. When Tom Blackburn finally arrived he did his duty manfully, taking me out every day. My first climb was Flake Crack on Dinas Bach, an undistinguished climb on a scruffy little crag, but to me it was the ultimate in excitement and difficulty.

When the weather began to improve Tony Moulam showed signs of emerging from his long hibernation; he offered to take us climbing. We started on Crackstone Rib, a route of *very difficult* standard, that was more steep and airy than anything I had been on up to that time. Having acquitted ourselves well on this, Tony decided to take us up a climb in the next standard, a *severe*. This route had a nondescript name – The Crevice – that gave little indication of what it had in store for us. The first pitch led easily to the foot of a deep-cut vertical corner, roofed by a big overhang, with a narrow chimney up its back. Tony went up first; he climbed with a slow precision, very much in keeping with his personality, resting for long periods, then trying a move, coming back down for another rest and then up again. I was most impressed by the way he safeguarded himself with cunningly contrived running belays, so that if he fell he could only have fallen a few feet. In the overhang his progress was still slower as he jammed his body into the crack and by sinuous wriggles eased his way up, but his progress was always positive and he seemed part of the rock.

Then it was Tom's turn to go up and the comparison between a really good climber on peak form and a lesser one immediately became apparent, for Tom had done little climbing in the last few years. Where Tony had seemed to slide up Tom fought and grunted, but with the help of a pull from the rope, he finally got up; and then came the moment of truth – it was my turn. I felt so alone on the end of the rope; the chimney loomed up above me, threatening and inhospitable. The rope at my waist came taut, pulled from above; a cry to come up sounded very far away, thinned and distorted by the wind, as I started worming my way up the chimney. At first it was not too difficult but soon the rock arched out over my head and I could find no holds to pull on. In my fear I jammed my body firmly in the inmost recesses of the chimney, but then, though I could certainly not slip down, I could make no upward progress. I started to fight the hard, unyielding rock, exhausted myself to no avail, edged my panting body up the chimney and out over the overhang, my feet kicking helplessly in space below me; the rope pulled at my waist, threatening to pull me in two. At last I was up, lying on a small ledge, completely exhausted, sobbing for breath. It was the only time I have ever been pulled up a climb and it was agonizingly uncomfortable, but it was also useful, for I had become over-confident even in my first few days of climbing, and this showed me all too clearly how much I had to learn.

That same afternoon, Tom Blackburn had to return to London, to cope with his mump-ridden family, so that evening I was left once more with

Tony Moulam in the hut. I planned the next day to walk over to the Ogwen Valley, where there are many more easy climbs than in that of Llanberis and where I could hope to find other people of similar ability to myself.

That night, in front of the fire, I summoned up all my courage to ask Tony if there was any chance of joining the Climbers' Club – it owned Ynys Etws and was one of the senior clubs in the country, having a long and distinguished history dating back to the last century. I wanted to stay in this warm and comfortable hut, and, much more important, to belong and feel part of the body of climbers. Tony must have been thoroughly embarrassed by my request – he talked about my youth, that I was too young anyway to be allowed into the club, and the fact that I had only just started to climb.

'You know, Chris, there are a lot of lads, just like yourself, who start to climb with just as much enthusiasm. They're keen on it for two or three years and then they give it up and go on to something else. Whatever you think now, you might do the same. If you are still climbing in five years, that's when you should start thinking of joining the Climbers' Club.'

I sat and listened in a state of dumb misery. It sounded like a sentence of eternal banishment.

A few years later Tony told me that at the time he thought I would either kill myself in the next few months or go on to do great things. I had plenty of narrow escapes during that period, but in many ways it was the best I ever had. Everything was strange and new, a constant process of discovery. My first *v diff.* lead, my first *severe*, the first trip to Scotland, the first iced gully on Tryfan, were all tremendous adventures that had a freshness one only seems to experience in one's teens.

A year after my first visit to the Llanberis valley, I returned with a friend of my own age, also still at school. We slept under a boulder below Dinas Mot and climbed with all the fanaticism of youth, doing at least three climbs each day; I always felt cheated if I got off the crags before dark and never dreamt of going drinking in the pub at nights. Apart from anything else we couldn't afford it. We slowly worked our way through the *VS*'s in the Llanberis guide book and made our first timorous visit to the dark flanks of Cloggy – to us it was as frightening as the North Wall of the Eiger.

Climbing now completely filled my interest, not only when on the crags but back at home as well, where I read everything I could lay hands on. At the same time, I realised that I had to find a career, and was now entering my final school term with A Levels at the end of it. It had always been assumed that I should go to University, and I even had a place at University College, London. After that I was not at all sure what I should do, but took it for granted that I should have to find some kind of conventional occupation.

But I failed one of my A Levels – one that I had been convinced I could pass. I felt disillusioned, wanted to get away from home, and after another term at school decided to do my National Service. At least it meant I could spend a couple of weeks in Scotland climbing under winter conditions while I waited for my call-up papers.

CHAPTER TWO

Winter in Scotland

The lorry panted slowly up the hill leading to the Moor of Rannoch. My excitement had steadily increased ever since leaving the drab streets of Glasgow and Dumbarton, and making my way into the hills along the winding road beside Loch Lomond. I had been this way twice before but it had been summer; the road packed with cars; tourists everywhere, and though, at the time, the hills had excited me to a degree I thought could not be exceeded, now, with a covering of snow, they seemed so vast, so utterly remote that I knew I had never seen anything more beautiful.

Each bend in the road brought a new view, higher and wilder mountains, an ever increasing feeling of the unknown. As we reached the crest of the hills, Rannoch Moor stretched before us, the whiteness of the snow patterned with black waters and beyond it, rounded hills, untouched, pure and desolate. The road winds round the edge of the moor and one has the feeling that nobody ever ventures into its midst – it is so featureless – and this adds to its fascination, to make it, in a way, more exciting than the mountains, for one's eyes are drawn inevitably to their tops and one knows that many people have stood there, while on the moor there is nothing on which to focus the eye, no place to reach, just rolling, snow-covered peat hags and water.

We swept round a bend, and Buachaille Etive Mor came into sight, its shapely mass and steep flanks dominating the other hills. The road ran past its foot in a long, straight stretch, before dropping into Glencoe. This was my objective, for I had arranged to meet a friend at Lagangarbh, a climbing hut owned by the Scottish Mountaineering Club, that stands at the foot of the Buachaille. John Hammond arrived the following morning and we spent the next few days floundering in the deep powder snow that completely covered the hills. We saw no one else – it was mid-week – but one evening on our return to the hut we saw a light in the window. Three rough-looking climbers were sitting round the fire, drinking tea, our tea I noticed, for there was no sign of any of their belongings. They ignored us; continued talking quietly amongst themselves.

John tried to break the ice.

'It's been a superb day, hasn't it?'

'Aye.'

'Have you done anything today?'

'No. Only came up this afternoon.'

'You're stopping here?'

'No. We're in the bothy by the road. It's free.'

'Haven't I seen you before?' John asked the largest of the three, a wild-looking individual with straw-coloured hair, hollow cheeks and eyes that for ever peered into the distance. 'Wasn't it in Chamonix last summer? You had your leg in plaster and your head was bandaged.'

'Aye, that'd be me. I had a bit of trouble on the Charmoz. I was doing the traverse solo and abseiled from some old slings on the way down; the buggers broke on me and I fell about fifty feet. I was lucky to get away with it – landed on a ledge. But I only cracked my skull on that. We got pissed the same night and I tried to climb the Church Tower. The drain pipe came away when I was half-way up. That's where I broke my leg. What did you do last summer?'

The conversation now became more friendly. I was still much in awe of established mountaineers and was quite content to listen. I guessed this must be none other than Hamish MacInnes, already a legendary figure in Scottish circles, though he was only in his early twenties. He had started climbing as a lad, hitch-hiked to the Alps just after the war with only £5 in his pocket and had spent his National Service in Austria. There he had earned the nickname 'MacPiton', having acquired a taste for pegging, from the Austrians, on the steep limestone walls of the Kaisergebirge. In the early fifties the use of any artificial aids was still frowned on, but Hamish hammered his pegs into Scottish crags with gay abandon, much to the disgust of the staider members of the Scottish Mountaineering Club. This never worried him, however, for he had a complete disregard for public opinion and was in every respect an individualist.

His two companions were members of the Creagh Dhu Mountaineering Club, a body even more legendary than Hamish himself. It had been started on Clydeside before the war at the height of the Depression. Its members had a fine tradition of deer poaching behind them, had fought the Zermatt guides in pitched battle when they had set up their own guiding agency, and prided themselves on their toughness. There was even a story doing the rounds that, on a rescue, several members of the Creagh Dhu had fought over the dead man's boots; though no doubt many of the tales about them had been exaggerated in the telling.

At the end of the evening John asked:

'Where are you going tomorrow?'

'Up the Rannoch Wall. We're going to try to do the first winter ascent,' replied Hamish.

'Do you think we could follow you up?' asked John.

A calculating look came into Hamish's eye.

'You can, if you take the gnomie with you. I'll go in front with Kerr.'

The gnomie was the youngest of the three. He had only just started to climb and was not yet a full member of the Creagh Dhu; he had to complete his apprenticeship, and so was at the beck and call of all the members, doing the cooking and making endless brews of tea. Climbing as a party of three is never much fun, it is so much slower than a party of two, but we should never have been able to undertake a first winter ascent by ourselves, since we had neither the experience nor sufficient knowledge of the area, so we agreed with alacrity. If we had known just how slow the gnomie was, we might have had second thoughts.

Hamish and his party came for us the next day – we had got up early because we thought it important to make maximum use of the short hours of daylight, but Hamish evidently had no such worries for they arrived at the hut in the middle of the morning. On the previous day the weather had been perfect, with a clear sky, brilliant sun and a hard, invigorating frost, but during the night a scum of high, grey cloud had hidden the sky and there was a cold wind that carried a few stray snowflakes. The Buachaille looked grim and menacing in the dull, flat light, much bigger, more dangerous than on previous days. It was warm and comfortable in the hut; I had no desire to go out into the wind and the cold, was suddenly afraid of the mountain, full of forebodings and yet excited at the same time.

'Do you think it'll go, Hamish?' asked John, voicing my own fears. 'The weather seems to be brewing up. There's some snow in the air.'

'It'll be all the more interesting,' replied Hamish cheerfully. 'There's a stack of powder snow on the crag already; a bit more won't do any harm. Anyway, we'd better be getting off – it's dark at six.'

We set out, plodding slowly through the deep snow in single file. It's a long way to the Rannoch Wall, nearly to the top of the mountain. We worked our way round the bottom slopes of the Buachaille and Hamish paused only to point out a long slide of water ice, which we had to cross.

'A nig-nog tried it solo last week and came unstuck at the top. He landed down there. We had to shovel his brains back into his head; it was quite messy.' I found myself clinging to the hand-holds a little harder and thinking regretfully of the fire we had just left. We were now climbing the Curved Ridge, one of the easy routes up the Buachaille, and I should have loved the security of the rope but was too proud to ask; anyway, everyone else seemed perfectly at ease.

At last the Rannoch Wall came into sight; it looked impossibly steep, jutted into the cloud base just above, with a fluted structure of ribs and grooves, bristling with little overhangs, and from below there seemed to be no ledges at all. Hamish confidently kicked steps across a snow gully to the foot of the wall, and before I caught up with the rest of the party, had already started up the first pitch – he was planning to follow Agag's Groove, a comparatively easy but fine line that started at the lowest point of the Wall and led to the crest of the Crowberry Ridge, near the top of the Buachaille. It had been done hundreds of times in summer and was not particularly hard – but now all the holds were covered with snow and ice; the gully we had crossed to reach its foot, dropped away steeply below us in a snow-chute between steep rock walls, giving us a sensation of isolation.

By the time we had untangled our ropes and tied on, Hamish had disappeared round a corner, somewhere above us. There was a long pause and we soon grew cold huddled together in the snow. We could hear Hamish singing an Irish rebel song high above. The rope to him crept out through Kerr MacPhail's hands with maddening slowness. At last there was a thin cry; another pause and the rope began to move quickly until it was taut, pulling at Kerr's waist. He started to climb and soon vanished into the flurries of snow that were now pouring down the crag.

We soon discovered why Hamish had been so happy that we should follow him up with the gnomie; he was the ultimate of slow climbers. Leading each pitch was all right; I was much too gripped to notice the cold, even enjoyed clearing the holds, balancing up the ice-glazed rock, but the waits in between were sheer agony. Then I had ample time to notice how cold I was, how slow the other two were in coming up. Each pitch was the same. We were following a series of shallow grooves and seemed to be getting somewhere near the top. The other pair had vanished entirely; we could not even hear their shouts and I felt weak and inadequate against the size of the wall, the strength of the wind and the driving snow. Our windproofs were frozen into suits of armour, and our clothes underneath, warmed by body heat, were by now wet and clammy from melted snow. The groove dwindled into nothing and the face steepened; a feeling of near panic grew inside me as I searched for the route, clearing away snow, only to find sloping ledges.

There was a lull in the wind and much to my relief I heard a shout from below – it was Hamish; they had finished the climb and were on their way down.

'Are you planning to spend the night out?' he yelled. 'It'll be dark in another hour. You'll have good bivouac practice for the big North Walls.'

I was not amused. 'Where the hell does it go from here?' I shouted.

'Traverse left,' he replied, 'and you'll find a peg. There's a bit of ice on the wall that makes it a wee bit hard.'

Across to the left it looked frighteningly steep but there was no time to waste if we were to get off before dark. I started to edge my way across, grateful for the hand-holds that Hamish had cleared from the ice. I could just see the piton about twenty feet away. My fingers had long ago lost all feeling and I was shivering so hard I felt I was going to shake myself off the holds. I was very glad to reach the peg. After that I felt more confident and a few more feet led to the top. It was now nearly dark but I felt reassured for Hamish had settled down on the Ridge below to wait for us. John quickly came up to me, and then the gnomie slowly followed. We were impatient to finish, to move swiftly and freely, to get some warmth back into our limbs. When Gordon reached the peg, we discovered why Hamish had waited for us.

A yell wafted up from the depths.

'Mind you get the peg out, Gordon.'

We heard the sound of hammering from below.

'I can't get it out, Hamish. It's bent in the crack and my hands are frozen solid,' he cried.

'You're not going up till the peg's out,' came the implacable reply. 'A night out will do you no harm. Don't let him up, Chris, till he has got it out.'

Bugger the peg, I thought. I want to get down. But Hamish has a strong personality and the 'gnomies' in the Creagh Dhu are used to an iron discipline, so we sat and cursed and shivered while the unfortunate Gordon hammered at the peg.

At last, a weak gasp of triumph.

'I've got it out, Hamish.'

'Well, you can go on up now. Next time you should take a heavier hammer,' replied the hard man.

By the time Gordon reached us it was dark. We hurriedly coiled the hawser-like frozen ropes and stumbled across easy-angled but snow-plastered rocks to the top of the Curved Ridge, which was to be our way down. We were greatly relieved that Hamish had waited for us, for, by ourselves, we should never have found the way. The three Scots went back to Glasgow that night saying that there was too much fresh snow to do any climbing, but Hamish said that he might return at the end of the week and told us where to find him.

John and I did some more climbs that week but they were of no particular merit for there was too much fresh powder snow blanketing the rocks and filling the gullies. Wading through it, thigh deep, was an exhausting business. At the end of the week John left for London and on the Friday night, Hamish arrived at Lagangarbh.

'It's no good going for the gullies,' he said. 'There's too much powder snow. We need a good thaw followed by a hard frost before we can go for the big stuff – but I know a nice little problem that's just waiting to be done on the Crowberry Ridge. We'll do the Direct tomorrow – it's never been done in winter.'

I was happy to follow him anywhere for I had complete confidence in him and still could hardly believe my luck that I should be climbing with one of Scotland's best mountaineers. We set out next morning and scrambled to the start of the difficulties, which was fairly high up on the Crowberry Ridge – this was the famous Abraham's Traverse. Hamish quickly uncoiled the rope and tossed me an end. I started to search for a good bollard on which to belay but could not find one.

'Don't worry about that,' said Hamish. 'You'll be fine sitting down there; it's a grand stance.'

I was much too in awe of the master climber to demur, so I sat where he pointed, feeling decidedly unsafe. Hamish stepped round the corner out of sight – the rock above was smooth and sheer, and the route lay round to the left. I was sitting on a small rock-pedestal, my feet braced against a block. Looking down, the ridge that had felt pleasantly easy-angled as we had scrambled up, dropped away steeply below my feet.

There was no movement from the rope in my hands, just the sound of Hamish's nails scraping on the rock round the corner. I began to wish that I had a proper belay, to imagine what would happen if Hamish fell off – the sudden violent pull of the rope that would surely tear me from my stance. I then began to pick out the line we should take as we hurtled downwards: we should hit that snow-covered ledge but inevitably bounce, and so on to the boulder-strewn slopes over a thousand feet below. Ten minutes went by, no movement, just the sound of scraping, of metal on rock. The rope acted as a telegraph wire, transmitting Hamish's struggles out in front even though he was out of sight. There was nothing I could do but sit and wait; I was more worried about being pulled off the ledge than about his safety. Another twenty minutes went by and the rope crept out a few inches. I restrained my longing to ask what was going on, whether it was difficult.

At last, a shout from above: 'It's a wee bit hard. I'm coming down for a rest. Take in the rope.' A clatter of nails and Hamish appeared.

'There's ice all over the holds. They are all sloping and I can't find anywhere to get a peg in.'

'Well, how about finding me a belay,' I protested.

'You should be all right as you are, but we'll give you something,' and he made a big loop in my rope and dropped it over the pedestal on which I was sitting; it was better than nothing, but if he fell off I should be pulled off my stance before it held me. I resumed my nerve-racking wait – another half-hour and he was back again. I was now on the point of open rebellion but Hamish's enthusiasm disarmed me.

'I've nearly got it,' he asserted, full of optimism, 'but I'll have to take my boots off – the nails skid straight off the holds, but I might just stay on in socks.' He set out once again in his stockinged feet; at least there was no more scraping of iron on rock, though perhaps this was even worse for the silence allowed my imagination even more play. The rope ran out slowly; there was a sound of hammering, the rope continued to move, and then a shout: 'I'm up.' I had been sitting in the same position for an hour-and-a-half, and when I stood up to follow, it was all I could do to move my limbs, there were so frozen. I soon discovered why he had found it so hard: the rock was covered by a thin but tenacious skin of ice that did not shatter under the blows of our axes. The place that Hamish had found so difficult was a gently sloping slab. He had managed to hammer a piton half an inch into a hairline crack, while his feet had been steadily slipping down the slab, and then, handling the peg with loving care, had stretched for the top where the holds improved. His position had been even more precarious than I had imagined. In comparison, the rest of the climb was easy and we quickly reached the top of the Buachaille.

That night Hamish was in high spirits.

'Conditions are much better than I had expected. Tomorrow we'll go on to the big-time stuff,' he told me.

'What's that?' I asked, full of apprehension.

'We'll have a go at Raven's Gully. It will be the best winter route in the Glen, if we can get up it. I've tried it a couple of times already.'

I had heard of Raven's Gully; there was a note in the Hut log-book describing Hamish's last attempt when he had been rescued from it. It was the steepest of the gullies on the Buachaille and the only one that had not had a winter ascent, though it had been climbed in summer. Huge boulders blocked the gully bed, forming fierce overhangs and the climb, even in summer, was rated as *very severe.*

'We tried it last year,' Hamish told me. 'I went up with a big group of Creagh Dhu lads. We got over the first overhang and I was just trying the second one, with the lads waiting on the snow below. Big Bill was fooling around unroped, and must have stepped backwards. One moment he was there and the next he was whistling down the gully. He must have gone a thousand feet before he stopped – we thought he was a goner. He just got up and shouted: 'Come on down – it's great down here.' There were a lot of boulders sticking out of the snow on the way down, so he was lucky to get away with it. We didn't follow him.'

'You had a narrow escape yourself last month, didn't you? Weren't you pulled out of the gully?'

'I wasn't pulled out. They dropped me a rope and I climbed out. I was only ten feet from the top anyway. I went up with Charley Vigano and John Cullen, two Creagh Dhu lads. The gully was heavily iced but we had got over the crux and just had a couple of hundred of feet up an icy groove to get out. I ran out a hundred feet, using a few pegs; it was bloody thin climbing and pitch dark by that time; then the rope jammed. The lads wouldn't leave their ledge, said they couldn't get up without the help of the rope. They were all right where they were, for they had heavy motor-cycle suits and were sitting on a big ledge, but I only had my jeans and a thin shirt under my anorak. I had to get up or freeze to death, so I took off the rope and went up solo. I got to within ten feet of the top; I was jammed across a little chimney. There were no real holds and it was all covered in verglas. I couldn't get up or down so I just stayed there. I thought I'd had it, it was so bloody cold and I was there for eight hours. Fortunately someone in the valley saw the torch signals the lads were making and a rescue party came up and gave me a top rope and then pulled the lads up.'

I was impressed by his story at the time but when I saw the spot where he had remained precariously jammed for over eight hours in a temperature that was well below freezing I understood just how tough Hamish was. The slightest loss of consciousness, or even relaxation of his muscles, would have caused him to fall, his position was so insecure. It was characteristic of him that he was so lightly clad, for he never seemed to feel the cold.

We settled down for the night, Hamish on the floor, though there were fifteen unoccupied beds in the hut, for he believed that a hard bed was essential for health. He was also very keen on health foods and advocated a diet of brown, stone-ground bread and honey; he was so persuasive that he even got some of the Creagh Dhu on to this diet.

The next morning it was a fine, warm day; perfect, Hamish claimed, for attempting the Gully. We set out early to make the maximum use of daylight, and weighed down by a rucksack full of pitons, crampons and spare clothes, plodded up the lower slopes of the Buachaille. The Gully is in an intimidating setting; it is a deep-cut, dark gash, flanking one of the most impressive walls in Glencoe, so steep that there was no snow to vein the rock, just black streaks of water ice. On the other side of the Gully was a steep but slender buttress; it was obvious from below that there was no easy escape out of it.

At first we cramponned up a slope of easy-angled ice but it quickly narrowed and steepened into a chute, enclosed by sheer walls, that was finally barred by a big overhang formed by a boulder jammed in the gully. This was the first obstacle. I was ensconced in the cave formed by the boulder; it was like being in a refrigerator. Hamish set to work on the ice-coated walls below the overhang, chipped away the ice and hammered in several pitons. The time dragged slowly; it took him an hour-and-a-half to climb this pitch; but worse horrors were in store. Above the overhang there was a stretch of simple snow climbing, but then the gully steepened and narrowed; there were several boulders jammed in the chimney, and the route seemed to go inside these, but everything was covered with a thick coat of ice. I had thought my stance at the back of the cave unpleasant, but this was infinitely worse for a stream of water was pouring down the back of the gully and the only possible stance was in its bed. We were both soaked to the skin. Hamish unroped and threw the end over the boulder just above our heads and tied on again. With this protection, he began cutting hand and footholds in the thick ice and slowly worked his way up the chimney. The water poured over him, running down his legs in streams. A grunt of relief, and he was able to pull out on to the wall, clear of the torrent – but a steep groove barred his way.

'I'll have to take my boots off, Chris,' he shouted. 'Bring them up with you. I'll leave them on the ledge.' I paid out the rope slowly, winced away from the stream of water and gazed out through the slit formed by the walls of the gully at the sunlit hills on the other side of the valley, longing to be there. My enthusiasm for first winter ascents had been washed away by the shower-bath of icy water that hammered on my head, and my one ambition was to escape the dank confines of these steep walls – I even began to regret ever having met Hamish.

The rope was now tugging at my waist. I could not hear Hamish shouting for the sound of falling water, so assumed he was belayed and nerved myself to plunge into the full force of the torrent. I was glad to feel the rope pulling at my waist: I could hardly co-ordinate the movement of my limbs, they were so cold, and the ice-covered gully wall was vertical. After a few feet I escaped the waterfall, and reached the ledge on which Hamish had left his boots. The groove above was steep and holdless, with the occasional knob of rock protruding from the black ice. Hamish had balanced up these in his stockinged feet; I followed in crampons, the points scratching ineffect-ively on rock and ice alike, very glad of a tight rope. I found Hamish standing on a snow ledge in his stockinged feet, showing no sign of cold though my teeth were chattering like a machine-gun.

'Aren't your feet cold, Hamish?'

'No, I can't feel them. I won't bother to put my boots on; I think I'll be needing socks again for the next pitch. It's a grand climb, isn't it?'

I agreed, without enthusiasm. At least we were now out of the waterfall, the rock above was less steep though very smooth, and the gully had opened out a bit, giving us a feeling of greater freedom. Hamish had started to edge his way across the smooth left-hand wall of the gully; he hammered in a couple of pitons on the way, as there was a thin glaze of ice over it – a shout of triumph and he reached the top of the pitch.

'Let's have my boots,' he called.

He had led two iced pitches and had stood on the stance in between for over an hour in his stockinged feet. It seemed a miracle that he was not frostbitten. I was quite sure I would have been, in his place; my feet were like blocks of ice, though I was wearing boots and two pairs of socks.

It was now my turn to follow him; my boots skidded on the iced rock and the rope gave me little help since it was running up from me at an angle. I reached the last peg; had I come off, once I had unclipped from it, I would have swung some thirty feet into the rocky bed of the gully.

'Make sure you get the peg out,' cried Hamish.

'I can't. I need it to hold on to.'

'Use the holds, man – they're there if you look for them. A swing won't do you any harm. That peg cost two bob.'

'I'll pay you for the bloody peg. I'm coming across.'

I teetered somehow across the wall, more off than on, but just managed to maintain contact with the rock.

The gully now deepened into a dark chasm.

'This is where the lads waited when we got stuck last time,' Hamish told me. 'I had to solo up those grooves to the right. That's where we go now. They don't look too bad today. Would you like to go in the lead?'

I jumped at the chance, for the rock was almost entirely clear of snow; there even seemed to be a few proper holds.

'It was completely covered last time,' Hamish went on. 'That's where I ended up – in that wee chimney up there.'

I could see why he had been stuck; the walls were as smooth as a bottomless coffin, about three feet apart and seemingly holdless. It was difficult to conceive how he had survived eight hours jammed across it.

'You should be able to get out to the left,' Hamish shouted from below. 'I took the chimney because the ordinary way up was covered in ice.'

I was only too glad to avoid it and started to traverse across broken rocks towards a welcoming band of sunlit snow. A few minutes later we were both standing near the top of the Buachaille, our wet clothes steaming in the sun.

CHAPTER THREE

Between Air Force and Army

My call-up papers arrived shortly after my return from Scotland, and in early March 1953, I joined the Royal Air Force to do my National Service. Much to my surprise I found that I enjoyed Service life. Perhaps after leading a rather solitary, fatherless childhood, when I had always felt oddly different, in some ways inferior, to other boys at school, I was now an integral part of a large organisation, in effect a family, in which I could submerge myself.

Because I had the right academic qualifications I was automatically put up for a National Service commission, and passed the selection board; questioned, I was asked if I wanted to apply for a permanent commission and decided to have a try, choosing the R.A.F. Regiment, which sounded more exciting than one of the administrative branches. One of the selecting officers on the Regular Commissions Board talked me into trying for a flying commission.

'Why don't you want to be a pilot?' he asked.

I didn't like to say that the idea had little appeal for me, as I thought this would doom my chances from the start: flying tends to be a holy word in the Air Force.

'I don't think I've got fast enough reactions, sir,' I told him.

'We've got experts who are paid to find that out. Shall I put you down for Air Crew?'

'Yes, please do, sir. I've always dreamt of flying.'

It did not really matter what I said, as I was sure I should never get through the aptitude tests.

I passed the board, and to my amazement, got through the aptitude test. It was quite a job conditioning myself to the thought that I was going to be a pilot. I went to Cranwell, the Royal Air Force College, in the autumn, but for the first two terms we got no nearer to an aircraft than the planes constantly buzzing over our heads. We were submitted to an intensive and very unpleasant basic training. The only thing that kept us going was dreaming of the pleasures ahead, when we would become full flight cadets, each have a room of our own, and learn to fly.

Once we did start flying, however, my own doubts about my aptitude proved more accurate than the tests of the experts. I was ham-handed in the cockpit of the aircraft and was completely incapable of judging height and distance in relation to the manipulation of the controls. My instructor couldn't even trust me on the ground after I nearly ran the plane, a Chipmunk, into a petrol tanker!

One by one, the other members of my term were judged to be sufficiently competent to go solo, and soon I was the only one to be flying with an instructor. I never really enjoyed flying; it was too foreign to me. I was like a person with a strong aversion to heights, trying to climb. Nevertheless, I hated the thought of being beaten, and wanted to make a success of this.

At last I was told I was going to have a flight with the Chief Flying Instructor; this was usually the last step before getting the 'chop'.

At first it went quite well; I even had hopes of being able to put up a creditable performance. I got the plane off the ground without too much trouble and was ready to take it on the old familiar circuit round the airfield. I knew it off pat – that I had to turn over the cricket pavilion, cut my engine above the clock tower, and lower the flaps above the parade ground. I should then have been at just the right height to bring the plane down at the end of the airfield.

But the Chief Instructor was full of guile.

'We'll go for a bit of a run,' crackled over my earphones. 'I'll take over for a bit.'

He took me to another airfield.

'You can put her down there,' he told me.

I knew none of the landmarks, but thought I could manage it. The landing strip looked absurdly small from a thousand feet as I made my circuit, came into the final leg, and realised with a blank horror that I had not lost sufficient height; I was still five hundred feet up, when I came opposite the caravan at the end of the runway, when I should have been just above the deck. I did another circuit, firmly kept cool, but it was no good, I was still a hundred feet up.

I was getting desperate; I had forgotten all about passing or failing; I just wanted to get the bloody plane on to the ground. I did an extra long circuit, was limping along at stalling speed only fifty feet from the ground when we were still some miles from the field; my passenger displayed immense powers of self-control in remaining silent. At last we reached the end of the field; one wing was lower than the other, we were askew to the runway, but the only I could think of was to get her down at all costs. I slammed back the stick, we lost airspeed and dropped to the ground, bounced crazily from one wheel to the other, much too fast, nearly out of control.

A tired voice came from the back.

'I think I'd better take over.'

We roared away from the airfield and back to Cranwell. I could not stop the tears coming to my eyes for I knew that this was the end of my flying, that I had failed.

I was given the chance of becoming a navigator or transferring to the ground side of the Air Force, but realised that I could never enjoy being entirely dependent on machinery, or cope with the wealth of technical knowledge one needed as a navigator, and the ground jobs were even less attractive, being entirely desk-bound. I had been happy at Cranwell, however, and had enjoyed the Service life; I therefore decided to transfer into the army and try to get into Sandhurst.

It was now midsummer and the Sandhurst term did not start until September; for two months I was in a happy limbo between Army and Air Force. I received the princely sum of £3 a week and was technically on duty at home – this meant that I could not leave the country. I spent the entire summer in North Wales, in the road-menders' hut by the Cromlech Boulders in the Llanberis Valley. During the week there were never more than a couple of other inhabitants, but at weekends there were sometimes up to fifteen, squeezed sardine-like on its floor. We were happy enough to put up with the discomfort, however, for the weekenders usually left a good stock of provisions to fill our own scanty larder; after nightly visits to the Pen y Gwryd Hotel, there was little money left for food.

The other permanent inhabitant of the hut was Ginger Cain. He was in his early twenties and had just left university prematurely. In a way we were both in the same boat, for we were both awaiting 'Boards', mine the Regular Commissions Board and his the Conscientious Objectors' Board. He was a born rebel, with a shock of undisciplined ginger hair, a big nose and a quick, wolf-like grin. Our routine in the hut could not have been further removed from service life, and Ginger could never understand why I wanted to give it all up and return to bondage; looking back, neither can I, but at the time, although I loved the feckless, irresponsible way of life in Wales, I felt I had to have a steady career, and, in fact, actively looked forward to life in the army.

I was summoned before the Regular Commissions Board at the end of July. We spent three days crossing 'crocodile-infested rivers' on the lawns of a large country house, competed in discussion groups and worked on intelligence tests. I now felt quite an old hand, having survived two similar boards. My final interview was with a colonel who was a caricature of the traditional Colonel Blimp. He had a swollen, red nose, a bristling mous-tache, and a black labrador who barked at regular intervals. When I was in full flight, describing why I wanted to make the army my career, he would roar – 'Shut up, you bastard! No, not you – the dog.'

After the Board I returned to Wales, and a few days later learnt that I had passed. Ginger also was successful, being registered as a conscientious objector, so we both got drunk in celebration of our mutual success. We quickly settled down into a pleasant, easy rhythm of existence; there was little incentive to climb, for that summer was an unusually wet one, even for Wales. The crags were rarely dry, and Clogwyn du'r Arddu was swathed in slime for the entire summer. We snatched our climbs between showers or on the odd fine day, but since we had no transport and little enthusiasm for walking, were restricted to those within easy reach of the hut. Each night we made a pilgrimage to the Gwryd, not so much for the beer, as for the favours of the girls working there.

The history of climbing in the Llanberis Valley is fairly recent: the crags are steep and vegetated, merging into the hillside, and until the 1930s were avoided by climbers; but then Menlove Edwards, a man of immense strength and pioneering zeal, who was fond of steep and mossy rock, put up a number of routes on them. In many ways he was the real father of modern climbing in this country. There was a pause during the war, but in 1947, Peter Harding and Tony Moulam filled in some of the obvious gaps left by Menlove Edwards. They were able to push the standard a little higher, making full use of their technical competence gained in practising on gritstone outcrops and of the improvement in equipment – the use of nylon ropes and running belays. Peter Harding produced a guide-book to the valley in 1950 and in recognition of the increased difficulty of his new routes, introduced two new standards – *extremely severe* and *exceptionally severe*.

In the previous three years, I had slowly worked my way through the new guide-book, ticking off routes with a youthful enthusiasm, and that summer I ventured on to the extremes. I had now nearly finished the book and so nerved myself to take a step into the unknown, to attempt some of the routes put up by Joe Brown.

In 1954 a fog of myth surrounded his name; he had made a large number of first ascents in the Llanberis Pass and on Clogwyn du'r Arddu, on stretches of rock that seemed so steep and intimidating that they had been dismissed as impossible by other climbers. The Cenotaph Corner on Dinas Cromlech, a right-angled gash between sheer walls, that from below looked completely holdless, was typical of his climbs. He had made many of these routes as early as 1951 and yet no one outside his own close circle had plucked up courage to repeat them. I had never seen him, for the Rock and Ice, the club he belonged to, tended to keep to themselves, and anyway I was only on the fringe of the climbing world, never having climbed on gritstone from where this new wave of climbers originated. There were any number of stories told about him, that he was small and light, that his arms hung down to his knees, that he had superhuman strength; one imagined an ape-like creature. It was said that no one of normal build could possibly repeat his climbs; a depressing thought, for I was nearly six foot tall and of very average strength. Nevertheless, I resolved to try one of his routes and chose Sickle, on Clogwyn y Grochan, because it was rated as only *very severe* and not *XS*. This did not do much to reassure us, however, for we took it for granted that a 'Brown *VS*' would be much harder than anything that had ever been done before.

In the course of the summer we did a few more of his climbs, but familiarity made them no easier or less intimidating. They still held an aura of mystery and terror that is difficult to comprehend today, in 1966. Although few other climbers were trying them, their ascent did not require the build of a superman; it was more a question of a refined, very precise technique. Brown's routes tended to take lines that at first glance looked impossible and had been dismissed as such by earlier climbers, but once on them we found that there were just sufficient holds.

Our best effort was Surplomb, another route on Clogwyn y Grochan, up a series of particularly savage grooves. It started up a blank wall, which was crossed by standing in a sling, balanced on a spike the size of a thumbnail; then came a fiercely overhanging crack, followed by a V groove that slowly opened out, until at the top I was barely braced across it by my toes and the small of my back, and felt that it was about to spew me out. There was no protection and it was now necessary to pivot round on one's toes to grasp the smooth, square-cut edge of the bulge that thrust one out of the seeming security of the groove. It was the hardest climb I had ever done, and I was a good hour braced at the top of that groove. Our bubbling egos were slightly deflated when we learnt that Brown had made the first ascent in nailed boots during a snowstorm. Even so, the climb still has the reputation of being one of the hardest in the Llanberis Pass.

Towards the end of August, the weather went from bad to worse; it was almost a relief to leave Wales for the next stage in my career. Before going to Sandhurst I had to be absorbed into the Regular Army as a recruit. I had chosen my own county regiment, the Royal Fusiliers, whose depot was in the Tower of London. I spent three days there as a private, employing every dodge I had learnt in the Air Force to avoid doing any fatigues. It was certainly an interesting time – the barracks, of Victorian vintage, are on one side of the Inner Bailey of the fortress, immediately opposite the White Tower. We recruits felt like prisoners in the Tower, for we were not allowed in any parts of it which were used or even in view of the public – this put everywhere out of bounds except a narrow lane between the walls and the back of the barracks; its entire length was in full view of the regimental policemen, whose mission in life was to terrorise newly joined recruits. The barracks, in 1954, were full of the atmosphere of the past. Tiny windows, one lavatory for about thirty recruits and no hot water. We ate in a vault that would have done good service as a dungeon. The other recruits, who came from the East End of London, were not quite sure what to make of me, but treated me with good-humoured indulgence and gave me any amount of advice.

After three days, dressed in ill-fitting khaki, I went on to the Royal Military Academy, Sandhurst. We spent most of the first two months on the drill square, being bellowed at by Guards sergeant-majors.

We each had our own small room, a great luxury, and six of us shared a servant. Most of these were nearing retiring age and had been at the Academy for years; Jack, my servant, was the second oldest, with over thirty years service to his credit. A confirmed snob, he delighted in telling me of the young gentlemen who had been through his hands in the past.

'They were a much better class than we get today, such nice young gentlemen, all from the best public schools. The Academy just isn't the same today,' he'd murmur, looking at me reproachfully. I am afraid I did not measure up to his standards. My next door neighbour came closer to his ideal, for he had been to Winchester, rushed off to London in mid-week to attend deb parties and was going into the Scots Guards.

There were many others like John, and they naturally formed a well-knit group within the Academy. They had the same backgrounds, went to the same parties, all knew each other or had mutual friends, and were going into the same kind of regiments – the Brigade of Guards, Cavalry and so on. They were full of self-confidence, at times were arrogant and had a firm though unspoken code of what was, or was not, good form. They undoubtedly had a strong influence on the rest of the Academy. For a start, one could not help being a little envious. I also should have liked to flit off to London to deb parties, to attend hunt balls, to have the same self-confidence. As a result, many of us with very ordinary, middle-class back-grounds aped some of their ways, conforming with the atmosphere that pervaded Sandhurst. I hid in the back of my wardrobe the unfashionable, double-breasted blue suit which I had bought whilst at Cranwell, and acquired the Sandhurst leisure uniform: tight cavalry twill trousers, plain coloured waistcoat and tweed jacket. I even equipped myself with a bowler hat – bought second-hand, and an umbrella, for my forays in London which rarely got farther than my home in Hampstead. My only girlfriend at the time, a straight-thinking, Northern lass, who was at a domestic science college in Leicester, was, I think, slightly appalled by my affectation. I became acutely conscious of my own social limitations and quite unconsciously began to add an exaggerated public school veneer to my ordinary south-country accent. I, and many others, were simply conforming to the Sandhurst mould, not consciously but because we were adaptable and wanted to be part of this society.

I thoroughly enjoyed my stay at Sandhurst, and flung myself into everything with immense enthusiasm; the study of war had always interested me, and playing at soldiers in the woods behind Camberley was great fun, just like cowboys and Indians, except that we had real rifles and thunderflashes. I was even made an under-officer in my final term – this meant that one carried a sword around on parade – and passed out quite high in the Order of Merit.

I had chosen to join the Royal Tank Regiment, and, after a short introductory course, was sent out to Germany to join the 2nd Tanks. It was a real awakening, for suddenly I realised that the two years spent learning to be an officer had taught me nothing of how to handle a small group of men and supervise the care and maintenance of three fifty-ton Centurion tanks. I was full of ideas learnt at Sandhurst, was very keen, impatient and headstrong; shy and unsure of myself, yet determined to impose my will, to have complete command. My predecessor, a National Serviceman, had been happy-go-lucky and fairly idle, yet had had a sound mechanical knowledge of his tanks and a likeable, friendly personality. I knew the tanks were badly maintained, were not sufficiently clean, that the crews were lazy, but I did not know how to put things right. I plunged into the fray, often with insufficient thought, too proud to ask my sergeant's advice. As a result, I often demanded the impossible and then had to back down. I was too conscious of the pips on my shoulders and my own dignity – I hesitated to work in with the lads, thinking that my job was to supervise.

It took me a good year to repair the damage done in those first weeks. A troop of tanks is a small, close-knit unit, and the crew of each tank a still smaller one – just four people with different jobs, one to drive, one to fire the gun, one to load it and operate the wireless, one to command and help the other three members whenever necessary. At Sandhurst we had been warned of the dangers of 'familiarity breeding contempt', but in the close confines of this mobile, steel box, one had no choice. One's crew were soon familiar with one's personal habits, weaknesses and character. It was no good erecting a stockade of discipline, of stiff upper lip; one had to earn their friendship and, at the same time, maintain their respect – discipline and obedience followed quite naturally from that.

Being an armoured regiment, there was never much likelihood of our going into real action – tanks were not used for internal security of the Malayan and Cyprus variety. We therefore trained in Germany for a full-scale war. If one paused to think, it all had a touch of make-believe; our equipment and organisation could not possibly stand up to a full-scale nuclear fight. But in exercises, atom bombs were flung around with gay abandon and we reluctantly dug our six-foot-deep trenches with eighteen inches overhead cover, or cowered for hours on end, inside our tanks, all hatches closed to gain protection from enemy fall-out. It was then that one's powers of persuasion were most needed to convince the soldiers that it was all worth while.

But for the most part, tank training was a really magnificent game, the best I have ever played. The big exercises were the best. They often lasted several days and we got little or no sleep, reaching a state of complete exhaustion. I always felt sorry for the unfortunate infantry plodding along through the fields with very little idea of where they were going or what was going on beyond their own narrow field of vision. They were the pawns in the fight, but we raced across the country – Juggernauts encased in steel, smashing through walls, scything through young trees, the wireless crackling in our headphones with messages to other tanks or troops, giving us a picture of the course of the battle.

Although I enjoyed my work as a troop commander, I began to wonder after a time, if I fitted into the Regular Army, or anyway, into this particular regiment. I soon found that I had little in common with the other regular officers, with the exception of a couple who had the same doubts as myself. But, most of all, I missed the company of climbers, even more than the actual climbing. We were stationed in the centre of the North German plain, there were no hills for miles around and I had been unable to find anyone even remotely interested in climbing. There could not be a greater contrast than between the free-and-easy relationships of mountaineers and the rank-consciousness of a foreign garrison. In England, while at Sandhurst, I had been able to escape at weekends, but in the Regiment, I was part of a tightly knit community. We worked together during the day, saw each other every mealtime and went to the same cocktail parties. We might just as well have been stationed on an oasis in the middle of the desert, we had so little social contact with officers from other Regiments – and none at all with our German neighbours. In a country with a large surplus of women, some of us fought a highly competitive struggle for the favours of a handful of English nursing sisters and the rest bottled up their sexual instincts until they returned home on leave – very few had German girlfriends.

Unless one was completely immersed in the regiment, its work, social life and intrigues, one could not help finding it all a bit empty; but there were no other outlets, no escape. I was unable to plunge myself into its life, much as I wanted to; my companions spoke a different language, had different values. At times, in my first year, I felt very lonely.

CHAPTER FOUR

First Alpine Season – on the Eiger

There was a distant clatter of falling stones; the gurgle of running water. My ears still tingled with the maniacal buzz of flies from the Alpine pasture we had just left. The sun was hot on my neck, my clothes wet with sweat. My foot slipped on a patch of steeply banked scree and I cursed under my breath; cursed the heat, the smooth, rounded, grey rock, the piles of debris and, above all, Hamish who was scrambling so quickly, with such confidence, just ahead. Beyond him and all around, stretched the rock, grey, yellow, black, more of it than I had ever before seen. The scale was so vast. Even on that hot, still afternoon the Face held a lurking threat. I asked myself yet again what I was doing on the North Wall of the Eiger.

Back in Münster, a few weeks before, I had received Hamish's letter suggesting that we should attempt it. I suppose I should have laughed outright at his suggestion and refused, for I had not yet been to the Alps and had little experience of ice climbing, but back in 1957 the Eiger was not nearly so much in the news as it is today, and I had read very little about it. I knew it had claimed several lives before the war when fanatical young Germans had hurled themselves at its defences, and that was all. I had great confidence in Hamish's ability, however, so shrugged my shoulders and thought, 'Well, it'll be a good start to my Alpine career.' In fact, at that time, it had been climbed twelve times and had claimed fourteen lives. Perhaps, had I known this, I should not have been so blasé.

I travelled down from Germany in early July, to meet Hamish at Grindelwald, the village below the Eiger. I craned out of the open window of the crowded little train that rattled its way up the deep, pine-clad valleys of the foothills, past precipitous limestone walls larger than any crag in Britain – yet here no one had even thought of climbing them. At the head of the valley I caught exciting glimpses of snow peaks; but it was only just outside Grindelwald, when the train crept round a spur, that I saw the North Wall of the Eiger. It was in deep shadow, tier upon tier of dull grey ice and dark rock, on a scale greater than I had ever imagined. Perhaps I had been ridiculously naïve, over-confident in my ability as a rock-climber, to think of pitting my strength against such a face, but one glance at it was enough: I felt afraid and began heartily to regret ever having agreed to go on to it.

There was no sign of Hamish at the station. Only a couple of days before I had received a cryptic telegram: 'Meet me Grindelwald 7 July Manx Norton.' Who or what was Manx Norton? Could it be the name of a chalet or restaurant in Grindelwald? It did not seem likely but I could think of no better explanation. I had imagined Grindelwald as a tiny Alpine village, packed with climbers. In fact it was a rambling little town crowded with tourists and had all the amenities of a resort. Prices were high and there were very few climbers in the streets. I searched for Hamish all day and began to wonder if I should ever find him. I even asked at the tourist bureau if there was a place, or person, called 'Manx Norton'.

That evening, quite by chance, I met him coming down the path from the Kleine Scheidegg – the hotel immediately below the Eiger. He was full of enthusiasm, greeting me as if we had parted only a couple of days before, rather than three years.

'Ah, hello, Chris. I'm glad you got here all right. I've been up to the Face today; it's in perfect condition. We'll go on it tomorrow.' His enthusiasm was overwhelming. He had discovered a flat in a chalet at only three francs a day, had found the only cheap food-shop in the town, and had picked up any amount of gossip about the Face. I have never known anyone get himself settled into a place so well as Hamish does. I even discovered the identity of 'Manx Norton'.

'Oh, that's my bike. I thought it might help you to find me. There can't be any like it in Europe. It's stripped down for racing. Did a hundred on it all the way down the Autobahn. The only trouble with it is there's no silencer, so you have to be careful in the towns, and I've taken off the lights, so you can't ride it at night,' he told me.

That night we sorted out our gear. I was blissfully ignorant of the equipment needed for a major Alpine climb.

'Have you got a duvet?' he asked.

'What's that?' I replied.

'A down-filled jacket. You can take a sleeping-bag, it will be just as warm if not warmer. How about a bivvy sack?' I looked blank. 'You'll need something in case the weather breaks. I've got a plastic bag that I made specially.' He got it out. It was big enough to cover him in a long, waterproof cocoon. 'But there is no room for you in it,' he went on. 'Let's see – you'll be all right in this.'

He produced a length of plastic material in the shape of a tube, about four feet long. In the event of bad weather I could use it to protect either my head and shoulders, the lower part of my body or my legs. Such was the force of his enthusiasm that I accepted it without a murmur. We had no ice-pitons, but bought a couple the next morning; we should have had at least six. My anorak was made of light nylon and was more suitable for skiing than tackling a hard climb. Hamish borrowed my commando frame-rucksack since his was falling to pieces.

Our only clue to the route was a postcard he had bought that day. I was happily ignorant of how badly equipped we were, while Hamish was quite accustomed to climbing with the bare minimum. In the three years since I had seen him, he had emigrated to New Zealand, made many first ascents in the New Zealand Alps and had taken part in a two-man Himalayan Expedition, operating on a shoe string.

'We had hoped to try Everest,' he told me. 'The Swiss, who were on it in 1952, left big dumps of food all the way up to the South Col and we were going to use these. It's a pity that John Hunt and his boys got there first. All the same we went to Khumjung and tried Pumori – carried 190 pounds each on the approach march. We could only afford one Sherpa and he wasn't much good, he didn't carry much at all but was a good sort. When we paid him off at Namche he offered to give us his knife, fork and mug. We paid him for them as eating with pitons and tent-pegs wasn't very hygienic. We reached over 22,000 feet on Pumori but the weather was bloody awful and our equipment was none too good: my sleeping-bag was a thirty-shilling, boy scout model and even colder than I had expected.'

Hamish was a hard man but I was not sure if I was. That night I got very little sleep as I thought round and round every possible disaster and began to wish that I had chosen a slightly less formidable companion. If only we could have some bad weather before we were established on the Face!

Unfortunately, it was a perfect morning with not a cloud in the sky, so we completed our preparations and early that afternoon caught the train to Kleine Scheidegg. The Face drops straight into Alpine pastures; there are no introductory ice slopes or glaciers. One moment you are walking through lush grass, the air heavy with the smell of moist hay, and the next you are embarked on the lowest rocks.

The first thousand feet or so give relatively easy climbing and we were planning to scramble as high as possible that afternoon, ready for a quick start the next morning on the first difficult step. Or, at least, Hamish was hoping, for I was still praying for a miracle; anything to give us an excuse for retreat. As I struggled up behind him I took careful note of the way back and on seeing a good ledge protected by an overhang and still fairly low on the Face – well below the top of the First Shattered Pillar – I persuaded Hamish to stop for the night. We had only climbed about eight hundred feet but I was already tired, for our rucksacks weighed forty pounds each and I had never before climbed with a sack on my back.

As Hamish prepared our evening meal, I gazed down at the comforting safety of Grindelwald sprawled far below us, and across the rolling foothills towards the setting sun. Just before dark my prayers were answered: a thin scum of cloud spread over the western horizon and slowly crept towards us. The clouds were not particularly threatening in appearance, and since that time I have often started a long Alpine climb in very much more threatening weather, but that night they were the heaven-sent excuse for me to remark: 'Hamish, I reckon the weather is breaking. Look at those clouds.'

'They're nothing to worry about. They will probably have cleared by morning,' he replied.

'Well, I don't want to be caught out in bad weather. We could easily be trapped here if it breaks during the night. I'm going down now.' And I started to pack my rucksack. Hamish followed suit, no doubt thinking dark thoughts about cowardly Sassenachs.

We stumbled down in pitch dark, our head-torches throwing small pools of light around us. A drop of three feet vanished into deep shadow just the same as a drop of three hundred. The scree skidded under our feet and the little walls and slabs that had seemed so easy when we had scrambled up them, now felt treacherously holdless. It was past midnight when we reached the final drop above the bergschrund at the foot of the Face. I only began to feel safe again as I took the last jump on the rope over the gap between snow and rock. We were off the Eiger. The Face loomed above us: huge, black, menacing.

We spent the night in the meadow immediately below the Face. Next morning, to my relief, heavy clouds hid the tops of the peaks and there could be no question of returning immediately to the Wall. I, certainly, had no desire ever again to set foot on it. Given good conditions I think we might well have climbed it, for Hamish had sufficient experience and ability to contend with all the complex mountaineering problems the Face set and I was capable of following him up it and of taking a share in the lead on the rock pitches, but if the weather had turned while we were on the Face, something that happens all too often, we had nothing in reserve. Our equipment, as I have said, was appallingly inadequate and the lack of balance in the party would then have told to our cost. When struggling for one's life in a maelstrom of rushing snow and wind, every member of the party needs to be equally capable, for one slip can bring disaster to all.

However, at the time, my ignorance was so complete that I did not fully realise just how great a risk we had taken. My fears were more a matter of instinct: I had become used to taking the lead on climbs, to making the decisions. But on the Eiger, or for that matter on any Alpine climb, it was inevitable that I should be out of my depth. The scale of everything was so great; there was snow and ice to contend with as well as rock. I wanted to go on easy climbs where I could gain experience as a leader and then progress to harder routes, in the same way as I had done on British hills. But Hamish was still full of ambition. Having escaped one great North Face, he wanted to take me on to another: the Walker Spur of the Grandes Jorasses.

'But it's rock all the way, Chris. You'll have no difficulty at all. Nothing on it is harder than *very severe*. It's just like one of your Welsh rock-climbs but a bit longer.'

In fact, 4000 feet longer but we had to find a compromise somewhere, so, with some misgivings, I agreed to our new venture. We set off for Chamonix that afternoon, Hamish on his Manx Norton and I on foot, intending to hitch-hike, being short of funds.

The atmosphere of Chamonix was completely different from that of Grindelwald. The former hugged the bottom of a sombre valley dominated by the jagged teeth of the Aiguilles and the massive snow hump of Mont Blanc, whose glaciers seemed ready to engulf the town. Grindelwald, on the other hand, was set in spacious meadows, a pretty toy village looking across to the mountain. Once in the streets of Chamonix the contrast was even greater. There was nothing beautiful about the town and it was crowded with trippers who had come in coaches for the day. It had the atmosphere of a third-rate seaside resort, but for all that it was a real climbing centre. The camp site in the woods at the back of the town was filled with the tents of climbers – it was easy to recognise the British for they were by far the most untidy. In the streets, too, there were climbers of every nationality, reading the weather forecast in the C.A.F. bureau, drinking at the bars, lounging in the pavement cafés.

Hamish was anxious to reach the foot of the Jorasses that same evening for the weather was once again perfect and the local experts told us that the rock was free from snow. There was no time to be lost, therefore, for the Walker Spur rarely comes into good condition, since it only gets the sun in the early morning and late evening and the Face is one of the highest in the Alps. As a result, snow takes a long time to clear from its smooth, granite slabs, which are impassable when covered with a veneer of ice. In some seasons, it never comes into condition.

But before setting out we had to buy food and get some better equipment. Hamish also found any number of acquaintances with whom to discuss the weather and other mutual friends. As morning crept into afternoon, I began to wonder if we should ever get away.

'We'd better hurry, Hamish, or we shall never reach the Leschaux Hut before dark,' I ventured.

'It's all right, Chris, I know the Aiguilles like the back of my hand. I'll find the hut all right. We'll just go and see my old friend Contamine. He might have some useful information about the Walker,' and we went to see Contamine, one of Chamonix's outstanding guides.

It was five o'clock before we were finally ready to leave, catching the train up to Montenvers, about 3000 feet above the town. From there we had to walk. The Grandes Jorasses stand at the head of the Leschaux Glacier – a tributary of the huge Mer de Glace that forms the main high road into the centre of the Mont Blanc massif. We shouldered our way through the crowd of tourists who were thronging round the picture-postcard stalls and trooping down the path to see 'the wonders of nature' in a man-made ice grotto.

The top of the North Face of the Grandes Jorasses, its rock a rich brown in the evening sun, jutted above some lower, intervening mountains. It looked remote, untouchable, but it did not have the air of menace that I experienced when I looked up at the Eiger. I felt a little apprehensive, but beyond that was excited at the thought of feeling the rough granite; of finding a way up the huge Face. Even the walk to its foot was exciting for I had never stood on a glacier before. As we scrambled down the steep bank, I could feel a breath of cool air, from the expanse of bare ice, brush my cheek. The surface under foot was rough, and crunched crisply. Everywhere was the gurgle of running water: from the bowels of the glacier, from little runnels down its surface. There were others beside ourselves, all walking purposefully towards their different objectives, yet united in the same aim, the same feeling of expectation and hope.

Distances were deceptive. From Montenvers our turning had seemed close at hand but as we plodded up the glacier it never seemed to get any closer. Meanwhile, the light was rapidly fading. By the time we reached the Leschaux Glacier and had negotiated the piles of boulders swept together by the junction of the two rivers of ice, it was totally dark, but Hamish was still full of confidence; he was now on his home ground.

The novelty of walking over crisp ice was beginning to pall, my rucksack to feel heavier, its straps to bite into my armpits; and the angle of the ice began to steepen. Deep shadows of open crevasses appeared on either side and a dusting of fresh snow thickened into a heavy covering.

'We're nearly there now, Chris. It's on the left-hand side of the glacier. There it is' – pointing to a dark mass some distance away. We increased our pace but as we drew closer, we saw that it was only a boulder.

'It can't be far, Chris. It's just a matter of keeping going until we hit on it.'

At that point he vanished from sight. He had fallen into a covered crevasse. Fortunately it was a narrow one and he was able to jam his shoulders on its lip. I helped him up and we continued our plod with greater care. I felt as if I was in the middle of a mine-field where one false step could spell disaster. Even Hamish's invincible optimism seemed slightly shaken and he admitted that we might have gone past the hut.

'We had better doss out for the night, Chris. We can sleep under this boulder. I've slept in a lot worse places,' he said, when we stumbled on a rock, jammed across a half-filled crevasse. Having made the decision, Hamish dived under the boulder, formed a platform in the snow and in a matter of minutes was completely encased in a plastic cocoon. I did as best I could with my short tube. We had sleeping-bags, so were sufficiently warm. Hamish immediately dropped into a deep sleep; he never seemed to notice either discomfort or cold. I took longer, for our position was cramped and I was unable to keep the snow from touching, and therefore wetting, the sleeping-bag. Also, there is something claustrophobic about sleeping in a crevasse: I can never help fearing that the walls are going to close in during the night, making an icy trap. To add to our discomfort, it began to rain and by dawn the entire sky had clouded over. We could see the foot of the Walker Spur only a few hundred feet above us, and far below we could just discern the Leschaux Hut, a tiny blob, clinging to the hillside beside the glacier. I consoled myself with the thought that I had experienced my first Alpine bivouac, though the circumstances could not have been much more ignominious.

The weather was much too threatening to think of going on to the Spur and anyway, everything we had was wet, so we walked back down to the hut. It was little more than a shell, for an avalanche had swept it some years before. The roof was left standing, supported by a skeleton of wooden struts, but the walls had vanished save for a small, box-like enclosure in one corner that gave shelter from the wind and rain. It was derelict in a pleasing way: there was just room for two in the tiny compartment, and it was warm and cosy inside. We stayed there for three days and in that time I felt very close to the mountains.

Most Alpine huts are packed with people, throb with activity and, strongly built against the forces of weather, are bastions of man; but the Leschaux hut had fallen to the power of the mountain, had been abandoned by its guardian and, as a result, this crazy pile of wood and corrugated iron seemed part of the hillside. Lying in my sleeping bag, the rain hammering on the roof, I was soon asleep.

It quickly became obvious that we should be unable to attempt the Walker Spur, for this high face takes a long time to clear of freshly fallen snow, but opposite the hut, on the other side of the glacier, was a smaller peak – the Aiguille de Tacul. Its upper part offered a fine rock buttress which, after carefully examining the guide-book, we found had never been climbed. Hamish had always loved new routes so he decided to wait out the weather and tackle it on the first fine day we had.

I now had my first lesson in patience: much time in the high mountains is spent waiting for the right weather; and the higher the mountain, the longer the wait. In this case we had little food and no books to read, but Hamish was fine teacher and a good companion. He could spend hours, just lying in his sleeping-bag in a state of semi-coma. I, on the other hand, have always tended to be restless, impatient for action. The hours passed slowly, broken only by mealtimes when we had all too little to prepare – a quarter packet of spaghetti or soup with a slice of stale bread. We had brought with us enough food for three days on a climb, and were now trying to make it last four days while we waited. On a climb there is no time to notice hunger, but lying in a small hut all day, there is not much else to think about.

For three days, it rained. We were down to our last hunk of bread and half-packet of soup when, on the third evening, the clouds began to break up and the Grandes Jorasses, all plastered in snow, were dyed an unbeliev-able crimson by the rays of the setting sun.

'It'll be fine tomorrow,' said Hamish. 'We'll have a crack at that buttress over the way. It should be quite a good climb and we'll be on new ground.' I was only too happy to agree, for the proposed climb seemed very much more suited to my limited experience than our other ventures. It was a fine rock buttress of about fifteen hundred feet, perched on top of a steep little glacier.

We set out early the following morning on my first proper Alpine climb. The fact that we were attempting a new route made it all the more exciting. I felt at home on the rock. The scale, though much bigger than anything in Britain, was nothing like so vast as that of the Eiger. In fact, the summit of our little peak was barely higher than the base of the North Wall of the Jorasses. We climbed all day under the hot sun, slowly working our way up grooves and slabs. It was by no means a great climb, or even particularly difficult. We were not painstakingly following a description in a guide-book, but were picking out our own route, so there were no man-made limitations between us and the mountain, and our freedom was therefore the more complete. The course we took, and our success, depended entirely on our own judgement. To me this has always been the principal attraction of making a first ascent.

We reached the top just before dark. The pleasure of standing on the summit of my first real mountain was short-lived, for we now had to get back down. To any climber trained on British hills, this can be a terrifying experience. I was used to reaching the top of the crag and walking down round the side, but now we were perched on a real summit. Hamish had no doubts. 'Come on, Chris, we'll be benighted if we don't hurry up. We might as well take off the rope. We'll go quicker without it.' Yes, I thought, right to the bloody bottom at 'thirty-two feet per second per second', but I took it off and started to follow him down.

On steep rock I had been more agile than Hamish but now, as he scrambled down piled boulders and steep little walls, he showed his ability as a mountaineer, moving with a confident, easy rhythm. I was thoroughly frightened, tired by a long day and unaccustomed to climbing down. Hamish was always drawing away, disappearing into the gathering gloom.

'Come on, Chris,' he yelled, 'if you don't want a bivouac,' and I forced myself on, but the glacier far below never seemed to get any closer. When we at last reached level ground it was totally dark. A slow tramp across the glacier, a last, back-breaking little climb to the hut and we were able to collapse into our sleeping-bags, to lie back and listen to the purr of the primus as we brewed some tea. There was nothing left to eat but that did not matter.

I had to return to my regiment the next day. My sole climb had been an unconventional introduction to the Alps and in many ways a dangerous one. Hamish had perhaps been over-optimistic in planning to take a complete Alpine novice on such long and serious routes. On the other hand he was an excellent and extremely cautious mountaineer once he had embarked on a climb and I learnt a great deal from him.

On the train, as it raced across Germany, I began to dream of the next summer. Now I wanted to climb some of the easier routes, to gain confidence so that I could feel self-sufficient and at home on the granite walls and icefalls of the Mont Blanc massif.

CHAPTER FIVE

Fiascos on the Aiguilles

The following summer Hamish was even leaner and harder. He had spent the winter in the Himalaya, chasing non-existent Yeti through the valleys of Kulu. His face was frighteningly gaunt and he had grown a thin goatee that emphasised the hollowness of his cheeks. He even admitted to feeling run-down but was as full of ambitious plans as ever.

We arrived in Chamonix at the start of July and set up house in a tiny shepherd's hut a few minutes walk from Montenvers, 3000 feet above the town.

'There will be less temptation to spend any money,' said Hamish, 'and it's nearer the crags.'

It was much too early in the season and even the lowest peaks of the Aiguilles were plastered with snow, but at least this gave Hamish a chance to recoup, for there was nothing we could do but wait patiently. He seldom stirred from his sleeping bag, ate vast meals of army compo that I had plundered from my regiment, and spent hours examining every diagram in the guide-book for spaces unsullied by dotted lines.

'There's a grand route here, Chris. It'll be a real plum,' he announced one afternoon.

'What have you found this time?' I asked, full of suspicion.

After my experience of the previous year I was determined to avoid being involved in any more wild-cat ventures. I wanted to tackle some good, established routes, to find my feet in the Alps gradually.

'This really would be good,' he replied. 'Right up your street, rock all the way, fairly low and no objective dangers. Have a look. It's up the south-east éperon of the Pointe de Lépiney. Nothing's been climbed anywhere near it.' I was not going to give in that easily.

'I'll go on it, but only after we have done a practice climb. How about the West Face of the Pointe Albert?' I said.

'Right, that's a bargain. You can lead me up it and I'll get all the pegs out. It'll be like a pin-cushion. We might as well get something for our trouble and we could do with some more pegs once we get on to the new stuff.'

The Pointe Albert is a small peak, near the end of the Chamonix Aiguilles, whose west face is about seven hundred feet high and very steep. As a result, it is a popular training climb, particularly amongst British climbers, for it is not much higher than one of our own crags and yet gives good practice in the use of artificial techniques.

We intended to rake in the harvest, as pegs are expensive items to buy. I salved my conscience with the thought that the West Face was used as a training climb and that we were therefore doing a good service. It would be much better practice for the parties that followed us if they had to hammer in their own pitons. Hamish worked manfully and removed every peg on the climb. At the end of the day we were thirty the richer. But it was now up to me to meet my side of the bargain, to attempt Hamish's new route.

We walked up to the Aiguilles de l'Envers Hut one afternoon a few days later; the path runs steeply from the Mer de Glace up the south side of the Charmoz. The hut is like a small château, perched on a rocky promontory at the foot of the Tour Verte. Its castellan and only occupant was a young maid of Chamonix (in best story-book fashion). During the evening she displayed a hearty dislike for the English but thought the Scots were very gentle people.

We left the hut just before dawn and set out across the glacier. It was a fine, starlit night; the walls of the Aiguilles, black and jagged, towered to our right; below us swept the Mer de Glace, a great frozen river, gleaming faintly in the light of the quarter moon – its crevasses, like huge ripples, scored the surface.

Getting up in the middle of the night is a painful business; there is a moment when you ask yourself why on earth you do it and wish yourself in a warm bed. But once out in the cold, clear night, your senses are more than normally alert. Excitement at the thought of the climb ahead surges through your body as you stride across the glacier, crampons crunching into crisp snow, and plod, panting hard, up the final snow slope. Eyes search for the faint shadow of a hidden crevasse, pick out the best line through the chaotic shadows of an ice fall.

We had an hour's walk across the glacier and, just as the sun hit the top rocks of the Aiguilles far above us, we came round a buttress and saw our objective. One glance was enough to realise why it had never before been climbed: after a couple of hundred feet of steep slabs, the spur thrust out and upwards in a monstrous overhang.

'We'll never get up that,' I exclaimed.

'It always looks a lot worse from below,' Hamish replied cheerfully.

'Anyway, we can always find a way round it. Let's get our teeth into it and see what it's really like.'

We roped up and started up the bottom rocks but after a few pitches were forced off to the left. Soon we were in the gully that bordered our peak. I was almost relieved: we could follow it to the top and perhaps get back to the safety and comfort of the shepherd's hut that night, for it seemed quite easy all the way up, but Hamish was made of sterner stuff.

'We should be able to get back on to the spur from here, Chris. We must be above those big overhangs by now. Those slabs should give some interesting climbing,' said the master.

'But what's the point? We've been forced off the route and can easily get up the Col. We might just as well admit defeat and follow the natural line. It's bloody pointless looking for difficulty on a big face like this. Besides, the weather looks as if it is brewing up,' I replied.

'But we're going back to the natural line. You don't want to miss a grand new route, do you, when you're nearly up? Don't worry about the weather, that's just afternoon cloud.'

I surrendered and we left our nice, easy gully for the smooth, inhospitable slabs on the right. Progress now became desperately slow for there were few holds on the slab and we had to hammer in pitons. As Hamish struggled above, I gazed with longing at the gully we had just left. We were obviously not going to reach the top before dark, for the higher we got the steeper everything became, until our way was barred by a belt of overhangs. Below the overhangs was a fair-sized platform.

'We might as well spend the night here; it looks as if the weather is brewing up after all,' announced Hamish. The entire sky was covered by a scum of grey cloud and there were a few flakes of snow in the air. Everything around us was grey and black. Hamish dived into a hollow below a perched boulder and began mining his way into the ice that packed it. Soon only his feet were showing. Feeling rather disconsolate, I searched for my own shelter for the night and ended up in a coffin-like recess at the back of the ledge. With a shroud formed by my plastic bag, I felt anything but cheerful and spent the night brooding over gloomy thoughts. I was much too cold to sleep.

The dawn was dull grey, and a light dusting of snow covered our ledge, but the storm had not yet broken. After eating a slice of stale bread and some dried fruit, washed down by tea which we had boiled over a spirit stove, I attacked the overhang above our resting place. It thrust my body out over the void, but there was a good, wide crack in the back of a groove and I edged my way up this, hammering in wooden wedges; dangling in my étriers, I quickly forgot the cold of the night and began to enjoy myself.

Hammer another wedge in above, clip in the étrier, swing on to it – and suddenly I'm falling, head first, my legs caught in the rope somewhere above me. There's a violent jerk and I'm gazing into Hamish's upturned eyes and beyond him to the glacier a thousand feet below. My foot is still caught somewhere behind me.

'Your wedge came out,' stated Hamish. 'Are you all right?' and he lowered me down to the ledge. One of the lower wedges through which the rope ran had remained in place. I was trembling with shock; my heart pumped furiously; and then I was angry, with myself for making a mistake, with the rock for spurning me. My foot was numb and I wondered if I had broken anything. I cautiously took off my boot and worked my toes.

'There's nothing wrong with that,' said Hamish. 'A bit of a sprain; it might give some trouble if it stiffens up.'

'I'll have another go at the bastard,' I said, 'otherwise I might lose my nerve.' I went up again, hammered in another wedge until it was firm in the crack, but this time I used the rock rather than trust my entire weight to the étrier and the wedge. I jammed a hand in the crack, cocked my foot far to one side and, panting with exertion, heaved myself over the overhang on to a tiny ledge. The rock still bulged above my head: if anything it looked more difficult than the stretch I had just struggled up, but at least I had beaten the part I had failed on.

'Come on up, Hamish. It's your turn now.'

'What does it look like beyond you, Chris?' he called.

'Bloody awful. It's all overhanging.'

'It's going to take a lot of time then,' said Hamish, 'and I don't like the look of the weather. Even when we get up, there's going to be too much fresh snow on the other side of the ridge. I think we had better get back the way we came.' I did not need any persuading for there was very little fight left in me, but I hated the thought of trying to get back the way we had come. 'We should be able to escape on that easy-looking rock over to the left,' he added.

That was enough for me, and I abseiled down to him. At first our retreat went smoothly, over the easy-angled, broken rocks on the lower slopes of the Pointe Chevalier, but then we reached a deep-cut gully that plunged down out of sight towards the glacier. Hamish abseiled into it and I followed. Once in its bed we were trapped. The walls on either side were smooth and sheer, a waterfall tumbled down its bed. We started down it. The doubled rope dropped out of sight. Hamish went first; there was a long pause after he had vanished from view and I could hear nothing for the sound of rushing water. At last the rope went slack in my hands and I guessed he was down on the next ledge. It was my turn to follow. At first, I was able to keep out of the stream of ice-cold water, bridging with my feet on either side, but then I came to a bulge, a huge boulder wedged across the bed of the gully. Hamish was about fifty feet below, hanging from a piton hammered into a crack in the smooth wall. The rope hung completely free down to him, and I was soon spinning gently in mid-air with the water thundering about my ears. Hamish was also in the direct line of the waterfall and I had no choice but to share his peg and single foothold. I couldn't help wondering just how secure it was.

'Get a move on, Chris. If we don't get out of this bloody shower-bath soon, we'll freeze to death. Give me the end of the rope and I'll pull it down.' I handed it to him and he heaved on it. 'Give me a hand. It's a bit stiff,' he cried. We both heaved on the end of the rope, put all our weight on it, but it was no good, it just stretched a little but did not budge an inch.

'I'll try to climb out to one side and pull from over there,' said Hamish, 'that might free it.' He moved with desperate slowness and then came to a stop on the steep slab just beyond us. The water hammered on to my head, spread a freezing numbness over my body. We seemed so helpless and insignificant against the strength of the mountain: I began to think of death. I hated Hamish for being so slow, for landing us in this predicament.

'Let's have a try, Hamish. If I stay here any longer, I won't be able to move at all,' I shouted, longing to move, to escape from the pounding of the water. He came back and I took his place. Desperate with cold, I leapt at the slab and managed to get up it. From my new stance I was still unable to shift the rope, but free from the waterfall I could at least think, and I realised I should have to prusik up the doubled ropes. This is a technique in which a form of slip-knot is tied round the doubled ropes; it grips them when a body's weight is on the knot, but can be slipped up the ropes once it is free of weight. With two knots, used alternately, ropes can be climbed in perfect safety. Using this technique, I hoisted myself laboriously up the gully and cleared the ropes where they had jammed. We were not free of trouble, however, for we were still at least one rope-length above the glacier. The rock bulged out just below us, so we could not see the foot of the crag.

It was now my turn to go down first. As I started out, down the rope, I imagined the worst. Would I reach the end to find myself dangling in space, with no cracks in which to hammer a piton? Soon I stood poised on the bulge: the end of the rope dropped straight into the cavernous jaws of a huge rimaye. It was at least twelve feet wide and I could not guess how deep: it just vanished into impenetrable gloom. Fortunately, just above the gap was a narrow ledge and I slid down to this.

I have always been afraid of jumping, and here was something that seemed beyond my capabilities. Hamish was somewhere far above, and the end of the rope dangled in mid-air. Safety was just twelve feet away but what if I missed the jump, if the edge of rimaye broke under my feet? Even if I maintained my hold on the rope, I should be dangling, helpless, in the depths of the crevasse. I knew I couldn't do it.

'Hamish, there's a bloody great rimaye. Come on down.' At least he'd be company. It was heartening to see him sweep down towards me. He was not daunted by the rimaye but took a bold leap, swinging out on the rope and letting it run through his hands. Even so he landed on the very brink. I followed, very glad to have him on the other side, ready to field me.

The weather had now cleared and it was a brilliant, sunny afternoon. We presented a sorry sight as we plodded back to the hut, soaked to the skin. People who passed, looked at us strangely. What on earth could we have been up to on such a perfect day! It was nearly dark, but we could not face the prospect of seeing the young guardienne at the Aiguilles de l'Envers Hut; we had cut much too fine a figure the previous night, so we went straight down to the Mer de Glace.

Our trials were not over. The Mer de Glace is a main road, a mountain motorway; hundreds plod up it every day, but at night it looked different. Great shadows turned the glacier into a maze. A mere crease on the surface of the ice looked the same as a crevasse hundreds of feet deep. We were soon hopelessly lost. We could see the point where we should leave the glacier, but turn where we would, there was always a gulf between us and our goal. We were so tired we could have lain down and slept on the ice, but our clothes were sodden and there was a hard frost. Eventually we found the way: what normally takes half an hour, had taken us three.

Another fiasco – I swore to myself not to go on any more new routes until I had some solid experience behind me. At the time I felt depressed but in fact it is this kind of experience that gives some of the richest memories. You quickly forget the agony of icy water hammering on your head and remember only the humorous side of it all.

CHAPTER SIX

South-West Pillar of the Dru

The war of attrition continued. Hamish had not been daunted by our experience on the Pointe de Lépiney and the following morning was planning the next step in the campaign. I was buried in my sleeping-bag in the darkest corner of the hut for I had a bad cold: my head bulged with catarrh, a never-ending stream of phlegm flowed from my nose and I felt miserable.

'You should be fit by now, Chris,' he said. 'Here's just the route for us – The Shroud, up to the left of the Walker Spur. There must be a couple of thousand feet of ice on it and we could finish up the summit rocks of the Walker. There might be some stuff coming down it during the day, but we could climb the ice in the dark.'

'Look, Hamish, you can keep your new route and stuff it. I couldn't care less if it's the last great unclimbed problem in the Alps. I just want to be sure of getting to the top of one or two good, standard climbs. I can't do anything, anyway, until I've got rid of this cold.'

And so the argument went on for the next few days, while I snuffled away in my sleeping-bag and the rain hammered on the roof outside. At least our controversy provided a never-failing topic of conversation. For however heated we became, we continued, somehow, to enjoy each other's company and even the argument itself. At last we came to a compromise.

'I'll go on any route you name, provided that it has been done before,' I told him.

Hamish thought it over. 'Well, how about the South-west Pillar of the Dru? It's rock all the way and should clear quickly.'

In fact, it also had the reputation of being the hardest rock climb in the Mont Blanc massif.

From Montenvers, the Petit Dru is like the steeple of a Gothic cathedral, towering at the end of the mass of the building formed by the ridge of the Flammes de Pierre. Its West Face completely dominates the mountain scene with an upthrust of 3000 feet of sheer, seemingly featureless, granite. Its ascent in 1952 by a French party marked a major step forward in Alpine techniques. On the right or west, the face is bounded by a spur, the South-west Pillar; this was climbed in 1955 by Walter Bonatti, an Italian and one of the greatest climbers of this century. It was even more difficult than the face and yet he went on it by himself. It would have been a considerable feat for a strong party but as a 'solo' effort, it was incredible. Most of the way he could use artificial techniques for there were plenty of cracks into which he could hammer his pitons. He could get some degree of protection by threading a length of rope through several pegs and then attaching both ends to his body so that it formed a big loop; if a peg came out or he slipped, the rope would still be attached to some of the other pegs and would therefore hold him. But there must have been times when he could not give himself this kind of protection, when a single slip would have meant a fall of some thousand feet.

In effect he had to climb the Pillar twice, for, having made a few feet of upward progress, hammering in pitons as he went, he had to climb back down to take them all out, a labour normally shared between two. In addition, he had to carry nearly as much equipment as a party of two. There is a telling photograph he took when half-way up the Spur, of a rucksack dangling on the end of a rope – rock around it, rock below – entitled: 'My only companion – a rucksack'.

Solo climbing of this kind is a supreme test of mountaineering skill and self-reliance. Bonatti had five nights by himself, perched on tiny ledges: plenty of time to review the dangers that faced him. Had he lost his nerve he would have had little chance of survival. To add to the strain, he was on new ground, so that he did not even have the benefit of other people's experience on the same route. He had to find his own way, never certain if he could surmount the next obstacle or if he would have to retreat and try another line.

By 1958 four other parties had repeated his route and several more had retreated from it. The fastest party had spent three days on the climb. In the light of these subsequent ascents, Bonatti's achievement seemed all the more unbelievable.

I was both frightened and excited by our plans to attempt the Pillar. It seemed a vast undertaking but at least it was reputedly firm rock all the way and someone had been there before us. My confidence was further increased when our party was reinforced. Two young Austrians came to live in the room just below ours. They also were interested in attempting the Pillar and were obviously good mountaineers. We got on well together and soon established a firm friendship. Walter Phillip, the eldest, was studying at university in Vienna. Already he had quite a reputation, with several outstanding new routes in the Eastern Alps to his credit. In the previous year he had climbed the West Face of the Dru in a particularly fast time. Richard Blach, his companion, was only nineteen and slightly built, but we were soon to find that he was a brilliant climber.

We walked to the foot of the Dru on the first fine afternoon, across the Mer de Glace and up a long moraine ridge to a pile of boulders immediately below the face, where we planned to spend the night. The Pillar, grotesquely foreshortened, stretched above us, dyed a rich brown in the light of the setting sun. On the other side of the glacier we could just see the tourists, like black ants, milling round the station at Montenvers. The whistle of the last train, clear and sharp in the evening air; the gurgle of running water; the purr of the primus; all strengthened the feeling of peace around our bivouac.

Just before dark I noticed two small figures toiling up the moraine ridge that led to our boulders.

'I wonder if they're going for the Pillar as well?' I commented.

'That'll be Whillans,' said Hamish, 'or I'm very much mistaken. I heard in Snell's that he was asking about the Pillar. We are going to have quite a party.'

I wasn't sorry to see them – I was glad of any addition to the party. I had heard a great deal about Don Whillans; about his prowess as a climber and his reputation for toughness. Three years before, with Joe Brown, he had made the fourth ascent of the West Face of the Dru.

We watched the two figures slowly come closer. The foremost, cloth-cap on his head, was short and powerfully muscled – it was Don Whillans all right. He was carrying a huge rucksack bedecked with French loaves. His companion, also short but less strongly built, was Paul Ross, a well-known Lakeland climber.

They paused, talked a little: no doubt Don weighed us up, and then the pair carried on to the top of the Rognon.

'See you tomorrow,' Don called back from the gathering dark.

We set the alarm to two o'clock and settled down for the night. We had carried up our sleeping-bags, and so were warm and comfortable, but I did not sleep. I listened to the quiet breathing of the others and envied them their peace of mind. My own mind leapt from one thought to another: perhaps the weather would break when we were half-way up; was I capable of climbing nearly 3000 feet of difficult rock? I was wildly excited by the prospect of our venture, but was too conscious of this conflict between fear and anticipation.

At last the alarm jangled.

'There is much cloud,' muttered Walter.

'Aye, and it's too warm. I don't like the look of the weather,' added Hamish. 'It could do anything.'

'I think we should wait till dawn to see if it clears,' said Walter.

I was secretly relieved. It felt like a last-minute reprieve and I promptly dropped into a deep sleep, only to be roughly awakened after what seemed a few minutes.

'Wake up, Chris!' shouted Hamish. 'The clouds have cleared. It's going to be a good day.'

I peered out of my sleeping-bag: there were still some high clouds to the west.

'What about those?' I asked. 'It looks pretty changeable to me.'

'If we waited for a completely cloudless morning, we'd never get anything done. Those will clear during the day. We'd better get a move on. It's five already,' he replied.

We hurriedly cooked some breakfast, packed our sacks and started up the snow slope leading to the couloir which marked the start of the climb. To reach the Pillar we had to follow the gully for nearly a thousand feet.

'Don had a late start as well,' said Hamish, as we plodded up the crisp snow. 'Look, he is just starting the couloir.'

I could discern two small figures in the shadow of the gully.

'We climb solo at first,' announced Walter. 'It is not difficult and will be quicker.'

He stepped on to the edge of the rimaye, to stride across the gap which was only a couple of feet wide, but the edge promptly collapsed and Walter only saved himself by throwing himself backwards. It was an inauspicious start, but undeterred, he hurled himself once again at the rock on the other side and literally leapt up it. The other two followed and I brought up the rear. The angle was not very steep but the rock was worn smooth by ice and falling stones. The holds were all sloping and dusted with gravel that slipped under our feet like ball-bearings. I noticed that Don and Paul were roped-up and heartily wished that we were. I was soon left far behind and then I heard a shout from above. Walter had just raced past Don, slipped and landed on top of him. He was lucky not to go down all the way. I felt even more unhappy and was greatly relieved when I caught them up at the start of some steep ice, for at last they had got out the ropes. Hamish now came into his own and took the lead, cutting steps all the way with a steady, easy rhythm. Don and Paul were out to the left, but were able to move faster than we, for they both had crampons whilst we had only one pair in the entire party.

Pitch followed pitch. It was an oppressive place – everywhere there were signs of stone-fall: rocks embedded in ice, the snow grey with debris – and above us towered the Flammes de Pierre ready to engulf us. It was dark and bitterly cold in the gully, but high to our left we could see the plunging skyline of the Pillar, a golden brown in the morning sun. I longed to move swiftly to escape from our icy prison but had to wait for the others. Everything had to be so slow, so methodical, as we worked our way, one at a time, up the ice slope. It was eleven-thirty before we reached the top of the gully and could traverse out on to a small ledge on the crest of the Pillar. We were in the sun: I caressed the warm, rough granite, felt the hot rays of the sun probe through my shirt. I should have liked to have basked in the sun for the rest of the day but the real work was only just beginning. We had over 2000 feet of sheer rock in front of us.

'You go in front, if you like, Walter. Paul and I can follow and take a turn in the lead if you get tired,' suggested Don.

'Aye, we'll bring up the rear,' said Hamish. 'Chris can do the leading and I'll take the pegs out with the "message".'

The 'message' was Hamish's extra heavy, chrome-plated, piton hammer. In fact he had volunteered to undertake one of the hardest, yet least exciting, jobs of all. It is very much more awkward taking pegs out than putting them in.

Walter and Richard climbed very quickly and soon disappeared from sight. Then Don and Paul vanished up a steep crack that marked the start of the real climbing. Suddenly I felt very lonely, even though I could hear the sound of a peg hammer far above. What did Bonatti feel with the entire face to himself?

I put away my fears and started to climb, eager to catch the others up. Crack followed crack; steep and sustained. My arms began to ache after the first two hundred feet. Could I keep it up for two thousand? This was rock climbing the like of which I had never before known. The granite was cleaved into smooth cracks and grooves: it swept endlessly up, and around us, and below it dropped sheer into the gaping mouth of the gully we had just left.

I heard shouts above, poked my head over the brink of a ledge and found Don and Paul resting in the sun. Above them leaned a big roof overhang. Richard was swinging below it, across a steep slab, in étriers; then he disappeared round a corner. He was still carrying his rucksack.

'That looks too much like hard work,' said Don. 'I'll leave my sack here and pull them all up when I get to the top.'

He started the pitch with a magnificent display of climbing, for he did not use étriers but just pulled up on the pegs and wedges in the crack, and then seemed to walk across the slab on which Richard had dangled. He did not hurry: each move was smooth, calculated and seemingly effortless, and yet, when I came to follow, the rock thrust me backwards. At the end of the overhang Don had swung across a steep slab on the rope clipped into a peg above him, and had vanished. I followed, and found myself in a bottomless groove. Looking down, the first thing I saw was the glacier 2000 feet below. Far above, quite unattainable, a pair of legs were swinging in the air. A crack, smooth, sheer, unadorned with pitons or wedges, stretched upwards; it was barred by two small overhangs.

'Did you go up here?' I shouted to the legs.

'Yes,' came a voice.

'Is it hard?' I asked.

'It's a bit strenuous,' came the reply, in a flat Lancashire accent, and the legs kicked idly against the rock.

I thrust myself into the groove. It was vertical but the crack was the right size for a hand-jam, and the toes of my boots just fitted it. Always retaining three points of contact, I clung limpet-like to the rock. At the first bulge the crack was a little wider, I could not jam my hands so firmly. Legs trembling, panting hard, I thrust an arm deep into the crack, leaned out and stepped over the bulge; but there was no rest, nothing to stand on, only another overhang just above. The legs dangling over the ledge looked closer now, but still unattainable. The rope which ran back to Hamish dropped away cleanly for over fifty feet to my last piton. If I came off, I would fall a long way. Should I ask for a top rope? It wouldn't take a minute to drop one. But I was proud, determined to climb on my own. I reached the second overhang. A stone was jammed in the crack just below it and I struggled, frantic, to thread a sling behind it, hanging on one arm. But I could not coax the loop behind the stone. I muttered to myself – I always do when I'm in difficulty – 'Can't get it on. Must push on before I plop off. It's only six feet.'

I pulled up over the overhang. Another few feet and the dangling legs merged into a body seated comfortably. Once over the edge I collapsed, panting, next to Paul Ross.

'Did you like Don's little variation?' he asked. 'The bugger went off route. Look, he should have gone up there,' and he pointed down another groove, next to the one I had just climbed. It was bristling with pitons and wooden wedges and would have been comparatively safe and easy to climb.

That was one of the hardest pitches I had ever climbed, and I wondered, with a sinking feeling, if there were going to be many more like it. If so, my strength could not possibly last the course. But that afternoon, as pitch followed pitch, my confidence was restored and I began to enjoy myself again. There were many difficult pitches, shallow chimneys, giddy traverses over bottomless slabs, but none had the unrelenting smoothness, the complete lack of protection, of the Whillans variation.

Late that afternoon we heard a shout from above. 'There's a ledge like a ballroom up here.' When I poked my head over the top of the last chimney,

I saw that Don had hardly been exaggerating. On the very prow of the Pillar was a platform the size of a night-club dance floor. Don had already unpacked his rucksack and was melting a dixie-full of snow over a gas stove. The ledge was scattered with ropes, climbing equipment and food.

'We might as well stop here for the night,' said Don. 'There's only another couple of hours of daylight and we shan't find a ledge as good as this higher up.' I was only too happy to agree, for I suddenly realised how tired I was. It was the height of luxury just to sit down and relax in the evening sun. The two Austrians were still working, a hundred feet above us.

'We'll peg another pitch and spend the night up here,' shouted Walter. Meanwhile, we prepared the evening meal. We pooled our resources. Hamish and I had some nutritious, though totally unappetising, survival rations, while the other two had more conventional food: bread, bacon, sausages.

It was nearly dark and we were just savouring our last brew of tea when the quiet of the night was shattered by a thunderous roar. We craned over the edge of the platform and, through a cloud of dust, watched several tons of rock pour down the bed of the gully we had climbed that morning. Sparks flickered in the dim light and, as the sound died away into an expectant silence, there was a heavy smell of sulphur in the air. None of us said anything for a few minutes and then Don voiced all our thoughts.

'Just as well that little lot didn't roll this morning. There wouldn't have been much left of us.'

The silence of the night was even greater than before, and then, suddenly, it was broken by a thin, high-pitched whine from directly above. I knew instinctively that it was aimed at us. We all ducked. There was a dull thud, and we looked up. Hamish was crouching by a boulder in the middle of the platform, his hands on his head. Blood was gushing through the gaps in his fingers. Fortunately I had a bandage in my rucksack: the only piece of first-aid equipment in the entire party. We strapped it in place but a black stain appeared within seconds, though the bleeding stopped after a few more minutes. Hamish was feeling weak and dazed. We were all stunned by the mammoth rock-fall followed by that single deadly stone. It was the only one that fell anywhere near us during the entire climb.

The platform, which had seemed so safe and comfortable, now felt hideously exposed. We huddled against the rock wall at its back, and without further talk prepared for the night. There was no question of being comfortable. Three of us wedged ourselves into a niche at the very edge of the platform. Paul Ross was standing in the back of it and Hamish sat between his legs, while I jammed myself below Hamish with my legs straddled across the front of it. I was wearing a down jacket but the cold slowly ate into my feet and spread up my legs. From time to time Hamish slumped on top of me, threatening to force me out of the groove. The night dragged endlessly and I gazed, full of envy, at the chain of lights in the valley far below. People were eating in the restaurants, sleeping in soft beds. I shifted my buttocks from one lump of rock to another. My teeth chattered uncontrollably and I consoled myself with the thought that this was a natural bodily function to help raise one's temperature.

Would day never come? All too slowly the sky outlining the plunging silhouette of the Pillar and the ridge of the Flammes de Pierre, changed from a deep black to a thin, watery blue. Suddenly a white flame of light struck the dome of Mont Blanc; slowly the line between dazzling light and grey shadows crept down the mountain and finally touched the spire of the Aiguille du Midi, colouring it a rich brown. We longed to move, to warm our limbs with exercise, but were so numb with cold that it was difficult to make a start. Facing the west, we could not hope to be in the sun for some hours to come.

We hobbled round the platform like old men, sorted out the litter of equipment carelessly scattered the previous night and made a brew of tea. After that I felt better but Hamish was in a bad way; he was very pale and streak of dried blood ran down one side of his face.

'How are you feeling?' I asked him.

'Bloody awful,' he replied. 'I keep feeling dizzy but I think I'll be all right. Once I get going it'll be better.'

'Do you think you can make it to the top?' asked Don. 'I don't fancy going back down that gully after last night.'

'I might need a tight rope some of the way, but I can keep going,' he said.

I knew that I should never be able to give Hamish all the help he would need. It was all I could do to lead each pitch of the climb: I had nothing left in reserve so I suggested to Don – 'Do you think it would be a good idea if you took Hamish? I am sure you will be able to help him better than I. Paul and I can stay at the back and take all the pegs out.'

'Fair enough,' agreed Don. 'We'd better get going.'

The two Austrians had already started and were now far above us, hammering their way up an impossibly smooth-looking groove. On the previous day we had worked our way up a system of cracks, weaving from side to side in search of the easiest way, but now there was only one possible line, up a series of long grooves that stretched up the smooth prow of the Pillar. The rock was just off the vertical, rough to the touch but it offered no incut holds. Walter had hammered pitons into the crack in the bed of the groove at full arm's reach and we pulled from one to the next as if we were climbing a giant ladder. Every now and then you could climb free, jamming fingers into the crack, legs bridged across the walls of the groove. It was wonderful, exhilarating climbing that made all the discomfort of the night seem worth while.

Hamish from time to time had fits of faintness, but with a tight rope from Don, was able to climb quite quickly. We were all full of optimism. Sometimes Paul and I caught the others up on a stance, sometimes we were left behind so that we felt we had the entire face to ourselves. At midday we reached a fair-sized ledge. Don and Hamish were lounging in the sun which was now beating down with a cruel strength. Richard was paying out the rope, and, glancing up, I could see Walter dangling in the middle of a great bulging wall. The only sound was the sharp clatter of his piton hammer.

'I've run out of pegs,' he shouted. 'Can you send some more up?'

We tied a bundle of ironmongery on to his spare rope and he hauled it up. More hammering from above and he slowly crept up the rock. We lay on the ledge, deadened by the heat of the sun, tired from our sleepless night. There was no snow or water and we were desperately thirsty.

'Can you send any more pegs?' yelled Walter.

We sent up our remaining stock, but he seemed little more than half-way up the wall. It was now late afternoon; the day was slipping by with a frightening speed and we were still a long way from the top.

'I'm sure the route doesn't go up there,' said Don. 'Hold my rope, Hamish. I'll have a look round the corner.'

He shot out of sight, there was a long pause and then a yell of triumph: 'I've found it. There's a bloody great overhang round here with pegs all the way up it. Come on round.'

We called Walter down. He had to abseil from his top peg and remove all the pitons on the way down, for he had used up our entire stock.

It was a great relief to move once more, to feel we were getting somewhere, particularly since it was no longer warm: we were now engulfed in cloud.

Don might have found the right way but it was not reassuring. I had never seen such a huge overhang; it thrust out above our heads into the swirling cloud, dark and forbidding. Don was already half-way up it, swinging from peg to peg like an agile monkey, and quickly disappeared from sight.

'What's it like beyond the roof?' I shouted.

'Steep,' he replied, 'but it will go. I'll need some pegs. There aren't any in place up here. Get some from Walter and send them up.'

'It's nearly seven o'clock,' I replied. 'It'll be dark soon. Are there any ledges there?'

'No,' came the reply.

I hated the thought of splitting the party – of some being left below the overhang. I think everyone else felt the same but it would be dark before we could possibly get the whole party and all the rucksacks over the roof.

'I'll come down,' shouted Don. 'We can stop the night on the ledges.'

He pulled the ropes up through the pitons and dropped them down: their ends were swinging in mid-air some feet out from us, the overhang was so big. At the bottom he had to swing back and forth, a human pendulum, to reach us.

We then all climbed back down to the ledges where we had spent most of the afternoon. We had made discouragingly poor progress; the big overhang, like the jaws of a trap, still loomed above us and we were only a few hundred feet above our last bivouac. Hamish, who never complained, and always had a wry joke to crack about his predicament, was obviously feeling very weak. Don, that day, had pulled him up every pitch on a tight rope.

We settled down for the night. Hamish had elected to stay by himself on a minute ledge about fifty feet above us.

'I'm not going to loose any height,' he said. 'It's been hard enough gaining it. Anyway, I'll get a good night's sleep away from you lot. See you tomorrow.' He always was an individualist.

I shared Don's plastic bivouac-sack. There was just room on the ledge to sit down, backs to the wall, feet over the edge, or knees drawn up to the chin. Either choice was uncomfortable and we both constantly shifted our positions to avoid getting cramp. We dropped the sack, a large plastic bag, over our heads. Inside it we generated a surprising amount of warmth, though at times I wondered if we were going to suffocate since there was no ventilation and Don smoked continuously all night.

'It'd be a good way to die, anyway,' Don remarked stoically. 'Better than freezing to bloody death.'

The night passed more quickly than the previous one. We talked in a desultory fashion, occasionally dropping off into a doze. I dreamt of foaming tankards of beer, for we had not had anything to drink since the previous morning. We were so thirsty we were unable to eat what little food we still had.

In the morning we were impatient to start, but it was so cold that it took time to sort out tangled ropes, repack rucksacks, force feet into frozen boots. We nibbled an oatmeal block for breakfast and were ready.

'You go first, Walter. It's going to take Hamish a bit of time to climb the overhang,' said Don. I was impressed by his refusal of the lead. He had found the right way the previous evening and had climbed the roof. Making the route out in front is by far the most satisfying part of any climb, but he was content to concentrate on his exacting task of nursing Hamish up the Pillar, and to let the Austrians press on in front.

Paul and I were to remain at the back with the job of taking out the pegs the front pair had hammered in. We had a long wait while the others climbed the overhang. I followed Hamish up, just a piton behind, swinging completely free in my étriers. Hamish had a desperate struggle for he could get no help from Don as the rope was running through so many karabiners. He sagged in his stirrups, panting hard: a desperate heave, and he lunged for the next peg at full arm's reach, clipped his étrier into it and dragged himself up. At times he went limp, hanging like a corpse chained to a gibbet. Only his raucous breathing showed that he was alive. Although I was just behind him there was nothing I could do to help but mutter the odd word of encouragement. I just followed from peg to peg, swinging in my étrier and breaking off the long icicles that hung down from the roof; but sucking them did little to alleviate my thirst. Paul, deep in the shadows below, had to wait patiently.

At last we reached the top of the roof. Another overhanging groove stretched above, but its angle was easy compared to that we had just climbed. We were still in shadow and it was bitterly cold; I had, therefore, kept on my down jacket, but half-way up the groove I came into the sun. Suddenly I was sweating. What little strength I had left seemed to evaporate in the heat. By the time I had struggled, panting, to the next ledge, my clothes were soaked and my mouth even drier than it had been before. I stripped off my jacket and lay exhausted for about ten minutes before I could even start to bring Paul up. By the time he had reached me, having taken out as many pegs as he could, we had been left far behind. The bright, sunlit rock stretched as far and steep as ever above our heads: below, it shot into the deep shadows of the couloir. I felt horribly alone and longed to catch the others up. I was not even sure which way they had gone. I shouted and my voice echoed but there was no reply.

I left the stance and worked my way up a ramp, over a wall, to the start of a slab. It was smooth, featureless except for a peg transfixed in a crack half-way across. I could never reach it. My rope dropped out of sight behind me. I almost sobbed with loneliness and fear as I started to edge my way across the slab. I don't think it was particularly difficult but I had got close to breaking-point and only just managed to reach the peg. I clung to it, afraid to leave its safety. I shouted in despair and this time had a reply from just above. Hamish poked his head from round the corner.

'Let's have a top rope,' I gasped. I have never been so glad to see a rope-end slide down towards me from above. I tied on, crossed the slab and climbed the last little wall before reaching the ledge. As I climbed it, I heard a steady purr and then, when I poked my head over the top, I saw, most wondrous of all sights, the stove with a pan-full of tea on top of it. They had found some ice in the back of a crack. There was gravel and sediment mixed in with the handful of tea leaves but it tasted like nectar: it was our first drink for over thirty-six hours. It required an effort of will to drink only a couple of mouthfuls, to leave Paul his fair share, but that drop of tea made all the difference.

I had come close to breakdown in the middle of the slab but now I had a new lease of strength. I still felt tired but for the rest of the climb I knew I could keep going. There were still many exacting pitches; the rock was more broken and this made the route-finding more difficult. On two occasions Walter had to come back and try another line. But at last, in late afternoon, the angle began to relent and we made rapid progress.

At last Walter shouted down: 'I've reached the Shoulder. I can see the top.' Just one more overhanging chimney barred the way but with success in sight we quickly stormed it. Easy rocks now led to the summit, but it was getting dark. There was no hope of getting down that night.

We had climbed the South-west Pillar but I felt no sense of exhilaration. I was much too tired and hungry; and too worried about our chances of getting down alive. Unnoticed by us, the weather had changed during the day. A cold wind was blowing, heavy clouds had crept across the sky, hiding the tops of Mont Blanc and the Grandes Jorasses, and a few flakes of snow swirled across the shattered rocks near the summit. I dreaded the thought of another cold, comfortless night.

Our only food was a packet of soup which we shared between the six of us: three mouthfuls each. I spent the night in a cradle of rope. Every time I dropped into a doze, I slid down the steeply shelved ledge, to wake hanging on my safety rope, but I was so tired that I slept for most of the night, waking occasionally to hear the snow patter on the surface of my plastic bag and to feel the cold bite into my feet and legs.

It was an ominous grey dawn. Tattered clouds covered the glacier below us; a dull, grey ceiling pressed down on our heads, engulfing us by the time we were ready to start. The wind tore at our clothes, drove the snow with agonising force into our faces. We could see the dark shapes of rocks a few feet in front of us but everything else was white: cascades of snow down the mountain, snow piled high on ledges, snow driving through the air.

'Can you remember the way down, Walter?' asked Don.

'I think so,' he replied. 'We came down this side last year, but it is difficult to see anything now.'

'Well, push on anyway. If we wait here we'll still be here next year, in the middle of blocks of ice,' said Don.

The descent was a nightmare. The rocks, plastered with freshly fallen snow, plunged into grey cloud. The ropes were like wire hawsers, stiff and frozen to the touch, and yet seemed to have minds of their own, twisting themselves into impossible knots which had to be patiently untied with numb fingers. There was no feeling in my feet nor in my hands, but I knew I could keep going. Hamish, also, had had a new lease of strength, but Richard, the youngest member of the party, was on the point of collapse: he could barely talk and just sat, slumped against the nearest rock.

We were abseiling down a series of grooves which we hoped would lead us to the ridge of the Flammes de Pierre, but after three rope-lengths, Walter admitted he was lost.

It was now that Don Whillans came into his own. He looked and behaved just the same way as he had at the beginning of the first day – a tough, self-contained, little man who would let no one or thing hurry him.

'Give us a rope, Chris,' he commanded. 'We're too far to the right. I'll have a look down here.'

He shot out of sight. There was a long pause and then a shout:

'Come on down. This is it.'

Don had once again found the route and led us down towards safety. We still had a long way to go but the wind dropped and it stopped snowing. We caught a glimpse of the Flammes de Pierre through the clouds and knew for certain that we were going the right way. Suddenly, in spite of our fatigue, we felt light-hearted and started to talk of the mammoth feast we should have when we got back to civilisation. We were at the most dangerous stage of any descent. Unconsciously, we had all relaxed our attention in the moment of our elation. Walter dropped a sling over a razor-edged spike of rock, threaded the abseil rope through it and started down with a bold leap. There was a twang: the sling had been cut through on the sharp edge and he somersaulted downwards, hit a snow slope twenty feet below, rolled a few feet and came to rest on the brink.

No one commented on his narrow escape but I for one went on down with redoubled care. The glacier, far below, never seemed to come any closer. Abseil followed abseil. Slowly we crept down slopes of soft, wet snow, smooth rock slabs or hard ice. I longed for the safety of flat ground, to stride, unencumbered by the rope. At long last, almost unnoticed, a traverse brought us down to the glacier. More slushy snow, crevasses black and gaping below, an easy snow slope and the Charpoua Hut – and safety.

It was nearly dark, but we were determined to get back to Montenvers that night, to eat a hot meal, to change into dry clothes. We forced ourselves on, down to the Mer de Glace, across it and up the other side, slowly pulling our aching limbs up the steel ladders. They were only a couple of hundred feet high but they seemed to go on for ever.

That night we gorged ourselves in the Montenvers Hotel and then, happily bloated, tipsy with wine and exhaustion, rolled into our sleeping-bags. No meal had ever tasted so delicious. Our appreciation of every simple comfort was heightened by our experience of the last four days. A sleeping-bag on a hard floor was to us the very height of luxury. I slept solidly for twelve hours and then next morning, after a leisured breakfast, began to think of what I should do next.

There were many times in those last four days when I longed to be anywhere but on the South-west Pillar; when I swore that I should never again go on a route of its calibre, never again submit to such discomfort, cold and fatigue; and yet the morning after getting back to safety I was planning to risk repeating the experience. People who have never climbed, particularly those who have an instinctive aversion to heights, find it difficult to understand the motives of anyone who ventures on to a vertical rock face, let alone those who choose to undergo an orgy of discomfort and pain lasting several days. I shall try, anyway, to analyse my own reasons for tackling such routes.

I had been climbing our small rock faces in Britain for six years before visiting the Alps and have already described the pleasure I gained in doing this: the sheer physical enjoyment of climbing a stretch of rock. To gain this pleasure to the fullest degree, I had to climb to the limit of my ability. To strive always to coax my body up places that were ever steeper, that had fewer holds, and, in doing so, to discover new things about myself and the rock I climbed. The element of danger was an important factor: the knowledge that if I made a mistake I should fall, perhaps to my death. But I did not court danger and certainly did not relish it, for in many ways I am timid. I hate being afraid, hate getting into a situation where I have to fight for my life. This sounds contradictory but in undertaking a climb I do everything I can to make myself safe: by using carefully contrived running belays; by working out every move in my head before attempting it; by turning back if I think it is too hard. In doing this I am cheating the danger – reducing what is inherently hazardous to something completely safe.

In the Alps it was the same but because it was all on a grander scale, one's every feeling was stronger. At first, I was afraid, for there were too many questions I could not answer. What would happen if we were caught by bad weather; if we lost our way on one of these huge, 2000 foot faces; if one of the party were injured? I had little experience of snow and ice, even the glaciers held lurking threats of hidden crevasses and tottering seracs. Like most British climbers when they first go to the Alps, I was more worried about the descent down the easy side of a mountain than the difficult rock climb to its summit, which uses techniques with which I was more familiar.

It made no difference that I was with an experienced and competent mountaineer who did know the answers, for I had become used to taking the initiative and I could not feel happy unless I knew that I was capable of at least sharing in the decisions and judging the best course of action in any situation. When we went on the South-west Pillar, I was afraid before starting it, and even more so on the climb itself, when things started to go wrong, for it was all so new to me. I could not know just how serious our troubles were; whether I was capable of lasting out for several days on end; whether it was possible to get up the climb in bad weather. We got up alive because Don Whillans and Walter Phillip knew what they were doing. Their self-confidence encouraged me at the time and I also learnt a great deal from them. My experience on the Pillar taught me that however bad conditions become, whatever goes wrong, I could extricate myself. I never again suffered the blind fear of unknown dangers for, on all subsequent climbs, I was able to appreciate the extent of any danger that threatened, and find a way of avoiding it. I was still frightened at times but it was a fear that was quickly banished by action.

But why seek out situations that are frightening? Does one enjoy being cold at night; desperately thirsty; exhausted? I certainly don't. Sitting on a stance, taking in the rope, or during the long hours of the night when there is plenty of time for reflection, I long to get back to the comforts of civilisation, but the moment I start to climb this is all forgotten and I am lost in the all-absorbing business of coaxing my body up the stretch of rock immediately in front. It is then that adverse conditions become a further exhilarating challenge: a problem to be overcome. And so it goes on. There are these moments of exhilaration and a few minutes later, waiting on the stance, there is time to notice parched lips, or, if the weather has broken, the trickle of icy water down the neck. But at the end of it all, back in Chamonix, the discomfort is forgotten; in retrospect it adds a piquant flavour to your memories and so you start planning the next climb...

CHAPTER SEVEN

Direttissima

'That's where they usually come off,' murmured the German climber lying beside us.

We could just discern the arms and legs of the man spread-eagled on the yellow rock a thousand feet above. He was like a tiny black ant on the wall of a huge windowless warehouse. About fifty feet below him, stationary, was another minute figure. The rope joining them looked like gossamer thread, and the wall stretched above, below and to either side: grey, compact, yellow, featureless.

Suddenly the leading dot shot downwards. It was all over before the impact of the fall registered on my mind. The climber was dangling twenty feet from his original position, presumably held by a piton. He rested for a few minutes and then started up again, soon reaching the point from which he had fallen. A long pause, the faint thudding of a piton hammer and he was up.

I was sitting with a group of Austrian and German climbers on a boulder at the foot of the North Face of the Cima Grande in the Italian Dolomites. The two performers, far above, were on the 'Direttissima', a route that had only been opened the previous year and which was reputed to be the hardest in the Dolomites.

A year had passed since my holiday in Chamonix and my ascent of the South-west Pillar of the Dru. I was climbing with Gunn Clark who was still a student, slightly younger than I, but with very similar mountaineering experience.

'It must be a good peg, anyway. What do you think, Gunn? Shall we have a crack at it?' I asked.

'Let's see how they get on at the traverse. It looks bloody terrifying to me,' he replied.

We had been camped below the Tre Cime for a week and had done several of the easier climbs in the area, but from the start, the Direttissima had fascinated us. Four young Germans had made the first ascent, taking five days to complete it. They had used several special techniques. The wall was so continuously overhanging that it would have been impossible to retreat from it in the normal way, by abseiling: at the end of the rope they would have been swinging in mid-air several feet out from the rock. They therefore had to leave in place all their pitons, several hundred of them, so that if they had to turn back owing to a change in the weather, they would be able to climb down. This of course meant carrying heavy loads for they also had to carry water and food. To overcome the problem, they took with them a thousand-foot length of line so that they could haul loads up from the bottom of the cliff. This was only possible because the face was so steep that the bundles nowhere touched rock on the way up.

It was much easier, of course, for the parties that followed, since all the pitons had been left in place, but even so the face maintained its reputation for difficulty. When we arrived that summer there had been a dozen ascents, mainly by German and Austrian parties. I was both attracted and frightened by the climb for I had done comparatively little artificial climbing and certainly nothing of the length or standard of the Direttissima. No other British party had done it and this made it seem even more formidable – there was no one with whom we could compare our own capabilities.

We heard any number of stories about the climb; there were plenty of other candidates camped around the Tre Cime waiting to go on it. They told us of the huge overhangs in the middle of the face and showed us various pieces of specialised equipment: drills for making holes in the rock where there were no cracks, expansion bolts to hammer into them, and even a hook for pulling up on pitons that were out of reach. But, more alarming, we heard that a member of the party that had last attempted the climb, had had a fall and had pulled out two expansion bolts. No one had been hurt but they had been unable to get up without the bolts in place and did not have any of their own. Since we did not have any either, we had decided to wait until another party did the climb. I think everyone was playing the same waiting game for no one went on to it for several days, until at last two Germans plucked up courage. We were watching their efforts that afternoon.

An hour went by and the two little dots slowly, almost imperceptibly, edged their way across the wall.

'They're on the traverse now,' said the German who had already done the climb. 'This is where the bolts came out.' We watched with double interest. The leader stayed in the same place for a long time, went back, crept forward. We could hear faint shouts as he talked to his second. He moved again and there was a whoop of triumph: he was across.

We decided to go on to the climb the next morning and spent the rest of the day preparing our equipment, but that evening clouds began to build up and there was even a little rain in the air. That evening we drank late into the night in the Rifugio Laveredo, confident that the weather would be bad the following day, before tottering, very drunk, back to the tent.

Someone was shaking me; I kept my eyes closed and pretended to be asleep.

'Wake up, Chris. There's not a cloud in the sky. The Germans next door are getting ready. I think they must be going for the Direttissima,' said the voice. I peered out of my sleeping-bag, hating to leave its pleasant warmth, and resenting Gunn's enthusiasm; but then I saw the thin blue of the sky and the two Germans bustling round their tent with last-minute preparations. The sight of them roused my competitive instinct.

We quickly cooked our breakfast, finished packing our sacks and set out for the face. It was only half an hour's walk from our campsite and along a good path all the way. It was eight in the morning when we reached the foot of the climb. There was no introduction to it, no glacier or snow couloir, not even the easy broken rocks that are found at the foot of most Dolomite walls.

It rose, sheer and uncompromising, straight from the path. Our way lay up a thin crack that was adorned with a solitary piton about thirty feet up. I have always hated climbs with difficult first pitches for there is no time to warm up, to find any kind of climbing rhythm. At the first step from the path I was hanging on my arms, thrust backwards by the steepness of the rock. I muttered to myself, cursed my rucksack which I had been too proud to leave at the bottom, fought the crack, clinging to it fearfully, until I reached the piton, clipped in and rested a moment. I was now more relaxed and felt my way up the rock, realising that it was not too difficult, just steep, and reached the stance. Gunn followed up quickly and I then set out on the next pitch, for we had decided that I should do all the leading. I was very happy with this arrangement – I love being out in front. (When second on the rope, I lose concentration, am aware of the danger of falling off, even though it would not matter if I did, and climb too quickly, without thinking out each move before making it.)

The first three hundred feet gave straightforward climbing to the top of a buttress that flanked the great, blank, yellow wall. The two Germans who had set out before us, were already a hundred feet ahead. It was reassuring to see them. The wall was so smooth and sheer that it was difficult to believe that anyone could climb it without pitons, and yet there were very few in sight, just one every twenty feet or so.

'What the hell do you do in between the pegs,' I asked plaintively.

'You'll soon find out,' the German replied.

Our route lay diagonally across the wall, so we were soon above unclimbable rock that dropped away to the path far below. The climbing was all-absorbing, the most airy and spectacular I had ever undertaken. Miraculously, the holds appeared: tiny, square-cut ledges that the toes of one's boots just rested on, that fingertips could curl over. There was no rest for the arms as nowhere did the angle relent. We were heading for a roof that jutted horizontally from the face. This gave me my first taste of A3 – almost the top grade of artificial climbing. The pegs were anything but reassuring, hammered into tiny holes and blind cracks, at the most an inch of steel biting into the rock. I handled each peg with loving care, eased my weight on to the étrier step, pulled delicately on the next one, and tried to avoid swinging too much as I heaved over the lip of the roof.

I had hardly noticed that we had nearly caught up the Germans. Suddenly there was a yell from above. I glanced up to see a body, all arms and legs, rush down towards me. Instinctively I ducked, clung to the rock, but he never reached me. I looked up and saw him dangling on the end of the rope, about ten feet below the peg that had held his fall. He also had come off in the 'usual' place. With hardly a pause he climbed back up, stepped cautiously into the top rung of his étrier and, precariously balanced, hammered in a piton above his head. The dull thud of the hammer inspired little confidence, but he clipped in his étrier and was soon standing on the ledge above. His second followed up quickly and all too soon it was my turn to start.

The rock was even more smooth and compact than it had been before. There were no cracks for pitons and, from the stance, I could see no holds. About fifty feet above, at the foot of a shallow groove, I could just see a tiny black ring protruding from the blank wall, obviously an expansion bolt. I slowly edged my way up towards it. There were just sufficient holds but I had to weave my way from side to side, sometimes coming back a few moves when I had taken a blind alley. On reaching the groove I found some more pitons and a couple of expansion bolts. They were all at extreme reach: climbing on pegs might be compared to going up an iron ladder with rungs six feet apart and rotting away with rust.

Another twenty feet and I reached the point where the German and many of his predecessors had fallen off. There was an expansion bolt and then, a good eight feet above, the piton he had hammered in, a minute Cassin peg protruding downwards from a hole. I cautiously climbed the étrier until I was standing in the top rung, my left foot bridged out on a crease in the surface of the rock, my arms spreadeagled to keep me in balance for there was nothing to hold on to. My fingers crept up the rock towards the peg but they were still a couple of inches too low. I tried to stand on tiptoe on the étrier rung, it slipped and I was off.

Before I had had time to think, I found myself hanging a few feet below the expansion bolt which had bent over in a graceful curve. I felt no sensation of shock or fear for my entire concentration was devoted to that piton only a few feet above but seemingly out of reach. I went up again and this time placed my foot more carefully on the rung, stretched as far as I could but was losing my balance. My finger-tips brushed the ring of the piton; another effort – the top joints of my fingers curled round it. My foot on the étrier scuffed round and I was hanging with all my weight on the two fingers. I now had to clip in a karabiner with my left hand and somehow extract the fingers of my right, which were trapped and extremely painful. My hands were tiring. All that existed in the world was a piton, a karabiner and a few inches of rock. A last struggle and my fingers were free: I was able to clip in my étrier and rest, panting, on it. Then a difficult move enabled me to pull up on to a narrow ledge.

Another pitch of free climbing, which was easy compared to the groove we had just climbed, led to the traverse where the expansion bolts had been pulled out. A line of pegs ran across a horizontal fault.

'It doesn't look too bad, Gunn,' I shouted, for ever optimistic as I started out. But after twenty feet the pegs came to an end – the last one was a long channel peg, resting loosely in a crumbling hole, that held when pulled sideways but could be plucked straight out with a direct pull. A few feet farther to the left, and at a lower level, was a small peg jammed by a piece of paper into the hole left by the missing bolt. Farther still to the left a ring piton drooped from another hole. I did not feel like trusting my weight to any of them but there was no other way, for the wall was gently impending and completely holdless.

I am not often aware of the drop below me, and certainly am not worried by it, but here I was unpleasantly reminded of it as I leant down, hanging on the long channel peg, to place an étrier on the paper-plugged bolt – my eyes inevitably strayed down the giddy drop of the wall to the screes six hundred feet below. Stepping on the top rung of the étrier, held in balance only by the tension of my rope running back to Gunn, I breathlessly reached across to the next peg, clipped in my other étrier and stood on the rung, fully expecting the peg to plop out as I put my weight on it. Another tensed move and I was across on good rock holds that I could grasp and pull on. I felt a surge of relief and the rich satisfaction gained from completing a particularly thin piece of climbing.

I could hear voices just round the corner and a few minutes later we reached the bivouac ledge, the only one for eleven hundred feet. The two Germans had already settled down but there was plenty of room. There were two ledges each only two foot wide but to us they seemed as big as railway-station platforms. For the first time that day we were able to relax, to sit down. It was only four o'clock in the afternoon and there were still several hours of daylight, but the wall now reared over our heads in a series of jutting roofs and it was obvious we should never be able to get up through them before dark. It was pleasant anyway to sit in the afternoon sun and to eat for the first time that day – we had had no thought of anything but the climbing earlier on. We had two pints of water with us, and brewed tea, greatest luxury of all, over a solid fuel tablet. We spent the rest of the afternoon making our ledge more comfortable, shifting loose blocks and dropping them to the screes seven hundred feet below. A group of spectators, sitting near the foot of the cliff, quickly scattered as our bombardment crept towards them.

This was undoubtedly a four-star bivouac ledge: we could actually lie down, moored to the rock by a complicated system of belays. For the first time on a bivouac I slept really well, only waking with the dawn. There was no hurry, anyway, as we had to allow the two Germans to get away. We sat on the ledge watching them at work above us. Most of the time they were swinging clear of the rock in their étriers. Below we could see two tiny figures at the start of the climb. The German leader ran out a hundred feet of rope, and took a stance hanging in étriers immediately below the huge roof. His second followed up with surprising speed and, passing the stance, soon disappeared over the roof. We could hear him calling down from somewhere out of sight but the rope moved slowly and the pitch was obviously difficult.

Three hours went by and we were still sitting on the ledge. I was restless, wanting to get to grips with the problem, so finally started up the pitch. The previous day most of the climbing had been on vertical rock but now it was all overhanging and one relied entirely on the pitons that were already in place. I arrived below the German and made myself a cradle of rope to sit in. I had to stay there for a further hour, immediately above me the German's backside, below – space. I pulled loose a stone. Without touching anything, it dropped to the ground eight hundred feet below.

At last the German moved on and I was able to bring Gunn up to my belay. Changing stances was a nightmare of dangling bodies and tangled ropes that tried my patience to breaking point. This type of artificial climbing was something that neither of us had ever met before: it demanded a machine-like methodical approach. The ropes were threaded through anything up to forty karabiners and it meant concentrating the whole time on which rope to use, how to thread it, whether it was likely to cross the other or get jammed in a crack. I was for ever haunted by the fear of the rope jamming immovably when I was half-way up a pitch so that I could move neither up nor down.

After traversing a few feet to the right, away from Gunn, I had to pull up over the first roof. My view was immediately constricted to a few feet of rock. Below I could only see the scree, the entire face being cut off by the overhang, and above, the rock jutted out once again, hiding the sky. I felt utterly alone, frightened by the immensity of the face. Swinging in my étriers, feet well clear of the rock, I pulled into an overhanging chimney whose back was lined with loose blocks. I was already running short of karabiners, and the rope was beginning to drag – tugging remorselessly at my waist – but there was still no sign of a stance or even a piton on which I would dare to belay.

It never seemed to end; then at last, when I had used up all my karabiners and most of my strength, I reached a foothold and three expansion bolts which were obviously used for belaying. Gunn now had to come up. It was just as hard for him as it had been for me: the rope passed through so many karabiners that he got little help from it. There were long periods when there was no movement at all and I boiled with impatience, though in fact he was taking no longer than I had done.

The change-over on the stance was even more awkward than on the previous one, and the pitch above every bit as long and tiring, but it did lead to a ledge of sorts, about nine inches wide, on which I could just stand in balance. By the time I had brought Gunn up, it was nearly dark and it was obvious that we would be able to get no further that night. It had taken us an entire day to climb three hundred feet. There was just room for both of us to sit on the ledge with legs dangling over the void. It was impossible to lean back for the wall behind us was gently impending. But our worst trial was thirst: we had only half a pint of water left and this did not begin to satisfy us. There were some drips falling from the overhangs above and we spent much of the night trying to catch them in a mess tin. It was a frustrating game for no drip fell in the same place twice, and the chances of one landing in the waiting pan were slight. Still, it helped to pass the time and we knew that we were now nearly up the steep section of the cliff, that we should be able to get out the following morning.

We started as soon as it was light – there was no temptation to linger. It was surprising how refreshed we felt after our uncomfortable night, especially since both of us had been exhausted at the end of the previous day. The overhangs above were not as severe as the ones we had already climbed and we soon reached a large ledge where we could have spent the night in luxury. Resting on it was a small lead case holding a book in which everyone who had climbed the 'Direct' had signed their names. We could not help feeling some pride as we added ours to the list.

The angle now relented – it was merely vertical – and our way lay up a deep-cut chimney that cleaved the face. The rock was grey and firm to the touch, offering cracks in which to jam our hands, and ledges and pockets. It was a delight to put away the étriers, to climb on rock, once more obeying the natural instincts of our muscles instead of the complex rope engineering of the previous day. Pitch followed pitch, through deep chimneys and over great boulders jammed in the bed of the gully. We were now climbing with real enjoyment, carefree in our confidence that we would soon be at the top.

Another hundred feet and we were there, lying in the sun below the great cross that marks the summit of the Cima Grande, but we did not linger long. The pile of empty tins that littered the summit rock reminded us of our own hunger. We coiled our ropes, packed away all the ironmongery and raced down the broken rocks of the descent, our mouths watering at the thought of spaghetti bolognese and bottles of Chianti.

CHAPTER EIGHT

Outward Bound

Back in Germany, I was browsing through Routine Orders one day in the Squadron Office, when I noticed a paragraph advertising for instructors to the Army Outward Bound School. I had never before heard of it but it immediately caught my imagination. I knew something of the civilian Outward Bound Schools and this presumably was much the same. The thought of working in the mountains, of teaching climbing, was immensely attractive. I immediately made inquiries about the school – I was determined to get myself posted there – but equally quickly met with opposition.

'You know, it won't be good for your career,' my colonel told me. 'You would be much better off with a few more years in the regiment and then a junior staff job or perhaps a secondment to the Trucial Oman Scouts.'

But I could think of nothing worse than spending any longer with my regiment. I detested paperwork, and even the thought of adventure in the Oman was not over-attractive: there would be no climbing, the company of only a few other regular officers with whom I was unlikely to have much in common, and a complete dearth of women. So I persevered, and fortunately my Commanding Officer, who was a sympathetic man, agreed to let me go.

I left the regiment at the end of January 1959. I had few regrets, and though I wasn't prepared to admit it at the time, knew I would not return. After a few days' leave in London, I caught the train up to Towyn in Central Wales to start my new job. By the time the train had reached Shrewsbury there were plenty of other young soldiers on board, all bound for the same destination as I.

At Towyn, a short, thickly-built sergeant, in the uniform of the 17/21st Lancers, was waiting for us on the platform. We all trooped out of the train, but there was none of the shouting I had become accustomed to in the army.

'Go over the bridge, lads, and form up in the station yard,' said the sergeant in a pleasantly normal voice and herded them good-humouredly but effectively off the platform. I just tagged on behind.

Outside the station was another man in uniform. He wore a kilt and had a short bristling moustache; on his shoulders were the insignia of a lieutenant-colonel and under his arm he carried a pair of bagpipes. I guessed that this must be Colonel Churchill, the Commanding Officer of the School.

'Ah, you must be Bonington,' he greeted me. 'I've got to see to this lot first. I'll see you later on in the mess.'

By this time the young soldiers, looking a bit sheepish and very unmilitary, had been formed into three ranks. The colonel marched to the head of the column and to the skirl of bagpipes we set off down the road.

After a few hundred yards we turned into a typical army camp, collection of drab brick huts with corrugated iron roofs, on a disused airfield. The column came to a halt, the bagpipes gave a last wail and another course of the Army Outward Bound School had begun.

I was not sure what to make of it all and I don't suppose the other newcomers were either; after all, when you attend a course in the army you are not often welcomed by the commanding officer playing the bagpipes, but I soon began to see what a good introduction this had been, for everything about the school was different – outside the run of normal army life.

The other instructors were waiting for the new course in a small laughing group; there were seven of them, one subaltern of about the same age as myself, and six sergeants. I was quickly introduced and told that for the first course I should be with Sergeant Cooper, after which I should have my own patrol. He was the youngest of the instructors, quite small but well-built, with a look of dedicated determination on his face; I winced inwardly and wondered how hard a time I should have trying to keep up with him.

Names were called out and the lads were divided out, ten to twelve in each patrol; they collected some extra equipment from the store and were then shown their huts – badly in need of decoration, with battered iron bedsteads and concrete floors.

'This is your home for the next three weeks,' Sergeant Cooper told his charges, 'I'll be down after supper to tell you something about the course. Come and have a drink in our mess,' he added, turning to me.

In the mess, I immediately noticed the friendly, easy relations between the officer and sergeant instructors; they were all on Christian name terms, something unheard of in the army as a whole. When one thought about it, however, it was quite logical, as we were all doing exactly the same job.

The school had been in existence for just over a year, and had been built with close co-operation from the entire staff. Typically of the army, neither the Commandant nor the chief instructor had had any experience of

Outward Bound training or even of elementary mountaineering before being told to form the school. The only man on the original staff with any knowledge of either subject was Sergeant Mick Quinn, who had spent some years with the Royal Marines Cliff Assault Wing. He was a brilliant talker, fixed you with a pair of bright blue eyes that carried absolute conviction, and could prove to most people that two and two made five, but it was his enthusiasm and knowledge that made the school a going concern. The fact that everyone had joined together, had often had fierce arguments over policy, and had finally got the school on its feet, had built this strong feeling of unity without any of the normal inhibitions that must exist between officer and NCO in other branches of the army. I recognised that this division must exist in the normal unit, but at the same time my experience of the freedom that existed in the school made me all the more loth to return to my regiment.

That night I went down to the patrol's hut to hear Ian Cooper tell the boys about the course.

'You've all heard a lot of tall stories about the school from other boys in your units who have done the course. I suggest you forget them, and I'll tell you what I shall expect of you for the next three weeks.

'For a start, after tomorrow morning's assembly, you don't wear uniform again until the end of the course.' Loud cheers from the lads.

'In the next three weeks you will be doing a lot of things you haven't done before. This first week we'll concentrate on teaching you how to look after yourself in the hills and we'll tone up your muscles. In the classroom, we'll brush up on your map-reading, do a bit of first-aid and teach you what to do in the event of an accident. You'll have plenty of practice on the assault course, a few runs, a morning on a small rock face just near the camp and some canoeing. At the end of the week we go into the hills for thirty-six hours, to do some walking and map-reading and have a night out in tents.

'Next week we shall go to Snowdon, where you will all have a chance to do some real rock-climbing and a lot of walking. Then in the third week is the final scheme. This is the climax of the course, when you will be able to put into practice all you have learnt. You will be out on your own, in groups of three, for three days and will try to complete a route we set you across about forty miles of hill country.

'Well, that's what you will be doing in the next three weeks. You might well ask what it's all in aid of. Some of you, no doubt, have heard that Outward Bound builds character; well, I wouldn't try to build any of your characters in just three weeks, but what you can do is find out something about yourselves. You will do things that you never thought you could. On the final scheme you might think you can go no further, but with some determination, you can force yourself on. There won't be anyone to drive you on, as there is back in your units, it will be up to you, on the final scheme and, for that matter, throughout the course. It's up to you to do your best at everything we show you, and provided you do, you will pass the course.

'This all sounds a bit grim, but in fact, I can assure you that you will all enjoy the course and the harder you throw yourselves into it, the more you will get out of it in the end.

'Well, that's enough for one night. I'll see you tomorrow morning at seven and we shall go for a dip in the sea.' Loud but cheerful groans from the audience. 'It's not nearly as bad as they all make out,' added Ian with a laugh. I felt my hackles rise. There seemed to be something unpleasantly hearty about early morning dips in the sea at the beginning of February; but next morning, in the cold dawn, it was not nearly as bad as I had feared and I even had to admit to myself that it did wake me up.

That first morning, at breakfast, it was pleasant to look out of the window of the mess, over to the guard-room and see the sergeant-major hold his early-morning parade of a dozen cooks and drivers. It was a reminder of the army, of which I was now delightfully free. The sergeant-major was in the Welsh Guards, he was just over five feet tall, and as dapper as any guardsman could be. He wore his black peaked cap with immense pride. I was only too happy to forget that I was a soldier and plunged into my new role of Outward Bound instructor.

The days passed quickly, periods in the class-room teaching map-reading, racing round the assault course, climbing on the sea-cliff a mile or so from the school, and then days in the hills, walking with the boys or, having sent them off on their own, wandering alone from top to top. This I enjoyed most of all and much more than the climbing – I quickly discovered that I was too interested in my own climbing to become a good teacher. I found it frustrating to take learners up the same easy climbs over and over again, and longed to escape on to harder routes which would tax my ability to the full, but for most of the boys the climbing was the highlight of the course, probably because it was exciting without being physically too arduous.

I soon became involved and found myself working harder than I had ever done in my regiment. Although the syllabus of each course was the same, no group of boys was identical and each required a different approach. Our students were from Junior Leaders' regiments and Army Apprentice Schools; they had joined the army at the age of sixteen or so, planning to make it their career. Our best students were usually from the apprentice schools. They had a much higher degree of intelligence, and I suspect a more stimulating course of training, than the boys from the regiments, the band boys and the lads from the Guards' boys' company, most of whom were right out of their depth in the hills. Some were practically illiterate, and a map merely a confusing pattern of lines and colours to them. You could spend hours teaching a simple knot, say the bowline, and at the end they would still be unable to tie it. Fortunately there was rarely more than one such boy in each patrol.

The final scheme was a really exacting test. The boys were on their own for its three days' duration, except when passing through instructors' checkpoints. They all went round a course that took in Cader Idris and the Arans in Central Wales, about forty miles across country with over 11,000 feet of climbing. In bad weather, when the cloud was down, it called for a high standard of map-reading to avoid getting lost, and a great deal of determination to keep going, particularly after a wet night, when sleeping-bags, tents and clothing were soaked. The ones that did keep going and managed to finish their route all agreed afterwards that it had been well worth while, whereas the comparative few who had given up when only half-way round suffered disappointment.

I have often had doubts about some aspects of Outward Bound training and have heard the criticism that in making the mountains a place of harsh testing, the students are put off them for life and would never want to return, that they struggle through their three weeks, breathe a sigh of relief and return to normal life in much the same state as when they started the course. I think this is the danger in Outward Bound or in any form of training, and that the final impact on the student will depend on the methods of the instructor. We were given a free hand in our interpretation of the syllabus, and each instructor had his own method. A sergeant like Spike Jones, who was in his late thirties and had several children, took his patrol at a much steadier rate than younger men, like Ian Cooper or myself, though the final result, as far as the boy was concerned, was probably very much the same. I believed in setting the boys tasks that extended them, but which were well within their physical capabilities, whatever they themselves might think: whether they went for a walk over rough country, or got up before dawn to take full advantage of the day's length. I tried to make it exciting and enjoyable. Mixed in with the hardship was plenty of sheer fun: the rock-climbing, that nearly all the boys enjoyed; canoeing; even a grindingly long walk, a race down scree or some hilarious boulder-hopping down the course of a mountain stream. It all added up to three weeks that were different from the normal run of their training or anything they had ever done before.

Beyond this, some students got a long-term benefit from the course. Often the boy who was shy and retiring in his unit, because he was good neither at games nor drill but was intelligent, gained a good deal in self-confidence when he found that he could walk as well as if not better than the brilliant games-player and could take an active, even vital, part in the control of a group in the hills: he might be the only one capable of reading a map and navigating the party to its goal. Surprisingly, too, outstanding performers on the course were often habitual trouble-makers in their units: their uncurbed spirits had rebelled against military discipline; but in the hills, finding something that was both challenging and interesting, they entered into everything with enthusiasm and had the force of personality to carry with them their less volatile fellows. I very much doubt if we ever changed anyone's character but students often discovered things about themselves that either they had not known or were not prepared to admit – from the boy who gained self-confidence on the one side, to the one who tried to free-wheel the course, but was caught out, on the other.

During my two years at the Army Outward Bound School I returned to the British climbing scene. I felt rather like Rip van Winkle: there were new faces in the climbing huts and pubs, the hills were very much more crowded, but above all there was a different atmosphere.

In 1955 the routes put up by Joe Brown inspired a superstitious respect; only a handful of climbers were venturing on to even the easiest ones. I could remember gazing up at the smooth cleft of Cenotaph Corner in the summer of 1955, tentatively trying the bottom few feet, but without any real conviction, and at the first hard move, coming scuttling down. At that time it had not had a second ascent, but now in the summer of 1959 any number of people had climbed it. I can remember hearing above the babble of voices, one night in the bar of the Pen y Gwryd Hotel:

'Did Cenotaph today.'

'What was it like?'

'Piece of duff, nothing to it. I don't know what they were making all the fuss about. You can put a runner on every six feet, all the way up.'

The climbs that only a few years before had been thought impossible for all but men of superhuman strength were now being done by the run of competent climbers, many of them in their teens. The barrier that had stopped us in '55 had therefore been largely psychological, a fear of the unknown.

On Clogwyn du'r Arddu, for instance, eleven major routes had been made before 1951 and then, between 1951 and 1959, Brown, Whillans and Ron Mosely put up another twenty-five climbs, all of which were considerably harder than anything done before. During this period only one other person, outside the Rock and Ice Club, put up a route of similar calibre. This was John Streetly, a man of much the same physical proportions as Whillans and Brown, even shorter than either of them and superbly built – but from a very different background. He was at Cambridge University – the stamping ground of many traditional mountaineers. A brilliant athlete, holding three blues, he erupted on to the climbing scene, repeated many of the Brown routes, and then made his own contribution, the Red Slab on Clogwyn du'r Arddu, before returning to his native Trinidad. It was only in 1959 that any other climbers began putting up such routes. Hugh Banner, a wiry, almost delicate-looking Liverpudlian, put two more routes on Cloggy, the Troach and Ghekko Groove; the former up a sheer, seemingly featureless wall. He was the forerunner of many more young climbers who that summer were gaining confidence on existing routes.

I, too, was content to tick off the Brown routes: there seemed no point in trying to do new ones before catching up on this great breakthrough and gaining confidence in the new standards. I went climbing on every available weekend and even in the long summer evenings after a day's work. On one such night I did Cenotaph Corner: only a few years before, the Corner had seemed impossibly huge, as smooth as the corner of a giant concrete building, but now, confident in the knowledge that many others had climbed it, and in my own experience on other climbs in the new idiom, it seemed to bristle with hand-jamming cracks and small holds. I was climbing no better than I had done earlier, but now had the reassurance that many others had also found it easy; there was no longer any mystery. Even on climbs that had not yet been repeated, that still had a reputation for great difficulty, the barriers were down. Setting out to attempt routes like the Woubits, a savage-looking groove, high on the Far East Buttress of Clogwyn du'r Arddu, you felt that this was just one more difficult problem, perhaps harder than anything you had done before, but in the same kind of class. The very fact that the rest of the cliffs were criss-crossed with the ropes of climbers, that there was a subdued babble of voices, that you could see a group of girls sunbathing on the shores of Llyn dur Arddu, made the undertaking seem less serious.

Our equipment had improved. In the old days my running belay technique had been rudimentary: I had carried a few line-slings that I draped over the odd spike of rock; and if I had fallen the chances were that they would either have slipped off or been cut through. But now I carried a dozen or more slings and a pocket full of pebbles. A sling could be threaded round a pebble forced into a crack, and would then give protection for climbing to the very limit of ability with a fair margin of safety. With ingenuity, running belays could be contrived even where there were no spikes available, thereby reducing the risk of damage in a fall; this technique of inserting chockstones was one at which Joe Brown excelled and even if he did not invent it, he did much to develop it. On the one occasion I climbed with him I was amazed by his patience and skill in slotting stones into a seemingly featureless crack.

Footwear had also improved. In 1955 we had all climbed in skin-tight gym shoes, but that summer I bought my first pair of P.A.'s, a tightly fitting boot with a very thin but rigid sole of smooth rubber, which adhered to wrinkles in the rock that a gym shoe would have just rolled off. To achieve maximum adhesion a great deal of comfort had to be sacrificed, for a really tight fit was needed with toes bunched into the pointed front of the shoe. At the end of each pitch it was a relief to take off the shoes, and walking down hill at the end of the climb was sheer agony; but, like a woman enduring the discomfort of smart, high-heeled shoes, it was worth it.

My first summer at the Army Outward Bound School was wonderful. I enjoyed the work, was fitter than I had ever been before or since, and felt I was once more in the climbing world. I now realised how much I had missed it when stationed in Germany. True I had had my long Alpine holidays but that left me with the greater part of the year away from the company of climbers. The thought of returning to my regiment, now transferred to Libya, clouded the future: I began to realise just how out of place I had been, how alien I had felt amongst my fellow officers. As a result I began seriously to think of leaving the Army. But it was a difficult decision to take, for I am lazy at heart, and in many ways the army encourages inertia: everything is done for you; you live at a high and extremely comfortable standard and the future holds no real worries. It was all too easy to drift along, and, anyway, what could I do if I left the Army? Almost immediately I dismissed the thought of becoming a climbing instructor at an Outward Bound School or similar establishment – I enjoyed my climbing too much. Once you start teaching climbing, you are not climbing to your own standard, but at that of your pupils; to be a good instructor, one's vocation for teaching must outweigh one's love of climbing, and in my case this was certainly not so. At the Army Outward Bound School, I even felt some frustration because I could only escape to go climbing at odd occasions: one weekend in three, and for the occasional evening at the end of a day's work – though, even then, I should probably have stayed with my patrol of boys if I had been giving absolutely everything to my job.

I therefore began to think of going into commerce, for I was used to the idea of security, and felt that I should aim for a high salary. At least in an office job I should have my weekends free and would be able to choose my own circle of friends and lead the kind of life I enjoyed.

My mind yo-yoed from one plan to another in my indecision and then, in the summer of 1959, it was temporarily put at rest: I was invited to join a Services expedition to the Himalaya. Its objective was Annapurna II, a 26,041 foot peak in Central Nepal, some ten miles east of the highest summit of the group which was climbed by a French party in 1950 – the first peak of over 8000 metres to fall. For the next nine months I had no time to think of anything else but the expedition; dreams of the Himalaya entirely filled my mind and, on a practical level, I was up till three o'clock most mornings doing my share of the work in putting it on its feet.

CHAPTER NINE

Annapurna II – the Build-Up

There was a smell of woodsmoke in the air and the rounded forms of the hills blurred into the evening haze. My body tingled with a feeling of love for the sounds and shapes around me – a feeling of voluptuous excitement that just wanted to absorb everything so new and strange. I was sitting on the top of a bank above the path, a few minutes from our camp. It was our first day out of Kathmandu; the expedition was really under way.

A few of our porters straggled past. They walked with a hurried jerky motion, legs perpetually bent under their sixty pound loads – scrawny stunted men, their necks knotted with muscle from the strain of their head-bands, which took the entire weight of the loads. They came from the valley of Kathmandu; you could tell from their dress – dirty, once-white shirts, with tails flying over ragged, cotton trousers. More colourful were a couple of hill men from West Nepal. They were in their early teens, their limbs smoothly rounded, covered by a short tunic of sack-cloth material, but their ears were gay with gold rings and they wore necklaces of beads and brightly coloured bangles. Their hair was shoulder length, but there was nothing effeminate about them; they had a look of devil-may-care virility, and carried wicked kukris stuffed into their waistbands.

The porters dropped their loads in a pile at the end of a narrow terraced field on which we had made our camp, and hurried off into the gathering dark to find lodgings for the night. I could just see the first houses of the village at the end of the path, squat buildings with reddish-brown walls and thatched roofs, dwarfed by the stately spread of a banyan tree. Someone started singing, a high pitched wail, that was strangely beautiful in the dusk. A girl walked past me, very pretty with long black hair in plaits, a gold star pierced into one nostril, a brass water jar tucked into her hip. She had an easy, graceful stride. For a few moments I felt I was part of the land, and then there was a shout from the camp.

'Grub up – come and get it.'

I walked over diffidently, feeling shy and withdrawn from the others. Wrenched away from the night and sounds around me, this was reality, the expedition of which I was a member – though we hardly knew each other and perhaps had little in common.

There were nine of us from three different countries, Britain, India and Nepal. None of us had met before the inception of the expedition and we had been brought together more by political expedience than on a basis of friendship or even climbing ability. Amongst the British, each of the three services had its nominee; then the Indians had been brought in for the sake of Commonwealth solidarity and the Nepalese to make things easier for us in Nepal.

I could see Jimmy Roberts, our leader, his face lit by the fire – a cross between that of a wrinkled boy and a petulant monkey. His voice was highly-pitched, particularly when he was excited, and one felt he was essentially shy, in spite of his job as military attaché in Kathmandu. He had at first seemed reserved and rather distant, but one couldn't help liking and respecting him – a feeling that grew ever stronger in the course of the expedition. That night, he had good reason for seeming reserved: here he was, leading a group of complete strangers, with a dubious set of qualifications as mountaineers, on an expedition to a 26,000-foot unclimbed, Himalayan giant. Only one of the British party, Dick Grant, had been in the Himalaya before. Stewart Ward and Bill Crawshaw had only limited Alpine experience, whilst I was young for Himalayan climbing – only twenty-five – and was primarily a rock climber. Of the Indians, Jagjit Singh had been to the Himalaya several times, but had tackled nothing of great height. The two Nepalese, Prabaka and Gadul were so slightly built, that it was difficult to imagine them on a mountain.

That night, Jimmy's main consolation must have been the Sherpas he had selected: nine of the most experienced in the business, all of whom he knew and trusted. Their previous expeditions covered every major peak in Nepal – Everest, Kangchenjunga, Makalu and a dozen others. As they served our dinner one noticed their affection for Jimmy, as they joked and chatted with him. There was no subservience, just a friendly respect. Urkein, the cook, went round asking every one if they liked the meal, obviously getting pleasure from our approval. His enthusiasm was so great that even when the porridge was burnt or the tea tasted of Yak-dung smoke, one did not like to complain.

After the meal I was glad to crawl into my sleeping-bag, though it was a long time before I dropped off to sleep. I was wakened with a cheerful 'Char Sahib' and looked up to see a grinning Sherpa leaning through the sleeve entrance of the tent with a mug of steaming tea in his hand. It was a wonderfully clear morning, and now from the tent door I could see the rolling green and brown hills merge into a rampart of snow peaks across the entire Northern horizon. I scrambled out of the tent and joined Jimmy Roberts, who was gazing at the line of mountains with an expression of ownership – they were so familiar to him.

'That's Himul Chuli over there,' he told me, pointing to a distant, shapely pyramid of snow, 'and that must be Annapurna II, though you can hardly see it.'

You couldn't – it was little more than a pimple to the far west, a hundred miles away, but that moment was one of the most exciting of the expedition. Suddenly the whole thing became real. This first sight of your goal is even more exhilarating than the moment when you reach the top: then there is the sense of anticlimax – it's all over – you've just got to get back down in one piece and go home. Looking across to our objective, we still had before us all the interest and pleasure of the approach march. There were still any number of unknown problems to solve. There was the same element of excitement and self-doubt that I had had when I hitch-hiked up to Wales and saw Snowdon for the first time in my teens, the whole world of moun-taineering before me. I wondered how I should perform, whether I should acclimatise well and above all, should I get to the top. Even though I told myself that all that mattered was that the expedition should be successful, and that someone should climb the mountain, I wanted desperately to go there myself.

For the next fortnight we made our way across the foothills of the great peaks, and then up the Marsyandi Khola, a precipitous gorge leading round the back of Annapurna II to its northern side – on the south, its defences seemed impregnable. Himalayan approach marches have been described many times over in expedition books and ours was probably much the same as any of them. But for me it had all the joy of a new experience – the easy tempo of walking a dozen miles a day, the constant change of scenery, of different people and customs, and the steadily increasing size of the mountains as we drew closer to them. The luxuriant sub-tropical vegetation of the foothills, the rich red earth, mud-walled thatched houses; it all changed almost imperceptibly to harsher surroundings – forests of pine and larch, dry stony earth, stone walls and stone villages of flat-roofed windowless houses, terraced into the hillsides. Even the people became more rugged, coarser, more Mongolian of aspect, than the people of the lower foothills.

Our destination was the valley of Manangbhot, a desolate place of stones and windswept scrub. It lies close to the Tibetan Border, which is separated from it by a range of low mountains to the north, while to the south, it is barred from Nepal by the sprawling mass of the Annapurna range. To the

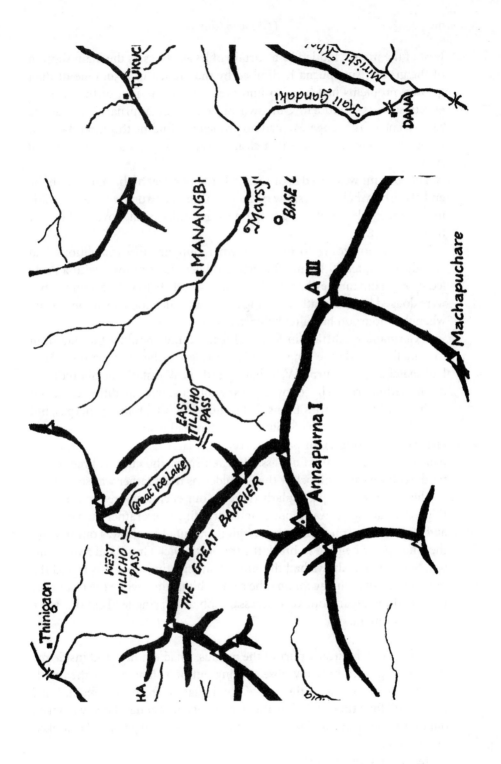

west of the massif, hidden by a curtain of lesser peaks, is the main summit of the group, Annapurna I, climbed by the French in 1950. One of their greatest problems had been to find their way to the foot of the peak, so effectively was it hidden. Our own objective, Annapurna II, lies at the eastern end of the range. We had no problem in finding this mountain, for it towered above the valley in a clean sweep of glaciers and buttresses of snow.

The summit was a wedge of rock at least 2000 feet high, perched on the end of a great whale-back snow ridge which seemed to offer the only feasible line of approach, but it was a long one – five miles in all – over a shoulder of 24,000 feet.

We were not going to an unknown mountain; five expeditions had already attempted it. Jimmy Roberts had been there in 1950, with a party led by Bill Tilman; they had got to a point shortly below the Shoulder, but were dogged by bad weather, having come out much too late in the season, when the monsoon had already started.

A German expedition in 1956 had reached the Shoulder but had been too small to tackle the long, undulating ridge to the final pyramid; they had snatched Annapurna IV, a shapely little peak just off the Shoulder, as a consolation prize. The following year another small expedition came out to the mountain, Charles Evans and Dennis Davis with three Sherpas, but they also, on reaching the Shoulder, felt they had insufficient in reserve to tackle the long ridge. Our party was certainly large enough and in addition had oxygen sets for the final assault. Even so, at the end of three weeks' hard work we were still below the Shoulder, as the weather was so bad.

The going was not particularly difficult; our enemies were the wind and thigh-deep snow – it was monotonous, grinding work rather than exciting and one day was much the same as another. But at least I was out in front the whole time helping to break the trail with Dick Grant and two of our best Sherpas. We always had the spur of anticipating what was round the next corner; of each day forcing the route a bit farther, while the rest of the party had the dreary, but very necessary job of ferrying loads in our wake up the mountain.

I woke to hear the steady purr of the primus. I had got my head inside my sleeping-bag, with only my nose sticking out of a small gap at the top. It was uncomfortable with the wet of condensation from my breath, but I just lay still for a time, dreading the start of yet another day. Finally I looked out of my bag, and could see Tachei crouched over the primus. He looked up, smiling.

'Tea ready soon, Sahib.'

'What's it like outside, Tachei?' I asked.

'Some wind, some snow. Very cold,' he replied cheerfully. It had been like that for the past fortnight, but somehow I felt encouraged by his optimism. He was in his mid-fifties, had been on some of the pre-war Everest expeditions and on many since. In the weeks we had spent together I had come to love him'; 'like' is too weak a word for the feeling of warm respect and affection both Dick and I felt for him. He had looked after us, indeed spoilt us for the entire time we had been on the mountain. At the end of a long day, when we had slumped into our sleeping-bags, he had struggled with the Primus and made the supper; this is something that any of our Sherpas would have done, but it was the warmth of his friendship and his never-failing loyalty that we valued so specially.

I glanced around our snow hole – it was about six foot high and ten long. The temperature was a degree or so below freezing, but compared with a tent it was sheer luxury. For a start there was no sound of wind – after a time the constant hammering of canvas drives you berserk. There was also space to move around, to stand up. We had carved shelves in the walls for our food and other equipment. In the passage we had even dug a small hole to use as a lavatory – basic, but it's no joke going out into the cold wind in the middle of the night. It had taken a day of hard work to build the cave on the crest of the ridge, but it was amply worthwhile. This was to be our jumping-off point for the summit, still five miles away.

Ang Nyima, lying in his sleeping-bag like a long grey slug, broke into a fit of coughing that seemed to tear deep into his chest. He had suffered from a bad chest cough for the entire time we had been on the mountain, and yet had always insisted on going out with us, even though his face was grey with fatigue. He had been on the successful Everest expedition and had carried a load to the top camp. Since then, he had joined the British Army and had been serving as a mess waiter in Malaya. The transition from the tropics to the Himalaya must have been particularly hard, but he was determined to keep going, I think largely because he realised he had a good chance of being in the summit party, owing to his position in the Services. We never got as close to him, however, as we did to Tachei; there was something aloof, almost disdainful, in his manner; I couldn't help feeling that he despised us.

Living in a cave, it was easy to get organised for the day – you could even put on your crampons before going out. Once out, we found the weather was the same as it had been for the past fortnight – clouds building up in the south, and a bitter wind blasting across the ridge. We hoped to establish a camp half-way up to the Shoulder, so that the next day, Dick and I could press on over the crest, and see the ridge that links the Shoulder with

Annapurna II for the first time. We would then be poised for the final phase of our assault.

First we had to cross a knife-edged section of the ridge. Ang Nyima and I had reconnoitred it the previous day: to the north the slope dropped away steeply to the Marsyandi Valley, while to the south, we looked down into a plunging gorge that ran right to the foothills of Nepal. On the other side of the gorge was one of the most beautiful mountains of the Himalaya, Machapuchare. Embraced by the cirque of the Annapurna Range, it tapered into a fluted fish-tail of ice.

We pressed on, slowly but steadily, as the slope began to steepen.

'I'll take a go in front,' I muttered to Dick, and plodded past him. I was panting hard, but felt I was going well, glanced up and saw the top of the slope only fifty feet above – we could have a rest there. Suddenly, like stepping through an invisible barrier, my strength, my very will to keep going seemed to ooze out of me.

The rest of the day was a nightmare – it never seemed to end. I was now bringing up the rear of the party. The rope, linking me to Dick, tugged at my waist whenever I paused for a rest. I repeated to myself, over and over again, 'I mustn't give in. I mustn't give in.' The only thing, I think, that kept me going, was the thought that if I did pack in, I obviously would not deserve to go to the summit. If Dick slipped there would have been no chance of my holding him, for my entire strength and concentration were directed to just putting one foot in front of the other.

At last we came out on to a shoulder.

'We'll make camp at the end of this,' said Dick. 'We can't go much farther today.'

'Thank God,' I told myself.

The ground stretched out in front of us in a level plateau, an antarctic waste of frozen snow.

'We can take the rope off here,' Dick said. 'You just follow on in your own time.'

The others quickly drew ahead, while I stumbled on, a few paces at a time. At this stage I was getting some slight, rather twisted satisfaction from my performance, dramatising to myself the efforts I was making, basking in a feeling of heroism in face of supreme effort, for my mind seemed partly detached from my body. I had spent many hours as a child telling myself stories of heroic endeavour, with myself in the principal part, fighting against limitless odds. As I plodded across the plateau I was back in those childhood days, in a dream world, that at the same time was true; my mind alternated between euphoria and despair. As I stopped for the twentieth time in a hundred yards, I began to wonder about my chances of ever reaching the summit. I asked myself if I had reached my height ceiling – perhaps I just would not acclimatise to higher altitudes, and anyway what right had I to be with the trail-breaking party out in front – perhaps one of the others could go more strongly.

By the time I had caught up the others they had nearly finished pitching the tent. The canvas was flapping in the wind with demoniac force. It took all our strength to pin it down.

Once the tent was pitched the two Sherpas turned away to return to the lower camp. We felt very small and lonely as we watched them disappear into the swirling clouds of wind-blown snow. We were now at a height of about 23,000 feet; above us the ridge stretched endlessly, in a graceful sweep, to the Shoulder immediately below Annapurna IV. It was a discouraging thought that our summit was another three miles beyond that. But now my only thought was to escape from the wind, to rest and find a little warmth. I struggled with my crampon straps – they were like steel hawsers – and then waited while Dick brushed the loose snow off his clothing before he dived into the tent. I shouted silent curses into the wind. At last it was my turn, and I wriggled through the sleeve entrance. Even though we had been careful there was snow everywhere inside. For a few minutes we just lay down, then we had to force ourselves into further activity.

'Come on, Chris, let's get this lot sorted out,' Dick said at last.

Everything at that altitude seemed an insurmountable problem – even unpacking a rucksack or getting out a sleeping-bag.

'Well, we can't complain,' grinned Dick. 'This is the first night on the expedition we've had to cook our own supper. If you like, I'll do it tonight and you can do breakfast. You seem to be more lively in the mornings.'

'That's fine with me,' I agreed with relief.

I lay back in my sleeping-bag, while Dick struggled with the Primus – the more tired you are, the more trouble they give. He cursed, pumped wildly, and yellow flames gushed around him, only to die away to nothing.

'Where's the bloody pricker?'

I searched amongst the heap of frozen clothing and food tins and at last found it. He pricked the infernal machine, pumped like a maniac and lit it once again. The thing once more burst into flames. After several more attempts he got it burning with a steady roar, reached out of the tent to gather some snow, and we settled own to wait for our brew of tea. One learns to be patient in the Himalaya – everything takes such a long time, and a panful of snow slowly melts down to only a few spoonfuls of water. We added more snow, until we had enough. At this stage Dick succeeded in upsetting the primus and our precious water went over my sleeping-bag. I could only laugh – it was just one more thing in an appalling day.

At last we had our tea and even some stew, but though I felt ravenously hungry, the taste of the tinned meat turned my stomach, and I could only manage a few mouthfuls. I longed for tinned fruit, for baked beans, for tuna fish, for things that we didn't have with us.

By the time it was dark, we had eaten. I was too tired to read and just dropped into an uneasy doze, but that night we never really went to sleep – the wind was too violent.

'We'll be lucky if the tent stands up through the night,' said Dick. 'Make sure your rucksack is packed before you go to sleep. We might have to move into the nearest crevasse at this rate.'

We just lay and listened to the mad hammer of wind on canvas, watched it flap with an uncontrollable force. It seemed impossible that the tent would last the night. The hoar frost that formed on the walls, the condensation of our breath, was immediately shaken off on to our sleeping-bags where it melted and then, later in the night, froze.

Somehow the tent stood up to the wind. When morning came it was my turn to cook breakfast. I promptly evened up the score by spilling the porridge over Dick. It said something for our friendship, that neither of us lost his temper. In fact, in the five weeks that we were together, sharing a small tent, I don't think we ever got on each other's nerves. We never said very much, but felt a real bond of sympathy – or at least I did for Dick: he was the kind of person who could get on with anyone: he had an evenly balanced temperament and was completely unselfish – I couldn't say the same for myself.

Breakfast was even worse than supper. Washing greasy pans is just about impossible at altitude – there is never enough water and the exertion is too tiring. As a result all food soon assumes a neutral flavour: the morning tea, a muddy grey liquid with icebergs of undissolved milk powder floating in it, tastes of yesterday's stew.

'Well, I suppose we had better try to get up to the Shoulder now that we have come this far,' said Dick.

I agreed without enthusiasm, wondering how I should perform today. I had to force myself on, somehow, if I was to remain in the trail-breaking party and eventually go to the summit. Getting ready to start was even worse than settling in the night before. Our outer clothes were frozen into suits of armour, boots, which were made of rubber, were stiff and cold to the touch, and once out, it took ten minutes to put on crampons.

The wind was as savage as ever, blowing in a constant blast across the ridge. We slowly stumbled towards the start of the slope – I felt as listless as the day before, wanted only to get back into the shelter of our snow cave at the start of the ridge. I silently prayed that Dick would turn back, but did not dare to suggest it. Even Dick was going slowly. After only a hundred yards, which seemed as many miles, he turned round.

'We'll go back. It's bloody hopeless against this wind,' he yelled into my ear.

I hardly replied, just turned and bolted for the tent. We dragged our gear out, and pulled it down, poles and all – we could never have folded it up in the high wind – and then started back for Camp III. Walking downhill seemed effortless after our struggle of the previous day. It felt like a return to real safety, and the snow cave a luxury hotel compared to our tent. Bill Crawshaw and Stewart Ward were there with half a dozen Sherpas; everyone was packing rucksacks.

'Jimmy Roberts has called us down for a rest until the weather improves,' shouted Bill.

I felt a wave of relief; I suddenly realised just how much I wanted to escape from this world of discomfort, perpetual glare and blasting wind. We wasted no time: having had the order to retreat, Dick and I decided to get back down that same day – we could not have stood another night on the mountain. It had taken us three weeks of hard effort to reach the site of Camp IV; it now took us a mere eight hours to get down to Base Camp, 12,000 feet below.

When we had walked up the long wooded valley from our base camp at the beginning of April, the ground had been covered in snow, but now, on our return, Spring was bursting through the warm earth. The feel of young grass underfoot, the smell of pine needles, the sight of soft browns and greens was inexpressibly delicious.

We spent a week down at base camp and for the first day or so it was a delight just to do nothing, to have a bath or lie in the sun, but soon I became impatient to return to the mountain. The moment we left the mountain the weather began to improve – there was hardly a cloud in the sky and, more important, none of those tell-tale plumes of wind-blown snow on the ridge far above us. Jimmy stuck to his guns, however; having brought us down, he was determined to give us a good rest before returning for the final assault.

It must have been a hard decision, and one that showed his quality as a leader. He admitted afterwards to having been gnawed by doubts lest he had sacrificed our only chance of good weather. But we were all in desperate need of a rest.

I also had my own doubts – I could not forget how badly I had performed on our last day on the mountain. Had I reached my height ceiling at 22,000 feet? Would I be chosen for the summit party? I was on tenterhooks until Jimmy gave us our final briefing for the assault.

CHAPTER TEN

Annapurna II – the Summit

It was like an 'O' Group on a military exercise. We were sitting in a half-circle round Jimmy Roberts, pencils and notebooks in our hands; we might just as well have been attending a briefing on a company attack against Redland, as one for the final assault on Annapurna II. It brought home the similarity between planning a campaign in war and on a mountain.

'Dick, Chris and Ang Nyima will go for the summit,' Jimmy told us, and I felt a tremendous feeling of relief and elation. 'They will be supported by six of the Sherpas, right up to the top camp. Bill, Stew, Prabaka and Jagjit, you will go as far as Camp III and help ferry loads to Camp IV. You can then wait at Camp III until they have got to the top. Once they have done this, you can have a go at Annapurna IV.

'I want to streamline the assault as much as possible. This spell of good weather can't last for ever. You can move up to Camp III in two groups, on successive days. Stop at Camp II on the first night and then press straight on to III. You should all be at III on the 11th May. On the 12th you can ferry loads up to IV, and then on the 13th the assault party with the six Sherpas can move in there. The next day they can ferry loads up to the Shoulder, and on the 15th establish Camp V there. On the 16th you should be able to push your top camp to the end of the ridge below the final pyramid, and on the 17th, with a bit of luck, make your assault.'

'You two,' pointing to Dick and me, 'can start using oxygen at Camp IV. Ang Nyima should need it for the final assault.'

'I wish I could come with you, but with my stomach in its present state, I should only be in the way. You'll be in charge, Dick, and you can alter the plan as circumstances dictate. Are there any questions?'

For the first six days we moved up the mountain with machine-like precision. The weather was perfect, not a cloud in the sky or a breath of wind. I was delighted to find that the oxygen-set brought my own performance

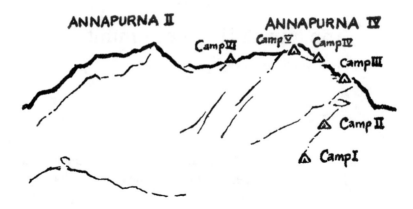

to sea-level standard. The strength-giving flow amply made up for the extra weight: the set and cylinder alone weighed thirty pounds, and by the time one had added some equipment or one's personal belongings it weighed a good fifty. Without oxygen-sets the Sherpas were going nearly as strongly as we were. I couldn't help feeling a twinge of guilt that we had this aid and they didn't.

We made our camp on the Shoulder according to timetable, but that night clouds were building up in the south, and by the morning a full-blown storm was raging outside.

'We'll go out on to the ridge, anyway,' Dick decided. 'We can always dump the loads for Camp VI and come back if it doesn't clear up.'

I thoroughly enjoyed that day. At last we were venturing on to ground that had never been touched by man – not that we could see much, for we were in dense cloud all day. We just felt our way along the south side of the ridge, crossing a snow slope of about 45°. We didn't dare get too close to the crest of the ridge for there were huge cornices on the northern side.

After a few hundred yards we came to a sheer drop, a step in the ridge that had stopped Charles Evans in 1957. In the cloud we couldn't even see the bottom, but managed to work our way down it, slithering in treacherously soft snow. We must have been a strange sight, Dick and I in front, like two men from outer space with our goggles and oxygen masks, and the six Sherpas strung out behind, all tied on one rope.

A further few hundred yards and we came to yet another step. We were now several hundred feet below the Shoulder. It was late in the afternoon and the weather seemed to be deteriorating. The Sherpas were grey with fatigue – they had no oxygen to help them on. Dick was in a bad way, as well. There was something wrong with his set so that he was only getting a trickle that barely made up for the weight he was carrying.

'We'll dump everything here,' he shouted, 'It's no good staying here. This might last for days and we should only be using up rations. Let's get back to the Shoulder.'

On the return we were going uphill for most of the way, into the full blast of the storm. The Sherpas were stumbling like drunken men, exhausted by their efforts. But for the bamboo wands we had left every hundred yards or so, we would have had great difficulty in finding the camp at all.

That night we all felt near defeat.

'I think we've had our spell of good weather. We should have come up earlier,' I said to Dick.

He was crouched over the Primus, trying to thaw out the regulating valve of his oxygen-set. There was probably some ice in it that had reduced the flow.

'It's not that bad,' he replied. 'We've got plenty of food and fuel up here. I'll send some of the Sherpas back tomorrow. We can sit it out for another couple of day, and then if it doesn't improve we'll have to go back as well.'

'Do you think your oxygen set is going to be all right? Why not send down for a spare?'

'I shall. But I'll manage somehow,' he replied. He had never complained during the day, though I could see that it had taken all his endurance to keep going – I knew that I could never have kept on in similar circumstances.

That night we slept well. There was none of the usual tension before going on a big climb – we were just looking forward to a day in our sleeping-bags, waiting out the storm.

It was daylight when I woke. At altitude, one's reactions are slowed down to a snail's pace. I had been lying awake for some time before I realised that there was no wind drumming against the tent. I poked my head through the sleeve entrance.

'What's it like?' asked Dick.

'There's a lot of high cloud coming from the north,' I replied. 'It looks as it if might brew up later on.'

'Where did you say it was coming from?' he asked excitedly.

'The north.'

'Do you realise, man, this is the first time since we've been here that it's come from that direction? It might mean a change.'

'I hadn't thought of that. We might as well push on to Camp VI today.'

'Bugger that, we'll go for the bloody summit. The Sherpas can follow on and put up the camp for us.'

Having made the decision, we wasted no further time, had a quick breakfast, and by 7.30 had set out. The route that had seemed so forbidding in the storm the previous day, was straightforward in the bright sunlight.

The three of us plodded steadily on, along the ridge, just below the crest; it dropped away below our feet, in a clean sweep of snow to the jigsaw of a hanging glacier several thousand feet below.

Although his set was still not working, Dick insisted on taking his turn in the lead. Whenever we paused he could hardly speak for panting, he was getting so little oxygen.

It took us only a couple of hours to reach the place where we had dumped our loads the previous day. It was a sobering thought that we still had over a mile to go, and a good 2500 feet to climb. As we approached the final pyramid, it seemed to loom above us: it looked frighteningly steep.

'You can take a go in front,' gasped Dick, and I moved into the lead.

Huge cumulo-nimbus clouds were building up to the south and from the north poured a flood of low grey cloud, washing against the ridge that we had just crossed; none of us said anything, but we were all secretly worried about a change in the weather. It never occurred to us to turn back – on those last stages of climbing a high mountain you are prepared to take any risk to reach the top.

The angle now steepened. A few hundred feet of hard snow led to a rock band, all hideously loose like the tiles of a roof on a derelict house. There was no time to take belays; we just eased our way over on loose flakes, careful not to touch the huge poised blocks above. Beyond, a fragile ribbon of snow clung to the crest of the ridge. A slash of the axe, step up, pant, another slash of the axe. It went on endlessly.

Again the angle steepened, the snow was all soft, slipping away under my feet; my hands burrowed frantically but found nothing. I glanced behind me; Dick was trying to find a belay, but could never have held me if I had come off. Somehow, I floundered on to firm ground, the blood pounding in my head, heart beating a mad tattoo.

'You bloody fool,' Dick muttered. 'You could have killed us all. There's an easy way just round the corner.'

I pressed on, round a small gendarme and up another ribbon of firm snow. With the oxygen, I felt I had plenty in reserve – I even enjoyed climbing over a boulder that barred our way on the crest of the ridge. I no longer glanced over my shoulder at the boiling clouds, but just kept my eyes on the snow in front. I thought we were coming to the summit, only to find the ridge stretching on beyond to a higher point. It was a surprise when I realised that the slope dropped away beyond a small cone of snow just in front of me.

'We're there,' I shouted to Dick, who was stumbling behind, head down – he had somehow kept going on a bare trickle of oxygen. We both stopped to allow Ang Nyima to catch up, and then, without thinking, thrust him up on to the summit. It was a tremendously moving movement, and the only time I have been so moved at the end of a climb – perhaps because this was my first big unclimbed peak, but more, I think, because we had worked closely and well together for such a long time. At that moment I was not aware of the other members of the expedition, whose efforts had, in fact, enabled us to reach the top – there were just the three of us on a small cone of snow with boundless space around us. We were cut off from the rest of the expedition – from the rest of humanity, for that matter – by the swirling flood of cloud that now filled the valleys to the north and south. Slowly it crept up the causeway running back to the Shoulder below Annapurna IV. To the south towered great mountains of cumulo-nimbus, dwarfing those snow peaks that had not been engulfed by it.

'Down going, Sahibs.' Ang Nyima, for ever practical, brought us to our senses. It was now past four o'clock and we had a long way to get back.

The moment we started down, all my elation left me. I just wanted to get down in one piece, moved cautiously, afraid the steps might break under me, that rock would come away. On the way up there had been no room for such fear; nothing had mattered except reaching the summit, and at that last stage, we would have taken practically any risk to reach it. Our oxygen was now nearly exhausted and we were getting only the smallest trickle. It was all I could do to climb down myself, let alone watch the rope leading down to Dick.

Suddenly he was falling; before I could do anything I was tugged off my feet, and shot down the steep snow. Automatically, I used the pick of my axe as a brake, but it was no good, for it just cut through the snow. There was no time to think – I was past thinking anyway. I was going faster, suddenly shot past Dick, and the rope came taut with a violent tug. He had somehow managed to brake himself and had then held me. We stumbled to our feet, and continued down. No one said anything about the fall – I didn't even feel a sense of shock, I was too tired.

Once we got off the summit pyramid, the ridge seemed endless: we had to cross a couple of waves before reaching the site of our tents which Urkein and Mingma had brought along the ridge earlier that day. It was sheer heaven to collapse into sleeping-bags, eat a can of fruit (melted over the Primus), and drink tea. This had been the finest day's climbing I had ever had, more than compensating for all the sweat and the grind of the last few weeks; but now there was a feeling of anticlimax, and my one ambition was to get off the mountain as soon as possible. I was horribly aware of the physical discomfort I had previously ignored, my sore throat and hacking cough. That night, I even succeeded in convincing myself that I was in the last stages of pneumonia and about to die – I woke Dick up, so that he could share my last hours, but he was singularly unsympathetic and assured that I would survive the night.

Three days later, back in base camp, I had the same feeling of anticlimax: my nerves felt raw with the prolonged proximity of the rest of the party and I longed to escape, if only for a few days. Jimmy Roberts' plans for our return gave me the opportunity.

'We'll have a change of scenery on the way back,' he told us. 'I'll send the porters back the way we came, while we, with a few Sherpas, can travel light over the pass to Muktinath, and then down the other side of Annapurna past Tukche to Pokara.'

'Could I take Tachei with me, and go across the Tilicho Pass?' I asked. 'We could meet you at the other side.'

'All right,' he agreed, 'but don't get lost; there aren't any accurate maps of that area.'

'That would be grand,' chipped in Bill Crawshaw, 'I'd like to come, too.'

My heart dropped – I wanted at all costs to get away from the others; fortunately he changed his mind and decided to go with the main party.

A walk across a Himalayan pass probably sounds an anticlimax compared to the ascent of a major peak, and yet the three days I spent crossing the Tilicho Pass, in many ways meant much more to me than our ascent of Annapurna II. This was the pass that Maurice Herzog had crossed in 1950 in his search for Annapurna I. Its position, marked on the Indian Ordnance Survey map, bore no relation to the actual configuration of the ground. The Grande Barrière, a chain of 20,000 foot peaks barred the way, and the Tilicho Pass was to the north of these. There was no path over it and it had never been used by the local people. The only map I had was the sketch-map in the back of Maurice Herzog's book.

It was three days before I could tear Tachei away from Base Camp: the Sherpas had settled down to a celebratory binge, consuming huge quantities of rakshi, a potent spirit distilled from barley or rice. They deserved it; their untiring efforts on the mountain had made our success possible. Two of them, Urkein and Mingma, were even celebrating the first all-Sherpa ascent of a Himalayan peak: while we were climbing Annapurna II they had slipped up Annapurna IV, leaving a dirty handkerchief tied to a bamboo wand as token of their achievement.

It was a delight to escape at last from the confusion of base camp, from the too-familiar sounds and voices. Tachei was looking decidedly the worse for wear as we walked up the wide, stony valley towards the village of Mananbhot. However slowly I walked I pulled a long way ahead of him after a few minutes, and would then settle down to read by the side of the track until he caught up.

'Sorry, sorry, Sahib. Very bad head. Rakshi, no good,' he would mutter as he staggered up to me. Each time I took something from him until I looked like the Sherpa and he the Sahib; but it didn't matter – the sun was shining, we were leaving the expedition, and an unknown world was ahead of us. It was late afternoon when we reached the head of the valley and stopped in a village. The houses, with dry stone walls and flat roofs, were terraced into the hillside. There were no windows, not even chimneys, and smoke from the cooking fires found its way through the doors. The village street, not much wider than a footpath, wound its way through blank walls broken only by the occasional door.

We were soon followed by a troop of grubby, barefoot children, who nevertheless looked happy and well fed. They directed us to a house where we could buy rice and eggs. I sipped a cup of rakshi, while Tachei bargained and gossiped with the woman of the house, a plump matron with a ready twinkle in her eye. But we departed with bare hands; she claimed that there was hardly any food left in the village and that their hens were no longer laying.

That evening we walked up to the yak pastures, about a thousand feet above. Two boys, who were looking after the herd, collected wood for us in return for a Mars Bar. They also brought back half-a-dozen eggs, green speckled with brown. They were the same size as European hen eggs, much bigger than anything you get in Nepal.

'What are they?' I asked Tachei.

'Rham Chicaw eggs, Sahib. Very good to eat.'

We bought these with another Mars Bar. I insisted on cooking the supper that night – an omelette from the eggs of the Rham Chicaw and thick, creamy milk straight from one of the Yaks – it was wonderfully rich in flavour. You could imagine it on the menu of an exclusive London restaurant at thirty-five shillings a portion. The two lads crouched by the fire and watched our every movement – I don't suppose much ever happened up there at the head of the valley and I was probably the first European they had seen.

We didn't bother to put up the tent, but lay in our sleeping-bags by the fire. We talked a little, though conversation was very restricted as Tachei could only speak a few words of English and I a little Hindi. A great deal of our conversation took the form of mutual adulation:

'Sahib, very, very good Sahib,' Tachei would assure me.

'Ah, but Tachei a very, very good Sherpa,' I would reply. I certainly missed a great deal, not talking the language, for Tachei was constantly telling me about the country and people around us in a strange mixture of Hindi, Sherpa and English that was almost totally incomprehensible. I just answered with the occasional non-committal grunt, which kept the conversation going.

The next morning we set off for the pass. I had decided to avoid the gorge leading straight to it, where the going was obviously going to be difficult; so we kept to the high ground and headed for a col over the ridge, running down to it. This was straightforward walking, but we had the interest of picking our route through unmapped ground. To reach the col we had to climb a treadmill of scree – two paces up, one back down. At its crest, we looked across to the huge ice wall of the Grande Barrière. It was a strange, desolate place, a wide basin of undulating, stony ground surrounding a huge frozen lake, whose surface was a jigsaw of dark cracks. We took a last look at Annapurna II, now partly hidden in cloud, and started down the other side across the snout of a dying glacier. It was nearly dark when we reached the shores of the lake and put up our tent. We were now a dozen miles from the nearest human habitation, not much really, compared even to the North of Scotland, but there was a sense of remoteness about the place that was emphasised by the size of the peaks around us.

The next morning we followed the shores of the lake to a line of cliffs. Herzog in 1950 had crossed the lake, but now the ice did not seem strong enough. We ended up by climbing the cliff though we had no rope, and it was a good five hundred feet high. Tachei was not very impressed by his introduction to the sport of rock climbing – the rock was unpleasantly loose and we had forty-pound rucksacks on our backs. Another few hours hard walking brought us to the head of the pass.

I felt sorry to leave the mountain solitude, but had already begun to dream of the chicken we would buy that evening. We were now above the Kali Gandaki, the valley running between Dhaulagiri and Annapurna. In violent contrast to the land of grey-brown rock that we were leaving, the fields formed a patchwork of brilliant green in the valley bottom. For the rest of the afternoon we picked our way down towards the valley, across high pasture land and then through dense scrub, losing ourselves in a maze of earthy gorges. That night we stayed in the village of Thinigaon. The houses were flat-roofed like those of Manangbhot, but they were much more spacious and clean, and built round a courtyard, with verandas looking into the centre.

We were given a room on the first floor; it was impeccably clean and well, though sparsely, furnished, with carved chests round the walls and ironware pots on the shelves. In the centre of one wall was a dried mud hearth for the cooking fire, and the smoke found its way through a hole in the roof.

That night we feasted on chicken curry, washed down by quantities of chang, a beer, white in colour, made from fermented rice. Happily drowsy, I listened to Tachei talk with our host, and felt sad that on the morrow I had promised to rejoin the expedition, that once again I should become part of an alien group in a strange land.

CHAPTER ELEVEN

Nuptse

Before setting out for Annapurna II, I had been invited to join another expedition – to Dhaulagiri, then the highest unclimbed peak in the world. It was civilian, organised by Joe Walmsley, a well-known climber from Manchester, who had already led one expedition to the Himalaya. I had been tempted, but it seemed unlikely that the army would release me two years running; then I heard that a Swiss expedition had been attempting Dhaulagiri at the same time that we were on Annapurna. They succeeded in reaching the top and I put all thought of Joe Walmsley's expedition out of my mind.

On my return to England, I had only a few more months left at the Army Outward Bound School before it was time to return to my regiment. As the weeks went by, I became more and more unsettled, hating the thought of returning to regimental soldiering, but not seeing clearly what I could do in the future; then, in early October, at a dinner of the Climbers' Club in North Wales, I met Joe Walmsley once again.

'We've now got permission for Nuptse,' he told me. 'It's the third peak of Everest – 25,850 feet high – and it looks as if it'll give some hard climbing.'

'Have you got everyone you want?' I asked tentatively.

'Why, do you want to come along?' he replied.

I hardly thought, but made up my mind on the spur of the moment – to hell with the army!

'Yes, if you've got room for me.'

'I can't say straight away. I'll have a word with the others and let you know next week.'

Having made my decision, I was on tenterhooks as to whether I should be invited. The letter arrived at the end of the week – I was in the party.

I suppose I could have tried to get permission from the army to join the expedition, but somehow the idea never occurred to me. I started to hunt for a civilian job. I was so used to being in a large organisation – the absolute security of the army – that it never occurred to me that I could do anything but go into another large organisation.

I wrote round to Shell, I.C.I., Unilever and B.P. One of my first interviews

was with Unilever. I passed the initial one with flying colours – ego pleasantly boosted, for only a small proportion of applicants even survived this –
and went on to their selection board. This was a more intellectual version
of those of the army and air force, though instead of crossing alligator-
infested rivers, we played with an imaginary soap-manufacturing company,
had discussion groups and even psychological tests. I surmounted this
hurdle, and the next thing was an interview with my future employer – the
managing director of Van den Berghs Limited, an associate company of
Unilever, that markets margarine.

I was confronted by the managing director flanked by two other directors.

'You know, you strike me as being a drifter,' said one of my inquisitors.
'First you tried the air force, then the army, now us. What makes you think
you are going to settle down here?

'I have only changed my career once,' I replied hotly. 'It wasn't my fault
that I couldn't fly. The army was a straight alternative to the air force. As
for my change now, it's all too easy to make a mistake in your choice of
career in your early twenties. Surely the important thing is to recognise it,
and then do something about it.'

'Yes, but why choose marketing?'

'I'm interested in selling things, and the whole process of marketing. For
instance, my job in getting the equipment for the Annapurna expedition
was a form of counter-marketing – persuading the manufacturers to give
us their goods free of charge. I thoroughly enjoyed this and the planning it
involved.'

'Sound's more like begging to me. But anyway, how do we know that
you are not going shooting off on another expedition in a couple of years'
time.'

'No, Nuptse will be my last expedition. I realise that I can't base my
career on climbing all my life. I want to get stuck into a worthwhile job
with a future.'

And so it went on. I don't know how far I succeeded in convincing them,
but I certainly succeeded with myself. I was determined to settle down
into a commercial career once I got back from Nuptse. I had taken the
precaution, however, of giving myself a long climbing swan-song: I was not
going to join Unilever until the September of 1961, which would mean I
could have a couple of months in the Alps on my return from Nuptse.

We were due to set out in early February, some by road, travelling in two
Standard Vanguards, and the rest by sea or air. I was lucky enough to go
out by sea – one of the best parts of the trip – but was to return overland
with the car party, and planned to stop off in the Alps.

The entire party, nine of us, assembled in Kathmandu at the end of

February. Three weeks later we had established our base camp below the South Face of Nuptse, and two of us were out in front, making the route up the lower slopes.

'We're wasting our time, Dennis. My feet are frozen solid. It's no good going on in this weather.'

'I think we should, at least, get round this bluff and see what it's like on the other side. I won't be long now.' And he continued chopping steps in the hard ice. I cursed him with everything I could think of – imagined the satisfaction of smashing a fist in his face.

'You can bloody well carry on by yourself then; I'm going back down,' I shouted up after him. He returned slowly.

'If we don't keep pushing on, we'll never get up this arête,' he reasoned. I realised I was in the wrong, but was infuriated, not so much by the cold, as by the man himself. We had been cooped up in a small tent for nearly a week now; had worked each day, foot by foot through tottering séracs and knife-edged arêtes; up ice that was like the skin of a rotting banana, ready to peel off its rocky flesh at the least touch. A blow of the axe opened gaping holes, and even a hundred feet below the crest of the ridge, you could, in places, look straight through a hole to the other side. The work was nerve-racking: this would not have mattered if we had been well attuned, but we were too different in temperament to climb together happily.

Dennis Davis was a wiry man of average height in his mid-thirties. His face was seamed by perpetual worry, emphasised somehow by his military moustache. He had a passion for hard work, driving himself perpetually to the limit, whether he was climbing a mountain or doing his job as a site engineer. Even at night in the tent he never relaxed, but had everything in apple-pie order. These, of course, are all commendable qualities. If you don't share them, however, they can quickly become maddening, especially when they are rammed down your throat. I am sure Dennis didn't mean to do this, but he always succeeded in giving me an uncomfortable guilt-complex when I was with him.

I am the very reverse, slightly lazy, often indolent, happy to do the minimum to keep things going. Not a matter of doing less than my share, but preferring to lie in the comfortable squalor of an untidy tent at the end of a long day, rather than spend the evening putting it in order, and preferring to eat off a dirty plate to avoid the trouble of washing up. Fortunately, many climbers are like-minded, but Dennis wasn't – hence my own guilt-complex bursting, under strain, into active conflict.

As we turned to go back, I felt a mixture of shame and anger. I changed my mind.

'Come on. I'll lead the bloody pitch; at least I won't take all day over it.'

I hurled myself at the ice bulge. We were trying to get round a gendarme of ice barring the arête; there was a narrow shelf down its side that Dennis had been trying to cross. I slashed at the ice, getting rid of some of my frustration in the violence of my blows, and quickly passed the obstacle. Beyond, the angle was easier, though the ice was as hard as ever, dropping away to a glacier a couple of thousand feet below.

We pressed on in silence for another few hundred feet, taking turns to lead. It was a slow business: we had to cut steps all the way, and hammer in ice-pitons every few yards, to hold the ropes we had left in place for the entire length of the route. We had already used 2000 feet, even though we had gained only 1000 feet in vertical height above the start of the arête.

'This'd be all right in the Alps,' Dennis muttered as he passed me, 'but it's bloody ridiculous here. We'll have to fix-rope the whole mountain at this rate.'

'It should be easier once we get into the middle of the face,' I replied.

'For a bit, but what about that rock band. It's all very well for you rock gymnasts to dream of doing VS climbing at 24,000 feet, but I think you'll find it a bit different from the Pass when you get there.'

'We'll see when we get there. Let's push off down.'

This time Dennis agreed. We were both overwhelmed by the size of the problem and felt claustrophobic on the narrow confines of this flying buttress that leapt so crazily up the side of the South Face of Nuptse. True, it opened out into a sweeping spur in the centre of the face, but that was somewhere above. Each time we reached a crest on the arête there was more beyond.

But at least that night we came closer together than we had at any other time that week. On the way down I apologised for my outburst. It was nearly dark when we got back to the tents. They were perched on a lip of ice that clung to a rock prow. For the first few nights I had lain awake wondering just how secure it was; the ice was honeycombed with holes – but soon we all just took it for granted. This was our third camp, though it was only at a height of 19,000 feet. The ground was so steep and difficult that we had found it necessary to keep the camps close together. Even so, finding sites was a desperate problem. There were few ledges large enough to take a tent and it would have meant hours of cutting to hack a platform out of the ice.

The rest of the party were ferrying loads across the glacier up on to the col at the foot of the arête. We could see the lights of Base Camp far below us; to the east was Makalu, black and massive in the gathering dark, while just opposite was the soaring spire of Ama Dablam, climbed only a few weeks before by Mike Ward and other members of Hillary's scientific expedition. They had wintered at a height of 20,000 feet and had slipped out to climb it in the early spring. They caused quite a furore, for they had not bothered to get the permission of the Nepalese authorities who inflicted a heavy fine on the expedition.

The next morning it dawned fine and we set out with renewed hope. Once the fixed ropes were established, ground that we had found terrifying when we first crossed it seemed easy. We didn't even rope up, just clipped karabiners, attached to our wait-loops, on to the fixed rope. In this way we were able to climb a stretch that had originally taken several days, in a matter of hours. We pressed on farther, and were now in urgent need of another camp-site but, if anything, the arête became even steeper. On our return, we found Les Brown. He was the youngest member of the party, tall and gangling, almost ungainly. He was an outstanding rock climber, having put up many hard, new routes in the Lake District. On the approach march, I had spent a great deal of time with him. Our attitude to and enthusiasm for climbing was very similar.

'John's coming up the day after tomorrow, and Joe says that you two can come down for a rest while we move through to the front.'

'That suits us fine,' replied Dennis. 'We've been out in front quite long enough. I could do with a good wash.'

'What about tomorrow, though? Someone should go out on the arête. I wouldn't mind going up with Les, and I can come down tomorrow night,' I suggested.

'Suits me, provided you *do* come down,' said Dennis. 'It's no good sticking out in front the whole time.'

Dennis went down that night, leaving Les and me in possession of Camp III. The next day was the best I had had on Nuptse. We quickly got on to new ground, and reached some rock gendarmes. Climbing on firm brown granite was a delight, but more than that, with no feeling of strain in our relationship, we enjoyed each other's company. It was just like an easy Alpine day. We came to a level part of the ridge and could see what we thought was the last barrier before reaching the centre of the face.

'You should be up that in a couple of days,' I told Les, feeling a twinge of envy. Although I felt in need of a rest, I hated leaving the front. I longed to see over that barrier myself.

John Streetley was in his sleeping-bag when we got back – he was small, bubbling over with vitality. I have already mentioned him as the only climber outside the Rock and Ice circle to have climbed at their standard in the early fifties. Since then he had returned to his home in Trinidad, and had built up a prosperous engineering business. He was the kind of person

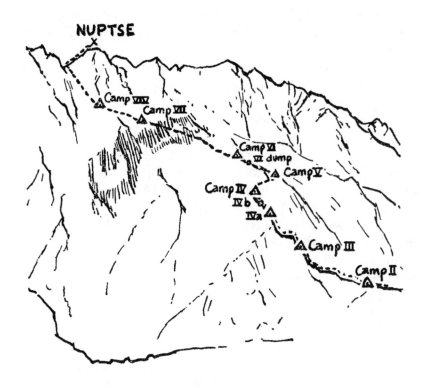

who was successful at anything he attempted, yet his dynamism had nothing ruthless about it. He had a wry sense of humour and an unending fund of stories that really were funny, but he had a reserve that, I imagine, few people broke: in spite of his warmth and friendliness, I never felt I knew him.

'How did you get on?' he shouted.

'We got in sight of the top,' replied Les. 'There's just one more rise in the arête, but it's a big one.'

'That's great! Did you see a decent camp-site?'

'There's bugger all. We were looking all the way.'

'Oh well, we'll just have to cut one out tomorrow, and we can push through to the top next day.'

'I'll give you a hand tomorrow,' I told them – secretly loth to go down.

The next day I went with them, carrying some food, to the site of their camp and left them cutting manfully into the ice – there were no platforms anywhere. I should then have gone down to Base, but once again found a good reason for staying up. Two of our Sherpas were now at Camp III and had carried loads with me, that day, to the site of Camp IV. I decided to stay with them, ferrying loads behind Les and John. I enjoyed the company of the Sherpas, and anyway it meant being spoilt: I could lie back and wait to be fed.

Each day I carried a load up the arête, but the two in front seemed to be making no progress. John had hardly acclimatised and had some kind of fibrositis in his back; Les and he, rather like Dennis and myself, seemed not to have been on the same wavelength – perhaps there was too great a difference in age and temperament.

After a couple of days they returned; Simon Clark and I moved up to take their place. I had already done some climbing with Simon in the Alps. Dark-haired, very intense, with pale face and horn-rimmed spectacles, he had done well at Cambridge, led an expedition to the Andes while still at university, and was now a management trainee with Shell.

By the time we reached the tent that Les and John had pitched, we were bubbling over with righteous indignation.

'It's a bloody shambles inside,' shouted Simon. 'What the hell have they been doing for the last three days?'

'Eating up the rations we carried up,' I replied dourly. 'Joe should never have let them out in front.'

We settled down to a grumbling session, criticising the leadership of the expedition and everyone in it; no doubt, at that moment, someone else was giving us the same treatment. I don't think our expedition was unique in the amount of backbiting that went on. It can happen all too easily on a large mountain, when people are under heavy strain, and often working in small isolated units, dependent on others above or below, but without adequate communications with them. In these circumstances it is easy to imagine that your own little party is doing the vital and by far the most unpleasant job of the entire expedition – and that because supplies are slow in coming up, or the people in front are not pushing forward, they are slacking.

The following day Simon and I made the big breakthrough. It took us six hours to climb a few hundred feet, leaving fixed ropes behind us all the way. The expedition had now nearly run out of rope; we were using our climbing ropes, and had even bought, at an extortionate rate, some old hemp rope from the Thangboche monastery. On the arête alone we had put nearly 5000 feet in position. We edged our way over blades of rock embedded in ice, conscious always of the steep drop below, now getting on for 3000 feet, to the gaping crevasses of the Nuptse glacier. A last wall of ice, and the angle began to ease, the slope opened out before us and we were on the col – level, crunchy snow with room for a few tents. After the confines of the arête it felt like a football pitch.

For a moment we felt as if we had climbed the mountain; that it was all over. But then we glanced up at the snow slope stretching above us: a band of steep rock barred the way into the upper ice-fields and summit gully, and we realised just how far we had still to go.

Sobered, we returned to the camp-site. I had a feeling of flat anticlimax. I had put too much of my strength and enthusiasm into getting up the arête. Now that we were up it, I seemed to have lost the urge to press on. I was full of plans. Simon and I spent most of our time planning streamlined assaults on the summit, and grumbling about the slowness with which supplies were trickling up the arête, but when it came to action I was hopelessly lethargic. We had intended to move up to the col the following day, but instead stayed in our sleeping-bags. I became obsessed with my own health, was coughing a lot, and had a pain in my chest that Jim Swallow, our doctor, assured me was merely from strained muscles. I didn't believe him, however, and imagined diagnoses of pneumonia or the like. Finally, after a lot of dithering, I decided to go down to Base Camp for a few days rest. As I scrambled down the arête, I had a feeling of guilt, mixed with fear that I should miss the final assault altogether.

I spent the next three days in my sleeping-bag in Base Camp. It was a depressing spot, not a touch of green anywhere, only stones and glacier debris. John was down there, still recovering from his fibrositis. The only other occupant was Jim Lovelock. He was a freelance journalist and had come out to look after Base Camp and write newspaper reports for the *Daily Telegraph*. He did much in those few days to bolster my morale by his unfailing cheerfulness and repertoire of bawdy stories.

It was agony watching the tiny black specks of the others creep ant-like up the shoulder on to the snow dome. I longed to be up with them. At this stage the weather began to break – it had been remarkably settled for the past three weeks – and the mountain was plastered in heavy cloud; snow fell every afternoon. Down at base we could only guess at the progress of the others as we caught glimpses of the upper slopes through rifts in the cloud. Dennis Davis and Jim Swallow were now out in front, at Camp V, about five hundred feet above the col. It was here that Dennis showed his dogged tenacity. Each day he went out in the storm to force the route a bit farther on, very often on his own, for Jim was not feeling too well. He didn't achieve very much, but the mere fact that he was up there and still trying, kept every one else going. Joe Walmsley and Les Brown, with a couple of Sherpas, were on the col, in Camp IV. In those few days enough supplies were ferried up to Camp V to make a summit bid possible.

After three days in Base Camp, I was still feeling weak and tired, but John decided to go back on to the mountain. I hated the thought of being left behind while everyone else was doing something, so I went with him. We stayed at the foot of the arête for the next few days. There seemed no point in going any nearer the front in bad weather, when it would just mean that more people were wasting rations without making any forward progress.

The weather had been bad for over a week and it was now well into May.

'It looks like an early monsoon to me,' I said gloomily to John.

'Certainly looks like it. We'll be lucky to get up at all if it doesn't improve soon.'

Already the arête was nearly impassable with freshly fallen snow. It certainly would have been if we hadn't fixed ropes all the way up it. John and I had the toughest but most enjoyable day of the expedition when we carried a couple of loads of food up it in a blizzard. We were out for ten hours, and got back in the dark after being swept away several times by avalanches of powder snow; we were saved by the fixed rope into which we had clipped.

The day after our epic ascent, when we were still trying to dry out our wet clothing, Simon Clark came down from Camp IV.

'It's bloody murder up there,' he told us. 'The wind just never stops; it's been hammering the tent, day and night for the last three days. I think you get a bit of shelter down here.' Later that evening he dropped a real bombshell.

'I'm getting worried about my wedding,' he told us – he was planning to get married on his return. 'If I don't start for home soon, I'm not going to have time to make all the preparations. I must leave on the 12th May.'

'You might as well start straight away, in that case, for we're certainly not going to climb the mountain in the next few days,' I observed.

'You know, I think I might come with you,' John added. 'I've got a hell of a lot to do back home – I've been away too long already.'

And so it was decided that they should set out in a few days' time. I was sorry to see John go, as I had particularly enjoyed climbing with him; but they were not leaving us in the lurch – the mountain was overcrowded as it was.

Climbing a Himalayan peak requires a pyramid of effort, with plenty of people at first to help ferry loads to about half-way up the mountain; but there comes a time when the party needs to be thinned out, when more people high up, simply means that more food and fuel are consumed, and that, therefore, more has to be brought up. Already there were four climbers and two Sherpas at Camp IV and beyond: enough to reach the top, if only the weather changed. Simon's and John's departure was, however, symptomatic of the spirit of the expedition. Somehow we had failed to forge any bonds of real friendship and affection while climbing together. I didn't go home with them, more because I personally wanted to reach the top of Nuptse, than because I had any unselfish desire for the eventual success of the expedition as a whole. I rather think that was the feeling of nearly everyone else, with the exception of Joe Walmsley, the leader, who devoted himself throughout to the prosaic but absolutely essential task of ensuring that our supplies were ferried up the mountain behind the party out in front.

The morning after John and Simon had made their decision, the weather showed signs of improvement and I decided to go up to Camp IV, since it should now be possible once more to make some real progress on the mountain. I wasn't made over-welcome when I arrived.

'What do you think you're doing?' asked Les.

'I thought I'd come up and see what's happening up front. Dennis has had a good spell up there.'

'Yes, in the rough weather. Why not ferry some loads up from III. We could do with some more food up here. You've done bugger-all load-carrying.'

I lost my temper.

'And you've done bugger-all in the last week except eat up food. When you were out in front you made precious little progress.'

Fortunately Joe put a stop to our stupid quarrel, and agreed that I should come up. There was a lot of justice in what Les had said. Perhaps in going down for a rest I was motivated by self-interest. Anyway at that moment I was determined to get up to the front and knew I was now going strongly – certainly as well as Les.

A couple of days later, Les and I went up to Camp IV just below the rock-band that Simon and I had seen when we reached the top of the arête. As far as we knew, Jim Swallow and the Sherpa – Pemba – were at V; Dennis and Tachei at VI. The previous evening we had seen the top pair go right to the foot of the rock-band. As we plodded up, I prayed to myself that they had found a way through it. If we could only surmount this last obstacle, we should be able to reach the summit.

Jim and Pemba were already ensconced at Camp VI when we arrived, so we hacked out another platform and settled down to wait for Dennis. It was a magnificent evening. We were at last creeping above the surrounding mountains. Ama Dablam's slender spire merged into the background peaks, as we looked down on it; to the west the rounded dome of Cho Oyu seemed not much higher than we were; and beyond stretched the ragged skyline of the Rolwaling Himal.

It was after dark when Dennis got back to the tent. His face was even thinner than when I had seen him last – haggard with weariness – and yet there was a look of triumph in his eyes.

'We've got through the band,' he announced. 'It doesn't look too bad beyond.'

'What was it like?' I asked.

'Nothing like as hard as we thought it would be. You don't have to go straight up it; there's an obvious traverse line with just one hard pitch – a chimney bunged up with ice. That was bloody thin. You know what Tachei's ropework is like. I might as well have done it solo. I've left a fixed rope on it.'

'How's Tachei going?'

'Really well. It makes all the difference having him with me; anyway I was getting bloody tired of looking after myself; it's great having someone who'll make the early morning tea.'

'I reckon we're in a position to make a dash for the summit now, don't you?' I suggested.

'I don't know about that; it's still a hell of a way to the top. We're not much higher than 22,500 here. I was beginning to wonder what had happened to the rest of you – nothing much has been coming up for the last few days. I was thinking of pressing on with Tachei. It looked as if we should have to do the whole bloody lot ourselves.'

I had an idea that this is what he would have liked most of all, he seemed almost sorry to see us; but I felt warm respect for him and the way he had kept battling on, all these days, in appalling condition with very little support from anyone.

'Well, now that we are here, don't you think we could get things moving. If you like, Les and I could have a go out in front,' I said.

'All right. You two can go and stay at the top of the rock band tomorrow and you could push on towards the foot of the summit gully the day after. We'll go with you with a load, and come back here. We'll come up and join you the day after tomorrow.'

'What about me?' asked Jim.

'Could you and Pemba ferry some loads up from below – we've got precious little up here in the way of food and fuel,' replied Dennis.

The next morning, the four of us set out for the rock band.

It quickly became obvious that Dennis and Tachei were much more fit than we were. They pulled away from us steadily. Both Les and I were feeling lethargic and took rests every few yards. The rock band, which had looked such a formidable obstacle from below, proved to be quite straightforward. Just above it, was the site of our camp – a small spur of snow on the end of the ice-field. It took us all afternoon to cut out a platform. We took it in turns to work: each cut for a few minutes and then collapsed exhausted while the other took over. Every now and then there was a deep-pitched whistle and a rock hurtled down from the huge black cliffs above us. We just had to hope that they would go to either side of our spur, but we felt hideously exposed.

We tried to put the tent up too soon, before we had cut a sufficiently large platform; we were so tired, we decided that it would have to do. It sagged crazily over the drop, poles askew, guy lines all at the wrong angle. That night, we felt that the least breath of wind would blow it away. In the morning, getting ready was sheer hell. The Primus wouldn't work and the inside of the tent was a sordid mess of dirty pans, spilt food and clothing. Les was never at his best in the morning and lay in his sleeping-bag – a pallid corpse – as I struggled with the breakfast.

It was impossible for both of us to get dressed at the same time in the tent so I volunteered to do it first, and wait outside. Les seemed to take hours to get ready as I stamped around in the bitter cold, trying to get some warmth into my limbs. I could see Dennis and Tachei at the foot of the rock band and the last thing I wanted was to be caught in camp by them.

At last we were ready, and started across the ice-field. We had to cut steps all the way. I trended too high and got on to some awkward rock, cursed myself, and had to start cutting down the slope. Les was feeling the altitude even worse than I, therefore I had to do all the step cutting. It was back-breaking work in an uncomfortable position; our progress was desperately slow. The slope seemed endless, until we could actually look up into the summit gully of Nuptse and see, far above, where it joined the summit ridge.

'I reckon we've done enough for one day. Let's get back,' I suggested to Les, and we started down. It was dark when we reached Camp VII, but very comforting to see the other tent up; to know that we weren't alone that night.

'Come in and have some tea,' Dennis shouted. My heart warmed to him but, as so often happened, he added a barb.

'Why, on earth, did you go so high; you couldn't have chosen a worse line.'

I knew we had gone too high, and that I had made a mistake, but we had put everything we had into making any progress at all. Over supper, we discussed plans for our assault.

'If you and Les could carry the tentage and food, Tachei and I could go up the gully tomorrow. I think we'll need at least a day's work cutting steps up there, before we can go for the summit and you can move up tomorrow. We can then all go for the summit together,' Dennis suggested.

It seemed the best scheme. There was no doubt about it, Dennis and Tachei were going much better than we were, and as he observed, even the foot of the gully was a long way below the summit.

The next morning Les and I carried about forty pounds each up into the gully, and left Dennis hacking out a platform on a narrow rock ledge – it was an inhospitable spot. As we turned to go, I had an uneasy feeling that they would try for the summit the next day. I was tempted to stay there myself, bivouac, and go up with them; but in doing this there would be little chance of a second attempt if we all failed. My commonsense told me it would be better to go back. After all, if they succeeded, we could always follow up the next day, and if they didn't, we should be fresh for the second assault. It was the old battle between being unselfish, thinking only of the success of the expedition, and my own personal ambition to reach the top. Not just to be the first on top, but also to enjoy the full climax of weeks of effort – the day when you force your way to the summit, see the top slowly get closer, and finally stand on it. Being the second party up could never be the same.

That night I lay awake thinking of how Dennis must now feel in the top camp, and wishing I were there. I half prayed that they wouldn't try for the summit, but was ashamed of myself for doing so, knowing full well, that in their position, I should go. There were now four of us at Camp VII, for Jim Swallow and Pemba had come up the previous night. I must confess, we were not over-glad to see them – the top camp would be a squash with four, let alone six people.

On 16th May, we all went up into the gully and spent most of the afternoon hacking out a platform barely large enough for two tents. By the time we had finished, it was nearly dark; still no sign of Dennis.

'The bastard's gone for the top,' I told Les. 'They'll have a bivouac if they don't hurry up.'

It was past eight o'clock when we heard shouts in the gully. A few minutes later they staggered down to their tent.

'Did you do it?'

'Yes.'

'Bloody well done, you deserved it,' and I really meant it. I should have loved to have been with them, but in face of Dennis's greater determination and fitness, he so obviously deserved to get there.

'How did it go?'

'The gully was the worst part of it. We started at six and didn't get any sun all the way up. It took us six hours to get up it cutting steps all the way. Old Tachei went great guns, did his full share of step-cutting – you'll be able to tell the ones he cut, they're enormous. We wanted to cut them big enough to get down easily; bloody glad we did, or we'd have never got back in the dark. The summit ridge is quite easy. We reached the top at three-thirty. Never thought it was coming; there were several false summits.'

None of us slept that night; a combination of excitement and acute discomfort kept us awake. I was on the outside berth of an Italian assault tent that seemed to have been designed for one small person. I spent most of the night having a pushing match with Jim to avoid being thrust over the abyss. He had a definite advantage, for he had a large lilo that filled most of the space, while I was lying on a small sheet of foam rubber.

Combined with my excitement at the thought of going to the summit, were some sneaking doubts about the safety of our situation. We knew there was no one else on the mountain above Camp IV, but worse, that there was hardly a scrap of food or fuel on any of the Camps. With us we had just enough for a meagre breakfast. If the weather turned, it would have been impossible to get back across the long ice-field to the rock band for it would be swept by avalanches from the rocks above.

When we set out in the morning, we found the line of steps, cut by Dennis and Tachei, so good that we were able to take off the ropes and climb solo. I soon pulled ahead of the others, with Pemba on my heels. The gully seemed interminable, and was deep in shade. Far above, at its top I could see a tiny triangle of sunlight, but it never seemed to get any closer. My feet had long lost any sense of feeling and I wondered if I had frostbite.

It was sheer delight when I eventually got into the sun; a few minutes later I could see over the top of the ridge. This was a bigger moment than actually reaching the top. For six weeks we had only been able to look south, had been enclosed by the great Wall of Nuptse, but now I was looking straight down into the Western Cwm; Everest – massive and black – was just the other side, its summit only 3000 feet higher. But most impressive of all was a rolling sea of brown hills broken by the occasional snow cap. It was utterly desolate and yet inexpressibly beautiful.

Pemba and I turned to the final ridge leading to the summit. As Dennis had told us, it was set at quite an easy angle. We were able to move comparatively quickly, though every hundred feet or so I found that I had to lie down, my heart rattling like an old car-engine whose big-end had gone.

We were on the top by midday, but there was no real feeling of emotion; we had just followed in someone else's footsteps. More than anything else, I had a sense of relief – it's all over, let's get the hell out of it.

By all appearances, we had been completely successful on Nuptse – six of us had reached the top. But at the finish of the expedition, I had a feeling of personal inadequacy, not because I had failed to be first on the summit, rather because I had lacked determination, had gone down to Base Camp thinking myself sick. I spent many hours in painful self-analysis, going back over events, hating my weakness. I also became very aware of my own failure to forget individual ambition and prejudice for the good of the party as a whole.

No one could have described us as a happy expedition – there was too much backbiting for that – but at the end of it none of us was an enemy for life, as has happened after quite a few Himalayan expeditions. Similarly, few friendships were cemented. We had remained throughout, nine individuals – at best several small groups – but never a complete team.

Immediately after the expedition I longed to go back to the Himalaya, just to prove to myself that I could do better, both physically and morally; the memory of the hardship and boredom of it all was too close to think of Himalayan climbing as pleasant. But when, after a year or so, as one always does, I had forgotten the unpleasant part of it, or at any rate, no longer rated it important, I longed to go out again for the sheer excitement of finding my way up a great unclimbed mountain.

CHAPTER TWELVE

Eigerwatching

I had been stuck in the same position for nearly ten minutes. My arms felt weak, my legs were shaking; my body seemed heavy and useless, and I was frightened by the steep rock above and below.

'You're climbing like a bloody nana,' came from my second, fifty feet below. 'At this rate we'll have a bivouac.'

We were on the Menagaux Face of the Aiguille de l'M, a standard little training climb, popular with all the British.

I had arrived in Chamonix the previous afternoon, at the end of the 7000-mile journey from Kathmandu. The trip was a vague blur of dusty roads, flies and punctures. I suppose it should have been a highlight of the expedition, but we were all too tired of travelling, too tired of each other, to absorb anything of the countries we had passed through.

I had arranged to meet Don Whillans in Chamonix at the beginning of July. We planned to spent the summer in the Alps, our main objective being the North Wall of the Eiger. It said something for our timing that we arrived below Mont Blanc within twenty-four hours of each other. Don had hitch-hiked out from Manchester, taking three days to do it – his rucksack was nearly as tall as he himself.

It was I who had insisted on going on the North Face of the Aiguille de l'M; I wanted to find out just how unfit I was. When eventually we reached the top I told him.

'I don't think I've ever been so unfit; I'll never get up the Eiger at this rate.'

'You'll be all right. When Joe got back from Kanch he was nearly as bad,' he replied.

'How about doing a few more training climbs before going over to Grindelwald? Sitting in a car for five weeks is no training for the Eiger.'

'You can do your training on the face. By the time you get to the top you'll be fit – or dead! Anyway, we haven't enough money to hang around. How much have you got?'

'Ten quid, but John Streetley has promised to send me another twenty.'

'That won't go far. You'll just have to tighten your belt – anyway, it'll get you used to civvy street. You don't know how soft you had it in the army.'

We left Chamonix early the next morning. We were lucky enough to scrounge a couple of return halves of tickets to Grindelwald from Geoff Oliver, a climber from Newcastle, who had just come back after an abortive skirmish with the bottom few feet of the Eiger. Grindelwald was the same as it had been four years before, spotlessly clean and smug, frowning on penniless climbers.

'Don't want to stay in this place longer than we have to,' Don remarked. 'They charge you even to breathe round here.'

To save money, I walked up to Alpiglen, while Don caught the train with all our gear. We had decided to camp there, since it was not as crowded as Kleine Scheidegg at the end of the line, and the walk down to Grindelwald to get food was relatively easy. It was an hour's walk up, and I found Don sitting in the forecourt of a small, wood-built hotel, the Hotel des Alpes. From a distance I could see he was fuming.

'Even the ticket collectors think they're God Almighty round here. One of the bastards tried to throw me off the train. I got a first-class compartment by mistake. I wouldn't have minded if he had asked me civil like, but he started shouting his head off, and then grabbed my shoulder – I just gave the bugger a push – that was enough. The sooner we climb the face and get out of here the better.'

We pitched our tent a hundred yards from the hotel and settled down to wait. If you want to climb the North Wall of the Eiger, it's not just a question of going straight on to the face and up. You are lucky if it comes into the right condition more than once in a season. You need settled weather, and the Wall should be clear of freshly fallen snow, but being a north face it takes several days to get into condition. That summer the weather followed a regular pattern – one day of stormy weather with heavy falls of snow, next day the clouds would slowly clear, the next would be beautifully fine and our hopes would begin to rise, but just as we began to prepare our equipment it would cloud over once again.

A couple of weeks went by, but the pattern never changed and we dropped into a pleasant, if monotonous routine. We were equally lazy, and who should do the cooking often became a real test of will power that I usually lost.

'The trouble is, Chris, you're too greedy. You'll always crack before I do.'

This was at four o'clock one afternoon, when we hadn't cooked anything all day and I had just started to peel some potatoes.

'What's on the menu, today?' asked Don.

'I'll curry them for a change,' I replied.

Our diet consisted of potatoes and vegetables – you could boil them, fry them or curry them for variety. We couldn't afford meat, but had the occasional egg and plenty of cheese. Each night we sat in the Hotel des Alpes, eking out a bottle of beer between us. Funnily enough, though, I found all this enjoyable and could feel my strength, drained by the climb on Nuptse and the long car journey, slowly come back. We didn't do any climbs – the weather was too unsettled to do anything serious, and anyway, Don wasn't prepared to go on a snow slog, just to get fit.

'I'll only do a climb if I'm really interested in it,' he observed. 'It's got to be a good line – not just hard – but one that catches my imagination.'

This summed up his entire attitude to climbing – all the routes he had put up in England and Scotland had been superbly direct, uncompromising lines – ones that hit you in the eye as obvious, but at the same time were too difficult, or more often too frightening, to have been done by anyone else. To this day, some of his climbs rank among the most formidable in Britain.

His attitude to climbing in the Alps was much the same – he made up his mind about what he wanted to do, and then stuck to it.

In fact, this summed up his attitude to life. He had a rigid code of his own, that no one could make him budge from. He always thought carefully before committing himself, and then once committed could be relied upon absolutely. He was intensely aware of his own rights, perhaps because he had to fight hard for them, and was bitterly aware of the limitations that his primary school education and upbringing in Salford, had imposed upon him.

'I'll meet any bugger half-way,' he often told me, 'but I won't go any further. I'm not going to be imposed on by anyone.'

This chip on the shoulder often made my relationship with him hard work; it meant that I had constantly to go more than half-way to find any point of contact. We couldn't have been more different in personality – where he was cautious, I tended to be impetuous, all too often undertaking something that, on mature thought I found I could not fulfil. In the mountains I enjoyed making last minute changes of plan, dashing off to climb this route or that, was restless if there was no climbing to be done. Don, on the other hand, decided the routes that he wanted to do, and was then quite happy to wait for them to come into condition, and was not prepared to fill in with anything second best.

Yet once we got on to a mountain we became a complete team, a single smooth-functioning machine. We never talked much, never seemed to waste any time, built up a rhythm of smooth, steady movement that, to me, is the height of pleasure in climbing. I have certainly never enjoyed climbing with anyone as much as I do with Don.

After sitting below the Eiger for a couple of weeks, we were both getting restless.

'I could do with a change,' said Don, 'anything to get away from this dump.'

'How about doing a climb round here?' I suggested, without much hope.

'No, it's not worth the effort; I'd rather fester here.'

'Well, let's get a change of air, anyway. We could hitch to Lucerne and see Max Eiselin. I met him when he came to Manchester to lecture on Dhaulagiri. He said I should call in on him. He might be good for a decent meal.'

Don took the bait and we set off for Lucerne; we never got there and very nearly didn't get any farther than Grindelwald. We had been sitting by the roadside for two hours trying to hitch a lift.

'I'll give it four more cars and I'm going back to Alpiglen,' announced Don. 'At this rate, we'll take ten days to reach Lucerne.'

But our luck changed and we got a lift down to Interlaken. We were just walking across the bridge, not even bothering to hitch, when a Volkswagen pulled up beside us.

'Do you want a lift?'

'Yes, please,' and we piled in; it couldn't have been better; the driver was a girl; what's more she was attractive, American, and on her own.

I had managed to seize the strategic seat beside her.

'Where are you going?' I asked.

'Only a couple of miles up the road, I'm afraid. Where do you want to get to?'

'Lucerne,' I replied, 'but let's have a coffee before we press on.'

Over coffee, we tried to persuade her to come with us to Lucerne, but ended by staying with her – she slept that night in the Youth Hostel, and we, under the stars. The following day, after a swim in the lake, she took us back to Grindelwald and spent the rest of the weekend in Alpiglen.

Things were looking up – Anne had to go back to Geneva after the weekend, but she promised to return, and for the rest of the holiday was our faithful chauffeuse, as well as being a good friend. She had only been in Europe for a few month, having come over to study French. She was a big girl, not conventionally pretty, dark-haired, but with a strength and warmth in her face that was attractive. From our first few words in her car I felt happy and at ease in her company; we could talk of anything and everything.

A couple of days after Anne had returned to Geneva, we acquired new neighbours: four Poles, also bent on climbing the Eiger. At first we regarded them with suspicion, resenting the fact that they might be on the face at the same time as ourselves, fearful that they might hold us up, that we could be involved with them in an accident. Their arrival acted as a spur for us to go and have a look at the face, to see just what was involved.

'Let's go up on the next fine day,' suggested Don, 'I think we'll have to come back down again, but at least we'll then know a bit more about what we're up against.'

A couple of mornings later, we were plodding up the grassy slopes above Alpiglen – it was still pitch dark, but we hoped to get on to the face just as it became light. I felt none of the fear I had experienced that first time I went on it with Hamish, as I had a better understanding of the difficulty and more confidence in my own ability, and, equally important, complete trust in Don.

We scrambled, silent grey shapes in the half light of the dawn, up the lower rocks. We soon had to put on crampons because every ledge was covered with iron-hard snow, and the rock was smeared with verglas. Nevertheless, we made quick progress up to the top of the first Pillar, a hundred feet or so higher than I had been in 1957.

'I reckon we must have got higher than any other British,' I suggested to Don.

'Doesn't say much for us,' was his matter-of-fact reply.

Beyond the Pillar there was even more snow – we were using the front points of our crampons the whole time. It was a wonderfully exhilarating feeling to stand poised on just two points which bit into the snow for only an inch, while a clean sweep of white dropped away to the dark shadows of the valley below.

We had climbed more than a thousand feet, though we had been going for only a couple of hours. Our way was blocked by the occasional short wall, plastered in verglas, but we still climbed solo to save time. We only paused to put on the rope when we reached the foot of a band of steep, overhanging rock that stretched across the face – we had reached the start of the serious climbing.

I found myself leading the first pitch, a traverse below the wall; it was all covered in smooth, hard water-ice. You could see the dark-stained rock through its transparent shield. I chipped away at it with my axe – it was about half an inch thick and absorbed my blows as if it were treacle. I placed a crampon point in the nick I had carved out fearful that it would peel away under my weight. There was no protection, no feeling of security; by the time I was half-way across the pitch, I was wishing I was anywhere else but on the North Wall of the Eiger.

I reached a ledge, and was able to belay.

'There's a rope been left here,' I shouted to Don. 'This must be the Difficult Crack; it looks bloody awful, it's completely plastered.'

Don left his rucksack with me, and started up the wall. It took him over an hour to climb eighty feet – it was like a vertical skating rink. The rope, left, I imagine, by the party that made the first winter ascent earlier that year, was no use to him – it carried an inch-thick sheath of ice. He had to clear each tiny handhold with his peg-hammer. The whole pitch was vertical so he had to hang on with the frozen fingers of one hand, while he hammered away with the other. When it was finally my turn to come up on a very tight rope, I couldn't help marvelling how he had led it, and feeling grateful that it hadn't been my turn to go first.

The angle eased as we traversed across a snow-field below the huge, blank face of the Rote Fluh – it was as big as most Dolomite walls, but here it was just one small feature on the North Wall of the Eiger. We reached another steep chimney piled with powder snow and an impossibly steep wall of snow.

'You know,' said Don slowly, with a dry grin, 'you and I are wasting our time; you could almost say that the face isn't in perfect condition. That's the Hinterstoisser Traverse.'

'Let's push off down,' I replied. 'You can't even see the fixed rope across it. I wonder how long it'll take to clear.'

'It'll be some days yet, if at all. Let's get back before the stones start coming down.'

We turned tail, abseiled down the steep sections and scrambled unroped down the rest. Just below the Difficult Crack, we saw four figures coming up towards us.

'Here come our Polish friends,' remarked Don. 'I wonder how high they'll get.'

We started down towards them when I noticed a cave in the face about fifty feet to our left – it was the Stollenloch, an entrance to the railway tunnel that pierces the Eiger leading up to the Jungfraujoch. Every day hundreds of tourists travel in this tube-train, happily unaware of the climbers clinging to the face outside.

We scrambled over to it, pushed open a solid wooden door and walked into the railway tunnel. The contrast was bizarre: one moment we had been on the dreaded North Wall of the Eiger, a place of rock and ice, a thousand-foot drop below our feet, and the next we were in the man-made safety of the tunnel. A train clanked slowly past – white gawping faces pressing against its windows stared down at us; a guard shouted and gesticulated, wordless, and the train ablaze with light rattled on up the tunnel leaving us in the dark.

'The buggers'll only make us pay, if they catch us,' said Don.

'I can imagine them chucking us back down the face, even in a blizzard, if we hadn't got the fare,' I agreed. 'Anyway, it won't take us long to get down outside.'

By the time we got back into the sun, the four Poles had reached us. Two of them were already starting to climb the Difficult Crack, while the other two sat at its foot, disconsolate.

'We've dropped our rucksack,' one of them told us. 'The other two will go on, but we must return.'

'You're not missing anything,' replied Don. 'Even the Hinterstoisser is plastered. The conditions couldn't be much worse.'

'All the same, we should like to have a look,' shouted down the men out in front, and continued to climb up the Difficult Crack. The ice had now melted, but nearly as bad, a waterfall was pouring down it.

We went down with the other two Poles, Somehow, meeting them on the face had brought us together. That night we cooked a communal meal and wondered how the other two had fared on the wall. Looking up we could see the glimmer of their light below the dark shield of the Rote Fluh.

Next morning the two Poles returned – they were a pathetic sight, their clothes still sodden, their equipment hanging in disarray around them. The temperature had not dropped below freezing; as a result they had spent the night sitting in the direct line of a waterfall on the only ledge they could find. That morning, being numb with cold, they also had gone through the Stollenloch, determined to walk straight down the line. They were picked up by the first train going up and were taken to the Eiger station where they had to wait for the next train going down. They were then made to pay the full fare up to the Jungfraujoch, and, because they hadn't any money with them, had to leave their cameras behind. Such treatment was probably correct on the part of the railway officials, but their complete lack of sympathy with the two Poles and their downright discourtesy, were less excusable.

After this little débâcle, we joined forces with the Poles – it certainly did a lot to raise our standard of living, for they had brought plentiful supplies from their home country. Tinned ham and sauerkraut were a welcome change from a diet of potatoes. Chesław, the only married man in their party, was appointed cook. He had a vivid imagination: we dined off villainous looking mushrooms collected from the woods, and one day he even brought back a tinful of snails – I don't know who it was who let them escape before he could try them out.

As soon as we returned from our reconnaissance, we had our first taste of the publicity anything to do with the Eigerwand seems to arouse. We were summoned to the telephone in the Hotel des Alpes that same afternoon.

'Were you on the Eiger this morning?' an excitable voice shouted down the other end. 'I'm from the *Daily Mail*.'

'Yes,' I replied, guardedly.

'Why did you come back – was one of you injured? – the weather seems very settled.'

'Yes, but the face isn't in condition. We just went to have a look.'

'When are you going back?'

'Depends on conditions. We might not be able to go on it at all.'

And so it went on. The next morning a Swiss freelance journalist arrived. He looked like a smoother version of Spencer Tracy – rugged good looks and grey hair outside, but in Don's words 'soft as shit' inside. He was dressed in the most immaculate climbing breeches I have ever seen – they had never been messed up on a mountain. He wanted to help us, develop our films for us, become our father confessor. I'm afraid we regarded him with the deepest suspicion.

'They all seem to want to get a story for nothing,' observed Don. 'I wonder how much they make out of it.'

'I don't see why we shouldn't make something out of it ourselves. If we get up let's sell the story to the highest bidder. The papers will make a story up even if we don't tell them anything – and God knows we need the money. There's only six pounds left in the kitty.'

Don hated having anything to do with everyday money transactions and I had therefore been appointed treasurer and chief buyer – I did all the shopping.

'Well, let's climb it first; we can then think about selling stories,' was Don's down-to-earth opinion.

Another fortnight went by, but the weather was no better; there were never more than a couple of fine days in succession. Towards the end of August, the snowline dropped below Kleine Scheidegg: it didn't look as if the Eiger would be in condition that summer.

'I think we're wasting our time here,' decided Don. 'Let's push off to Chamonix. Do you know anything about that Central Pillar of Frêney?'

'Robin Smith went to have a look at it in '59. It sounds as if it could be really good. Shall we have a go at it?'

'Aye, we could do that. If we got up, it'd be better than doing the Eiger. I fancy doing a good new route. It faces south so it should come into condition very quickly.'

The four Poles also decided to abandon the Eiger. Chesław was going to return home to his family – Stanny and Jan Mostovski wanted to go to Zermatt to try the North Face of the Matterhorn, and Jan Djuglosz, who spoke the best English of these three, asked if he could join us on the

Central Pillar. We had become very close to the Poles and were delighted. Jan was a professional mountaineer, making a living as an instructor and writer in his native Tatras. He was strongly built, and looked very purposeful with heavy horn-rimmed glasses and a jutting jaw.

A few days later, driven by Anne, we left Grindelwald for Chamonix and the Central Pillar.

CHAPTER THIRTEEN

The Central Pillar of Frêney

The refuge bivouac on the Col de la Fourche is a tiny corrugated-iron Nissen hut designed to hold eight people; it clings to a small ledge just below the crest of the ridge and from its door you get a giddy view of the great Brenva Face of Mont Blanc. In early July of 1961 Walter Bonatti, with two companions, Andrea Oggioni and Roberto Gallieni, arrived at the hut. They were on their way to the Central Pillar of Frêney, an unclimbed rock buttress high on the south face of Mont Blanc. At first glance this seems an unlikely approach, for the Central Pillar is at the head of the Frêney Glacier, and from the Col de Fourche they would have to cross below the Brenva Face and then ascend the couloir leading up to the Col de Peuterey, a new route and major ascent in its own right. Only then would they be able to start climbing on the Pillar, the most remote and highest Grade VI climb in Europe. The more direct approach up the Frêney glacier was even more difficult, for the glacier is seamed by crevasses and threatened by tottering seracs.

To their surprise, the three Italians found the hut occupied by four Frenchmen. Bonatti recognised one of them as Robert Guillaume, a young climber who had already put up several important first ascents. The others were Pierre Mazeaud, an extremely experienced mountaineer, Antoine Vieille and Pierre Kohlman. There could be no doubt where they planned to go. Bonatti must have been bitterly disappointed to find them there: he had had his eye on the Central Pillar for nine years and had already made one attempt on it, but it is an indication of his character that he immediately offered to go on to another climb since the French were there first. They rejected this offer, however, insisting that the Italians should join them.

They set out in the middle of the night, and in cold, clear conditions crossed the head of the Brenva Glacier, over the Col Moore and up the Peuterey Couloir, reaching the Col de Peuterey just after dawn. That day they managed to climb about two-fifths of the way up the Pillar; so early in the season the cracks were still heavily iced, making progress slow.

The Central Pillar has a smooth rock obelisk about four hundred feet high, that rests on a 200-foot plinth of broken granite. They reached the foot of the obelisk on their second day, but during the afternoon, wisps of cloud had been forming, and suddenly the storm broke around their heads – an inferno of snow, thunder and lightning. Kohlman was struck by one of the flashes and was badly shocked.

They settled down for the night, confident that a storm of such violence could last only a few hours and that they would then be able to scale the few hundred feet of steep rock that were between them and safety. But the next morning the storm was as furious as ever, and they resolved to stick it out. Retreat in those conditions didn't bear thinking about, especially down the icy chaos of the Frêney Glacier.

They sat it out on the ledge for three days and nights, and still the storm showed no sign of letting up. In this type of bivouac it is impossible to stay dry – snow inevitably seeps into the bivouac tent, condensation from the breath soaks everything. They could eat only limited quantities for it was practically impossible to light their cooker in the storm. The French were even worse off than the Italians for they had no bivouac tent but relied on plastic sheets which they wrapped around themselves. Quite apart from the mutual warmth you gain in a tent, it is much easier to maintain morale when huddled close together, able to talk to each other.

Bonatti very quickly emerged as the natural leader of the party, closely supported by Pierre Mazeaud. On the fourth day, their fifth out from the Col de la Fourche, he decided that they must retreat, while they still had the strength to do so.

The snow was falling as thickly as ever, as they abseiled, rope length after rope length, down the Pillar – the ropes must have been like hawsers, their clothes frozen into armour plating. Once off the Pillar, however, it was even worse; they were up to their chests in powder snow and could only see a few feet in front. Bonatti, with an uncanny sense of direction, guided them to the Col de Peuterey, but by that time it was nearly dark, and they had to resign themselves to another bivouac in the bowels of a crevasse.

There was no question of getting back the way that they had come; the couloir leading down to the Brenva Glacier was a death trap, continuously swept by avalanches. They made for the Rochers Gruber, a rock rib running down into the lower basin of the Frêney Glacier. Near the top of the rib, Vieille, the youngest member of the party, was unable to go any farther – they tried to haul him along, but he died in front of their eyes from exhaustion and exposure. Down on the glacier, Guillaume collapsed – they were unable to carry him for they were all near the end of their tether; their only hope was to reach the Gamba Hut and send back a rescue party. Without Bonatti it is unlikely that they would ever have picked their way through the crevasses of the Frêney Glacier, but eventually, when it was already getting dark, they reached the couloir leading up to the Col de l'Innominata. Oggioni, who had taken up the hardest position of all throughout the retreat, at the rear of the column where he had retrieved all the abseil ropes and had helped on the others, was now able to go no farther. Mazeaud stayed with him at the foot of the couloir.

From the top of the Col de l'Innominata they had 2000 feet of steep descent to the Gamba Hut. Kohlman was now showing signs of delirium, threatening to take Bonatti and Gallieni, tied to him on the same rope, down with him. They tried to drag him along, but eventually, when he actually attacked them, were forced to untie from the rope and flee down to the Hut.

When the rescue party went out to pick up those who had been left behind only Mazeaud was left alive. So ended one of the most long drawn out and at the same time heroic tragedies in Alpine history. It was a miracle that anyone survived at all; this was largely a tribute to the determination and skill of Walter Bonatti.

Only a month later another party set out for the Pillar – Pierre Julien, an instructor at the École Nationale in Chamonix, and Ignazio Piussi, a leading Italian climber who was attending an international meet at the school. They caused some criticism by using a helicopter to reach the top of Mont Blanc and then just descending the Peuterey Ridge to the foot of the Pillar. That same day they climbed as far as the smooth section near the top, but dropped a rucksack containing their gear; as, anyway, the weather was beginning to look threatening, they made a quick retreat.

When we set out to try the Pillar for ourselves we knew no more than the bare outlines of the stories of the previous attempts and had only seen a photograph of it, taken from a distance. On reaching Chamonix, our first problem was to find a fourth member for our party – three is an awkward number on a long rock climb.

'How about asking Julien?' suggested Jan. 'I know him quite well from a course at the École I attended last year.'

'Might as well ask him,' agreed Don, 'we might get a bit of information from him, if nothing else.'

We walked over to the School that afternoon and asked for Julien. He wasn't much taller than Don, but was more heavily built – dark glasses, a smooth V-neck sweater and immaculate breeches; he oozed an aggressive, bouncy self-confidence.

After the preliminary introductions, Jan told him of our interest in the Central Pillar and asked if he would like to join us.

'It is impossible,' he replied. 'I have too much guiding to do, but I should be happy to give you any help I can.'

'What is it like where you turned back?' asked Don.

'There are some cracks out to the left. You need plenty of big wedges,' he told us.

On the way back to the camp-site we met Ian Clough. He had just arrived from the Dolomites. Neither Don nor I had climbed with him, but we knew him by reputation. Although only in his mid-twenties, he had done as much hard climbing in the Alps as anyone in Britain. He came from Baildon, in Yorkshire, had served three years in the R.A.F. Mountain-rescue Team at Kinross, and had then decided to devote his entire time to climbing. For the last few years he had eked out a precarious living as an instructor for the Mountaineering Association. He had just climbed the North Face of the Cima Ovest di Laveredo by the French Direttissima route. It was continuously overhanging for seven hundred feet and he had spent two nights sitting in his étriers – we decided that this was ample qualification for a place on our team.

A few days later, the weather seemed settled and we caught the last téléphérique up to the top of the Aiguille du Midi. Just as the doors were about to close, three heavily laden climbers piled in. I immediately recognised Pierre Julien.

'The others are René Desmaison and Poulet Villard,' Jan muttered to us.

'I don't think there's any doubt where they're going,' said Don.

For a few minutes we pretended to ignore each other, glancing across occasionally with lowered eyes; then Julien walked over to us.

'You go to Frêney?' he asked.

'Perhaps, and you?'

'Perhaps.'

At the top of the Midi the three Frenchmen took one of the tele-cabins going across to the Torino Hut. I couldn't understand this, for the obvious way to the Col de la Fourche is to walk down on to the Vallée Blanche from the Midi.

'I wonder what they're up to?' asked Ian.

'They've probably got a helicopter waiting for them,' suggested Don. 'Anyway, there's nothing we can do about it. Let's get to the hut before it's dark. We'll only have a couple of hours' rest as it is.'

On the way across the Vallée Blanche, just below the dark spire of the Grand Capucin, we noticed a solitary tent, but at that stage were unaware of its significance. The hut, when we reached it, was crammed to bursting: there were already a dozen people packed on to the two-tiered bunk that almost entirely filled its interior. As we cooked our meal in the open doorway, I kept glancing across the expanse of the Brenva Glacier to the vast bulk of the Brenva Face and across it to the sheer silhouette of the

Eckfeiler Buttress, climbed only a few years before by Walter Bonatti. You couldn't see the Pillar from here; it was hidden by the upper part of the face, but the sight of the ground we had to cover that night was frightening enough. Behind the Eckfeiler Buttress I could just see the couloir leading up to the Col de Peuterey; it looked impossibly steep and long – a major climb in its own right and we had to get up it in the dark.

As I looked, my eye caught a puff of smoke high up on the face of the Eckfeiler Buttress; it quickly spread into a plunging torrent of swirling brown cloud that completely enveloped the face; almost at the same time came the noise, a deep-pitched thunder that hammered at our ears, filling me with an instinctive fear. I have never seen such a rock-fall – it seemed to stretch into minutes, though in fact it could have only lasted a few seconds, but even when the sound had vanished into the stillness of the night a heavy sulphurous smell lingered on, though we were nearly a mile away from the Buttress. Later that night we intended to pass below the very same place.

To me it seemed an omen; before a big climb I have always felt some fear, but that night my imagination was working overtime as I thought of our prospects of survival should the weather break when we were high on the Pillar. There was little chance of sleep, anyway, for we were packed together like the inmates of a concentration-camp barracks; you couldn't possibly turn round, or even lie on your back, there was so little room.

But the evening's excitement was not over. At about eleven-thirty, the door swung open, and in strode a big, handsome-looking man wearing a domed crash hat. He had an air of absolute self-confidence as if he owned, not only the hut, but the entire mountain. He went straight to the hut book, which we had filled in a few hours before (Frêney Pillar with a big question mark), glanced at it, wrote his own entry and walked out. As the door closed we dived for the book – there it was – Walter Bonatti. He was with a client on his way to the Brenva Face.

'Well, at least he can't get up on to the Pillar for a while,' observed Ian.

'Put yer heads down. Let's get some kip,' said Don. 'We'll have to start in an hour.'

I don't think any of us slept, we just lay and waited for the alarm. At last it was time to get up; the other occupants were also stirring. We had a quick brew of coffee, loaded our rucksacks and set out. A couple of parties had already left. We could see their lights slowly move across the glacier below. We put on crampons straight away, and scrambled down steep snow and rocky steps to the glacier. High up on the Brenva Face we could see tiny pinpoints of light – Walter Bonatti and his client.

The sky was a deep black, glistening with a myriad of stars; there wasn't a breath of wind and yet I felt there was something wrong; subconsciously, I think, wanting any excuse to avoid going on to the Pillar. I heard a trickle of water running down the rock.

'You know, it can't be very cold. There's some running water over there. That could mean that the weather's changing. I wonder if we should just go up the Major.'

'It's as settled as it ever will be,' replied Don. 'We've come this far, let's go on.'

We crossed the Col Moore, and then left the beaten track to the Brenva Face and dropped down to the other fork of the Glacier. Now that we were committed, my fears seemed to vanish and I began to enjoy myself; we came to a bergschrund at the bottom of the slope. Don jumped across without hesitation, rolled a couple of times on the other side and stopped himself with his axe. I paused on the edge for a minute – I have always hated jumping – and then for fear of seeming a coward launched myself into the dark, bounced and rolled down the slope.

We roped up for fear of hidden crevasses, and were soon picking our way across the glacier. As we approached the dark bulk of the Eckfeiler Buttress we could still detect a heavy smell of sulphur in the air: we had to clamber over the debris of the rock-fall a full hundred yards out from the face.

The couloir now stretched above us. An awkward ice-bulge at the bottom fell to Don's axe, and we were then able to make our own way up the firm snow, climbing quickly and silently in pools of light from the head-torches. It was a good 2000 feet long, but we reached the top well before dawn. For its last few feet it reared up steeply, a wall of mouldering rock held together by bonds of clear ice. It was my turn to lead; a boulder rattled away under my foot, narrowly missed Don fifty feet below, and bounded out of sight into the deep shadows of the couloir. I jerked my head, and my head-torch went out – I must have disconnected the battery. In complete darkness I felt my way up the rock – it was unpleasant, as dangerous as anything we were to find on the Central Pillar, but not unenjoyable. A few more feet and I was standing on the Col.

We had taken only four hours to reach the Col de Peuterey, and it was still dark. There was now no question of it being too warm – we were all chilled to the marrow.

'There's no point going to the foot of the Pillar before it's in the sun,' decided Don. 'Let's have a brew.'

We crouched around the gas stove, trying to capture a little of its warmth, and stamped up and down the level plateau of the Col. We were there for over an hour before the line of dazzling sunlight slowly crept down the length of the Pillar to its foot. The rock, a rich brown in the sun, looked warm and inviting.

'Someone's coming up the couloir,' shouted Ian.

'It must be the French,' said Don. 'How many of them are there?'

'Just two.'

'That's odd, I wonder what's happened to the other. Anyway, we'd better get started before they arrive.'

We quickly crossed the snow slope of the Upper Frêney Glacier, found a way through the big bergschrund at the foot of the Pillar, and started up the rock. Don and I went first, followed by Ian and Jan. It was some of the best climbing I have ever done. The rock was superbly sound, warm to the touch, and we had all the excitement and interest of being on new ground. There were no signs of our predecessors and we just picked our own route, winding our way through thrutchy chimneys, up jamming cracks, over steep walls.

The shattered tooth of the Aiguille Noire had been far below us at the base of the Pillar; soon we could look over the corniced summit of the Aiguille Blanche to the haze-covered foothills of Italy. The couple we had seen in the couloir had now reached the Col; about an hour later another pair arrived. They made no move to follow us, but put up tents and seemed to be waiting to see how we fared. We assumed that these must be the French, and that somewhere they had picked up a fourth person. We were wrong, however. The first pair had been two Americans, Garry Hemming and John Harlin, complete outsiders to the Frêney stakes, but formidable climbers. They had spent the previous night in the small tent we had seen below the Capucin. The second pair were Desmaison and Poulet Villard. They had had a hard time of it: they had climbed the couloir after the sun had come on to it, when the snow was dangerously soft, and they were constantly bombarded by stones dislodged by the two Americans.

The three French climbers had gone over to the Torino Hut the previous night, hoping to find there Ignatio Piussi who had been summoned by telegram to join the team. He had hired a car and raced across North Italy from his home near Trieste, but had been delayed on the way and missed the last téléphérique up from the valley. Julien had therefore stayed behind while the other two pressed on. Piussi and he set out first thing that morning but only reached the couloir in the late afternoon. So, late that evening there were six camped on the Col de Peuterey.

By that time we didn't worry about them; we were fifteen hundred feet up the climb, and it seemed a fair lead. At four o'clock we had reached the foot of the final tower. The Pillar now slimmed down from a broad, crack-seamed buttress to a slender, monolithic candle of rock, girdled at half

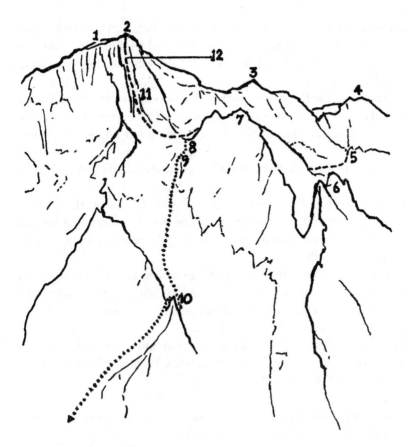

The South Side of Mont Blanc
Illustrating the Frêney disaster and our own ascent

– – – – – – – – Approach and ascent line of the Pillar by both parties

. . . . Line of retreat used by the Franco-Italian party

1 Mont Blanc
2 Mont Blanc de Courmayeur
3 Mont Maudit.
4 Mont Blanc de Tacul
5 Col de la Fourche
6 Aiguille Noire de Peuterey
7 Aiguille Blanche de Peuterey
8 Col de Peuterey
9 Rochers Grubers
10 Col de l'Innominata
11 Central Pillar of Frêney
12 Highest point reached by Bonatti and his party

height with a belt of overhangs. There were few cracks up it, and what there were all petered out. Gazing up at it, we each had a twinge of doubt – we had no drills or expansion bolts with us – if there were no cracks, no holds, we should be defeated.

Resting against the Pillar was a rock pedestal some fifty feet high. Bonatti and his party had sat out the storm on top of it. There were a few sad relics of their ordeal, an empty gas cylinder, a cooking pot and some wooden wedges.

'We've time to have a look up there before it's dark,' said Don. 'Hold the rope.'

The rock was smooth and sheer, but up to the line of overhangs there were some cracks, and Don made good progress, hammering in his own pegs and using a few left by our predecessors. On reaching the overhang, he edged his way to the left.

'I reckon this is as far as the others got,' he shouted down. He disappeared out of sight and the rope lay still in my hand for nearly twenty minutes. At last he reappeared. 'There's bugger all round here,' he shouted.

'What about Julien's wide cracks?' I asked.

'Not a sign of them – the cracks are all blind and just vanish above the overhang – you'd never get up her without bolts. What's it like to the right – can you see round the corner?'

'Can't see much – there seems to be a chimney up through the roof and there's a corner leading up to it. There might be some cracks in it, but it looks as if it'd be bloody hard getting into it.'

'I'll have a look.'

Don worked his way back and was soon directly over me, spreadeagled, crucified on an overhanging prow of rock. There were no cracks for pegs and he seemed to spend hours on end in the same position before inching forward imperceptibly. I longed for him to come down, so that we could put on duvets and settle down for the night. The sun had dropped out of sight round the side of the Innominata Ridge and it was bitterly cold – we were now at a height of over 14,000 feet.

'I think it'll go,' at last shouted Don.

'Well, come on down, I'm bloody freezing.'

Ian and Jan had caught us up and were sorting out their equipment on a ledge to the side of ours. The gas stove was purring steadily. Don threaded a rope through his top piton and abseiled down in the fast-gathering dark.

We settled down for the night – Ian, as the youngest and most easy-going member of the party, was appointed chief brew-maker; every hour or so during the night he made us some tea or soup. None of us slept much, it was too cold for that – our legs, unprotected by down clothing, were numb. From time to time I had attacks of the shivers when my teeth chattered with the speed of castanets. I couldn't help thinking of the isolation of our position, of the difficulty of retreat if we should be unable to climb the sheer tower above our heads. I could imagine how Bonatti and his party, seated on this same ledge only a couple of months earlier, must have felt – with safety so near, and yet so unattainable.

After a bivouac you are so chilled that it is difficult to start moving before the sun warms your bones. Fortunately, high up on the south side of Mont Blanc, we caught the sun early.

This time I went up the first pitch, using the pegs Don had hammered in the night before. I took a stance on a small foothold just below the overhangs, sitting in a sling. I felt I was poised immediately above the great ice-falls of the Frêney Glacier 3000 feet below. Don moved up past me and was soon thrust out of balance on the overhanging prow. The time crept slowly by and it was all I could do to stay awake in the warmth of the morning sun. A hundred feet below, Jan and Ian basked on the bivouac ledge, while, on the Col de Peuterey, the campers were showing signs of life. Two tiny figures set off down towards the Rochers Grubers and the other four started out for the foot of the Pillar.

Don was now out of sight round the corner of the Pillar. I could hear the dull thud of his peg-hammer – the cracks were all blind – and the hoarse pant of his breath. He was two hours on the prow: there was nowhere on it to rest; nowhere was it less than vertical.

'Give me some tension.'

My grasp tightened on the rope. Out of sight, poised, alone over the steep ice gully, he leant across the blank wall – there was nothing for his hands or feet, no crack in which to hammer a peg. His finger latched round a wrinkle; he was held in precarious balance by the tight rope stretched horizontally from round the corner. The farther he moved across, the more it tried to pull him back, to send him swinging, helpless, into mid-air far out from the overhanging wall. The corner, with a reassuring crack in it, was only six feet away, but it might just as well have been a hundred, the rock seemed utterly impregnable. He searched for a crack – relaxed, somehow, even though he had now been hanging on his fingers for nearly an hour. He found one low down to the right – little more than a score on the surface of the granite. He probed it with a tiny ace-of-hearts peg, tried to make the point stick in, for he could only spare one hand; then, oh-so-carefully, reached for his hammer, just tapped at the head to lodge it in the crack. The peg skewed to one side and shot down out of sight – hands getting tired, muscles aching, Don patiently tried to place another peg. This time it stayed in the crack – went in a good half-inch. Holding it gingerly, he edged his way across the wall into the corner.

He had said nothing for over an hour, but I could feel the tension transmitted through the rope by the imperceptible slowness with which it had run through my hands. The pegs now had a good resonant ring to them. There was obviously a useful crack in the corner. Another hour crept by – you need a lot of patience to be a climber.

'You'd better come on up to me,' came a muffled shout. 'The rope's dragging and I think I'll have to do the next bit free. The crack's too wide for the channels and too narrow for wedges.'

As I crossed the prow, I wondered how on earth Don had managed to lead it – it was all I could do to cling on. It was difficult to conceive how he had managed to place the pegs.

I found him ensconced half way up the corner, sitting in his étriers.

'You'd better stop down there. There's a bit of a ledge for you to stand on. There's sweet bugger-all up here.'

As soon as I was belayed, he started on the last stretch up to the roof. The crack in the corner was just wide enough for his fingers. The roof jutted out above him a good twelve feet, but in the corner of the roof the crack widened into a chimney actually cutting through its ceiling.

We were in heavy shade, and it was bitterly cold on the belay. The rope ran swiftly through my fingers – thank God he's nearly up – but then there was a long pause. I gripped the rope more firmly. He was now a good fifty feet above me – his shoulders jammed in the chimney, his feet pawing ineffectively on the smooth rock below. There was a crack sufficiently small to take one of his pegs, right in front of his nose, but he was unable to let go with either hand to grab a peg and thrust it in. He struggled to get higher into the chimney, but could get no purchase with his boots.

'I'm coming off, Chris.'

There was a long pause – not even a man as hard as Don resigns himself to falling. I hunched my belay, wondering what the impact would be, whether his pegs would stay in. A mass of flailing arms and legs shot down towards me, the rope came tight with a sudden, but not over-violent jerk and I found myself looking up into Don's face. He was hanging upside down a few feet above me, suspended from one of his pegs. He had fallen just over fifty feet.

'I've lost me 'at!' he stated.

'Are you all right?'

'Aye.'

'Shall I have a go at it?' Quickly. I was tired of standing in the cold, anxious to seize the opportunity to get out in front while Don was still stunned.

We changed over – that took a long time – and I started up the crack. I had no illusions about it. If Don couldn't climb it free, I certainly couldn't, but I hoped I might be able to engineer myself some kind of aid. There was nothing, however – as Don had said, the crack was too wide for our pegs, too narrow for the wedges.

I returned. 'Let's see if the others have anything,' I suggested, and shouted down to Ian and Jan. But it was no good, we had the entire stock of ironmongery with us.

Meanwhile, the other party had just arrived below the steep section, having climbed most of the way up the gully at the side.

'Ask the French if they have anything,' I shouted.

There was a long pause. When the reply came I could only just hear it – we were a hundred and fifty feet from the others round the corner.

'They say we can have some gear in a minute. They want to look at the other side first,' shouted Ian.

Another long pause – it was now late afternoon.

'Have they made up their bloody minds yet?' I asked.

'They say that we are on the wrong line – that it goes up the other side. They need all their gear for themselves.'

'Well, bugger them in that case; we'll get up by our own means. Have you any slings down there?'

'Yes, what do you want them for?'

'I'll try chockstoning the crack – show the Frogs some Welsh technique,' I replied.

It took us an hour to manœuvre the rope so that we could haul up the slings. I then collected some small stones from the back of the crack, jammed them into it, and, threading the slings behind them, clipped in my étriers and tentatively trusted my weight to them.

In this way I was able to reach the ceiling; standing in a sling, I hammered in a good peg. From there I had some of the most awe-inspiring climbing I have ever experienced. Above my head the chimney narrowed down to a dark slit, while below there was nothing but space, dropping away to the Frêney Glacier. If I had fallen I would have been dangling some ten feet out from the rock. At the end of the roof, the chimney thinned down to an ice-blocked crack; I had to arch myself out from its comforting confines and swing up on frighteningly small hand-holds. There was no time to pause – even to notice the fear that filled my body. I climbed those last few feet with a desperate speed, only conscious of the need to reach a resting place before my strength ran out.

I reached a ledge and let out a yell – we were over the main difficulties. Don followed me up quickly, and shot past round a ledge just above. It was now very nearly dark; we had climbed only two hundred feet in a complete day. Ian and Jan were still sitting on the ledge where we had spent the previous night. The French seemed to have made no progress round the corner and were preparing a bivouac site.

'You two had better prusik up,' Don shouted down to the others, 'It'll take too long if you try to climb. We'll drop a rope.'

We dropped a single rope and Ian went first, spinning like a spider on the end of a thread, as he worked his way up on slings. Just as Jan prepared to follow him, Desmaison offered him some pegs and asked him to take their rope up, so that they could prusik up the next morning. Jan agreed to do this.

We found a small ledge on the other side of the Pillar. It was sloping and only just fitted the four of us, but that didn't matter – we were nearly up. Nothing could stop us now. My position was at the lower end of the ledge, and I spent most of the night fighting to maintain it as the others slowly slid on top of me – at any rate it helped to keep me warm.

Next morning we climbed the last two pitches. A couple of light planes were roaring round our heads, taking photographs. We all had a feeling of wild exhilaration and triumph, heightened by the struggle we had experienced the day before. The Pillar ended in a slender tower; thence a short abseil took us down to a snow slope leading to the top of the Brouillard Ridge of Mont Blanc de Courmayeur. Another hour's plod and we were on the top of Mont Blanc. A French reporter, dropped there by helicopter, was waiting for us. More important than his congratulations was a flagon of red wine and tins of fruit juice. Slightly tipsy, we staggered to the Vallot Hut and then on down to Chamonix.

CHAPTER FOURTEEN

Eigerwandering

On our return we found Chamonix in a state of turmoil. That same day a jet fighter had struck one of the telecabin cables across the Vallée Blanche. The cabins nearest the break had fallen to the glacier several hundred feet below, killing the occupants, while the rest were stuck at intervals along the remaining cable. A major rescue operation was being launched to bring down the stranded passengers and as a result the town was buzzing with reporters.

The day after our return we had a celebratory champagne lunch with the three French climbers and Ignatio Piussi. After the lunch, when I had got over the initial excitement of doing a great climb, I began to think of what we could do next.

I was due to report at Van den Bergh's in just four days' time to start my new career as a margarine executive, but the weather was still miraculously perfect. Surely we could fit in one more climb before going back; but if we were to do this, I should have to fly, and I certainly couldn't afford the fare. I then began to think once more of the Eigerwand. It must be in condition after nearly a fortnight of perfect weather.

That night, in one of the bars, I met a reporter from the *Daily Mail*; he was a straight-speaking, cheerful Australian. Over a bottle of wine, I suggested they might like to finance our bid on the face and fly me home afterwards; he phoned Head Office and they agreed. Don and I were in the hands of the Press.

Time was vital, so next morning Anne ran us over to Grindelwald. By the time we reached Alpiglen, in the late afternoon, we were tired out but felt we must go straight on to the face. I had only three days left and, anyway, we wanted to use the good weather while it lasted. It was blazing hot as we tramped up in a cloud of buzzing flies; somehow it all seemed farcical and make-believe. Back at Alpiglen we had posed for photographs.

'Now let's have a picture of you and Anne together, saying good-bye – can't you make it a bit more personal than that? – come on, closer – they'll probably never use it – that's it – let's have a bit of real passion – lovely – just the thing.'

Inevitably the picture appeared – on the front page – titled 'A kiss before the Eiger'.

'Can I say anything about you and Anne? Any romance in the air? You are just good friends? Well, I suppose that's better than nothing.'

A photographer was following us up through the Alpine pastures, panting hard, cursing under his breath; he looked utterly out of place in a lightweight, Soho-style suit and winkle-picker shoes. Every hundred feet or so he collapsed, groaning.

'It's bad enough up this – how the hell you characters hope to get up there I just don't know. I wouldn't do this again for a hundred pounds.'

'We'll take you a couple of hundred feet up the face, if you like,' I offered, 'just think of the name you'd make for yourself in Fleet Street.'

'You know what you can do with that. This is as far as I'm going. Hold on a minute while I get my breath back – now turn round and give us a wave as you go up the slope – best of luck – bloody glad I'm not in your shoes.'

The Face seemed strangely peaceful and real after the hectic rush of the last twenty-four hours. Bargaining for the right terms, posing for photographs, answering questions, were now all matters of the past. We were on a climb that we wanted to do; relief at escaping all the hullabaloo below completely drowned any feelings of doubt or fear that I might otherwise have had.

We scrambled up the bottom slopes over easy-angled slabs and steep little walls. It was completely different from three weeks before. We were sweating in the heat of the sun – the Face had hardly any snow on it at all. We intended that afternoon to reach the Swallow's Nest Bivouac, at the foot of the first ice-field. We should then be poised, ready to cross the ice-fields in the early hours of the morning before the daily stone-fall started. We now felt we knew the Wall, had given a great deal of thought to climbing it safely and, by doing this, were confident that we could keep the danger factor to an acceptable level.

We roped up at the foot of the Difficult Crack. This time it was clear of ice – warm dry rock in the afternoon sun. Don made short work of it. The Hinterstoisser Traverse was also clear – a steep holdless slab, with a rope stretched across it. It was my turn to lead. I treated the rope cautiously, for who could tell how long it had been there? Another pitch and we reached the Swallow's Nest, a ledge about eighteen inches wide, at the side of the first ice-field.

We cleared some ice from it and settled down for the night, full of confidence, as we now felt on peak form and the face seemed in perfect condition. We couldn't lie down on the ledge, but were fairly comfortable, sitting crouched, close together; from time to time we had a brew, chatted for a few minutes, dozed off. But at midnight Don asked me:

'Can you hear all the running water? Even the bloody stones are still falling. You know, it can't be freezing up there.'

'It might do in the early hours of the morning,' I suggested.

For the rest of the night we waited for it to start freezing, so that the stones in the upper part of the face would be held safely in position in the clasp of the ice, but the gentle trickle of falling water interspersed with the distant rattle of stones continued.

In the dawn there were a few wisps of cloud to the west.

'I don't like the look of the weather,' said Don. 'If we push on now we're going to get stone-fall all the way up the face. It's just not worth it. I've no desire to give the papers a sensational story.'

'We could go up just a bit,' I suggested. 'The weather might improve.'

'What's the point? That's how half the accidents occur on the Eiger, with people pushing on just a bit farther, not knowing when to go back. We can always come back next year.'

Don's argument was conclusive, and a sign of his prudence as a mountaineer. We packed up our gear and started the long trek down. Although we had only been 1500 feet up the Face, the reporters were waiting for us in force. We spent the night in Alpiglen, and the next day I booked an air passage back to England – I should get back with a night to spare. The weather now seemed to be more settled and I longed to wait out for just a little longer. I half envied Don his freedom, he was staying out for a few more weeks, but I was obsessed with the importance of starting my new job on time, of creating the right impression.

Just as we were ready to leave Alpiglen, a tourist rushed into the Hotel.

'I have seen someone fall from the mountain!' he shouted, incoherently. At first we didn't believe him, but felt we had to go and just make sure, so plodded back towards the foot of the Eiger; we saw someone wave and walked over to a self-important German tourist.

'The body is over there,' he announced proudly. We walked hesitantly, averting our eyes – neither of us wanted to look – as we held the blanket we had brought up with us, ready to cover the corpse. We had a vague impression of blood and naked limbs twisted into grotesque shapes – the clothes had been torn to shreds in the fall, but skin is a tough covering – and then dropped the blanket over it. The German was hovering at our side; he lifted the blanket with the flourish of a showman, to show us how the head had been bashed in. I could have killed him at that moment – I couldn't help feeling that here was the fascination of the Eigerwand, the thing that makes the crowds gaze through the telescopes when someone is in trouble on the Face, the thing that makes the Eiger front-page news.

We went in search of the dead man's companion, but could only find the odd trace of blood – he could not possibly have survived, anyway, for he must have fallen from the crest of the Mitellegi Ridge, 5000 feet above. We decided to leave it to the guides, and returned to Alpiglen.

I had now missed my plane. I booked another for the early hours of the morning and drove through the night to Geneva, giving Anne a hurried farewell; we made plans to meet again, but somehow it seemed the end of the line. Those six weeks had been idyllic in their complete lack of any form of responsibility, in the tension of doing an exacting climb and the absolute relaxation of lazing in the valley; but now, that was all over. I was both excited and nervous at the prospect of my new career.

The pace at which I was moving was too great for me really to appreciate the change. Five hours after saying good-bye to Anne in the empty airport lounge, I was standing, scrubbed, shaved and dressed in a dark suit outside the doors of a huge skyscraper office block. It was nine o'clock, and a flood of men and women poured in around me through the doors. I went in hesitantly, found that I had lost the letter telling me to whom I had to report, so went up to the porter:

'I've come to work here – who do you think I should go and see? I'm afraid I've lost the letter telling me.'

'Well, I don't know – I suppose it could be Mr Smith. I'll try to find out.'

Half an hour later he discovered the right man and I was welcomed into Van den Berghs.

The first six months as a management trainee were spent looking round the firm, tramping from department to department, sitting in front of innumerable desks and hearing about the occupants' jobs. Having listened for a couple of hours, you were expected to ask intelligent questions – I could rarely think of anything to say. In the army I had detested office work and in civilian life there seemed to be little difference. Still, it was only for six months. Then I was given my first real job – as representative in Hampstead. I had to go round the grocers' shops taking orders for margarine, putting over the company line, and persuading the grocer to accept display material. We had learned the process at training school. You walked through the door, brief-case in one hand, display material in the other, contrived to raise your hat and give the grocer a cheerful good-morning. He ignored you, being busy or naturally bad-tempered. It was part of the job to assess the margarine the grocer required, and make the order for him. Some of my clients were happy to let me do this, others were passionately possessive about their shops, trusting no one. In my case they were probably very sensible – working out the quantities you had to put in was very simple, but somehow I always got it wrong – the rage of the shopkeeper knew no bounds when he discovered that he had fifty or so boxes of surplus margarine, or conversely, that he ran out in the middle of the week.

The Company was not averse to the closing of accounts with some shops, provided new accounts were also gained in others. I was only too successful in the first venture, closing over a dozen in six months, but I never actually opened a new account. It was less work that way – by the end of my tour of duty I had only three calls to make on Fridays, which helped towards a long weekend.

As the winter drew to a close, I became increasingly restless. Although I told myself that I would only be a representative for a few months, that in a couple of years I should hold an interesting and responsible job as Brand Manager, or perhaps District Manager in charge of an area of South-East England – I just couldn't see it; did not really like the work. With the coming of spring I began to fret over the idea of only three weeks' holiday in the Alps, and turned over the tempting thought of accepting an invitation to join an expedition to South Patagonia – one that I had regretfully refused only that autumn when I was still fresh and keen in my new job.

Practically speaking, I should have settled down happily in Unilever, for I had just become engaged. I met Wendy at a party (very conventional) in the New Year. She was small and dark, wore a little black dress, and rubbed herself up against me when we danced with the ecstatic pleasure of a kitten being stroked. Fortunately, she wasn't in the least bit conventional, and was even more appalled by my future in the margarine business than I. The prospect of being a suburban housewife had little attraction for her. She was an illustrator of children's books, had never been out of the country, never even been north of Leicester, but had a powerful urge to see more of the world. When I met her she had just written off to answer one of those advertisements asking for crew members on a yacht sailing to the Far East, but had begun to have second thoughts when she was asked for a photograph and her vital statistics.

Soon after we were engaged, I bought her a pair of climbing boots and took her to the hills. We went on Gritstone: her first climb was to be on Froggatt Edge. She was full of enthusiasm, but looked a bit apprehensive when I tied the rope on.

'This is only a Diff,' I assured her. 'You'll find it a piece of duff.'

'What's a Diff?' she asked, bemused.

'Difficult.'

'Couldn't we do something easy to start with.'

'Difficult is easy – I know it sounds contradictory, but beyond Diff there are four more grades – anything easier than this would be a walk. You won't have any trouble on this and we'll soon have you doing VSs.'

I started up the slab.

'Now, watch how I do it – keep your body well out from the rock, just like walking upstairs – this is too easy; I'll just do a little variation – just step up on to this little hold here – that's more interesting – right – I'm belayed; come on up, love.'

Wendy started up the slab cautiously; almost immediately she looked tensed and frightened, and hugged the rock. Even so, she reached the scene of my variation without too much trouble. The rope was now at a slight angle and if she had slipped she would have swung across the face. I suddenly realised that my belay wasn't much good, my stance worse, and wondered if I could hold her, if she did fall.

'For God's sake don't slip, love – I'm not sure that I can hold you.'

That was the last straw! The poor lass dissolved into tears, lunged across the slab and grabbed one of my boots – with a struggle I managed to pull her up.

That was the first and last time Wendy ever tried rock climbing. But she enjoyed being in the mountains and was quite happy to sit at the foot of a crag while I climbed. This suited me well – better, in fact, than if she had acquired a passion for the sport. If she had wanted to be taken climbing, she could probably not have followed me up the routes that I wanted to lead, and even if she could, I could never have felt certain that she could hold me if I came off. In the Alps, the difference in strength and endurance between a man and a woman becomes even more evident. I was pleased that we each had our own strong interests – Wendy's were painting and singing – that we could each follow to the full.

We got married in May, only five months after our first meeting, and shortly after this I made my decision to go to South Patagonia, knowing full well that my firm would probably refuse to let me go. I had taken ten years to make up my mind to put climbing first, rather than a conventional job, though during those years climbing had always been my first real love. I soon got my firm's reply – the letter that I have used to open this book. I had spent many hours of indecision before taking the final step. I was still not quite sure how we were to make a living but had a wonderful feeling of freedom as I wrote my letter of resignation. An Alpine season was before us and then an expedition to South Patagonia. I was even planning to take Wendy with me, though at this stage we had only fifty pounds in the bank, barely enough for me, let alone her.

That summer, Don and I planned to have another look at the North Wall of the Eiger. I now realised the potential value of the story of the first British ascent and intended to make the most of it. This sounds rather like doing the climb for money, something that leaves a slightly unpleasant taste in the mouth, particularly in mountaineering circles. But I was happy in my own mind that I wanted to do the climb for its own sake; if I could make sufficient money out of it to go to Patagonia, to take Wendy with me, to retain my freedom to climb, then so much the better.

I also thought of my responsibility to Wendy, not so much in the context of the Eigerwand, but as a mountaineer generally. As far as the Eiger was concerned, I felt, and I know Don did, that we could climb it relatively safely by going on it only in the most suitable conditions and then avoiding the stone-fall areas at the times when they were swept. We had already turned back twice because conditions had not been right. We didn't look at the Eiger as a unique climb, suggested to the public by the sheer weight of sensational publicity surrounding it, but rather as a potentially dangerous face that needed extra care and planning to negotiate safely.

As far as I was concerned, if I went on climbing at all now that I was married, I might just as well go on the Eiger. Wherever one climbs in the Alps, and at whatever standard, there is a certain degree of danger – much higher than on the rocks of this country – but the greatest danger is not so much on the difficult faces, when nerves are taut and concentration at a maximum, but on the easy stretches, where a momentary loss of concentration can cause a slip which can all too easily prove fatal. Comparatively few good mountaineers are killed on hard routes; they lose their lives on the easy ways down. Herman Buhl walked through a cornice; Robin Smith and Wilfred Noyce slipped on bad snow on the way down from a peak in the Pamirs; Toni Kinshofer, one of the four to make the first winter ascent of the Eiger, was killed on a tiny practice climb in Germany. There are many more examples.

When she married me, Wendy knew that I could never give up the mountains, they were too much a part of me. Nor could I start climbing at a lower standard, for, to me, the joy of climbing is to stretch my powers, my experience, my ability to the limit, and yet still have something in reserve. I don't enjoy danger for its own sake, certainly hate being afraid, as I inevitably am if things get out of control – if, say, I am out of condition on a climb that is too hard for me. But when on peak form, the exhilaration of climbing is at its greatest when I am in a potentially dangerous position yet feel in complete control.

It is difficult, probably impossible to equate this attitude with the full responsibilities of a married man, but I know I could never give up climbing. All I can do, is to take every possible precaution to keep the risk factor to a minimum. As July approached I made my preparations for another attempt on the Eiger.

CHAPTER FIFTEEN

Rescue on the Eiger

There was water everywhere. It trickled down the slabs and walls, staining them a gleaming black in the afternoon sun, and poured down the cracks and chimneys in foaming white waterfalls. This time the Difficult Crack was swept by a torrent. Our waterproof mitts were of little avail: it poured down inside our sleeves, and thundered about our heads as we climbed. By the time we had reached the top of the Crack we were both soaked. It was the end of July and once again we were going up the lower slopes of the Eiger, planning to stop the night in the Swallow's Nest.

We reached the chimney leading up to the foot of the Hinterstoisser Traverse. I was belaying Don, with the rope round my waist; I flicked it over my head as he reached me and it caught the head of my ice axe tucked into the shoulder-strap of my rucksack. Out of the corner of my eye I saw something flash down, glanced round and watched with a numb horror my axe cartwheel out of sight down the face.

After the first shock I felt a heavy shame. I had committed the cardinal sin, shown myself utterly incompetent.

'I've dropped my axe,' I shouted.

'I know. I saw it. I was expecting something like that to happen. You've been with the fairies all afternoon. Are you feeling all right?'

'I'm OK The rope flicked it out. Shall we go back down for it?'

'We'd have to go down too far. Anyway, we'd probably never find it. I've had enough of trogging up and down the bottom of the Eiger. Whoever's out in front will have to use my axe. For Christ's sake, don't drop that or we really will be in the cart.'

Neither of our peg-hammers had picks, so that we were now relying completely on Don's axe. Perhaps we should have gone back, but we had been on the face too many times to contemplate that.

When we reached the Swallow's Nest, we found that water was even trickling down the overhang above it.

'Let's hope it freezes tonight,' observed Don, 'or we're going to have a wet bivouac.'

We did – if anything, the flow of water increased in strength during the

The author in Patagonia (*photo Don Whillans*).

Above: The author at the age of sixteen, just after he had started to climb.

Left: The author at Harrison's Rocks, a sandstone outcrop near London.

Below: Hamish MacInnes preparing the evening meal on our bivouac ledge on the lower slopes of the North Wall of the Eiger.

Above: End of the second day on the South-West Pillar. Hamish in background with a broken skull, Paul Ross in the foreground.

Left: Approaching the Walker Spur up the Leschaux Glacier. We spent the night in one of the crevasses immediately below the Spur.

Below: Don Whillans in the lead on the South-West Pillar.

Top: Annapurna II from the north.

Above: Sherpas resting on the Shoulder: the Summit Pyramid of Annapurna II in the background (*photo Major R. Grant*).

Tachei.

Les Brown on a gendarme on
the arête between Camps III
and IV on Nuptse.

Central Pillar of Frêney
from the Col de Peuterey.

Clough and Djuglosz
on our first bivouac –
the site of the disastrous
bivouac of Bonatti
and his party.

Don and Chris setting out from Hampstead for the Eiger in the summer of 1962 (*photo Daily Express*).

Brian Nally at the top of the Second Ice-field, at the moment we reached him to bring him back to safety.

Ian Clough at the bivouac below the Difficult Crack.

Chris at the bivouac below the Difficult Crack (*photo Ian Clough*).

Right: Chris on the Hinterstoisser Traverse (*photo Ian Clough*).

Far right: Cutting steps into the White Spider from the end of the Traverse of the Gods (*photo Ian Clough*).

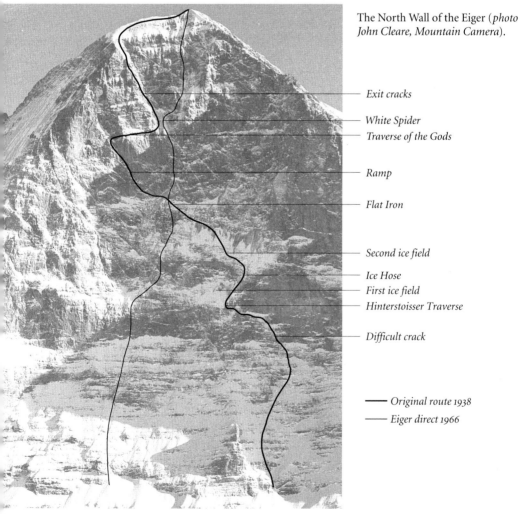

The North Wall of the Eiger (*photo John Cleare, Mountain Camera*).

Exit cracks

White Spider
Traverse of the Gods

Ramp

Flat Iron

Second ice field

Ice Hose
First ice field
Hinterstoisser Traverse

Difficult crack

—— Original route 1938
—— Eiger direct 1966

night. We dropped the bivouac-sack over our heads, but this didn't really improve matters: its inside was soon wet from the condensation of our breath. In the morning there were a few wisps of cloud – if anything it looked more threatening than it had done the previous September. We should have turned back straight away – stones were even bounding down the First Ice-field – but we had been on the Face too often, and hated the thought of another retreat, of having another night in the Swallow's Nest. We took our time in the morning – both thinking along the same lines but not voicing our doubts.

'We might as well start up the Ice-fields,' I suggested, 'and get a bit farther than last year.'

'Aye,' agreed Don. 'It'll be easy enough to turn back.'

We climbed up the side of the First Ice-field. It was set at an angle of about fifty degrees and was ice all the way. The front points of our crampons bit in about an eighth of an inch – just enough to hold our weights, but it felt precarious – one false step, a momentary loss of balance, and we'd be off. Even so, this was safer than cutting a grand staircase, because the time taken to cut large steps would increase the chances of being hit by falling stones.

At the top of the Ice-field, we reached the Ice Hose, a short gully joining the First and Second Ice-fields. It was jammed with near-vertical ice. I broke out on to rock on the right where the holds were all sloping, covered with a thin veneer of ice. Soon I was a hundred feet above Don, with no sign of a ledge, not even a peg crack – I had no runner, and if I had slipped, would almost certainly have taken him with me. A stone sliced past me with a thin, high-pitched whistle – we really were on the North Wall of the Eiger.

I had run out a full hundred and fifty feet before I reached the foot of the Second Ice-field and was able to put in an ice-screw. Don came up to me quickly; we looked across the field – a grey expanse of steep ice – another stone whistled down – we felt small and helpless against its monstrous threat.

'I don't like it – I think the weather's brewing,' I told Don.

'Aye – we've come far enough – let's push off down.'

We turned to go down. We saw two climbers coming up towards us. The one in front shouted something in German – I couldn't understand what.

'We're English,' we shouted.

'Two of your comrades are injured,' he replied. 'Will you help us to rescue them?'

Of course we agreed and turned back up the slope. At this stage we didn't know just what had happened. The previous day, through a telescope at

Alpiglen, we had seen two climbers moving very slowly across the Second Ice-field; we didn't know who they were.

We only heard the full story when we got back down. The pair were Brian Nally and Barry Brewster, two climbers from Southern England. I had met Barry once before; he was a student at Bangor University – one of their tigers. I was impressed, and a little frightened, by his intense seriousness as he talked about climbing. He had done all the hardest routes in Wales, climbing many of them in tricounis just to improve his technique. His experience on ice was limited: he had had several seasons in Chamonix, but, like most British climbers, had tended to do rock routes. Brian Nally, a house painter from London, was the ice specialist of the party. The previous year he had made the first British ascent of the North Face of the Matterhorn with Tom Carruthers, a Glasgow climber. Before going on the face, they had agreed that Brewster should be the rock expert, while Nally should take the lead on the ice-fields. In Nally's words – 'he was the brains of the team – I the navvy.'

They set out just twenty-four hours before us, bivouacked in the Swallow's Nest and, like us, were soaked to the skin. That morning they started out up the side of the First Ice-field, but instead of going into the Ice Hose, they followed Heinrich Harrer's description from the back of his book, *The White Spider*, and attempted the wall, about a hundred feet to its left. In doing this they lost the route and wasted several hours. As a result it was getting on for midday when they reached the Second Ice-field. Here they decided to cut steps diagonally across it, and so their progress was slow.

It was four o'clock when they reached the end of the ice-field; the stone-fall was by now violent as the afternoon sun loosened the rock in the upper part of the face. Looking up at the Eiger, it is difficult to get any idea of scale, the top is so foreshortened, but the entire upper 2000 feet of the Eigerwand are in the shape of a huge amphitheatre round the White Spider. Every stone that falls inevitably goes into the Spider, which then acts as a funnel, concentrating the bombardment down the centre of the face on to the Flat Iron. This place is a death trap after midday.

Barry Brewster took over the lead at the foot of a rock pitch – the start of the Flat Iron.

'There's a pitch of V Sup. up here,' he remarked, as he took off his crampons.

He ran out about eighty feet of rope, and clipped into a couple of pegs. Nally, who was belayed to a ring peg at the top of the ice-field heard him shout –

'Stones!'

Brian ducked into the rock instinctively, for he was now hardened to the constant bombardment that they had experienced from the start of the Second Ice-field.

Suddenly, the dark shape of a body came hurtling down. Both peg runners were pulled out by the force of the fall, and Nally was only just able to hold the rope – the peg to which he was belayed bent to a frightening angle. The rope held, and Barry was lying suspended on the end of it on the steep ice a hundred feet below. When Nally reached him, having secured the rope to the peg, Barry was unconscious. Brian Nally then did everything that anyone could have done in the circumstances. He cut out a ledge for his friend – no easy matter in hard ice, with the stones continuously whistling down – gave the injured man his crash hat, wrapped him up in all the available spare clothes and then settled down for the night: his second in wet clothes.

The following morning we learnt of the accident, and turned back up the ice slope. Don led out the first pitch, slowly cutting steps – it was no good moving fast now, we had to have a line of large steps on which to retreat with an injured man.

'I think I can see someone,' Don called down. 'Look, at the top of the ice-field.'

I could just discern a small red figure moving slowly along the top.

'Stop where you are,' shouted Don. 'We'll come up to you.'

He didn't reply, but took no notice and continued for thirty feet or so; then he stopped on a small spur, and seemed to be lying down. This gave us some idea of the vast scale of the face, of the distance we had to cover to reach him – he was just a minute blob of colour in the dull grey of plunging rock and gleam of ice.

We were now getting used to the sound of falling stones which were coming down the whole time: a high-pitched whistle, then a thud as they hit the ice around us and bounded on down the face.

'It's as good as a bloody war film,' remarked Don, after a particularly bad bombardment.

But then we heard a deeper sound – it seemed to fill the wall with its wild keen. I looked across and saw the tiny figure of a man shoot down the ice into space. It was like being hit hard in the stomach – I just hugged the ice and swore over and over again – then got a grip of myself – became aware of the danger we were in, of the man who was still alive at the end of the ice-field – the little red blob of colour was still there; it must have been the injured man who had fallen.

We shall never know exactly what happened, but probably Brewster had been swept from his perch by stone-fall. Mercifully, he was dead when he fell, for Nally had been with him when he died early that morning.

If he hadn't died, I am not sure what we could have done to bring him down. Although fourteen Swiss Guides had come as far as the Gallery Window, it is doubtful if they would have crossed the ice-fields, and anyway, it would not have been justifiable. Nally told us that Brewster was paralysed below the waist, probably with a broken back; in trying to carry him back we should almost certainly have killed him. To carry him, we should have needed at least eight people, and with such a number and the time it would have all taken, someone else would inevitably have been hit by stones.

We could certainly rescue the remaining climber, however, so Don and I continued cutting across the ice-field. It wasn't so bad while you were actually moving – your attention was completely taken up with the job in hand – but it was a different matter on the stances; you then had sufficient time to wonder about the chances of being hit by stones, to notice that the weather was closing in. The sky was now completely overcast; wisps of grey mist were reaching round the side of the face. I pressed myself against the ice, tried to vanish under the protective cover of my crash hat, to present as small a target as possible; stones whistled and landed all round me: one bounced off my helmet, another hit my shoulder – is anything broken? I worked my arm up and down – it felt numb but I could move my fingers – just a bruise, nothing more. And so it went on –

'Come on, Chris.'

I left the ice peg in place for our retreat, and hurried to join Don. I could see the line of the other party's steps just above us – they had been partly washed away by the streams of water pouring down the ice, and, anyway, seemed to wander haphazardly across the face.

'It's no good following their line,' Don remarked. 'It'd be too difficult getting back along it. We must cut across in a dead straight line.'

Pitch followed pitch – it just never seemed to end; all this time Nally was lying inert on the small spur of rock. I wondered if he also was injured, whether he would be able to help himself on the way back. Don and I now felt very much on our own, for the two Swiss Guides had vanished – there was no one else on the face and I couldn't help wondering what would happen to us if we were hit by stones.

One last rope length and I found myself only a few feet from Nally; I had run out the full length of rope, so turned round to tell Don to come up so that he could lead the last few feet.

'It's all right,' Nally called out. 'I can come over to you.'

I had never met Brian Nally before. At first glance he seemed unaffected by his ordeal. He was wearing a red duvet that clung wetly to him, and he moved slowly, methodically, as he cut steps across to me. Round his neck, in a tangle of knitting, was his climbing rope; an end of it trailed behind him. His features were heavy with fatigue. He had a look of simplicity, yet in his eyes there was a wildness.

'Are you going to the top? Can I tie on to you?' he asked.

My nerves, already stretched, exploded.

'We've come to get you down, you bloody fool.'

'But why not go on up, now that you've come this far.'

'Your friend is dead! Do you realise that? We're taking you down.'

It was only then that I realised how shocked he was, how misplaced my anger. He was like an automaton, did what you told him, but was incapable of thinking.

'We'll have to put you in the middle, between us. We'll use your rope. Give it to me.'

I spent the next twenty minutes untangling the rope – it was knotted as only three hundred feet of nylon can be. Each knot had to be undone separately, the rope was sodden, it numbed and cut my hands, but at least I was doing something. Don, a hundred and fifty feet below, was in the line of some of the worst stone-fall. All he could do was to wait patiently and watch the storm gather about our heads.

At last the rope was untangled. I tied Brian into the middle and he started back towards Don. Our progress was painfully slow – most of the steps had again been washed away by streams of water pouring down the ice – and stones were still coming down the whole time. Brian had given his crash hat to Brewster; a stone hit his head with a dull thud, he teetered backwards, and I grabbed his arm, pulling him back into the ice. He shook his head and seemed all right, or, at least, no more shocked than before.

At the end of the ice-field the storm broke: there was a deafening blast of thunder followed by a torrent of hail. Like a river in spate, it completely covered us, tore at us with steadily increasing force. We were all suspended from the same ice piton which was submitted to a seemingly impossible strain. Then, as suddenly as it started, the storm stopped.

'Let's get a move on,' Don shouted, 'before it starts again.'

We abseiled carefully down the Ice Hose, and then Don demonstrated yet again his genius as a mountaineer. Instead of branching back right, the way we had come up, the way used as a line of retreat by countless parties in the past twenty years, he led down to the left, to the brink of a sheer drop. Just a hundred and fifty feet below was the end of the Hinterstoisser Traverse – if only Hinterstoisser and his companions, who discovered this line in 1936, and in doing so, the key to the Eiger, had found this way down they would have been alive today; instead they tried to get back across the traverse, having failed to leave a rope in place behind them to safeguard their retreat. Without it, the traverse was impassable and they lost their lives in trying to abseil straight down the sheer wall below it.

Once down by the side of the traverse, we began to feel more safe, though I didn't relax till we reached the Stollenloch Window, where a reception party was waiting. We were pulled through the window, blinded by the flash bulbs of press cameras, and the whole ghastly nightmare reached its climax. On the face, things had been very simple – a straight question of survival. Don and I had a job to do, and we did it. There was no time to feel afraid, no place for fear. I should imagine it was rather like soldiering in the First World War – after a time you become accustomed to being under fire, fatalistic about the chances of being hit. But now, back in safety, it was different; a couple of Swiss journalists had laid on the special train to take us down, just to make sure of getting the story first. Inexplicably, the train remained stationary in the tunnel for nearly an hour, in spite of the fact that we were soaked to the skin and near exhaustion. In that time they got the full story from Nally, taking advantage of his shocked condition.

A couple of days later he was presented with the bill for his rescue – one for several hundred pounds, covering the employment of fourteen guides, the hire of a special train and the loss or damage to the guides' climbing equipment. He didn't have the money; he could probably have sold his story for a large amount immediately after the accident but the Swiss journalists had already prised it from him, and, anyway, the very last thing he had thought of was to sell the story of his friend's death to the highest bidder.

The whole question of rescue on the Eiger is a difficult one and has caused endless controversy, from the early attempts before the war, right up to the present. In all Alpine Districts the local guides are responsible for mountain rescue and are obliged to go out if anyone is in trouble. The North Wall of the Eiger has been made an exception to this rule and the Grindelwald guides are not obliged to go on to it. I can sympathise with their attitude. The North Wall is a dangerous face and any amateur venturing on it does so with this knowledge. It seems hardly fair to expect a man whose job it is to take tourists up the easy routes of the Oberland, who in all probability is not technically skilled on steep ice and rock, who has a wife and family dependent on him, to take the serious risks that an Eiger rescue would entail. Inevitably, however, many guides feel guilty in refusing to go on to the face, and this guilt leads to an aggressive attitude towards anyone else attempting the Eigerwand, or, as in 1957, even against the amateurs who organised the rescue attempt of Longhi and Corti. In this case, the chief of the Grindelwald rescue section, Willi Balmer, refused to co-operate in any way with the rescue.

In the case of the Nally-Brewster rescue, the Guides had at least set out, and two of them came as far as the foot of the First Ice-field. Presumably, if they had not caught up with us, they would have crossed the Second Ice-field, to the injured man. As soon as Brewster fell, however, they all retreated, leaving us to bring Nally down on our own. We should have been perfectly happy if some of them had stayed in safety at the end of the Second Ice-field – we should then, at least, have had some kind of support if anything had gone wrong. Instead, they all went down and then six of them picked up Brewster's body from the bottom of the face. We couldn't help feeling that they were putting their priorities in the wrong order.

In view of their behaviour, their bill seemed particularly unreasonable – if they had actually joined us they would have deserved every penny they took.

'I've had enough of the Eiger for this season,' observed Don that night in our hotel bedroom. 'All this publicity and money-grubbing is enough to make anyone sick. Let's push off to Austria and do some real climbing.'

I was only too happy to agree, and the next day we piled on to the motor-bike and set off for Innsbruck.

CHAPTER SIXTEEN

The Walker Spur

We spent three weeks around Innsbruck. Our two wives, who had come out from England separately and had been trailing behind us as we dashed from peak to peak, now caught us up. We climbed on the limestone faces of the Kaisergebirge and Karwendel – pleasant lighthearted routes on warm dry rock – and put all thought of the Eiger out of our minds.

Towards the end of August Don had to return home; by this time we had both nearly run out of money, and since we could not afford the girls' train fare, asked them to hitch-hike back to England while we travelled back on the bike.

'We might as well do a climb on the way,' I suggested. 'The girls are going to take longer than us to get back.'

'Aye. I've always fancied the North Face of the Badile. We'll go and do that,' agreed Don.

We sent most of our climbing equipment back in a friend's van, for the Badile is a rock route and we didn't expect to have to bivouac on it; we wanted to travel as light as possible on the bike. At this stage I had no thought of doing any more climbs before going home with Don.

We drove over to the Badile in a day. It is situated in the Bregalia – a soaring shield of smooth granite slabs. It was once rated as one of the great rock climbs of the Alps, but now, with the overall rising standard of rock climbing, it has almost become a 'Voie Normale' – certainly among British climbers. It was in perfect condition when we arrived, without a spot of snow on it. We bivouacked below the face and climbed it the next morning in six hours. There was no doubt about it, we had both reached peak form – something that only comes at the end of a long season.

On the way back to England we decided to look in at Chamonix, and arrived there a couple of days after climbing the Badile. The town, now somnolent at the end of the season, basked under a heat haze; the Aiguilles, a rich brown in the afternoon sun, were blemished by only the odd streak of snow.

'Even the big stuff must be in condition. How about one more route?' I asked Don.

'No. I must be back in three days. Anyway, we haven't got any gear. You stay on if you like. I don't mind driving back alone.'

'If I can find anyone to climb with, I think I shall.'

There weren't many climbers left in the Camp Site, but that evening in the Bar National I met Ian Clough.

After doing the Frêney with us the previous year he had stayed on in Chamonix and had done the complete traverse of the Chamonix Aiguilles, had gone home to spend the winter working as a Student Teacher in metalwork, and intended that Autumn to go to Training College.

'It's high time I settled down,' he told me. 'You can't bum around all your life.'

'Who are you with?' I asked.

'Geoff Grandison and Wilky,' he replied. 'We're going back in a couple of days.'

'How about doing a route with me before you go?' I suggested.

'I'll have to ask the others. What are you thinking of doing?'

'The Walker Spur should be in condition. How about that?'

'I'll let you know in the morning.'

I was now in a fever to go climbing. I had always wanted to do the Walker Spur of the Grandes Jorasses, ever since that first abortive attempt with Hamish in 1957. I also had a dream, that I tried to dismiss as impractical, to finish the climb by doing a traverse across the Jorasses and the Rochefort Ridge, all the way to the Torino Hut. It seemed an exciting finale to a great climb, better than just going down the easy way at the back. I had never mentioned this to anyone – didn't suggest it to Ian: it seemed too far-fetched, on the end of a 4000 foot rock climb that ranked as one of the most serious in the Alps.

Next morning, Ian came over to our tent.

'The others have agreed to wait for three days, so I can come.'

'Grand. Let's go up this afternoon. I'll try to borrow some gear from someone.'

I spent the rest of the morning scrounging gear. Fortunately, nearly everyone was on their way home and by lunch time I was once again fully equipped with borrowed duvet, pied d'éléphant, bivouac sac, axe and crampons.

We caught the last train up to Montenvers and walked up the Mer de Glace in the gathering evening. Just as we came through the moraine at the juncture of the Leschaux Glacier with the Mer de Glace I saw a couple of figures also hurrying towards the Jorasses.

'Come on, Ian. They must be going for the Walker. We'll drop into this gully and try to get in front of them. I think we'd better miss out the

Leschaux Hut and bivouac at the foot of the face to make sure of being first in the morning.'

We hurried, almost ran, up a small valley in the glacier, and pulled ahead of the other pair. I have always hated being behind other parties on a long climb in the Alps.

We were just congratulating ourselves on being at the head of the queue, when we reached the foot of the Walker Spur. A couple of French climbers were sitting on a slab of ice, obviously settled for the night; they already looked chilled and thoroughly disconsolate. They waved up at the face, and said something that we couldn't understand.

'We'd better climb a bit up the face,' suggested Ian.

'It'll be a lot warmer than sitting on the glacier,' I agreed. 'I've had one night like that already with Hamish.'

We scrambled, unroped, up the first hundred feet of the spur, up a short icy gully and then over slabs. Soon we discovered what the two Frenchmen had been talking about: every single ledge on the lower slopes of the Walker was already occupied by climbers; there were at least four parties out in front of us. This is a mark of just how popular the hard climbs are becoming: the Walker is so rarely in condition that, when it is free of ice, literally dozens rush to it.

We spent an uncomfortable night seated in a slight depression in the surface of the slab. It was impossible to relax, for we were both constantly slipping off it. As soon as it was light, we started up the climb, spurred on by the shouts coming from below – we certainly weren't at the end of the queue.

We caught up quickly with the pair immediately in front of us – three Parisians. On the stances we chatted together, discovered mutual acquaintances, discussed climbs we had both done. The lower part of the Walker Spur offers a series of vertical steps up steep grooves, divided by traverses across easy-angled slabs. I found that we could overtake the climbers immediately in front on these traverses. Perhaps this was contrary to climbing etiquette, but there is nothing more irritating than to be held up by a slower party in front.

Our climb now began to resemble a car trip from London to Brighton on a Bank Holiday, as we slowly jumped the queue, overtaking whenever an opportunity offered. On the vertical steps we had to wait our turn, but even this was quite pleasant – there was someone new to talk to each time: on this ledge an Austrian who knew Don, on the next a Swiss whom I had met a couple of years before in Chamonix. In such an atmosphere you didn't feel that you were on a serious climb; the actual technical standard of the climbing was not very high, and the number of people on it made it feel more like Cloggy.

We had reached the foot of the first great landmark of the Walker, the famous point of no return – the Grey Tower. We had at last fought our way to the front, though, in our hurry, we had gone too high. We should have traversed across at a lower level, and then done a short pendule across a wall to reach the only line of weakness up the Tower. It was reputed that once across this you couldn't get back.

Unnoticed by us, a bank of grey cloud had been creeping over the sky from the north-west. Suddenly the sun was obscured; I noticed the cold wind, the dark threat of the clouds. We had grown used to the shouts of the other parties – it was like the Tower of Babel, with everyone yelling at the tops of their voices in several different languages – but now the sounds were receding. We were on our own; the rest, twenty other climbers, were all going down in face of the threatening weather.

It never occurred to me to retreat – I didn't reason it out – Ian and I didn't discuss it. We both instinctively felt that the weather would not break, and were so confident in each other that, even if it did, we felt we could cope with it. It wasn't a form of foolhardiness: we had merged into a single unit, thinking almost as one person. This is something that I had never experienced before, not even with Don. In climbing with him, although we always shared the lead, I knew he was a better mountaineer – that in the final resort I should always defer to his decision. With Ian, I found an equality that made us, I think, a near perfect team.

The cloud now lapped around us, cut us off from the others, and enclosed us in a small world of our own – a world of grey cold rock dropping away into the grey swirls of mist. We climbed without a pause, without a word being said, leading through on each pitch. Because we had come too high we had to make a series of spectacular tension traverses, from pegs we hammered in, across a blank wall to the foot of the Grey Tower. Back on the route, we passed the odd piton, clipped into it, worked our way up through the murk.

It was getting lighter – a break in the cloud appeared above, a patch of blue. We had reached the foot of the Red Tower high on the buttress. The rock was now more broken, and in places covered by ice. We had established a steady rhythm of climbing that made short work of each difficulty: it was impossible, later, to remember one pitch from another, in retrospect they all seemed the same. This is climbing at its best – a drug more exhilarating than any purple heart or jab of cocaine and every bit as addictive in its after-effects; once you've tasted this feeling you can't live without it. An icy gully, broken rocks, the glimpse of a cornice through a break in the cloud, and we were standing on top of the Walker Spur. We had taken thirteen hours from the foot, at least two of which had been wasted, waiting to pass the parties in front of us.

With the drying up of new routes in recent years, an increasing importance has been placed on the times taken on different climbs – people just can't resist the competitive element in the sport however much they deplore competition in mountaineering. I certainly find a great deal of satisfaction in doing a fast time up a climb, not so much for its own sake but because it is a sign of competence; also it is safer, for the quicker you are, the less likely you are to be caught out by bad weather. To me, though, the greatest attraction of putting up fast times, is the rhythm of movement that is built up: nothing exists but the climber and the mountain. Once you start wasting time, losing the route, getting the rope in a tangle, this feeling vanishes and frustration sets in.

We paused on the top only for a few minutes – a cold wind was blowing from the north, and there was still a great deal of cloud about. I didn't mention to Ian my idea of a long traverse, the weather was much too threatening, so we started down the south face, now in Italy. We had got about fifteen hundred feet down, to the foot of the Rochers Whymper, a rock spur running down from the Pointe Whymper; the weather was looking more encouraging, and, anyway, there was only half an hour of daylight; I suggested to Ian:

'How about stopping here for the night. It's a hell of a slog right down to the valley and we'll then have to pay for the téléphérique to get back up to the Torino Hut. If it's fine tomorrow, we could have a crack at traversing the Jorasses and then going along the Rochefort Ridge. Hermann Buhl has done it as far as the Col de Grandes Jorasses, but I don't think anyone has done the whole traverse as a finish to the Walker.'

'All right by me,' he agreed, 'how about going the whole hog and doing a traverse of the whole bloody range – finish on the top of Mont Blanc?'

'That'd be great. We can always have a day's rest at the Torino. We could then do the Major. I've always wanted to do it.'

It was wonderful climbing with someone who could respond so spontaneously to an impromptu change of plan – who had exactly the same enthusiasm as I had. We settled down for our second bivouac on a comfortable ledge. We both felt pleasantly fresh, were warm in our duvets and pieds d'éléphant and had sufficient to eat – the greatest luxury of all, however, was that we cold even lie down on our ledge.

Next morning dawned fine, and we decided to do the complete traverse – we had a pleasant feeling of madness as we plodded back up the arête we had descended the night before. There was nothing very difficult on the ridge – we only put the rope on for one short section – but there was some of the most enjoyable climbing I have ever had, over airy pinnacles, round tottering gendarmes, on tapered snow arêtes. To the south, in a heavy haze, stretched the brown hills of Italy; to the west, the rounded dome of Mont Blanc; while to the north the massive buttress of the Jorasses dropped away below our feet to the glacier, a crazy jigsaw of crevasses, four thousand feet below. On a face you spend all day, or even several days, with the same view, but here on the crest of a ridge, crossing summit after summit, the view was for ever changing, there was limitless space around us.

We had scrambled over the pinnacled summits of the Jorasses, and the ridge now dropped steeply towards the Col de Jorasses. A couple of abseils took us down. We found a pleasant surprise: on the col was a small, newly-built bivouac-hut roofed in gleaming metal. There was no question of spending the night in the hut – it was too early – but inside we found a packet of spaghetti which made a welcome lunch as we had now very nearly run out of food. Above the Col, the Calotte de Rochefort rose steeply in a rock buttress. Perhaps we lost the route here for we found this short section harder than anything on the Walker Spur. Once up, however, it was easy going once again along a snow arête; we were able to put the rope away, and climb solo.

I noticed that our speed was dropping – I began to feel I had had a hard day.

'How's it going?' I asked Ian.

'I'm buggered,' he replied.

'Me too,' and we plodded on.

There were still two summits to cross – the snow was now soft from the afternoon sun, and at every step we sank in to our knees. On any long day there comes a point when you are getting tired and your one ambition is to get to the end of it, to have a good meal and lie down; it is always the same, but, in retrospect, it is this very period that seems the most worth-while.

Our progress was no longer easy: each step required an effort of will. We slogged on: one more summit, the Aiguille de Rochefort; an awkward crevasse – to hell with it – jump and hope for the best; some unpleasant wet snow over ice – not worth putting on crampons – we slowly teetered across, rubber soles sliding on the ice; we struggled over a small crest – will it never end? Then the Dent du Géant, a blade of granite, rich brown in the rays of the setting sun, was immediately above us.

'We can just nip up the South Face to show we're real hard men,' said Ian.

I managed the weakest of laughs.

'I couldn't walk up a bloody mole-hill, let alone climb. Thank God we can get past it without climbing. Anyway, it's not really on the ridge – it's just a subsidiary summit.'

It was now downhill all the way – I led off, feeling a new burst of energy with the end in sight, but skidded on a piece of soft snow; I stopped myself with the axe just in time.

'Steady on,' Ian murmured. 'You don't want to go down that fast. I reckon you're getting a bit bloody dangerous. This is where Arthur Dolphin was killed.'

Ian's warning brought me back to my senses; Arthur Dolphin, one of the best climbers that the Lake District has ever produced, had been killed on this same descent only a few years before. With doubled caution we scrambled down the last slopes to the huge, flat snow-field leading to the Col du Géant and the Torino Hut. Darkness had fallen: we had been on the go, with hardly a pause, for sixteen hours.

The danger was over – it was just a matter of putting one foot in front of the other, heads down, each immersed in his own thoughts. The lights of the Torino glimmered warmly, but never seemed to get any closer. I dreamt of litres of watered Chianti, succulent spaghetti – great long coils of it, greasy with meat sauce – filling my mouth, of the clean flavour of a salad, above all of bed; just to lie in bed for days on end. Another glance up at the light showed it still no nearer. Time seemed to stop altogether – the walk was endless and would go on to the end of all time – yet only a month before, Don and I, on the way to climb the South Face of the Géant, had bounded across this same plateau, hardly noticing it.

The refuge finally took us by surprise – it was suddenly in front of us. Push the door open, stand blinded, confused in the light – people sitting at tables, eating, laughing. The Guardian jabbers at us in Italian – have we Alpine Club Cards? – can't find them – just want something to drink, lie down, go to sleep. A bottle of Chianti – can't eat anything – too tired – can't keep my eyes open. I stagger up to bed, pull off my boots, feel the rough embrace of old blankets, relax to the sound of the other occupants' snores. The best two days' climbing I have ever had were over.

CHAPTER SEVENTEEN

Success on the Eiger

My whole body ached with fatigue, yet I was at that state of exhaustion when I was too tired even to sleep. I lay awake in the darkened bunk room, my mind flitting from image to image – incidents of the last two days – had Wendy got home all right? – where was she now? And then I thought of the Eiger – I'm not sure how it started, but suddenly, with a dazzling clarity, I realised that we could do it. It must be in condition. The weather had now been perfect for over a fortnight, and we were both on peak form. All the grim associations of the Eigerwand had been washed away by the climb we had just done. I thought of it as the magnificent route that it is, and one that we were ready to tackle.

The rest of the night, waiting impatiently for the dawn when I could tell Ian, I turned over plans. As soon as there was a glimmer of light, I rolled out of the bunk and shook him –

'Ian, wake up – I've just had an idea.'

He rolled over, burrowed under the bedclothes; I persevered.

'Come on, Ian – it's important; how about going for the Eiger?'

'Fuck off. Tell me about it later.' And he burrowed down still further. I had to contain my enthusiasm and return to bed. A couple of hours later I had another try, and this time he was more receptive.

'Might as well have a go,' he agreed. 'I've always wanted to do it but never had the right partner.'

That morning we walked down the Vallée Blanche to Chamonix, and the following day caught the train across to Grindelwald. Less than forty-eight hours after arriving exhausted at the Torino Hut, we were sorting out our gear at Alpiglen.

I had a feeling of foreboding – stronger than I had ever had before. There were a few high clouds in the sky – could this mean a change in the weather? surely not, the weather forecast was excellent, but it had been wrong before now. Down in the village we had heard that only two days before Diether Marchant, a brilliant young Austrian climber, had fallen from the Ramp when trying to climb the face solo. In the excitement of rushing across to Grindelwald, I had no time to think of Wendy, but suddenly I began to think of the dangers of the Eiger, and became convinced that our attempt was doomed; what if I were killed? But I had gone too far – I had talked Ian into coming with me – there was no turning back now.

We left Alpiglen at half past four in the afternoon – rather late, but we intended going only as far as the foot of the Difficult Crack: I had had quite enough of the Swallow's Nest bivouac and had noticed a good ledge protected by an overhang at this lower level. As we scrambled up the lower rocks I noticed a trail of blood stains, a piece of flesh clinging to a small bone; looked away, shut it out of my mind and didn't mention it to Ian for fear of putting him off. Later he told me that he also had seen it, but hadn't told me for the same reason.

We reached the ledge just before dark, glanced down and saw two figures climbing up towards us. We were not glad to see them. On the Eiger it is much better to be on your own with the companion you have chosen and in whom you have complete trust. Everything is very simple – if you get into trouble, you get yourself out of it. I should never expect anyone to come to my help on the Eigerwand – in most cases a rescue operation is impractical, and anyway, what right have I to expect others to risk their lives when I have chosen to go into a place, knowing full well its dangers. If there is another party on the face with you, whether they are competent mountaineers or insufficiently experienced, you are tied to them. If they get into any kind of trouble, you would have to go to their help; if you were in trouble, they would feel the same obligation, even though in doing so they might sacrifice their own lives. Whether we liked it or not, there was now another party. The next thing was to find out who they were.

As soon as they came within hailing range, Ian called out.

'Hello. Who are you?'

The man in front replied in German, but then to our surprise his companion called out in broad Scots.

'And who the hell do you think you are?'

'Chris Bonington and Ian Clough,' I replied. 'Are you Tom Carruthers, by any chance?'

I knew that Tom Carruthers, a well-known Glaswegian climber who, the previous year, had been with Brian Nally on the North Face of the Matterhorn, was planning to go on the Eiger.

'Aye,' he replied.

'Who's your mate?' asked Ian.

'I only met him today. I was hoping to go on the face with Bill Sproul but he sprained his ankle and had to go home. This bloke's partner backed down at the last moment so we decided to team up.'

'Do you know anything about him?'

'He's pretty good, I think. He's been to the Caucasus.'

'What's his name?'

'Anton Moderegger – he's Austrian.'

We were astounded by the whole business. Not only were they complete strangers, but they could hardly speak a word of each other's language. Nevertheless, I suggested –

'If we are climbing at the same speed, we might as well join forces, but if one party is faster than the other, I think the fast one should press on.'

'That's fair enough by me,' agreed Tom, and the two settled down on a ledge just around the corner.

Conditions seemed perfect for the Eiger. As soon as the sun dropped below the low foothills to the West, it grew cold – there was no doubt about it – it was freezing hard: there would be no stones coming down early the following morning. Ian and I settled down for the night with a feeling of complete confidence – in each other and in the weather. All the early fears I had experienced were now gone, replaced by a pleasurable anticipation of what lay in wait for us in the next day or so.

'We might as well have a feast tonight,' I suggested. 'We're carrying miles too much food – I could hardly lift my sack this afternoon.'

We cooked a thick stew over our small gas cooker, opening all the tinned food we had brought with us. I have found on long climbs in the Alps that I can go for several days with very little solid food, provided that there is plenty to drink at night – well-sugared tea and soup. During the day there is no time to eat; you are keyed up to such a pitch of nervous tension, your concentration is so complete, that you feel no desire for food.

The pool of light from Ian's head torch and from the steady purr of the cooker seemed homely and peaceful. Our ledge was positively luxurious – we could spread our equipment over it, could even lie down, and were protected from the threat of falling stones by an overhang jutting overhead.

'I reckon this is the best bivouac I've ever had,' observed Ian.

'It's a lot better than the Swallow's Nest – I doubt if we'll be as comfortable tomorrow night,' I replied.

'How far do you think we'll get?'

'It's hard to say; I suppose we could just make the top. It's been done in a day. Anyway, let's get some kip.'

We both had down jackets and pieds d'éléphant. We were dry and sufficiently warm. I quickly dropped off into a dreamless sleep, happily unaware of the thousand-foot drop a couple of inches behind me.

We slept too well! It was past dawn when we woke up; we could hear the other pair moving just round the corner.

'Come on, Ian,' I urged. 'We want to be sure of getting away first.'

We were at the foot of the climb, it would be safe and easy to turn back; at this stage, therefore, I felt no compulsion to join forces with the other party. If we had overtaken them half-way up the Face and they had been in trouble, it would have been a different matter.

After a hurried breakfast, we packed our sacks and I started up the Difficult Crack – it was the first time I had led it, this had always been Don's pitch. I had a momentary pang of guilt as I looked up at it, wondered what would be Don's feelings if we succeeded, but then put the thought aside for I knew he would have done the same in similar circumstances.

The crack was both dry and clear of ice – a pleasant augury of what was to come. We crossed the Hinterstoisser Traverse, moving quickly and easily.

'I've never seen it in such good condition,' I assured Ian. 'If we don't get up this time, we never shall.'

'Don't count your luck too soon,' he muttered.

Beyond the Hinterstoisser, conditions remained good. We were able to scramble on rocks up the side of the First Ice-field, where the ice had shrunk from the face, and then at the top of the Ice Hose, across bare rocks to the foot of the Second Ice-field. The atmosphere was different from what it had been when I was with Don just a few weeks before. There was not a cloud in the sky, but, more important, the face was still and silent – no rattle of falling stones.

'Last time we cut right across the ice-field,' I told Ian. 'This time we'll go straight up. There should be a good gap at the top which we can use as a handrail.'

It was much quicker going straight up. We cut the odd step, but for the most part went up on the front points of our crampons, sharing the lead all the way. At the top I was pleased to find a good gap between ice and rock and we traversed across quickly with hardly a pause. It was only nine o'clock in the morning. But things were going too easily: we had to cross the entire length of the Second Ice-field, a distance of some hundred yards, and it was here that I made a stupid mistake in the route-finding. The vast scale of the face caught me out. We were sharing the lead and now it was Ian's turn to go in front, up a little gully which seemed to reach the Flat Iron. Without thinking, I accepted his judgement, in spite of the fact that I had been beyond this point when we rescued Brian Nally; then I led up a thin crack in a corner. Something was wrong here – it was as hard as a Gritstone problem, and there were no pegs in place. I was soon a hundred feet up and extended near my limit – a fall would have been fatal. There were some loose blocks in the back of the crack – be careful with those – I cocked a foot out behind me, swung out of balance and could feel the weight of my rucksack dragging me down. There were another fifteen feet of difficult climbing, and I had nearly run the rope out before I reached a ledge.

'I'm bloody sure this isn't on the route,' I shouted down. 'You'd better come up all the same.'

Once Ian had joined me, we traversed across a series of ledges and soon saw that we were too high; there was nothing for it but to abseil down to the ice-field. We had wasted at least an hour on our little excursion; the only consolation was that others had made the same mistake – we could see a rusty peg in a crack just above.

Back on the ice-field we were soon at the start of the climb to the Flat Iron. A fantastically twisted piton marked the point where Brian Nally had held Brewster's fall. It was my turn to lead. I took off my crampons and pulled up a steep wall. This was the route all right, it was much easier than where we had just been. After a few feet the steepness relented and I reached a region of easy-angled slabs. It all looked deceptively safe, but this was the most dangerous spot on the entire Eigerwand – the Flat Iron. After midday this place would be a death trap subjected to a constant bombardment of falling stones; everywhere I looked the rock was scarred by their impact. As I brought Ian up towards me my eye was drawn by the trailing loop of the climbing rope, to a small patch of white on the grey ice-field a hundred and fifty feet below – the ledge where Brewster had spent his last night. There was something lying on it that I couldn't make out, a rucksack, or perhaps an anorak. All the way up the Eiger there are these grim tokens of other people's misfortune – a tattered piece of material, a broken axe, a piece of old rope; and this all combines to give the face an atmosphere of brooding menace, even when it is in perfect condition and no stones are coming down.

At the top of the Flat Iron we looked back to see how the other pair was getting on; at first we couldn't see them and then, straining our eyes, could just discern two tiny dots at the end of the Second Ice-field; they were moving so slowly that it was difficult to distinguish them from rocks embedded in the ice.

'I wonder why they're going so slow?' asked Ian.

'God knows, but if they don't hurry up they're going to reach the Flat Iron when the stones start coming down. Look, they're trying to cut across the ice-field. They'll take too long.'

We shouted to them to cut straight up to the top, but they were too far away to hear.

'Come on,' I urged. 'It's no good waiting for them. There's bugger all we can do; we'll be sitting ducks ourselves if we stay here much longer – it's right in the line of fire.'

'You know, I reckon their morale's cracked,' Ian suggested. 'This face is so bloody terrifying that I reckon you need someone with you whom you really know and trust. It must be desperate if you can't even speak each other's language. You might just as well do it solo.'

We watched them for another minute: two tiny ants on a sweep of grey ice. Even at that distance we could sense their uncertainty; it was infectious for we suddenly realised the danger of our own position, and turned without speaking to the Third Ice-field.

'We'll have to cut steps here,' Ian called back. 'It's bloody steep.'

He hammered away rhythmically, the pick of his axe scattering particles of ice that hissed out of sight down the slope. It was a relief to reach the shelter of the Ramp, a narrow rock-gully stretching up into the Face.

On the ice-fields we had felt naked and exposed; it was pleasant to feel rock around us once more: our world confined to rock walls on either side, rock soaring above our heads. I bridged up a chimney – no more delicate teetering on the points of my crampons, but back against one wall, feet against the other, thrusting with all my might against the hard unyielding rock. It had been cold on the ice-fields, but soon we were warm as we struggled pitch after pitch up the Ramp. The chimney opened out into a bay at the back of which was a deep-cut corner that closed down near its top to a narrow gash. This was the famous waterfall pitch. I remembered reading of the struggle that Hermann Buhl had to climb it when he fought his way against the weight of the water thundering about his head. Today it was still – there seemed to be not a drop of water on the entire face. It was Ian's turn to lead, and he started up confidently, but suddenly his progress slowed.

'It's plastered with verglas!' he shouted down. 'Watch the rope.'

He now had to chip away the invisible film of ice from every hold; even so it was impossible to clear it completely, for it clung to the rock with the tenacity of treacle. Slowly, patiently, he cleared the holds, eased his way up the chimney. This was by far the hardest part of the Ramp. The next pitch was easier, but a bulge of opaque overhanging ice barred the way.

'You're getting all the good pitches,' I told Ian, with a trace of envy; with dry clothes, and being certain of the weather, we could relish technical difficulty for its own sake as something that made the climbing all the more interesting. He now had to cut foot and hand holds in the ice, hanging back out of balance. Fortunately he was able to use the wall of the gully behind him to get some support. When he pulled out of sight over the bulge I could still hear the thud of his axe but the rope was running through my hands more swiftly.

'Come on up, Chris.'

I negotiated the bulge and found myself on the narrow ice-field that we knew marked the top of the Ramp. Somewhere up there was the start of the Traverse of the Gods – the way back into the centre of the Face. We had to find the right line: if we went too high here, we could land ourselves in serious difficulties. To make matters harder, we were now in cloud, an eerie silent world of plunging rock and dirty, rubble-strewn ice.

There was a shout from above; we glanced up and saw a figure outlined against the cloud on the arête high to our right. We hadn't known that there was anyone climbing above us, and immediately wondered what they could be doing, how we had come to catch them up. Could they be in trouble? If so, what on earth could we do about it; this was the most inaccessible part of the entire Face.

As I climbed up a steep wall towards the figure, I couldn't help remembering our experience with Nally only three weeks before; I poked my head over the ledge, and found two climbers seated there, grinning a welcome. They just weren't the kind of people you would expect to meet half-way up the North Wall of the Eiger. One of them, as far as I could gather from his stream of broken English, had only been climbing for a year, though he had trained hard for the North Face by cycling to work every day throughout the winter. His companion seemed more experienced; but their progress that day had been pathetic: they had climbed only three hundred feet, having spent the previous night in the Ramp. At four o'clock they were going to settle down for the night.

'We are tired,' they told me.

I couldn't help feeling responsible for them; I didn't like the thought of leaving them behind, any more than I liked the prospect of taking them with us. But I offered:

'Would you like to join us – we can all go up together. I think we should push on tonight as far as possible.'

'No. It is quite all right. We shall stay here and go on tomorrow.'

We left them with a feeling of relief mixed with guilt, and started across the Traverse of the Gods, a line of rubble-strewn ledges, clinging to the sheer wall. We could hear the cow horn at the Kleine Scheidegg blow a lugubrious tune and, nearer, the rattle of the rack railway; the sounds emphasised the isolation of our position more than the wildest mountain could have done. We seemed so close to safety, and yet, if anything went wrong, nothing could help us. At the end of the Traverse, I started into the White Spider, a terrifying place of converging walls and steep ice. As I edged round the corner, there was a high-pitched whistle. I ducked instinctively and a stone bounded past my head: the afternoon bombardment had begun. I retreated hurriedly.

'There's no point going any further today,' I told Ian. 'We'd be asking for trouble. It should be safe here for the night, and we can press on in the morning when the stones have stopped.

'This is as good a place to bivouac as any,' he agreed. 'We'll have plenty of time to get sorted out.'

It was little more than five o'clock. We could probably have reached the summit that night, but the risk of being hit by a stone was too great for it to be worthwhile – the only justification for fast ascents is greater safety; in trying to climb the Eiger in a day the danger factor is definitely increased, for its upper parts must inevitably be climbed after the stone-fall has begun.

We had no sense of urgency: the weather seemed settled. The rock was bathed in a warm yellow light from the slowly sinking sun, a sea of low cloud engulfed the valleys and lapped around the tops of the foothills. At the other end of the Traverse we could just see a tiny red blob – our two Swiss friends. Contentedly we prepared our resting place, cleared stones from the narrow ledge and searched for patches of snow to make a brew. We had dry clothes to sleep in, enough food and plenty of gas for our stove – what more could a climber want. As night fell we watched the myriad of lights in the valley below, feeling detached from the rest of the world. The bivouac wasn't quite as comfortable as our first – we couldn't lie down on the ledge – but we dozed off for long periods, occasionally waking and brewing tea or coffee. The night didn't drag as it does on a cold, wet bivouac, and all too soon the horizon to the east began to pale with the coming of dawn.

I started, once again, into the Spider. There was no stone-fall, but the very silence suggested a lurking menace. I have never been in such an oppressive place on a mountain. On three sides, dark walls converged on the triangular strip of ice; looking down, the rest of the Face was cut away and only the Alpine pastures 4000 feet below were visible. Around me stones embedded in the ice were a reminder of the bombardment we should suffer if we didn't get out of the Spider in time. I suddenly realised that I was cutting large steps, moving slowly, oppressed by the threat of the place. I forced myself to move up on the points of my crampons, kicked hard into the ice, teetered up on an eighth of an inch of steel – a hundred and fifty feet of rope ran out, and I seemed to have barely started on the ice slope. Ian came up to me, said nothing; I think he had the same feeling of oppression, almost claustrophobic, in these close confines.

Looking up from the bottom it had seemed only a couple of hundred feet, but we ran out five lengths of rope before reaching the top. Suddenly, once out of the Spider, we had a wonderful feeling of release – the top of the Exit Cracks, a network of gullies seaming the final rock-wall between us and safety, looked quite close. We read the description, 'Climb easy slabs for two hundred feet, then a steep black nose. (Grade V)'. Ian ran out the first rope length, a full hundred and fifty feet; I led through and started looking for the black nose; a pitch of grade V – it must be hard, for there are only two or three others of that standard on the mountains. I quickly scrambled up another hundred feet, shouted down to Ian:

'I wonder if we're on the wrong line – this is dead easy – it can't possibly be V. Can you see any steep black noses down thee?'

'There's a horrible looking groove just above me,' he replied doubtfully. 'It's certainly steep enough, looks bloody desperate. I suppose you could say that it was on a nose – the rock's black.'

I came back down – we both gazed up at the groove – it would give some hard climbing, there was no doubt about that. It was about sixty feet high, near vertical, bunged up with ice. If you are not quite sure of the way it is all too easy to convince yourself that a certain line is the right one; you then fit almost any rock feature to the route description, turning arêtes into gullies to substantiate your reasoning. Ian and I very quickly convinced ourselves that this was the route.

The next thing was to decide whether to tackle it in crampons or ordinary boots, for there were pieces of rock projecting from the ice. Since I have always been a rock climber rather than an ice expert I decided to trust to my boots and what rock there was.

It was one of the hardest pitches I have ever done – much harder than it looked from below, but after the first few moves there was no turning back. I couldn't possibly have climbed down and there were no cracks for my pegs – the rock was either compact, or so shattered that the peg would have been pulled straight out. I balanced up from one rocky projection to another, soon realised that it was even steeper than I had thought, found myself thrust backwards out of balance. I knew that if I slipped I should almost certainly be killed and take Ian with me; yet this was climbing at its best – I was right at the edge of my own limits and at the peak of my form. I had no feeling of fear. I caressed a shattered flake, calculated whether it would take my weight, decided it could, pulled gently, and was bridged across the groove sixty feet above Ian, the rope dropping straight down to him without a runner. The rock was covered by a glass-like film of ice, there was nothing solid to hold on to – all one could do was to use the balance of limbs counterpoised on two rugosities. I didn't notice the time but when I reached the top Ian told me I had been an hour. He followed up quickly, calling for a tight rope.

'You got your hard pitch,' he gasped. 'It was more like VI to me. Are you sure that was on the route – there should have been some pegs in it.'

'They might have been covered by the ice. Anyway, we'll soon see – there's another crack over there.'

Ian climbed over towards it – everything was plastered in ice, making progress desperately slow.

'We're definitely off route,' he called back. 'I'm now on the wrong side of the Spider – it must go up where you turned back.'

Meanwhile the two Swiss had caught us up. It was quite obvious that they would never have succeeded in leading the pitch I had just climbed so I gave them a top rope and hauled them up the groove. Now all four of us had to abseil back down. We discovered, at this point, that our two Swiss friends had no idea of how to abseil. It seemed unbelievable that they could have ventured on the Eiger with such a scanty knowledge of any rock techniques, though in all fairness to them they were thoroughly competent on ice. Ian gave them a hurried lesson in the elementary principles of abseiling and soon we were all back at the foot of the groove.

After this pitch the Exit Cracks seemed child's play. Once again we were very lucky with conditions: they were free of ice. I could imagine just how hard they might be in bad weather, for the route ran up a series of smooth, polished gullies of compact rock. When free of ice, it was just a scramble, and after a time we even took off the rope, but when heavily iced it would be a different story: all the holds were sloping and there were no cracks for pitons; the easy gullies would then turn into glassy chutes.

We were still unroped when we reached the summit ice-field. I suddenly noticed the clean sweep of ice dropping away below my feet, straight down to the woods and valleys 6000 feet below, and felt naked and exposed without the security of a rope.

'I reckon we could do with a rope,' suggested Ian.

I agreed wholeheartedly; we cut out a proper ledge, roped up and finished the climb in orthodox manner, using peg belays, moving one at a time. Only a few years before, two Germans had fallen to their deaths at this very point, just a stone's throw from the top.

Ten minutes and a hundred feet later, we were on the Mitellegi Ridge, following the well-marked trail of footsteps left by other climbers. It was all over; we had climbed the North Wall of the Eiger. My strongest feeling was one of gratitude for our good fortune, that the face had been in such perfect condition, and above all that we had been able to enjoy the actual process of climbing, while on it. It was not just a question of retrospective satisfaction at having survived a stern struggle, a feeling of relief at the end of several days' acute discomfort and danger. This must be the feeling of the majority of the people who climb the Eiger, for all too often the Ramp and every other chimney or gully on the face is a torrent. Once you are soaked to the skin there can be no question of enjoyable climbing and the nights are then sheer purgatory; there is a real satisfaction in this kind of strife over hard conditions, but to me, this cannot compare with the sheer physical pleasure of climbing over difficult terrain, of picking out a complex route when I am sufficiently warm and dry to appreciate it. We were always aware of the potential menace of the face – I have never been on a climb with such a grim atmosphere, partly gained of course from our knowledge of its history and my own experience on it, but also from its very structure, the sheer compact walls, plunging slopes of grey, rock-scarred ice, and the dark shadows contrasting with sunlit woods and pastures below. We were aware, too, that an unexpected change in the weather could turn the face into an inferno, that suddenly we could find ourselves fighting for our lives, that then we should have to use our last reserves of strength – all the skill and experience we had ever gained in the mountains.

But all that was over. We sat on the summit, munched some dried fruit, basked in the sun, enjoyed the exquisite pleasure of having space all round us, of seeing mountains on every side, and no longer confined to the one view from the prison we had just escaped. Another few minutes and we left the summit – it was a joy to be able to scramble unroped down the easy slopes of the West Ridge. We heard a shout from below, and saw the two Swiss work their way up the final ridge; they would soon be on the top.

We reached Kleine Scheidegg in a couple of hours, and then all the elation was knocked out of us. Herr von Almen, the proprietor of the hotel, asked us into his study.

'Could you tell me the names of the two climbers who were behind you?'

'Yes – they were a Scot, Tom Carruthers and an Austrian. I think his name is Moderegger. Why do you ask?'

'I'm afraid I have bad news for you. They are dead.'

'But – how?'

'We do not know. The face was covered in cloud all afternoon. I watched them on the Second Ice-field in the morning. They were very slow. Then, when the cloud lifted in the evening, I couldn't see them.'

'Couldn't they be out of sight in the Ramp?'

'No, I'm afraid not. I searched the lower part of the face with my telescope and was able to pick out their bodies. The guides are going up this moment to bring them back.'

Even in those seemingly perfect conditions, the Eiger had made its claim.

EPILOGUE

The ship was slowly pulling out from the wharf; tugs hooted, people were waving, a woman near me was crying. I held Wendy closer to me, just to convince myself that she really was there beside me, that we were both on board this ship bound for South America. The previous month had passed in a breakneck whirl of lectures, telling the story of my ascent of the Eiger, building the foundations for a new freedom and earning enough money for both of us to go to Patagonia.

We were on the threshold of a new life; there was to be no more compromise between leading a conventional career and my love of climbing. I could not quite see what the future would bring, at times I even had moments of doubt, but beyond that I felt a deeper happiness than I had ever known. I was at last basing my life on the things that I loved.

THE
NEXT
HORIZON

To Conrad, Daniel and Rupert

CONTENTS

ACKNOWLEDGEMENTS

I owe a great deal to all the people who appear by name in these pages, in many instances for their forbearance. I owe my special thanks to John Anstey, Editor of the *Daily Telegraph* Magazine, who showed confidence in my ability to produce photographs and to write. He started me on a new stage of my life as adventure journalist; to George Greenfield, my Literary Agent, who has done a great deal more than negotiate contracts, and has been my adviser and friend over the two most important expeditions in my life so far; to Livia Gollancz for her editorial advice and her patience in waiting for a book which was finished literally in the last hours before flying out to Kathmandu, en route for Everest; to Betty Prentice, who typed the manuscript, corrected the spelling and improved my grammar; to my mother, who thought of the title and lastly, and most of all, to Wendy for her love and her courage through these years and, on a more immediate level, for her selection and layout of the pictures.

C. B.

CHAPTER ONE

Chilean Expedition

The two trucks rattled and bounced over the rough dirt road in a swirl of dust that was instantly whipped away by the blast of the wind. On either side of the road was a forest of dead trees, a graveyard of whitened skeletons with limbs twisted by incessant wind and bleached by sun and weather; a sky filled with a fleet of great sausage-like clouds, brown-grey zeppelins driven in from the Pacific by the constant fury of the Roaring Forties. In the distance, just visible above the petrified forest, were the mountains – jagged dark shapes that seemed dwarfed by the high vault of the sky.

It was the 28th November 1962 and we were on the last leg of our journey to climb the Central Tower of Paine. It didn't matter that we were cold and uncomfortable in the back of the lorry, sandwiched between packing cases and the canvas roof, for we were very nearly at the end of our journey, soon to see the mountain we had to climb. This first glimpse of the objective is one of the most exciting moments of any expedition. Up to that point there is always a feeling of unreality about the entire enterprise. It is difficult to believe that one will ever overcome all the mundane problems of raising money, begging equipment; it is even more difficult to imagine the jump from England to mountains in some distant corner of the earth.

We had spent over three weeks travelling from England, firstly by passenger liner to Valparaiso in Chile, then on an exhilarating flight down the spine of the Andes to Punta Arenas, a small windswept town on the Straits of Magellan, and now we were driving north, across the pampas, towards our objective.

The truck pulled up a small hill and round a shoulder; the ground, grass clad, with only the occasional lonely finger of a dead tree, stretched down into a shallow valley, rising gently on the other side to a low ridge. The pampas was like an Atlantic swell, rolling away into the foothills of the Paine Massif, dusty green, and yet the air was so clear that you could pick out each windswept shrub and protruding spine of rock. And there, some twenty miles away, was the Central Tower of Paine – a slender blade of rock that at this distance seemed dominated by the squat mass of the mountains round it.

It was this peak that had triggered my resolve to abandon a conventional career and make a living around climbing, but at that instant, as we gazed at the distant nobble of rock which was to be the focus of our lives for the next few weeks, I was filled with a simple excitement at the prospect of tackling it. One of the features of climbing is the intensity of concentration it exacts. In its basic form, if you are poised on a rock wall a hundred feet above the ground, all other thoughts and problems are engulfed by the need for absolute concentration. There is no room for anything other than the problems of staying in contact with the rock and negotiating the next few moves. In this respect, climbing offers an escape, or perhaps it would be better to describe it as a relaxation from everyday worries of human relationships, money or jobs. This relaxation lasts for longer than just those moments when you are actually climbing and life is in jeopardy.

Sitting on a ledge, belaying one's partner, senses are extra acute; the feel of the rock under hand, of the wind and sun, the shape of the hills – all these are perceived with an extra intensity. Absorption in immediate surroundings once again excludes one's everyday life. On an expedition the same withdrawal from everyday affairs takes place, but here the expedition becomes a tiny little world of its own with, in microcosm, between its members, all the tensions and conflict that can take place in the larger world. The all-consuming aim is to climb the mountain of one's choice and this transcends in importance anything that might be happening beyond it.

For the next few weeks nothing mattered to me but this distant tower of rock and the small group of people who were concerned in climbing it.

There were nine of us altogether, seven climbers, two wives (one of them my own), and a three-year-old child. Wendy, Elaine and young Martin were not part of the expedition but inevitably filled part of the story. Barrie Page, the leader of the expedition, was a geologist and had visited the Paine Group two years before as a member of a scientific expedition. With him had been two other members of our group, Derek Walker and Vic Bray. They had made a map of the area and carried out a geological survey, but they had been enthralled by the Towers of Paine: three magnificent granite spires, set in the midst of some of the most exciting rock scenery in South America. The smallest, the Northern Tower, had been climbed by an Italian expedition in 1958, but the Central and Southern Towers were unclimbed. The Central Tower was especially attractive, forming a perfect rock spire, sheer on every side. They didn't have the equipment to tackle it but resolved to return. Barrie had invited Don Whillans and myself. I had at first refused because of my new job with Unilever, but had then realised that I could not resist the opportunity. The sixth member of the team was John Streetley, who had had a mercurial climbing career in the mid-fifties while studying at Cambridge, and had then returned to his native Trinidad to build up a successful business. He was going to join us later in the expedition. Ian Clough, with whom I had climbed the North Wall of the Eiger that summer, had joined us at the last minute, giving up a place he had at a teachers' training college, and paying his own fare out.

Our little convoy came to a halt at a police check-post – it was like a small Customs point, with a hut by the road and a red and white drop-bar barring our way. There were two carabineros in neat grey uniforms with pistols at their sides. They seemed almost to expect us. The chief, lean, tough-looking and very tanned, asked Barrie something in Spanish. He got out some papers; the carabinero looked at them but didn't seem satisfied and started to grill Barrie. The other carabinero, a great slob of a man who reminded me of pictures I had seen of Hermann Goering, just looked bored.

At first the rest of us had taken no notice, thinking that our passage through the check-point would be a routine matter, but we could quickly sense Barrie's growing excitement and the hostility of the carabineros. We gathered round, tensed and anxious.

'What's up, Barrie?' asked Don.

'Oh, just a bit of bureaucracy,' said Barrie, and kept arguing.

'Seems to be more than that to me,' said Don. 'Why won't the buggers let us through? We've got permission to climb the Tower, haven't we?'

'Of course we have,' said Barrie.

'Well haven't you got it with you in writing?'

'We don't need it. We've got blanket permission to go into the Paine Massif,' said Barrie. 'They're just being awkward.'

'Well they should bloody well know, shouldn't they? Either you need permission or you don't.'

There was something about Barrie's manner – he was a born salesman, effervescent, fast talking and very difficult to pin down – that was the very opposite to Don, who likes everything spelt out in black and white. The argument developed into a three-cornered battle between Barrie, Don and the carabineros, with very little communication between any of them. The post was at the Estancia Castillo, a big ranch managed, as many of the estancias are, by an Englishman. He eventually came to our rescue and talked us through the police post, calming our ragged nerves with a very English afternoon-tea in his home. Set in the great empty space of the pampas, Mr Saunders' house was what I imagine an English country house of forty years ago must have been like, with its array of servants, tea in a silver service and big soft armchairs nestling on a thick pile carpet. Our own appearance, modern-day climbers, must have seemed a little incongruous. We were still agitated by the brush with the police, the possibility that having come so close we could be stopped from reaching the Tower. We had already heard that an Italian climbing expedition was coming out later in the season. Don read Machiavellian plots into what had just happened.

'The Italians could be behind this,' he said. 'Are you sure you asked for permission to climb the Tower, Barrie?'

'Of course I did; it was all tied up in the general application. I was talking to the authorities in Santiago about it.'

'Yeah, but what about having it down in black and white. Cut out the waffle, and let's see your application.'

'What on earth's the point? I haven't got it here anyway.'

'Well, there you are, if you haven't got permission in black and white I reckon those Itis are behind this. They'll try to stop us any way they can; I've seen it before.'

One obvious problem was the ambiguity of the title of our expedition. When Barrie, Vic and Derek had been to the area before, they had called themselves the South Patagonia Survey Expedition. To maximise on any goodwill gained by this earlier expedition, Barrie had named ours 'The South Patagonia Survey Expedition II 1962/3'. Don, therefore, had grounds for his suspicion that Barrie could have failed to make a specific application to climb the Central Tower.

And the argument went on and on; it had developed into a witchhunt against Barrie with, I suspect, very little justice; but we all wanted a scapegoat to ease our fears. The Saunders' just looked bewildered and seemed quite relieved when we continued our journey.

Another twenty miles over open grassland, with the massif of the Paine getting ever bigger on the horizon, and we reached Estancia Cerro Guido. This was run by another British family, the Neilsons. By European standards it was huge, with 100,000 head of sheep and covering 300 square miles. Both the Estancias, and indeed the bulk of Chilean Patagonia, were owned by a single company that had originally been under British control but had been turned over to the Chileans. The Chilean Government had then forced the British to sell off some of its lands, but it remained a landowner of immense power. Most of their farms were still managed by Britons, who lived at a high standard of living with practically no security. Their pay was not particularly high, yet they received their keep and a lavish entertainment allowance so that they could look after guests sent down by the company. In this way they were professional hosts as well as sheep farmers.

Theo Neilson was a tall, distinguished-looking man, with an air of sadness, almost defeat, about him. His wife, Marie, bubbled with vitality and obviously loved plenty of people around. They gave us a wonderfully warm welcome, put us up for the night, and that evening we had a magnificent dinner; yet it seemed strange to be sitting around a formal dinner table, being waited on by uniformed waitresses, here in the middle of the pampas. I felt guilty about my impatience with the long-drawn-out meal and conversation; an impatience caused partly by the fact that I am shy about talking in a big group. But more than this was a longing to be beneath the open sky, close to the grass and earth, without the need to make polite conversation to one's next-door neighbour.

But the next morning we set out on the final leg of our journey to the base of the Paine. The rough dirt track curled through undulating hills, past little rock outcrops and the skeletons of dead trees. Pink flamingo rose laboriously from a small lake as our truck rattled past. Big woolly sheep browsed on the short coarse grass, and horses, temporarily free, gambolled over the pampas. I had a feeling of release and excited anticipation in the clear morning air, glimpsing, at each bend in the road, the mountain we had come so far to climb. As we drew closer, the spire of the Central Tower seemed as slender as ever, the rock compact, without any sign of weakness. I just prayed that Barrie was right and that there was a way up the other side.

The site of our base camp was near a small estancia nestling immediately below the mountains. It reminded me of a Scottish hill-farm, with its little two-storied stone-built house, corrugated iron buildings and wooden sheep-pens. It seemed to blend into the landscape, becoming an integral part of this wild and lonely country. Our own camp was in a coppice of stunted trees and scrub, sheltered from the wind by a couple of low hummocks. As we unpacked boxes of gear and food, all the tension of the previous day was replaced with the excited anticipation of the climb to come. We had chosen Barrie as a scapegoat for our own uncertainty when it had seemed that we might be prevented from attempting the climb, but with the uncertainty removed these doubts were put aside. As leader of the expedition, Barrie was in an invidious position anyway, since Don, Ian and myself knew each other well and had considerably more climbing experience than he had. However, because of the compact size of the expedition, this barely mattered. A party of six on a comparatively small mountain can afford to come to decisions in a democratic way, allowing leaders to emerge through the natural process of personality and experience. Through the course of the expedition, decisions were reached through discussion with comparatively little argument.

For the rest of that day we were immersed in the process of unpacking, and that evening were invited to a barbecue by Juan Radic, the owner of

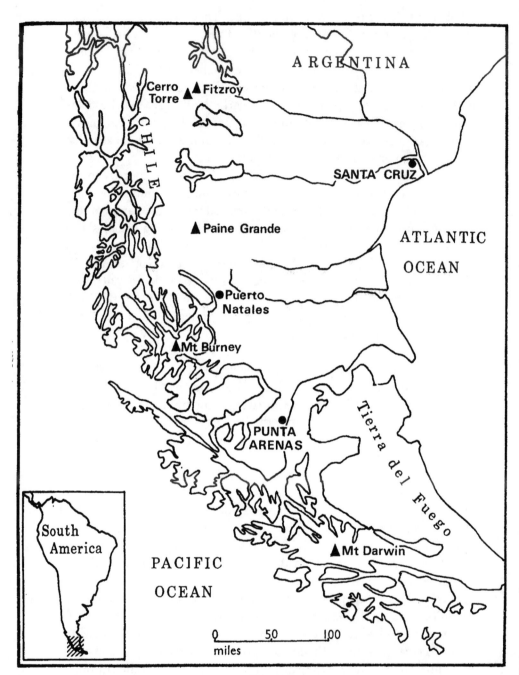

Patagonia

the neighbouring estancia. It was a magical experience, in complete contrast to the formal dinner-party we had had the previous evening. It was held in a sheltered arbour of trees at the side of the house. Cows' horns were nailed to the trunks; chairs were formed from tree stumps and in the centre of the glade was a smouldering wood fire, over which a spitted lamb, opened out on a frame, was turned from time to time. The aroma of the lamb mingled with the wood smoke, the scent of the trees and of the earth.

Juan Radic was a big man, now going to fat with the hint of a pot belly. He was of Jugoslav stock and had started the farm from scratch, but now he was able to spend most of his time in Punta Arenas, leaving the day-to-day running of the farm to his brother, Pedro. One felt he was more a businessman than a farmer, but Pedro was everything that one imagined a gaucho to be: tall, lean and hard, with a face battered by the winds; strong yet lonely, with a strange tinge of melancholy. He could have stepped straight out of a cowboy movie, with his scarlet shirt, black baggy breeches and sombrero, and bristling black moustachio. That night it was Pedro who tended the meal, basting the sizzling meat with a sauce made from mint and garlic, passing round the skin sack of wine which we squeezed to send a fine jet into the backs of our throats. There were no glasses, no knives or forks. The only concessions to civilisation were some chipped plates and a big bowl of salad: the only available vegetable in that part of Patagonia, a form of coarse, pleasingly bitter-tasting lettuce.

All the newcomers were initiated into Patagonian life by trying to squirt some wine down their throats from the wine sack – a knack which took some acquiring. Pedro then sprinkled a few mysterious drops over each of our heads and made the sign of the cross. And then the feast began. We tore the meat from the carcase with our fingers, sat in the cool dark, warm-lit by the smouldering fire, and gorged ourselves on succulent tender meat; squirted wine down open throats. Next morning in my diary I wrote:

> The real thing about the night was the feel of it – the atmosphere. Eating because you want to eat, tearing the meat, held in greasy hands, with your teeth. Drinking when you want to, talking naturally, because you have something to say; listening because you are interested. This was a real enjoyment that went to the depth of my being.

And next morning we had splitting hangovers, but we set out all the same for the Central Tower of Paine. The Towers were hidden from our base camp by the rounded bulk of the Paine Chico. To reach them we should have to follow a long valley to the back of the Towers, where Barrie assured us we should find a comparatively easy slope, leading up to the col between the Central and Northern Towers. It was about twelve miles to the

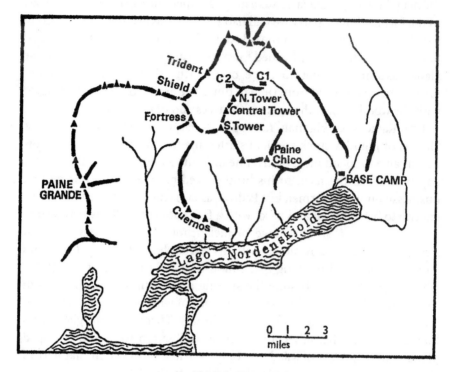

The Paine area

foot of the Tower and we would have to carry up all the food, climbing gear and tentage we were going to need. This, obviously, was going to take several days. The weather was perfect and apparently had been so for the past fortnight.

'That could be the whole season's good weather gone,' Don remarked dourly; but to me, on my first visit, it seemed difficult to believe that it could ever get really bad. We were all talking of climbing the Tower in the next few days.

That morning we plodded slowly up the grass slopes that led up the side of a gorge leading out of the valley we were going to follow. It was stupefyingly hot without a breath of wind; flies buzzed round us, attracted by the sweat trickling down our faces, and every few yards we stopped for a rest, unfit, boozed-up from the night before. From the top of the rise, the valley was laid out before us, steep scree slopes leading down to dense scrub-like forest. There were no traces of paths or of anyone ever having been there before, though to our knowledge three expeditions had been this way.

We stumbled and hacked out a route to the base of the glacier which guarded the eastern flanks of the Towers. From this angle the Central Tower seemed invincible, a magnificent monolith, presenting a sheer face of about 3000 feet – a face that today might be possible, but which in 1962, with the gear we had available, was out of the question. We dumped our loads and plodded back towards base camp. On the way we discussed tactics. We were still two days' carry from the foot of the Tower and were obviously going to have to ferry a large quantity of gear to its foot, but we were keen to take advantage of the good weather and start climbing as soon as possible. We therefore agreed that Don and Barrie should go out in front, establishing our second camp on the glacier immediately below the Tower and then push up to the Tower itself, while two of us ferried gear from Camp I to the glacier and the other two stayed at base camp. That night in my diary I wrote:

> Obviously I should like to have gone on the recce party, but I feel that Don could be better qualified in a way. He has a good eye for a route and anyway I want to try to hold myself back a bit. I want to be out in front, I love finding the route and making it, but at this stage it is more important to establish our camps and get up all the equipment we shall be needing.

We agreed that Ian Clough and I should toss for moving up to the first camp to do the carry up to the glacier; I lost the toss and therefore was to stay behind at base camp with Vic Bray, to ferry loads up to Camp I. In the next few days I was afire to be out in front, dreamt of what Don and Barrie might be doing on the Tower itself, even imagining that they might have climbed it, with me still back at base – and yet it was a pleasant, easy rhythm, each day plodding up the 'grind' – the long slope leading into the Ascencio Valley – and each day finding it a little easier. Vic was a good companion; he was older than the rest of us, being in his thirties. He was not a brilliant climber, but had spent some years with the Royal Air Force in Mountain Rescue, and was a good steady goer. A confirmed bachelor, he was self-contained and yet most considerate of other people, always ready to lend a hand even if it was thoroughly inconvenient to himself at the time. During this period Wendy was still staying with the Neilsons and I only saw her for one short visit. She was bursting with vitality, and yet her greatest love of all was frustrated. As a child she had been devoted to horses, spending her entire time in the local stables. Here in Patagonia horses were still the principal means of transport, but she hadn't been able to ride, and in fact never did.

The weather stayed fine for a further three days, just enough to enable Don and Barrie to reach the 'Notch', the steep col between the two Towers. 'It'll go all right,' Don told us. 'There's a crack line practically all the way up, with only one gap on a slab at about quarter height.'

They were keen to go down for a rest, and at last it was to be my turn to go out in front with Ian Clough. Wendy had now moved from the Neilsons, and the two girls were staying in the Estancia Paine, the agreement being that they should look after the house for the Radic brothers and do the cooking. The rest of the team were opposed to their staying at Base Camp, and they had only come out on the understanding that they were to stay at one of the estancias.

Young Martin, the Pages' three-year-old child, was the principal problem. He was a pleasant enough child, but none of us, at this stage, had any children and as a result we were completely intolerant of his natural need for attention and his spirit of inquiry. Even Wendy now admits that she had no concept of the trials that Elaine must have gone through, trying to keep Martin from under the feet of a crowd of resentful climbers, and at the same time amused and out of mischief. My own loyalty was constantly split between Wendy and my enjoyment of having her with me, and my need to feel part of the expedition. Looking back, it all seems incredibly petty, but at the time it was very real, in the little, slightly neurotic, world of the expedition. Most expeditions find a scapegoat and in our case it now became three-year-old Martin – in some ways this was fortunate, since he remained happily unaware of our feelings, though undoubtedly they must have affected Elaine. She is a down-to-earth, practical person, who one felt would be more at home running a suburban house to a nine-to-five routine than trying to cope with the involved politics of a climbing expedition and the problems of looking after a three-year-old in the middle of the wilds.

But the focus of our small world remained the Tower. On the 4th December, Don and Barrie had reached the col between the Central and North Towers and Don had deemed the climb feasible. They had returned to the glacier and the following day, since the weather had deteriorated, had returned to our camp in the Ascencio Valley. Meanwhile, Ian and I moved up for our turn to go out in front. The way to the west of the Towers led through dense scrub forest and then up through a chaos of boulders on to the lateral moraine of the glacier. At the head of the glacier towered the huge walls of the Fortress and Shield, two magnificent peaks that were still unclimbed. On our left was a long scree and boulder slope, leading up to the foot of the Central and Northern Towers, that stood like Norman keeps on the top of a giant earth mound. That afternoon Ian and I carried tentage and supplies up to the site of a camp a few hundred feet below the foot of the Tower, and left the gear on some platforms built by a former expedition to the North Tower.

The following morning we set out to make our first attempt on the

Central Tower. Up to this point the weather had been unbelievably mild, with plenty of sunshine and practically no wind. But now, as we picked our way over broken scree slopes, a few snowflakes scudded down and the wind began to stab at our faces. Broken ledges led across the foot of the North Tower and then a gully blocked with great rocks swept up between the smooth, sheer walls of the two Towers towards the col.

Its crest was like a wind tunnel that seemed to concentrate all the fury of the gale blowing across the Patagonian ice cap. Below, we had some protection, but now we were battered by its full fury. Even so, I could not help looking, enthralled, around me. Immediately in front, through a split in the rock that might have been the castellated wall of a crusader's castle, I could see down to the jumbled rocks of the East Paine Glacier, across to the shapeless mound of the Paine Chico, and beyond to the pampas, its lakes set like jewels of copper sulphate, blue, slate grey, brilliant green, on an undulating mantle of rough, grey-green tweed, that stretched to the far horizon.

On either side, the walls of the Tower reared above, brown and yellow granite, solid, unyielding to the pounding gales; and behind us, the driving hammering wind that raced past the massive, square-cut walls of the Fortress and over the smooth white shawl of the ice cap.

For an instant I felt a heady exhilaration to be here in the arms of the elements, far from other people, from the rest of the expedition; but as soon as we started to sort out gear for the climb, my pleasure was doused by the numbing cold and driving wind. A pedestal of rock about a hundred feet high leaned against the Tower – a clean-cut crack up its centre invited us – but to reach it we had to climb a short step immediately above the col. I set out, belayed by Ian, but immediately wind tugged at my body, hands were numb, and resolve drained out of me. Having climbed the initial step, I hammered a peg into the crack behind it and abseiled off – at least we had climbed the first twelve feet of the Central Tower.

We turned tail and fled back to our camp site, chased by the wind. There seemed no point in staying there, eating food we had so wearisomely carried up, and so we collapsed the tent and plodded back to the floor of the glacier, but even as we went down I began to wonder if I had made the right decision. That night in my diary I wrote:

If tomorrow is good we shall have wasted half a day in coming back up again, and a lot of energy. Having taken a decision, I have the terrible habit of reviewing it and re-reviewing it – often deciding that I had taken the wrong decision after all. As in this decision, there are so often equally important factors on both sides. The thing I must realise, and then practise, is that a positive decision, once taken and then pursued, is more right than dithering from one thing to another.

As it turned out, our decision was right, for the next morning it was blowing and raining even harder than it had been the previous day, and so we returned to Base Camp.

Our attempt to climb the Central Tower of Paine now slowly degenerated into a struggle with the weather, in which the Tower itself took a second place. A temporary improvement in the weather tempted Ian Clough and me back up to our highest camp on the 13th December. We pitched a Black's mountain tent, built a dry stone wall round it, and prepared to sit out the storm, still convinced that somehow we must remain in easy reach of the foot of the Tower so that we could seize the first available opportunity to snatch a few hours' climbing if the wind dropped, rather than waste the good weather in plodding up to the camp site. That night the wind just strummed across the tent, and we both slept long and deep. The following morning snow scudded down and the wind seemed to be rising, but I determined to sit it out. Ian was a fine companion for this type of long wait; quiet, easy-going, and always ready to do more than his share of the day-to-day drudgery of cooking and washing-up. On the boat trip out I had been irritated by his almost naïve enthusiasm for everything new, but now, cooped up in a tent about 2000 feet above the rest of the team, I felt his real worth.

During the day, the weather steadily deteriorated. It was rather like having one's tent pitched across the tracks in a railway tunnel. The air would be quite still, and then, in the distance, would come the roar of the wind, tearing through the Towers above us and down the slope until it hit the tent with a solid force, bellying out the thin cotton, stretching the seams until it seemed impossible that it could resist the remorseless force. And then, with equal suddenness, the wind would vanish and we were left, lying limp and helpless in our sleeping bags. That night we got very little sleep, and it seemed impossible that the tent could stand up to this kind of punishment for very much longer. The following morning, relieved at having survived the night, we packed up, collapsed the tent and fled down to the glacier.

But as we walked down, the wind dropped, blue sky appeared, the sun peered out from behind a cloud. Had I made a mistake? Should we go back? Could I suggest it to Ian? But he, mind made up, was heading down. I followed in agony from indecision. The others were obviously surprised to see us. The wind had barely reached the glacier. Don immediately made his decision.

'Barrie and I might as well go up,' he commented, and they started to pack their rucksacks. We were now very low on rations and fuel, so Ian and I, with heavy hearts, agreed to go down and get some more supplies. But that night I wrote in my diary:

I felt a great wave of lost opportunity as I watched them prepare to go up. If only we had waited there a bit longer, if only we had had more determination. What are my motives on an expedition? There is an awful lot of desire for personal glory. I want to be out in front. I want to be taking the lead. Is it an inferiority complex that makes me need the assurance of my success? I wish I could control it – cut it out. To have a major part in climbing the Central Tower, and then to reach the top in the first party, means a tremendous amount to me. I know it shouldn't, but it does.

I was longing to be back on the mountain, and yet, as we came down the last slopes of the hillside above the estancia we bumped, by chance, into Wendy and suddenly all the doubts vanished in my pleasure at being with her once again; until later that night, when a sky studded with stars in black velvet reminded me again of the mountain – how I longed to be at grips with it, feeling the brown granite, hammering in pitons, immersing myself in all the rich simplicity of climbing. Even in Wendy's arms, gorged with love-making, the driving urge to climb was greater – an urge caused partly from my love of the actual process of climbing, partly from my competitive drive to be out in front.

But we had something more tangible to worry about, for John Streetley, the seventh member of our expedition, had arrived at Base Camp that day, and armed with the scantiest information about our whereabouts, had set out to find us. Ian and I should have met him on our way down, but somehow we had missed him – easy enough in the dense scrub of the Ascencio Valley.

'He might well have gone up the wrong valley,' I commented. 'He can't come to any harm, anyway: he knows how to look after himself.'

The next morning we set out for the mountain, laden with stores for the rest of the team, confident that we should find John at our camp on the glacier. The weather had turned bad once again and so all my own secret worries about having gone down had been proved pointless. The wind was now reaching down even to the glacier, chasing over the boulders, blowing clouds of dust that penetrated every chink of clothing. Don and Barrie had been forced back down the mountain, their tent blown over in the middle of the night. They had even had to collapse the tents on the glacier, and I could see them at work under a huge boulder, trying to dig out a cave.

As I scrambled up to the boulder I hoped desperately that John Streetley would be there. I suddenly felt guilty about taking it for granted that he had found the others, but yes, there he was, just behind Don. I formed some kind of attempt at a humorous question about his wanderings, but as I groped, saw that I had been mistaken – it was Vic Bray.

'Where's John? Has he arrived?' I asked.

I was greeted with blank looks. A great wave of guilt overwhelmed me. He had now been out for two nights, with a third coming on, and I had only wandered back up to see the others. I could visualise him lying in the boulder field with his foot trapped by a fallen rock.

'Why, when did he arrive?' asked Don.

'Afternoon before last. He just asked the girls where we were, and pushed on up.'

'He could be bloody anywhere,' commented Don. 'He's probably just wandering around, looking for us. Anyway, I suppose we should have a look for him. He might be in the other valley.'

We divided into two parties and searched either side of the valley on the way down to Camp I. We had succeeded in selling the story of the expedition to the *Daily Express*, and I was the official correspondent. I took this very seriously, as it was my first assignment with a proper newspaper. The *Daily Express* had bought the story of my ascent with Ian of the North Wall of the Eiger, but they had used one of their own writers and had sensationalised the entire business. I had hoped to be able to redress this in the reports I sent back telling our story on the Central Tower of Paine, but now, faced with the possibility of a disaster, I dreaded my obligation to have to report it.

Full of doubt and worry I worked my way down, across the boulders of the glacier, and then through the dense scrub of the lower part of the valley. Don was just in front of me, and as we approached the dump of supplies which made up Camp I, he let out a shout. As I arrived, I saw that the tarpaulin covering the dump had been made into a bivvy shelter, and there was John's head, impish and grinning, sticking out from under it! Suddenly, in our relief, we were all shouting and joking. He had wandered up into the wrong valley, had bivouacked up there and had then returned to the dump, and next day was planning to walk round to the western valley, where we were ensconced.

That night we stayed at Camp I, crowded under the tarpaulin, and the next morning discussed what we should do.

'I reckon we're due for a rest at Base Camp,' said Don. 'But I think we should try to keep a pair up on the glacier to take advantage of the weather if it does improve.'

'Well, I'm keen to have a go at the Tower,' said John. 'I don't mind going up.'

Everyone else remained silent.

'How about you or Ian?' suggested Don. 'You've just been festering at Base Camp.'

Impulsively I agreed, and almost immediately regretted it – split between my desire to climb and hunger for the flesh-pots of Base Camp and Wendy. The mountains were once again clad in cloud, and even here, in the woods, the wind was hunting in the trees. With regret I watched the others heading down the valley, and started with John back through the dripping woods to the glacier. We could barely stand upright in the wind. There was no question of pitching a tent and we spent the rest of the day digging away at the cave under the boulder in an attempt to make a weathertight shelter for the night.

As so often, once committed, the very wildness of conditions became attractive. There was a satisfaction in hauling and pulling rocks to make walls for our shelter – it was back to the fun of building shelters as a child, and, as it turned out, our shelter was not very much more effective than the rickety lairs I had built many years ago. The fine, swirling glacier dust covered everything in a grey film; but no matter: we were in the mountains, twelve miles from the nearest human being.

John was a good companion. Small and stocky like Whillans, he had a similar personality in many ways – a quick dry wit, forceful, immensely strong, more relaxed than Whillans – easier to get on with, perhaps through success or a more comfortable upbringing. His family originated in Trinidad and he had had a traditional education at public school and Cambridge. At university he had starred as an athlete and sportsman, getting blues for boxing and running. He took to climbing casually, showing a natural genius for it, making a few brilliant ascents, and then returned to the Americas where he built up a successful business. At a time when Joe Brown and Don Whillans held sway over British climbing, he was the only person to put up a new route of comparable difficulty to theirs – on Clogwyn du'r Arddu, finest and most well known of all the Welsh cliffs.

He had a self-sufficiency and lightning wit that made it difficult to feel you ever really got to know him, but as a companion, on that basis, he made pleasant and easy company.

That night we cooked a magnificent meal, lightly garnished with glacier dust, and settled down for the night. I began to dream I was lying in a waterfall and then, slowly, reality merged with my dream-world, and I woke in the pitch dark to hear the sound of running water, to feel cold rivulets running down inside my sleeping bag. I fumbled for the torch; couldn't find it; woke Streetley to share my discomfort – he had a lighter. Eventually we got a candle going, and saw that the cave on which we had worked so hard the previous day was neatly channelling water down its sloping roof and over all the flat spots on the floor. We spent the rest of the night curled into niches which were out of range of the prying streams.

There was an element of the ludicrous in our struggles with the elements: here were seven experienced mountaineers, defeated time and time again, not by the technical difficulty of a steep mountain but by a mixture of wind and rain. Perhaps if we had shown greater stoicism in the face of discomfort, we could have achieved more, but somehow I doubt it. There is a sapping power to the force of continuous wind that can only be borne for a limited time.

But we were still determined to stay in range of the Tower, and the following morning started trying to construct a new shelter, this time a hut with dry stone walls roofed with the tarpaulin. By the end of the day we had a hovel with barely sufficient head-room to sit up. The tarpaulin roof thrashed over us in the wind, slowly tearing itself to bits on the rocky walls. Before the first night was out holes had appeared in it and every time a gust hit us it threatened to take off. I dozed intermittently through the night, planning my retreat to the dubious shelter of the boulder, and wondering if we should ever be able to get to grips with Big Ned. We had vested in our objective a definite personality, regarding him with a mixture of hostility, yet at times affection; we had the same kind of relationship with the Central Tower that a primitive tribe might have with an implacable forest god, who could destroy them at any moment, yet who was also responsible for their wellbeing.

But that morning the god was kind, and the sky cleared; though serried streamers of cloud marching across it, high over the Central Tower, were a sure sign that more bad weather was on its way. We resolved, anyway, to go up to Camp III and at least sort it out and stock it with some more food. As we plodded up the long boulder slopes, the clouds came scudding in, round the walls of the Fortress. The air was full of fine racing snowflakes. But I wanted to press on, up to the Notch, in spite of the weather. I was convinced that we needed to try to climb in these bad conditions to make any progress at all, so that when, at last, the weather did improve, we should be sufficiently high on the Tower to make an immediate summit bid.

Camp III proved to be a depressing place. Half-eaten food was floating in pools of water on the floor of the collapsed tent; everything was wet and soggy. We put up the tent and had a brew. I suggested rather tentatively that we went up and had a try at climbing, and John, keen to get to grips with the mountain, was agreeable.

By the time we reached the Notch, a full gale was howling through it, hammering our senses and making every movement a painful effort. It was strange looking down through the Notch to see gently rolling pampas, bathed in sunlight. Down there it was warm and dry; the others were probably lying in the sun; Wendy, perhaps, was painting, while here on the Notch, life and our own efforts seemed very puny against the force of the elements. But once I was in harness, and at the foot of the crack, submerged in concentration, all was forgotten.

Clip in étrier, step up, look round for a place for the next peg, hammer it in. Hell, my gloves are in the way; take them off; my hands are quite warm. Concentration – nothing in the world except the rock, all brown and rich, and the crack. Holds now; feel them; can I pull up on them? Yes. Where should I put my foot? Over there – use an étrier to help; I stick my foot out, but the étrier is swinging in the wind at 90 degrees to me. Cock my foot up above my head and field the étrier; step up. Then an awkward hand jam; it hurts like hell, but I'm up a bit more. Time for another peg; the crack is opening up inside, so that only half an inch of rock is in contact with the peg; but it holds my weight. And so, up and up and up, timeless, oblivious of cold and wind, of Streetley stamping with cold down below. At last I pull on to a ledge. To me, it had seemed only a few minutes, but it had been one and a half hours and I had completed only eighty feet of climbing.

'Do you want to come up, John?' I shouted.

'I'm bloody frozen down here. I don't think I could move if I tried,' he replied.

'Okay, I'll come down. Can you tie those ladders to the rope?'

We had brought out some electron caving ladders and these seemed ideal for the steep bottom step. Today we should have used jumar clamps to climb the rope, but in 1962 these aids were almost unknown. It was nearly dark by the time we had rigged the ladder, and I had returned to the Notch. We were tired and cold, yet we felt jubilant at our tiny success. We had at least climbed a single pitch on Big Ned after four weeks' struggle with the weather.

But the weather was winning. That night we tried to sleep at Camp III, and spent most of it watching the seams of the tent stretch and contract as they were battered by the wind. In the morning we fled downhill, and pushed straight back to Base. For the time being, the weather had won. Our tents would not stand up to the wind, and even the boulder camp on the glacier was untenable. There seemed nothing for it but to wait for a spell of fine weather at Base Camp. And anyway, it was the 20th December, only a week to Christmas.

CHAPTER TWO

Christmas in Patagonia

Christmas in Patagonia meant roast mutton, quantities of booze and a friendly visit by the Neilsons from Cerro Guido. We had been at Base Camp for over a week and the big saucer-like clouds that cruised over the Paine Massif were a sure sign that it was windy as ever in the mountains. The team sank into a restless inertia. Don, John Streetley and I made a foray to attempt to climb the Cuernos, an attractive peak about eight miles down Lake Nordenskjold, the huge glacier-fed lake that lay alongside the Paine range. A rainy bivouac in the woods cooled our ardour, however, and we returned to Base Camp.

It was a restless, disturbing period for me. Wendy and I had planned to wander up through the Americas after the expedition, spending the money I had made from climbing the North Wall of the Eiger. It had seemed an attractive scheme, but now my basic caution and need for stability began to affect me. I longed for solid roots, was worried about getting stuck into a new career and writing the book which had been commissioned just before I left England. I decided, therefore, to go back with the others rather than spend another six months travelling. Wendy was bitterly disappointed, for in many ways she is more adventurous than I. She is the product of a home that had always been unstable financially, yet had remained a close-knit unit. Her father, Leslie, is an amazing man with a free-ranging intelligence, spirit of inquiry and basic strength, that has enabled him to emerge through a series of personal crises that would have overwhelmed a lesser person. Like mine, his father pulled out when he was still young, leaving his mother to bring up four children in Birkenhead. He left school at the age of sixteen to join the art department of Newnes, where he showed special promise as a cartoonist. He would probably have followed a steadily developing career in the magazine world, but then, at the age of eighteen, he was caught by evangelism. This eventually led him into the Baptist ministry. But he had ideas that were years ahead of their time, especially for his parishioners in Buckinghamshire. He tried to apply a psychological interpretation to their problems; I should imagine his sermons went straight over their heads, for he has a philosophical bent, constantly inquiring about the nature of his own belief and that of others, trying to get to the roots of a problem, rather than skating over the surface in the way that I suspect most of his churchgoers would have preferred. Eventually, he fell out with his parishioners and fellow churchmen. Disillusioned, shaken in his beliefs, he left the church and faced the problem of making a new career with practically no qualifications. He started working as a medical artist and then progressed to illustrating children's books and magazines.

He had married shortly before going into the church and had two children, Neville and Wendy. Money had always been short, with disaster looming just around the corner, but Les somehow managed to give the two children a good education and a stable home life. Wendy went to Brighton High School and then on to Art College, where she stayed for only three years, just getting her intermediate certificate before leaving to earn some immediate money, like her father, as a freelance illustrator.

In many ways she had a lonely childhood, isolated by lack of money, which made her different from most other children at school. This gave her a superficial shyness, yet hidden beneath it was a real strength that enabled her to do without the conventional props of economic security.

I, on the other hand, had had a childhood that was relatively secure financially, but very much less stable emotionally. My parents' marriage had broken up before I was a year old and my mother had been left, without any help from my father, to bring me up at a time when jobs were hard to get and salaries for women painfully low. Fortunately, as an advertising copywriter, she managed to achieve a reasonable earning capacity and compared to Wendy's family we were positively wealthy. But the fact remained, she was very much on her own in a thrusting, unstable profession. Because she had to go out to work I was brought up, until the age of five, by my grandmother. Then, on the outbreak of war in 1939, with the scare of bombing, I was sent to boarding school. I was there till 1942, when I was brought back to London and lived alternately with my mother and my grandmother. They were strange, lonely years, for my mother had few friends and there were none of the conventional family contacts with other family groups. I had plenty of love but at times there was a tussle for possession between my mother and grandmother. I suspect this left me with the feeling of insecurity and a need for family existence that made service life very attractive, and tempted me to prolong my National Service into a regular commitment. When I became disillusioned with the army, I had needed another big organisation to jump into and had secured a management traineeship with Unilever. It was largely meeting Wendy, and her contempt for traditional security, that gave me the courage to abandon a conventional career and plunge into the unknown; but a conflict between my desire for security and love of freedom remained. In addition, I don't think I was ready for wandering in the sense that Wendy was. I had little perception or awareness outside the narrow field of climbing; my entire ambition and concentration was focused on the Central Tower of Paine and my own part in the expedition, to the exclusion of almost everything else. My senses were alive to the feel of the wind and sun, the empty beauty of the pampas, the architecture of the mountains, the mystery of dark pools and tangled glades in the forest below the Paine. But it got no further than my immediate senses. I absorbed the beauty and atmosphere of the place but was lacking in curiosity; I learnt little of the life of Pedro or the gauchos who worked on the estancia. I was too tied up in the climb and my own problems to be able to gain much from a sight-seeing adventure through the Americas.

It was a hard time for Wendy. She was so close to everything she had dreamt of doing, yet was unable to fulfil her dreams. The expedition was a man's world; so was the estancia, and she had become an unwilling append-age. If Elaine had not had a child with her, the two girls could probably have gone off exploring on their own, becoming independent of the exped-ition, but in the circumstances this could not be.

Just after Christmas the situation changed once again. We were told that Juan Radic, the owner of the estancia, was bringing his wife and family up from Punta Arenas, which meant that the girls had to move from the farm-house. Much later, I learnt from Derek Walker that this was only an excuse; in fact Juan and Pedro had become tired of having someone else's small child running riot in the house, and did not really appreciate the girls' housekeeping. Meals were seldom on time and they weren't served the vast quantities of food to which they were accustomed. Another irritant must have been the presence of Barrie and me when we were resting at Base Camp. I always felt uncomfortable invading the privacy of their house, but naturally wanted to sleep with Wendy.

There was considerable opposition to the girls' staying at Base Camp from the very start. This was largely because it had been understood back in England that Barrie had made arrangements for them to stay in an estancia for the entire trip, and therefore the others, quite naturally, had a feeling of being misled. Not having women or wives of their own with them, one could hardly blame them for resenting the ones who had. The communal mess tent had a feeling of a London Club in its male exclusivity, and I could hardly blame them for wanting to retain it. Wendy and I set up camp in a little two-man tent about a hundred yards from the other tents. I was torn between two emotions: one part of me wanting to immerse myself in the expedition, to be part of the tribe, and the other part enjoying my love for Wendy. At the time I wrote:

> An expedition is very much a living, single unit. I find it myself in many ways, and I think Wendy feels it. An awful lot of you goes into the expedition and the mountain you climb. I hope to God it does not mean that I am just not passionate because the depth of my love for her is total and complete, and yet I feel I can't give her everything; somehow, at times my sexual passion seems to be drained, I think – I hope – by the efforts of the expedition, my own channelling of enthusiasm.

This was when I was tired after our return from the Cuernos, and worried about my relationship with the rest of the expedition because of the girls' presence in Base Camp, yet in the constant pendulum of emotion that I have always been prey to, the next day, refreshed, I wrote:

> We woke up to hear rain pattering on the tent and a distant roar of wind. Although the sun spread a dappled pattern of leaves on the roof of the tent, I felt that the weather had changed once again. It had, and got progressively worse during day.
>
> But Wendy and I spent a delightful morning, in fact a whole delightful day, just loving each other with a great, warm, fresh, light-hearted love. It's strange, all the aspects of love that you plumb; light-hearted, bubbling, idiotic love that is all coloured and playful; deep love that goes right into your emotions; doubtful love, when you just want to be loved, but can't imagine anyone loving you.
>
> I think that on this trip we've gone through a big range of loving, and of doubts about the present and future, but never doubts of our own love for each other. I know that every day that goes by, my own love, and the confidence that I have in that love, gets stronger and yet each day I feel that I have reached an absolute optimum of loving.

We had known each other for less than a year, had been married for only six months, and were still in that tentative, finding-out stage of a relationship. In spite of the pressures caused by my own split loyalties, the general feeling of resentment against the girls, and Wendy's sense of lost opportunity, we had some wonderful times together during that fortnight, as we wandered down by the slate-grey waters of Lake Nordenskjold, making love in the soft grass of the pampas, confident that no one would pass our way, and overlooked only by a condor, soaring high above our empassioned limbs.

In face of the continuous bad weather the team seemed to have lost much of its single-minded push to lay siege to the Central Tower. Don was planning to make another attempt on the Cuernos with Derek Walker, though I was surprised that he was prepared to miss a chance of fine weather on the Central Tower. The rest of us were planning to return to the foot of the Tower yet again, to try to build a storm-proof camp where we could wait out the weather. But there was little sense of urgency, or even real unity, in the team at this stage – and then something happened to shake the team out of its fast-growing apathy.

We had known all along that an Italian expedition was on its way to climb in our area, but somehow, until they actually arrived, we never took the threat seriously. On the 28th December, the day that Don and Derek were due to set out on their mini-expedition, we heard that they had reached the Estancia Guido, and the following day they pitched camp about half a mile from ourselves. Derek and Don immediately cancelled their plans, and that afternoon we went over to size up our potential rivals. They were an impressive-looking bunch, slightly older than we were, very neat in matching sweaters and breeches that gave them an almost military air. They gave an impression of disciplined single-mindedness, very different from one that any stranger would have gained from our own motley group.

They greeted us with wary courtesy, and a spate of introductions followed. There were seven of them altogether; their leader, Gian Carlo Frigieri, was grey-haired and could have been in his late forties; a non-playing captain, I suspected. Their star was undoubtedly Amando Aste, dark-haired, rather sullen, who obviously resented our presence in the mountains they had come to climb. He had a reputation for hard solo climbing in the Dolomites, with many well-known routes to his credit. It was undoubtedly a strong team – on average experience probably a good deal stronger than ours.

Unfortunately, they could speak little English, and we no Italian. Barrie produced a postcard of the Towers and pointed to the Central Tower.

'This is our Tower. We have climbed high on it with much fixed rope in place.' He pointed to a spot considerably higher than our real high point, a puny eighty feet above the col. They did not seem very impressed; Amando Aste scowled even more fiercely and muttered something in Italian.

Barrie tried once again. 'South Tower very good, just as steep as Central.' It looked good in the photograph, if anything more slender than the Central Tower, but it had been taken face-on and did not show that the Tower comprised a long, comparatively easy-angled knife-edge ridge. The Italians were not impressed; they had obviously seen photographs of both Towers from more revealing angles.

Before leaving we invited them round for a drink that night and then returned to our camp for a council of war. As we talked, I could sense the growing unity of purpose caused by this threat of competition.

'Those buggers'll go for the Central Tower,' said Don.

'You never know,' said Barrie. 'I think I talked them out of it. They can't possibly use our fixed ropes, and we've got the only line up the Tower.'

'I shouldn't be so sure of that,' I said. 'All they've got to do is climb one of the cracks on the side of the pedestal, and they could come out above the ladder. If they get into that central dièdre, we could never get round them.'

'Well, we'll get them well wined up tonight, and persuade them that there's a good route round the back of the Tower,' said Barrie.

'You're not going to shift them by giving them a bit of booze,' said Don. 'In one way, you can't blame them anyway; calling ourselves the South Patagonia Survey Expedition! How the hell did they know we were going to be a climbing expedition? If you haven't got proper permission for us to climb the Tower, Barrie, they might well have us moved off altogether. I reckon that's what they're up to now.'

'In that case let's move up to the foot of the Tower,' I suggested. 'I can't see a policeman walking all the way up there. Anyway, unless we find a way of living immediately below the Tower in this bad weather, we're going to waste the first windless day in getting back up there. How about pulling Camp II back into the woods, just below the glacier, and sitting it out there?'

'I think that's still too low,' said Don. 'What we could do with is some kind of hut where Camp III is, just below the Tower. You could then keep a pair in it the whole time, and they could just nip out as soon as the weather got fine, and be on the Tower in a couple of hours.'

'It would be a hell of a job getting materials up, though, wouldn't it?' said Derek.

'I don't know,' said Don. 'All you need is a solid framework, and you could make the walls out of tarpaulin.'

'There's a lot of timber in Juan's wine store,' said Vic. 'I'm sure he'd let us use it. It would be ideal for the frame. We cut it to size down here and then carry the whole lot up.'

Don and Vic went off to find materials for the box. Thus was born an important new concept in expedition tentage, which was to enable us to beat the high winds of Patagonia on this trip, and which, eight years later, in a more sophisticated form, was to play a vital part in our ascent of the South Face of Annapurna.

The presence of the Italians had acted as a catalyst, giving us a stronger sense of purpose and unity than we had had for some time. That night, as we prepared the communal tent for our reception, there was an atmosphere of almost childish gaiety. Wendy, wearing a pullover of brightly-coloured patches, looked positively seductive, curled up on one of the camp beds.

'We'll have to leave you here on your own to receive the Italians,' suggested Derek. 'You might be able to turn their thoughts to other things.'

Meanwhile, Don and John Streetley were fooling around, Don climbing on John's shoulders, dressed in a long cagoule, to resemble a misshapen seven-foot giant. We were all excited, talking louder than normal, getting a kick out of the potential threat of the situation. It was the feeling of people about to go to war – a little apprehensive, yet excited at the same time.

And then the Italians arrived. There were more handshakes, a pretence at bonhomie, but the conversation soon lagged – apart from anything else, we spoke too little of each other's language.

I found myself sitting next to an Italian called Nusdeo. We talked in broken French, our only mutual language, and quickly exhausted the normal conversational gambits of what each had climbed, and whether we had any mutual climbing acquaintances. He had been on the North Wall of the Eiger only a few days before Ian and me, making the first true Italian ascent. And then the conversation lulled. Because I couldn't think of anything else to say, I asked if they intended to tackle the South Tower. He looked embarrassed, muttered something about being obliged to go for the Central, for this was the objective their club had sent them to tackle. There was a strained silence in the room, and the Italians left soon after.

As they trooped out of the tent there was an even stronger sense of unity and determination in our group.

Don summed up everyone's feelings when he said, 'If those buggers think they're going to push me around, they've got another think coming to them.'

I don't know what the Italians made of us. They must have noticed the huge pile of empty beer-bottles outside the tent. We had been in the area for a month, and had obviously made very little progress; at this stage, they had no concept of how savage the weather could be – that the principal problem of climbing in Patagonia was mere survival in the high winds rather than technical difficulty. We were a good deal younger than they, and seemed less well-organised. I suspect we had much the same appearance as Britain did to the Germans in 1940 – disorganised, few in numbers, and fairly contemptible.

'We've got to have it out with them,' said Don, 'and find out just what they're planning to do. If we're not careful, they'll be shinning up our fixed ropes.'

'How about formulating some simple questions with a "yes" or "no" answer?' I suggested. 'We can then go over to see them tomorrow and nail them down to some kind of commitment.'

'That sounds all right,' agreed Don. 'What we want to know is – are they going for the Central Tower or not. If so, do they intend to use our col? And if they do, are they thinking of using our fixed ropes? If they do, some bugger's going to get a bloody nose.'

Next morning, Don, Barrie and I went over to the Italian camp. Barrie acted as spokesman, asking the questions we had formulated the previous night. Their leader repeated Nusdeo's assertion that they had to tackle the Central Tower, since this was what their club had financed them to climb. He also complained bitterly that they had no idea that an expedition called the South Patagonia Survey Expedition could possibly have designs on difficult rock peaks.

Barrie ignored this complaint and went on to the next question. 'Well then, are you going from the Col Bich?' This was the col between the North and Central Towers. It also gave the only obvious route up the Tower. The answer was 'yes' once again.

'But we are already established on the Col Bich with fixed ropes going up one crack line. You don't intend to use our fixed rope, do you?'

They showed every sign of indignation that we should even make such a suggestion. Taldo, a big tough character, who was the most friendly and outgoing of the Italians, was very positive, smashing his fist into his hand to emphasise his assertions that they wanted an Italian route, a solely Italian route, up the Central Tower, totally separate from any 'voie Britannique'. There was no sign of Aste; and Aiazzi, his climbing partner, just sat it out in the corner, his face expressionless.

We returned to our camp and Don, Vic, John Streetley and Ian Clough, the practical men of the expedition, began building the prefabricated hut – our secret weapon to beat the Tower. Don Whillans and Vic Bray were the craftsmen, cutting the timbers to the right length and marking out the tarpaulins. At the end of the day, they had completed the hut, tacking the framework together and fitting over it the tarpaulin shell. Even the hinged door was complete, with its written inscription, HOTEL BRITANNICO – MEMBERS ONLY. Each component was then numbered and the hut was dismantled, ready to be carried to the foot of the Central Tower.

It was New Year's Eve, and that night the bachelors welcomed it in with a hard drinking session. The feeling of unity in the group, engendered by the presence of the Italians, was still not sufficient to overcome their resentment of the girls' presence, and they preferred to celebrate in masculine seclusion. As a result, I slipped away early, and was asleep well before the arrival of 1963. I woke early to the sound of rain pattering on the tent.

The weather was as bad as ever, but I was anxious to get the prefabricated hut established as soon as possible so that we could take full benefit from the first break in the weather. There was a risk that the Italians, reaching the col and forcing the crack line to the side of the pedestal which we had climbed, would establish their route in the big groove that was the main feature of this facet of the Tower and, seemingly, the only way up it.

Capturing the enthusiasm of the rest of the team was no easy matter. The Base tent was surrounded by the debris of the night before, and they all had splitting hangovers.

'What's the point of going up in this kind of weather?' said Derek. 'The Italians aren't going to do anything on a day like this. Remember, they don't even know the way up through the forest yet.'

'But we've got to keep our advantage,' I replied. 'God knows, it's little enough. They've only got to push one pitch up from the col and they'll be out in front. Short of having a dobbing match half-way up the Tower, we'd never get past them. We must get a pair established below the Tower as soon as possible.'

'I agree with Chris,' said Don. 'Now that we've got the box made we want to get it into position quickly.'

'In that case, how about getting our camp on the glacier pulled back into the woods today? That will give us a secure intermediate camp. We can then carry the box up tomorrow and erect it at the site of Camp III,' I suggested.

'Sounds all right,' said Don.

And that settled it; with Don on my side, the rest soon agreed to abandon the comfort of Base Camp, and return to the front line.

It was nine o'clock in the morning before we were ready to set out. The dismantled hut weighed, with all its timber beams and heavy tarpaulin, about 250 pounds, but divided amongst the seven of us, the loads were a reasonable weight, though some of the timbers were awkwardly long. We left camp surreptitiously, anxious to avoid being seen by the Italians with our secret weapon. Progress up the Ascencio Valley was slow; the rest were suffering from severe hangovers, and the seven-foot-long timbers kept getting caught in the branches of trees and undergrowth. Once out of the forest and on the glacier, it was even worse. The wind whipped across the snow, treating the timbers of the box as sails. It was difficult, anyway, to keep one's footing on the snow-covered boulders of the moraine, and in the wind we were blown about like a helpless flotilla of dinghies, capsizing in hidden snowdrifts and foundering amongst the jumble of hidden rocks. It was three o'clock before we reached the camp on the glacier. The cave we had excavated under the boulder was full of snow and the gear and food were buried beneath it, a mess of unwashed pans and broken food boxes.

'You left the place in a hell of a mess,' I told Barrie. 'Couldn't you have washed-up and sorted the place out before coming down?'

'You'd have left it in no better state,' he replied. 'It's all very well to talk, but it was all we could do to keep the tent up, the wind was so bad.'

'So bloody what! You could still have done a bit of tidying-up. We're not on a Boy Scouts' picnic, you know.'

But almost as my temper flared, I felt ashamed of my lack of control. It was an anger born from the cold driving wind, and my resentment of the invidious position in which I had been placed in relation to the other members of the expedition because of Wendy's presence in base camp. In the micro-world of an expedition the pettiest details, like an unwashed pan or an irritating mannerism, are blown up out of all proportion.

But there was no time for anger now. We were battered and half-frozen by the winds, and only had a few hours of daylight to retreat to the woods and put up a new camp. We grabbed tents, cooking stoves and a few dirty pots and pans, and fled back down the glacier to the woods. In these conditions, the mere act of living, trying to stay dry in a waterlogged tent, lighting a fire from wet wood, took up all our energies. During the entire period we had been in the vicinity of the Central Tower of Paine, we had had only about two hours of technical climbing; the rest of the time had been taken up in our losing struggle with the weather.

When we woke in the morning, everything was muffled and quiet. We were near the height of the southern summer, and yet the scene outside the tent could have graced a classic Christmas card, with every branch weighed down by snow. We were so exhausted from the previous day that it was eleven o'clock before everyone had emerged from their sleeping-bags and breakfast was cooked.

'I think we should try to get the hut up today,' said Don.

'Christ, have a heart,' said Derek. 'I'm shattered, and I think we all are. Can't we leave it until tomorrow? The Italians won't get in front of us in this.'

'Okay. Fair enough, but we must get it up tomorrow.'

'We're going to need some more food as well,' I suggested. 'Someone had better go back for some.'

'Well, what about you and Barrie?' said Don. 'You've got your women waiting down there for you.'

And so it was agreed. Barrie and I set out through the forest, all silent, rather mysterious and very beautiful under its mantle of snow. We heard the sound of distant talking.

'Could be the Italians,' said Barrie.

'We'd better avoid them,' I suggested. 'The less they know about our movements the better.'

And we slunk through the trees like a pair of partisans; I must confess, I've always had a fondness for playing at soldiers and, on the whole, found the Italian threat thoroughly stimulating.

We returned the following day with big loads of food, to arrive just after the others had returned from putting up the box. They were all jubilant. It had been a savage day, blowing hard and snowing in gusts, but in spite of this they had lugged the timbers up to the site of Camp III, and had erected the hut in position. That night I felt a tremendous feeling of affectionate loyalty to the others. We seemed, at last, to be on the way to beating the elements. The camp in the woods was well sheltered and storm-proof, and, with a bit of luck, the hut would stand up to anything the wind could do round the foot of the Towers.

'We've put it up, so you and Barrie might as well go and sleep in it tomorrow,' said Don.

'That's all right by me,' I replied, and let myself drift off into contented sleep. Next morning I woke to the sound of the wind howling through the tops of the trees and the patter of snow on the roof of the tent. I stayed in my sleeping-bag, reading, delaying the moment of decision when I should have to leave the comfort of the camp in the woods for our vigil high on the flanks of the Paine.

Don shook me out of my lethargy. 'Well then, are you going up the hill today?'

It was two o'clock in the afternoon, and we'd barely have time to reach the hut before dusk. The weather seemed to be clearing, with patches of blue being torn in the high flying cloud; and then the clouds themselves began to disintegrate into broken gossamer that merged pearly grey with the brilliant blue of the sky. The covering of snow that had made the going so difficult two days before had now been blasted away by the wind to fill the dip between the moraine ridge and the slope leading up to the Towers. Following the crest of the ridge we were able to reach the site of our former Camp II quite easily, but in a matter of minutes the weather changed yet again. As we collected a few extra tins of food from the dump we had left in the cave, there was a roar of wind. It raced down the slopes of the Paine, its front defined by a crest of swirling powder snow, and hit us with a solid force, hurling us to the ground. All I could do was cling to a rock, fearful lest I should be blown away – load and all. Our progress became little more than a crawl between gusts, as wave upon wave of wind rolled down and engulfed us in its demonic fury. I was tempted to turn back, but kept going on two scores: partly out of anxiety for the state of the hut, wondering whether anything might have worked loose in the wind, but more, I suspect, from a fear of appearing to be weak in the eyes of the others.

The hut was still standing, a solid haven against the fury of the wind. It was about seven feet long, five feet broad and four feet high; squat, ugly, yet completely functional – the only habitation that we could have carried up from the valley and which would stand up to the winds.

We spent three nights in the hut and each day tried to make progress on the Tower. I was convinced that we had to climb in the bad weather and high winds, even if it only meant making token progress, so that the moment the weather did improve we should be poised to make a bid for the summit. It was easy to formulate such a plan in the comfort of Base Camp, but the reality of wind-battered rock and ice vanquished resolution. It was all we could do the first day to struggle up to the foot of the Tower and improve the line of ropes we had left on our previous visit. The following day it had started to snow, but hoping that this might be accompanied by a drop in the strength of the wind, I persuaded Barrie to come out once again. The rocks were covered by a white blanket; what had been a walk the previous day was turned into a precarious climb; ropes were concealed and, once discovered, were coated in ice. It was as bad as climbing the North Wall of the Eiger in a winter's blizzard. We reached the Notch, to find the rocks ice-plastered and ropes frozen in wire-like tangles. My resolve faltered, faced by the sheer immensity of discomfort and cold, and the snow that plastered the rocks, penetrated clothing, froze hands. So often, climbing becomes a battle between resolution and self-indulgence. How far can one force one's body on in face of such discomfort? My emotions said 'fight on', but commonsense counselled retreat. After all, we could only climb a few feet beyond the high point on a day like this, and with a good 2000 feet to go, it became pointless when balanced with the risk and suffering we would undergo for so tiny a gain. We turned back, and as we went down the clouds began to scatter, the wind dropped and the sun began to warm us. Should we turn back and have another go at making progress? I looked at Barrie, wondered if I dared suggest it, but then abandoned the idea. The best part of the day was gone and we were established in retreat.

Don Whillans and Ian Clough were waiting for us at the hut. It was their turn to stand sentry, and it looked as if the weather might at last show us some favour. We pressed on down to Base Camp for a rest – I, torn between the pleasure of seeing Wendy and the longing to be back on the mountain, obsessed by the fear that Don and Ian might snatch a couple of days' fine weather to climb it while I was resting.

They did have one fine day – enough to make the first real progress after six weeks on the Tower. This was the first sunny, windless day we had experienced since the first few days after our arrival. The snow vanished in a matter of hours; the rock was warm to the touch and it was as pleasant as climbing in the Llanberis Pass on a hot summer's day. They quickly scaled the wire ladder that John and I had left just before Christmas, and then reached the top of the pedestal which leaned against the main mass of the Tower. Their way was now barred by a region of smooth, steep slabs, leading into the centre of the face where a great, open corner swept up into its upper reaches. This seemed to be the only obvious line.

Don spent the entire day working his way across the smooth, blank slabs. There were few holds for hands or feet; hardly any cracks to hammer in a piton for running belays. A slip could very easily have been fatal. He reached the foot of the great corner just as dusk was falling. He was tempted to spend the night there and carry on next day, but they had barely adequate bivouac kit, and a line of high-flying clouds was building up over the ice cap – a sure sign that the weather was reverting to normal. Next morning the wind was hammering once again on the walls of the Whillans Box.

The Italians had used the one fine day to carry a tent up to a ledge a few hundred feet above our Box, close under the base of the Tower. But they soon learnt, the hard way, that no tent can stand up to the fury of a Patagonian gale. It was blown down during the night, and the following morning, discomfited, they retreated to the woods.

A few days went by. John Streetley and I had another sojourn at the hut, tried to force a route beyond Don Whillans' high point, but were beaten by the cold and wind. You could only climb rock as steep and hard as this in perfect conditions. We too retreated to the woods, pursued by the fury of the wind, which, even in the shelter of the tree trunks, threatened to destroy our tents. We were now running short of food, but no one was keen to go down to Base to collect more, for fear that the weather might improve while he was away, and the Tower be climbed in his absence.

'How about tossing for who should go down?' I suggested.

'I don't know. If two go down, every bugger might as well go down,' said Don. 'This weather isn't going to improve for a few days.'

Eventually Derek and Ian decided to continue the siege at the hut, hoping for a further good day, but the rest of us abandoned the camp in the woods, and headed back for the flesh-pots of the estancia. That night we had a drinking session. Don and I happened to go out for a pee at the same time. We stood looking up at high cloud, scudding across the moonlit sky. We looked at each other.

'I don't think we've miscalculated,' he said.

'You know, Don, we've avoided each other up to now – I think we'd best get together.'

'Aye, I've been thinking on the same lines. We'd better do the next spell on the hill together.'

I had a tremendous feeling of relief after this conversation. During the expedition Don and I had sensed a definite strain in our relationship. This had stemmed, in large part, from the previous summer, which we had spent together with our wives in the Alps. The main objective had been the North Wall of the Eiger. We had made one attempt together, had become involved in the rescue of another British climber after his companion had been killed at the top of the Second ice-field, and had then gone off to Austria.

We had pitched our tents next door to each other at the camp site in Innsbruck, and then led almost completely separate existences, except when we came together to climb. Once on the mountain, we climbed superbly well together, but in the valley we had too little in common, were too different in temperament. I respected him, couldn't help liking him, but our backgrounds and attitudes to life were too different for us to achieve any kind of intimacy. Don is shrewd, very calculating, makes up his mind after careful thought and then sticks to his decision to the point of stubbornness. On the other hand, I tend to be impulsive, very often plunge into a commitment on an emotional impulse, and then feel forced to change my mind after more mature reflection.

At the end of the summer the weather had, at last, shown signs of improvement, but Don had agreed to give a lecture in England at the beginning of September. In his position I should probably have cancelled the lecture, but Don had settled in his own mind that the climbing holiday was over, and that, as far as he was concerned, was that! The girls were to hitch-hike back, while Don and I took his motorbike, planning to complete one last climb, the North Wall of the Badile. We then drove back to Chamonix; the weather was still perfect and I, therefore, decided on impulse to stay on, and snatch another climb. Ian Clough was also without a partner, and so we went up to climb the Walker Spur of the Grandes Jorasses, realised how well we were going together and dashed off to the North Wall of the Eiger. We completed it in near-perfect conditions. It represented a superb climax to a long summer, both in terms of climbing experience – for I don't think I have ever been so much in tune with the mountains, moving so well, or being so very fit – and also as the means of launching out into a new career. The successful ascent had brought a commission to write a book, lectures and newspaper articles. It had also shown the risks involved in selling a story to the popular press, when one's own words can be taken out of context, and sensationalised.

Don had written me a very bitter letter, accusing me, with some justice, of having cheapened the entire climb by what I had said afterwards. Inevitably, I think there was some bitterness as well. Don had always, at that time, seemed to have missed the boat. In his partnership with Joe Brown he had been overshadowed, and it had been Joe, not he, who had been invited to go to Kangchenjunga. He had been on two Himalayan expeditions at a later stage, but these had lacked the aura of romance and importance that surrounded the third-highest summit of the world. Through no fault of his own, the first expedition, to Masherbrum, had failed. On the second, to Trivor, he had worked so hard in the early stages he fell sick at the time of the summit assault, and therefore had to stand down.

I think my opportunism and material success inevitably acted as a barb to a relationship that was fragile anyway. At last, under the stress of circumstances, and the sheer scale of the problem that the Paine presented, our differences seemed unimportant. Climbing together on the Central Tower of Paine we should undoubtedly be faster and more effective than if we split up and climbed with any other member of the team.

And so, that night, on the 13th January, we agreed to climb together.

All we needed now was a fine day.

CHAPTER THREE

The Central Tower of Paine

We returned to the camp in the woods the following day, as Derek and Ian came down from the hut after spending two more days sitting out the bad weather. The wind was still gusting hard, but after another two days had dragged by it showed signs of dropping.

'We might as well move up to the hut,' said Don. 'No point hanging around here.'

'If you and Chris climb together, John and I can come up in support,' said Barrie.

And so it was settled. We walked up that afternoon. For the first time in weeks there was hardly a breath of wind. The clouds had vanished and the sun blazed down as we sweated our way up the long moraine slope leading to the hut. As we pitched a second tent beside the hut, we heard a rattle of stones from below us. Two Italians were also coming up. They passed without saying anything, and plodded up to the site of their camp, about 500 feet above us.

'We'll have to be bloody careful they don't get out in front of us,' I suggested, always suspicious of the intentions of others. 'Let's make a really early start in the morning.'

'I don't think we've got too much to worry about,' said Barrie. 'They can't know just how far we have got up the Tower.'

'All the same, I'd rather be on the safe side. I'll try to wake up about four o'clock.'

It was a perfect night. The contrast to what we had experienced in the last six weeks was so great that it was difficult to believe that these were the same mountains. It was still and silent, and the sky was a clear blue that slowly darkened to the deepest of violets. To the west, high above the snow-clustered cone of the Paine Grande, was a band of cloud that slowly changed colour from grey to a rich yellow-brown, merged into orange and, as the blue sky deepened, turned to crimson, cut by the massive black silhouette of the Fortress. It had a feel of peace and beauty that belittled our own internal rivalries and our race with the Italians. None of us said much that night; our sense of unity was cemented by the sheer grandeur of our surroundings. As the cloud slowly lost its fluorescence to merge with the dark of the sky, we climbed into sleeping-bags and settled down to the tense wait that comes before any big climb.

The sense of exultation, though, gave way to a mixture of excited anticipation and some fear at the thought of the morrow's venture. What will happen if the weather breaks while we are on the upper reaches of the Tower? Can we possibly get back in high winds? Will I, personally, be up to the difficult climbing we shall undoubtedly have to face?

I poke my head out of the tent; the stars glitter, cold, silent, windless. I look at my watch, 2.50; wait patiently for what seems an hour, and I look again at 3.00; John Streetley tosses at my side.

'Are you awake, John?'

'Yes.'

'I reckon we should start cooking.'

'I don't know. It's bloody early yet.'

'Okay, we'll give it half an hour.'

The time drags slowly past, and on the dot of 3.30 I crawl out of the tent to wake the others. Big Ned, dark and solid against the sky, stands patiently waiting. In the months of skirmishing at his feet we have given him a live personality. 'Big Ned's won again. He's in a bloody awful mood today.'

The others wake quickly, a hurried breakfast and we're off, plodding through the quiet half-light of the dawn. Tiptoe past the Italians – we don't want to wake them – then up the fixed ropes in the gully, hand over hand, feeling the weight of the packs on our backs. The Italians have been to the Notch; no sign of any progress on the Tower, but a great pile of gear that looks newer and better than ours.

'Shall we chuck it down the other side?' I suggested jokingly.

'No need. We'll beat them by fair means,' said Don. 'They can't get in front of us now.'

And up the fixed ropes. Compared to today's climbing techniques we were in the dark ages. Our fixed rope was made from ordinary hemp; we had no jumar clamps or other aids to climb the rope but had to pull up hand over hand. There were no modern hard steel pitons, harnesses or expansion bolts. As a result, our adventure was, perhaps, the richer.

Don went first, and I followed. We climbed the ropes one at a time, belaying each other with our climbing rope. It was just as well. As Don pulled up the blank slab just below our high point, the rope parted in his hands. It had had a tremendous battering from the wind, and the fibres of hemp must have simply disintegrated. That he stayed in contact with the rock was a miracle. Most people would have heeled back from sheer shock, but he somehow kept his balance on the steep slab, managed to remain standing on a couple of sloping rugosities, didn't drop his end of the rope, and then calmly joined the two ends in a knot. He was about eighty feet above me and I, not expecting a crisis, had been happily dreaming of the climb ahead. If he had fallen, he would have gone down 160 feet before I felt the impact, and I doubt if I could have held him. It was a remarkable escape – an indication of Don's uncanny power of survival.

I followed up the rope, more shaken I think than he was, and looked up at the new ground ahead. An open groove led up to a square-cut roof overhang. Above this the groove soared out of sight round the corner. But there were crack lines for our pitons. It might be hard, but it was possible.

This was the climax to weeks of frustration. The rock was warm and dry to the touch, rough-textured, solid, satisfying. I climbed the crack leading up to the square-cut overhang with the aid of pitons. I could hear vague shouts below, but ignored them. All that mattered was the rock a few inches in front of my nose.

But at the foot of the Tower, events were dramatic. Derek Walker and Vic Bray had spent the night at the camp in the woods and had left before dawn with the aim of getting a grandstand seat. They passed the Italian camp at about seven in the morning, a time when we were already near the top of the fixed ropes on the Tower. The two Italians, Nusdeo and Aste, were just emerging from their tent. They, obviously, had no sense of urgency and, at this stage, I suspect they had no idea that we had made so much progress on the Tower. Derek called out to them, and pointed upwards. He could just see us, two tiny dots on the sunlit rock of the Tower, below the big groove.

'Look, there they are,' he called out.

They looked, were obviously appalled by what they saw, and started to pack their rucksacks. At that moment the rest of the Italian party arrived, and immediately went into a huddle. There was obvious disagreement about the best course of action, but after a few minutes of fierce discussion they grabbed a load of gear and set out up the hill in pursuit of us. In the heat of the moment, they had forgotten their claims that they wanted a purely Italian route, and immediately started climbing our fixed ropes.

The climb was developing into a bizarre race, with Don and me in the lead. There was always a risk, however, that if we took a wrong line, and were forced to retreat, they could profit from the mistake and get ahead of us on the right line. We had intended to leave a line of fixed ropes behind us to safeguard our retreat, in the event of bad weather and high winds, but in the face of this threat of competition, Barrie Page and John Streetley pulled up the ropes behind them.

Meanwhile, out in front, I was climbing, happily oblivious of the drama down below. A couple of pitons hammered into the roof of the overhang above me, and I reached over the top. I have always preferred free climbing to artificial climbing; this, and the traditional British aversion to an excessive use of pitons, has always made me use as few as possible. At this point I overplayed my purism, trying to reach up over the overhang and pull up on a rounded ledge; my feet, standing in étriers, but jammed at an angle against the rock to give me a little more height, suddenly swung free, and the next instant I found myself hanging upside down, fifteen feet below the overhang.

I wasn't hurt – just angry at having made a mistake. I was so tied up with the climbing that I don't think I was even shocked by the fall. I swung back on to the rock, put in an extra piton, and pulled up. I spent over two hours on this 150 foot pitch; it was the best piece of climbing I have ever done: steep, sustained, on magnificently firm rock. On either side, the granite dropped away, smooth and sheer, and we seemed to be on the only possible line up this part of the Tower.

A shout from below. Barrie and John had realised that they would only slow us up if they tried to follow in our steps, and therefore, very unselfishly, they elected to go back down. Meanwhile, the Italians were just coming into sight on the slab leading up to the long groove. But somehow their presence seemed to matter no longer. It was insignificant, compared to the scale of the rock around us – the immensity of the Patagonian ice cap stretching out to the west. We could hear the cries far below, but they were thin and reedy, lost in the clear sky above.

And we were a close-knit pair, united just for a few hours by our mutual efficiency and common drive to reach the top. We said hardly anything to each other; there was no need for words; each knew what the other had to do. Our differences in background, personality and outlook on life were temporarily submerged by the scale and gripping absorption of the problem in hand.

I had reached the end of my pitch, tired, nerves extended, yet elated. Don followed up. Gave me the accolade:

'That was 'ard.'

He carried on up the next pitch, a square-cut corner as steep and high as the famous Cenotaph Corner in North Wales. He bridged up it with beautiful confidence, legs straddled on the walls in continuous, deliberate movement. Above, the angle dropped back and we began to climb more swiftly. Pitch followed pitch, and we were on the shoulder that was a major landmark from below.

'It doesn't look too bad from here,' said Don.

'Yes, but what about the time? We can't have more than a couple of hours of daylight, and it looks a hell of a way to the top. I think we'll have to do a lot of traversing.'

'We'll just have to go a bit faster. We should be able to get back here by dark. We'll leave our bivvy gear and travel light.'

We dumped the gear and set off over broken rocks towards the crest of the ridge. The angle was now much easier, but there were other problems. Every crack was gummed with ice, and there was snow on all the ledges. Don led a particularly frightening pitch, balancing up iced rocks. He used no pitons for protection and climbed with amazing speed. When I followed, he was out of sight and the rope was at an awkward angle. Had I slipped, I should have spun across the slab to come crashing into a rocky corner at its side.

I crawled fearfully up the iced cracks, full of wonder at how Don had managed to lead them in such fast style. Our way was now barred by a smooth rock tower; an abseil down the side, a scramble over a snow slope, and we were back on the ridge, with yet another tower in front. The light was beginning to fade. Don even dumped his camera to give him greater freedom of movement. It was steep, awkward climbing, but we were now barely aware of it, our sense of urgency was so great. We were in a race, not against each other but against the fast-falling dusk: the sense of euphoria and single-minded concentration that grips the long-distance runner at the end of a race must be very similar to what we now felt.

Another rock tower barred our way. Surely it must be the top. I pulled over the crest but there before me was yet another. Don went into the lead, balanced across a short, steep wall, stepped up round the corner and let out a shout. He was on the top.

I followed, and found him sitting on a block-like summit the size of a small table. The sun, a red orb, was dropping into the snow-white mantle of the Patagonian ice cap; a huge glacier like a grey speckled puff-adder curled down from the cap to an ice-dotted lake, now fast fading in lengthening shadows. At last we could see all round us, the ephemeral reward for weeks of struggle: the Cuernos' sharp beaks down to the left, the Fortress and Shield, solid, seemingly impregnable, to the right, and in front, across another glacier, the Paine Grande, an ice-encrusted pyramid.

It was difficult to believe that the winds that had held us at bay for seven weeks could ever have existed, the feel of silent peace was so great, and yet our own memories were not so short. In the moment of elation there was still the worry of how we were to get down, the threat of what could happen to us, should the weather break.

We hammered into the summit block a Cassin Piton, just to show the Italians that we had been there, and then, I'm not sure whose idea it was, shouted in unison, 'Big Ned is Dead!'

As we shouted I knew a second of superstitious dread. Were we tempting the fates in decreeing the death of the personality we had built these last few weeks? But there was no time for delay; the light was fast fading and we had a long way to get back to our bivouac gear on the shoulder. We left the summit, having spent a mere ten minutes on it, scrambled and abseiled back down towards the shoulder, reaching it in the gathering dusk.

We had been on the go for fifteen hours, without anything to eat or drink. It was now that we realised that when Barrie and John had turned back, they had all the food and the gas stove with them. They had even called up to ask if we wanted anything passed up to us, but at that point, all we could think of was the summit, and we shouted 'No.'

We were parched with thirst; there was plenty of snow, but without a stove it was useless. We went through our sacs.

'I've got a can of sardines and two Mars Bars,' I said.

'Fat lot of good that is. I can't find my matches. I'm dying for a bloody smoke.'

Don made another search and found them. He was content for the night, thirst and all. It was a perfect, cloudless night, the sky clear and black, glittering with stars. Thirst and hunger seemed unimportant, to be savoured as a prelude to the food and drink we should have at our victory feast.

The snows of the ice cap were cherry pink in the light of the early sun, as we coiled ropes and packed our rucksacks. We were on the way down, full of victory, but part of me called out for caution. There was still 1000 feet of sheer rock between us and solid ground. Fix the abseil rope, check the anchor, slide down, full of fear and caution. Will it pull free at the bottom? Thank God, it does; fix the next abseil, and so we go down.

Two rope-lengths from the shoulder, we meet the Italians. They spent the night in the groove, crouched on tiny ledges. First, there's Aste and Aiazzi. They glower at us, but then, on the next ledge, is big friendly Taldo. He grins happily, shakes hands and says in broken English, 'It is good you getting to the top. This is your route. We should not be here.' In fact the Italians reached the summit at 5 p.m. that afternoon, the same time as Ian Clough and Derek Walker arrived (twenty-two hours after us) at the top of the North Tower.

We laugh and smile – we can afford to now – and carry on down. It's the very last rope length. Derek, Ian and Vic are waiting for us at the Notch.

'We've got some booze for you to celebrate with,' shouts Derek, waving a bottle.

Don throws down the doubled ropes. They don't quite reach the bottom. We slide down all the same, stopping on a square-cut block about fifteen feet from the base of the Pillar. Don starts pulling down the doubled rope – all 300 feet of it. It comes down in a tangle, its end jamming in a crack just below us.

The end in sight, raked by thirst and fatigue, it seemed too much trouble to untangle so much rope to descend that last little step. A piece of hemp rope was lying on top of the block – it was the same that had broken when Don pulled on it on the way up. We picked it up, gave it a tug.

'Should be all right if we go carefully,' said Don.

He tied it to a piton and started to slide down it – oh, so slow and cautious. He was down, and it was my turn.

I eased my way down the rope, transmitting as much of my weight as possible through my feet on to the wall. I came to the place where our 300-foot rope had jammed in the crack, paused to free it, and in that pause – or perhaps as a result of the tug I gave to the other rope – I put too much strain on the hemp rope. It parted and suddenly I was somersaulting backwards.

A lightning thought: 'I'll hit the snow at the bottom.' I did, but didn't stop and rolled on down.

'God, I've had it.' Scrabbling with my hands, rolling over and over, frantic, clawing at the rock. And I came to a halt on the brink of a 500-foot drop. I was trembling violently, panting with pain and horror. The others sat around, giving me time to simmer down; someone handed me a water-bottle. I became aware of my limbs, noticed the agonising pain in my ankle and was convinced it was broken. I took my boot off and tried to wiggle my toes.

'Looks firm enough to me,' said Don encouragingly. I rested for an hour or so, and then we set off down; for me, there was no more exhilaration, just slow, painful movement and the realisation of how close I had been to death. But even that was engulfed by the reality of a pain-filled present. It took us two hours to get back to the hut.

I was on the point of breakdown from fatigue and shock, yet still felt compelled to write a report, for the *Daily Express*, of the successful climb and my near-accident. Once I had finished the report and had given it to John Streetley to take down, Don remarked, 'You'd better do the cooking, Chris. I'm no good at it.'

It could have been a piece of fine psychology – and certainly worked out that way – but I suspect it was Don's laziness. He really did hate having to cook. Anyway, I started cooking a magnificent spaghetti and Don did his best to cheer me up.

'Tonight it'll be agony; once the shock wears off. I had five days on my own on Masherbrum with a sprained ankle. It was bloody awful trying to get out of the tent for a shit. I ended up just sticking my arse out of the door. I reckon you'll have to stay up here till the swelling goes down.'

'Perhaps one of the others might feel like staying up here too,' I said hopefully.

'I very much doubt it. They'll all want to get down to Base. What's the point anyway? We can leave you plenty of food.'

Having had his spaghetti, Don pushed on down to Base Camp, leaving me to doze in the tent. Later on that afternoon, Derek Walker and Ian Clough, just down from the North Tower, came to the hut. I was relieved when they decided to spend the night there, and resolved, come what may, to stagger down with them the next day.

It should have taken less than an hour to reach the camp in the woods; it took me four hours of unmitigated agony. There was no question of getting all the way down to Base Camp, but the others were keen to get back to comparative civilisation – to gallons of white wine, fresh roast mutton and all the other fruits of our victory.

'I've got to get a bit more film up here,' said Vic. 'I might as well stay up here with you and we can go down together tomorrow, if you're fit.'

I suspect he made this excuse to salve my pride. He had a rare sensitivity and kindness in his make-up. I was deeply grateful for his company that night. Next morning the swelling had lessened and I felt sufficiently rested to tackle the long plod back to Base Camp. I tried to ignore the pain and, as a carrot to keep me going, fixed on a vision of Wendy coming to meet me.

At last, on the long grass slope leading down to the valley, I saw her. I had kept a tight hold of myself up to this point, but now, in her arms, we both let ourselves go. The others had tried to underplay my narrow escape, but she had heard them talk about it amongst themselves. Somehow, this had made it worse. We clung close to each other in the hot grass; Wendy cried in agonised relief, and my tears mingled with hers. And then slowly we walked down, past the skeletons of dead trees, back to Base Camp.

My ankle was badly sprained – perhaps broken – and I obviously needed to get an X-ray. I resigned myself, therefore, to going to Punta Arenas, while the rest of the team began to think of a further objective. The weather seemed to have settled into a good spell, and they therefore decided to make an attempt on the South Tower of Paine.

Meanwhile, we cadged a lift into Cerro Guido, and then got the bus down to Punta Arenas. The town has a feeling of empty neglect; it is a place of greys and browns, of swirling dust and corrugated iron roofs. The general atmosphere reflected my own mood, for I longed to be back in the Paine, at grips with the South Tower, could imagine the others climbing under the hot sun, could almost feel the rough texture of the granite under my hands. The moments of joy and excitement of climbing the Central Tower were past and finished. The present was a swollen ankle, a sparse hotel bedroom and a drab hospital. I was X-rayed one evening and they discovered a hair-line fracture on my ankle bone. I was put in plaster for a week, and had to eke out the time around Punta Arenas. Wendy and I spent much of the time in bed, playing interminable games of Scrabble, which Wendy invariably won. I have always been an appalling loser and ended up in a fit of temper, hurling the Scrabble set out of the first-floor window. Fortunately, the board didn't hit anyone walking in the road below.

My gloom was temporarily lifted when we met Eric Shipton, who was passing through Punta Arenas after one of his many exploratory trips in South Patagonia. I had never met him before, but he had been one of my heroes in the early 1950s when I had started climbing, and his book *Upon that Mountain* had been my bible. His appearance certainly lived up to my early dreams. He was in his late fifties, with a mane of silvery hair, balding in front to reveal a high forehead, and sweeping back behind quite large but neat ears. But his commanding feature was his eyes – a brilliant blue, that forever seemed searching some distant horizon from underneath a pair of bushy grey eyebrows. There was an asceticism in his mouth, which was pursed, almost prim, and yet somehow this was softened by a manner that was distant, yet had a gentle warmth about it. He was a person that I felt one would never be able to claim to know well, yet at the same time could be a delightful companion in any venture. He gave the impression of a man at peace with himself – who had discovered the life-style that he wanted to adopt, and who would just go on quietly following it. With three companions, he had been investigating Mount Burney, to discover whether it was an active volcano. Characteristically, the weather had been continuously bad, and in the month they had spent in the vicinity of the mountain, they never actually saw its top, or enough even to work out a reasonable route to the summit. Shipton is not a man to remain idle, and they therefore circumnavigated the mountain, carrying all their gear on their backs and remaining on the move for seventeen days, in appalling weather.

Their daily ration was porridge for breakfast, a bit of chocolate and cheese for lunch, and a concentrated meat bar for supper. They had forgotten to take any salt, and I shall never forget Shipton's look of quiet satisfaction when he remarked: 'You know, we hardly noticed its absence at all. I think we might well leave it behind on our next trip.' The remainder of his team did not seem quite so enthusiastic at the prospect of saltless porridge.

I couldn't help comparing our two ventures. We had spent two months in one area, laying siege to a supremely difficult mountain. Without this persistence, we should never have attained the summit, for we had to lie in wait near at hand to snatch the odd fine day. Shipton, on the other hand, had covered a couple of hundred miles of exciting, unknown country, in the same period. He hadn't reached the top of any mountain, had barely tackled anything harder than scrambling, but through weeks of grinding effort and discomfort, he had come into closer contact with the romance of wild country than we did. Our climb also had its mysteries, had certainly stretched us to the limit, had very nearly killed me, but the mystery was one of technical problems. We knew the way to the foot of the mountain – Derek and Barrie had already been there – the sense of discovery was in looking up at a stretch of rock and saying, 'Yes, I think there is a route up there', and then tackling it, using our skill and experience to confirm our prior judgement. In a way, it was just an extension of attempting a new route on a crag in Britain. The scale was bigger, the weather much worse, the risks greater, but the principle remained the same.

The mountain traveller is looking for something different – he wants to see what is beyond a mountain range, and having reached the watershed, and looked down the other side, he is driven on to the next horizon. Facets of individual mountains, even the summits, cease to have such importance. He is interested in a mountain range as a whole.

Shipton was on his way down to Tierra del Fuego to explore the Darwin Range. It was obvious that I would not be able to climb again in the next few weeks, so I resigned myself to taking on the role of the tourist and wandering across Southern Chile and the Argentine with Wendy, to meet the rest of the expedition in Buenos Aires on their way back.

I now kick myself for my lack of curiosity, but I was too tied up with climbing, wanted too much to be on the South Tower. Even so, once we had made the decision, had our rucksacks packed and a flight booked to Puerto Montt in Southern Chile, I couldn't help catching Wendy's excitement, for this was her voyage of discovery. We were well laden, being equipped for almost any eventuality, with a heavy mountain tent borrowed from John Earle (one of Shipton's party), Wendy's guitar, a box of oil paints and easel, a huge rucksack, a suitcase with our respectable clothes, and various string bags full of bits of food, cooking pots and other items.

From Puerto Montt we followed the tourist trail through the Chilean

Lakes, beneath the volcano Orsino, to Bariloche. Sometimes we stayed in cheap hotels, sometimes we camped. Soon I was able to forget the Paine, stop envying the others on the South Tower, in the idyllic present of our wanderings.

We spent three weeks on our own travels, wandering through the lake country, catching steamers and local buses. For a couple of days we camped on a volcanic shelf that jutted into the clear, limpid waters of Lake Orsorno, cooking over a wood fire, drinking cheap local wine and swimming nude, unworried at being overlooked. Then on to Bariloche, and up to San Martin Los Andes, where we stayed with an old friend of Eric Shipton who ran a little guest house. We went riding through scrubby hills, sunbathed below the blazing sun, and just absorbed the country around us. It was all over too soon – time to return to Buenos Aires to meet the others. In those weeks of happy-go-lucky wandering, the Paine had already receded from my mind, and I had ceased fretting about the superb climbing I might be missing.

As it turned out, I had missed little. They had been forced to turn back from the South Tower after making a lightweight push up its South Ridge, hoping that this would give the easiest route. But they found it to be a great whale-back of a knife-edge ridge, with serried gendarmes, each of which would have taken a long time to surmount. At the same time, the Italians had tackled it from the north, which was steeper, and displayed difficulties of a more concentrated nature. In addition, perhaps, they were more forceful, having been beaten in the race for the Central Tower. They reached the summit, and our team then turned their attention to the Cuernos, the other attractive unclimbed peak quite near our Base Camp, but failed on this as well.

I must confess, I could not help feeling relieved that I had missed nothing. It made the retrospective enjoyment of our own little holiday that much greater. I was looking forward to our return to England, to finding a place to live, with a new career – of what, I wasn't sure – to carve out.

CHAPTER FOUR

Woodland

'Where shall we live? How about Wales? Or the Lakes? Or perhaps even the Peak District?' This was a freedom I had never known before and which, I suppose, comparatively few people ever know. Where I lived had always been conditioned by my work, first for the army, and then for Unilever.

But now I was a freelance – in what, at this stage, I wasn't at all sure. We got back to England at the end of March. Our possessions consisted of a few clothes, plenty of books, Wendy's guitar and paints and my climbing gear. I had spent most of the money I had made from climbing the North Wall of the Eiger on taking Wendy with me to South America. I now had an advance of £500 for the book I had been commissioned to write by Livia Gollancz of Victor Gollancz. But most of this went on our first essential, a vehicle to get around in. We bought a brand-new Minivan – the first vehicle I had ever owned.

The immediate future was quite clear: I had my book to write and in the autumn I had some lectures. Beyond that I wasn't at all sure, and, in fact, downright frightened. People had a habit of asking, 'How long can you keep up this climbing business?'

'Oh, well into my forties,' I'd reply.

'Yes, but what are you going to do then?' they'd ask.

I'd put on a brave front and reply, 'Well, I'm going into the communications game – to learn how to write and talk about climbing. If I can do that successfully, I'll be able to make a real career of it.' They'd look sceptical, and I'd felt little conviction in what I had explained.

But in the present, there was a book to write – my first venture in the communications game – and I put off starting it time and again, frightened of the sheer scale of the project, of all those words I should have to spew forth. At that stage my total writing experience consisted of four articles in mountaineering club journals; and so I chased after easy alternatives, and there were no shortage of these.

Immediately on our return I was involved in making a commentary to Vic Bray's film of the Central Tower. Don and I had taken no film at all on our push for the summit, and Vic had been down in the valley; we were therefore desperately short of climbing footage, and so the BBC hinted that perhaps we might try to 'find' some film of the summit assault – good, close-up material of pitons being bashed in, hands going on to holds, and so on. Time was short, money shorter, and so we decided to shoot the necessary sequences near Don's home.

'I know just the place,' he said.

Our 'Potted Paine' was in a quarry high above a Yorkshire valley, near the village of Heptonstall. Below us, the chimneys of the mills jutted like granite needles out of the smog. The rock itself was steep enough, though it was stained black by centuries of pollution and the texture was coarser than that of granite. Most embarrassing were the initials and messages carved into the rock. Vic had his work cut out to avoid filming either the factories in the background or the graffiti on the quarry wall – even so, there crept into the corner of one of the sequences used in the film to depict our summit assault, a rough-hewn heart inscribed 'Kate loves John'.

To bolster our lack of film still further, the BBC built a ten foot high replica of the Tower, round which I had to peer as I made my commentary direct to camera. It was the first time I had ever been in front of a TV camera, and I was so nervous I could barely keep the quaver out of my voice as I read the script from the auto-cue.

While I was in London I met a long-lost cousin who was something – I'm not sure what – in television. He was quite a bit older than myself, very sophisticated, and had all kinds of important connections. My appetite for filming had been whetted, and I mentioned to him a scheme that was in my mind.

'How about making a film on the North Wall of the Eiger – a documentary of a complete ascent?'

My cousin knew just the man to finance such a venture, a man who had various television interests in the former Commonwealth. I went to a sumptuous office off Sloane Street, and was immediately in a strange world – it seemed almost straight out of a TV spy thriller. I was very much at sea as we talked of a £50,000 budget, production companies, and so on. But I went ahead and invited various climbing friends to join the bonanza – Whillans, Clough, Patey, MacInnes and several others. We were all going to spend the summer below the Eiger, playing at film stars. It seemed too good to be true – it was. I was handed over to an assistant, who handed me on to someone else, and from buoyant enthusiasm they became more and more cautious, until eventually the entire scheme fizzled out. This was a period of enjoying an ephemeral little glitter, of being a minor celebrity – something that had never happened to me before. I was eager to snatch at every opportunity to get myself established as a writer, film-maker, what-have-you, in an effort to find a clearly defined career.

Making a living around climbing was nothing new, even in 1962. Frank Smythe had done it successfully before the war, through his writing, photography and lecturing. Edward Whymper could, perhaps, be described as the first climbing journalist, though of course his income was primarily based on his profession as proprietor of a wood-engraving firm. In the post-war period, Alf Gregory and some of the other Everest climbers had made a fair amount of money by lecturing, but there was still a strong feeling of amateurism in the sport. I was often asked at lectures, 'Are you using the fee to finance your next expedition?' as if there were almost something slightly nasty about using the fee as part of one's income.

We had still not decided where to live. Wendy, at this stage, was uncommitted to any one area, provided that it was deep in the country. We had had six months together in a furnished room in Hampstead before going to Patagonia, and that was enough for her of London living. I felt the same, and obviously wanted to live in a mountain area. Originally, we had planned to settle in Wales, with the hope that I could get into the University College of North Wales at Bangor, but this seemed no longer necessary.

I was attracted to the Lake District, partly perhaps because I had done comparatively little climbing there, but also because it has a quality of beauty lacking in Wales. Snowdonia has a grandeur that is difficult to match anywhere south of the Border, but it is a beauty that is somehow alien to man. The farms and cottages suggest harsh austerity, unsoftened by hedgerows or gardens. Somehow, they don't seem to belong. The Lakes, on the other hand, are altogether softer, and more varied in their appeal. Each valley has its own special character. Man has succeeded in becoming an integral part of the country, with the cottages and houses blending into the hills as if they were an essential part of the landscape. There are more trees in the valleys, hedgerows intermingle with stone walls, and even on the open fell, there is a lighter, warmer quality.

And so we settled for the Lakes, loaded our brand-new Minivan with our few possessions – sleeping-bags, Wendy's guitar and paints, my climbing gear – and drove north. We were under the happy illusion that we should be able to find a charming country cottage for about £1 per week. We were soon disillusioned. The summer season was nearly upon us and holiday cottages were at a premium. Even a two-roomed cottage could cost as much as £10 per week.

We stayed with friends in Keswick and started hunting. After a week, we had looked at a dozen cottages, had chased after several long-odds tips, had even applied for a council house in Mungrisdale, though, not surprisingly, failed to get it.

We were beginning to give up hope of finding something that we could afford, and were even thinking of looking for a cottage in the Peak District, when we called in at the Royal Oak, in Ambleside, one Sunday lunchtime to have a drink. I began talking to the barman, and it emerged that he was a climber. After working through the normal climbing gossip of mutual friends, we mentioned that we were looking for somewhere to live.

'If you're really desperate, I know a place near here,' he said. 'I stayed in it myself last winter. It's a single room over a garage on a farm. It's pretty rough, but at least it's a roof over your heads.'

This was to be the first time I had met Mick Burke, and it was to be another two years before we met again. At this stage, he was just one of the lads who had chucked up regular jobs to live in the hills with the minimum of work and the maximum of climbing. He came from Wigan, had started as an insurance clerk, but had quickly tired of a routine nine-to-five job, and had spent the previous year around Ambleside, doing a bit of labouring, or working the bar in the Royal Oak when he felt in need of a rest.

We left without further delay, and drove to Loughrigg Farm to see if the room was still vacant. The farmer warned us – 'It's a bit rough, you know.'

It was. An outdoor staircase led up from the farmyard to a small balcony. A peeling wooden door opened into a fair-sized room, lit by a couple of windows. The walls were of bare plaster, brown with dirt, and traced with a network of cracks. The floor was covered with rotting linoleum, which had long lost its colour, and the room was furnished with a few pieces of battered furniture that had probably been rescued from a refuse dump. The nearest water was from a tap in the yard and the sanitary facilities were limited to an earth closet, most primitive and smelly of all toilets, placed at the back of a pigsty. Set in the backstreets of a city it would have been unbelievably sordid, but here, in the heart of some of the most beautiful country either of us had ever lived in, it didn't seem to matter.

Loughrigg is on the southern edge of the Lake District, nestling amongst the broken foothills that spill down from the Langdale Pikes. From the balcony outside the door we could gaze across the farmyard, over the spring green grass of a field, dotted with clusters of Scots pine and larch, to the still waters of Loughrigg Tarn. A scattering of elm, still bare of leaves, ringed the lake, and beyond it, breaking up the fields and part-concealing other farm houses, grey-barked spinneys' arms intertwined, merged with the darkling green of spruce forest. This, in turn, mingled with the open fell leading up to the Langdale Pikes, picked out by the waning snows.

We lived in Loughrigg for three months, and were able to watch the explosion of colour, of every shade of green, that takes place each spring in this part of the Lake District. I did comparatively little climbing, in part surfeited by our expedition to Patagonia. I was still working on my project to film the North Wall of the Eiger. When that fell through, I thought up a more modest scheme, with the hardy Scot, Hamish MacInnes, to make a low-budget film of the North Wall of the Matterhorn. This was to fill the summer of 1963.

In the meantime, we continued a desultory search for a more comfortable home, and eventually stumbled on one through the good offices of Heaton Cooper, the Lakeland artist. We had never met the Heaton Coopers, but a mutual friend had told them about us. They called on our garret one afternoon when we were out, and left a note inviting us round for coffee.

Several other people were there, and soon the conversation turned to finding somewhere for the Boningtons to live. Fenwick Patterson, another artist, who had abandoned the rat-race and settled in Coniston, thought he knew where we might find a furnished house. In a few days this led us to Woodland – to me, and happily to the vast majority of Lakeland visitors, an unknown corner of the Lake District. It is down in the south-west corner of the Lakes, between Coniston and Broughton-in-Furness. The road runs beneath Coniston Old Man, barely wide enough to take two cars, between a mixture of dry stone walls and hedgerows. You pass Torver, and on either side is the open fell – in no way mountainous, but with mysterious little hills clad in bracken – and then, round a bend, past a farm, you come to the signpost to Woodland, down a steep little tree-clad hill. It's off the road, an oasis of green in the midst of the russet browns of bracken-clad hills. A newly-grown fir forest jostles with coppices of fine old deciduous trees, a few houses and farms spread on either side of the lane; you reach a signpost marked Woodland Hall, a makeshift cattlegrid, a rough, potholed drive; continue through a wood of young birch, past an artificial lake, full of weed, willows brushing the surface of the water: everything is overgrown, wild, attractive, up to the Hall itself.

We're after the Lodge. It's owned by the Dicksons, seed farmers from Essex, who have made their money from market gardening, and have now succumbed to the romance of the Lakes. They have bought the Hall, its attendant farm, and the Lodge, a cluster of buildings clinging just below the crest of a low ridge that bounds Woodland on its western flank. The Lodge is T-shaped, with the base of the T dug into the bank. In the front are two rooms on either side of the hall, and all look out on to Blow Knot Fell, a hump of hill that has an endearing beauty which grows on you as you look at it through the seasons; through the deep browns of autumn to spring, to the light, glistening green of the new sprouting bracken that dulls so very fast as the bracken grows, and which, even at full maturity, when it is a drab grey-green, ripples in the wind to make the hill seem live, capable of responding to the love it evokes.

And Woodland did evoke love – Wendy's and my love for each other, and our love for the place itself. It was a backwater, hidden away from tourists, standing back from the bigger hills of the Lakes and looking across at them. The northern horizon is dominated by Coniston Old Man, framed in trees from the cottage, a graceful, near-symmetrical cone, unbalanced by the sweep of the ridge that embraces Low Water and hides Dow Crag in its grasp. From the top of the ridge, just below the houses, you can look across a marshy valley to another ridge, lower, field-clad, which guards the secret little valley of Broughton Mills. Beyond it, slightly higher, a third wave-like ridge, breaking here and there with rocky surf, guards the Duddon Valley. And then you look down the valley to the Duddon estuary – brown sands and mud flats only covered at high tide. At night there's an angry glow at the end of the estuary from Millom Ironworks – ugly perhaps from close up, but from a distance, strangely beautiful.

But we hadn't yet been accepted as tenants. We walk up to the door of the big house where we meet Ivor and Beeny Dickson – the Pattersons have warned them of our arrival. Ivor is a big, rather sleepy man who has learned to stay silent and allow the constant flow of his wife's talk to continue, unheeded, past him; and Beeny, as we came to know her, is small, birdlike, with endless energy and a great capacity to be interested in the affairs of others. She had been planning to rent the Lodge as a holiday let, but on the promise of at least a year's stay, to include the winter, she agreed to let us have it for £3 a week, fully furnished. We had been paying £5 a week for a single room in London.

And so we moved into Woodland Lodge. It had become increasingly important to find a firm base, for we were fairly certain that Wendy was pregnant. We had already had one false alarm on the boat back from South America, when she had missed a period. This had seemed appalling in the limbo we were in at that time, with no knowledge of where we were going to live, or what I was going to do. Wendy certainly did not want a child at this stage; she wanted a few more years of freedom, to develop her own work as an artist and, more to the point, to see something of the world. I, on the other hand, had mixed emotions. When I viewed the prospect of parenthood logically, it appalled me, but whenever I was drunk a deep-rooted desire to procreate took hold of me.

We were both superbly ignorant of the complexities of pregnancy, but Wendy took a series of ultra-hot baths and went in for violent exercise, on the offchance that this might cause a natural miscarriage. To our vast relief, she had her next period just after getting back to England, and in celebrating our narrow escape, using the laxest of lax rhythm methods, she conceived in earnest.

Now that we were established in the Lake District, parenthood became an easier idea to accept. We were quickly resigned, and then excited, at the prospect. Wendy was due to give birth around Christmas, 1963, and we decided that she should come out to the Alps for the summer, while we made our film on the Matterhorn. I succeeded in getting a small advance, and our film stock, from the BBC. Meanwhile, Hamish got everything else organised. I had known Hamish, off and on, over a period of ten years. On my first trip to Scotland, at the age of seventeen, I had met him and had been taken up a series of winter climbs. At this stage I had never climbed on snow and ice, and I was employed as a portable belay. We made the first winter ascent of Raven's Gulley (described in *I Chose to Climb*), and a couple of other routes.

Our paths had then split, mine into the army, while Hamish, always the lone individualist, had temporarily emigrated to New Zealand; had set out to climb Everest with another hard Scot, John Cunningham, and had then returned to Britain.

In 1957 we had climbed together again in equally bizarre circumstances. It was to be my first Alpine season, and Hamish had talked me into making an attempt on the North Wall of the Eiger. Fortunately for me, we did not get very far up the Wall before I found an excuse for retreat. It was a matter of out of the frying-pan into the fire, for he then persuaded me to try the other great North Wall of the Alps – the North Wall of the Grandes Jorasses. This attempt also ended in fiasco, when Hamish fell into a crevasse in the pitch dark.

The following year we climbed together once again, and ended up by making the first British ascent of the South-west Pillar of the Dru. This was the first time that I had met Don Whillans. Our present project was very different from these early adventures – then, we had been climbing for fun, now we were trying to make a film. In a way, this was to be my introduction to the problems associated with making a living out of the mountains.

Wendy and I drove out to the Alps in our Minivan, stopping at Chamonix on the way. The weather was perfect, and I was sorely tempted to snatch a climb before starting work in Zermatt – we were due to meet Hamish the following day – but my sense of duty won, and I thrust the temptation aside. Hamish was waiting for us in Zermatt and had already done some superb ground work. He had enlisted the support of the head of the local tourist office and, as a result, we had unrestricted free-access to all the téléphériques, subsidised accommodation in a chalet in the village, and a special concession for hut fees.

We had everything – but the weather. It broke a few days after we reached Zermatt, and never really improved throughout the summer. Hamish filmed goats, cows, tourists and the familiar local life of Zermatt. Ian Clough arrived to take part as one of the 'stars' – I being the other – and we all sat and ate and drank through the long, wet summer.

The only climb I did was an ascent of the Matterhorn by the Hörnli Ridge, climbing solo with Hamish, jostling with the long queue which trailed its way to the top of the most famous mountain peak in Europe. On a good day up to 300 people have been to the summit – the majority of them tourists, who are hustled to the top by the local guides, and then raced down to enable the guide to get some rest before taking up the next pair. That summer the fee for an ascent of the Matterhorn was £14, and so in theory the guide could make a fair amount by shuttling clients from the Hörnli Hut to the summit, getting back to the hut at midday, having an afternoon rest, meeting the next client and setting out at two o'clock the following morning. The amount he made, though, depended entirely on the weather, and during 1963 the guides must have had a lean time, for even the Hörnli Ridge was out of condition for most of the summer.

The profession of guiding has changed a great deal in the last fifty years. In the old days, the local guide was very much the leader of the party, invested with the respect of his clients who, in their turn, were experienced mountaineers. In recent years, however, particularly since the war, the vast majority of climbers have ventured into the hills without guides. A few outstanding mountaineers, such as Walter Bonatti, Gaston Rébuffat, René Desmaison and Michel Darbellay, the Swiss climber who made the first solo ascent of the North Wall of the Eiger, have managed to preserve a select clientèle of wealthy amateurs, who are also competent mountaineers, but the vast majority of guides are now dependent on the casual tourist, who would like to be taken to the top of a well-known mountain – Mont Blanc from Chamonix, the Matterhorn from Zermatt. As a result, both the status and ability of guides have declined. A man who spends most of his moun-taineering career hauling clients up the Hörnli Ridge of the Matterhorn, can gain only limited experience, and this must inevitably diminish the level of his prowess on the hills.

That summer saw the start of my real interest in photography. Up to this time I had always taken a camera with me on my climbs, but had been little more than a holiday snapshooter. Hamish was very interested in photography, and had his own firm ideas on the ideal camera – a massive, old, folding $2\frac{1}{4}$-inch square Zeiss Ikon which, inevitably, he had picked up at bargain price in a sale. Fired by his enthusiasm, I sank all our savings in a second-hand Hasselblad, which Hamish assured me was a fantastic bargain. It couldn't have been more unsuitable for climbing. It is the Rolls-Royce of $2\frac{1}{4}$-inch square cameras – a single lens reflex camera, shaped like an oblong box, with interchangeable lenses and backs, to enable one to shoot different types of film without having to finish the spool.

It was bulky, heavy, and even the lens alone was worth about £100. In the hands of someone as unmechanical as myself, it was doomed to a hammering. But for the rest of that summer in Zermatt, I wandered round the foothills above the village taking chocolate-box pictures of mountains framed by trees, or reflected in little lakes. In doing so, I became more visually aware.

By early September, all the climbers had packed up and gone home, the snow was creeping down towards the valley, and an early winter seemed to have arrived. We returned to England.

A wasted summer? In a way, yes; but I had learned a great deal. Wendy, now six months pregnant, was beginning to bulge, and we could feel the movement of her babe in the womb. We were both becoming increasingly excited by our looming parenthood. In the past, I had always had a feeling of anticlimax at returning to England – there had been nothing there for me – but now, with Wendy, the prospect of returning to our little lodge at Woodland was immensely attractive. We were tired of the ordered prettiness of Switzerland. On the way back we stopped for only a day in London, and then hammered towards the Lakes. In the next two years I was to learn the way to Woodland all too well, as I drove, tired, rather depressed after frenetic lecture tours. But I came to know the landmarks of the return, and always felt a rising excitement as I got closer and closer.

The home stretch started at Leven's Bridge, at the turning off the A6, on to the Barrow and Ulverston Road, round the southern part of the Lake District. The next marker was Newby Bridge, at the foot of Windermere – wooded hills, rocks breaking through – and then the dyeworks at Back-barrow. The road narrows and winds through the works itself – everything stained blue – and then on the right an old iron works which must be one of the oldest, and certainly the most decrepit, in England, with rusty machinery that blends into the landscape. I'm getting excited now, in spite of tiredness; swing round the bends, up the long straight, across the head of the Cartmell Estuary, take a short cut on to the Broughton Road, up narrow lanes, round blind corners, and then back to the main road – now narrower, like the upper reaches of a great river – up to Broughton Fell, swing right on the moorland road to Woodland – we're nearly home – I feel a warm love of the place – could almost stop the car to get out and feel the turf at the side of the road. The fells are bracken-covered and the road winds across, unfettered by walls or hedge, over a final rise, and there's Woodland beneath – the Hall and Lodge a squat, grey mass of buildings, clinging to the crest of a low ridge; beyond, in rolling waves, the hills of the Southern Lake District. This isn't grand, awe-inspiring country, but neither is it pretty. There is a secret intimacy about its little valleys, tree-clad, winding their way into craggy fells.

We race down the hill, the engine, raucous, noisy, past the corrugated iron bungalow where we bought all our eggs, and then up the winding tree-covered drive to the Lodge.

The Lodge wasn't a handsome house; the kitchen was incredibly damp, the rooms were box-like, with ceilings that were too high for their small size, and the sheets on our bed always felt a bit damp – but it didn't matter, for the setting of the place was perfect. We both came to love the changing colours and tones of the bracken-clad hill opposite.

Back at Woodland, it was time for me to start writing my book – but there were also lectures to give, for we had now spent the advance, and were flat broke. Through the autumn and winter I made frequent forays to the south, lecturing about the Eiger until I knew the lecture parrot-fashion. It was lonely, depressing work, for I frequently spent several days, even weeks, away from home, living from my van, staying at a different place each night.

I felt very vulnerable, uncertain of the future, aware that my only asset was an ascent of the North Wall of the Eiger. My activities of the summer heightened these worries, for we had really failed in my first creative venture – we had not produced a film for the BBC. I had little idea of film technique, and my dreams of directing Hamish, who was the cameraman, had proved abortive – Hamish is eminently undirectable. He knew a lot more about filming than I, anyway, and knew exactly what he wanted to do.

We were becoming entrenched at Woodland, building up a circle of friends who, like us, had withdrawn from the conventional career game. There was Tony Greenbank, tall, lank, immensely enthusiastic about every scheme and project. He was my age, had been a librarian, but had always had an ambition to write. It was much harder for him to get started than it had been for me, for he was just an average climber, who got a great deal of enjoyment from his sport, but was in no way a celebrity.

He abandoned his job as a librarian and went to Eskdale Outward Bound School as an instructor, with the intention of using it as a tool to get established as a freelance writer. He was already married, which made his step still bolder. He soon became unpopular with some of his fellow instructors, who resented the fact that he was making money on the side by contributing articles to regional papers such as the *Yorkshire Evening Post*. It was this constantly recurring resentment of professionalism, and particularly of contributing to the media, and hence to the popularisation of climbing, that I had encountered. I suspect that there was often an element of jealousy in it – that you were making money out of something that was just a pastime for the majority. In Tony's case, his fellow instructors' resentment could hardly be based on grounds of professionalism, since they were also making a living out of climbing; I suspect it was a combination of straight jealousy, aligned with resentment of someone publicising their own private world.

Tony took a correspondence course in writing, and then resolved to give up his job at the Outward Bound School and work full-time as a freelance writer once he had reached a self-imposed target of annual earnings. It said much for his determination and sheer hard work that he reached this target in two years, whilst working at a job that was both physically exacting and time-consuming. He then bought a caravan in his native Yorkshire Dales, had his first child there, and somehow still managed to churn out his work. When I first met him in 1963, he had progressed to a small cottage at Arnside, near Kirkby Lonsdale, on the fringe of the Lake District.

Another aspirant writer we came to know was David Johnstone. Very different from Tony, he was small and slight, with a shock of dark hair and delicate features. He was an adept at judo. While Tony had few intellectual pretensions and was essentially a popular writer, David wanted to be a serious writer, and had already written several plays and a novel, sadly, all rejected.

He was the son of the local optician in Ulverston, had been sent to Rossall, a public school near Blackpool, and on leaving it had decided to devote his life to writing. For a time he had survived in London, writing during the day and busking with his violin in the evening – this was before the time when it became fashionable for hippies to pick up a living folk-singing in the passages of Underground stations.

He met his wife-to-be, Caroline, a big voluptuous girl, while flitting on the outskirts of the deb scene, and once they had married they took off to Northern Italy, where for a time they lived an idyllic life under the hot sun, with David writing and Caroline earning a little money by teaching English. Eventually, they were forced to return to England, and when we came to Woodland were living in a caravan near Coniston. Shortly after we arrived we were offered a farmhouse high on a hillside near the foot of the Duddon

Valley. We were content with Woodland and so told David about it, and he moved in with his newborn child. They furnished the house from the pickings of a single auction sale, for the magnificent sum of £25. He needed much greater courage than I. He had no publicity to help him, was trying to establish himself as a serious playwright, and fought in the face of repeated rejection by publishers and theatres. He had to earn a living somehow, and so took a job in forestry – back-breaking, hard work, for a minimal wage. He lost this job when the foreman found him asleep in a ditch; and then, after a period on the dole, he found work in the tannery at Millom, hauling maggot-ridden hides and plunging them in the steaming curing-baths. There was no question of writing any longer – just one of brutish survival, of being penniless, desperately tired every night, and somehow trying to maintain a prickly pride in the face of seeming defeat.

Things at last improved when he managed to get the job of Duddon roadman. The pay was £10 a week, barely enough for food and rent, but he was comparatively free, could start the day when he wanted, and wander the roads with his broom and shovel, thinking his own thoughts.

On a fine day I often tempted him from the path of duty, and we would go off climbing on Wallabarrow Crag, nestling amongst trees in the bed of the Duddon, or disport ourselves on the Duddon School of Bouldering – a little array of crags I had discovered near the road.

And so 1963 slipped into 1964. The changing year was marked by the arrival of Conrad, our first child. He was born in the early hours of New Year's Eve, 1963. I had wanted to be with Wendy at the birth, but had been confronted by the solid conservatism of a small local maternity home.

'No one's ever asked for anything like that,' said the iron-willed matron. 'We haven't got the facilities, and anyway you've got to think of the feelings of the midwife.'

I wasn't going to stop there, and phoned the chief gynaecologist of the area.

'My dear chap, I've nothing at all against the husband being with his wife for the birth – it's a personal matter and, I must say, as far as I'm concerned, I think it's best to let the wife get on with it on her own. I've four kids, and I've never been with her – but that's purely a matter of choice. I'd be delighted for you to be with your wife throughout, but I'm afraid we just haven't got the facilities and, in her interests, I've got to say "No".'

I didn't have a leg to stand on; they allowed me to stay with Wendy during her initial contractions, but as soon as she went into the second phase she was wheeled into the delivery room and they tried to show me the door. I was probably unnecessarily stubborn, but I insisted on staying at the home. Wendy had a long and painful delivery, perhaps aggravated by the tension caused by the reliance she had placed in having me with her. She spent long hours awake through the night, a lot of the time on her own, unattended, while I spent the same long hours sitting upstairs waiting, helpless – it was all so unnecessary, since she needed me and I could have helped her and the midwife, but we were confronted by the solid prejudice of tradition.

In the later stages I could hear her crying out in pain, gasping and groaning. Had I been with her it would not have been frightening, since I would have been working with her, reassuring her and helping her in what small way I could; but sitting in an empty, cold little room, I could only imagine the worst. I became convinced that Wendy was dying, and, for about the first time in my life, actually knelt down and prayed, from my own absolute helplessness. At the same time I felt a tinge of shame, that I was only doing this as an emotional last-resort, for I cannot claim to be a Christian and, if anything, am agnostic. There seems much that we cannot explain in purely physical and scientific terms; there might well be some kind of spiritual force, but it seems sheer wishful thinking to believe that this force is particularly concerned with mankind's wellbeing – there is so much suffering in the world, so much ill done in the name of good, so much crime that does seem to pay. But that night, faced with the fear of losing Wendy, I was snatching at straws and went through an emotional hell, until at long last, at five o'clock in the morning, her raking gasps ceased and were replaced by the persistent raucous cry of a newborn child.

I was allowed down to see her, pale, exhausted, but wonderfully tranquil, and our tiny babe, freshly washed and incredibly ugly. After bandying a lot of names about, we settled on Conrad.

Once she returned to Woodland, life went on very much as before. We got around a lot, carrying the baby in his pram-top in the back of the van, on occasion leaving him in the van when we went to a pub. I had my lectures through the winter, and Wendy accompanied me to some of them. I also skirmished with the book and, as winter changed to spring, snatched every fine day to go climbing.

In many ways it was an idyllic life. Work pressures were few, since I only had the book to write and had not yet succeeded in getting established as a photo-journalist. Once the lecture season was over, I had long periods at home. In the evenings we played canasta, and at weekends, when friends arrived, endless games of Risk, a splendid game of world conquest. Wendy learned to drive and then became interested in folk-singing. She already played the guitar and had a pure, haunting voice with an extraordinary emotionalism in it. After practising for some time, she screwed up her courage to sing at a folk-song club in Keswick, run by Paul Ross, a well-known Lakeland climber, with whom I had made the first British ascent of the South-West Pillar of the Dru back in 1958.

Those years of 1963 to 1965 were, in some ways, a limbo period. I had reached a peak in my Alpine career, with the ascent of the North Wall of the Eiger, and was now casting round to try to find the next step forward in my life. As far as climbing went, I had reached a plateau. I had attained a high level of competence in general mountaineering, but to push beyond this level needed a greater degree of organisation and a greater awareness of technical developments, especially those taking place on the West Coast of America in the Yosemite National Park.

That summer of 1964, I hoped to achieve the same level of satisfaction and excitement that Ian Clough and I had achieved in 1962, but I was destined to be disappointed.

CHAPTER FIVE

Alpine Summer

May 1964. I had barely got half-way through my book and was already six months over deadline, but the Alpine season was pressing close and, after the previous year's fiasco, my dreams turned increasingly to getting some good climbing. But what to climb – and with whom? Because of the pressures exerted by my commitment to the book, and my own lack of organisation, I had left everything up in the air.

Then I had a phone call from Tom Patey. 'Would you like to come to the Alps with Joe and me? We've got some good new routes lined up; if you're interested in coming I'll let you know where they are.'

'But who'd I be climbing with? A party of three's no good.'

'I've just the right man. His name is Robin Ford; I climbed with him last week in the Cairngorms.'

'I've never heard of him.'

'That's because he hasn't done much on the English scene, but he's got what it takes to make a great Alpinist – you'll have your job cut out to keep up with him. Anyway, have you got anyone better in mind?'

I hadn't; and so it was settled that I should climb with Tom Patey and Joe Brown that summer. I had only climbed with Joe once before, back in 1962. I was still working in London at the time, had come up to North Wales to climb with Don Roscoe, one of the original Rock and Ice members. When I had arrived he told me that he was unavoidably engaged but that Joe, who was working at Whitehall, the Derbyshire outdoor activities centre, was up for the weekend and looking for a partner. I had never met him and was intrigued at the thought of climbing with the living legend of British mountaineering.

Joe was keen to finish a new route he had started the previous weekend on Castel Cdwm, a steep little crag on the south side of Snowdon above Llyn Cwellyn. We walked up to the crag, Joe was agreeable but not talkative; I was slightly on edge. I thought I was climbing well at the time, had made early ascents of many of Joe's routes, and had often liked to think that I was in the same class as he, as a rock-climber. I have always been intensely competitive and could not resist wondering how my climbing would compare with his.

'Do you want to have a go first?' said Joe 'I had to turn back last week; you might have a bit more luck. You'll need a lot of chock-stones.'

This was in the pre-nut era, when, to protect themselves, climbers still relied on what the rock offered – rock spikes for slings (often only nylon line with a breaking strain of a bare 1000 lb.) or chockstones jammed in cracks. Joe was probably one of the earliest, and certainly one of the most sophisticated exponents of the inserted chockstone – you carried a pocketful of stones with you and jammed them in the crack. It was a fiddling, intriguing business, demanding a fair level of skill.

The year 1962 was when someone – I'm not sure who – had the idea of stringing bolt-nuts of different sizes on to a sling and using these in place of chockstones. Since then, these nuts have been refined into a series of shapes, tailor-made for their purpose. In many ways, I suspect that this was a retrograde step, for it enabled the climber to gain protection from running belays in places where protection would have been impossible with inserted chockstones or the traditional flake runner. One of the attractions, indeed reasons, for climbing, is the element of risk involved, of pitting one's own judgement against the mountain, with a fall as the price of a mistake. In its purest sense, the solo climber is getting the most out of the sport since he is staking his life on his judgement. Without companions or rope, he has a good chance of being killed in a fall. The majority of us, however, prefer to hedge our bets, climbing with a companion, using a rope and then contriving running belays to reduce the distance we fall if we do come off. The problem is in deciding just how far we should reduce this risk before losing a vital element in the sport.

There has always been a tradition in British rock climbing that has renounced the use of pitons. Since the war, with rising standards of difficulty, and with the progressive encroachment on to every available piece of rock in the country, pitons have become increasingly used when no other means of protection or of natural ascent have offered themselves; but there has always been a stigma attached to their use, and credit has gone to the man who has succeeded in repeating a route with less such aid than his predecessors. The development of the nut and metal wedge has not been accompanied by any such stigma, even though its resemblance to a piton is very close. Both pitons and nuts are metallic foreign bodies that are being slotted into cracks. The obvious difference is that pitons are driven in by a hammer, while the nut, in theory, is only hand-inserted. It is all too easy, however, to apply a few taps of a hammer to the nut to lodge it more securely. Does this turn it into a piton? I wonder. On the other hand, a piton can, on occasion, be hand-inserted. Does this make it a nut?

The development of the nut was a gradual, insidious process which, as a result, roused little controversy and today, in 1972, it is difficult to imagine any kind of effective rejection of nuts proving practical; but back in the early 1960s they could have been rejected in exactly the same way that the pitons had been and still are. If an ethic or rule had been established that any foreign body, metal or plastic wedge, jammed or placed in a crack, should be regarded as cheating, the sport might have maintained a higher level of adventure or risk, and at the same time, I suspect, would have reached the same level of technical difficulty in the routes being pioneered. The difference would have been that fewer climbers could have repeated the hardest routes, simply because the risks involved, and therefore the self-confidence required, would have been greater. I must confess, though, that I use as many nuts as anyone and certainly depend on them to maintain my own climbing standard.

But I have digressed. Joe and I are standing below Castel Cdwm. The rock juts steeply above, in a series of bristling overhangs, cut by a broken crack. If I had been with anyone but Brown, I think I would have suggested we went somewhere else, but I wasn't going to back down in his company. I collected my pocketful of stones, jammed a hand in the crack and pulled upwards – at least there were holds, but it was all overhanging. I began to tire. Ten feet up, the angle lay back to what, from below, had seemed a slab, but once on it I found I was off balance and I couldn't find any holds.

'Where did you go from here?' I shouted down.

'Up the slab,' came the reply. 'You can get some good inserted chocks in the crack above.'

But how the hell to get to the crack above! Suddenly, the cliff seemed to grow above me as my arms progressively weakened. I hammered in a peg.

'What do you think you're doing?' came from below. 'I got above there last time without a peg.'

I dangled on it; my arms felt like stretched spaghetti. The climb was undoubtedly impossible.

'You'd better have a go,' I conceded.

Back down, I took over Joe's rope, and spent the rest of the day watching him at work. It was an impressive sight. He was very methodical and completely relaxed. He drifted up the holdless slab, then at full, elongated arm's reach, placed a tiny stone in the crack above, threaded a sling behind it and sat in the sling. And so he slowly worked his way up the climb.

When I followed him, I got up the pitch quite quickly, cursed myself for turning back, for surely I also could have inserted all those chockstones. It's just a matter of patience – or is it? It was beyond my conception before the start of the climb that chockstones could be used so ingeniously. It was also beyond my ability to relax sufficiently in a lead position to keep going.

On that first acquaintance I had found Joe easy-going, friendly, yet somehow withdrawn. There is something inscrutable about both his features and his personality. He once admitted to me: 'I don't think anyone really knows me – not even my wife, Valerie.'

He was very different from Don Whillans, and you could see why they had fallen apart. Joe and Don between them had made a revolution in British rock-climbing, putting up a series of routes, most of which held a legendary aura of being impossible for any but a breed of supermen of much the same shape and size as Don and Joe – in other words, fairly short and prodigiously strong. They were probably equally good as climbers; Don was attracted by obvious, very direct, usually vicious lines up crags that were often very poorly protected. Joe tended to go for more devious lines, less obvious, but nevertheless superb routes. In sheer volume of new routes, Joe climbed by far the largest number. This was partly because Don began to lose interest in British rock-climbing, preferring the sterner and fresher environment of the Alps, and then the Himalaya. Although Joe has always admitted that he prefers lighthearted rock-climbing to greater mountaineering, his record is impressive. In 1955 he went out to Kangchenjunga with the comparatively lightweight party led by Charles Evans, and went to the summit. The following year he joined Tom Patey, Ian McNaught-Davis and John Hartog, on an expedition to the Mustagh Tower, and also reached the summit. This must rank as one of the outstanding mountaineering achievements of the fifties, for the Mustagh Tower is 23,860 feet, and one of the steepest and most shapely mountains in the world. Climbing it with a party of four, and all four getting to the top, was a magnificent achievement. Don, on the other hand, while being a superb mountaineer, seemed to have an unlucky streak. He had been on two Himalayan expeditions by 1962 (one to Masherbrum and the other to Trivor) but on neither reached the summit, and his expedition to Gaurishankar, in the autumn of 1964, was equally unsuccessful. This disparity in success, the fact that Joe was hailed as Britain's greatest-ever rock-climber, the fact that he, and not Don, had been invited to Kangchenjunga, had undoubtedly eroded their relationship, and they had ceased to climb together.

I knew Tom Patey much better than I knew Joe. We had had a superb, happy-go-lucky climbing holiday together in Scotland, in the summer of 1960. Tom told the story of our adventures in a climbing journal shortly afterwards, and it is now published in a collected volume of his works,

One Man's Mountains. He had a rich and complex personality, with a bewildering variety of talents. He was undoubtedly one of the outstanding British mountaineers of the post-war period, with a host of new routes in Scotland and the Alps to his credit. He was also a brilliant Himalayan performer, having reached the summit of Rakaposhi as well as that of the Mustagh Tower. He was no technician, wasn't even a brilliant rock-climber, but on mixed ground of heather, earth, rock, snow or ice, I have never seen an equal. He moved with an easy speed and confidence over this type of ground, as happy unroped as roped. He had an easy contempt for style and elegance, whether in climbing, appearance or general way of life. There was little grace in his movements as a climber; he just swarmed up a rock face, inelegantly perhaps, but in complete control. His general appearance showed equally little regard for fashion or style. Off the crag he'd dress in an old ready-to-wear suit, obviously quickly purchased from a multiple tailor, and always crumpled. On business, or a formal occasion, he'd wear a tie that had been purchased with equally little regard for fashion, but at the first opportunity he'd pull it off, stuff it in a pocket and open the neck of his shirt. He didn't look an athlete, smoked heavily, constantly took drops for his hay-fever, and had limbs that seemed to have been hung on to his body with as little regard as the clothes that covered them. His face was that of a man who had seen life – the perfect Raymond Chandler tired-and-battered-private-eye face – grey, creased, hard worn, yet somehow compassionate.

But Tom was more than a mountaineer. He had a boundless, impish imagination and a superb command of the English language. He had that very special ability to satirise lightly without hurting his victim unduly. He was also a good musician and carried his accordion with him wherever he went. He could play anything on it from hearty German marching songs to Highland jigs and reels, but his most unique ability was as a song writer. He composed a series of songs about climbers and climbing which were a form of musical cartoon. His favourite riposte, whenever anyone grumbled at being the target of his pen was:

> The highest compliment that anyone can pay you is to make you the subject of satire. It's better to be written about under any circumstances than to be ignored.

You could always guarantee that a holiday, or even a short weekend, with Tom would be full of surprises – that it would develop into a magical mystery tour of pubs, people and mountains. That summer in 1960 we had climbed fifteen new routes, all discovered by Tom who had an encyclopaedic knowledge of the Highlands. We had started several impromptu ceilidhs, and had met a whole series of bizarre personalities, whom, I am sure, I should never have got to know without him around.

I was full of great expectations and a few misgivings, therefore, when Tom suggested we climb together that summer of 1964. We could be sure of plenty of new routes to climb, for Tom had prepared a dossier of unclimbed lines in the Alps, but they would be routes of his choice.

We drove out to the Alps in his battered Skoda – it was a replica of its owner, unfashionable, untidy, but very rugged. At an early stage of the journey Tom surrendered the wheel and retired to the back seat to play his accordion as we rolled down through France on our way to Chamonix. This was the first time I had met my own climbing partner, Robin Ford. He was in his early twenties and at this stage had done most of his climbing in Britain; almost immediately it became evident that we had little in common. There was too big a gap in age and experience. He would have been better off climbing with someone of the same range of experience, rather than plunging in with quite a high-powered team which had already discovered a great deal about the mountains.

Soon, it also became evident that Tom's approach to Alpine climbing was very different from mine. I liked big, exciting objectives, but once having decided on an objective, preferred to plan out the attempt very carefully, leaving as little as possible to chance. Tom, on the other hand, regarded the trip as a light-hearted holiday, enjoyed drinking and singing, in the Bar Nationale and at the camp site, into the early hours of the morning, and then would rush up the hill at the last possible moment to snatch a new route, relying on his flair and speed to get up the climb in the day, and back down to Chamonix for another carousal. He was not interested in the multi-day epic, or the highly technical rock-climb. He was a superb mixed Alpinist with a genius both for picking out a good line up a mountain and the ability to climb it, only putting on a rope when the difficulties became acute.

We completed two new routes in this style: one up the South-West Ridge of the Aiguille de Leschaux, a beautiful and very isolated peak at the head of the Leschaux Glacier, and the other on the North Face of the Pointe Migot, a subsidiary of the Chamonix Aiguilles. They were both tributes to Tom's genius for smelling out new routes. He had a big black book full of photographs, often purloined from books and journals loaned to him by friends, in which possible new routes were marked. This was quite an achievement, even in 1964, for almost all the obvious lines in the Chamonix area had long been climbed.

We talked to Lionel Terray, the famous French climber, about our plans for new routes, but he dismissed our ambition with the comment, 'The virgin climbs around here are like dried-up old spinsters. They are not worth taking.'

There was a lot of truth in this, for all the major ridges and walls had been climbed, but an essential facet of climbing is the desire to seek out new ground. This was particularly strong in Tom, and he was happier searching his way up a comparatively undistinguished rock wall, tucked away at the back of a subsidiary glacier, than following a well-worn trail up a climb of much greater quality. I was less satisfied, however, for these new routes we were doing were Tom's routes, not mine. In addition, Joe and Tom were a faster pair than Robin and I. As a result, we were simply following them up the climbs without any of the satisfaction and thrill of picking out the route for ourselves.

On the North Face of the Pointe Migot, Robin and I made a firm bid to get out in front. We had been drinking and singing late into the night in the Bar Nationale, and had caught the first téléphérique up to Plan d'Aiguilles, the half-way station on the way to the Aiguille du Midi. We left the ugly shell of the téléphérique station, and started up the path that led to the Glacier de Blaitière. The Pointe Migot is little more than a nobble on the ridge that sweeps north from the Aiguille du Plan, towards the Chamonix valley. At its end is the shapely tower of the Aiguille du Peigne, which boasts several classic rock-climbs, on which British climbers habitually sharpen their teeth before venturing on to harder things. Beyond the Peigne is the Aiguille des Pélerins, another granite tower, and hidden behind that is the Pointe Migot, whose North Face, black and virgin, drops down into the head of the Glacier de Blaitière. The North Face of the Migot was a coy, and undoubtedly plain old spinster whom no one had yet bothered to court. Only someone with Patey's appetite for untouched ground would have sought her out.

But that morning our team were in anything but good shape. Patey was muttering about his hay-fever and Joe, recovering from a hangover, was sick half-way up the Glacier de Blaitière. I had retreated to bed early and consequently was feeling moderately fit. I chivvied Robin out into the front, so that we should at least have a chance of taking the lead.

The pace quickened. Patey and Brown obviously guessed what we were up to and tried to reduce our lead. We scrambled up jumbled ice below the Pélerins, and up the gully that led up towards the North Face of the Fou. On our left, the frozen cascade of the hanging glacier on the North Face of the Plan loomed over us. It was a grim place, full of lurking threats of stonefall. The North Wall of the Pointe Migot was very steep, broken at about

The North Face of Pointe Migot

half height by a sloping shelf that ran up diagonally from right to left. A system of cracks seemed to lead up towards it.

'Come on, Robin,' I said, sufficiently quietly for the others not to hear. 'If we can get roped up first and into those cracks, Tom and Joe'll never get in front.'

I spurted towards the foot of the cracks and pulled ahead of Robin who was less used to this competitive climbing. The trouble was, he had the rope. We were still fifty yards in front of the other pair. Robin reached me; I grabbed the rope and started to uncoil it – the damned thing was in a tangle. I cursed. Tom was only twenty yards away. I tossed the rope on the ground – should come free – 'You untangle it while I run out the first pitch,' I said.

It was a grotty crack, quite steep, filled with ice. I started up it, climbing fast, ran out twenty feet and the rope tugged from behind. I looked back to see Robin struggling with what looked like a tangled skein of knitting. Patey and Brown were now with him, already roped up. Patey started up the cracks. He reached me.

'I'm glad to see you've a sense of urgency,' he said complacently. 'Very commendable in a place like this. I'm sure you won't object if Joe and I climb past you while you sort out your little troubles.'

'Not at all,' I replied.

By the time Robin had sorted out our rope, Tom and Joe were on the next pitch. I had resigned myself to following them up yet another climb. We climbed two more pitches, and the groove we were following divided, one branch going off to the left and the other going straight up. Tom was belayed at the dividing point and Joe was leading up the left-hand groove.

There was just a possibility that they had taken the wrong branch. The groove going straight up was steeper, but it looked as if it might lead directly up to the foot of the gangway in the middle of the face.

'I'll just have a look up here,' I told Tom. 'It'd save a bit of time if Joe's going up a blind alley.'

As soon as Robin reached me I started up the groove. It was filled with ice at the back which pushed me out of balance, but there were sufficient holds for three strenuous pulls and the angle eased off; the groove ran easily straight up to the gangway. We'd won. We were out in front once again. I ran out the rope and called Robin to come out. There was an interminable delay as he fiddled around with his belay. I glanced over to the right and could see Joe belayed at the top of his groove. Tom had already joined him and was now swinging across towards me, using tension on the rope.

'What the bloody hell are you doing down there?' I shouted to Robin. 'Get a bloody move on.'

No reply, but at least he was climbing now. The rope trickled through my fingers. Patey had nearly reached me, a couple more ape-line swings, and he was in the groove just below me. He didn't wait, but climbed straight past, giving me an easy grin. I managed the weakest of weak smiles, and yelled down to Robin to hurry up. But by the time he reached the stance Tom had got to the top of his pitch, and Joe was already on his way across. We had lost Round Two.

The bottom of the gangway was guarded by a small snowfield. Tom launched on to this, kicking into the snow with his boots. He hadn't bothered to put on his crampons – no time in the competitive climbing game. He got about half-way up, and suddenly there was a sloosh, and he came shooting down the steep snow. It was only a few inches thick, lying on hard ice.

Tom fell about thirty feet, but was held by the rope. He obviously hadn't hurt himself, and I couldn't resist letting out a cheer – but how was I to profit from their misfortune? Robin was leading up towards Joe, and was going much too slowly to give us any chance of passing them before they sorted themselves out.

Tom returned to the fray, climbed the snow more cautiously, reached the rock gangway and followed it up to a point where it steepened. I resigned myself to following, and concentrated on enjoying the climbing. This was excellent, being steep and tricky, with the minimum of protection. The whole climb had taken us only four hours, and just after lunchtime we pulled over the top to stand on the summit.

The climb had been fun, the competition had added spice to what was a mediocre route, and we were back in Chamonix that evening. I felt dissatisfied, however, and wanted something bigger and more challenging. Above all, I wanted greater control of the initiative. There was little satisfaction in being on a new route if it was not your own concept and you were just following another pair up it. But that summer I was destined to be disappointed, partly because the weather remained unsettled, but mainly, I suspect, because I was not clear on what I wanted to achieve – either in climbing or in my own life. Tom and Joe were now due to go home, and so I teamed up with two Americans, Jim McCarthy and Dick Williams, in an attempt to make a new direct route up the North Wall of the Civetta, a 5000 foot limestone wall in the Dolomites. Jim McCarthy had conceived the idea. He had just finished Law School in New York, and was the most outstanding climber on the East Coast of America. Strangely, our paths had already crossed back in 1958, on Jim's first visit to the Alps, when we had met on the lower rocks of the East Face of the Grand Capucin. My companion, Ronnie Wathen, and I had completed the route, but unfortunately Jim had been forced to retreat after his partner had dropped their rucksack.

Jim had come over to Europe with a formidable array of the newly-developed American hardware – the chrome molybdenum pitons that had enabled a small group of Californian climbers to conquer the huge granite walls of Yosemite. A few of them had already made their marks on Europe. In 1962, Royal Robbins and Garry Hemming had made a direct start to the West Face of the Dru, up a series of superb crack-lines in the lower part of that face, and the following year, Tom Frost, another Yosemite pioneer, had made the first ascent of the South Face of the Fou, with John Harlin, Hemming and a Scot, Stewart Fulton. Jim wanted to apply the same Yosemite style of climbing to the North Face of the Civetta. He was aware, however, that his team was on the weak side. He had climbed in Yosemite himself, but his companion, Dick Williams, had never been farther afield than the New Yorkers' local crag, the Shwangunks. These are a 200-foot high line of outcrops in upstate New York – the American equivalent of a glorified Shepherd's Crag, or Three Cliffs of Llanberis.

I met Jim one night in the Bar Nationale, and he immediately asked me to find another companion and join him. I had been making plans with Brian Robertson, a young Scots climber, full of big ambitions. He was a leading-light in a group of Edinburgh climbers who called themselves the Squirrels, after a famous Italian climbing group called the Cortina Squirrels. Brian was rather like a squirrel, short, strongly-built, with a squirrel-like persistence. He was a great enthusiast, becoming near-incoherent in his enthusiasm for whatever happened to be his latest project. He happily agreed to join us, and the next day we all piled into Jim's newly-purchased Volkswagen Varient, and were whisked over to the small town that nestles below the North Wall of the Civetta. McCarthy is a great fixer; he already had introductions to one of the senior guides and great pioneers in the area. We spent the night in his barn, and next day, thanks to his good office, had our mound of baggage, ironware and food whisked up to the hut on the little service téléphérique, whilst we wandered up, unladen, through woods fragrant with flowers and the hot resin of pine trees. We stayed in a newly-built hut, immediately opposite the face. The more I looked at the wall, the less happy I felt. The line that Jim had chosen was to the right of the Phillip Flamm route, straight up a huge, blank, overhanging wall of grey and yellow rock. There were cracks all right – indeed, the scale was so vast they were probably chimneys – but it all seemed awfully steep. I had not undertaken such a big artificial route before and felt unsure of my own ability and, never having climbed with Jim, felt little confidence in him either.

I insisted on doing a training climb first, and the next morning we all set out to complete the North Face of the Torre Val Grande, a classic route on the far left of the Walls of the Civetta. Brian and I quickly pulled away from the two Americans as we scrambled up the broken gully that led to the start of the real climbing. It was an enjoyable fun-climb, with a thrutchy roof overhang which we swung up in étriers, and then a few good pitches of free climbing. We got back to the hut that evening to find the rest of the team at a low ebb in morale. Dick had never climbed on the loose rock that guards the approaches to most Dolomite climbs. He was unaccustomed to fast soloing, and eventually they had turned back before even reaching the foot of the climb proper.

This boded ill for our plans on the New Direttissima on the Main Wall of the Civetta. Dick wasn't keen to commit himself to such a major undertaking, and nor were we. That afternoon, however, we had passed the tent of another British climber, Denny Morehouse. I didn't know him personally, but had heard a lot about him. He had spent a lot of time in the Dolomites, mainly climbing with continental climbers, and had an impressive array of hard routes to his credit.

Sitting in the mouth of his battered tent, he looked a bit like the mad professor in an early surrealist German film. He wore heavy horn-rimmed spectacles, one lens of which was starred, presumably from a falling stone; his gear was in tatters and he had been living for the previous fortnight on a diet of pasta and plain bread.

I suggested inviting Denny, and Jim agreed. We brought him up to the hut, gave him a good meal, and the next day planned to carry all the gear up the face to the start of the difficulties.

The moment we started working together, things went wrong. Big wall climbing demands a high level of teamwork, rope management and awareness of the job in hand. We didn't have a clue. Jim understood the new American methods; was accustomed to the high level of discipline adopted on the walls of the Yosemite; we were blissfully unaware of these techniques. Soon the rope was tangled into an inextricable mess. Denny, out in front, dislodged a boulder the size of a table, and it narrowly missed Jim. I dropped a peg-hammer; a few stones whined down from above and we all retreated for the night to the hut, full of doubts about each other. We were going to set out for the face at three in the morning. I felt half-hearted as I organised my gear, snuggling into my sleeping-bag as a haven of safety, dreading the moment of commitment when we set out for a climb that I don't think any of us felt up to. I dropped off into an uneasy sleep, to be woken all too soon by the jangle of the alarm. No one moved – and then Jim jumped down from the bunk, looked out of the window and called: 'The goddamned cloud has come in – you can hardly see the bottom of the face.'

I suspect we were all secretly relieved. I rolled over and immediately dropped into a deep sleep. By morning the cloud had begun to break up, and by midday it had turned into a good day, but the delay had done the trick. With hardly a word said, we abandoned the attempt. Jim and I climbed the Andrich Fae route, a classic free rock-climb to the left of our proposed line, and then we all set off for Chamonix, I anxious to get back to the main scene of action, to snatch at least one good new route before the end of the season.

But our return to Chamonix coincided with the arrival of bad weather. Our little group, that had never coalesced into a team, broke up. Jim and Dick went down to the Calanques, Brian went home, and I stuck it out in Chamonix, just hoping for one good route to make the summer seem worthwhile.

Three weeks went by; three weeks spent hanging around Chamonix, living in other people's tents, listening to the sound of rain drumming on the roof and eking out my beer money in the Bar Nationale, until near the end of the season, I became involved in a BBC documentary on the North Wall of the Eiger. Amongst my plans for that summer had been an attempt on making a new Direct Route up the North Wall of the Eiger. This was the current last great problem of 1964, and already several leading Continental climbers had tried and failed on it. John Harlin, an American climber, was leading contender, and had already made a couple of attempts. My own plans were little more than pipe-dreams – I had neither sufficient equipment nor the right companions for such an undertaking.

I trekked over to Grindelwald to meet the BBC team at the start of September. I should have liked to have talked about my original ascent of the original route on the Eiger North Wall – a climb full of good and exciting memories. The producer wanted something that was more immediate in its appeal, and I allowed myself to be talked into showing all the gear I should have used on an attempt on the Eiger Direct, as if I were about to go on the route. Having abandoned all thoughts of attempting it that summer, I felt cheapened. It emphasised my own vulnerability and made me doubt my own integrity. At the end of the interviews I returned to Chamonix, washed out and depressed.

But the weather was, at last, looking up, as all too often it does in early September – there wasn't a cloud in the sky, and the Chamonix Aiguilles were clear of snow. At last, here was the chance to recoup a wasted Alpine season – one great, exacting route and I could go home happy, my confidence restored. And yet, perhaps, in those weeks of waiting and worry, I had lost sight of the very reasons why we should climb – had lost the sheer spontaneous joy that climbing should entail.

I met up with Mick Burke in the camp site. He, also, was without a companion and we agreed to tackle the South Face of the Fou, a route that still awaited a second ascent, and had the reputation of being exceedingly difficult. I had a few American pegs, sold to me by Jim McCarthy; there weren't nearly enough, and I suspect we could have got ourselves into a precarious situation if we had ever launched ourselves on the climb. Anyway, Mick and I went into Chamonix to get some bivouac food before setting off for the hut that evening.

It was in the supermarket, between the dried-soup shelves and the refrigerated cabinet holding dairy foods, that I suddenly realised that I had drained myself of all my drive and ebullience – I felt an irresistible longing for home, to hold Wendy close to me, to see and play with Conrad. I had already half-filled a basket with bivouac food; I stood there in an agony of indecision, and then just dumped the basket on the ground and walked out of the shop. I found Mick at the camp site, packing his rucksack.

'Y're ready then?' he said. 'There's only ten minutes before the last train to Montenvers, you know.'

'I'm sorry, Mick, I'm not going. I think I've been out here too long. I feel bloody stale, and wouldn't be any use on the climb anyway.'

Mick took it wonderfully stoically, without any recriminations. Having made up my mind, I had the homing instinct of a carrier pigeon. I caught a train for Paris that evening, spent most of the night pacing up and down in the corridor, in a fever to get home; reaching Paris, I was so impatient that I got a taxi to the airport terminal and took the next available plane to London. I phoned Wendy and caught a train that took me as far as Preston. Wendy drove down in the middle of the night, with Conrad asleep in the back of the van, to pick me up.

That return to the Lakes was a return to reality, to the joy of our life together, to a newly-found satisfaction in getting down to the book, which at last seemed to flow with some prospect of, one day, being finished – even to a renewed and fresh enjoyment of climbing, unsullied by worries of maintaining a reputation, or building a career round the mountains.

CHAPTER SIX

Home Ground

A Lakeland autumn: the hill opposite turning a rich golden brown, leaves falling in the little artificial lake at the bottom of the drive, and rock warm to the touch under an autumnal sun. I had three weeks before my lecture season started – three weeks to skirmish with my book, lie in the sun and climb when the will took me, or friends arrived to drag me – all too willing – away from work. Two of our most regular visitors were Mike Thompson and Martin Boysen. Mike was one of my oldest friends. We had first met at Sandhurst, back in 1956, when he joined my company. He was already a climber, having been born and brought up in Cumberland. He went to St Bees, a school more renowned for prowess at rugby than academic learning, and had wandered the hills in his spare time, either with or without permission.

He also had gone into the Royal Armoured Corps – into the cavalry – spending three years in Malaya and then returning to this country to complete a university course at the Royal Military College of Science, Shrivenham. Mike was getting tired of army life at the same period that I was becoming discontented. His problem, however, was that having started the science course, the army insisted on getting their money's-worth from him and therefore insisted that he complete at least another five years after finishing at Shrivenham. At this stage, Mike was determined to escape, wanting to get a place at university to study anthropology. He struck on an ingenious solution to his problem by standing for Parliament, since no member of the armed forces can become involved in politics, and yet it is anyone's constitutional right to stand for Parliament if they so desire. In 1962 he stood as Independent candidate for Middlesbrough West. Much to his surprise, he got around fifty votes, but lost his deposit. This freed him from the army.

In the autumn of 1964 he was just starting his final year at University College, London. Besides his interest in anthropology he had a flair for property – many of our Lakeland climbing trips had been spent exploring ruined barns as possible conversions. He had spent a couple of summers converting one such ruin above the Duddon Valley, and, in London, had secured the lease of an unfurnished flat high above Dean Street, living in it for three years nearly rent free, by sub-letting rooms to friends. In Mike's make-up there is a property tycoon and an anthropologist sometimes working hand in hand – at other times in conflict. He is one of those people who never seem in a hurry, never seem to do very much, yet quietly and effectively succeed in carving out a life of their own choosing.

Martin Boysen had slotted into a more conventional mould. He was one of the most brilliant rock-climbers that this country, or to be more accurate, Germany, had produced since the war. Born in 1941, at Aachen, of a German father and an English mother, he spent a terrifying infancy, of which he could have barely been aware, with his mother under constant surveillance by the Gestapo, and constant threat of arrest. After the war they came back to England, and Martin was brought up in Tonbridge, near Harrison's Rocks. He started going to the rocks when he was fourteen and it was here that I first met him, a shy, gangling boy who drifted up the most difficult problems with an easy grace, showing no visible effort. He went to Manchester University in 1961 to study biology, met Maggy in his first term, took her climbing and they have beeen together ever since. Maggy, slim, vital, dynamic, compensates for Martin's easy indolence. We spent many delightful weekends with him when they visited us at Woodland. They both had a deep abiding love for the hills which went further than just a passion for rock-climbing. Martin had an extensive knowledge and interest in the fauna and flora of the mountains – and this was how one of the best routes I helped to put up in the Lake District came to be called the Medlar – named after a rare tree, reputed to be found only in Southern England, but growing at the foot of our climb.

Martin and Mags arrived one weekend shortly after I had got back from the Alps. Mike was over in the Duddon Valley, working on his cottage at Bigert Mire. The weather was perfect and Martin knew of the ideal new route for us to try.

'I had a go at it a couple of weeks ago,' he admitted, 'but I wasn't climbing well, and turned back.'

'Where is it?'

'Wait and see – we'll have to make sure it's fine tomorrow.'

Such is the secrecy that surrounds any possible new line – there are so few left in the Lakes.

The morning was fine and Martin revealed that our planned ascent was on Raven Crag of Thirlmere. From the road it is lost in the conifer woods that cling to the slopes of Thirlmere – the crag is a good 600 feet up the hillside, steep and slender, with jutting, angular overhangs. A light green lichen clings to the rock, making patterns similar to amoeba or bacteria seen through a microscope. The crag was discovered, in 1952, by Harold Drasdo and Pete Greenwood. Its very character, yielding bold lines on very steep rock, attracted some of the outstanding post-war climbers to its flanks. Pete Greenwood was a leading light of the Wall End Barn mob, a group of climbers who temporarily opted out of the rat race, long before beatniks or hippies had been thought of; they raced round the Lakes on high-powered motor-bikes, and went in for prodigious drinking sessions. As with many of the hard climbing groups, their members later settled down to successful careers in a number of widely differing fields. Pete Greenwood, finally deciding that he had had enough of bumming around, worked his guts out as a labourer on the Spade Adam project, saved enough money to buy a plot of land, built a house, borrowed more money, and is now a property tycoon in Cumberland. Jack Bradley, who made the first ascent of Necropolis, an attempt to tackle the huge cave that is carved out of the centre of the crag, seemed to be one of the wildest members of the Wall End mob. He became a successful financier in Leeds, floating companies with the same *sang froid* that you or I would display buying a few premium bonds.

Communist Covert, a fine line that works through the big overhangs of the cave, and airily across the upper part of the buttress, fell to Arthur Dolphin, a climber whose brilliant career was cut short in 1954. He was Lakeland's leading rock-climber, making the same impact in the Lakes that Joe Brown and Don Whillans were making in Wales. Even today, some of his routes rank as the finest and most difficult in the area.

The final stamp of recognition for the crag came in 1956, when Don Whillans forced the overhangs of the cave with his route, Delphinus. It was a typical Whillans route, a direct onslaught at the most obvious, and certainly the most formidable, challenge of the cliff.

And now, on a fine September's day, Martin Boysen, Mike and I were picking our way through the sweet-smelling woods towards the foot of the crag.

'That's the line,' said Martin. 'Up that undercut ramp to the left of the cave.'

'It looks bloody hard,' I replied. 'Are you sure it's possible?'

'Oh yes, you'll do it all right. I'd only just recovered from glandular fever when I tried it.'

And so I found myself at the sharp end. I was well armed with a wide selection of nuts. We were still in the primitive nut era, when you simply scrounged a collection of nuts from the local garage and threaded them on a few slings. The smallest were meccano style nuts on thin bits of line that would barely have held a man's deadweight, and the biggest were over an inch across and weighed a pound a time. The purists drilled out the threads, but I hadn't bothered.

I didn't feel like leaving the ledge – the rock leaned back the wrong way; the holds seemed minute, tiny flakes, cracks that took a finger tip and no more; and after forty feet or so, a nasty little overhang jutted out at least a foot.

'I'm bloody sure I won't get up this. There's nothing for protection.'

'Course there is,' replied Martin. 'I got a good spike runner about six feet up – look, you can see it.'

With a careful look I could – and it was minuscule, but at least it provided some kind of haven to head for. I balanced up gingerly, weight on fingertips slotted into horizontal cracks; a couple of moves and I'm at the spike; it's just big enough to balance a thin line sling round. Another move and I manage to slot a small nut into one of the cracks. I begin to feel better. Even if I fall off, I shouldn't hurt myself.

My arms are beginning to ache, but the long disappointing season in the Alps is beginning to pay off. I am at least fit and mentally attuned to the rock. I am even beginning to enjoy myself; I stop threatening to turn back; edge my way from hold to hold, relaxed, wary, looking for possible runners. Forty feet up, and the base of the overhang, a perfect thread belay, just big enough for a piece of line. I untie the knot of a sling, using one hand and my teeth, push the end of the line into the crack and get out my wire threader to thrust and manipulate the nylon string behind a bulge in the crack – I'm like a safe-breaker, playing the tumblers of the safe in the Bank of England – total concentration – a touch of exhilaration. And the sling is through. More one-handed contortions to tie the knot – my other hand is getting tired. I'm safe again and happy – a master of the steep rock around me, master of my mind and muscles. I jam a hand in the crack beneath the overhang, place a foot in just the right place to give me leverage, and swing up, reach up; fingers play over the ledge above the roof, slot naturally on to a dimple in the rock – it'll suffice – and I step up on to the ledge with ease, muscle and mind tensed, knowing it's hard, yet everything slipping into place. This is the joy of climbing, the absolute freedom of mind and body, a short-bloomed euphoria that flowers in the process of climbing, and can be savoured while resting on the stances before another pitch, lasting through to the top of the climb and down to the pub that evening – the logical end to every Lakeland climbing day. And then next day, with the confrontation of work, of day-to-day problems, the euphoria fast vanishes and the climb is just one more incident docked up in the past. But still it has an importance, as a moment of total relaxation, of unspoilt joy, the repetition of the experience, a goal to seek for other days, till one day, when muscles will no longer respond to the command of mind, this precious euphoria might prove unattainable. I wonder what then?

But I'm at the top of the overhang; a black groove beckons me on, and Martin shouts out from below:

'How about belaying there, Chris?'

He's worried I'll get the whole climb. Fair enough, after all the line was his concept, not mine. And so I hammer in a piton, slot in a couple of nuts and, half hanging off my belay, take the rope in. As Martin climbs up, I gaze down over the dark tops of pine trees, across Thirlmere, a twisted sword stabbing at the vitals of a Lakeland Valley. Not so many years ago there were no sombre pine trees; farmhouses nestled in the bed of the valley and a Lakeland road, narrow, between dry stone walls, wound across the valley bed. This has now been changed by the hands of man – the valley bottom was flooded, forests were planted on the slopes, and a new beauty has emerged, more sombre, brooding, but nevertheless with its own attraction. I can feel the heat of the sun on my face; feel the warm rock against my back; rub a little patch of dried moss into a powder and watch the specks of dust float down towards Martin, as he moves slowly, but oh so easily, up towards me.

And then it's his turn to go out in front. He tries the groove behind me but makes no progress, swings out on to the wall. It's steep and flaky, with tiny spikes for finger- and toe-holds. Another few feet, he pauses, goes back a bit; most unlike Martin, but he's still recovering from glandular fever. I'm bored, the rope begins to cut into my back and I think of pints of cool beer, the reward for victory.

Martin seems to be struggling; a tension is transmitted down the rope. He's standing in a sling balanced over a small flake; the flake breaks off, Martin slips, seizes a hold and somehow manages to remain hanging on to the rock; another struggle and he's up. I quickly bring up Mike Thompson to join me, and then, in turn, we climb to the top of the crag.

Pints of beer, jubilation at snatching a fine new route and talk of other possible lines. Mike is the great strategist. We've been climbing together for nearly twenty years, and on hard ground I have done most of the leading, but almost all the new routes we have done together have been Mike's discoveries. In the same way that he quietly seeks out interesting old houses, he searches for new lines on the crags. That day he had seen another possible route, straight up the centre of the crag. We returned, just the two of us, a couple of days later, to complete a route which was slightly easier than the Medlar, but longer and with a more satisfying line, straight up the centre of the crag to the barrier of overhangs that guard the top.

And so September slipped into October, a gently vanishing Indian summer that blended imperceptibly with the chill clouds of late autumn, and the start of a new lecture season – our sole source of income, £20 a time at luncheon clubs, lecture societies or mountaineering clubs. I hated the nomadic existence – the series of one-night stands, the driving, the filling in of time before another lecture, and, above all, the worry that I was getting nowhere. The carefree joy of a summer's climbs vanished in the reality of making a day-to-day living.

CHAPTER SEVEN

Hogmanay

It is not always the mammoth successes or the major ascents that are the most memorable. Sometimes an epic failure – a combination of struggle with wind and storm, and the inter-action with one's companions – turns what could have been a very minor, low-key incident into one that will never be forgotten. This was the case over New Year, 1965. It started normally enough. We had been invited to see the New Year in with some friends just north of Glasgow, and were then going to meet Tom Patey on New Year's Day, to get in some climbing. But I should have known better – things happened when Tom was around. Mary Stewart, our hostess on New Year's Eve, also has this catalytic quality.

Mary is a vet who lives in the most wonderfully chaotic house I have ever known, with her five children, dogs, other animals, and a succession of friends – often flotsam from the competitive society, who finally end up under the ever-open hospitality of her roof. The house is in the middle of a golf-course outside Glasgow, was once a stable but now has a couple of big rooms and a kitchen downstairs and a warren of rooms upstairs.

After graduating, Mary, an American by birth, came over to Scotland to do postgraduate work and had fallen in love with the hills and the country. She had taken up climbing and had married a member of the Glasgow Mountaineering Club. Unfortunately the marriage had not worked. Her husband was a solicitor, and Mary was a warm-hearted Bohemian with little interest in being a suburban housewife.

Strongly built and wiry, with a hand grip as firm as a man's, Mary would have been the perfect frontierswoman on a ranch at the edge of Indian territory in the Far West. Her hair is a rich copper, long and thick, and her face seems perpetually weather-beaten; but there is a rare warmth and kindness in her face that cancels out any danger of over-masculinity. I can always see her in my mind's eye – bare footed, clad in a pair of old Levis and a simple sweater worn outside her trousers, ornamented by a big, broad, patterned belt.

Wendy and I drove up to Scotland on New Year's Eve, with Conrad, now one year old, asleep in the back of the van. The trip was starting badly; I could feel depression creep over me – the result, I suspected, of the proximity of a New Year and its festivities, with my own doubts for the future. The book was barely half-finished. I had just completed a gruelling lecture season, giving the same lecture on the North Wall of the Eiger, which was now two years old, over and over again. It wasn't just the boredom of repeating the same lecture, it was the worry that this was something of the past – that I was leaning backwards, unable to go forwards.

The party was well under way when we arrived. A record player throbbed out its beat. People were dancing, dark gyrating shadows in a candle-lit black-draped room. We were deafened, confused, out of tune with the rhythm of a party that had been under way for some time. Martin and Maggy Boysen, who had been staying with us at Woodland, were already there. So was John Cleare, a climber who was also a professional photographer; he had with him a statuesque, very extrovert, very blonde girl-friend, and seemed the symbol of the success and self-confidence which at that time seemed to be eluding me. He had a real skill – a positive career. This shell of self-confidence probably hid much the same uncertainty that I felt, but that night it seemed real enough to me.

Another friend, who seemed to have found happiness in another way, was Eric Beard. Slightly built and wiry, with an attractive ugliness about him, big ears framing a crew-cut head of hair and a gnomish face that was one big grin, he had devoted his life to becoming a brilliant fell runner. He held the records for running the Welsh three thousanders, and a host of other records. Stripped off, he was all legs – strongly muscled, bonded to a lean, compact body and topped by his big grin.

He had no qualifications, had spent some time as a Leeds clippy, before abandoning steady jobs for a nomadic existence, instructing at climbing centres, or working as an odd-job man. He was the traditional life-and-soul-of-the-party, joking, singing, exuding a simple warm-heartedness, and yet behind this there was an indefinable wistful sadness, as if, in his complete freedom from material pressures and the ties of family or a fixed base, he also was a lost soul, searching for some kind of fulfilment.

I sat on the floor in a dark corner, and tried to drag myself out of my own mood of depression. But it was no good – the New Year was very nearly on us and the spontaneous enjoyment of the others was alien to my own feelings; the New Year was full of foreboding and before it arrived I sneaked up to bed. Wendy, upset, confused, tearful, followed me, trying to understand the depths of my mood, trying to pull me from its dark trap, till at last love and sleep curled round us, and we were lost in oblivion.

We woke to a bright sun, cloudless sky and a hard, keen frost. No depression could survive against such a stimulus – New Year's Day, 1965, didn't seem so bad after all, and anyway, who cared about the distant future when, with a bit of luck, there would be some good snow and ice conditions in Glencoe? I had one plus from my mood of the night before – I had drunk comparatively little and had gained a lot more sleep than the others. We got up, helped clear the debris of the party, and planned the rest of the weekend. Tom Patey was going to meet us that day in Glencoe, and soon we had three car-loads of climbers ready to set out for the hills. Even Wendy was coming, leaving Conrad behind for the first time ever, with Mary's children.

As we drove up to Glencoe, she looked anxious and worried, like any animal taken away from its newborn litter. But I had now recovered completely from the previous evening's low. There was a sprinkling of snow on the foothills as we drove round Bearsden to Balloch, and then, as we came to the foot of Loch Lomond, we could see Ben Lomond near its head, serene, magnificent, plastered in snow.

It was like one's first trip to Scotland, as we careered round the bends on the shores of the loch and then chased over the great sweep of Rannoch Moor. Buachaille Etive Mòr, a cathedral of black rock interlaced with snow, beckoned us on our way. We stopped at Altnafeadh, a stalker's house with a couple of barns by the road, and wondered what to do. It was already past midday, and it would be dark by six that night. There were three of us, Mary Stewart, a friend of hers called Jock, and myself. It was obviously too late to tackle any of the harder routes, and anyway we were too polyglot a party. I suggested the Left Fork of Crowberry Gully – the guide book assured us: 'It is fairly certain that this fork will provide an exciting finish to the gully.' The Right Fork is one of the great classic gully climbs of Glencoe – comparatively straightforward by modern standards, but nevertheless sufficiently long and difficult to trap the unwary into enforced bivouacs.

The Left Fork is slightly shorter than the Right, but makes up by steepness, being a narrow fissure capped by a jutting roof overhang. It was a joy to leave the car and walk through a light covering of powder snow towards the towering mass of the Buachaille. Soon we were at the foot of Crowberry Gully itself. Lined with firm snow, it curled up between the steep, dark rocks of the Crowberry Ridge and the North Buttress – and on this sunny New Year's Day, there seemed little threat or foreboding about the climb. We put on crampons and started soloing up the lower snow-slopes in the gully, boots kicking with an easy assurance into the firm snow. As we gained height, and came to the first little step, we put on the rope – and on we went, till we reached the foot of the Left Fork, a narrow gash in the upper rocks leading on to the crest of Crowberry Ridge. I was itching to tax myself, to get on to some hard climbing.

The Left Fork was little more than a wide chimney, lined with ice, and blocked near its top by a smooth roof. I swarmed into the chimney, wriggled and thrutched up its narrow confines, to a point below the roof. The capstone jutted smoothly over my head – there were no holds, and the chimney widened so that I was nearly doing the splits in my effort to straddle both walls. Providentially, someone had left a piton in place, so that I had some protection in the event of a fall; I was now nearly a hundred feet above the other two. It was the kind of climbing that I have always enjoyed, gymnastic, contortionist, and yet, by using either side of the chimney to the best advantage, I could avoid putting too much weight on my arms – just as well, for there was nothing to pull on anyway. The holds above the roof were all sloping, glazed in ice. The jut of the overhang forced my body backwards; I was dimly aware of the situation as I was forced out of the secure confines of the chimney, but I knew no fear. My concentration on those few feet of rock in front of my nose was too great. Crampons scraped on rock, dug a fraction of an inch into the glaze of verglas. The world contracted into those few feet immediately above me – a pull, a straddle and I was up; a few more feet and I was in the gap just below Crowberry Tower. I knew a delicious sense of achievement – of freedom – of pure, simple joy at my situation; how different from the dark mood of the previous night. Climbing, the great healer, had restored my self-confidence.

It was now the turn of the others. Mary was justifiably apprehensive; although strongly-built and a good climber, her family and work commitments had kept her away from the hills, and this was obviously going to be considerably harder than anything else she had ever tried.

Jock swarmed up the pitch to join me; and then it was Mary's turn. I got into a good position to give her a tight rope. By this time I was getting worried about having brought her on a climb which was obviously too difficult for her. She started up steadily enough – slow, but steady progress – the sound of panting and scraping of crampons on rock drifted up the fissure, getting stronger as she came nearer. The scraping and panting got louder, the rope crept in more slowly as she came up to the roof overhang and came to a dead stop. I was getting cold and gave the rope a reassuring heave.

'For heaven's sake, don't pull, Chris, you're pulling me off,' came a shout from below.

The rope was arched over her head round the roof, so that any pull tended to pull her outwards and off what precarious holds she had managed to find. There was another long pause, a lot more scraping:

'Come on, Mary,' I shouted. 'We're bloody freezing up here. Straddle across the chimney and just bridge up. As soon as you get free of the chimney, we'll be able to pull you out.'

'I can't make my feet stick on the rock,' came the reply.

'Just slap them on,' I shouted. 'They'll stay there. Come on; one big effort.'

'Okay, I'll try now. Hold the rope tight.'

Another long pause and the rope moved a few inches – more scraping from below, and suddenly the rope tugged at my hands and body, pulled me off my stance, and I found myself hanging on the belay with the rope nearly cutting me in two. Mary had lost contact with the rock, had spiralled out into mid-air, and was now hanging in space below the overhang – even with the correct knot, it's no joke hanging on the end of a rope. You can survive about ten minutes before losing consciousness and suffocating.

'For God's sake, let me down,' shouted Mary.

'Hang on, we'll have a go at pulling you up,' I replied. There were three of us, and with a bit of luck we should be able to haul her up to the holds above the roof overhang.

'Be quick, I'm being cut in half,' she shouted.

Jock climbed down to me and we both heaved on the rope, but it was no good. There was too much friction as it went over the overhang, and anyway it is nearly impossible to haul up the deadweight of a person without some kind of pulley system. We heaved and hauled with very little effect, until the pleas from below, to be lowered back down, became irresistible.

Reluctantly, we lowered Mary about thirty feet, till she came in contact with the ice once more. I then gave the rope to Jock and climbed down to a point where I could see her. She was slumped, exhausted, on the ice.

'Come on, Mary,' I shouted. 'I'll talk you up. You'll be all right.'

'Okay. I'm sorry, Chris, for being such a nuisance, but I just couldn't stay on, and I think I'd have been cut in two if you'd kept hauling much longer.'

It was typical of Mary to apologise for a situation that was mainly my fault. Anyway, she soon started to climb again and, exhausted, cajoled and shouted at, she struggled over the overhang.

By this time it was beginning to get dark and in the dusk we scrambled, well content, down the Curved Ridge, back to the cars. We drove down to the Clachaig Hotel, where we had arranged to meet Tom Patey, Martin and the others. So far, the weekend had been enjoyable, but in no way specially memorable from any other winter's weekend. But Tom had a way of turning the ordinary into the extraordinary, and this was to be no exception. Tom was a great traveller; he thought nothing of driving from his home in Ullapool to Speyside, in the Cairngorms, a good hundred and fifty miles on narrow roads, for an evening drink and a sing-song. His standard weekend could include an itinerary that most mortals would spread over a week – a lecture on the Friday night in Cambridge (to pay the expenses), then a quick flip over to Wales to see Joe Brown, and on the way back he would often make a fifty-mile diversion to call in at our cottage in the Lakes. He was a genius at concocting complicated plans for a party's enter-tainment, which might include a ceilidh a hundred miles away, followed by a day's climbing in the opposite direction. In fact, climbing with Tom Patey was a kind of Magical Mystery Tour, in which no one, except perhaps himself, knew what was coming next.

He was already ensconced in the bar at the Clachaig, his squeezebox out, a dram of whisky at his side and a cigarette in his mouth.

'The snow conditions are no good here,' he greeted us. 'They'll be a lot better on Creag Meaghaidh and I've got a good line you'll be interested in.'

'I don't know,' I replied. 'The Buachaille seemed in great condition to me.'

'Ah, but on Meaghaidh it'll be even better, and we'll be able to drink at the Loch Laggan Hotel.'

And so we drank and argued till closing time at the Clachaig and, well oiled with beer and whisky, were ready for anything. We left Glencoe at eleven o'clock, and raced in convoy round Loch Leven, through the still, silent streets of Kinlochleven and Fort William, past Ben Nevis, massive, squat, gleaming in the moonlight, and up to Glen Spean, over a road white and shiny with hard-packed snow. This was Patey country, and he drove his Skoda like a Timo Mäkinen, careering round the bends at a steady fifty. I followed, dogged, rather nervous, but determined not to be left behind – apart from anything else, I didn't know where we were bound.

At last we came to a stop outside a hotel. It was dark and silent, but there was a bothy, Tom said, down by the side. The bothy was an old hen house, with holes in the floor and gaps in the door, but it had a roof and walls, and we all got sleeping-bags out and snuggled down. Wendy muttered about the cold, and snuggled close to me. She's a comfort-loving girl with an appalling circulation. It was three in the morning when we got off to sleep; even so, we woke quite early. There was little temptation to stay in bed – it was too cold, draughty and uncomfortable.

Breakfast in the hotel with bowls of porridge, Aberdeen kippers and plates full of toast; time slips by and it's midday before we get away.

'It's only a wee walk to the crag,' Tom reassured us. I suspect he enjoyed the perpetual confrontation with time, the game of brinkmanship, of leaving at the last minute, and then snatching the chosen climb from the oncoming night. Tom didn't believe in coolly laid plans – his climbing was one of instant pleasure, based on his own close knowledge of the hills and the most intimate details of almost every crag on the Scottish mainland.

But it was more than a wee walk to the foot of the crag – snow was knee deep, in places thigh deep, and our progress soon slowed to the laborious plod of the man in front who was making the route. There were six of us – Martin Boysen, Tom Patey, Eric Beard, Mary Stewart, John Cleare and myself. Only Tom had ever been to the crag before – but he, of course, knew every foot of the way, every indentation on the crag. We didn't need a map or guide-book, for we were with the local expert. And so, thoughtlessly, chatting, joking, wading, we walked towards Creag Meaghaidh.

This was just another light-hearted day in the hills; it was too late to think of trying any of the more difficult climbs, and in any case we were all feeling tired after only a few hours' sleep the night before. The weather was overcast with a ceiling of featureless grey, merging with the grey-white of the upper slopes of the cliff. There was no wind, no sound; everything was muffled by the snow. It took us two hours to reach the foot of the crag – it seemed lost, smothered in the mountainside. At three o'clock in the after-noon there were only two and a half hours to dark.

'Do you think Martin and I have time to do South Post?' I asked Tom.

'Och yes, it'll only take an hour if you move fast,' he replied. 'You go straight up that tongue of ice above the big gully in the centre.'

We waded through the snows into the gully. There was no sense of perspective or scale; everything was black or white, black rocks and snow merging into mist, merging into snow. We stumbled through the snow with the exaggerated slow-motion movements of a cinematic dreamworld – raise one leg, plunge it into the snow, transfer weight to it and sink, down, down, down into the clinging morass of soft powder snow. It didn't matter how much you cleared with your hands, you still sank into it; we never reached the foot of the climb – it was only fifty feet away, but we just never seemed to get closer to it. Martin lost patience first, suddenly erupting into a frustrated rage at the soft, cloying mass, hammered it with his axe and cursed at the top of his voice, curses that were instantly muffled in the snow around us.

'Come on, let's bugger off from here – we're wasting our bloody time.'

I agreed, and we turned round to flounder back down the gully to the foot of a snowy ramp which the others had followed to complete an easier route. We soon caught them up, near the top of the ramp, at the foot of the head-wall of the cliff. A steep ice pitch spiralled upwards into the mist, and we could hear Tom hacking away somewhere up above. Flakes of ice, loosened by his axe, tinkled down the rock, and we sat huddled at the foot, waiting for him to finish his work.

It was now four-thirty, only an hour to dusk. At last, there was a shout from above and Mary, who was tied on to Tom, followed him up on a tight rope. I went into the lead, trying to keep up with Mary, but the ice was steep and I found that I needed to cut the odd extra hold. As a result, I soon got left behind. By the time I reached the top of a narrow scoop that led out on to the summit plateau, Tom and Mary had already vanished. I could just discern a line of footsteps, fast drifting over in the wind. John Cleare and Beardie had tied on to our rope, which meant that Martin and I had to wait until all four of us were on top. It was very nearly pitch dark before John Cleare reached the top.

I had been getting increasingly worried. Tom was the only person in the team who knew the way down. Neither Martin nor I had map, compass or torch. We didn't know the general configuration of the mountain with any degree of certainty. 'Has anyone got a torch?' I asked.

'Not me,' admitted John.

'I've got one,' said Beardie, and dug it out of his sack.

'We'd better keep on the rope,' I said. 'We could go over a cornice too bloody easily in this light.'

I started to follow Tom and Mary's tracks, but after a few paces they vanished, drifted over by the ever-shifting snows. We stopped in the pitch dark, somewhere on the top of Creag Meaghaidh.

'Has anyone got a map?'

'No.'

'No.'

'No.'

'Compass?'

'I've got one,' said Beardie, and produced it with the aplomb of a conjuror. It turned out that he had some food as well. He, who had least experience as a mountaineer, was the only one who had the bare essentials of equipment.

But a compass without a map is of only limited value. We sat down on the snow and I tried to draw, with the tip of my glove, the configuration of Creag Meaghaidh from what we could remember from a glance at the map on the hotel wall, and from what little we had seen on the way up.

'I think the line of the cliffs should be north and south,' said John.

'I suppose Tom went down one of the gullies,' suggested Martin. 'We could try to find it and go down it ourselves. It would be the quickest way back down.'

'How do we know which is the right gully, though?' I pointed out. 'I think we should try to get to the col on the north of the crag and cut down that to the gully bottom. If we follow the line of the top of the crag on the compass, as soon as it starts curving round to the east we should know we are heading for the col. Then all we've got to do is keep going down till it starts climbing again, and that must be the col – we turn right and we'll get back down into the corrie.'

It sounded simple, but we weren't even sure if the cliffs did lie in a north–south line. Cloud merged with snow at the end of the torch-beam – it was very difficult to tell where snow ended and space began; it was like being in a white box. I started off leading, the others following at intervals of about fifteen feet, all linked by the rope. It was a strange, elating feeling – the situation was undoubtedly serious, for a bitterly cold and gusty wind was playing across the undulating surface of the plateau. We had no bivouac equipment, very little food and only one torch which we couldn't expect to last for more than a couple of hours' continuous use.

In addition, Martin had only recently recovered from a bout of 'flu, and was already feeling tired and weak. Without Beardie's food, the position would have been even more serious.

'You'd better take the torch,' I told Martin, who was just behind me. 'If I go over a cornice, there's less chance of us losing it if you have it.'

We peered into the mist, trying to differentiate between the edge of the cliff and space, kept checking the compass, and advanced slowly and carefully, keeping what I thought was a safe distance from the cornice edge. But it was very difficult to tell just where it was. Martin shone the torch from behind. It cut a bright swathe through the snow-filled clouds, so that the line of light also looked like the line of the slope.

'I think we've come to the place where we can start dropping down,' I shouted. 'Martin, can you come up to me so that we can see just how far this slope goes down?'

Martin came up to my side and altered the angle of the torch so that it was shining straight down. We were standing on the very lip of a huge cornice, looking straight down into a bottomless void. Had the cornice collapsed, the pair behind us would have had very little chance of holding both of us, and almost certainly, all four of us would have fallen to our deaths.

It didn't take a second to sum up the situation. We both scuttled back to safety, and resumed our tortuous progress, trying to follow the top of the line of cornices to where we thought the slope should drop away to the col between the two mountains – and imperceptibly the ground did begin to drop away – we were losing height in our tiny cocoon of dim torchlight. Surely, we must be heading for the col – but were we? Our blade of light was no longer a brilliant white; it had faded to a smoky yellow – a sure sign that the battery was dying. Once dead, we should be unable to read the compass – unable to see the line of a cornice – and should have no choice but to stop where we were and wait for the long night to end. But would we all survive it? The wind was now gusting hard, tearing gaps in the thin layer of cloud above us, to give glimpses of a black, star-studded sky.

With hope buoyant, we plunged down the easy slope, trending eastwards as we had visualised the descent to the col. But there was no sign of any col. We could just discern what seemed a steep drop to the right, and on the left and front, the slope dropped away, undulating gently.

'Are you sure this is the col?' asked John.

'I don't know,' I had to admit. 'It could be a depression on the main ridge line, or I suppose we could have missed it altogether. Anyway, we'd better keep going while we've got a bit of light left in the torch.'

We kept plodding on, now going gently upwards. Suddenly, glancing at the compass, I realised that the steep drop was now to our west. Had we somehow doubled back on ourselves? Surely not – the steep slope was still on our right. But where the hell were we? Without a map, without any more than a vague impression of the configuration of the land, we were basing all our movement on a series of guesses – an edifice of decisions as fragile as the proverbial card house – but once we stopped reasoning out each move based on these fragile hypotheses, we should be totally lost. I was uncomfortably aware that the mountains to our north and west stretched for miles, without road or human habitation. We might have been in the middle of the Antarctic, our situation seemed so isolated, the immediate surroundings so bleak.

Looking at the compass, it seemed just possible that we had crossed the col we had been seeking, and were now on top of the hill immediately opposite Creag Meaghaidh. But if this were the case, were the slopes immediately below us precipitous, or would we have an easy run off? There seemed only one way of finding out – to start down and hope for the best. The torch battery had, at last, died on us and we could just see the ghostly glimmer of snow against rock. I worked my way to the brink, fearful that I might be trying to step over a cornice, prodding the snow in front of me like a blind man with his stick. It dug into snow – I was on a straight slope. Slowly, we worked our way down – each little drop assumed the scale of a major cliff – even three feet seemed a bottomless pit, and it was only by lowering oneself gingerly down each step that one could find just how extensive it was.

At last the angle of the snow around us began to level out, and we came out of the cloud to see, spread below us, dark and ghostly, the corrie we had left so thoughtlessly the previous afternoon. It was nearly midnight, but we still had an hour of floundering in front of us before we could get to the road. Beardie now came into his own. Throughout our adventure he had kept up a patter of jokes and sensible suggestions. Now he forged into the lead and broke trail almost all the way back, wading thigh deep through the snow. Just short of the road, we saw the glimmer of torches. Patey was there with the beginnings of a rescue party. He, also, had had his share of adventures.

'Why didn't you follow my tracks?' he asked.

'They were covered over by the time we got up.'

'I'm sorry about that. I never thought you'd have any trouble following them, and I wanted to get Mary down the gully before it was pitch dark.'

On the way back down the valley, Mary had fallen through a snow bridge into a stream. She had been soaked to the skin, and her clothes had frozen solid on her. Tom, who had just recovered from a bad attack of 'flu, had been on the verge of collapse.

Altogether, we were all lucky not to have had at least one serious casualty from exposure. We had, undoubtedly, broken just about every rule of mountain safety that had ever been made.

And yet I am unrepentant – it had been an extraordinary, rather wonderful experience. Half the attraction of climbing is playing with danger and the unknown. It would have been lunatic to have consciously sought the particular set of circumstances that faced us, but having landed ourselves in our predicament through lack of forethought, extracting ourselves from what could have been a dangerous situation presented an intriguing challenge.

If we had been taking out school students our conduct would have been unforgivable – but we weren't. All of us were experienced mountaineers who should, perhaps, have known better. Each individual had his own responsibility, to wife and child in my case, to girlfriends or parents in that of the others. If we had died, it would have been our own responsibility. It would have been more difficult to define our responsibility to a search party, if it had been called out. Had we got ourselves well and truly lost, and then collapsed from exhaustion, it could have needed the efforts of several hundred searchers to find us. In this instance, we should have come in for a lot of justified criticism for causing others inconvenience entirely through our own lack of preparation. But we had got away with it, and I suppose, rather like mischievous schoolboys, who have successfully played truant, were filled with the excitement of the experience, feeling closely united through the way we had worked together.

It was two o'clock in the morning before we got back to the hotel. Tom played his squeezebox, and we all dissected the experience with as much satisfaction as we would have done a major first ascent. Wendy and Maggy had spent a chill day in their sleeping-bags in the bothy, getting more and more worried by our non-appearance, but neither was prepared to show her fears to the other; neither wanted to increase the worry of the other. In every way, they had had the most trying time, as I am afraid women almost always do in such circumstances. There was none of the excitement of being involved in danger – just the long, cold wait, with nothing to do but worry. They needed much more self-control and courage than we might have shown, and yet it was all too easy for us to take it for granted. Fortunately, they were so glad to have us back, uninjured, that they chose to put aside the agonising hours of waiting.

Are we being selfish or irresponsible if we go on climbing once we are married? I suspect we are, but equally, I know – and Wendy knows – that I would not be the same person if ever I were to give up my climbing. I think this is something that every girl who marries a climber has to come to terms with. At the same time, the married climber should probably take greater precautions to avoid unnecessary risks and danger, though this is difficult to undertake, as was demonstrated by our own near-débâcle which occurred because we had taken the hills for granted – something one can never afford to do in Scotland in winter.

But we survived, and we learned a lot and, in a strange kind of way, thoroughly enjoyed our experience.

Thus the New Year of 1965 was launched, in a way symbolically; for out of depression and near-disaster had emerged great experience. And 1965 was to prove a turning-point in my own new-found career as a freelance climber, writer, photographer and lecturer.

CHAPTER EIGHT

Tele-Climbing at Cheddar

There was no telephone at Woodland. If anyone wanted to contact me in a hurry they had to send a telegram and I would then go to the nearest phone, which was about half a mile away. One morning, shortly after getting back from our New Year in Scotland, a telegram arrived:

PLEASE PHONE BRISTOL 43112 ABOUT POSSIBLE TELEVISION
PROGRAMME – KELLY.

Ned Kelly was a producer working for TWW – Television Wales and West.

'We're thinking of the possibilities of making a film of one of your climbs in the Avon Gorge. Would you be interested?'

'Of course I would. What were you thinking of doing?'

'Well, that would be very much up to you. We want something that will be easy to film, with good camera positions and which, at the same time, looks impressive.'

'Could I think about the best climbs, and then come back to you?'

'Okay. Give me a ring as soon as you've thought of something.'

I have made comparatively few first ascents in Britain – a small fraction of the number made by someone like Joe Brown – but the one place where I did help to make a breakthrough was in the Avon Gorge during the mid-fifties. I was at Sandhurst at the time, and the Avon Gorge gave the best climbing of any area within reasonable range. Set within a couple of miles of the centre of Bristol, immediately above the busy road to Avonmouth and the muddy waters of the River Avon, it had an atmosphere of its own. It can claim none of the magic of a high mountain crag, and yet it has a unique fascination.

The River Avon cuts its way through a line of hills: the Clifton Heights on one side and the Cleveland Hills on the other. It carves out a gorge dominated by quarried cliffs, which is spanned, in one splendid leap, by Brunel's suspension bridge. Today, the river is a trail of muddy effluent, carrying the sewage and polluted waters of the city of Bristol. At high tide, small coasters nose their way up and down the river, drowning the steady roar of traffic with the occasional ear-splitting shriek of their klaxons. In 1956, only one cliff had been fully explored by climbers; this was a buttress of quarried limestone that swept at a comparatively gentle angle down towards the road, its flanks guarded by smooth clean slabs. Hugh Banner, Harry Griffin and Barrie Page, all at Bristol University, had put up most of the early routes on the crag, and these were the ones that we first tackled from Sandhurst. You parked your car at the foot of the cliff and at the top, as you poked your head over the brow of the climb, and scrambled over a barred railing, you found yourself on a footpath, often having disturbed a courting couple. From the top, a brisk five-minute walk took you to the Coronation Tap, where you could down a pint of scrumpy cider and eat home-made pies.

We had exhausted the possibilities of the existing routes after a few weekends. Inevitably, our eyes were drawn to the steep flanks of the Main Wall, a 200 foot bite out of the Clifton Downs, quarried without leaving any of the broad ledges that graced some of the other cliffs in the gorge. It looked blank, loose and frightening. We skirmished around its base for several weekends, making tentative half-hearted attempts to get off the ground before I, at last, committed myself to a frighteningly loose and steep wall in the centre of the cliff, pushing myself beyond the point of no return. We managed to reach the top and named the climb Macavity, after T. S. Eliot's cat, who defied the laws of gravity. In some ways, this first route was the least obvious line on the entire wall. A few more routes followed, some put up by myself, and others by friends at Sandhurst, amongst them Mike Thompson, and Jim Ward, a wonderfully eccentric and very untidy officer cadet, destined for the Gurkhas.

At the beginning of 1965 the Main Wall still held its mystique. Mike Thompson and Barry Annette had made an exciting girdle traverse of the cliff, and Barry had put up several more hard routes up the Wall itself. One feature of the Avon Gorge climbs is that, being man-made, without the weathering of centuries, the rock structure has a characterless uniformity, with very few crack-lines. All the climbing is similar: balancing up on sloping holds, using small, incut ledges for hand-holds, and stepping delicately up little roof overhangs. It certainly would not provide drama for filming – it was difficult enough getting interesting still photographs on it.

But Cheddar Gorge – that could be very different. Cheddar Gorge is a true gorge in every sense – certainly the most dramatic in Britain – squeezed between a steep crag-dotted slope on one side, and sheer, vegetated walls on the other, winding from Cheddar Village into the Mendips in a series of sinuous curves. On a summer's weekend the bottom of the gorge is crammed with cars and the Cheddar Village end is packed with crowds of tourists flocking to see the caves. This can present a real problem for the climber, for the cliffs overhang the road and any rock that is dislodged will inevitably hit it. The cliffs, for the most part, are festooned with ivy and every ledge is overgrown with vegetation. As a result, the climber has no choice but to tear down great swathes of ivy and unpeel the heavy moustaches of grass that cling to the smallest ledge; these, in turn, can dislodge rocks and all end up somewhere near the road.

The safest time for climbing in the gorge, therefore, is mid-week in the winter. Then, there is a lurking, exciting mystery about the place. The gorge, empty, has grown somehow in stature, and is as mysterious as any high mountain crag.

Surely there must be a route to be climbed in the Cheddar Gorge, which would have the attraction of being virgin and, at the same time, be very much more dramatic than anything in the Avon Gorge!

I suggested this to Ned Kelly, and we arranged to meet in the Cheddar Gorge the following weekend. My next problem was to decide on a climbing partner for our TV spectacular. I was anxious to keep it to someone who had been involved in the development of climbing in the region, rather than go for one of the great names, like Joe Brown or Don Whillans. Mike Thompson seemed the obvious choice; he was one of my oldest friends, had done as much as anyone to develop climbing in the Avon Gorge, and was a very pleasant companion. We also wanted a support team and someone to take still photographs, so I phoned John Cleare.

One weekend in late January, I drove down to the gorge with Tony Greenbank, having arranged to meet John Cleare there. Unfortunately, Mike was in bed with 'flu, and couldn't make it. We were to find the perfect television route on the Saturday, prior to meeting Ned Kelly on the Sunday morning.

A light sprinkling of snow covered grass and vegetation, turning the gorge into a stark, black, grey and white study, skeletal black arms of the leafless trees reaching into the flat grey sky; grey rock etched with the black of cracks; and the white of snow on every ledge and slope.

The challenge was obvious. Near the lower end of the gorge, just above the commercial caves, is a huge, 400 foot wall, certainly the biggest in Southern England, and one of the largest stretches of continuously vertical rock in the country. It goes to the top of the gorge in a single leap from a newly-completed car park at its foot. Immediately above the car park, the rock is sheer, and seems unpleasantly friable, stretching up to a band of blank overhangs which, in turn, lead to a band of weakness which is guarded by an entanglement of brambles clinging to the near-vertical rock. To the right of the main wall is an ivy-filled groove that seemed to provide the only breach in the wall's defences. This had been climbed some years before, by Hugh Banner, and had been named Sceptre, but it avoided the main challenge, making an escape to the right on to steep and heavily vegetated rocks. Graham West, a Derbyshire peg-climber, had made an attempt on the Main Wall, trying to peg his way straight up it but had been defeated after a hundred feet or so by the scarcity of cracks and the friability of the rock. The previous year, Barry Annette had straightened out Sceptre, continuing directly up the groove system above the climb's initial corner, but his route still skirted the High Rock.

We looked up at it – in awe – slightly appalled by its challenge.

'There's a line all right,' I said. 'Look, you've got a bit of a groove going out to the left of Sceptre. Peg over that overhang, up that overhanging corner, and then you could traverse left along that break into the centre of the face, and the big groove leading to the top.'

'Looks great,' agreed John. 'But what if the rock's bad? It's bloody steep. Do you think you're on good form?'

'Bloody sure I'm not; I haven't done any proper climbing yet this year.'

We delayed the moment of commitment, and went down to the café at the caves to have tea and sandwiches.

'It might be an idea if we did something else – just to warm up,' I prevaricated.

'It's a bit late to start on the big wall, anyway,' said Tony. 'How about looking at the top of the gorge? I noticed a good line there on the way down.'

We all walked up to the head of the gorge with a comforting feeling of release from what was obviously going to be a serious and nerve-racking climb. Near the head of the gorge was a fine rib of rock, rising above a small, covered-in reservoir; it was only 150 feet high, and looked ideal as a training climb. It was just the right standard of difficulty – just hard enough to give us confidence for our effort the next day.

We met Ned Kelly on the Sunday morning. He had a perpetual boyish look, is of medium build, with a pleasant smile and a ready enthusiasm in his manner. He came from London originally, and had done a little climb-ing. Having started in television as a cameraman, he had progressed to directing. The programme had been his idea, and would be squeezed in amongst his run-of-the-mill work organising quiz programmes and beauty contests.

'What I want to do is a form of live broadcast,' he told us. 'We'll record the climb on videotape the day before it actually goes out on the air; to all intents and purposes, though, it'll be a live broadcast, because we'll have the cameras in position, and I'll be mixing the pictures – we'll be sending it out exactly as it happened.'

The difference between a film and this type of broadcast is that with a film probably only one camera is used, with the facility of switching to a dozen different positions. Thousands of feet of film can be shot, in any sequence, taking close-ups of hands on holds, and fingers curling round pitons which, of course, might be conveniently situated at ground level. The whole lot is then edited, and the resulting film is probably more perfect than a genuine, live broadcast. But the public, all too used to seeing stunts in films, view anything they see with a fair level of scepticism. In a live broadcast, on the other hand, there is no room for this type of cheating. The cameras are already set up, and only the action of the climbers at the time can be recorded. To the viewer the thrill, no doubt, is one of – will he fall off? This is the kind of emotion that dominates the watching of motor racing, though in either sport, there is the fascination of watching someone mastering a skill which the viewer knows he could never accomplish.

There had already been a few live climbing broadcasts put out by the BBC, but I had never been involved. The first was a joint Franco-British production in 1963, an ascent of the South Face of the Aiguille du Midi, above Chamonix. The only Briton to take part was Joe Brown. Though very dramatic, it must have been comparatively easy to put on. A téléphérique goes to the top of the Aiguille du Midi, and another goes, in a single giant span, right across the Vallée Blanche, giving superb views of the South-West Face. The South-West Face itself is little more than a small rock buttress, under a thousand feet high, but its position, dominating one of the greatest glacier basins in the Alps, is unique.

The programme was such a success that the BBC decided to do a repeat of their own, this time bringing a single French climber, Robert Paragot, over to England, and using three British climbers. They chose Clogwyn du'r Arddu, the finest crag in Britain south of the Scottish Border; Joe Brown, Don Whillans and Ian McNaught-Davis climbed with Paragot. This was a very logical choice since Joe and Don, in their early partnership, had made the great post-war breakthrough in high-standard climbing on 'Cloggy', and Mac was undoubtedly the best, and funniest, talker on the climbing scene. He had already become a climbing spokesman on radio, and combined a flamboyant personality with a strong sense of humour. He was also a very competent mountaineer having been with Joe Brown and Tom Patey on their four-man expedition to the Mustagh Tower in 1956; he had always succeeded in maintaining a fair climbing level, at the same time as following an exacting and successful career in the computer business. He is an interesting example of the amateur professional, since he has a career outside climbing and is essentially amateur in his attitude to climbing – that it should be great fun and an escape from day-to-day work – but makes a certain amount of money as a climbing commentator on radio and television.

I had happened to be climbing in North Wales that weekend, and must confess I was envious of the climbing actors cavorting across the mist-enshrouded walls of Cloggy. And now I had my chance. Ours was not to be a full-blown live broadcast, but a cut-price substitute. In some ways it was the more satisfying for that, being on a small, informal and friendly scale, and we were just dealing with Ned Kelly who, rather like myself in my role of a professional climber, was getting himself established in the world of television. We were doing something different, for we were looking for a new route to present as an outdoor broadcast – a line which, as we gazed up at it that morning, looked feasible – but only just. The whole concept was immensely exciting, for up to this point, outdoor broadcasts of climbing had been made on established routes. I suppose the truest film of all would have been a live presentation of our efforts to make the first ascent, though the trouble here is that climbing tends to be a very slow process, especially when pioneering new ground. We had to show the public how we climbed, but at the same time we had to make it visually interesting, and to do that, we had to be able to climb quickly, to a set schedule.

Climbing broadcasting has evolved rapidly over the last eight years, and in 1965 we were still in the very early stages of live, or semi-live, presentations of climbs. Our first problem was to make our new route. Once made, we would then be in a position to climb it for television. It was bitterly cold, certainly not the weather for high-standard rock-climbing, but our audience, in the shape of Ned Kelly and his girlfriend, were waiting, and we had to show him that the wall could be climbed. John Cleare was going to act as my second, and we got our gear together for our first winter ascent.

The groove of Sceptre which led up to the point where we hoped to break into the steep, unclimbed wall of High Rock, was smothered in snow. I was hoping that this part of the climb would prove quite straightforward, while the upper, unclimbed part was so steep that it held no snow and so, except for the cold, would be no harder than it would have been in summer. P.A.s on, draped with slings, pitons and nuts, I started up the bottom rocks, clearing snow from every hold, and soon my hands had lost all feeling. The smooth soles of my P.A.s skidded on snow-dusted rocks.

'It's too bloody cold,' I shouted down. 'We'll never get up it today.'

'Course you will,' shouted John. 'Just keep going, and it'll work out.'

I kept on going, grumbling and muttering to myself, as I tend to do when I am climbing. Once I'd got used to numb fingers there was even a strange enjoyment in picking my way up the groove. I avoided the snow where I possibly could – a little like those games you played as a child, avoiding every other paving stone on the pavement, the only difference here being that it was a game in the vertical. The route had originally been tunnelled through a barrier of ivy and the strands, now weighed down by a clinging layer of snow, were on either side of the groove, ever pressing in, in a hopeless battle with the invading climbers.

The slow progress I made upwards seemed quick to me, because time races by for the leader on a climb. But the others, down below, were stamping in the snow. I reached a small ledge, about a hundred feet up the groove, just below the point where it bifurcates. The original Sceptre route went up to the right, our new line to the left, up an improbable corner to a square-cut, smooth, triangular roof, that looked as impregnable as a ceiling at home. There weren't even any cracks in it.

I brought John up to me, left him belayed to a piton and started gingerly towards the roof. I was weighed down with about twenty pounds of ballast, a wide assortment of pitons and nut runners, for we fully expected our route to be high-standard peg-climbing the whole way. I bridged across the groove, prepared to find it near impossible, but somehow, all the holds fitted into place. They weren't obvious – a side hold here, a bridging movement, a pull on an invisible little jug, and I was below the overhang. I leaned out and felt over it – I couldn't find a hold, but there was a crack. Time to put in my first peg: I got out a small one, nudged the tip of it into the crack, gave it a tap and it bounced straight out, tinkling down to the ground, 150 feet below. Have another try; arms now tiring, legs aching and beginning to tremble from my bridged-out position. This time the peg held, another half-dozen whams of the hammer, and it was in to the hilt. I clipped in a karabiner, pulled gently on it, just to get a bit of height, to see what was over the lip of the overhang. I could straddle out still higher; the angle above dropped back just enough to allow me to pull over the overhang without using an étrier. I pulled up, balanced on to the slab, and let out a victory yell. We'd cracked the first problem.

The slab led up to a niche below a ferocious-looking overhanging chimney, comprising a whole mass of blocks that seemed morticed into each other, but there were cracks in between the blocks, and surprisingly, the structure seemed sound. I slotted in a nut, felt more confident, and once again straddle out. This was the kind of climbing that I have always enjoyed – steep and technical, where one could use one's skill to avoid putting too much weight on one's arms. The bridging holds kept arriving; another nut runner – it was going free. I could hardly believe it. I now seemed straddled out over the car park more than 200 feet below, and

Cheddar Gorge: Coronation Street

could see the ground between my legs. A hand over the top, a final heave, and I was standing on top of a flake, only twenty feet below the line of overhangs that led back into the centre of the face. The time seemed to have gone in a matter of minutes, though in fact I had been working for two hours. John followed up slowly, because he was frozen stiff from the long wait below. As he worked his way towards me I kept glancing behind me; a crack jammed with earth led up to the great jutting roof above, but characteristically there was a line of weakness below the roof, a horizontal dyke that would give hand-holds, and what seemed to be another inter-mittent crack line that relented to give the occasional foot-hold. This led to a great shield of rock that jutted out from under the roof, and barred the way to the start of the groove which we knew led to the top.

John poked his head over the top of the overhang I'd just led. He was as bemused as I by the fantastic nature of the climbing. It had not been desperately hard, just wonderful, sensational climbing, in a magnificent situation.

But it wasn't over. The day was now drawing to a close – only a couple of hours to dark, and we still had a long way to go. I started up the crack behind the pedestal – it was just the right width for hand-jamming, but I had to clear the earth before I could slot in my hands. I was now cold and stiff from the delay while I had brought John up to my position. There is an additional nervous strain while doing a new route which one never experiences in repeating a climb, and on this one in particular, the scale and steepness, combined with the cold, almost gave the climb Alpine proportions.

I was nervous and a little frightened as I struggled up the crack, making heavy weather of something that should have been easy. By the time I reached the overhang I was trembling with exertion and my own nervous tension. I had now reached the traverse into the centre of the Face – at first quite easy, but very steep to tiring arms. Step carefully, swing across, and then the Shield. Close up, it looked even less reassuring than it had from below.

'There's a crack this side of it,' I shouted back.

And I hammered in an angle piton, just under the overhang in the solid part of the rock. Swinging out and across on it, I was just able to reach across the Shield to feel round the other side.

'There's a bloody crack going right back behind it; it's detached from the rock,' I shouted again.

'Looks pretty solid to me,' said John from below. He's a very reassuring second.

'It's all very well for you, you don't have to try swinging round it. If it came away, I'd have a ton of rock on top of me.'

I tapped it with my peg-hammer. It sounded hollow – but it didn't shift at all. About six feet high and four feet across, it seemed cemented to the sheer wall immediately below the roof in some completely inexplicable way. There was a good line of hand-holds along its top, but I was frightened to trust them; I could imagine, with dazzling clarity, myself clinging to the top of this shield of rock, and feeling it keel outwards and then crashing down with me beneath it.

I hovered and teetered on the edge of the Shield, trying to summon some courage and then John released me.

'You'd better do something soon,' he remarked. 'It'll be dark in half an hour.'

That settled it – we couldn't possibly get to the top before dark. We'd have to try to escape – no question of abseiling back down. However, there was the possibility of traversing right instead of left, into the top of Barry Annette's Direct Finish to Sceptre. It wasn't easy, but anything that avoided that terrifying Shield seemed welcome, and I thrutched up the final crack that led to a small pinnacle on the edge of the High Rock. I got up as it was growing dark, and John felt his way up behind me to the top.

We hadn't succeeded, but it had been one of the best days' climbing I had ever had. We soon convinced ourselves that there was a way across the Shield, that it was a lot more solid than it looked – and then we began to plan when we could return. There was no question of finishing the climb the following day; John had an assignment as a photographer, and I had a lecture to give in the North – but what if someone else came and snatched our route.

'I know of at least three others who've got their eye on it,' warned John. 'Pete Crew was talking about it only last week, and I believe Chris Jones has been sniffing around the gorge.'

Pete sounded the most formidable competition. In the early sixties he had established himself as one of the best young rock-climbers in the country, and was certainly the most prolific. Perhaps not as brilliant a technician as Martin Boysen, he had a restless dynamism and drive which enabled him to snatch a huge number of good routes, often in direct competition with others. He came from Barnsley and his father had worked on the railway. Pete had got a scholarship to Oxford, had been bored and irritated by the academic strictures of the University, and had abandoned his university career to start a small mail-order climbing business in Manchester, in partnership with another Oxford man, Pete Hutchinson. After a time, Pete Crew had tired of this and had gone into computers, working in London. Most of his climbing was based in North Wales, but he had made one or two very successful forays into other areas to snatch the odd 'last great problem'. He had done this very successfully, a few years before, in the Lake District, when the local Lake District climbers, led by Lakeland's most formidable modern pioneer, Alan Austin, had been laying siege to the prominent unclimbed pillar on Esk Buttress. This had already defeated several parties, and one of the contestants in the Austin team, Jack Soper, while drinking in a Welsh pub, had been unwise enough to mention the fact that they were going to try the climb on the next fine weekend. Crew overheard this remark, and the very next weekend set out, hot-foot for the Lakes. The Soper/Austin party, blissfully unaware of any competition, had made a leisured start for the crag, only to find Crew and Baz Ingle, his normal climbing partner, embarked on their carefully planned line. The moral of the story is that all's fair in love, war and bagging new routes, and if you want to preserve a new line, the only solution is to guard it with a mantle of security that would shame MI5!

We all swore each other to secrecy, and arranged to meet in three weeks' time, when we hoped the weather might be a little warmer – but only two days had gone by when John phoned me from Guildford, where he lives.

'I think we'd better get moving,' he told me. 'I've heard that Crew has been talking about our line, and is planning to go down next weekend, to climb it.'

'Does he know about our effort?' I asked.

'I don't think so, but he's had the line itself in mind for some time. I think he's planning to do it with Chris Jones.'

'I can't possibly get down till next week; I've got a couple of lectures, one on Thursday, and the other on Saturday.'

'Well, it could be too late by then; they could easily have a go at it this weekend.'

'We'll just have to hope for the best; I can't possibly make it. Could you get away early next week though?'

'Yes, that would be okay.'

'Right. How about trying to find out whether Pete is planning to go down. You know him pretty well, don't you?'

'Don't you think there's a risk of his smelling a rat? He still mightn't know anything of our plans.'

'That's true – we'd better just hope for the best, and hope they don't go for our route. It's still bloody cold.'

And we left it at that. I phoned Mike Thompson and Tony Greenbank, arranging to meet the next Wednesday, and then went through agony, imagining that the rival team might be on our climb.

At last Wednesday came, and Tony and I drove down in my Minivan. It was still very cold and a fall of fresh snow covered the hillside and car park. Our route looked reassuringly virginal, but how could we be sure until we had made a closer investigation?

There was no point in repeating the lower part, and so we abseiled down our escape route, to a small and uncomfortable stance immediately below the overhang. Mike Thompson was looking ill, and complained that he still had not recovered from 'flu, but none of us took much notice; we were too intent on trying to complete the climb, and I was already tensed by the thought of that big, seemingly precarious shield of rock that I would have to swing round.

Reaching it fresh, at the beginning of a day, it didn't seem quite as frightening as on the previous occasion. The peg I had left by the side of it was still there, and somehow, because it was already in place, seemed sounder than when I had first hammered it in. The Shield looked more solid. Even so, I didn't like the idea of swinging round it, hand over hand. I tapped a piton into a crack in the middle of the Shield – it didn't shift at all – clipped in an étrier and gingerly put my weight on the rung. If it does come down, I reasoned, I should be swung to one side by the rope, out of its path, and with this prayer I trusted my weight to the step of the étrier, reached round the other side of the Shield, and swung across, on to a small ledge the other side. These days, the move is made free by a hand traverse over the top of the Shield. It has stood the test of time, and is probably as solid as the cliff it is cemented to – but on a first ascent, you view the rock in a different perspective, everything being unknown, untried. As a result, you, the climber, are keyed up to a degree unknown if you are following a guide-book ascent. There is always the doubt as to whether the next move is possible, the worry of how to get back down if it isn't. And that is the joy of making first ascents – one way we can taste the thrill of exploration on our cluttered, over-developed planet – a pioneering experience that can be had above the Cheddar car park, on a cliff in Wales, or on a secluded crag in the heart of Scotland.

The groove stretched above me, both threatening and inviting. It looked hard. First, I had to set up a belay and bring Mike across. He had been feeling progressively more ill as I had teetered and struggled on the Shield.

'I don't think I'll be able to make it,' he called. 'I feel bloody weak. It'll be better if one of the others could do it.'

Tony Greenbank had been looking after John Cleare's rope while the latter took photographs, and so, after a lot of manœuvring, Mike and he changed over and Tony came across to join me. One of Tony's special charms, and a quality that makes him a brilliant second, is his enthusiasm and ability to flatter.

As he swung around the Shield, he kept up a constant barrage of 'Great, man, great. You must feel terrific about leading that.' 'This'll be the greatest route ever.' 'You're climbing fantastically.'

My ego swelled accordingly, and as we changed over the belays I had another look up the groove. It was vertical all the way, with a couple of small overhangs protruding, at about thirty and sixty feet. Surely, it couldn't possibly go free – or could it? There was certainly a good finger-jamming crack to start it; you could bridge out on either wall of the groove, which even on this vertical rock meant you could stay in balance.

I started out, wafted upwards by a barrage of enthusiastic praise by Tony. It was superb climbing – I could look straight down between my straddled legs, to Tony half hanging on his belay on the narrow ledge, and then on down to the car park, now nearly 300 feet below.

A few cars had stopped; Mike, below, tried to persuade their drivers to move out to a safe distance from the base of the cliff. But our figures must have seemed too remote to pose a threat. I reached a small ledge, with a boulder perched precariously on it. I couldn't possibly get over it without dislodging it, and perhaps hitting Tony.

'Look out, I'm going to drop a rock,' I shouted.

The onlookers just gawped.

'Get out of the way, I've got to chuck a rock down.'

They didn't seem to hear me – I had to push it outwards to get it away from my second. I gave it a heave, and it described a graceful arc down to the ground, landing with a resounding thud about twenty feet from the nearest parked car. The onlookers moved back to a respectable distance, and I continued climbing.

I had reached the first overhang – miraculously a hold appeared round the corner – a pull and I was up round it; more bridging, another nut runner in, the next overhang – concentration, yet a sensation of acute enjoyment, of being in control over mind and muscle. Another few movements, a ledge in sight, and it's finished. And then, a feeling of pure ecstasy, at the end of a superb piece of climbing. One more pitch that was interesting, but not as hard as the previous pitches, and we were on top of the gorge. We had completed our climb. What had started as a route for a television broadcast had turned out to be the most satisfying I have completed in this country. It had all the makings of a classic route. It was a magnificent line up a stretch of unclimbed rock; there was only the one escape on it, and somehow, that didn't detract from the feeling of commitment while climbing. Most satisfying of all, it had yielded almost entirely free climbing, with only the odd piton for direct aid or protection. In subsequent ascents by others, even this comparatively small level of aid has been eliminated.

The idea of the climb had been evolved from commercial motives, but did this destroy any of the pure enjoyment that one should experience from climbing? I don't think so. I have often been asked whether I can continue to enjoy climbing when I know I am dependent upon it for a large part of my income. I think this shows a confused interpretation of motives and values. I certainly couldn't tolerate teaching other people how to climb, or even taking less competent people climbing, as a guide. But it is not the payment which would spoil it for me, it is merely that I like stretching myself to my own limits in climbing, and one can only do that when climbing with someone of similar calibre.

To do the things I love doing and get paid for them at the same time seems the perfect answer and, I imagine, is the motive for professionalism in the majority of sportsmen. However, I was worried about one facet of this type of career: I disliked the idea of total dependence upon being a performer, or gladiator, in high-standard climbing. For a start, one's career would be limited to the period whilst at the top of the sport; and there was another objection – that of being pressurised into climbs which were outside the boundaries of risk that one was prepared to accept. I wanted to develop my own powers as a writer and photographer so that I should become more broadly based in my career.

But finding our way up the High Rock on Cheddar gave us everything that climbing can offer – even down to a bit of healthy competition, in the shape of the threat (which, in the event proved baseless), of someone else snatching our route from us.

Having got the route in the bag, we now had to wait until May, when we were due to climb it in front of the cameras. In the meantime, back at home in the Lakes, I was storming through the final stages of my book, and we were looking for somewhere else to live. We were tired of the inevitable restrictions imposed on anyone living in furnished accommodation and, not having enough money to buy a house, decided to try to rent an unfurnished cottage. But hunting for unfurnished cottages in the Lake District is like searching for the lost Grail. Having given in our notice for Easter, we were beginning to contemplate erecting our tent in a field somewhere, when at last our search bore fruit. I was tired of the South-West corner of the Lake District. It is very beautiful, but is outside the main climbing area. I fancied getting closer to Keswick, which is the closest the Lake District has to a climbing centre.

One morning, at the end of a wild goose chase to the north of Keswick, we saw an advertisement in the paper for a cottage at Kirkland, near Ennerdale. It was farther into West Cumberland than I had originally intended, and would obviously present problems in getting out of the Lake District to give lectures. Even so, we were desperate, and therefore went over to see it.

West Cumberland is a small world of its own, isolated to the west by the Irish Sea and to the east by Lakeland fells. As a result, it has developed its own special character, charm and problems. In the space of a few square miles are concentrated some of the most beautiful and remote valleys in the Lake District, rolling fell country where, even on a bank holiday, you won't meet anyone all day. As you approach the coastline, dead slag heaps rise from little mining villages of terraced houses, brave in the face of dying pits, with bright-painted door lintels and woodwork. On the coast itself, a trinity of industrial seaports combine some of the worst relics of indus-trialisation with a peculiar fascination of their own.

The route from Keswick to Kirkland goes through no-man's-land, between the fells and the industrial belt, through sleepy, unspoilt Cock-ermouth and then over a winding hedged road, to Cleator Moor and Egremont. Kirkland itself is like most of the little mining villages whose original purpose for being there has long vanished with the closing of the mines. It is a terrace of houses, perched on the crest of a hill, as if dropped there by a careless god. Somehow, they do not belong to the patchwork of pastures around them; are not sculptured into the land, as are Lakeland's farms and cottages. The road, fast narrowing, winds down a hill towards Ennerdale village. To the east is the great sweep of Ennerdale, with its lake and pine-clad slopes, which culminates in the rounded mass of Pillar Mountain.

Bank End Cottage was on a lane through two gates, tacked on to the end of a farm. This was part of the land, cradled in the arms of two grassy spurs that framed an ever-magnificent view of the hills around Ennerdale. The lake and valley bottom were hidden by dimpled hillocks to our immediate front, but above them rose the fells, a view more limited than the one from the road down from Kirkland, but in its way more attractive, with a tantalising quality of hidden secrets that I came to appreciate; and at Bank End Cottage we were to know a stronger feeling of homemaking than we had before experienced. But first, we had to rent the house. The owner lived at the farm at the end of the track – a quiet man, whose life, and probably those of his children, would be devoted to farming the land immediately around him. He had advertised the cottage at thirty bob a week. It had two bedrooms, a bathroom, kitchen, a big living-room downstairs, and a small dining-room to the side of it, which was tailor-made for my study. The staircase was a half spiral of stone; the floor was stone flagged; the walls three feet thick; there were small, deep-set windows and a low-beamed ceiling. Even the garden was perfect – a little patch of deep, sweet-smelling grass, bounded by a high hedge with an old wooden seat, softened with age and wood-rot, in the corner. The fact that there was only an Elsan for a toilet seemed unimportant when balanced with the beauty of the cottage.

'I've had twenty applications already,' he warned us.

'But we're desperate,' I replied. 'We've got to move out next week, and have nowhere to go.'

Fortunately, Conrad, now eighteen months old, was on his best behav-iour and looked cherubic.

'I'll have to think about it. Could you give me a ring at the end of the week?'

We were on tenterhooks. We phoned him that afternoon and offered £2 a week for the cottage. Whether this clinched the deal, or whether we had managed to capture his sympathy, I don't know, but at the end of the week he told us we could move into Bank End Cottage. We were to live there for two years, the first year of which was to be idyllically happy. Conrad was growing into a rare, self-contained, adventurous yet gentle child. We went exploring together in the fields around the cottage and I shall never forget one wild, windy day, when I took him in the papoose, and we walked over the fields to the open fell and climbed Murton Fell, a 1400-foot hummock. The wind hammered at our faces, and great grey clouds scudded across the rolling fields from the sea to break on the high fells of the Lake District. To the north we could see Ennerdale's slate-grey waters, torn with flecks of white by the fierce wind, and back below us, a mile away, our own haven, almost lost in undulations of the land. Then, back home to a coal fire and mugs of tea, to a cottage in which, slowly, we were implanting some of our own individuality. We had started with a single desk – the only piece of furniture we had owned at Woodland – slept on the floor, used a camping stove for cooking; then, slowly over the months, we picked up some furniture at sales and were given even more by relatives and friends.

Our proudest acquisition was our cat. He came with the cottage, but in fact, acquisition is the wrong description, for Tom Cat was more a distinguished guest than a pet. He was a magnificent tabby with a white blaze on his chest, who could boast that no one would ever own him. One morning, shortly after we had moved in, he walked through the door and gave a firm but courteous mew to indicate that he expected to be fed. Most of the time when we were at home he stayed with us, though on occasion would vanish for a few days at a time, always returning sleek and immaculately clean. When we left the cottage – even for quite long periods – a day or so after our homecoming, Tom would slide in through the door, plump, self-possessed and friendly in a remote kind of way.

It was shortly after we moved into Bank End Cottage that I went down to Cheddar Gorge to perform in the television broadcast. Wendy and Conrad came too, and we set up camp in a field in Cheddar Village. The broadcast was exciting in the sense that this was my debut as a climbing television performer, that I had to become accustomed to climbing with a pair of headphones crackling in my ears and that I had to talk while I climbed. We practised the climbs many times over, however, so that I knew every move backwards and, in the process, of course, lost a great deal of the spontaneity and adventure which, ideally, one should pass on to the viewer. But that first time, it was sufficient challenge in itself.

Our week at Cheddar was hectic and exciting. I was meeting and working with experts in the communications field; was constantly learning from them. The climax – the actual broadcast of the climb – becomes in a way, an anticlimax compared with those nerve-stretching moments in January, when we had made the first ascent. That, whatever the motivation initiating the attempt to climb the High Rock, had had all the ingredients of climbing adventure. The television performance was a job of work – but was an enjoyable, exacting and very interesting job. To me, the climbing took second place – there was no mystery, because I had done it before. The challenge was to try to put across to the lay viewer what climbing entails – not just the obvious sensationalism, but how I, the climber, feel, as I work my way up a stretch of rock which is commonplace to me, but unbelievably difficult and dangerous to the beholder.

Finally, to tidy up the whole affair, we had to think of a name for the climb. We decided to call it Coronation Street – because it was next to Sceptre, and we were doing the broadcast for ITV.

CHAPTER NINE

Rassemblement International

Things were looking up. At long last, a mere two years behind deadline, I had finished my book. My fee from the Cheddar broadcast provided a little money in the bank and I was full of ambitious plans for an Alpine summer, with some good partners to share them. In addition, Wendy was going out with me, and we had bought a large, Agincourt-style frame tent, especially for our family holiday.

And then, a few weeks before we were due to leave, I had a call from Tom Patey.

'I've just been nominated by the Alpine Club as the British representative for this year's International *Rassemblement*. They've left me to choose my companion. Joe can't make it this year, so I wondered if you'd like to come.'

I accepted immediately, arranging for Wendy to join me later, as planned. A holiday with Tom was guaranteed to be unusual, varied and exciting. The previous year, when Tom had been climbing with Joe, the arrangement had not been satisfactory since, as a team, they were so much faster than Robin Ford and myself. But this time Tom and I would be climbing as a team. In addition, we should be living it up, for the International *Rassemblement*, or meet, was based on the École Nationale de Ski et Alpinisme in Chamonix. The function was held every two years, and national clubs from all over the world were invited to send their representatives. I had already heard tales of superb food, free lifts on all the téléphériques, and free stays at the huts.

The international meet was due to start early in July, and I drove out with Tom. We had with us Tom's bible of potential new routes; in it were a few additions to the previous year's collection, the products of his ingenious research. The cuisine at the École Nationale lived up to its reputation, with succulent steaks for lunch, unlimited red wine and masses of vegetables. The actual meet was a cross between Noah's Ark, with pairs of different nationalities, and the Tower of Babel. Already a healthy element of competition was springing up between the big league climbers of the Alpine countries, fostered by the custom of listing everyone's ascents as they were made. This was a little like a league table, which we all examined with care as we decided what to do next. An ascent of the Bonatti route on the Grand Pilier d'Angle would have rated ten points, probably by virtue of the fact that it was by Bonatti and had not yet had a second ascent, while that of the South-west Pillar of the Dru, once the most prestigious of all Chamonix rock-climbs, was little more than a trade route, and therefore would only rate two points in the prestige stakes.

Climbing with Tom, I was on safe ground – he was interested in nothing but new routes, which really defied any imaginary point count system.

The range of ability assembled at the *Rassemblement* was impressive. From Italy came Roberto Sorgato, one of its finest climbers – among many other routes, he had made the first winter ascent of the North Face on the Civetta, and had also made a couple of attempts on the Eiger Direct – at that time the most outstanding unclimbed problem in the Alps. Never bothering to indulge in competitive stakes, he was happy to eat, drink and flirt with the girls down in Chamonix. Equally uncompetitive were a pair of Mexicans, with neat little black moustaches. They wore beautiful blazers bearing their mountaineering club badge, but had no climbing equipment at all. To every invitation by their French hosts to actually go out climbing, they replied that the hospitality of Chamonix was so delightful and they were gaining so much from meeting their fellow mountaineers that they were happy to stay within the confines of the École Nationale. We shared a room with two inscrutable, but immensely courteous Japanese.

The International side of things started well, with two Americans, Steve Millar and Lito Tejada Flores, going up with us to do a new route on the West Face of the Cardinal, an elegant little rock spire above the Charpoua Glacier. Having cut our teeth on a comparatively small peak, I was keen to get on to bigger things. Ever competitive, I had my eye on the international point count. Tom, ever easy-going, agreed, and we worked through the Patey bible.

'How about the Right-hand Pillar of Brouillard?' I suggested. 'Crew and Ingle failed on that last year. They couldn't even get to the foot of the Pillar.'

'Aye, that could be pleasant enough.'

The Right-hand Pillar of Brouillard, one of a trinity of three, is a rock buttress at the head of the Brouillard Glacier, the widest and most difficult glacier in the Mont Blanc region. Walter Bonatti had climbed the Red Pillar of Brouillard in 1958, and the chapter in his book devoted to this ascent comprises a hair-raising description of his crossing of the glacier and then dismisses the actual ascent in a couple of paragraphs – a tribute to the horrendous difficulty of the glacier. Crew and Ingle had fared no better, getting lost in a maze of giant crevasses, and finally, after falling into one, they retreated before even reaching the foot of the Pillar.

That afternoon, we happened to call in at the Bar Nationale, at that time the meeting point of all British climbers in Chamonix. Crew and Ingle were sitting at one of the tables.

'Just arrived?' I asked.

'Yes. Conditions aren't much good, are they?' Pete replied.

'Hopeless,' I agreed. 'What are you thinking of doing?'

'Probably push off to the Dolomites,' Pete replied.

'You might just as well; nothing's in condition.'

And then we had some beers and started talking about the south side of Mont Blanc. Tom, less competitive than I, even mentioned our interest in the South-west Pillar and then went on to suggest we joined forces. I kicked him under the table, and Crew looked nonplussed, muttering something about preferring the idea of climbing in the Dolomites, and shortly afterwards made his excuses and left.

'I'll bet you anything they're going for the Pillar,' I told Tom.

We crossed over to the south side of Mont Blanc the next morning, availing ourselves of the free téléphérique tickets given to us at the *Rassemblement*. At this stage, judging Crew by my own competitive values, I was convinced he was probably on his way to the foot of the climb. I was all in favour of going straight up to the hut and, if possible, stealing a march on them – unless, of course, they were already ahead of us. Tom, the traditionalist, was convinced that no one could be guilty of such overt competitiveness, and insisted that we seek out their camp site in the woods of the Val Veni, and proffer our invitation once again.

We found them in a woodland glade, just out of bed and, over a cup of coffee, we quickly agreed to join forces. It was midday when we got away, plodding through the richly perfumed pine woods of the Val Veni and then up the winding path to the Gamba Hut. It stood on a grassy spur running down from the Innominata Ridge of Mont Blanc, flanked by the frozen cataracts of the Frêney and Brouillard Glaciers. On the other side of the Frêney Glacier soared the West Face of the Aiguille Noire de Peutérey – a petrified brown-yellow flame.

On we tramped, past the new Monzino Hut, solid and lavish, with granite walls and plate-glass windows, to the shell of the old Gamba refuge, a little wooden and stone hut which seemed part of the fell-side. It had seen a thousand exploits – some victorious, some tragic. Bonatti, with his client Galieni, had staggered here that June day in 1961, through a blizzard, after four companions had died in their retreat from attempting the first ascent of the Central Pillar of Frêney. This disaster had highlighted just how remote are all the climbs on the south side of Mont Blanc. Now the hut had been superseded, and was already partly demolished. I was sad to see it go, for it seemed in keeping with the wild beauty of that outlying spur of Mont Blanc. The new hut represented civilisation's cloying encroachment on the fast-shrinking mountain wilderness, when even the climbing huts begin to resemble hotels. Gone was the crusty old pensioned-off guide, who lived in a little cubby-hole at the end of the single, dark bunk and living-room.

But the ruins of the old hut still stood and, to save money, we stayed there. Next morning we watched clouds scudding over the summit of Mont Blanc; the weather was obviously unsettled and somehow our little team had not coalesced into a determined group. Perhaps it was too early in the season, and we were insufficiently fit, and so we turned tail, went back to the valley and then returned to the flesh pots of the International *Rassemblement*.

The next fortnight passed pleasantly enough, with another new route on the West Face of the Aiguille du Midi, a sortie into the Vercors with the great French climber, Lionel Terray (tragically, to be killed in the same area only a few weeks later), then the final party to close the *Rassemblement*. All the climbing dignitaries of Chamonix attended, and a list of everyone's climbs during the fortnight was displayed, giving full vent and satisfaction to our competitive instincts. There was plenty of champagne, superb food, and Wendy, with a grubby and bewildered Conrad in tow, arrived half-way through the reception. She had driven out from England in our Minivan, with the girlfriend of a friend of ours.

They had had their share of adventures; a broken fan belt, just short of Dover, caused the car to boil dry before they noticed anything was wrong. Then, reaching the ferry only just in time, they were turned back because we had forgotten to have Conrad put on Wendy's passport. They ended up sleeping in the van while waiting for the Passport Office to open, and then, next morning –

'Have you the husband's consent to take this child out of the country?'

'But I'm going out to meet him. He's already in France.'

'But how do we know? I must have a letter of consent.'

Wendy, near to tears with fatigue and exasperation, then remembered that she had my most recent letter in her handbag. I had written that I was longing to see her. She showed this to the Passport Control man, and Conrad was duly entered on to her passport.

Across the Channel, half-way through France, it was getting dark when the dynamo failed. With lights getting dimmer, dazzled by oncoming traffic, they arrived at a garage whose owner allowed them to sleep on the garage floor while waiting for the mechanic to arrive next morning. At long last they drove into Chamonix. In spite of everything, although sweaty and a bit bedraggled, Wendy, in a mixture of tears of relief at finishing the journey and smiles at being with me again, looked fabulous. We all got happily drunk and then I smuggled Wendy and Conrad up to our room in the *Rassemblement*, to have one last night under a roof, before spending the rest of the summer under canvas.

Next morning we drove over to Leysin, in Switzerland, where we had arranged to meet Rusty Baillie. Rusty was a Rhodesian climber who had come over to Europe in 1963, immediately making his mark with the second British ascent of the North Wall of the Eiger, with Dougal Haston. I had met him in Zermatt immediately after he had made this ascent, at the time when Hamish MacInnes and I were trying to make our Matterhorn film. Having spent the previous year in Kenya, Rusty had been doing various odd-jobs, acting as a life-guard at a beach club, working as a game warden, and enjoying the hot sun.

High on the list of our possible objectives was the North Wall Direct of the Eiger. This had undoubtedly become the current Last Great Problem of the Alps – one of the most over-used clichés in mountaineering literature and talk. In recent times, a new last great problem has been found, attempted and solved, almost every year. European Alpinists were beginning to run out of unclimbed ground – every face and ridge in the Alps had been climbed and had at least one route up it. Wherever there was room for one, a Direttissima, or Direct Route, had been made, straightening out the original route to follow as closely as possible the imaginary line a drop of water would describe in falling from the summit. In many instances, in the Dolomites, these routes had been engineered by drilling a continuous line of bolts, making a mockery of the natural configuration of the rock, and the entire concept of the Direttissima.

The possibility of putting a Direct Route up the North Face of the Eiger, however, did indeed have the ingredients for being the true Last Great Problem in the Alps. No other wall in the Alps combines length, intricacy of route-finding and objective danger to such a degree – a fact grimly proved by the ever-lengthening roll of accidents on the face. True, the original route put up by Heckmair, Vörg, Harrer and Kasparek was not technically extreme by modern standards – there was no pitch on the climb harder than Grade V, one grade below the top grade – but this fact ceased to have much significance to a climber caught in a blizzard, or confronted by rock covered by a thin and treacherous covering of ice; and all too often the North Face of the Eiger was either caught by bad weather, or was in a dangerously iced condition.

Strangely enough, it was Sedlmayer and Mehringer, the first serious party to climb on the face who, in effect, made the first attempt on a Direct Route up the Eiger. In the summer of 1935 they embarked on the bottom rocks of the face and took a fairly direct line up to the First Ice-field, climbing the first rock barrier near its centre. (On all subsequent ascents this line was turned, by the Difficult Crack and Hinterstoisser Traverse, well to the right.) They reached the Flat Iron, a prominent prow of rock in the middle of the face, and there their luck ran out. Hit by a savage storm, probably knowing they could never have got down, they tried to sit it out, and were frozen to death – the first victims of the Eiger.

Their deaths at least taught those who followed that the Eiger does not lend itself to Direct ascents, for the strata stretch across the face in a series of smooth rock bands and ice-fields in the lower part of the wall, and in the upper part the lines are all diagonal, seeking to lead the climber to the edge of the wall. The route finally completed in 1938 was, therefore, essentially a wandering line, searching out the lines of weakness through this huge maze of ice-filled chimneys and galleries.

Climbers did not start thinking of a direct ascent until early 1963, though on my own ascent of the North Wall in 1962, Ian Clough and I caused a great deal of excitement amongst the ubiquitous watchers at Kleine Scheidegg, by losing the route in the upper reaches, and making one desperately difficult pitch, straight up towards the summit from just above the White Spider, before realising our mistake and coming back down.

In the winter of the following year, two Polish climbers, Czesław Momatiuk and Jan Mostowski, made the first recorded attempt to climb the Eiger Direct. They chose winter, hoping to reduce the objective dangers, since the Direct line also goes straight up the main line of stone-fall on the face. In winter the stones would be frozen into still silence. Following the Sedlmayer-Mehringer line, they were forced to turn back by bad weather at the start of the First Ice-field. Between 1963 and 1965 several more attempts were made by various leading European climbers, with little progress; no one did better than Sedlmayer and Mehringer, thirty years before.

From the start, the name Harlin had been closely linked with these attempts. He climbed the original route on the Eiger in 1962, a short time before Ian Clough and I made our ascent. His thoughts had immediately turned to the possibility of making a Direct Route, and he had camped below the face in the summer of 1963, but the weather had been too bad to make an attempt. He did, however, meet the Italians, Ignazio Piussi and Roberto Sorgato, who were also interested in the Eiger Direct. In the winter of 1964 he joined them, and two other Italians, in an abortive attempt, returning in the following June with the famous French climbers, René Desmaison and André Bertrand. They reached the top of the Second Ice-field before being forced back by bad weather.

Harlin had already made for himself a considerable reputation with a series of revolutionary new routes, using the newly-developed technical climbing techniques which had been evolved in Yosemite. Tom Patey drove over to Leysin with us, and sociable as ever, suggested we should call and see John Harlin.

At this stage I regarded Harlin as a potential competitor for the Direct route, and was a little defensive, perhaps, since he had already made several attempts, and presumably knew more of the problems than I. I had already heard a great deal about him – he was known in some quarters as the Blond God – a nickname not entirely affectionate, for his flamboyance and drive had made enemies as well as friends.

His house in Leysin was perched on the hillside overlooking the broad sweep of the Rhône Valley, with the Dent du Midi, standing like a Gothic cathedral on the other side of an empty void, hiding Mont Blanc: the Verte, Droites and Courts, whose snow-clad North Faces, white-etched with the black of distant granite, peered from behind the Dent du Midi, like three sirens tempting the climber to their cold touch.

We knocked and John opened the door. His title was well earned – he had a Tarzan-style physique and looks, from his blond hair to his thigh-sized biceps. He greeted us warmly, and ushered us into his big downstairs living-room. It was sparsely furnished with a few brightly coloured rugs and cushions scattered over the floor, a low settee and some big, bold, rather brooding abstract paintings on the walls. I learned later that these had been painted by John.

In the course of our conversation, my own suspicions quickly subsided – he appeared outgoing, frank, and immensely enthusiastic. I suspect that he had also viewed me with suspicion, as a potential competitor, but as so often happens, now that we met, antagonism vanished in a decision to join forces in our attempt on the Eiger Direct. We decided to make the attempt as a threesome, since I had already involved Rusty Baillie; we resigned ourselves to waiting until the end of the season, when the weather is often more settled, and the long cold nights reduce the stone-fall down the face.

John suggested that we should camp in the quarry immediately behind his house. We could get water from his outside tap, and even have the occasional bath. And so it was all settled, and things at last seemed to be slotting into place. We had a pleasant base for the summer, our team had been strengthened with John's inclusion, and now all we had to do was wait, and climb, until the weather was sufficiently settled for the big North Wall. Our routine in Leysin became a leisured round of sunbathing in the quarry, playing on the abundance of boulder problems the crag offered and, in the evenings, wandering up to the Club Vagabond, the social centre for most of the English-speaking people there. It had been opened some years before by Alan Rankin, a Canadian who had tired of travelling in Europe and wanted to settle down. He had seen the need for a non-institutionalised, free and easy hostel, to provide cheap accommodation for travellers, without any of the puritanical overtones which tend to dominate Youth Hostels. The result was the Vagabond Club. It had a bar, discothèque and comfortable bunk accommodation. Regular habitués, many of whom eked out a living by working in the Club, were mainly Americans, Canadians or Australians who had, at least temporarily, opted out of the rat-race. Its shifting population encompassed thousands of young people wandering round Europe. Some stayed a few nights, others longer. It was a good place to drink at night – if you were alone, there was an ever-changing supply of attractive girls and a timeless atmosphere of slightly aimless pleasure-seeking, one which could be satisfying for a short period, but which could, perhaps, cloy over a longer one.

In the following week I saw a lot of John Harlin, and came to know him well. He had an extraordinary mixture of qualities, mirrored, perhaps, in the contrasts of his life and career. He had always been a brilliant natural athlete, excelling at almost every game and track event in which he took part. Since his father was a pilot with TWA, he had had a nomadic child-hood, constantly on the move from one city to another in Europe and the United States. At Stanford University, where he first started serious climbing, he flirted with the idea of becoming a dress designer, even knock-ing on the doors of Balmain and Dior, to no avail, finally ending up at the other extreme as a fighter pilot in the United States Air Force. At university he had met and married Marilyn, an attractive blonde girl studying marine biology, and by his early twenties had two children, a boy and a girl.

He had made little impact on the American climbing scene, mainly because in the early fifties, when he was at Stanford University, climbing in Yosemite (which was later to become the cockpit of world rock-climbing) was still in its infancy. It was not until the late fifties and early sixties that a small group of American climbers were to develop fully the new equipment and techniques, which were to enable them to tackle the sheer granite walls of Yosemite, and then to revolutionise rock-climbing throughout the world.

John was posted to Germany in 1960, and it was in Europe that he established himself as a mountaineer. Strangely, he was not a brilliant natural climber. On a trip he made to Britain in late 1960, he climbed with Ron James, who, at that time, ran an outdoor activities centre in North Wales. John was at a loss on British rock, and did very little leading. In the Alps, however, his ambition was boundless. He walked to the foot of the Central Pillar of Frêney in 1961, at the same time that Don Whillans and I, with Ian Clough and the Pole, Jan Djuglosz, made our first ascent, and turned back only because there was already too big a crowd there, in the shape of a rival French party. In 1963, he established his reputation with his first ascents of the South Face of the Fou (in the Chamonix Aiguilles), and the Hidden Pillar of Frêney. John had been the architect, the driving force behind the venture, though Tom Frost, a brilliant Yosemite climber, had led the most difficult pitches of the climb. This was to be the pattern of many of John's ventures – he provided the inspiration and drive, often using climbers who were technically more skilled than he, to lead the key section.

Taking the step I had taken two years before, he left the United States Air Force in 1963 to become Sports Director of an American private school in Leysin. Even with Marilyn teaching biology at the school and, in fact, earning a higher salary than he, their incomes suffered a considerable drop from his Air Force salary. That summer of 1965, when I came over to see him, he had taken a further step in commitment, leaving the American school to start his own International School of Modern Mountaineering. With an impressive brochure and a few students, recruited entirely from the United States, the new school was launched.

He had invited Royal Robbins, one of the leading exponents of Yosemite climbing, to be chief instructor, and the two men, both prima donnas in their own right, could not have offered a greater contrast. John, flamboyant, assertive and impulsive – Robbins, very cool, analytical, carefully avoiding any ostentatious show, yet every bit as aware as John of his own position in the climbing firmament. The pair planned an attempt to make a super-direct route up the West Face of the Drus, a line which John had attempted on several occasions with a variety of weaker partners, with consequently little success. With Robbins he was to succeed, and in doing so, to complete a route which to this day ranks as one of the most difficult and serious rock routes in the Mont Blanc Massif.

After the climb, Robbins had devoted himself to running John's climbing school, whilst John himself put in spasmodic appearances, dreamed up new plans and snatched training climbs for our planned ascent of the Eiger Direct.

One such was on the Dent du Midi – a direct start to one of its ridges. The climb itself was undistinguished, but our way of climbing it was indicative of the nature of the team. We set out spontaneously after a fondue party in our tent in the quarry, which was followed by a long night's drinking. In the early hours of the morning, staggering back from the Vagabond Club, we noticed that it was a superb, clear night – the first for some time.

'We could do a route tomorrow,' I suggested.

'I know a new line on the Dent du Midi – how about trying that?' suggested John.

'How long would it take?'

'We could be up and back in the day, if we started early enough.'

'That'll have to be now. It's two o'clock already. We'll have to pack some gear, and we've got to get there.'

'What are we waiting for? Let's go.'

And go we did; having packed the sacks, we piled into John's Volkswagen bus, driving through the dark, down into the Rhône Valley and up the other side to the foot of the Dent du Midi. We reached the top of the road and walked through the woods to the sound of the dawn chorus, then up above the tree-line, and by seven in the morning we were at the foot of the vertical step in the North Ridge of the Dent du Midi, which had never been climbed direct. It was our intention to try out the American Big Wall climbing technique. In this technique the lead climber attaches the rope to a piton and then the second man climbs the rope, using jumar clamps. While he climbs, the leader can either rest or haul up the rucksack carrying all the gear for the climb. This was the technique we proposed to use on the Eiger, even though I had never used jumars before. We tossed up for who should have the first pitch, and I won. It gave pleasant straightforward climbing, leading up to a huge roof overhang. Rusty led the next pitch, disappearing round the corner of the roof and climbing a long groove. He reached the top. John was to follow him, being taken up on the rope, while I was to have my first try at jumaring.

'Nothing to it,' said John, as he climbed off the ledge, and disappeared round the corner. 'Just clip on, and swing out on the rope.'

The trouble was, the rope was going straight over the lip of the overhang which jutted a good fifteen feet outwards above me. We had scrambled several hundred feet up steep broken rocks before starting to climb and, as a result, there was a giddy sense of exposure. I clipped on to the rope and stood poised like a trapeze artist under the big top. Had Rusty secured the rope correctly? I had to trust him. Did it pass over any sharp flakes of rock? God knows. I hated the thought of committing myself to that slender strand of rope – was even more determined not to show I was frightened, especially to the Blond God – and so, with a shudder, I stepped off the ledge, and went spiralling into space. The rope dropped with a sickening jerk – it had been caught round a flake. My own heart, already pounding, seemed to plummet down into my stomach. And then my swings decreased – the rope was intact, and all I had to do was climb it.

I now discovered that the length of the slings, which connect the jumars to one's waist-loop and foot, is of vital importance. Mine were all wrong.

They were too long, and incorrectly proportioned to each other. As a result, climbing the rope, especially with a rucksack suspended from my waist harness, was a murderous struggle. Later, I learned that an essential precaution for any jumaring is to tie a knot in the rope, so that if the jumars do slip on the rope, you don't slide straight off the end. This was a precaution of which I had been blissfully unaware. Climbing with Harlin was a hard school – a constant game of Chicken, with no one prepared to call off first.

The rest of the climb was a romp, and we were back late that night, tired and happy, having completed a 2000-foot climb and having walked round the entire Dent du Midi – about fifteen miles in all.

And so the summer wore on – the Eiger Direct always in our thoughts, but the weather never settled enough for us even to think of going over to Grindelwald. Rusty and I did, however, attempt a climb which was to give one of the most tense and memorable experiences of my climbing career. There was a fine weather spell in mid-summer and John used this for his ascent, with Royal Robbins, of the Direct on the West Face of the Dru. Rusty and I decided to have another try at the Right-hand Pillar of Brouillard.

We sorted out our gear one morning, assembling our meagre supply of American pitons. I wanted to travel light anyway, hoping to get away with a fast ascent. So much of the pleasure of climbing can be destroyed if you are weighed down by too much equipment.

When John saw our equipment layout, he raised an eyebrow and commented: 'You guys sure do believe in travelling light.'

He was destined to be proved unpleasantly right.

CHAPTER TEN

The Right-Hand Pillar of Brouillard

And so through the Chamonix tunnel once again – car lights, psychedelic, wink in front, automatic speed controls flash their warnings, and we're excited, like small boys escaping from parental control. At the end of the tunnel, a distant blink of white suddenly rushes up on us, and we've passed under Mont Blanc – under a thousand million tons of rock, ice and snow, and back into the dazzling sunshine and a cloudless sky. This was the perfect weather we had been awaiting all summer. It was difficult to believe that it had ever been bad – could ever be bad again.

Before racing up to the old Gamba Hut we go to the little cable station which carries food and supplies, and send up our packs. Both Rusty and I are intensely competitive; there's already a tension in our relationship – I am the established climber, with sufficiently obvious weaknesses to make stardom questionable, while Rusty, the young climber still to establish himself, has enough good climbs behind him, together with the self-confidence gained from knocking around the world from an early age, to feel himself every bit as good as I.

I lengthen my pace, sweating hard, enjoying the undeclared competition. I have been out in the Alps a few weeks longer than Rusty and am therefore slightly fitter. Reaching the garish new Monzino Hut first, I am pleased at my hollow little victory. It is three o'clock in the afternoon, and I want to get high on the Innominata Ridge tonight, ideally to the little bivouac hut which is opposite the foot of our objective. Rusty, swept along by my enthusiasm, agrees, and we collect our sacks, leave the soft comfort of the new hut, pass the site of the old one, now sadly cleared down to its last timber, and start plodding up the long scree slopes leading to the crest of the ridge which bars the view of our objective.

A fine weather forecast aided my decision to press on as far as possible that afternoon, though this was hardly borne out by existing signs. An even ceiling of dark grey cloud clung to the top of the Pic Innominata and completely hid the main mass of Mont Blanc. From the crest of the ridge we could look down on the chaotic jumble of ice towers forming the Brouillard Glacier – obviously a place to avoid if we possibly could. The route up to the Eccles Bivouac Hut lay over comparatively easy-angled snow-slopes, below the crest of the ridge, up towards the Col de Frêney, and then up a slightly steeper slope. We could just discern the hut – a tiny box, clinging to the slope of the Innominata Ridge, just below the cloud ceiling. From there, we could see that a straightforward traverse led into the upper Brouillard Basin, from which we should be able to reach the foot of our Pillar.

We started wading through wet, sugary snow towards the Col de Frêney. This was obviously the wrong time of day to be crossing these slopes, but unless we wanted an unnecessary bivouac, we should have to keep going to reach the hut before dark. Reaching the Col de Frêney an hour before dark we were, finally, defeated. The steeper snow leading up to the hut was a bottomless morass of soft sugar, but having retreated to the Col we found a small island jutting out of the inhospitable snows, and settled down there for the night. At least the forecast had proved correct. As night fell the cloud ceiling disintegrated, and a myriad stars stabbed through it. It was reassuringly cold, always a sign of settled weather, and as dawn broke we began to cook our breakfast. Then began a chapter of accidents which were to dog our entire attempt. With frozen fingers I dropped the burner of our stove as I struggled to light it. I heard it trickle down into the dark void below. No longer did we have the means to melt snow for drinks – something that was even more serious than losing all our food. But it was a fine morning, and we couldn't possibly turn tail and return, so packing our sacks we started up towards the hut we had struggled so hard to reach the previous night. In the hard frost of the dawn, the snow was crisp and firm, crampons bit into it with a satisfying snick; no longer wallowing, we were able to move steadily, easily upwards, passing the hut, empty and silent, traversing across steep frozen slopes into the upper basin below the Pillar. We could now gaze across at our objective. The face of the Pillar was sheer, clean and dry, but the slabby flanks were dotted with snow patches and running with melt water. Cutting into the left-hand side of the face was a great clean dièdre, which ended in a number of huge roof overhangs, but to its left was a series of cracks that seemed to offer the easiest line. We resolved to try this.

Quickly, we crossed the firm snows that led to the base of the Pillar, and started up the broken rocks at its foot. These led to a steep rock buttress and two good pitches up a series of steep cracks which, in turn, led to a ledge that stretched across the Pillar. Above it, the rock stretched steep, smooth, seemingly impregnable. We traversed the ledge, trying to outflank this obstacle. Time slipped by. We were on the side of the Pillar; the rock, no longer red-brown and firm, was that dusty shade of grey that almost always means bad rock with a lack of crack lines. Suddenly, the climbing had lost its attraction, and we started fumbling around, wasting time in changing belays. We were hesitant, indecisive. It was now early afternoon, and we had still gained no height above our traverse line.

'This is no bloody good,' I said; 'we'll have to get back into the centre of the Pillar. At least there are some decent cracks there.'

As we travelled back into the centre of the Pillar, we felt hot, tired and thirsty. Looking up at the rock above, the line seemed obvious enough – up that big clean dièdre – but what about the overhangs above? We had lost too much time, and felt very small, weak and helpless as we sat on the ledge, still near the foot of the Pillar, in this remote spot.

'Let's bivouac here. We'll have a go at the groove tomorrow,' I suggested. Rusty didn't take much persuading, and we settled down for the night. A trickle of melt water gave us a little to drink, though barely enough to slake our thirst. Packets of soup and tea bags were a hollow mockery without the burner on the stove – but still, we had a good large ledge on which to sleep, and the weather seemed settled.

Next morning, we started up the gangway that led to the groove. Rusty led the first pitch up steep but perfect rock – the red granite of the south side of Mont Blanc is superb climbing rock. I followed up to the foot of the big groove. It curved up in a single sweep, just off vertical and without a ledge and hardly a single hold – only the crack in its back provided a mixture of hand-jamming and lay-back holds.

I sorted out some gear and realised just how optimistically light we had travelled. I had only four pitons large enough to use in the crack – over 200 feet of climbing; and what about those serried roofs above?

I set out, half-hearted, already beaten. I worked my way a few feet above Rusty, hammered in a peg, hung on to it, and stared upwards. The crack seemed endless, full of unknown threats.

'We just haven't got enough gear,' I shouted down.

'What are you going to do about it?' asked Rusty.

'There's only one thing – we'll have to go and get some more.'

Go and get some more! Go down 7000 feet of snow, scree and grass, all the way back to the valley and Courmayeur, just to get a few pieces of hardened steel – and then all the way back! That is what we did. We abseiled right down to the lowest rocks of the Pillar, for the way we had followed the previous morning was now being swept by a continuous hail of stones, dislodged by the afternoon sun. Abseil after abseil, until we were nearly down; nearly, but not quite, for between the foot of the Pillar and us was a monstrous bergschrund, a huge, mind-boggling chasm about fifteen feet across, with its lower lip about twenty feet below. The schrund itself vanished, seemingly bottomless, in dark shadows. Always frightened of jumping from heights, I hate leaping over crevasses. In theory, it is easy enough; you leap out on the rope, let it slide through your fingers and land on the other side. But what if it snags – if you miss the other side and go penduluming back against the sheer ice wall, to be left hanging in the void? I stood there, determined not to show Rusty how frightened of the jump I was. Pride giving me the necessary impetus, I leapt, reached the other side, let the rope go and rolled down the slope. Rusty followed, and we plodded back to the Eccles Bivouac Hut, to reach it just before dusk.

After sleeping in the comfort of a bunk, the next morning, in the dawn, we raced back down towards the valley. An afternoon was spent shopping for pitons, more food, and a burner for the gas stove. We were ready for another onslaught. We walked back up to the Monzino Hut that very same afternoon and spent the night in its lush comfort. No more wallowing in wet snow for us.

This was to be a serious, systematically organised attempt; we had a mass of high protein food; nuts, cheese, salami, chocolate, tea bags and tubes of condensed milk. The warden of the hut called us at three in the morning, with boiling water for our tea. Piling our gear at the side of the table, the food neatly packed in a single nylon stuff bag, we packed our rucksacks. We were being so methodical – so uncharacteristically efficient. I knew that Rusty had packed the food – he thought I had packed it – and we both left it, in its stuff bag, sitting on the table.

We set off through the night, head torches throwing small islands of light in a glittering black world as we progressed up the long scree slopes, cramponned across the snow slopes, and reached the Col de Frêney just as dawn broke – time for a first breakfast.

'Might as well have a quick brew,' I suggested. 'We've got enough food with us for a five-day siege.' We sat down and looked at each other expectantly.

'How about some cheese?' I asked.

'Good idea.'

'You'd better get it out.'

'But you've got the food.'

'Have I, buggery. You took it.'

'No, it was up to you to take it. I've got all the pegs.'

Recriminations followed quickly, each determined that it was the fault of the other. Having searched our rucksacks, we discovered we had six tea bags, a bag of sugar and a handful of almonds – we were back to normal – disorganised. But at least we had some means of melting snow for drinks, and enough pitons to climb the big groove.

The Right-hand Pillar of Brouillard

Swift easy movement over the hard, frozen snow was balm to our anger
and worry about the loss of the food. We soon reached the bottom rocks
of the Pillar and climbed to our highest point.

I set out, once again, up the groove. With sufficient pitons to hammer one
in every twenty feet or so, it no longer felt either so long or so committing as
before. It was certainly magnificent climbing. I ran out 130 feet of rope,
hung on a piton to bring Rusty up, and then led another pitch, up towards
the big roofs. The angle had steepened and the cracks had thinned down,
but the peg-climbing was straightforward, and I was happily lost in the
concentration that good, hard climbing always offers.

It was now Rusty's turn to lead. The way above was barred by the roofs,
and the only possibility seemed the crest of the buttress to our right. The
wall between was steep and blank and Rusty fussed around it. Holding the
rope I began to notice the passing of time and the big clouds that were
growing out of nothing in the blue air around us. Just afternoon cloud –
or something more ominous? The cloud line to the south, like the front
face of a giant tidal bore, seemed to carry a more serious threat, but with
its own wild beauty, enhanced by the very vulnerability and isolation of
our position. The maze of crevasses and chaos of ice towers in the Brouillard

Glacier were etched as black shadows drawn by the afternoon sun. Then, as the sun became diffused, blanked out by the fast-piling cloud, shadows also vanished, the snow and rocks around being flattened into menacing greys and whites by the even lighting.

The rope in my hand had gone still. Rusty had vanished round the corner. I cursed him, to myself, for his slowness and shouted:

'What are you doing? Have you reached a belay?'

But there was no reply.

At last – 'Come on, I'm belayed.'

The rope pulled in tight. I followed it, uncomfortably aware that if I did fall off, I should go spinning round the corner, as the rope was going away from me horizontally, offering scant support. Rusty was on a ledge round the corner; a crack line vanished upwards into the mist that now enveloped us. It was impossible to see if it led anywhere.

'I think this pitch is mine,' said Rusty very firmly. 'You had the two in the groove.'

'All right, but you'd better be quick, I think the weather's breaking.'

Rusty set out, hammering his way up the crack, at times nearly invisible as the mist swirled around us. I had sweated up the groove and now my clothes were cold and clammy. I shivered, cursed Rusty, and shouted up:

'If you can't get up any faster, you'd better come back down. We've not got long before dark.'

No reply, just the ping of the hammer. He was now sixty feet up. He paused, obviously enjoying himself, let out some rope and penduled back and forth across the face, trying to work out the best line. 'Bloody idiot,' I thought, 'what the hell does he think he's doing!' There was a roll of thunder in the distance to emphasise the danger of our position.

'It's great up here,' came wafting down. 'I think we can get across to the right. You'd better come up.' And so I followed.

It's strange: once you're out in front again, all fears vanish. We had nearly reached the top of the Pillar; a blank slab barred our way. I climbed a few feet, managed to place a peg and then tensioned out from it, working my way, though constantly pulled back by gravity, till I was able to reach a series of ripples in the smooth granite. I let go the rope and balanced up; six feet, and I was on a sloping ledge. Rusty followed up, and I began hunting for a way up those last feet. But our luck ran out. The mists suddenly turned to flurries of snow; snow ran down the rock, covering every hold and, in a matter of seconds, what should have been quite easy climbing was rendered impossible. The change had all the dramatic suddenness that makes mountaineering the exciting and exacting sport it is. At midday, we had stripped down to our shirtsleeves under a blazing sky. The transition from sun to blizzard had taken about three hours, but the final transition from cloud to scudding snowflakes had been instantaneous, turning a straightforward climb into a struggle for life.

I slithered down to the little sloping ledge, which was already banked up with snow, and we started preparing our bivouac, hammering in pegs, spreading the rope on the floor of the ledge to act as a rough cushion and insulation. It was now snowing too hard to think of dressing for the night, unless sheltered by the bivvy tent; so we got out our red nylon bag and Rusty got under it to get ready for the night. This meant slipping off his breeches to put on his long wool underpants, then removing his anorak to put on extra sweaters and a down jacket – the whole time being careful not to drop anything. The perpetual nightmare on any bivouac is of dropping your boots. I stood and stamped and shivered outside, as the storm which had hit us so quickly rose to a crescendo.

At last it was my turn to crawl into the bivvy sack. It was almost impossible to brush all the snow from my clothing – as fast as I brushed it off, more cascaded down from the rock above. Finally, I gave up and crawled into the tent-like sack – it was just a big bag of lightweight, proofed nylon, which we could pull over our heads. With me inside it as well as Rusty, there was hardly any room to move, let alone change my clothes. I managed to pull my boots off, slipped them in my rucksack and then pulled the pied d'éléphant over my legs, ending up with my feet in my rucksack.

By this time the storm had reached a new fury; it was nearly dark, and flashes of lightning lit the outside of the tent. Thunder crashed with ever-increasing reverberations. Our position was undoubtedly dangerous, but we felt a strange sense of security, almost contentment, while squeezed on that little ledge. The wafer-thin walls of the sack guarded us from the cruel talons of the wind and inside, uncomfortable though we were, there was an element of relative luxury, compared with what it could be outside.

We got out the gas stove and started melting snow which we collected from just outside the tent. We were already nearly buried in it on our ledge. After a few minutes, the flame went a dark colour, and then went out altogether. We had sealed ourselves in the sack too efficiently, and were fast running out of oxygen. The cold and snow gusted in, as we pulled up one side of the tent to admit some air. The flame of the stove flickered into life, and after half an hour or so we had a panful of lukewarm water in which to drop our precious teabags. The night passed slowly. We dozed, talked spasmodically, and tried to climb back up our sloping ledge, down which we were perpetually sliding. I thought (as no doubt Rusty also thought) about just how desperate our position was. There was the memory of the 1961 disaster, during the first attempt to climb the Central Pillar of Frêney, when four had died in a retreat after a storm very similar to the one which was striking us. There was, however, one big difference – we had the Eccles Bivouac Hut as a retreat – though even reaching that in a severe storm could prove a cruel test.

When morning came, the wind was as fierce as ever, and, to delay the moment when we should have to abandon the partial shelter of our bivouac tent to fight with tangled ropes and snow-buried gear, we had another brew and a handful of almonds. With no other excuse for delay, we struggled with frozen boots, and at last emerged from the sack into the full force of the wind. In an emergency like this, one must be very, very slow and systematic, checking everything twice, and three times, to ensure that knots are tied correctly, karabiners are clipped in, pitons secure. At last, with ropes untangled, a piton in place, we hurled the rope so that it disappeared down into the void. Rusty went first. There was a long delay – I couldn't hear anything – just stood shivering until the rope went slack. It must be my turn. I clipped in and started abseiling. We had never heard of the karabiner brake abseil, and were using the old-fashioned method, where you thread the rope through a karabiner clipped into a thigh loop, and then pay the rope over your shoulder. It offers the minimum of friction, and as soon as I launched myself out on it I realised there wasn't enough. The face of the rock was encased in wind-blown snow, the rope itself had an icy sheath, and I just went plummeting down, barely in control. It was just as well that Rusty had secured both bottom ends to a piton he had hammered in, otherwise I doubt whether I could possibly have stopped myself. How Rusty managed to stop himself, I just don't know.

'Nearly went off the end,' he stated tersely. There was no ledge, just a horizontal crack into which he had hammered a couple of pitons. We now suffered the nightmare: were we going to be able to pull down the doubled rope? We pulled one end; it jammed solid, and was so badly iced that even with jumars we could never have climbed back up to free it. We heaved again, and it gave a little, another pull and it started running through our hands. I threaded it through the piton for our next abseil as Rusty heaved. It was my turn to go down first, into the unknown.

Down and down we went in a succession of abseils, through the wind and snow and storm, building up a rhythm with a weird enjoyment at our sense of control in the face of the fury of the elements. I regarded Rusty in a new light. At ground level, even on the climb when things had been going well, many of the quirks of his personality had irritated me, in exactly the same way as I am sure I had irritated him. Now, confronted by the sheer scale of our struggle, we were closely united, and I was able to respect his calm, methodical approach to our problem.

We reached the great bergschrund at the bottom, hardly noticing its size as we leapt across and then groped through the white-out, towards the crest of the Innominata Ridge, where we knew the hut should be. But what if we couldn't find it? If we went too high or got on to steep ground? But then, in a break in the cloud, we saw the gleam of the tin roof below us.

We were tired and hungry, but with a few more hours to dusk, we kept on going down, hoping that the great piles of fresh powder snow would not avalanche under us. At the Monzino Hut, the guardian gave us a bowl of soup, but the goal of wives and food and sleep kept us going down, automaton-like, till we reached the valley and great mounds of antipasto, litres of red wine, and long, deep sleep. We had reached a point fifty feet below the summit of the Pillar, had come tantalisingly close to success, but somehow it didn't seem to matter. The experience had been exacting and rewarding, and at no time had either Rusty or I felt out of control of our own destiny, even though the margin for error was nil. This, perhaps, is what climbing is truly all about. You would never seek out the situation, but once in it, fighting your way out stretches nerves and mind and body to the limit, and in so doing brings new levels of awareness of yourself, and your companions.

We slept in the van and next day drove back to Leysin to two very worried girls. There, we had an interlude; the weather continued unsettled, and Rusty was getting married. He had met Pat, a practical, down-to-earth girl, while in Kenya – she had followed him to Europe. The ceremony took place in the Mayor's office and then in the church in Leysin; I was best man. Returning to John's house, we had a magnificent buffet lunch, prepared by Marilyn and Wendy.

Rusty did not have much time for a honeymoon. The weather improved after a few days, and we resolved to make another attempt at the Right-hand Pillar of Brouillard, this time increasing our team to four by including John and Brian Robertson, who had just arrived in Leysin.

Once again, the walk through the Alpine meadows, and up the steep path to the Monzino Hut; a night at the hut, and another dawn start – this one threatened from the beginning with auguries of bad weather. Wispy clouds of grey were playing round the dark sabre tooth of the Aiguille Noire, and an ominous mackerel-shaped cloud perched over Mont Blanc. It was too warm, and we wondered whether to set out at all, but the forecast was good and John, perhaps as a result of his Air Force background, had a fanatical confidence in the powers of weather forecasters. The ascent was untoward. This was the first big climb I had been on with John, and I liked the steady rhythm of his movement, the confidence of his decisions and his speed of climbing. We were on the same wavelength, climbing with the minimum of verbal communication.

We had reached the top of the Pillar by four in the afternoon; clouds, once again, were boiling up around us. Another storm was on its way. We left a rope in position for the other pair to follow up the last pitch of the Pillar, and began to climb together, up the broken snow-plastered rocks that led towards the crest of the Brouillard Ridge. Even when we reached that, we should still have over a thousand feet of climbing before we reached the summit of Mont Blanc. And as we climbed, the snow came gusting in, blanking out the peaks around us and enclosing us in our own little world. If we had just been a pair, I have a feeling we should have risked all and made a bid for the summit – we were climbing well and strongly enough. But there was no sign of the others – they were not as swift. So, with hardly a word exchanged, we turned tail and retraced our steps to rejoin them near the top of the Pillar.

Another storm-racked night in a small bivvy tent; a straight repetition of the previous experience, but now we were four and not two. We knew the way down, and our descent next day was merely an exercise in patience.

We had climbed the Right-hand Pillar, though total success still eluded us; we had not tasted that delicious moment when, on reaching the top of a mountain, the ground suddenly falls away on every side, and new vistas are opened before your eyes. We had been pinned within the close confines of the Brouillard Cirque, with its now familiar, magnificent views of chaotic icefall, the jumbled mass of the Pic Innominata, the split tooth of the Aiguille Noire and, to the south, the haze of the Italian foothills and the gentler peaks of the Gran Paradiso.

But we had gained all there was from the Right-hand Pillar, and we should not go back. Although we were supremely fit, ready for the Eiger Direct, and all it had to offer, the weather was not. August crept into September; October was approaching with commitments back in England.

There was no choice, we would have to delay our attempt on the Eiger Direct until the winter, and so, towards the end of September, Wendy and I took the tent down, packed the Minivan and set out for home. In some ways we were relieved to escape from the close confines of Leysin and from the demanding, all-embracing presence of John Harlin. For eight weeks I had been caught up in his dreams and plans, like so many others before me, having arranged to climb the Eiger Direct, help with the International School of Modern Mountaineering and with plans for a mammoth flight down through the Americas.

As we drove from Leysin, the spell lifted and the ideas seemed distant, far-fetched and improbable. Reality was the touch of Wendy, Conrad, and our cottage at the foot of Ennerdale, with Tom Cat waiting for our return. We drove hard on the way back, overjoyed to be in England once again. We couldn't wait to see our Lakeland hills.

CHAPTER ELEVEN

Eiger Direct: Preparations

Our return to the Lake District was like an escape from enchantment. Becoming too involved in John's fantastic schemes, I had felt my own individuality and freedom of action curtailed. From the sane quiet of Ennerdale, even John's winter plans for the Eiger seemed filled with question marks. For one thing, I had never climbed in the Alps in winter, and knew too little of the problems involved. John reckoned that the climb could take up to ten days in winter, and that there was usually a period, some time every winter, when the weather remained settled for ten or more consecutive days. My worry was the thought that you could not possibly tell, at the start of any one good weather spell, just how long it was going to last. What would happen if you got three-quarters of the way up the face after seven or eight days, and then the weather broke? Would you have the strength left to fight your way out or retreat – especially in a winter blizzard? I doubted it.

Nursing my doubts, I became involved in another expedition for the summer – to climb Alpamayo, a spectacularly beautiful peak in the Peruvian Andes. Conveniently, I put all thoughts of the Eiger Direct to the back of my mind, until one day in November the telephone rang:

'Is that Chris Bonington?'

'Yes.'

'My name is Peter Gillman. I work on the *Daily Telegraph* magazine and they want me to do a story about your planned route on the Eiger Direct this winter. Could I come up and talk to you? I'll bring John Cleare along as well, if I may, to take some pictures.'

'I suppose so. When do you want to come?'

'Day after tomorrow, there isn't much time.'

As I put the phone down, all my doubts welled up. This would commit me to the climb and, in facing this commitment, I realised just how worried I was about the entire concept. I could not bottle it up any longer and expressed my doubts to Wendy; doing so rendered it impossible for me to go on.

Wendy has always been prepared to accept any climbing project, providing she can sense that I am confident about it, but it would have been too much to have expected her to be stoical about something with which I was so obviously very unhappy. Quite apart from this, my own uncertainty rendered unwise any attempt to carry through such a scheme. This one seemed all wrong, somehow. Although I had complete confidence in John Harlin as a mountaineer, and had struck a rare accord with him on the Right-hand Pillar of Brouillard, I was less certain about his practical planning ability. With these doubts already in my mind, talking to a journalist about the planned climb would be impossible – I couldn't possibly let him see them. On top of this was the worry of becoming a gladiator, at the mercy of the watching public. It is one thing to exploit the interest of the media, and through them, the public, to carry out something you truly want to do, but quite another to feel forced to go on a climb about which you are not happy, because you have publicly committed yourself to do so. I was, perhaps, trapped in the cleft stick of the professional mountaineer, faced with the pressure to climb for the sake of a position in the climbing firmament, and it was a position which I abhorred. After an agonising day of indecision I rang up Peter Gillman to tell him that I had decided to withdraw from the climb. At the same time, I wrote to John telling him how I had let him down. It was now early November and he was not going to have long to find a replacement.

There followed a very flat few weeks. I had the nagging feeling that in standing down I had dropped out of top-class climbing – that, for the first time, I had rejected a climbing challenge at a time when my ability as a climber was my only tangible asset. As a writer and photographer I had had published only one short article in the *Daily Telegraph* magazine, together with a couple of pictures.

Just as my morale reached its lowest ebb, I had a letter from John Anstey, editor of the *Daily Telegraph* magazine, asking if I would be prepared to act as the magazine's photographer covering the climb. Having bought the exclusive rights to the story, they planned to send Peter Gillman out as their reporter, but wanted to get pictures from the side of the face and to have someone to meet the team on the summit, should they prove to be successful.

Suddenly, everything had changed. This was the very chance that I had been waiting for. I should be able to use my ability as a climber to exploit a creative skill which could put my entire career and life on to a sounder, and what seemed to me a more worthwhile course. I accepted immediately, and it was arranged that I should fly out to Switzerland as soon as John was ready to start climbing – probably sometime early in February.

Other opportunities then presented themselves. The BBC wanted to put on another live climbing broadcast, this time on the steep cliffs of Anglesey. Presumably as a result of my performance on Coronation Street, Chris Brasher, who had masterminded the BBC's outside broadcasts from the very start, approached me asking me not only to perform in it, but to help find a suitable site for the broadcast as well.

I was to meet him on the weekend of the 7/8th February 1966, on Anglesey, above the South Stack Lighthouse. The trip was ill-fated from the start. Wendy and Conrad came with me and we drove down early on the Saturday morning. Our little Minivan was now four years old and had done just under 100,000 miles. It was fast falling to bits, and on the way it developed some kind of distributor trouble. In spite of three years in the Royal Tank Regiment, and a driving and maintenance course, my mechanical ability has never gone further than opening the bonnet, pulling at wires and, finally, kicking the vehicle in exasperation, hoping that this would make it go.

We reached Holyhead that evening only to find that the BBC team had long departed. Tired and bedraggled, with Conrad bored and whining in the back, we drove to the Pen Y Gwryd Hotel, where the recce team were staying. We hardly had time for introductions when I was called to the phone. It was the *Daily Telegraph* magazine – John Harlin had just informed them he was about to set off for the face; could I fly out first thing the next day? John Cleare, a member of the recce party, drove me to Holyhead that night to catch the midnight boat-train to London. Leaving Wendy in the Pen Y Gwryd Hotel with a lonely bed, I was in the air by ten o'clock the next morning on my way to Zurich. I couldn't help being wildly excited at the prospect of covering the climb, and had no regrets about not being a member of the climbing team.

I reached Kleine Scheidegg that evening; there seemed little risk of the team having set off, for the sky was covered by a scum of high grey cloud, and the forecast was bad. The team, which numbered three, were comfortably installed. Dougal Haston and Layton Kor had joined Harlin and I found them all in the room which had been allotted to them, at cut rates, by Fritz von Allmen, the hotel proprietor. It was an attic in one of the outbuildings and presumably was used for putting up his staff.

I only knew Dougal in passing, and had never climbed with him. On early acquaintance he seems silent and withdrawn – even contemptuous of others. He dresses with an almost foppish elegance, in a very mod style, but any risk of effeminacy is avoided in the cast of his features. His eyes are hooded, his face long and somehow primitive – a strange mixture of the sensual and the ascetic. Relaxed to the point of laziness, he has a single-mindedness which, when the need arises, enables him to direct his entire powers in the desired direction.

Layton provided a complete contrast. Over six feet in height, he reminded me of a big, awkward cowboy in some kind of Western comedy. He had the biggest hands I had ever seen, and they were constantly in motion, drumming on the table, clasping and unclasping – not so much from nervousness, more as a culmination of restless energy which could not be contained. In background, Layton and Dougal were very different. Dougal, the son of a master baker, had studied philosophy at Edinburgh University, had been bitten by the climbing bug and as a result had never completed the course. Even so, he was basically an intellectual, widely read, intro-spective and essentially philosophic in his interpretation of life. Layton, on the other hand, was a bricklayer, never aspiring to much else other than his own climbing. Whereas Dougal gave the impression of being completely self-contained, Layton was like a big, slightly mixed-up puppy, in need of love and care. He was a brilliant rock-climber and was one of the few American climbers, outside the small Yosemite bred and trained group of climbers, who had actually tackled routes in the Yosemite Valley. As a potential member of the Eiger Direct team, I found him intriguing, for this was to be his first taste of winter mountaineering and he knew even less about it than I.

They made me welcome and told me that the face had been in perfect condition a few days before, but that the weather pattern had now changed, leaving them to wait until it was more settled before making their push. This suited me; I was in the pay of the *Daily Telegraph*, staying at a com-fortable hotel, with some of the best skiing in Europe on the doorstep – and I was very happy to spend a week or so skiing. There were problems, however. My relationship with John was no longer as easy as it had been, now that I had split loyalties between my paymasters and the team. I was the middleman. John wanted me on their side, getting as much support from the *Telegraph* as I could for the team. On the other hand, as rep-resentative of the *Telegraph*, I was hopeful that this would be the first of many assignments and I also wanted to ensure that my masters had a fair deal. This strain grew as the days slipped by without any sign of the promised spell of fine weather. I was becoming increasingly worried about the chances of the team. They had collected an impressive array of food, gear and clothing, but it seemed an awful lot for three men to shift up the face. John, recognising this fact, bent his own climbing ethics. The weight of the gear would have been particularly awkward on the lower part of the face, which was comparatively straightforward with long stretches of snow slopes broken by ice walls. At the top of this section, at the base of the First Rock Band, was the window of the Eiger Station. This was an eternal contradiction on the biggest, most unattainable wall in the Alps – that a man-made tunnel should spiral its way up inside the mountain, with a peephole from which the curious could gaze out on to the face.

John saw a way of utilising this. If we took all the gear up on the train, we could lower it out of the window and leave it there, thus saving two to three days' hard work, ferrying it up the lower part of the face. These two or three days could, at the end of the climb, prove crucial. This was the argument: they were trying to climb the face in the most aesthetically pleasing manner, not by laying siege to it with thousands of feet of fixed rope, and therefore, surely, they should be allowed to make their own rules. I wondered. If you want to lower gear out of a window, why not use the train yourselves and start the climb at the window? But it was their climb – not mine; it was they who were going to take the big risks once they set forth up the Rock Band. So I suppressed my own doubts and, one afternoon, with Dougal, caught the train up to the Eiger Station and lowered three rucksacks, full of gear and food, out of the window. And there it stayed – for the weather still showed no sign of improving.

We skied, did a few practice climbs on the little pinnacles above Eiger Gletscher, drank in the Gastubel in the hotel and, on occasion, danced to the stolid, slightly Teutonic music pumped out by the three-man band resident there for the winter. February was drawing to a close – and I began to wonder whether the team would ever get off the ground – when the weather showed signs of improvement. Then John had an accident. He loved being the centre of attraction, dropped easily into Tarzanesque poses, and enjoyed showing off the odd feat of strength. Skiing down the Lauberhorn, he tried balancing on only one ski, tripped and dislocated his shoulder – the Blond God immobilised! The team decided to retire to Leysin to lick their wounds, leaving me to hold the fort in Kleine Scheidegg.

A couple of mornings later, one of the waiters called me and told me that someone was starting up the face. Looking through the powerful binoculars kept by the hotel proprietor outside his private sitting-room, I saw a number of tiny figures at the foot of the Wall. One was undoubtedly starting up the first pitch. John had warned us that a German group was also preparing for the climb but we had never taken the threat seriously, having also heard that the team numbered eight. This was a ridiculously large number for an Alpine route – where on earth would they find sufficient bivouac spots for a team of that size? And so we had tended to discount them. But there they were – actually starting on our climb whilst our men were in Leysin with John out of action for some days to come. I telephoned him immediately. Though non-committal, he said they would return to Scheidegg immediately.

'You might as well get over there and have a look at what they're doing,' he suggested. Next morning I skied over – rather diffidently, since I am a very poor and timid skier – not at all sure of the kind of reception I could expect from the rival team. My fears were justified, for when I tried to get close enough to photograph them, one of their members started throwing snowballs. Retiring to a respectable distance, I carried on taking my pictures with a long-focus lens.

It didn't take long to work out why they had a team of eight. Their entire concept of the climb was different from ours. It was obviously their intention to lay siege to the face, fixing ropes as they went, hauling up a mass of gear. Superficially this seemed a logical approach, for they were able to start out up the face even though the weather forecast was poor and snow was falling, while we had been sitting impotent at the foot of the wall for three weeks, and might well have remained there for another three, before starting it up. I was impressed by the systematic approach used by the Germans – it was obviously slow, but nevertheless very effective.

That night I told John what I had seen, and we determined to start climbing the next day. John was still out of action, and so Dougal and Layton were to climb up to the base of the First Band in order to start finding a route through it. I led them across to the foot of the face the next morning, and waved goodbye as they started up the fixed ropes left by the Germans the day before. Following these for about 1500 feet, and using them part of the way, they made their own route in places. They reached the foot of the Rock Band in early afternoon and Layton started up. It presented very difficult piton-climbing and from a distance it looked completely blank – but this was the kind of climbing at which Layton excelled. At ground level he seemed gangling and awkward, barely able to control his great limbs whereas on rock he came into his own. He had an extraordinarily good power:weight ratio for a man of his size, with a delicacy and precision of movement that was a joy to behold. On the Rock Band he discovered tiny pockets in the rock, filled them with little wedges of wood and then tapped in a peg. He spent all afternoon making about thirty feet of progress and then retired to the small ledge that Dougal had cut out of the snow immediately below the Eiger Window.

That night the weather broke and they found themselves in the direct path of a constant torrent of spindrift which came pouring down from the upper reaches of the face. It penetrated behind their tent, and pushed them inexorably off their ledge, till they were hanging from their ropes. Inside a bivvy tent in bad weather it is almost impossible to remain dry – breath and steam from cooking condenses on the walls and inevitably runs into clothes and sleeping-bags. By morning their gear was soaked through, and they were beaten. They baled out at dawn and fled back to the valley. The Eiger – and the Germans – were winning.

The following day the weather improved and the Germans were back on the face, where they continued to work their way slowly up to the foot of the First Band. They dug out a snow cave immediately beneath it and this was to prove to be the secret of survival on the face. A tent bivouac sack is of limited use, since once the weather breaks, it is almost impossible to remain dry inside one – as Dougal and Layton had just discovered to their cost. In a snow hole, however, it doesn't matter what the weather does – once the cave is dug you can remain inside it for as long as your food lasts. There are no condensation problems and there is an inexhaustible supply of water from the snow that comprises the walls. Even if there is a hundred-mile-an-hour gale outside, the air is quiet inside the cave and the temperature remains the same – just below freezing mark.

But we still had to learn the snow-hole game. It was becoming increasingly obvious to me that our little team of three was inadequate for the style of siege operation which was seemingly essential if we were to have any chance of success. At the very least we needed four – two men to go out in front to make the route, and place a continuous line of fixed ropes, and two men to ferry loads behind. The entire concept of the climb had changed and with it my role. Before, there was no question of my venturing beyond the bottom of the face, since the team planned to cut adrift from the bottom and make a single push for the top. Now, with a continuous line of fixed ropes it was possible for me to go very much higher up the face, getting better photographic coverage of the climb and, at the same time, helping the team by being a fourth man. When they got high enough to make their bid for the summit, I could then either come back down again or accompany them all the way to the top. At an early stage of the climb, John had invited me to join them fully, but though I toyed with the idea, I never felt totally committed to the climbing; whether because of the strength of my own interest in the photographic coverage of the climb, or an awareness of the risk-level still involved in that final push, I am not at all sure. Having got out of the project once, I never really felt like committing myself totally to it again. Nevertheless, there was a part-commitment. We now had to adapt to the Germans' siege tactics, digging a snow cave at the foot of the Rock Band and laying siege to the Band. They had already started at a point about 200 feet to the right of the Eiger Station window, up an obvious fault. The line Layton had chosen was very much more direct, and also looked considerably harder. Layton, Dougal and I set out in the early hours of the 28th February, for the foot of the face. The Germans were already ensconced below the Rock Band. We climbed the fixed ropes of the bottom third of the face in the dark, reaching the foot of the rock-wall in the dawn. Whilst Layton climbed, and Dougal held his rope, I was to dig a snow hole. The first problem was to find the right kind of snow. I needed compacted old snow of sufficient depth to tunnel into till I reached the rock, and then to be able to make a room large enough for four to sleep in. It had to be in a place where the hard underlay of ice was well covered, for it is near-impossible to cut away large quantities of ice – in winter it is much too hard and it would take all day to dig away a small ledge, let alone a room.

I was learning the hard way. We hadn't thought of taking a shovel and I quickly discovered how inadequate an ice axe is as a tool for digging. But how about the Germans, next door? They had dug a vast cave which they called the Ice Palace. They had everything, and were sure to have a shovel. Could I ask them? If so, would I make our team beholden to them? What would John think of that? We were still deeply suspicious of each other and had had only the briefest of conversations to determine some kind of *modus vivendi* on the face.

We had agreed that both parties should use the line of fixed ropes from the bottom up to the foot of the Rock Band. Thus far, honours had been fairly even, for although the Germans had made the bulk of the route in the first 1500 feet, Dougal and Layton had climbed the last 500, which gave, technically, the most difficult climbing. Now we had chosen separate lines, ourselves going for a series of ice gullies once we had reached the top of the First Band, and the Germans heading up the line of a rock buttress to its right. The big problem would come above the Flat Iron Bivouac, in the upper part of the face, for there seemed only one feasible line up this, and whoever got there first would be able to stay in the lead. It was like Patagonia all over again, with our team once again outnumbered. This was not mountaineering in the pure, uncompetitive sense, but there was no doubt that the competitiveness added a touch of spice.

But now, on a more practical level, I wanted to borrow a shovel from our competitors – but should I? No, it could possibly put us in their debt; and so I chipped away with my miserable little axe for another half-hour. Or could I? What harm was there in it, anyway? They could only say No. Finally, I made up my mind, swallowed pride and crawled out of the short burrow I had dug, to borrow from the hated next-door neighbours.

There was a purr of a petrol stove from their burrow; a delicious aroma of fresh coffee wafted from its entrance. I poked my head through. 'Guten Tag.'

A grunt.

There was only one of them in the cave, looking very comfortable wrapped in a sleeping-bag on a foam mat. I tried some English. 'Do you think we could borrow your shovel?'

'I don't know at all. Why didn't you bring one up yourselves?'

'We never thought of it.'

'Perhaps this will make you think a little better before you set off,' he said, sounding very self-satisfied – the cat teasing the mouse. It was time to start a different tack – if he was going to be pompous, then two could play at that game!

'Don't you believe in some fellowship amongst mountaineers? I know you're not particularly glad that we're here, trying to do the same route as you, but what possible difference to the eventual outcome can it make if you lend me your shovel? It'll just make it either easier or a hell of a lot slower for us to dig out a bloody snow hole.'

'I cannot possibly let you have the shovel before consulting my colleagues,' he replied. 'I shall be talking to them on the walky-talky in an hour or so, and shall let you know then.'

I returned, mortified and very angry, to our miserable little burrow and vented my feelings on the snow – every blow of my axe plunging deep into a Teutonic head. The trouble was, you needed an awful lot of axe blows to clear very little snow. About ten minutes later, there was a little cough from behind me. I turned, and there, wearing a wicked little grin, was the German. I was to learn later that it was Peter Haag, co-leader of their team: 'I have been thinking; it is petty not to let you have the shovel. I haven't waited to ask the others. You can use it if you want – come and have some coffee cognac when you've finished.'

We had begun to establish a sensible relationship on the face, and as time went by, and we got to know each other as individuals, our lurking sense of competition was accompanied by a growth of real friendship. Peter was one of the few members of his team to speak good English. He had recently finished a degree course in engineering, and was a cheerful happy-go-lucky individual who could never have maintained a savagely competitive stance for long. Jorg Lehne, his co-leader, on the other hand seemed the typical Teuton – harsh in manner with a limited, beer-cellar style of humour, competitive to the end.

Peter and I talked for a bit until, with renewed vigour, I set to work on the snow hole with my borrowed shovel. It made all the difference. You could use the blade of the spade to shape out big blocks, and then could shovel them out from behind quickly and easily. By the end of the day I had a room big enough for two. From time to time I climbed out of the hole to photograph Dougal and Layton. Dougal was belayed about half-way up, hanging from a piton and, above him, Layton was slowly and methodically pegging his way up the wall.

Climbers are never easily impressed by the progress of others, but Layton's ascent was truly amazing, for the rock appeared to be completely blank, with no cracks for his pitons. Most climbers would have drilled holes for expansion bolts and, in fact, the Germans used several on what seemed an easier line round the corner. This big, gangling man, however, who seemed so ill at ease and awkward on the ground, was in his element, using every little weathering he could find on the surface of the rock. After taking a few pictures, I returned to the hole to dig out some more snow.

The weather seemed to be getting a little worse. It had started with a perfect dawn: a carpet of cloud at our feet shut out the intrusion of Kleine Scheidegg, its railways and ant-like skiers; overhead the sky was a clear pale blue. But the weather can change fast on the Eiger, and is always unpredictable. A line of high grey cloud had raced in from the west, settled on the summit rocks, and imperceptibly had slid down the wall. A few snowflakes drifted lightly round the grey air – first a flurry and then a steady fall. In a matter of minutes, the spindrift avalanches began to career down the face, their augur a dark shadow, a sibilant whisper, and then an all-penetrating, suffocating downpour of snow crystals infiltrated every chink of clothing and froze any exposed skin. It piled on top of the climber, trying to take him down, down, down into the snows at the foot of the wall.

Climbing was impossible in these conditions. Dougal and Layton started to bale out. Worried about them, I looked out of the hole. I could hear shouting, didn't want to leave the shelter of the hole, but the calls became insistent, with a raucous quality of emergency. I swung out on to the fixed rope and worked my way across in a lull between avalanches. Dougal was about a hundred feet above me, hanging upside down!

'I'm stuck,' he announced, very matter-of-fact. 'The bloody rope's jammed. I think I'll have to cut myself free. Can you get a knife?' At this point he disappeared in another spindrift avalanche. I hunched into the snow, waiting for the worst of the torrent to rush past and then swung across to the Germans' snow hole to borrow a knife. Dougal must have been hanging for about half an hour before I managed to tie the knife on to the end of the rope for him to pull up. His position was still risky. Had he made a single mistake, cutting the wrong rope, or unclipping himself incorrectly, he would have fallen, with little chance of survival. He suc-ceeded in cutting away the jammed rope, and got back to firm ground. A few minutes later, Layton, frozen solid and tired from his nerve-racking climb, joined us.

'I've had enough, man,' he told us. 'I'm going back down till this stuff clears up.' At this, he plunged down the fixed ropes and soon vanished in the swirling snows. Dougal and I decided to stay up there, spending the rest of the afternoon digging out the snow hole. Outside, the snow was gusting in a high, blowing wind, but inside we were happily unaware of it. Snow holes were, undoubtedly, the secret for tackling big walls in winter.

Next morning, on finding the snow scudding down the face, we did some more digging, to make the cave big enough for four, afterwards retreating to the bright lights of Kleine Scheidegg. The contrast was, at one and the same time, confusing and yet attractive. On the face life was simple – merely a question of survival. From there, the tiny black dots of the skiers skimming down the Lauberhorn and round the Eiger Gletscher Punch Bowl, were as remote from us as if we had been on another planet. Nearer at hand, the tourists who gazed down at us from the Eiger Window, like so many people goggling into an aquarium, were completely removed from our own private world of wind, snow and rock. What was real – their world or ours? I suspect it was theirs. Back at Scheidegg, we were still in a make-believe atmosphere – this time with a touch of MGM or Paramount included – a world of glamour-story fantasy, of Chateaubriands for two, eaten by one hungry climber, of bucketfuls of champagne, all paid for by the *Daily Telegraph* magazine, and the endless interest of the press and tourists.

This kind of atmosphere is meant to be totally abhorrent to climbers and climbing – men of the mountains should be seeking the quiet of the hills, escaping from the vainglory of press coverage – yet I wonder. My position was different from that of the other three. I was part of the media; was the exploiter rather than the exploited and, I must confess, I thoroughly enjoyed it, with the excitement of calls to London and the challenge of getting film, taken on the face, back as quickly as possible. Pete Gillman shared in his side of the story. His own report was factual and accurate. Certainly in no way did he sensationalise the story as so many reporters working for the popular press are tempted to do. Was what we were doing against the interests of mountaineering? I don't think so. It certainly made a lot of people aware of what climbing can be like. Some elements of the press played on the level of competition which undoubtedly existed between our team and the Germans, but this, in fact, was a competition that was slowly being reduced through our growing knowledge and interdependence upon each other during the climb itself. This also came through slowly in the press reports.

I sometimes wonder how John, Dougal and Layton felt about it all. John, undoubtedly, revelled in it. This did not mean that he was doing the climb solely for honour and glory – his love of the mountains, his need to extend himself to the limit, to find new horizons, went much further than that – but the glory was part of the attraction, as it is with most men.

Dougal on the other hand – silent, introspective – went through it all as though hardly aware of it. I think he accepted the circus at the bottom of the mountain for what it offered him – a comfortable bed, limitless food and booze – the means to carry out his ambition, to stretch himself to his own limits on the face. And Layton, very much the same, had the least ego-drive of the three. He just liked climbing, finding a fulfilment of his abilities and confidence in himself on a vertical rock face which he did not find in everyday life. At Kleine Scheidegg he ate huge meals, paid long and earnest court to the attractive, but perhaps a little straight-laced postmistress at the station and, after a few days, became impatient to do something – go up on the face – go skiing – go to Leysin – it didn't matter, but Layton was always searching, a little lost, with a touch of indefinable pathos in his make-up.

In those early stages of the climb we yo-yoe'd back and forth between Kleine Scheidegg and the Rock Band, forcing a few more feet, and then retreating through the bad weather. There was always the temptation of the comfort of the hotel. The only man of either team who firmly rejected this indulgence was Peter Haag, who steadfastly stayed on the face, living in the Ice Palace.

Back at Kleine Scheidegg, our own party was now increasing. Peter Gillman was permanently installed. I had asked for an assistant, and the picture editor of the *Telegraph* magazine had signed up Don Whillans, who was staying in Leysin at the time. He was working at the American School, as the sports master and proctor, the latter being the equivalent of house-master, or custodian of the pupils' morals. I felt a little apprehensive about the choice, since I knew that John Harlin and Don Whillans had little in common. Don had previously turned down John's invitation to join him on the face, distrusting his logistic planning and, I suspect, resenting his flamboyance. In Don's down-to-earth description – 'A load of bull-shit!' In the event, he was able to give only limited physical help, either to me or to the team. On the one occasion he ventured on to the face with me, he was troubled by an acute attack of vertigo, an illness which has troubled him from time to time over a long period, and he was consequently forced back down. He did help, however, in getting together much of the extra equipment which we now found we needed and, at the same time, providing a practical and at times drily humorous element of commonsense to our councils.

We had a courier, in the shape of Dougal's current girlfriend, an attractive Canadian girl called Joan. Her job was to carry my exposed film in a hired car from Grindelwald to Zurich Airport. Unfortunately, she was not the most brilliant of drivers, and after she had crashed the car twice, writing it off completely on the second occasion, we felt it was time to look elsewhere. This seemed a heaven-sent opportunity to get Wendy into the act, and I phoned her one night, to suggest that she fly out to Zurich to become the team's courier.

'But what about Conrad?' she asked.

'Can't you find anyone to look after him for a couple of weeks?'

'I don't know.'

'Please, love, it'd make all the difference in the world if you could get out here. I'm missing you like hell, and it's such a heaven-sent opportunity. The *Telegraph* will fly you out, and pay you whilst you're here.'

'I just don't know. I don't like leaving him.'

'Think about it. I'll phone you back this evening.'

Wendy thought about it and, finding she was able to leave Conrad with some friends in Moor Row, a nearby village, finally decided to come. However, when she arrived at Kleine Scheidegg three days later, thoughts of Conrad and how he was, constantly nagged at her.

I had desperately wanted her with me, but in fact we saw all too little of each other. When she was at Kleine Scheidegg, I was on the face helping the climb and taking pictures – and as soon as I got back down, she had to collect the film from me and dash off to Zurich, an exhausting three-hour drive on icy roads.

It was now early March – getting near the end of winter. The First Band had, at last, fallen to the onslaught of Layton, Dougal and John, now recovered from his dislocated shoulder. We were ready for the final push up the face. I was going with them, up to whatever should prove the high point of the fixed ropes; I would then leave them for their climb to the summit, race back up by the West Ridge, and meet them at the top.

CHAPTER TWELVE

Eiger Direct: the Climb

It was the 7th March and we were at last committed to the face; with a bit of luck the constant yo-yo between Scheidegg and the snow cave would be over. John and Dougal, out in front, had forced the Rock Band the previous day, spent the night in a small snow hole they had hollowed out under a rock overhang on the ice-field between the two bands, and were now climbing up towards the Second Band. Layton and I were hauling gear up the First Band. Ours was the support role. Layton had jumared up first, and most of the day went slowly as he hauled sack after sack up the face. I alternated between the snow hole and the foot of the slope. As in war, siege tactics on a mountain entail constant long periods of inaction, broken by spasmodic moments of frenetic activity. There is one big difference though: the moments of inaction are precious in their own way – you can gaze over the hills, feel the peace and silence of the mountains – peace that is the more real for the very presence of a lurking threat of change in the weather, or a mistake on a fixed rope.

Then it was my turn to follow Layton up the fixed rope – the second time I had ever been on jumars. The rock was sheer and the rope dropped down in a single span of 300 feet. Economising on weight, we had used 7 mm perlon, being the thickness of an ordinary clothes-line and, in theory, strong enough, with a breaking strain of 2000 lb. – in practice it inspired little confidence. Wherever the rope went over a sharp edge of rock, it flattened out under tension till it was not much thicker than a piece of tape; how much wear before it was cut through? Only time and experience could tell.

You clip the jumars on, one for your thigh harness, one for your foot. I got the lengths of the slings wrong again, and as a result turned that first ascent into a terrifying struggle. You have to first pull in all the spring in a 300 foot length of rope by putting your weight on it, then shooting down the ice slope about thirty feet, bouncing like a red ball at the end of a string, all the time imagining what is happening to the rope, high above your head, as it saws over sharp edges. But you can't afford to think of that. Blot it out of your mind and start jumarring, pushing up the clamps alternately, your life depending on that thin thread that stretches for ever in front of you. Glance over to the left; you're level with the Eiger Window. A train has just pulled in and the tourists are gawping through the window, just a few feet away – a few feet which might as well be a thousand miles, for your life and your whole world revolve round that thread of rope. You've moved above the window – no longer in sight – no longer exists – nothing does, except the need to push the jumars up, alternately, with your rucksack, attached by a sling to your waist harness, dangling spinning below your feet.

A jerk – you drop three inches. It's the rope – it's gone – broken; death, tumbling horror, fear, and a heart that pumps at twice its normal rate. But you're alive! The knot in the sling attached to the karabiner in your waist harness has jammed on the gate of the karabiner, and had then freed itself, letting you drop those few inches. Although this happened quite frequently, the jab of horror was always there – frightening in a way that climbing emergencies rarely are. You are so helpless, the pawn of a rope fixed in position by another man, the potential victim of a piece of rock that might be slowly sawing through your life-line as you, your own executioner, bounce and struggle your way up.

The angle began to ease. Nearly up, I reminded myself to adjust the length of the slings to my jumars for the next rope length, and then took stock. Layton was already near the top of the next rope-length, up a steep ice runnel. A cluster of rucksacks, all of them our responsibility, hung from a peg, and the evening sun was just touching a rocky spur over to the right. Clouds had come rolling in that afternoon, blotting out Kleine Scheidegg, and we were now alone in the world. John and Dougal were somewhere above – I could hear John's yodel. No sign of the Germans, they were somewhere to the right, but exactly where, I did not know. They had favoured the rock spur, but with a bit of luck they would now be in difficulties. We had chosen the short hard road, had conquered it, and now had an easy run out to the foot of the next major barrier, the Second Band.

No time to dream. Layton had reached the top of the next rope-length and I started after him. Swing across to the right, up over a short steep wall, and the angle eases. No need for two jumars here. One's enough – just kick into the snow and push the jumar up. Suddenly it is steeper, the rope's at an angle and the jumar jumps off; I begin to topple over backwards, but grab the rope with one hand – a moment's struggle, and the jumar is clipped back on again. A narrow escape, but I just keep going. A little hole in the snow – the cave where John and Dougal had spent the previous night and, presumably, where Layton and I would spend tonight. But there's more work to do in the evening sun, more loads to ferry up to the foot of the next barrier.

Now I can see John and Dougal, small insect-like figures against the white of a snow ramp cutting across a great rocky depression in the Second Band. The Germans are to their right, hammering away up an impossible-looking rock-wall, sheer, featureless and seemingly very high. There's a shout. One of the Germans has fallen – it happens too quickly for my straying eye to catch – one moment he is spread-eagled on the rock, and the next, he is dangling about twenty feet below. More shouting – he's talking and sounds cheerful, so he can't have hurt himself.

The sun fades fast, washing the rock and snow in a soft yellow glow which gives an illusion of warmth. John and Dougal, 300 feet above, are climbing into the dusk; they reach a ledge in the dark and have an uncomfortable, cramped bivouac. I return to our own little hole between the two Rock Bands, to find Layton already folded into it. It is very small, womb-like, reassuring. The petrol stove roars in the night, and we brew ourselves rose-hip tea to wash down our ration of *viandes sèchées* (a wafer-thin dried meat) and assorted nuts.

The raucous excitement and melodrama of Kleine Scheidegg has vanished. We are back on the big mountain wall, confronting our own special over-simplified reality. I love the rock and the snows, and these few moments of peace give me supreme comfort in my sleeping-bag. I lie curled in the tight confines of the snow hole, tired but able to rest, hungry and able to eat – sheer contentment for a few moments of time.

Next morning the weather was still fine, and we jumared up to the camp site prepared by the others. We were now to experience the fable of the tortoise and the hare. Undoubtedly, we seemed able to climb more quickly than the Germans, and tended to pick the better routes. This enabled us frequently to get out in front, but because of our fewer numbers, we were never able to sustain our advance and, on several occasions, the Germans were to move through us, taking advantage of their reserves in numbers and their greater carrying power.

This is what happened that morning. John and Dougal had had an exhausting day and little sleep that night, their bivouac having been so poor. As a result, we were forced to spend the day after their successful ascent of the Second Band consolidating our position, ferrying up loads and digging out a good bivouac site.

The Germans were better rested and, having failed on their line up the rock buttress, climbed our fixed ropes in the early morning. They pushed on through, up the easier ground that lay above the Second Band leading up the side of the Second Ice-field. That night their front pair bivouacked about 500 feet above us, to the side of the Flat Iron, having pushed on without leaving any fixed ropes behind them. This meant we had no choice but to reclimb the route they had followed, leaving the fixed ropes in position. In the meantime, Layton, ever energetic, had raced back down to Kleine Scheidegg the previous night to pick up some more supplies, returning in the dawn to join us for our push towards the crest of the Flat Iron.

Once again, John and Dougal took the lead, while Layton and I followed, humping loads. Jorg Lehne and some of the Germans were immediately behind us, using the same fixed ropes. It was strange: even though we were still undoubtedly in competition, with each party prepared to steal a march on the other, there was also a growing friendship as we came to know, and at times to help, each other. Peter Haag and Karl Golikow, a delightful, friendly character, who always wore a broad grin and had a few cheerful words for us, or for anyone, were out in front, tackling the rocks leading up the side of the Flat Iron. Dougal and John, alternating the lead, slowly worked their way up the side of the Ice-field, and I humped my big rucksack, taking the occasional photograph and chatting to Jorg Lehne or Layton.

At last, we seemed to be nearing a summit push, though I was not at all sure, at this stage, what part I was to take in it – whether I should continue with the team once they abandoned their fixed rope, or go back down. I had surprisingly little ambition to be out in front, with my mind attuned to the challenge of getting a photographic record and not to the climbing itself. As a result, I became more aware of the risks than if I had been more deeply involved in the climb.

The day slipped by and as morning merged into afternoon a few herringbones of cloud acted as forerunners to the smooth grey ceiling that was always a sure herald of snow. We had more loads than we could take in a single carry, and it meant that I had to go back down to haul the last rucksack up to the top of the Flat Iron. It was a heavy, awkward load and I was beginning to tire. By the time I reached the top of our line of fixed ropes, it had started to snow. There was less than an hour left to dusk, and we still hadn't found a deep enough bank of old snow in which to dig a snow hole. The Germans, who had got there before us, were already ensconced, their hole dug, petrol stove roaring, and the bleakness of our own position became more evident. We had felt care-free and confident that morning, but all this had vanished in the cold grey of twilight.

'There should be something on the top of the Flat Iron,' John suggested.

'I'll have a look,' said Dougal, always ready to tackle the hardest, most unpleasant job, especially if it meant leading out in front. He worked his way across the steep snow slope, immediately below the rocks of the upper part of the face. There was a thin layer of powder snow on top of hard ice.

His progress was painfully slow, his protection apart from the occasional ice piton, non-existent. It was nearly dark before he reached the crest of the Flat Iron, site of the infamous Death Bivouac, where Sedlmayer and Mehringer had frozen to death in 1935. He still had to find enough built-up snow to dig a snow hole and seemed to spend an eternity prodding about on the crest of the arête before finding the right kind of snow and, equally important, a place to anchor the rope.

'Okay, you can come across,' he shouted. 'Be careful on the rope, the peg over here isn't too good.'

It was impossible to pull the rope in tight, and it described a sagging arc across the rock-studded ice that lay between us and the crest of the Flat Iron. By this time, chilled to the bone, tired and apprehensive, I had lost much of my enthusiasm for the North Wall of the Eiger.

I was the last to traverse across. By this time it was pitch dark and I couldn't see where to kick in with my crampons. I slipped and hung sagging on the rope and, in my fear, cursed and swore into the blind night. Being a traverse, it was particularly awkward, with the constant risk of a jumar jumping off the rope. By the time I reached the others, Dougal had disappeared head-first into the snow, burrowing away like some new species of mole. There was no shortage of volunteers to do a spell of work in the snow hole; there was warmth in digging, shelter from the wind, and a comforting sense of enclosure in the bowels of the snow. Another hour slipped by, feet frozen, hunger gnawing, we dug away or awaited our turn to dig, crouching in the snow on the threshold of the hole. It was past midnight before there was room for all four of us. We piled in, crammed together between the rock-wall of the Death Bivouac and the outside snow wall, which seemed precariously thin. But there were still two sacks on the other side of the fixed rope – one of them Dougal's, for he had led over the crest of the Flat Iron without a rucksack. The other one contained our precious brew kit and stove.

'I guess someone'll have to get them,' said John.

There was a silence, each person dreading the prospect of another traverse on that sagging rope in the dark of the storm. We could hear the powder snow avalanches, soft yet menacing, swoosh down the face.

I was cold, frightened, and knew that under no circumstances did I want to leave the security and relative luxury of the snow hole.

'I've only come this far as photographer, and I've done a hell of a lot more than that. I'm sorry, but I'm not going back over that traverse!'

Layton muttered something about his feet being bloody cold; then Dougal, without saying a word, swung himself out of the hole to make the dreaded traverse. We sat there, in the cave, silent – each held by his own special thoughts. Mine were of shame at my cowardice – guilt that I hadn't volunteered – mingled with the relief of being still huddled in the snow, sheltered from wind and danger. As the time dragged by, John kept looking out of the entrance, shouting into the wind, but getting no reply. Then, at last, Dougal came back, fulfilled in the challenge he had accepted, in a state of peace that at that moment and for some time to come, Layton and I could not know.

John volunteered to get the other sack, and was back sooner, since Dougal had succeeded in tightening up the rope, thereby rendering the traverse much easier. At last we could have a brew, and we fumbled in snow-filled rucksacks for candle, matches and gas stove. Dougal lit the candle, tried to light the stove, but the cartridge appeared to be empty. He started unscrewing it; with a sudden whoosh, the gas, perhaps blocked in the jet, escaped. It ignited with a flash, and the whole cave seemed filled with fire. I was nearest the door, and the instincts of survival took over. Diving for the entrance, I only just stopped in time as I remembered there was a 3000 foot drop on the other side. At the same time, John, with a great presence of mind, grabbed the blazing canister and hurled it through the entrance.

I received a dark look. At that moment my stock was very low. I have often thought back on this incident. No one enjoys memories of a situation which became too much for him, of panic in the face of an emergency when he reached that fragile borderline of giving up. Compare this with my reaction to the storm on the Brouillard – a situation which, in actual fact, was potentially more dangerous than this one on the Eiger. Then, I had been in control; on the Flat Iron I was not. It all comes back, I suspect, to one's level of involvement and responsibility. In an emergency, I realised and felt I was just the cameraman – I did not intend to go to the top, having already opted out on grounds of risk, and therefore was all the more risk-conscious. John, on the other hand, behaved magnificently, reaching his own heroic stature to the full, and more, the depth of his involvement in the venture, his responsibility as leader. And so did Dougal, his involvement provided with a cutting edge of desire to explore the very extremities of his own potential.

Fortunately, the damage had been slight and the fireworks more spectacular than dangerous. We found a fresh cartridge, loaded it into the stove and in the early hours of the morning drank our first brew for nearly twenty hours. Then we all slumped into sleep, piled one on top of the other, like young wolves in a crowded lair. In the dawn, we could see the light glimmering through the walls of the snow cave. John poked an axe into the outer floor, and looked down through the hole it left. You could see Grindelwald – a good 8000 feet below. We had burrowed our cave into the curling lip of a cornice, and the outer wall actually overhung the slope of the Third Ice-field!

It had dawned fine, once again. The Germans were already at work on a line of grooves that led up to a gully in the centre of the face. Because of their greater logistic back-up, they had managed to get away early and stay out in front. We were going to have to find an alternative route if we were to avoid following them for the rest of the climb. The team now seemed poised for their summit bid. There was barely room for four in the snow hole, and I wanted to get my film back to Scheidegg, to send it to the *Telegraph*. There was little enough temptation to stay with the team and complete the climb with them. I don't think it was the risk involved that really deterred me, though awareness of it was ever present – perhaps more so than I have experienced on another route, before or since. It was primarily my lack of personal involvement, combined with concentration upon the photographic coverage of the climb.

I left that morning for the valley, after taking a couple of final photographs of Layton and Dougal setting out across the Third Ice-field to climb a groove leading to a ledge system at the foot of the prominent pillar in the centre of the face. The most obvious way up was by a gully on its right-hand side, but the Germans were already installed in this. Dougal, however, was doubtful about its feasibility, for it was barred near its top by a huge bulge of unstable-looking snow. They resolved to return the next day, and attempt a traverse of the base of the pillar, across steep blank-looking rock, where they hoped to find an easier gully on its other side. But their hopes were to be dashed.

That evening the clouds rolled back over the face and by morning a full-blown storm was raging. We talked over the problem, on the walky-talky, with me sitting in comfort in Peter Gillman's room at the Scheidegg hotel. The little radio crackled with static, and the voice of John Harlin was frequently smothered, as if it had been engulfed in spindrift.

'Layton's coming down this morning,' he told us. 'There's no point in three of us staying up here. Dougal and I'll sit it out. We can't afford to let the Germans reach the top of the Pillar in front of us; we'll never get in front if they do. Two of them seem to be staying up.'

'What's the hole like?'

'Not too bad. Quite a bit of spindrift gets in through the opening, but we're beginning to get it sealed off properly.'

'How much food do you have?'

'Should be enough for four or five days, if we're careful.'

'Well, good luck, I'm just off to a chateaubriand for two, all to myself, over and out.'

John and Dougal settled down to their meal of dried meat and nuts, followed by rose-hip tea. They had no books with them, but in the ensuing days found little time for boredom. Just fighting the insidious spindrift that crept through every chink in their defences, cooking and keeping their sleeping-bags dry, filled the day. Both John and Dougal had a wide-ranging philosophical bent. Perched in a tiny world of their own they had complete freedom to explore their own dreams, aspirations and interpretations of what they were trying to achieve in their lives.

Back at Kleine Scheidegg, the excitement steadily built up as more and more correspondents arrived – all avid for good sensational stories. John and Dougal, in their tiny eyrie, were secure, and deeply content – but to the lay beholder down below, they were trapped in the jaws of the Eiger. The journalists allowed their imaginations free rein, producing a series of sensational stories with headlines that read ... 'It started a race ... now it's a rescue.'

Each day at Scheidegg, we phoned Geneva Airport for a weather forecast. There was a high pressure system in the Atlantic, which seemed to be drifting slowly towards Europe, bringing with it omens of good weather. However, it remained sitting off the coast of Ireland, and the winds continued to batter the Eiger. After four days, when John and Dougal had nearly run out of food, John contracted a chest infection. At one point we had no less than six doctors, all on skiing holidays, in consultation at the end of the walky-talky.

We discussed co-operation with the Germans, joint relief operations in order to carry food to the beleaguered climbers – even skied to the foot of the face, in appalling circumstances, but all to no avail. No one fancied the thought of trying to fight their way up those fixed ropes, in the face of continuous spindrift avalanches.

At last the weather improved, but our decision had been made for us. John and Dougal had no food left, and John was too ill to think of anything other than retreat. On the 16th March they came back down. The Germans, having managed to stick it out, were already sending up a relief force, and this meant that in a matter of days they would be able to force their way to the top of the Pillar, then up what seemed the only feasible route into the famous White Spider.

I had no ambition to go back on to the face – even less to do any lead climbing – but now there seemed no choice. John and Dougal obviously needed a rest. I agreed, therefore, to go back with Layton.

We set out on the 16th, myself apprehensive, frightened of those all-too-thin fixed ropes that had by now been in position for over a month, had had dozens of ascents and been battered by several storms. Yet, as so often happens, once committed, I lost much of my fear, began to enjoy the feeling of my own fitness and the rhythmic, steady movement as I climbed the ropes, finally taking them for granted. After all, they'd been here for some time and I'd climbed them all before.

The height that had taken four weeks to gain, now, with fixed ropes in position, took a mere eight hours. The snow hole had a well-lived in look, with a rim of frozen excreta round the door, and holes drilled in the sides by urine. In a blizzard you don't open up the entrance to relieve yourself – especially as, living in a deep-freeze, there is no smell or risk of infection.

It was a good feeling to be back on the face in the quiet peace of the little ice cave – very different from the frenetic hurly-burly of the hotel below. The following day, the weather had brewed in once again, with more spindrift avalanches spewing down the face. No question of going out. I curled up in my sleeping-bag, reading a book. Layton lying beside me, tucked in nose to tail, was clenching and unclenching his great hands. He hated inactivity, was like a steam boiler, steadily building up pressure with no outlet to allow escape.

It was just as well that the next morning dawned fine. We set out early; but not early enough to beat the Germans, who were already at work high in the groove above.

'If you can't get across the Pillar, we've had it,' I commented to Layton. 'You'll have a dobbing match to get past those buggers.'

'Don't worry, it'll go all right,' he replied, quietly confident.

I climbed up the fixed rope Layton and Dougal had left in place before the storm. Jorg Lehne, looking rather like a wartime stormtrooper, was paying out the rope to Karl Golikow, who was out in front on their line.

'Morning, Jorg. Do you think Karl will get up?' I asked.

'Maybe. We do not like that snow bulge. It could be dangerous. What will you do?'

'We're going round the side. There's a better groove on the other side of the Pillar.'

'Ah, but the bottom of the Pillar looks very difficult. I don't think it is possible.'

'To Layton, anything is possible,' I replied with less confidence than I tried to put into my voice.

Layton came up and joined me at this point – gone was the cumbersome, rather diffident backwoodsman from the States, gone the nervously tensed companion of the previous day. He was now sure-moving and confident. He went straight into the lead, kicked up a few feet of snow to the foot of the rocks, hammered in a peg, clipped in a karabiner and étrier and stepped up. A short pause; gloved hands, searching, had found another placement for a peg, nudged one into the crack, tapped it with half a dozen sure blows and repeated the previous process. He knew exactly what he was doing and where to find the right placement for his pitons by glancing at the rock rather than by trying a dozen different places. He then knew how hard to hammer the piton into the crack – not too hard, yet sufficiently to hold his weight. He was a craftsman, superbly adapted to this highly specialised form of climbing.

He reached the line of weakness that stretched round the base of the Pillar. From below, it had looked easy-angled, but now I could see that this was a relative term. It was still desperately steep, and loose into the bargain. Clusters of icicles clung to every crevice in the rock, and Layton had to clear each one away before finding placement for his pegs. I don't think any of our own team, or that of the Germans, could have completed that traverse without drilling a succession of holes for bolts, but Layton, making maximum use of his long reach, and uncanny ability to place pitons, got across it, using the cracks and crannies which nature had provided in the rock.

This type of climbing is a slow process, and the morning slipped by as he moved and swung deliberately from étrier to étrier. I talked in a desultory fashion to Jorg Lehne, gazing down at Scheidegg, now 6000 feet below us, and watching the cavorting black specks of the skiers as they gambolled in their world of bright sunshine.

A cry came down from above. Layton had managed to get round the side of the Pillar, had pulled the rope in, and now it was my turn to follow up his pitch using jumars, and removing the pitons. Following Layton, this could be desperately difficult, because they were placed so very far apart. I found him perched on a narrow ledge which he had cut out of the ice. Above, an ice runnel ran between steep rock-walls to an even steeper ice-field. It looked hard. I belayed myself and Layton set out once again. At this stage, I had no intention of doing any leading – I had come along in an emergency, was getting some extra pictures, and was happy to hold Layton's rope.

But Layton was no longer moving with confidence. He, a master on rock, had little experience of snow and ice. He messed around, trying to put in an ice screw – you treat it like a corkscrew, and screw it in to its head in the ice, turning it by hand, or using the pick of your hammer for leverage. Sometimes they don't bite easily – there's a knack to it – one that Layton hadn't yet learned. But at last he got it in, climbed another few feet, cutting steps in the wrong places and getting tangled with his crampons.

'Can't get a bloody peg in,' he muttered.

I was getting worried. You can't afford to fall off on ice; the ice screw runners are of very doubtful value, and would almost certainly pull out. If he had a long fall, I might also be pulled from my stance, since his belay pegs seemed none to sound.

'Do you want me to have a go?' I offered. 'At your present rate, I don't think you'll get up before dark.'

'Okay, this just isn't my scene.'

And so I found myself out in front, for the first time on the climb – something that I had never intended to do. I couldn't help but get a thrill of excitement, mingled with apprehension. It looked a long, hard ice pitch, harder than anything I had ever attempted before.

Layton slid back down on the rope, and I set off, kicking carefully up to his top peg, and then pausing to take stock. He had reached the top of the little ice runnel and the ice now flared out, and up towards a band of rock about seventy feet above. It was around 70 degrees in angle, which was sufficiently steep to make it essential to cut hand-holds as well as foot-holds. The occasional island of rock stuck out of the ice, a sure sign that this was only a thin skin over the rock underneath.

You've got to be methodical on ice, working out the sequence of holds that you plan to create, cutting them with the minimum of effort, no bigger than absolutely necessary, all the time remaining relaxed, or aching calves and hand cramps will soon make steady movement impossible.

I cut my first steps; the apprehension slipped away. For the first time on the climb I was totally involved. Swing gently, not too hard or you'll shatter the ice and it won't form a perfect step; make three or four steps – all in the right places; make hand-holds to go for, and then step up, gently, delicately, with precision.

I'm thirty feet above my last runner, time for another, but the skin of ice is too thin to take ice screws. I clear away some ice. The rock underneath is as smooth and polished as a boiler plate – no cracks there. Just keep climbing, you can't afford to fall off. And the ice gets thinner, not more than an inch thick, with a gap between ice and rock, which is nice for fingers which curl reassuringly round the ice rim in the little holes I have cut. But it's frightening in another way. What if the ice around me breaks away? I'll be clinging to an icy toboggan – all the way to Grindelwald. The thought is only fleeting – there's no time any longer for fears, no room for the play of an over-vivid imagination. Just ice in front and the need to fashion a stairway. And a snow gangway, where the angle seems to ease twenty feet away, becomes the focal point of my very existence.

Now I'm a hundred feet above Layton, and the rope drops gracefully down to that one pathetic little piton that he managed to hammer in, some twenty feet above him. That would mean a fall of 160 feet. But I've reached the snow, good hard snow – you could go straight up it on the points of your crampons. I don't feel brave any longer, and cut little steps with my axe, kick my boots in hard, and move up the ramp, slowly, steadily, to the foot of a groove that runs up the left-hand edge of the Pillar.

Cut out a stance, find the rock belay, and I'm safe. We've solved the problem of the Pillar and a great bubbling wave of joy rolls over me. I look up the groove. It'll go all right – no problems there. I can see its top. That must be the crest of the Pillar and there's no sound up there – that means the Germans have failed to get up the groove on the other side. We might have beaten them. I yell down to Layton and bring up the rope. I daren't let him jumar up to me, since I can't trust my belays and am afraid that his deadweight on the rope could pull them away.

As he climbs, I gaze down, across the face, with a rich feeling of contentment. It had been the hardest, and certainly the most spectacular ice pitch I had ever climbed. The complete lack of protection made it, in effect, a solo ascent, for had I fallen, I don't think Layton could have held me.

It was nearly dark before he reached me. We hammered in some extra pitons and very gingerly abseiled back down the ice-field to the end of the traverse. The day's excitement was not yet over, however. Layton was the first to swing back across the horizontal rope of the traverse, and I followed. Half-way across, my jumar jammed, and I found myself in an inextricable knot. Whatever I did seemed to tie me more securely in position, so that I could move neither backwards nor forwards.

Layton was waiting on the other end of the traverse.

'Guess it's going to be pretty cold if you have to stay there all night,' he commented.

I continued my struggles on the rope, hanging free from the rock at the lowest point of a V formed by the horizontal rope under tension. The only way out seemed to be to untie completely, maintain my hold on the rope, and then reorganise my jumars and karabiners.

By this time, Layton had vanished back down to the fixed rope, towards the snow hole, muttering about his feet being cold. I felt very much on my own in the gathering dusk. Make a mistake now, and you're dead, Bonington. The thought of the fall was worse, more immediate, than death. At last I succeeded in getting the gear sorted out, and was able to pull myself across the end of the traverse. Tired and hungry, I abseiled back down towards the Flat Iron. On the way across to our snow hole, I passed the entrance to that of the Germans. Jorg Lehne was sitting in the entrance.

'How did it go?' I asked. He looked thoroughly discouraged.

'It is too dangerous,' he said. 'We had to turn back. We could get round by the side, but it would take a very long time. I wonder though, could we use your fixed rope to get to the top of the Pillar?'

'Seems fair enough, provided you wait for us, and follow us up,' I replied.

We had used each other's fixed ropes in the past, but now we had an advantage over the Germans, for we had been the first to reach the one vital bottleneck which offered the only feasible route into the upper part of the face. We had to make sure that we stayed out in front.

That night, I told John the good news. 'Sounds good – you guys have done a fine job. Dougal and I'll come up the day after tomorrow.'

'How do you feel now?'

'I've been checked over by the hospital in Interlaken, and they say the infection has cleared up. I feel fine.'

'Roger, good to hear. Layton and I'll go up again tomorrow, and have a go at reaching the Spider.'

'Sounds good.'

'The brew's ready now. See you day after tomorrow. Over and out.'

Our link with Scheidegg and civilisation cut off with the flick of a switch, we settled down to a victory feast of nuts, cheese and dried meat, with Calcatonic, an effervescent vitamin drink.

Next morning we were just getting ready to go out, when Jorg Lehne appeared. 'Chris, I would like to talk to you. We have an idea.'

'Go ahead.'

'We should like to see this competition end. Would it not be a good idea if today Karl climbed with Layton. Then you would have a truly shared rope, and we could go on like this with our teams climbing together. Then it could not be said that one or other team had been taken to the top by the other. Do you think it is a good idea?'

I was immediately attracted to the suggestion. True, we had everything in our favour, which of course was why Jorg Lehne was appealing to us now. He was making his suggestion from a position of weakness. I responded immediately.

'Sounds like a good idea to me, but I'll have to talk it over with John.'

'Why not let Karl climb with Layton today?' asked Jorg. 'It would give you a good chance to get pictures.'

'That's a good idea. Okay. Layton climbs with Karl today, but as for joining up on the route, John'll have to ratify that.'

Had I been weak in agreeing so easily? I've often wondered. The previous day I had enjoyed some of the most intensely stimulating climbing I had ever known, and had certainly had my best day, so far, on the Eigerwand. The day before us held the same promise, of good climbing which would almost certainly be safer and better protected than the lead I had already made. And yet, photography was still my main priority. I wanted to get the best photographic record that I possibly could of this climb, and when you're actually climbing, or even belaying someone and holding the rope, photography is very difficult. Perhaps this, more than anything, influenced my decision.

Another factor was that co-operation seemed to be the perfect way of ending the competition on the face. I had come to like and respect the Germans, as I know John, Dougal and Layton had, also. If we could all end up climbing together, it would be the perfect climax to the successful conclusion of the route.

There was still the dilemma, whether or not I should stay with the climbing team and go all the way to the top with them. At this stage, it looked as if the final push for the summit would be quite straightforward. I had no pictures in from the side, from the easy West Ridge of the Eiger. More, I had a dream of going to the summit of the mountain by the West Ridge, and then abseiling down the top ice-field on a long rope, to meet the successful team. Thus, I hoped to get the most spectacular pictures of all. I decided to go down, having photographed Layton from the top of the Pillar.

Layton and Karl set off together for our previous night's high point, and I sat and talked with Jorg Lehne. At eight, I opened up the wireless to talk to John.

'We've made a rather radical decision,' I told him with some diffidence, for I wasn't at all sure what his reaction would be.

'It's only a temporary one, until you actually ratify it. Layton and Karl Golikow are climbing together, up the Pillar, today, and I suggest that we let them do this until you get up here. We should then climb in conjunction with the Germans. This seems a good compromise to me, as it is inevitable that we are going to be following the same route to the top. What do you think?'

'Well, it's a lot to swallow at the moment, Chris,' said John. 'I'll have to think about it. Offhand it sounds good – except I think it should have happened later, after we had actually reached the top of the Pillar. How did this decision come about?'

I told him what had taken place and we left it at that. In a way, I had forced the decision on John and his fears were well grounded. There was always the risk that in the final analysis it might have seemed that we had got help from the Germans when, in fact, the very reverse had occurred. Had I climbed with Layton that day, and had we then actually dropped a rope to the Germans, it would have been obvious that it was they who had needed the help. But I was tired of all this manœuvring – wanted to get my pictures – so had made the decision.

Layton and Karl reached the top of the Pillar just after midday and dropped a 300 foot rope straight down the groove which had defeated the Germans. I jumared up it, while Layton started up the next pitch, a great rock corner that led to a huge roof overhang.

He moved up quickly and easily. It was very steep, but the cracks were deep and sound – it was just a question of hammering away. I hung on the rope just below Karl as he belayed Layton, taking my final pictures from the face itself. Layton, a hundred feet above, was spread-eagled below the overhang, the do-ing, do-ing, do-ing of his hammer had a joyful ring to it, and I think we all felt that the climb was very nearly in the bag.

It was time for me to start my long descent and I went down without regret. My ambitions were concentrated on the photographs I was taking, not on reaching the top of the Eiger Direct. And I spun down, down, down, precise, careful, for if you aren't, you're dead. Clip on the karabiner, brake on to the rope, check the gates are facing the right way and are closed, lean back, slide and zoom down the rope, in a single effortless leap to the next anchor piton – clip into that with a spare karabiner, remove the brake from the rope, replace it, check it, check it again, and down again.

It took only one and a half hours to get from 300 feet below the White Spider to the bottom of the face. Picking up my skis, I pointed them downhill, and with less grace than on the ropes, plunged through the deep powder snow of the famous White Hair Run below the Eiger, down to the rack-railway track that led up to Kleine Scheidegg. I had finished with the Eiger's face. In four days' time the whole climb should be finished. Next morning I would realise my ambition of climbing the West Ridge to photograph Layton and the Germans as they reached the White Spider. John and Dougal would be climbing the fixed ropes to reach the Death Bivouac that night.

March 20th. The weather still perfect. Mick Burke has now replaced Don Whillans as my assistant and we are scrambling up the broken rocks and snow slopes of the West Ridge. Dougal and John are on their way to the Death Bivouac and Layton is out in front, cutting the final steps up into the White Spider. We reached the crest of the ridge in the late afternoon, hot, tired and sweating. Winter had crept away during our long siege of the face, and spring had now pounced upon us. The afternoon sun had crept round the face, and was now bathing the summit rocks of the Eiger in its soft rays. I could see climbers in the White Spider, tiny little red flies, sitting – too complacently, perhaps – in the middle of the Spider's Web. Two of the Germans were spending the night there. John, Layton and

Dougal were at the Death Bivouac, all set for the summit push.

As Mick and I scrambled back down the West Ridge, in the gloaming, it seemed as if everything was, at last, fitting into place. Another couple of days and I should be taking those summit shots as John, Dougal and Layton cut up those last hundred feet or so of ice-field, to reach the top of the Eiger.

CHAPTER THIRTEEN

Eiger Direct: the Summit

When we reached the Kleine Scheidegg hotel, late that night, Peter Gillman had some disturbing news for us.

'There's a bad weather forecast, with a front coming in from the Atlantic,' he told me.

'Does John know?'

'Yes, I told him on the evening call.'

'What's he planning to do?'

'He wanted to make a push for the summit tomorrow, but he's worried now, and says he'll wait to see what the forecast is.'

Next morning we were ready for the radio call at 7 a.m.

'How're things?' John asked.

'Not good, I'm afraid. The front seems to be moving in to the west coast of Europe. Could be here tomorrow.'

'I don't want to be caught out on those summit rocks. We'll stay where we are and see what it's like at midday. Could you give me another call then?'

'Okay. Let's hope it's better.'

Up on the face, a restless Layton decided to come back down to Kleine Scheidegg for more supplies, to have a beer and see his girlfriend. He set off at about 9 a.m. Now, so close to success, all they had to do was to wait for two fine days, and then they could tackle those last 1500 feet to the summit. Back at Scheidegg I spent the morning preparing gear for my own coverage of the arrival at the summit, and then went through the daily ritual of getting the weather forecast. This entailed phoning not only the airport at Geneva but also the weather centre in London, in order to get a rounded pattern of the progress that frontal systems were making across the Atlantic. There was a touch of superstitious confidence in all this, as if we believed that the favourable interpretation of one forecaster might actually change the inexorable march of a storm – we were the modern-day suppliants to the gods.

The London forecaster was more encouraging than the man in Geneva, saying that the frontal system seemed to have slowed down, and might take another twenty-four hours to reach the Alps. I was just leaving the phone kiosk when Mick Burke came into the hall.

'Have you had a look through the telescope recently?' he asked.

'No.'

'You should. The Germans don't seem to believe in weather forecasts. I've just seen one in the Fly.'

'Christ. That means they could reach the top by tomorrow. I wonder what John will do?'

In the call at midday, we told John both about the improved forecast and the progress of the Germans. This altered the situation completely, for it meant that the going between the Spider and the Fly (the name we had given to the small snow field above, and slightly to the right of the Spider) must be quite easy.

John now had no choice. The Germans were obviously going for the summit, and if he chose to sit it out, waiting for the storm to pass, his own opportunity might well be missed. I urged him to move up the fixed rope to the Fly that afternoon, so that they could make their bid for the summit the next day. It was the obvious course, and one that he had arrived at on his own. He made his decision.

'I guess we'll go for the summit tomorrow. Tell Layton we're sorry we can't wait for him. He can always join the Germans; they look as if they're planning to put a second team up there, once the fixed ropes have been placed.'

John and Dougal sorted out their gear in the Death Bivouac and set out an hour later – Dougal first, followed by John.

Back at Scheidegg, Pete Gillman, who had just happened to come out to the big binoculars to see what progress they were making, swivelled the glasses towards the face, and began following the line of the fixed ropes from Death Bivouac, up towards the Spider. At full magnification the figure of a man could be discerned quite clearly – not just as a black dot, but as a real person, with arms and legs. You could even pick out the thread of the fixed rope through the eyes of these binoculars. The magnification was so great that it was very easy to get lost, having swung the lenses across the bewildering maze of rock and ice.

Suddenly, as Peter followed the line of rope towards the top of the Pillar, something flashed down across the lens. A dark shape; flailing arms – but were they? Could it have been imagination? Perhaps a rucksack had been dropped. A stone? Pete cried out, and soon a small group gathered around the telescope.

'I think someone on the face could have fallen,' he told us.

'Could it have been a rucksack?' I asked.

'I don't think so; I'm sure it had arms and legs.'

I gazed through the binoculars, first searching the face. There were two little figures on the Spider, one of which must be Dougal. Then, by searching the rocks below the Spider, I hoped to find John, slowly climbing the fixed rope, but could find no one. Perhaps he was hidden behind a buttress of rock, or in one of the gullies that led to the Spider. I dropped down the wall, through the eye of the telescope, to where someone was stirring outside the German snow hole on the Flat Iron, then on down to the foot of the face. Scanning the snows at the base of the Eiger, all the time trying to convince myself that it could only have been a rucksack that had fallen, I found something – a dark smudge in the snow. It could have been a rock, or a sack – but I knew, we all knew, that it was John Harlin.

The only way to find out for certain was to ski over, and I set out with Layton, taking with us one of the walky-talky radios. I still tried to convince myself that it was a rucksack that had fallen, but that even if it were John, there could be a chance of his having survived the fall by going into deep powder snow. We skied in silence, each dreading what we might find. We came to some gear scattered in the snow – the contents of a rucksack.

'It was only a sack,' I shouted, in a wave of relief that, somehow, I knew was not justified.

And then I saw something above us. We plodded up through the snow to where John Harlin's body lay, grotesque, distorted by the appalling impact of his 5000 foot fall, but still horribly recognisable. There was a strange, terrible beauty in the juxtaposition of the bent limbs of this man, who had devoted everything to climbing, and finally to this project and to the face towering above. It made a perfect photograph – a picture that said everything that could possibly be said about the North Wall of the Eiger. I was horrified with myself that I could even think in this way; I knew that I could never take such a picture.

We could not bear to look at him for more than a few seconds. I forced myself to feel his heart, though the fact that he was dead was painfully, totally obvious. Having turned our backs on him, I opened up the wireless, and in a voice that I found impossible to control, told Peter that it was John who had fallen. I asked him to arrange for a party of guides to come for the body, and then Layton and I returned to Scheidegg. I could not have borne carrying him down myself, I was much too upset.

Back at Scheidegg, I became involved once more with the climb as a whole. What had caused the accident? Was it a broken rope, or had he failed to clip in with his jumars correctly? The latter seemed unlikely. John, for all his ambitious schemes, was a supremely cautious and very competent mountaineer. We could only surmise. Now, what would the others do – Dougal and the Germans, poised so close to success but threatened by the change in the weather which was already showing itself with an advance guard of high cirrus marching over the western horizon? Late that evening, we made contact with Dougal on the Germans' walky-talky set. Karl Golikow had come down the fixed rope from the Fly to bring the radio to him.

'The rope parted,' Dougal told us, 'just above the Pillar. It went over a particularly bad spot just there.'

'What do you plan to do yourselves?' I asked.

'We've talked about this,' he said. 'Our first reaction was to come back down, but then we realised that if we did this, John would have thrown away his life for nothing. We want to finish the route. It's what John wanted to do more than anything, and we reckon that this is what he would have wanted us to do.'

'I think you're absolute right,' I said; 'but what about gear; did much go down with John?'

'All the food and our bivvy tent, but there's just enough up here.'

The next day was spent in getting reorganised for their summit push, and in getting their gear up into the Spider. There were four Germans, Jorg Lehne, Gunther Strobel, Siegi Hupfauer and Roland Votteler, with Dougal. As they worked, the clouds crept over the sky and built up for the storm. The safest course would have been to pull back to the Flat Iron bivouac to sit out the storm, for there was insufficient snow in the Spider or the Fly to dig a proper snow hole. But this was impossible on psychological grounds. After the tragedy they could never have continued the siege in cold blood – it was a matter of making one last desperate attempt, and in doing so they intended to preclude any possibility of retreat, for they had to lift the fixed ropes behind them, in order to give themselves enough for their summit push.

Action absorbed some of our grief. If they were going to make their bid for the summit, I had to be there, not only to record their arrival, but to act as the nucleus of a rescue party, in case they needed help. There was now barely time to climb all the way to the top of the Eiger, and anyway I needed more gear than Mick Burke and I could carry. I decided to use a helicopter, which would cost the *Telegraph* well over £200, but it seemed worth it.

Mick and I spent the rest of the day in preparation, and took off late that afternoon. The helicopter was flown by a squat, tough-looking little Frenchman, who couldn't speak a word of English. The machine itself looked ridiculously fragile, as we piled ourselves and our gear into it.

Clouds were now scudding over the Jungfrau, and the bowl, formed by the two edges containing the North Wall of the Eiger, was filled with cloud. Somewhere in there were Dougal and the four Germans. The helicopter buzzed crazily up the side of the Eiger.

'Est que possible au sommet?' I shouted.

He shrugged. 'Pas possible.'

We were now above the Eiger Glacier, a large cwm between the Mönch and the West Ridge of the Eiger. The higher we went, the less possible were the landing spots we saw; crevasses gaped, the slopes stretched up into the clouds.

The pilot muttered 'pas possible' once again, and pointed down towards Scheidegg. There seemed no choice but to go back.

As the helicopter darted downwards I had a sense of failure. We could not, must not go back down – but what else could we do? Obviously he could drop us, far below the summit, on a part of the mountain where I had never been before, but we could never have carried the mound of gear all the way to the summit. Nearly back at Scheidegg, I realised suddenly what we had to do. We could leave most of the gear in the helicopter and get him to drop us on the glacier. We would still be a lot nearer to the summit than if we had to walk all the way from Kleine Scheidegg. I tapped him on the shoulder, gesticulated upwards and he, with a resigned shrug, that said 'these mad English don't know what the hell they're doing', turned the helicopter back up the mountain. Mick and I quickly readjusted the loads, dumping most of the food, all the ciné gear, and some of the climbing equipment.

It was a crazy, exciting feeling as we skimmed back up, close to the snows. When high enough, we hovered at about six feet – it was too steep to land – and he gestured for us to jump out, a frighteningly final gesture. So what if there was a hidden crevasse at the point of landing – only one way to find out – jump! And I did. The snow leapt up at me, and I was there, in one piece, with the slipstream of the helicopter hammering at me.

Mick chucked down the gear and came after me. The pilot gave us a wave and the helicopter suddenly careered up into the sky, leaving us lonely and vulnerable, as it quickly shrank into a small speck. There we were, on the flanks of the Eiger, crevasses around us, the North Face of the Mönch, dark, dominating to one side, and a great snow slope in front, leading up towards the top of the Eiger. We shouldered our rucksacks and started up the slope; it wasn't particularly steep, but the snow conditions were most frightening. The crust of snow was firm and hard, beaten into position by the winds; but beneath, it was soft and powdery. As we made our way up it, the top surface on either side of us cracked, sending lines racing across the smooth surface of the snow, a sure sign that we were on windslab, the most dangerous of all avalanche snows. The crust was not anchored to the snow beneath, but was merely resting on steep powder and could break away in a single catastrophic slab, as much as a hundred yards across, with us on it. In a place like this, there could be little chance of survival, and none at all of a rescue party coming to dig us out.

We tiptoed up the snow, hardly daring to talk, as if the resonance of our voices might trigger off an avalanche. When, at last, we reached the top of the slope and the ridge connecting the Mönch with the Eiger, we were exposed to the full blast of the gale, and it was very nearly dark. Having scrambled up the ridge, finding no suitable spot for a snow cave, we knew we would have to look for a snow bank on the flanks. I stumbled forward in the dark, working my way across a steep snow slope. It was impossible to tell whether there was a drop below of five, fifty or 500 feet. Without somewhere to dig, we would have scant chance of survival.

Eventually I found a snow bank, brought Mick across to me, grabbed the shovel and started digging. At least I was able to keep warm as I worked away in the shelter of the snow, while all Mick could do was to sit, huddled outside, waiting for me to dig out enough snow for him to creep in behind me. There was an odd sort of enjoyment about the entire venture. Perhaps it was because we were on our own, with a simple, independent aim. And although now in the midst of a most savage storm, we still felt in complete control of our destinies. Our position was certainly more dangerous than it had been that night on the Eiger Direct when we had been trying to establish our snow hole on the Flat Iron. Then, I had been nervous, almost cowardly, partly I suspect because I was not in command of the situation, having type-set myself as the photographer. Now, I was in command. Mick depended on me, in much the same way as I had depended on Dougal and John. The very level of this responsibility made me forget any fear that I might have experienced.

It was nearly midnight before we finished. There was no sound of the wind in the hollow we had dug out of the snow, and we were able to relax and sleep. We woke in the morning to cool, filtered light. It was impossible to tell whether the storm was still raging, or whether it had cleared up into the perfect day. I discovered soon enough, by sliding down the short curved tunnel. Fresh blown snow, banked high in the entrance, had to be cleared by digging away with my hands before I could tell what the weather was like in the outside world.

If anything, it was worse than the previous night. Dense cloud surrounded us, and the wind, tearing blindly through it, made it impossible to tell the difference between wind-blown snow and cloud. Back in the hole I found Mick asleep, and gave him a prod to tell him that the storm was still raging outside. He just grunted, happy to be snug and warm inside his sleeping-bag. It was nearly eight o'clock, and we had agreed to give Kleine Scheidegg a call on the hour, every hour, if possible. I switched on the set and listened to the crackle of static; then Pete came up, very weak and distorted, as if talking from another planet – which, in our present position, he might well have been doing, he in his centrally-heated bedroom, and we in our snow cave a thousand feet below the summit.

'The Germans on the face got through last night,' he told us. 'They bivouacked in the Fly, but Lehne and Strobel fixed a lot of rope yesterday, and reckon they got somewhere just below the summit ice-field. They think they'll get out today.'

'Sounds great. We'll try to get up there ourselves. It's bloody desperate up here.'

'Have you got enough food?' asked Peter. 'We were worried when we found all that gear you left behind in the helicopter.'

'We're fine, thanks, specially if they get out today. Open up every hour, so that we can get you back if we want you.'

'Okay. Have a good trip. Over and out.'

We were on our own again. I couldn't help worrying that the Germans and Dougal might have got up early and, at that moment, could even be at the summit. This being the case, I would have missed my great opportunity of getting summit photographs. Quickly, I prodded Mick into wakefulness, got the stove going, and an hour later we were packed, ready to go. At this stage I thought we were only a few hundred feet below the summit, but once we started climbing, it became increasingly evident that we were very much lower. It was a savage day, much worse than the previous one, for the wind seemed even stronger and almost impossible to face into, because of the way ice particles were driven into our faces. It was also an almost total white-out, impossible to tell where the driving snow ended and the mountain began. We just picked our way through it, groping blindly upwards in an enclosed world of our own. It was exciting, stimulating work. A steep snow slope led up to broken rocks covered in snow, then to a wall of hard, green ice, up which I had to cut my way, all the time battered by the wind. Mick was a good companion, always ready with a touch of dry Lancastrian humour, whenever he caught up with me in this world of snow and cloud and wind.

We reached the summit. Had the others been and gone? There were no signs, but there probably wouldn't be anyway. We found a piece of hard, frozen orange peel, jammed between two rocks. Gazing down the steep icefield of the North Face, we shouted, but the words, torn from our mouths by the rushing wind, were dissipated in the airblown snow. It was difficult to believe that anyone could survive there, let alone complete a high-standard climb.

We ourselves were beginning to freeze, exposed as we were to the full blast of the wind.

'We'll have to find somewhere to snow-hole,' I told Mick. 'Come on, we'll drop down till we can find enough snow to dig in.'

We tried to keep as close as possible to the crest of the ridge, so that we could look over and peer into the mist and snow, in a vain hope of seeing the others. About 500 feet below, we found a bank of snow sufficiently deep to dig a cave. It was high time, for by now we were frozen to the bone, and I had lost all sensation in my feet. Once in the hole, we got out the wireless and called Gillman.

'We can't see anything down here,' he told me. 'I haven't managed to get any information from the Germans, either. I'll go over now – what's it like up there?'

'Bloody desperate. Let us know as soon as possible what progress the others have made.'

Mick and I got our boots off, massaged our feet, and then climbed into sleeping-bags. Fully expecting the Germans to arrive at the summit at the same time as ourselves, we had left all the food at the other snow hole. We now realised that we had only two tea-bags, no sugar, and a bar of chocolate – pitifully little to keep us going in these conditions.

An hour went by, and I switched on the walky-talky. Pete came up after a few minutes, sounding even more distant and distorted than on the previous call. We had to ask him to repeat what he was saying, over and over again, to get any sense out of the confused jumble of words. Eventually we gathered that, a couple of hours earlier, Jorg Lehne and Dougal had reached a point just below the summit ice-field. This meant they could be at the top in the next hour or so. Immediately closing down the set, Mick and I struggled to get back into our frozen outer garments. It was like trying to put on suits of armour. Out we went, up towards the summit. Each time I went out, I had felt that the weather couldn't possibly get worse, and each time it had. Hardly able to stand against the force of the wind, we certainly could not face into it. Slowly, we crawled up to the top, where we looked over the edge and into the face, where we could see nothing except whirling snow and ice dropping away into the abyss. Having stayed there for half an hour, at the end of which time we were scarcely able to move, it was time to return to the comfort of the snow hole. At least we had a retreat, but what of the climbers on the face? What had they? While we snuggled in our sleeping-bags, Dougal was abseiling down frozen ropes to the place where two of the Germans had prepared a bivouac site. Gunther Strobel had come up to the high point, carrying Jorg Lehne's and his own bivouac gear, so that they could bivouac where they were, leaving Dougal to return to the bottom, where his gear had been left with the other pair. He spent the night wrapped up in a bivouac sack, his sleeping-bag already frozen solid from the previous night. His stance was too small for him to even contemplate taking off his boots, though he did succeed in removing his crampons and, in doing so, perhaps saved his feet from frostbite.

It must have been a long, cruel night, though talking to Dougal afterwards, one could see that he had derived the same strange enjoyment from an extreme situation as I had experienced that day in wandering around the top of the Eiger in the tempest.

We woke at dawn and lay in our sleeping-bags, with nothing to do but wonder about the fate of our friends on the face. It seemed they could have little chance of survival in a storm as savage as this. Outside, the wind was as fierce as ever, with visibility as low. I switched on the wireless at 6 a.m. and Peter told me that three of the Germans, together with Toni Hiebeler (a member of the team which made the first winter ascent of the North Wall of the Eiger by its original route), were going to try to reach us, to bring us more food, and enough rope to lower someone down the face to try to help the climbers trapped on it. It was obvious that Pete couldn't hear my reply, and he ended up by telling me to press the send switch of the radio three times as affirmative and twice for negative, in reply to his questions. We, of course, unable to ask him anything, did gather that the Germans' radio had also failed, leaving Peter with no idea of their progress.

Having had practically nothing to eat on the previous day, we now ate two cubes of the chocolate left from the bar we had brought with us from the lower snow hole. We discussed the possibility of searching for our previous home, but quickly abandoned the idea. We could never have found it in the near white-out conditions we were experiencing. Although I dreaded the thought of another struggle to the summit, our consciences finally drove us out. We fought our way through the driving snows to a point where we could overlook the summit ice-field. No sign of anyone. We could try, however, to get a higher snow hole, and to this end we started poking about. It was late afternoon when there came a shout from below. I looked down, and saw Karl Golikow, grinning as always, in spite of the blizzard and the seven-hour struggle which they had experienced in fighting their way up to our assistance. He got out his walky-talky and spoke to the base camp man, talking fast and excitedly; then he hammered me on the back.

'They are nearly up,' he shouted against the wind. We abandoned the snow hole and crawled up to the top as fast as we could. Jorg Lehne and Gunther Strobel had just arrived, their faces masked in icicles. Jorg looked surprisingly fit, but Gunther, moving like a sleep-walker, was obviously badly frost-bitten. Grabbing hold of them we shook hands, and thumped them on their backs in our pleasure at seeing them alive. They had fought their way out of the grasp of the face and the weather, entirely unaided. They had, they told us, left fixed ropes behind them for the others to follow, and we helped and guided them back down, towards the other Germans who were now coming up towards us.

We didn't know then, that Dougal was struggling for his very life. There was one section where Jorg had run out of rope, and had left a gap of about a hundred feet. Dougal and the two Germans had no ice-axes – not even an ice-hammer. This was all right as long as they were following up the fixed ropes left by the lead pair. But now there was a gap, without even a trace of the steps they must have cut in the ice, for these had all been filled in by the driving snow. His crampons had become loose, and he was unable to tighten the straps because they had frozen into bands like strips of steel. The lead pair had disappeared and he could not even see the top of the ice-field though, in actual fact, he was only about 300 feet below it.

There was no point in staying where he was – all three of them would have died, and so he started out, on what must have been the most difficult lead of the entire climb. He moved, clearing the snow with his gloved hands until he found traces of the steps cut by the others; stepped up into them cumbrously, yet so carefully, always uncomfortably aware that if he did slip he would almost certainly pull the pair below off their stances and that they would all fall to their deaths.

He came to the top of the line of steps. The end of the rope had been blown about twenty feet to one side, and between him and the rope was a smooth ice slope, canted at about 50 degrees. In trying to balance across on the front points of his crampons, he found they were so loose on his boots, so blunt after weeks of climbing, that he obviously had no hope of getting across.

Most climbers would have given up, or made a mistake, faced with such an appalling situation. Dougal did not, and in solving the problem survived and, at the same time, displayed his own genius as a mountaineer. The only hope seemed to be a tension traverse. To complete this manœuvre you hammer in a piton, clip in a karabiner, and then swing across, almost horizontally, relying on the side tension of the rope to hold you in. Dougal had a piton – the ice-dagger which was his only aid; he had no hammer, but did have a Hiebeler clamp, a little lever of light alloy. He tried to hammer in the piton with this, but it only went in about an inch, then moved from side to side in its hole with frightening ease. It certainly would not have held a fall, and it was highly doubtful whether it could even have taken the strain of a tension traverse.

As Dougal worked his way across, leaning against the rope, placing his feet very, very carefully, he was well aware that a slip meant a plummeting fall of 6000 feet for both himself and the two others. But having managed to get across, he seized the rope, fastened his own climbing rope to it, and then climbed up towards the summit.

I got back to the top just in time to see him moving up those last few feet. I don't think I have ever been so glad to see anyone in the mountains, as I was to see him. My pleasure and emotion did not stop me taking photographs, although the cold very nearly did. My first camera froze solid and I had another half-frame camera round my neck but that was frozen as well. My last resort was yet another camera, which I had wrapped in a down jacket in my sleeping bag. It worked, and pointing it in the general direction of Dougal, I got half a dozen pictures of him as I manipulated the rewind and trigger with frozen fingers. When my fingers began to go white, I stopped, sucked my hands in my mouth until I got a bit of life back into them, and then shot a few more.

And then back down to the snow hole, moving slowly and cautiously, fearful that after so much had happened, now, in sight of safety, we should have another accident. There were shouts of pleasure as we thrust ourselves into the cosy confines of the hole. That morning it had barely been large enough for Mick and me, but the Germans had enlarged it slightly, until it was just big enough for four. Eleven of us were now crammed into it – there was no room to move, certainly insufficient to get into sleeping-bags. A gas stove was purring in the back, someone had a flask of schnapps, and we laughed and joked in our relief at the face team's success and, more to the point, at just being alive. Toni Hiebeler, jammed in the back of the cave, complained of suffocation as the air became thick with smoke and lack of oxygen; I took off Dougal's boots to massage his feet, which seemed cold, but were not frost-bitten. His hands, however, were in a bad way, being covered in great black blisters.

The dawn crept in, and we packed rucksacks. One by one, we squeezed out of the snow cave for the last leg down to Scheidegg – back down to newspaper men, flash bulbs, TV lights, but more important than any of this, as far as I was concerned, to Wendy. Once in the hotel, Mick Burke and I peeled off our boots, Mick grumbling that his were soaked. Rather self-satisfied about my own, which were a different make, I remarked:

'Mine are bone dry. My feet haven't been really cold once, during the whole business. You should throw those away and get a pair of these.'

By this time I was down to my socks, pulled these off to gaze at five blackened toes. I had been frost-bitten without even realising it. Mick and I collapsed into near-hysterical laughter at the come-down from my own pomposity – laughter that was short-lived. A brain surgeon, having a holiday in Scheidegg, volunteered his services and prescribed an injection in the artery in the fleshy part of my thigh. He spent over an hour trying to locate it, digging away with his needle until, eventually, Wendy who was holding my hand began to feel sick and faint, and even my own very limited level of stoicism ran out. We fled from the hotel that night to Interlaken, where there was a hospital. Wendy tearfully left me there to get back to Conrad in England. She had by now been separated from him for three weeks.

I managed to escape from the hospital after three days of boredom. The climb was over – eight weeks of intense excitement, tragedy, superb climbing, farce and the inevitable circus atmosphere that the Eiger always seems to encourage. The climb, undoubtedly controversial, excited criticism in both the popular press and in mountaineering circles. It was said that unfair means had been used to conquer an Alpine face. An extract from a British newspaper article sums up a surprisingly widely held opinion. 'In early March the circus came to Scheidegg again and we were subject to the ballyhoo that now accompanies each North Wall climb ... Certainly the courageous contestants were supreme technicians but some of them came down to Scheidegg to sleep at nights and this bears no more relation to climbing than taking a plane to Petersgrat does to ski mountaineering. One Wengen guide was heard to declare that he could have dragged his grandmother up the network of fixed ropes ...'

Even amongst experienced mountaineers there was a feeling that it was wrong to use expedition tactics in the Alps. I am convinced that the climb could not possibly have been completed by any other method that winter; it is quite possible that given the ten days of perfect weather that John had hoped for, they would have completed the climb as they had planned by conventional Alpine methods, but even so the likelihood of the weather breaking before they reached the top would have been so great, that I do not think an Alpine-type assault was, or would be, justified in winter.

Neither team planned the long-drawn-out assault that occurred – their frequent returns to Scheidegg both for rest and supplies were forced on them by the circumstances of bad weather. I do not think that this action caused a particularly dangerous precedent in the history of Alpine climbing;

just because these methods were used on one climb, because they were expedient, does not mean that they are going to be used on every subsequent first winter ascent or new route done in the Alps – apart from anything else, it is much more enjoyable going straight on to a climb and getting up it.

Only a few people would deny that the Eiger Direct was a great line, whatever methods were used to climb it. To the people who climbed on it, it became more than just a climb; it was a place where twelve people of different nationalities came together and from initial distrust and competition built up a very real friendship and understanding under stress and extreme difficulties. This friendship had been forged before John's tragic death – the two teams would have reached the top together in unqualified victory but for the breaking of a rope.

More important from a personal point of view, perhaps, there is the solid balance of experience that has enabled me, and the others who survived, to go on to tackle other challenges in the mountains and, in my own case, along different paths of adventure journalism. Alongside, is the loss of a powerful personality and brilliant climber – one more name to be added to an ever-growing list of close friends who have died in the mountains, doing something they wanted above all to do, for reasons that none of us have fully succeeded in defining.

Sangay from the East

My backside had never been so sore. I shifted in the wooden saddle, but this merely altered the point of pain as the mule I was riding took each jerky step through the morass of mud that pretended to be a path. A trickle of rain ran down my back, unpleasantly chill for the tropics. There was water everywhere, weeping from the grey sky, pounding on the foliage, cascading from the ceiling of leaves above us; it rushed in a brown foaming torrent over the entanglement of dead branches and leaves that covered the floor of the forest.

A far cry from the North Wall of the Eiger in winter, it was difficult to believe that just six weeks earlier I had been sitting in my sleeping-bag in a sub-zero temperature in the snow cave on the Death Bivouac. This was when I had first heard about Sangay. It was on the evening radio call, when Pete Gillman said, almost as an afterthought,

'Oh, by the way, John Anstey says "Do you want to go and climb an active volcano in Ecuador? You'd be the photographer." '

I didn't even think. 'Sounds terrific. Yes, I would.'

It was largely a question of out of the fridge on to the hot plate – but apart from the fact that anywhere warm seemed attractive, this could also be my big break – another job with the *Telegraph* magazine.

The following six weeks passed in preparation for my next assignment whilst sitting it out in hospital, recovering from frost-bite. I spent much of the time as a guinea-pig for a new method of treatment called hyperbaric oxygen, which entailed hours spent lying in a cylinder filled with two atmospheres of oxygen. You had to wear a special anti-static tunic, and were not allowed to take in with you even a book; apparently, in oxygen so pure and concentrated, even the slightest static electricity could have caused a fire that would have sent you up in a puff of smoke. As a result, I just lay there for hour upon hour, trying out patience as a potential guru – a role in which I failed miserably.

But at last I escaped and now, on the 16th May, a mere ten days after getting out of hospital, I was jogging through the jungles of Ecuador, bound for our volcano, when the mule in front came to a sudden halt and my own cannoned into it. Long ago I had resigned myself to the fact that I had no control over the beast – it went where it chose. Our way was barred by a fallen trunk, and one of the muleteers jumped into the mud, in an attempt to manhandle the mules over the barrier. Glancing back at Sebastian Snow, my companion on this adventure, I saw that his proofed anorak looked like blotting paper and a trickle of water, which was running down from the tip of his nose, passed his slightly pendulous lower lip. He looked peculiarly helpless, largely because his glasses were completely misted up and he was unable to see where he was going. He presented a very different picture from that of the dark-suited, smooth, old-Etonian to whom I had been introduced by John Anstey in London. This trip had been Sebastian's idea. One of a fast disappearing breed of gentlemen explorers, he had started his own career of adventure after leaving Eton by answering an advertisement in *The Times* to join an expedition to survey the true source of the Amazon. While wandering alone in the shadow of the Andes he had conceived the idea of following the Amazon all the way down to the sea, something that no one had ever done in its entirety. What made the adventure so attractive was the total lack of planning, combined with the sparseness of his knowledge of the problems involved and his relative lack of funds. Hiring a faithful Indian – Sancho Panza to his Quixote – he embarked upon a series of horrendous, yet slightly bizarre adventures in his journey to the Atlantic. This trip developed in him a taste for South American jungles, causing him to return time and time again to probe and explore, always in the manner of the Victorian amateur. By the time I met him, he had made another river trip, this time a north-to-south continental crossing up the Orinoco from the Caribbean, across the Casiquare link, a geographical phenomenon which joins the Orinoco to the Amazon, and then down one of the Amazon tributaries to link up with the River Plate and finish at Buenos Aires. He had made two attempts at this venture, the first ending in sickness, before eventually he completed his journey.

When I had met him over lunch in Quaglino's in early April, it was difficult to believe that he could possibly be a hardy jungle explorer: he was undoubtedly eccentric, probably neurotic and enjoyed making extravagant, and at times outrageous, statements, simply to watch the effects on his audience.

This was one of the first things I was to discover about the difference between going climbing with chosen companions, and carrying out a journalistic assignment. In the case of the latter, you go with whom your employer selects, and it is up to you to make the best of it. There was obviously going to be no shortage of adventure on this mission. Our objective was Sangay, a very remote volcano on the eastern edge of the

Andes, overlooking the Amazon Basin. It was also high, 17,496 feet, and very active, with a reputation for having had as many as 400 eruptions in the course of a single day. As an objective, this was one of the factors which had endeared it to both Sebastian and John Anstey, since Anstey wanted to be sure of having truly spectacular photographs, and it promised to satisfy Sebastian's unquenchable thirst for action which, at times, I felt was akin to a fanciful form of death wish.

In our venture, Sebastian was to be the jungle expert and writer, I the mountain guide and photographer. After only a week in Sebastian's company all my reservations about him vanished, leaving an easy relationship of mutual mockery, which hid a real affection. His affectations of neuroses, eccentricity and dyed-in-the-wool conservatism were little more than a shell concealing a whimsical sense of humour and a special organisational ability perfectly geared to the elaborate etiquette and principle of mañana (leave everything until tomorrow, in the absolute confidence that tomorrow will never arrive), which dominates all dealings in South America.

We had flown out to Quito via New York, Miami, and Bogotá weighed down with 400 lb of excess baggage, which included a high altitude tent, ropes, climbing boots, and a special Boots first-aid kit. The trip had started on the right footing when I, having succeeded in leaving the ice-axes in Miami Airport, with equal facility convinced Sebastian that it was his fault. Cables had criss-crossed, and eventually the missing axes had caught up with us. In Quito I had been even more impressed by my companion. He had a wealth of important contacts and our expedition had been organised in the course of a few days, mainly over endless cocktails and dinner parties. All the necessary permits, local food and other impedimenta materialised with an almost magical quality. Sebastian even succeeded in enlisting the help of a local climber, one Jorge Larrea, who worked in a bank and had climbed Chimborazzo with him some years before. He was to interpret and generally act as diplomat.

Without Jorge's services (neither of us spoke Spanish), as bargainer, and remembering all the things which both Sebastian and I invariably forgot, I do not think we should ever have come within a hundred miles of Sangay.

The volcano had had several previous ascents, and had claimed at least one life, but all of these had been from the west, where the volcano abuts on to the high grasslands of the Andean plateau. The approach from that direction is relatively straightforward; three days' march from the road-head over grass-clad foothills. This did not sound adventurous enough, so I hit upon the idea of tackling the volcano from the east – from the Amazon Basin. The nearest civilisation was the small town of Macas, on the banks of the Rio Upano, a tributary of the Amazon. It had an airstrip and although we could have flown in from Quito in a matter of hours, this, once again, would have destroyed the adventure. Why not go overland? – we should see so much more of the country and as a result get that much better story material.

And that was why we were jogging along on the backs of mules, through a tropical downpour in the middle of a seemingly pathless jungle, somewhere between the towns of Cuenca and Macas. Up to this point, the trip had been a magical kaleidoscope of colours, smells and zany experiences, ranging from the dinner parties in Quito, in modern apartments which might have belonged to the wealthy in any country in the world, to the earthy reality of our present situation.

Our journey started in Quito, its narrow streets filled with motor cars, neon signs, patient, inscrutable, poncho-clad Indians – a perfect Spanish colonial city, on which the trappings of modernity hung like fragile cobwebs ready to be brushed away. It is a city of churches with ornate cupolas and baroque columns, their interiors filled with gold and precious stones, a tribute to the rape and pillage of the Inca civilisation.

And then – the first stage of our Odyssey, the bus ride to Cuenca. Sebastian, still clad in dark suit and wearing his Old Etonian tie like a banner, presented a sharp contrast to myself, already scruffy in T-shirt and jeans. He was squeezed between me and a splendidly fat Indian lady nursing a small pig, surrounded by a cacophony of sound, of talk, of clucking hens, of the honk of the horn and the rattle of the engine. We were in the bus for twenty-three bone-shaking hours, as it bumped over paved roads, round hair-pin bends marked with little white crosses to commemorate the victims of accidents.

Cuenca was another old Spanish colonial town in Southern Ecuador, with less of the trappings of modernity than Quito. There was colour everywhere, with women washing clothes on the banks of the river, spreading a veritable coat of many colours over the grass to dry. The Indian market poured forth its noise, bustle and smells, guinea-pigs, fowl, turkeys, vegetables, cones of grain like dormant volcanoes, and people – women in wide sweeping flannel skirts of tangerine, purple and blue; heads shaded with panama hats; faces brown and impassive. I just wandered, absorbed, excited, stimulated by the challenge of transferring the atmosphere from reality to film. I'm not a natural tourist, have never enjoyed seeing a place or museum with the visit as an end-product in itself. But this was different. I was here with a purpose – to get a photographic record – and it was this very intention – the fact that I wanted to reproduce the pictures which were pressing on me, that made the impressions all the more important.

From Cuenca we took a taxi to the village of Gualaceo, one more step away from our familiar Western way of life – but only a step. We stayed at a *hosteleria* run by an enigmatic German – 'Martin Bormann without a shadow of a doubt,' Sebastian assured me. The hotel was at tourist standard, but the village itself could hardly have changed in the last 200 years – ever since the Conquistadors overran the country.

After Gualaceo the escalation into wilderness moved faster. A jeep over a muddy road to the road-head, an hour's bargaining with a group of dissolute, villainous-looking muleteers whose breaths stank of Aqua Diente, the local fire-water, and then we were on narrow paths, an up-and-down trip through banana plantations past small huts and through scrub, to the village of Limon, a collection of clapboard houses on either side of a dusty trail, that could have come straight out of any Western film. Sebastian had, by now, shed his dark suit, and he rode into town with the nonchalance of any gun-toting cowpoke. We looked up the best saloon in town and found it at least moderately clean. It had bare-board rooms upstairs, and on the ground floor an open saloon with a miniature billiards table which seemed to provide the sole local pastime, and a fly-blown bar. We certainly had little chance of living it up on our *Daily Telegraph* expense accounts. Supper consisted of a few lumps of tough meat, mixed into a mash of overcooked rice, washed down with the local wine. Our muleteers had insisted on being paid the previous evening, and evidently, having enjoyed an all-night debauch, were even more drunk than they had been when we had hired them. Jorge, therefore, sacked them and then succeeded in finding a quiet, dour-looking Indian, who looked altogether more reliable.

Whilst planning our trip, no one in Quito had been very certain whether there was a road, or even a path, to Macas – no sane person would ever dream of going overland when there was a perfectly good plane service. Even at Cuenca, it had been impossible to get any reliable information, and in many ways this was the charm of our experience. That night we stopped at our first jivaria – home of a jungle Indian. The Indians whom we had met so far came, had originated, from the plateau. They had been exposed and in bondage to the original Spanish invader for nearly 400 years, and their lives, dress and customs were influenced accordingly. The Indians of the forest had had less direct contact and their lives had not changed much in the last thousand years. We came across the jivaria in the late evening, at a time when I was beginning to wonder just where we should spend the night. It was a single building, in a small clearing in the forest, with a high, steep-angled roof of thatch. The walls were merely vertical bamboo poles, close enough together to stop an intruder or a large animal, but sufficiently wide apart to allow the chickens and small pigs owned by the family to run in and out freely. There were no windows, and the doorway was simply a gap, barely wide enough to squeeze through. Inside, there was just the one big compartment, softly lit through the gaps between the bamboo walls. From the two supporting timbers of the roof hung the worldly possessions of the family – an old gun that looked as if it would be a greater danger to the man who fired it than to the object of his aim, a few pots and, somehow out of place, a transistor radio. The man of the house wore a tattered shirt and trousers and his wife was clad in a grubby long frock that trailed in the dust and mud – standard wear for all Indians at this time, imposed by the prudery of the local mission. The children, and there were six of them, ran about stark naked, showing off distended bellies and pathetically thin little legs and arms.

Yet there was a quiet dignity in their hospitality; we were strangers in the forest, and we were welcome. I am not sure whether they expected anything from us, but there seemed to be no bargaining. They even offered us some of their evening meal – a bowl of yucca – a root vegetable which seemed a cross between a potato and a parsnip, and less tasty than either!

Next day it was raining, with the torrential deluge that I have already described. In its own way it held a greater fascination than any experience on the Eiger and, in some ways, was even more frightening: I thought I understood mountains but felt lost and ill at ease in the mystery of the forest.

Three days later we reached Macas, a dusty, lost outpost of Western man, dominated by a huge clapboard church and criss-crossed with power lines for an electricity supply not yet connected to a generator. It boasted a few tired little saloons which were still to be modernised for the ubiquitous tourist.

We were a mere thirty-five miles from Sangay, could see it from the top of a bluff, which also performed the duty of a cemetery, high above the river Upano. At first sight, the volcano seemed unreal, like a Japanese painting, its symmetrical cone silhouetted against a copper sky, and a gentle plume of smoke drifting from its summit.

It was the last view of our objective that we were to have for seven days, for we were now in the rainy season and most days the skies wept and Sangay was hidden from view. We could take our mules no further and Sebastian, the fixer of the expedition, produced an introduction to the only European in Macas. He was a German baron, who promised to do his best to help with porters, and to find a guide for our trip.

'But it might be difficult,' he warned us. 'Everyone here is frightened of the volcano, and no one has ever been on its slopes.'

Apart from anything else, the inhabitants of Macas were settlers from the

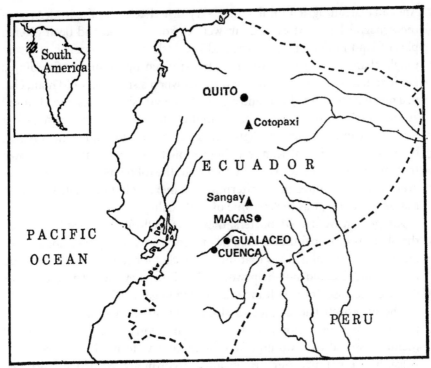

Ecuador: Sangay

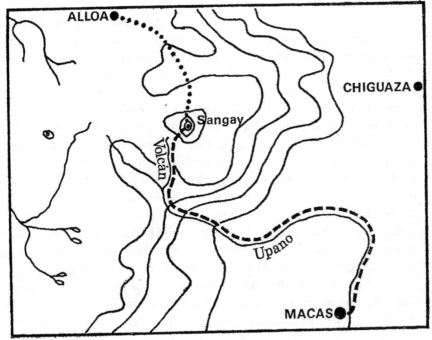

The route to Sangay

Andean plateau, agricultural pioneers trying to hack away the wilderness of the Amazon Basin. Most of them were ex-soldiers who had been given a plot of land in lieu of a gratuity, and had little more experience of virgin jungle than we ourselves. We had almost given up all hope of finding a guide to take us to the base of the volcano, when a small wiry old man, clad in a faded bush shirt, shorts and a pair of old gym-shoes, presented himself at our hotel. Through Jorge, he assured us that he knew the route as if it were his own back-garden. Eight years before he had guided an Austrian botanist up the Rio Volcan, a tributary of the Upano that flowed down from the base of Sangay. We were to set out the following day at dawn, and eventually left at three in the afternoon – a mere eight hours late which, by Macas standards, was the epitome of punctuality.

Altogether, we had six porters; they were well-built, cheerful lads. Like the Sherpas of Nepal they used a head-band for carrying their loads. One factor that worried me was that they were clad for the hot jungles around Macas, and I could not help wondering how they would fare once we reached the base of the volcano and started to gain altitude.

The approach had a spice of sleepy adventure to it, and this gained piquancy as we got closer to the mountain. Don Albino, our guide and mentor, assured us it would take only three days to reach the base of the volcano. We planned our provisioning accordingly. At first the way led along a footpath on the banks of the River Upano, through a hotch-potch of maize and banana plantations, virgin jungle and entanglements of undergrowth where the exhausted soil had allowed the jungle to encroach once again. Every now and then a Jivaro house would rear from rich vegetation and each night we stayed at one of them, always meeting with the same standard of dignified, slightly withdrawn, hospitality.

Then, after three days, we reached the last jivaria. Our porters were becoming nervous, and Don Albino was visibly losing confidence. He muttered about it being a long time since he had walked into the Rio Volcan; that the way had changed; of the unspeakable dangers that might lurk waiting for us. At last, he admitted frankly that he could not possibly guide us any further and we should have to find a local guide. He duly produced a Jivaro, whom he assured us had regularly been to the base of the volcano, and we set out on the last leg of our journey. We were now in real rain forest that had never been cleared and had the sepulchral look and gloom of a cathedral – but it was quite easy to walk through, there being little undergrowth. It also held an indefinable menace – the feeling that it stretched for ever, into the wild confines of the Amazon Basin. We followed our guide, whispering like so many tourists in the crypt of St Paul's, for two hours, walking through the forest until we came out once more into the open on the wide shingle beds that flanked either bank of the Upano River. We were just short of the tributary of the Rio Volcan, which flowed down into the Upano, at its confluence, over a series of shingle banks formed from black lava dust between high cliffs of gravel.

The sky was a leaden grey, and it had begun to rain as we trailed up the side of the river. Our porters looked singularly uncertain and unhappy in this strange environment. The rain already had a cool bite to it, and the porters' claims to be able to make themselves shelters from the boughs of trees began to ring somewhat hollow. They seemed to be just as helpless as any city dwellers confronted by the wilderness. We ended up by rigging a bivouac tent between a couple of trees for them, while the three of us retired to our two-man tent.

Next day we walked up the Rio Volcan, and as we walked the sides closed in, towering above us with an ever-closer proximity. There was no sign of the volcano; it was hidden in cloud, and I had the disturbing feeling of being in the middle of a vacuum, perhaps exaggerated by my own sensations of lethargy. Whether it was the altitude, a forest fever, or the result of my four weeks in hospital, I felt desperately ill and tired, yet was determined not to betray this to Jorge and Sebastian. At last we reached a point that seemed a dead end. The Rio Volcan spewed forth from a narrow gorge which would have been impossible to follow; our only hope seemed to be a steep gully, leading to the top of the cliffs and the upper jungle.

I retired to my sleeping bag that night, unable to control my shivering fit, worried that I might fail to complete this second, crucial, professional assignment. Our porters were crammed beneath the bivvy tent in a pile of humanity which at least enabled them to retain some warmth, for they did not even have woollen blankets to cover themselves at night but merely made do with a ragged cotton sheet.

To my relief, next morning, the fever had vanished, and I felt my strength renewed. Our Jivaro guides would go no further, but Don Albino, though obviously scared stiff, agreed to accompany us towards the base of the volcano. We were now gaining height fast, but every foot of the way had to be hacked from the impenetrable entanglement presented by the under-growth. That day we advanced only a couple of miles. It had rained non-stop all day; our porters were cold and miserable and food was nearly exhausted. Sebastian was obviously enjoying the situation. He loved melo-drama, and had a touch of the masochist in his make-up. I was sour and bad-tempered, worried about whether we should ever find our volcano, let alone climb it! And Jorge – patient, phlegmatic Jorge – who, I am sure, never ceased to be amazed by Sebastian and myself, did most of the cooking and somehow kept our porters going.

That evening, we stopped on the crest of an overgrown ridge; higher than the previous night's camp, it was also considerably colder. We had now issued all our spare clothing to the porters, but by this time everything was soaked and they had the greatest difficulty even in lighting a fire, the brushwood was so wet and rotten. Next morning, we were confronted with mutiny – Don Albino was the spokesman.

'The men are frightened and very cold,' he told Jorge. 'They want to go home. If we stay here any longer we shall all die.'

With promises of bonuses, Jorge persuaded them to stay for three more days at this camp, where they could, at least, find some firewood, help us to carry the tent to a high camp and then wait for us to return.

Reluctantly, Don Albino agreed and three of the youngest and fittest of our porters shouldered loads to help carry the gear to a point where we could, at least, see the volcano. The vegetation had now changed to a form of giant and leprous weed of huge umbrella-like leaves on soft fleshy stalks. It made me feel like a pygmy in a science-fiction film, and I half expected to be confronted, at any moment, with a giant sixty-foot high spider or a mammoth ant. We could have been on a set for Conan Doyle's *Lost World* – and it continued to rain as though it would never stop.

Our progress was slightly faster than the previous day; by dusk, we had emerged from the forest of Sachapalma, and had reached the grass-line – great tussocks of coarse, man-high grass, which were almost as impenetrable as barbed-wire entanglements. With some way still to go, it was obvious that we were going to need a higher camp. I persuaded Gabriel, the strongest of our porters, to stay with us. This meant cramming four into our two-man tent, while the other two returned to await our descent.

Just as dusk fell, all our efforts were rewarded. The clouds suddenly unrolled, and we were able to see Sangay, squat, foreshortened, towering over us. Even as we gazed, there was a dull, heavy rumble, accompanied by a great mushroom of ochre-brown smoke which welled up from near the summit. There was no glow, no pyrotechnics, just boiling, expanding cloud that was somehow more menacing than any amount of molten lava.

We settled down for a damp and very cramped night. The bottom of the tent was full of puddles and a strong sense of survival was needed to avoid getting one's sleeping-bag soaked. I wriggled and manoeuvred throughout the night, in order to remain dry, while Sebastian, the eternal stoic, lay still and silent, in the middle of a large puddle.

I suspect I was the only one to appreciate fully how serious our position could become. We now had no more than two days' stock of food, and although we were only thirty-five miles from Macas, that thirty-five miles had already taken a week to cover. More to the point, if anything should happen to us, there was no one in Macas who could, or, for that matter would, come to our aid. In the flat light of dawn, I could gaze back over our path. It was just possible to discern the swathe in the forest, cut by the River Upano, but apart from that there was a matt carpet of dull green stretching to the far horizon. Above us was the volcano, with featureless lava rubble stretching up into an even ceiling of cloud. Suddenly, I realised how easily we could get lost. It had taken three days to cut our way through the upper jungle to reach this point. If we missed this narrow thread of a path on the way back down, we should have very little chance of cutting our way back to the Rio Volcan. We were on our own, and the responsibility for the party was mine.

But we needed to get closer to the base of the volcano, and so, leaving a trail of wands marked with some torn-up red flag, we waded through the chest-high grass, towards the top of the grass line. Now we were faced with another problem. There was no running water and all the liquid we had was the contents of a single water-bottle. That night we camped imme-diately below a ridge of lava that stretched smoothly up towards the brow of the sky line. There could be no question of awaiting the perfect weather. We had no food or water, and there was some element of doubt as to whether our porters in the camp below would wait for us. I was not sure how high we were, but guessed our altitude to be about 10,000 feet – still 7000 feet below the summit, a long climb by any standards.

That night I was on edge, hardly slept and, at midnight, poked my head out of the tent to see a sky, velvet black, studded with stars.

'Come on Sebastian, wake up; it's a perfect night.'

He groaned and rolled over. Even so, I got the primus lit, boiled the half-panful of water, which was all we had, made some coffee, and thrust it into his hand. Jorge was still dead to the world.

Not wanting to waste any more time, I ordered Sebastian to get ready as quickly as possible. I got dressed and started out, up the lava slope, where I could see deep patches of cloud silhouetted against the glitter of the stars. I aimed to get to the summit by dawn, hoping to get those precious photographs of our objective.

The angle was easy, about 20 degrees, but the surface was covered with a thin layer of lava pebbles, which skidded underfoot on a compact base of lava mud. Even so, with a focused drive to reach the top, I just plodded on through the dark, occasionally flashing my torch to get an idea of my immediate surroundings. And then the lava changed almost imperceptibly to ice – it was dusted with lava dirt, embedded with lava bombs, but it was ice nevertheless.

Just as I reached the start of the ice, the stars blurred and then vanished –

the mountain was, once more, engulfed in cloud. There were no features –
no way for the others to follow my trail. I began worrying about them and
cursed myself for being so impatient in leaving them behind. I sat down to
wait for them until an hour had gone and there was still no sign of them.
Where the bloody hell can they be – what do they think they're doing?

I plunged back down in a towering rage; I had lost about 2000 feet in
height when I saw three shadowy figures emerging from the mist and gloom
of the dawn.

'Where the bloody hell have you been?' I asked.

'I'm frightfully sorry, Chris – all my fault,' said Sebastian. 'I'm afraid I
forgot the rope and had to go back for it. We were only ten minutes or so
behind you when we started, but we'd been gone for an hour before I
noticed it. Don't worry, I went all the way back for it.'

'You've wasted three bloody hours in doing so. Anyway, what's Gabriel
doing with you?'

'I thought he'd like to come to have a look at the crater as well.'

'God almighty, do you think we're on a bloody holiday jaunt? There's
some steep ice up there. Jorge, can you explain to him that it's too difficult
for him and that he'll need crampons?'

Gabriel, looking a little relieved, turned back and I drove the rest of my
team up the lava slope. It was like going up a giant slag-heap, and in the
swirling mist it could have been somewhere in the smog of a South Wales
coalfield. Then we came to the ice – time to put on crampons. Jorge and I
had put ours on, but when I glanced over to Sebastian – he was trying to
put them on back to front!

'I really am most frightfully sorry,' he said. 'I've never worn these things
before.'

I strapped them to his feet, tied a loop in the middle of the rope and
dropped it over his head, to attach to his waist. Jorge quietly tied on to the
other end and we set out once again. The slope was not steep, but had
anyone slipped it would have been impossible to stop, since the ice was too
hard for the pick of an axe to act as a brake.

'I'm terribly sorry, Chris,' Sebastian was always very apologetic. 'I can't
see a thing. My glasses are misted up.'

'Can't you take them off?'

'Well, no; that's even worse – blind as a bat without them.'

'Just follow the rope then – I'll tell you if there's anything to watch out
for.'

At that point we reached a gaping crevasse, guarded by a superb portcullis
of icicles. A narrow ice bridge led over it, and Sebastian felt his way across,
tapping his axe to either side, as if he were a blind man. I began to feel a

little like a guide-dog, as I sniffed my way up the slope, tugging at the leash, impatient to reach the top.

There seemed no end to it. We could have been in one of the circles of hell, destined to eke out eternity plodding ever upwards. The entire adventure had an unreal quality unlike any climb I had ever undertaken. The risk was there; I was a good deal more frightened than I had ever been on the fixed ropes of the Eiger Direct, but my fears were intangible, almost superstitious. I half-expected the entire mountain to explode suddenly beneath my feet. And the lava bombs were real enough. It was like being at the end of a long skittle alley, as lumps of rock, some the size of a small table, came bounding from out of the mists, bouncing and ricocheting down the slope past us to disappear once again. You could almost imagine a group of old Inca gods swinging their bowls at us from somewhere near the top. There was no sound, no interruption – just the ting and clatter of the boulders bouncing past.

As we climbed higher we were able to guess their origin. We passed through a museum of lava bombs, hurled from the crater during former eruptions and now, each one isolated on its own icy plinth, raised in monument by the action of the sun melting the ice around each separate boulder. And then the ice beneath the rock had melted and down the monument had fallen, to roll and rattle to the foot of one of the highest slag heaps in the world.

A chill wind, just above freezing-point, was blowing thin sleet across the slope, but suddenly a warm blast of air, slightly sulphurous, mingled with the wind. Underfoot the ice vanished, to give way to a fine brown powder, hot to the touch. We could not see anything, but there was a smell of sulphur everywhere – a smell which tortured the back of the throat and sent us into paroxysms of coughing. The slope dropped away to our right, and we were struck by the heat, like the blast from the opened door of a furnace. We peered into the mist – but what was mist, and what was smoke? We couldn't tell. There was a hiss at our feet, and little wisps of steam jetted from a crevice stained green and yellow by the sulphurous fumes of the fumarole. We stumbled on.

Sebastian pointed up the slope, to where it seemed to rise in some kind of crest.

'Follow me,' he gasped. 'We must place the Union Jack on the summit.'

Although we had no Union Jack, we followed him dutifully. On taking a few uncertain steps, he collapsed, overcome by the fumes. I grabbed him and, with Jorge to help, dragged him back down the slope. Fortunately, after a couple of minutes, he regained consciousness and we were all able to stagger back the way we had come. The heads of our ice-axes were stained a dull yellow-green, and I couldn't help wondering what effect the fumes had had on our lungs.

I trailed back down to the camp in the woods with mixed feelings – relief at getting away from this strange, unpredictable living beast of a mountain, but nevertheless filled with a sense of failure. My mission had been to get pictures – gaudy, lurid pictures of pluming red, hot lava fountains, and firework displays in the black night sky – but all I had managed to get were a few shots of Sebastian in the mist, looking like a bedraggled Outward-Bound schoolboy in the mists of Wales or the Lakes. I found it impossible to transmit on to film the feeling of uncontrollable, unpredictable power that the heat, and the hiss of the fumes and the swirling clouds had imparted to all three of us. I could not reproduce my own fears. I did not even know what I had on film. I had just clicked the shutter release of the camera, in the midst of the grey gloom, uncomfortably aware of the all-pervasive grit and water which covered not only the lens, but also my hands and clothes.

I should have liked to have returned to the summit – to have sat it out until at last we had a fine, sunny day – but having no food, and with porters who could be held from flight no longer, we had no choice but to retreat.

CHAPTER FIFTEEN

Sangay from the West

Our adventures on Sangay were far from over. That night we got back to the camp in the woods, where our long-suffering but faithful porters were awaiting us. The following day we dropped back into the bottom of the gorge of the Volcan river, but by now it had rained almost non-stop for a week, and the entire bed of the gorge was filled with boiling brown waters.

'We'll have to wait for it to subside a bit and then make a dash for it,' I decided.

'But what if the rains don't let up?' asked Sebastian. 'I've known them to go on for weeks at a time.'

'Well, we'll then have to cut our way out, along the top of the gorge.'

'If we don't make it, I suppose we could always make a second Fawcett story,' said Sebastian. 'Do you think John Anstey'd send anyone out to find our bones? I'll keep a diary to the very end, with a last, loving message to Laetitia and the children.'

We sat it out, on a lava sprit at the end of the gorge, for another day. On the second morning, the level seemed to have dropped a little and we made a hurried descent of the gorge, fording a couple of torrents which had been little more than trickles on the way up. In the process, we very nearly lost Don Albino, who, frail as he was, let go of the rope I had taken across the torrent, and was on the point of being swept away into the main stream when Sebastian, with great presence of mind, and considerable courage, dived in and saved him. The Indians, indifferent to death, just looked on and, I suspect, would have let him drown.

This proved altogether too much for Don Albino, who sat down and told Jorge that he would go no further – we could leave him where he was and once he had rested he would continue the journey. I felt it impossible to abandon him, and ended up by carrying him, piggy-back fashion, down the river bank. He was little more than a skeleton held together by a few sinews and a bit of skin. At first he seemed to weigh nothing, but as the miles crept by, his weight increased, and at the end of the day I felt exhausted.

We had now reached the end of the Rio Volcan, where it joined the

Upano. The gods were undoubtedly mocking us, for the weather had cleared, rewarding us with our first cloudless day since leaving Macas. Sangay, conical, serene, eternal, lay just ten miles up the valley down which we had fled the previous day. There was no question of returning, however, as we had to get more food before we could tackle the volcano once more. But determined to tackle it I was – I put it to Sebastian:

'Look, I know you've got a superb story – the trouble is, I haven't any pictures to back it up. My whole future depends on this story. Will you come back with me?'

'But how can you guarantee it won't be just the same, all over again?'

'There's no need to go in from this side again. We'll go in from the other side, where it should be a hell of a sight easier. If we take more food, we can sit it out until we get a good day. Do you mind?'

'My dear Christian, all I ask is a single hot bath in Quito, and I'll go to the ends of the earth to help you get your pictures.'

Sebastian, although a master of superlatives, really meant what he said, and so we trekked all the way back to Macas. On the last night, before reaching the town, we went to bed at dusk, as was our usual custom. We were told the next day that we had slept through the most spectacular eruption of Sangay in living memory. Had I only been awake, I could have photographed the perfect volcano firework display. Everything about Sangay seemed ill-fated.

We flew back to Quito, where we spent a week collecting food, sending for some money, and living it up in the aseptic luxury of the Intercontinental Hotel. There were letters from Wendy, full of love and her own adventures in the Lake District. She was, at last, beginning to gain confidence in her folk-singing – had sung at a folk festival and was full of plans for the future. I longed to get home to her, and dreaded the thought of going on to Peru to join the expedition to Alpamayo. I had had enough of adventure for the time being, and had become a homing bird. But first, I had to get my pictures on Sangay. From the west, it would be as if approaching a different mountain, on a different continent, for we would approach it from the High Andean Plateau: no jungle, no slimy forests of Sachapalma, just shoulder-high grass, spread over a switchback of sharp, knife-edge ridges, that guarded Sangay with an intricate network of ramparts, as if it were the citadel of an eighteenth-century fortress.

The road-head was at a hacienda called Alloa, set in an upland grassy valley which could have known little change in the past 300 years. One man owned the entire valley, and though theoretically the feudal system (with the Indians being treated as serfs) had been abolished, in practice the system remained. If the Indians wanted to stay in the valley, they had to work for the landowner on his terms – and these seemed fairly harsh. The homes of the Indians, resembling mouldering hay-stacks, were huts made from bunched grass, without windows, doors or chimneys. Each had a small patch of land for his own crops, and much of his pay was in kind – food and grain. For escape, he could go to the cities, but found little prospect of work, and a life which could be even harsher. At least on the hacienda some measure of security was provided, and the hardship of the life was made bearable by alcohol.

We arrived at the Hacienda Alloa on the second day of one of the many religious feasts which grace the Ecuadorian calendar. In the morning all the peasants went to church – a dark, windowless barn of a place, with none of the gold and glittering ornaments of the churches of Quito – just a stark wooden cross on a battered old table. But the room was packed to bursting, with an overflow standing around the threshold and the walls outside. There was a constant babble of voices, cries of children, as the priest celebrated Mass. At the end of the service they held a procession in two long parallel columns round the field immediately outside the church. One of these columns was formed by the major domo of the hacienda leading the menfolk, whilst his wife led the women in the other. There was something infinitely sad in the stoic, melancholy cast of their features, all of which seemed weakened and debauched by a life of hardship relieved only by alcohol and drugs.

At the end of the procession they all flocked to the village tavern, a bare mud hut and compound, which was soon packed with Indians – men, women and even children, all of whom proceeded to get more drunk than I have ever seen anyone before or since. The scene was Hogarthian – with a soldier lying flat in the gutter, blind to the world, his rifle beside him – a man offering his wife or lover a draught from his half-full bottle of Aqua Diente, in the middle of the street – a mother giving her eighteen-month babe a slug of the fire-water, to stop it crying.

The binge lasted three days, during which time I had no choice but to wait patiently until the porters we had been promised had recovered from their hangovers. When, eventually, they did, we set off on our journey, the first leg on horseback to an outlying ranch about fifteen miles from the foot of the mountain, followed by two days' march through the long, near-impenetrable grass, to the base of the volcano.

Away from the bottle, our porters proved wonderfully reliable – much stronger and more self-sufficient than our brave little bunch of lads from Macas, who were so much out of their element once in virgin forest. These men had spent their childhood and working lives wandering the sierra, in search of game or stray cattle. Dressed for the part, with broad, heavy felt hats, thick woollen ponchos and well-made boots, they knew how to make effective shelters by cutting the long grass and building little thatched huts – mini-replicas of their own hovels by the hacienda. They never complained of the incessant rain, nor of the heavy loads, nor the hard going through the pathless maze of grass-clad ridges.

Reaching the base of the volcano on the third day, we waited there for another couple of days, and then moved a camp up the side of the mountain, to an altitude of about 15,000 feet, on a shoulder immediately opposite a lava run. It was a strange, rather frightening place. By day the lava blocks, which were pushed down the slope by the remorseless power of the volcano, looked like dull, black coke. But at night these glowed a rich cherry red as they rattled and rumbled down the slope. Every few hours there was an eruption from the main crater. We could not see anything, for the entire summit was wrapped in cloud. We could, however, feel the mountain tremble beneath us, and it was all too easy to imagine a great river of molten lava, poised somewhere out of sight, above us in the clouds, ready to sweep down and envelop us.

We had some trouble persuading the Indians to help carry our tent so high on the volcano, and when they left us there, they had shaken our hands with a fervour which seemed to imply that this was the last time they ever expected to see us. Having lived in the shadow of Sangay all their lives, they had a healthy and perhaps superstitious respect for the mountain. In the two nights and days that Sebastian and I spent high on its flanks, we began to share both their fears and their respect.

And then, at last, I had one clear day. I raced to the summit, tailed by Sebastian, and took my pictures, which had a peculiarly anticlimactic quality. Although the crater was vast, it was filled with a dense steam and you could see nothing – you could only hear a steady hiss from its depth – a hiss which, to my untutored ears, sounded exceptionally sinister. I spent an hour on the brink of that crater, hoping for a clearance – even half-hoping for an eruption – to get some truly spectacular photographs, yet at the same time fearful of my own prospects of survival in such an event.

An hour went by. Nothing happened, and with a sense of relief, feeling I had done my duty, I fled down the slope, back to our camp. Our Indians welcomed us as if we had returned from the halls of the dead, but still I wasn't happy. I was worried in case I had not succeeded in getting suffi-ciently dramatic photographs of the volcano. Paradoxically, on the day of our return to its base, the weather once again cleared into a series of perfect, cloudless days, when even the interior of the crater seemed free from steam. I had just persuaded Sebastian – ever loyal and patient – to return with me to the summit for yet another attempt to get the perfect definitive picture of a volcano. We were to go up first thing in the morning, and I was sorting out my gear for what would be our third ascent of the mountain, when an Indian came running into the camp.

The moment I saw him I knew there was something terribly wrong. He had a message addressed to me. I dreaded opening it – fearing something might have happened to Wendy. I had an instant, appalling sense of relief that it was not Wendy – although it was Conrad. He had been killed in an accident. It was like a physical blow, instantaneous, believable and real – dreadful in its finality. I collapsed on to the ground and cried, with the Indians standing silent, sympathetic around me. Sebastian, holding my shoulder, gave me all the sympathy and strength that he could.

I did my best to pull myself together, knowing that I had to get home without delay. The accident had occurred over a week before, and the fact that I learned of the tragedy as soon as I did was entirely due to an old climbing friend, Simon Clark, who was now working in Ecuador. We had met in Quito on our way out, and later he had seen a mention of the accident in *The Times*. The *Daily Telegraph* had already cabled to the British Embassy, but there was no way in which they could get the news to me, since they had only a vague idea of our whereabouts. Simon knew even less than them, but immediately made inquiries about our route into Sangay. He drove to the Hacienda Alloa, and would have carried the message in person but for the fact that he had vital business commitments. He sent an Indian with a note to tell me of the tragedy, and I shall always be grateful to him for his efforts. He left a Land-Rover with a driver to take me to Quito, and this must have saved Wendy from several days' unmitigated hell in our loss, compounded as it was by my own absence on the other side of the earth.

I started back that afternoon, knowing that I could not sleep until I reached home. Our Indians, whose own lives are full of death, held a silent compassion that I shall never forget. We walked through the dusk, and as night fell I looked back at Sangay, that dark conical silhouette, against a star-encrusted sky – a flaming red snake of molten lava coiling down its slopes. Even in my grief I was aware of the intense beauty and peace of the scene. I walked and walked, drugged by fatigue, yet telling myself over and over again that I should never feel and see Conrad again.

They had horses waiting for us at the outlying station and we rode on through the night, over the hair-pin path which led to Alloa, reaching it at dawn. I shook hands with the Indians – their leader, a fine, grizzled old man, crying as he waved his farewell – and we drove on through the dusty little town of Riobamba, past Cotopaxi, snow-capped, conical and pink in the early morning sun, and into Quito. There, I was taken to some friends of Simon who were infinitely kind, and we held to that tight brittle edge of small talk that enables one to keep grief private. Then the plane to New York; long hours of waiting for the connection, longing for Wendy, keeping going till we could hold each other close, worrying about whether she was all right. And Heathrow, Immigration, baggage collection, Customs, then Wendy broke through and we just clung and clung together, isolated from the world in the totality of our grief and love for each other.

Wendy had been staying with Mary Stewart, and Conrad had gone playing with Mary's four children. At the bottom of the field abutting the garden was a stream. Normally it was little more than a trickle, but there had been a cloudburst. Conrad, ever independent and adventurous, had strayed from the others and must have fallen into the swollen waters. Wendy herself had found him. It was one of those one-in-a-million chances that you can never guard against. Mary's and countless other children had played by the banks of the stream all their lives, and then, for some unknown reason, by some chance, this had happened.

Now we have two fine children, and time, and the love of our children, has eased our grief, but it will always be with us in a closed quarter of our minds. There will always be the nagging questions; the asking of what Conrad might have done with his life – how he would have developed. He had a rare quality of gentleness tempered with intrepid independence. His was a happy, intense little life, lasting only two-and-a-half years, without any of the sorrows and disillusion that inevitably accompany the joys and challenges of a life which is allowed to follow its complete course.

Wendy had endured a hell that I could never know; for the fact that the news was a week old, that the accident had occurred so far away, meant that I had known only thirty-six hours of solitary grief compared with the long days of Wendy's suffering. Her parents and a host of wonderful friends had been a tower of strength to her, but neither of us felt whole without the other. Together we could admit our sorrow and Wendy was able to release, slowly, some part of the pain of our loss.

CHAPTER SIXTEEN

The Old Man of Hoy

'Life goes on' is an over-used, but very true, cliché. Even in the depth of our grief, Wendy and I knew a joy in each other. Desperately, we wanted and needed another child. Wendy quickly became pregnant again and was due to give birth in the early spring of 1968. Various assignments and climbs followed, some close on the heels of our tragedy and my own return from Ecuador.

Some weeks after my return, Tom Patey, always compassionate, phoned to tempt Wendy and me up to the Isle of Hoy in the Orkneys. He made a climb the excuse, but I suspect that as much as anything he intended to get us away from our immediate environment. The bait was the Old May of Hoy. 'The finest rock pinnacle in the British Isles,' Tom assured me. 'It's three hundred feet high, as slender as Nelson's Column, sheer on every side, and unclimbed. It'd make a great story.' I couldn't resist it, though Wendy decided she would rather stay in Haywards Heath with her parents for the few days I hoped the climb would take.

I caught the sleeper up to Inverness, where Tom met me at the station for the drive to Thurso in the far north of Scotland. It is a wonderful drive, up the eastern seaboard of the Highlands and then over the bleak heathered flats of Caithness, with thunder clouds like Spanish galleons sailing overhead, the hills of Ben Klibreck and even Ben Hope in the far west, etched clear in rain-washed air. Tom was full of legends of the Old May of Hoy – of obscure scandals he was happy to offer my journalistic pen, gathered from some of the colourful characters who lived in self-imposed exile amongst the Western Isles.

The remainder of the team were awaiting us at Thurso: Rusty Baillie, his wife Pat, their baby, a dog and an impressive pile of ropes and ironmongery. Rusty was to be the technical expert, I the photographer and Tom the stage manager of our venture.

In order to reach Hoy, I had to survive a sea-sick voyage to Stromness, well described as the Venice of the North, followed by a shorter, less painful trip in a specially chartered fishing boat to Hoy. A bumpy journey in one of the island's few cars (and only taxi) then took us to Rackwick Bay, where

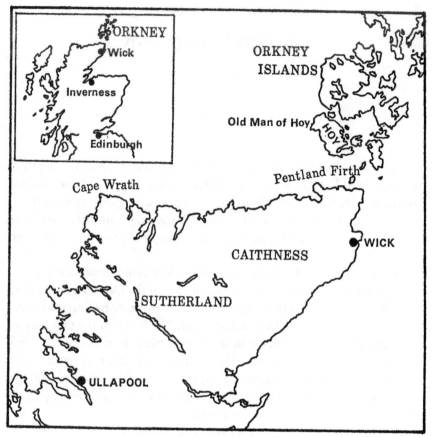

The Old Man of Hoy in relation to Scotland

a collection of single-storeyed crofts clung to a wind-swept shore. The Old Man of Hoy was the other side of the hill that rose in an easy sweep from behind the Youth Hostel, the former school-house of the dying community. Setting out to view our objective that same evening, we walked over the short, springy turf, while skuas wheeled and dived over us, their great wings and hooked beaks posing a tangible threat.

We came to a bluff, and there in front of us was the top of the Old Man of Hoy, truncated by the cliff top. It was square-cut, obviously slender, and yet gave little idea of just how tall it was until we reached the brow of the cliff, and could look down and across at the most remarkable monolith and summit in the British Isles. It could have been a fairy-tale tower, 450 feet high, with a grassy top that seemed little larger than a billiard-table.

'Looks bloody loose to me,' I commented. 'That sandstone'll just crumble away as you climb it. The whole issue could come toppling down.'

'Och, no. Where's your spirit of adventure? Those are no words from Bonington of the Eiger,' replied Tom. 'I can see I'll have to start amending some of the verses in your song.'

'That crack should go,' said Rusty, ever practical. 'Just the right size for bongs.'

We returned to the Youth Hostel, where Pat had already prepared the supper, and settled down to a long night of Patey songs, accompanied by malt whisky.

It was eleven the next morning before we were ready to set out, and we scrambled down to the foot of the Old Man. We saw that it was linked to the island by a neck of piled boulders, probably a natural arch which had collapsed hundreds or thousands of years earlier. From its base, the Old Man was slightly daunting, and had, undoubtedly, reached a stage of advanced senile decay. Indeed, it was difficult to understand how it had succeeded in standing against the buffeting of the storms of the Pentland Firth all these years. To the seaward side, a series of pendulous folds of wafer-like sandstone overlapped each other, like a whole series of double chins. No hope there. The landward side offered more scope – here, there was a series of steps leading up to a small ledge, and Tom started up this. Climbing solo, as was his wont, he got to about twenty feet above the ground, and in pulling up on to a seemingly sound step, pulled out a shelf-sized block. He retired to the ground and we made another perambulation round the Old Man – no one keen to commit himself to any one line. I had defined my own position very firmly, having cast myself as the photographer – a role reinforced by the battery of cameras I had slung round my neck.

We returned to the landward side of the Old Man.

'I think you should go up there,' I suggested. 'It's the only place where you can get started; and I can get some good pictures from the side. It'll look fantastic!'

Tom, this time armed with a rope, returned to the fray, stepping cautiously up the rickety staircase that led to a platform about eighty feet up. Beyond this, the line seemed to peter out. To the right, facing into land, the pillar leaned into a steady overhang, jutting out at least twenty feet from the wave-washed base. On the seaward side of the corner, the rock was sheer, featureless and repulsively yellow, a sure sign of bad rock. The only hope seemed to be a crack that probed through the overhangs.

'That's the line,' Rusty announced firmly, as he arranged himself in ironmongery, bing-bongs, and all the other appendages of the modern technical climber. Patey regarded these preparations with a philosophical patience, whilst I hovered around, changing lenses and trying out different angles. At last, Rusty, ape-like with his long, strongly muscled arms and crinkly ginger hair, swung on to the platform and lowered himself round the corner to get into the overhanging crack. I retired to the cliff side opposite to take pictures, and Tom smoked endless cigarettes, or searched through his rucksack in search of sustenance, preparatory to the long wait.

Tom had little faith in ropes, and no enthusiasm at all for rope management, being a great believer in the old school of climbing which laid down a maxim that the leader should not fall. He relaxed, therefore, noting Rusty's slow progress and the frequent tap of his peg-hammer, which indicated that he was using artificial aids and was, as a result, most unlikely to fall. They had no verbal communication because of the crash of the sea and were out of sight of each other. From my own perch on the side of the cliff, I had a seagull's-eye view of both climbers – Rusty spread-eagled over the crack, Tom dreaming in the sun – each in his own little world. The crack was overhanging, its side covered in a fine grit that was like a million ball-bearings. Rusty, emboldened by a slight easing of the angle, and a few rounded holds, moved up without the security of a piton. A foot-hold crumbled, his feet skidded off the rock, his fingers slipped on the powdery surface of the holds and he was left jammed solely by his shoulders in the chimney. Down below, happily oblivious of the drama round the corner, Tom was lighting up a cigarette. Rusty slid back to his last piton, secured the rope and abseiled back down.

The following morning we returned to the fray, thrusting Rusty into the battle once more, so that Tom could day-dream on the belay ledge and I could take my pictures. Rusty took six hours to lead the pitch, clearing away the loose sand, hammering in his bongs, till at last he was standing on a small ledge just above the overhanging chimney. It was time for action – I was going to have to do some climbing.

I scrambled down the cliff front, to the foot of the stack.

'You don't need a rope,' Tom shouted over the crash of the breaking seas. 'This first pitch is a piece of duff.'

I started up. It was the first time I had actually done any rock-climbing since I had been on the Eiger Direct – months before, in the winter. Although it was easy, I was frightened of the looseness of the rock, of the seas smashing into the base of the stack to one side, of the hard ground below. Poking my head over a flat step, I suddenly confronted a small, very indignant fulmar chick – a little bundle of down with a yellow beak. It squawked a couple of times and then, with unnerving accuracy, ejected from its mouth a gob of foul, slimy sick, that landed squarely between my eyes. The shock very nearly toppled me over, and I cursed the chick for its insolence yet somehow, at the same time, feeling a certain respect for its

The Paine Expedition: standing *l. to r.* Vic Bray, Derek Walker, Chris Bonington, our two cooks loaned by the Chilean Army. Sitting *l. to r.* John Streatley, Barrie Page, Don Whillans, Ian Clough.

Barrie Page looks out of the box shelter which Don Whillans and Vic Bray designed – the prototype of the Whillans Box on Annapurna – the only shelter that could stand up to the high wind in Patagonia.

Above left: Our first home in the Lakes at Loughrigg Tarn – one room above a garage.

Above right: Woodland Hall Lodge and our trusty Minivan.

Left: Bonington on Fool's Paradise, Gowder Crag, Borrowdale – one of the best routes in Borrowdale.

Above: Mick Burke.

Above right: Joe Brown near the top of the Old Man of Hoy.

Right: First ascent of The Medlar.

Below: Martin Boysen

Left: Coronation Street: the route (*photo John Cleare, Mountain Camera*).

Below left: Haston and Harlin after being trapped by storm in a snow hole.

Below right: John Harlin.

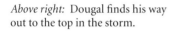

Above right: Dougal finds his way out to the top in the storm.

Below right: Sangay in eruption.

Below: Suave, sartorial Sebastian before Sangay.

Above left: An unusual view of the Old Man of Hoy.

Above right: Hoy: Tom Patey climbing the fixed rope up the Difficult Crack.

Left: The Huskies sleep while the igloo is being made.

Below: The end of the journey: Blashford Snell in command with flags flying.

Annapurna from Base Camp: Whillans' box in foreground.

Annapurna: looking across the Difficult Traverse on the ice ridge.

The Annapurna team.

Chris and Wendy Bonington with Daniel and Rupert (*photo Liverpool Echo*).

courage. I stepped carefully over it to reach Tom sitting on his perch. He was sharing it with another fulmar chick, but was astute enough to position himself just out of range of the gobs of vomit which the angry little bird ejected at him at regular intervals. The mother bird swooped and dived, just out of range, indignant at this invasion of her privacy.

'You might as well get all the pegs out,' said Tom. 'You're the expert in technical climbing, and I'm sure you'd do it a lot quicker than I would.'

'Wish I could,' I replied; 'but remember I've got to get the pictures. I'll jumar up, just above you, and photograph you as you climb up, and take all the pegs. It'll look fantastic. Just think of it – you'll be immortalised.'

And so Tom, grumbling, followed up behind Rusty, while I swung out on the rope Rusty had dropped from above, and jumared up past him, photographing his struggles with étrier, pitons and rope. Tom's forte was fast, free climbing with the very minimum of clutter of modern aids. He was totally unmechanical, delightfully unmethodical, and could guarantee getting any rope system into an inextricable tangle. Two sweating and cursing hours later we were all on a small ledge about 150 feet above sea level. But the day was already nearly spent.

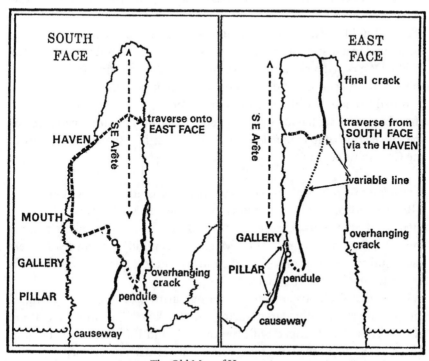

The Old Man of Hoy: routes

'We could bivouac,' suggested Rusty. 'It's only a few hours of darkness.'

'I don't mind – what do you think, Tom?'

'You must be mad – a hundred and fifty feet off the deck, with a good bed and a bottle of whisky half an hour's walk away! I'm off down. I'll happily give you a call in the morning.'

The flesh is weak, and the determination of Rusty and myself quickly waned at the prospect of spending a night sitting on a small ledge while Tom was back in his bed. We all retreated to Rackwick Bay, returning to the third day of our siege next morning. The climbing was taking longer than the North Wall of the Eiger!

We made an early start and it was now agreed that Tom should take over the lead, since the next section was peculiarly suited to his special talents. The angle had eased slightly to less than vertical, but the rock had softened to a consistency that was little firmer than hardened mud. There were no cracks for pitons, something that didn't really matter, since Tom could rarely be bothered to use them, and the rock was covered in a light mould. He swarmed up with reassuring speed, and a mere two hours later we were all assembled below the final pitch to the top – a splendid clear-cut open corner.

'It's my turn to have a lead,' I stated firmly, and started up. In some ways it was both the pleasantest and the easiest pitch on the entire climb. The rock had suddenly become firm and reassuring to the touch, there were big holds, and in a matter of minutes I was standing on the top of the Old Man of Hoy. We raised a cairn on the summit, lit a bonfire, and then waved to the solitary spectator standing on the cliff top opposite.

It had been an idyllic three days, far removed from the normal British climbing scene, yet having its own peculiar charm. The climb had given all the satisfaction of having reached a virgin summit as spectacular as any of the Chamonix Aiguilles.

A year later we returned, in very different circumstances, to take part in the BBC live broadcast of a multiple ascent of the Old Man. It was to be by far their most ambitious venture in this field, involving six climbers making three different routes up the Old Man. Two climbing camera-teams were used, and tons of equipment, and gantries had to be erected on the cliffs opposite, and even on the stack itself.

It was like a military operation, with an army assault craft carrying all the gear, together with a large tractor, into Rackwick Bay, whilst a platoon of the Scots Guards coped with the catering and the shifting of the gear. This was the advance guard for a whole host of BBC personnel to put on the climbing spectacular.

Joe Brown and Ian McNaught-Davis were to make a new route on the South Face of the Old Man, while Peter Crew and Dougal Haston, representatives of the new generation of technical climbers, were going to hammer their way up the South-East Arête. Tom Patey and I, the traditionalists, were to repeat our original route. We were to be the one sure factor in the proceedings, since the others were to attempt new routes on sight and, as a result, their speed of progress or even their success, could not be guaranteed.

The invasion of Hoy took place about ten days before the broadcast, but the BBC, ever careful of their budget, did not want more of the stars around than was absolutely necessary, and so Ian McNaught-Davis, Tom Patey and I were due to arrive only a few days before the transmission. In the meantime, we decided to snatch a couple of days' climbing in the North-West Highlands, near Tom's home, before joining the big circus. We could be sure of an interesting time with the Patey. Mac picked me up at Carlisle on a Friday evening, and we drove through the night to Ullapool, Patey's eyrie, where Tom ran one of the biggest medical practices, in terms of area-cover, in the whole of Britain. We arrived there, bleary-eyed, in time for breakfast, and Tom was already full of plans – almost before we had managed to get across the threshold.

'I thought we might polish off the Stack of Handa,' Tom suggested. 'It's not as spectacular as the Old Man of Hoy, but no one's actually climbed it, though I've heard that an intrepid egg collector managed to get there at the beginning of the century by having a rope trailed across the top.'

Having eaten a leisurely breakfast, we drove to Tarbet, a tiny hamlet that nestles at the bottom of a valley cradled between craggy, heather-clad hills. The far western seaboard of North-West Scotland has a special, wild beauty of its own. The mountains are isolated and very, very ancient in geological terms, well worn and hoary, standing in their solitude like hermits who have sought the wilderness. Tarbet was a row of little two-storeyed houses at the end of a narrow, single-track road, ending in the sea with a single jetty. It was a sheltered spot, guarded to landward by the low hills, and to the seaward side by the rolling bulk of Handa Island, which was uninhabited and preserved as a bird sanctuary.

'The Stack's the other side,' Tom told us. 'We'll get out there by boat.'

We called on Donald MacLeod, the Handa boatman responsible for taking parties of bird watchers out to the island. The bulk of his income, however, came from lobster fishing in the treacherous seas around Handa. Tragically, only two years later, he and his son, Christopher, were to be lost at sea, one wild, wintry day.

'Och, Christopher'll take you out to Handa,' he told us. 'You'll be wanting to climb the Stack, will you? I don't think you'll be doing that – it's sheer on every side, and there's nowhere to land.'

But Tom was not a man to be put off by any warning. We embarked in the MacLeod's boat, a solidly-built rowing boat, powered by an outboard motor. Even so, it seemed very puny for anyone to think of using it to venture out on the open sea in the winter storms. As we chugged round the point of land which sheltered Tarbet, even on this comparatively calm day, the boat quickly began bucking in the swell which perpetually sweeps down through the Minch.

On we sailed, around the Isle of Handa, past the teeth of reefs marked white by the swirl of the seas, and on which sat a host of gulls, which took off, plummeting and diving as we passed them. The cliffs began to build in height: sheer, dark sandstone, dropping straight into the sea, every ledge stained white from the excreta of the thousands of gulls which made Handa their home. And then – the Stack itself; at first it seemed to merge with the cliffs of the main island, for it was very unlike the Old Man of Hoy. This was no shapely obelisk, but a massive keep, standing clean-cut from the sea, filling a small bay formed by the line of the main cliffs. It might have been part of the island itself, but on closer inspection, you could see that there was a gash between island and Stack, a narrow passage-way filled with foaming seas and flanked by sheer cliffs. At its bottom it was around twenty feet wide.

'Do you want to go through the gap?' asked Christopher.

I would have declined, happily. I have always been nervous of the sea, but the Patey was made of sterner stuff. 'Aye, let's have a look; we might be able to find somewhere to get a footing on the thing.'

And so we swung through the gorge, white waters swirling to either side, and the walls black, dripping with water, stained with white streaks, stretching up, threatening, and obviously unassailable.

We cruised round the Stack, trying to find a chink in its defences. The gulls seemed to pose the greatest problem. Even if we managed to make a landing, every ledge, every possible hold, was filled with slippery, stinking excreta.

'You'll never get up that,' I pronounced.

'Ah, but you'll never achieve anything if you don't have a try,' replied Patey, the true pioneer. 'Do you think you could land us on that little ledge over there?'

'I'll have a go,' said Christopher, as game and adventurous in his own medium – the sea – as we could ever be on the rocks.

We edged our way into the base of the Stack, rocking crazily as we came in close. Patey took a prodigious leap on to a seaweed-covered rock, scrabbled in the weed with the waves lapping at his feet, and then pulled up on to a narrow ledge, just above the water-line. A fulmar ejected a stream of vomit at him, a dozen others went into the attack, but Patey was not to be deterred.

'Come on across – it's great over here, I think there might be a line we could get up just over to the right.'

I'm afraid Mac and I were made from a weaker mould, and so declined the invitation. Tom returned to the boat, but certainly was not prepared to admit defeat.

'If we can't climb it, we'd better try putting a rope across it,' he suggested, and we were duly landed on the island to walk over the close-cropped, springy turf, to the top of the cliff overlooking the Stack of Handa. Soon we had three 150-foot ropes tied together, and by taking either end and dragging them on along the cliffs flanking the Stack, we were able to drape them over its flat summit. Anchoring the rope to a couple of large boulders, we were all set to go or, to be more accurate, we were all set for Tom to go – for Mac and I had already made our own personal decisions that under no circumstances were we prepared to trust ourselves to such a dubious life-line. The Stack is about 200 feet high, and the gap between it and the cliff-top, over which we had draped the rope, was at least fifty feet. It was all set for the perfect Tyrolean traverse, as Tom launched forth, clipped on to the rope with a karabiner, with a jumar clamp to use as a handle in order to pull himself across. Inevitably, he got the ropes into a tangle, and by the time he reached the mid-point, he had tied himself into a nearly inextricable knot.

'Are you going to stay there all night, Tom?'

'We'll come back for you after the broadcast, if you like.'

Tom muttered and cursed, eventually disentangled himself on his high trapeze and slowly pulled himself across to the Stack of Handa, to become the second man ever to stand on its summit. One couldn't help wondering how that fisherman of former times had reached this point – had he used a thick old hawser; had he just pulled himself across hand over hand?

Tom let out a yodel on the summit and tried to entice us across – alas, to no avail – and then he returned to solid land. So ended a delightful little adventure – one of the hundred I had with Tom. There was always that light-hearted, carefree quality about anything you did with Tom – however serious the undertaking might have been. Perhaps it was due to his total lack of competitiveness, the sheer, boundless scale of his search for adventure for its own joyous sake. Tragically, he was killed abseiling from one of the stacks he so enjoyed discovering. In his death I, and all his many other friends, lost a source and inspiration to discovery that we shall never be able to replace.

Lagging behind the others as we walked back to the boat, I sat and gazed over the strip of waters that separated Handa from the mainland. In a way the land was an extension of the sea, a wild, stormy sea, petrified into stillness, the white caps, tips of rocks jutting through the heather, and peat hags of the foothills – the oft-repeated gleam of waters and the mountains – Suilven, Canisp, Quinag, jutting like rocky islands out of the storm-wracked seas. At that moment, I loved the hills and the sea and the sky, almost dreaded the next day when we were to go on to Hoy, with all the hurly-burly of the preparation for the big happening, the climbers and all the other people involved. I shrank from it as I had often done as a small boy when invited to a children's party, shy and a little frightened by exposure to so many people, yet knowing full well that, once involved, I should lose these inhibitions and enjoy myself.

And so to Hoy; the big circus – and it was tremendous fun. Dougal Haston and Pete Crew were hammering their way up the South-East Arête. It was obviously going to take such a long time that it was essential they got at least part-way up it before the start of the actual broadcast. Hamish MacInnes was in his element, as one of the climbing cameramen and consultant engineer for the erection of all the platforms needed for the big live-cameras and the complex set of pulleys required for lowering them into place. Joe Brown, relaxed as ever, had climbed the Old Man by our original route at the start of the proceedings, taking only an hour on the steep overhanging crack where Rusty had spent more than eight!

'It's not too difficult,' he reassured me. 'You can climb it free all the way.'

One of the features of the programme was that we were going to try to make the climb as spontaneous as possible by not rehearsing every move. As far as Joe was concerned, his climb would be a genuine new route. It was essential, however, that I should be able to guarantee climbing quickly on our route, so that if the other two parties became stuck for any reason, the cameras would be able to swing on to Patey and me, in the assurance that we, at least, should be showing some signs of action.

I was determined, therefore, to rehearse that long, overhanging crack. The fact that Joe found it easy did nothing to reassure me. I had no illusions about our disparate rock-climbing abilities – what he found easy, I might find bloody desperate!

Happily, in this case I did not. Secure in the knowledge that Joe had climbed it free, I approached the crack aggressively and to my amazement, in spite of its bristling overhangs, the holds slotted into place, so that I managed to get to the top in about half an hour. It was truly wonderful, sensational climbing.

I was less happy about my final role in the spectacular. Someone – I'm not sure who – had had the brainwave that the broadcast should end with an abseil, all the way down from the top of the Old Man of Hoy to the ground – 450 feet, in a single plunge, for the top actually overhung the bottom.

Coming in late to the meeting at which this was discussed turned out to be a definite mistake, for the team had, in my absence, voted me into the job.

'But the descendeur'll get so hot that the rope might melt if I stop on the way down,' I protested.

'Simple,' said Joe. 'Don't stop.'

'But what if I do? – it could jam or something.'

'It's all right, Chris,' said Hamish. 'I've got just the thing – a special friction brake which will absorb the heat, and won't melt the rope.'

He produced a slightly Heath-Robinson-looking device, made of alloy, with an asbestos cam built into it. This, he assured me, would absorb all the heat. I was not convinced.

'Have you tried it out?'

'Och aye. I did a two-hundred foot free abseil on it the other day.'

'But this is four-hundred and fifty feet!'

'Won't make much difference. Give it a try, anyway.'

'I don't want to do it more than once – I'll wait for the actual thing.' In fact, I did try it on a 150-foot abseil from part-way up the Old Man. By the time I got to the end of the rope, there was a frightening smell of burning nylon. I was not reassured.

The day of the broadcast arrived. The action was to be spread over the two days of the Whitsun holiday, with a bivouac thrown in for good measure. In addition, we had a spectacular pendule by Tom Patey, as he swung out from the base of the overhanging rock, to jumar up the rope to join me at the top of the pitch, accompanied by the racy repartee of MacNaught-Davis and even an attack by the odd fulmar. It was good climbing, in spite of the element of circus, and it undoubtedly made superb television. There were crises, when radios wouldn't work, when one of the climbing camera teams very nearly failed to get their gear into position in time, until finally, right at the end, when all six climbers had managed to finish their three separate routes on schedule and preparations were being made for the grand finale in the sunset – with Bonington abseiling into fame from the top of the Old Man of Hoy – my nerve failed!

'Would you do it, Joe?'

'No.'

'All I've got to do is jam a bit of clothing in the descendeur, and I'll melt the bloody rope. Could I have a top rope?'

'No good. You'll spin for certain, and the two ropes'll wind round each other. You'll be jammed up for certain that way.'

'I'm bloody well not going to do it!'

'Just think of your public,' said Tom. 'Seven million viewers are waiting for you. You can't let them down – anyway, think of the immortality you'll win.'

'Not much good to me if it's posthumous,' I replied.

'Only ten minutes to go,' said practical Joe. 'I know what, we'll lower you down a rope that's been secured at the bottom. That'll stop you spinning and it might even look better, because they can put it at an angle and you'll be silhouetted against the sky.'

And that was how it was done. I was lowered from the summit by the others, rather like an Admiral in a bo'suns chair, slightly apprehensive at first, and then, when it worked, I felt superbly, wonderfully elated, drifting down, talking away into the microphone of my radio, in spectacular circumstances but at no risk to myself.

Two days later, the camera platforms had been stripped down and the Old Man of Hoy was left to its regular inhabitants – the fulmars, puffins and cormorants who lived on its flanks. Climbers have often criticised these live climbing broadcasts on the grounds of the simplification, the popularisation and some of the cheating which must inevitably accompany them to make them technically possible. Whatever the rights and wrongs, these broadcasts are tremendously exciting for those who take part, and they do give the non-climber the best opportunity of seeing and feeling through the eyes and experience of others. The challenge of communication is very much in the hands of each climber taking part, for while the cameras are on him, not only can he show how to climb a stretch of rock, he can also impart his own particular feelings and even his own peculiar philosophy. A problem the BBC have is trying to find new climbs and new ways of presenting them; spurred on, perhaps, by a need for each broadcast to outdo the last, making each one much bigger, different or more exciting.

I suspect that the Old Man of Hoy broadcast will never be superseded as the perfect live broadcast. It had every ingredient – a perfect, very obvious summit, a scale which was also perfect, since the climbers clinging to the tower were dwarfed by its size, yet were not totally lost in its immensity. In the group of six climbers, our personalities jelled particularly well – Joe, silent, laconic, supremely competent; Mac, extrovert, clowning happily and stepping into the breach whenever the commentary seemed to be dying;

Pete and Dougal, both somewhat terse, workmanlike, practical – the modern climbers; Tom, the very antithesis, laughing quietly at the entire circus, poking gentle fun at my own earnest professionalism.

At the end of the broadcast, after a magnificent victory binge in Stromness, we all scattered our different ways: Mac back to London and his high-pressure business life; Dougal to Leysin and his climbing school; and Tom back to the mainland to search out another sea-stack. I couldn't help envying him, for in my relative success as a photo-journalist I had lost a great deal of freedom, was getting trapped into the very rat-race from which I had wanted to escape in 1962. But it was, at least, a self-sought race – one by which I couldn't help being enthralled, as I was sent on an ever-widening variety of assignments, learning more and more about my craft as a writer and photographer.

CHAPTER SEVENTEEN

Eskimoes

I knew I should ask Joanacee to stop the dogs so that I could take some pictures, but could not bring myself to do so. I was so cold.

The sun had dropped below the low line of hills to the south-west, but the sky was still red; tattered streamers of steam, rising from an open lead in the distance, were coloured a fiery crimson; the smooth surface of the ice around us was broken by petrified eruptions of ice blocks. A low pressure-ridge, like a neglected piece of dry stone walling, stretched into the distance and the shadows beneath a sprouting tumescence of ice were deep green.

The sledge pulled round the headland and the view was gone, but for the rest of the journey I was racked with guilt that I had not recorded those few moments. I sat hunched on the back of the sledge behind Joanacee, wriggled my toes, rubbed my fingers, but could not rid them of the cold that bit into them. The cold now crept through the double thickness of my caribou-skin parka, played gently up and down my back. We had been travelling since dawn, and had had little to eat; our bodies were running out of the fuel needed to combat the intense cold of minus 40 degrees Fahrenheit.

In front, the eleven dogs were trotting effortlessly, each one of them hauling on its own lead, all of which were clipped into the main lead only a few feet in front of the komatic or sledge. It was about twenty feet long, and eighteen inches wide, with our equipment, fuel and food covered by the caribou skins, securely strapped to it. Joanacee crouched in front, ever watchful, with his deadly twenty-foot-long sealskin whip trailing behind. A flick of the wrist and it snaked forward, cracking at the hind legs of a dog who had lagged behind the others.

Only a week earlier I had been saying goodbye to Wendy in our Lakeland cottage, then four days ago I had been sitting in an ultra-modern office in Ottawa, discussing with an official of the Canadian Department of Northern Affairs the problem of the Eskimoes' adjustment to modern society. Now I was sitting on the back of a komatic, near the head of Cumberland Sound in Baffin Island, just a few miles south of the Arctic Circle.

'Plenty of people have done stories of the far north in the summer,' John Anstey, editor of the *Daily Telegraph* magazine, had told me before I set off. 'I want you to go hunting with the Eskimoes in mid-winter. See what their lives are like today and how they are adapting to change.'

This time I was to take on the job of both writer and photographer. I had flown to Canada at the beginning of February, and then on from Montreal to Frobisher Bay, the administrative capital of Baffin Island, en route for Pangnirtung. Here I was going to spend three weeks hunting with the Eskimoes, at the same time collecting my story. On getting out of the plane at Frobisher Bay the place seemed totally hostile to man – it was dominated by machines. The cold hit us as if it were a solid wall as we hurried from the plane across a few yards of iced tarmac to the entrance of a building. From the reception hangar, I was taken by car to the Federal building – a vast, barn-like edifice comprising government offices, social centre, store rooms, repair shops and accommodation for all the unmarried personnel posted to this outpost of so-called civilisation. It appeared there were some people who never left the building throughout the winter, and I could well believe it, for there was no reason for them to do so – outside was a bitterly hostile world, with an icy wind blowing clouds of snow past neat rows of prefab huts, the homes of the Eskimoes. The lucky ones were employed about the station as drivers while those less fortunate were cleaners. The vast majority, however, had no employment at all, and just lived on Welfare – an aimless existence, spiced by alcohol when they could lay their hands on it. I was glad to escape from the claustrophobic confines of Frobisher Bay.

A big single-engined Otter aircraft took me to Pangnirtung, our route leading us over a sea of low rolling hills, flecked with the black of exposed rocks. It was a bleak, empty, inhospitable place and seemed as foreign to man as the surface of the moon. Yet in these hills roamed small herds of caribou nibbling the moss and lichen hidden by the shallow covering of snow. Then we came to the sea; tentacles of ice-cold water writhed into the coastline; the sea-ice stretched white and featureless into Cumberland Sound, then darkened towards the floe edge; grey mist covered the black waters and mountains jutted above the mist on the other side of the Sound. We were approaching Pangnirtung, flying up a long fiord with hills towering on either side. On first sight from the air the settlement looked like a handful of tiny matchbox houses that a child had scattered carelessly over a white carpet. The plane landed on the ice of the fjord and taxied to the group of people waiting for us.

Jim Cummings, the manager of the Hudson Bay Company store, was amongst them. He had agreed to arrange my hunting trip and to look after

Baffin Island: the hunts from Pangnirtung

me while I was in Pangnirtung. A quiet, stockily built man, he gave the impression of being quite shy, but lingering under what first appeared to be an abrupt manner was an impish sense of humour and considerable kindness. He was a bachelor, as are many of the Hudson Bay Company managers, for they spend long periods in isolated communities where there are few, if any, European women. Rightly or wrongly, the Hudson Bay Company do not encourage mixed marriages with the Eskimoes, though many managers, I am sure, have taken Eskimo girls as mistresses. Jim, however, was courting one of the school teachers, an attractive, strong-minded Scots lass, whom he has since married.

He showed me to his home, a single-storeyed, double-skinned building, heated by a magnificent oil stove. It was deliciously warm inside, and had a humanity about it that the Federal building in Frobisher Bay had lacked.

'What exactly do you want to do?' he asked.

'Have a good look at Pangnirtung, and then go hunting with the Eskimoes,' I replied.

'Well, looking at Pangnirtung won't take long,' said Jim. 'It's what you can see – a collection of prefabs, a few of the old Eskimo tents, the hospital and the school. As for hunting, there are not many Eskimoes that bother any longer. What do you want to hunt, anyway?'

'Caribou, if possible,' I said. 'That's what the editor wants.'

'I suppose I could find a couple of lads who'd take you,' he said. 'Do you want to go by Skidoo, or dog-team?'

'Dog-team, definitely; it's more romantic – I want to make it as original as possible.'

'Well, even that has problems; there aren't many decent teams left. The best hunters can afford Skidoos, and the ones who aren't so good don't keep their dogs in good condition. It's easier for them to hang around the settlement and live on Welfare. Still, I think I should be able to find something for you.'

Next day he introduced me to two young Eskimoes, Joanacee and Levi. They owned a dog-team each, and Jim assured me that they were reliable. Our food preparations for the ten-day trip were simple. Jim made a massive stew in a ten-gallon pan, poured it out on a plastic sheet in an unheated store-shed and, next morning, broke up the frozen mass with a hammer, packing all the lumps in a couple of sacks. These, a bagful of sugar and a bag of tea were our rations.

We left Pangnirtung that morning and all day our two komatics skirted the coast of Cumberland Sound, running over the flat sea-ice, past bare rocky islands and the occasional stranded iceberg. Every three hours or so we stopped and the dogs immediately curled up in the snow, or rolled ecstatically on their backs before settling down.

Joanacee lit the petrol stove and started to melt some snow. While it was melting, they sorted out the leads of the dogs, which had become plaited together during the run as the dogs had changed their positions. Once the snow had melted, the two Eskimoes turned over the komatics, and iced the steel runners, taking water into their mouths, and letting it run out in a steady stream over the metal. Once this was done we had some tea and hard tack biscuits to eat. Levi produced a hunk of raw, frozen meat, chopped pieces off it and popped them into his mouth. 'Tuctu,' he muttered. It was the meat of the caribou.

While the Eskimoes worked I felt extraordinarily helpless; they were so sure and quick in everything they did – I was so slow; the cold had a numbing effect, making even thought difficult. I quickly decided to allow myself to be mollycoddled by our two guides and to concentrate just on getting pictures. I was already having problems. The metal of the camera was so cold that if it touched my cheek as I held it to my eye, I received a cold burn. As soon as I brought the eyepiece anywhere near the warmth of my body, it misted and froze over, so that I could see nothing. Worst of all, though, the film was so brittle in the cold that it snapped at the least excuse. I tried to warm the camera inside my parka, but felt the heat drain out of my already chilled body, into this lump of metal, which had a temperature of around minus thirty.

Our first day brought us to Bon Accord, an Eskimo hunting camp near the head of Cumberland Sound. We reached it in the dark, for we had only eight hours' daylight at this time of year. I was glad to stumble into the warm tent, leaving the Eskimoes to feed the dogs. This was Levi's home, where he lived with his parents and four brothers and sisters. It was warmed and lighted by three seal-oil lamps, long wicks glimmering on the edge of an open dish of melted seal blubber.

We left in the dawn, the sun, a heavy red orb, hanging above the horizon. This tiny settlement felt like the furthest outpost of the world; five snow-covered tents clung to a rocky headland, surrounded by a waste of ice. The Eskimoes rounded up the dogs and packed the sledges; in a mad scamper we raced across the chaotic jumble of reef ice that bordered the land.

We picked our way through an archipelago of islands jutting through the ice. A biting wind whispered from the north, freezing my face, building long icicles on my beard and moustache, and yet I now felt I could contend with the cold, felt intoxicated by the empty desolation yet utter beauty of this world of ice and snow and granite, rich brown in the rays of the sun.

We stopped early that day on a small island. Levi and Joanacee immediately started probing the snow for a suitable site for our igloo; they were looking for a drift of hard, compact snow. Once they found one, they cut out the blocks for the snow house, and then built it up in a continuous round spiral. In just over an hour the igloo was completed, but there was still work to do. They shouldered their axes, and walked over to a pile of stones; the dogs, unleashed from the sledge, followed them, gathering around in tense expectancy, as the two Eskimoes levered off the stones to reveal a cache of frozen seal. The dogs lunged forward, but a lazy flick of the whip followed them and quickly drove them back, and they waited impatiently until the seal had been chopped into small pieces. Then they tore into the scattered meat, snapping at each other for choice bits, devouring it with the savagery of the wolves they were originally bred from. All our belongings were put either inside the snow house or on top of it, out of reach of the dogs, who would have a try at eating almost anything, including their own harnesses.

It was dark when, at last, we crawled through the low entrance and settled down for the night. In comparison with the cold outside, the igloo felt more comfortable than the most luxurious of hotels. The floor was covered with caribou skins, the cooker was roaring, making the air warm and heavy with fumes. Melt water crept down the walls; where it dripped between blocks, Joanacee made bridges of toilet paper. For supper we broke off some lumps of the stew we had pre-cooked in Pangnirtung, and as an appetiser we ate raw frozen caribou – no meal had ever tasted more delicious.

It was difficult getting to know my two companions – for the first day or two I even found it hard to link their names with their faces. The main trouble was that we could not speak a word of each other's language. Levi and Joanacee were both in their late twenties; like most Eskimoes they smiled a great deal, never became flustered, and yet I felt they never gave much of themselves away. During the journey I came to like and respect them, but I could never discuss anything with them or learn what they really felt about me, themselves or the life they led. Even so, we established a relationship that I found pleasantly restful. They were eager to teach me their language and we spent many an hour repeating Eskimo words – a whole string of gutturals that I found almost impossible to remember, one word from the next.

It took two more days to reach the area where we could hope to find caribou, first up a long fjord that plunged into the land, low craggy hills on either side, and then into the land itself, up through a winding defile, where the dogs laboured hard under the whip, sliding on smooth ice, catching their traces on upthrust rocks. I have never been anywhere so desolate; the snow-covered land was like the swell of a frozen ocean, bare rocks replacing windswept spume. It was difficult to imagine how anything could live in such surroundings and yet we could see the tracks and droppings of caribou. Beneath the shallow covering of snow was the moss they lived on.

We built an igloo in the middle of this waste and on the following day started the hunt, travelling in a huge circle round our base. I could not help wondering how my two guides would find their way back, it was all so featureless. It was bitterly cold, for we were now forty miles inland – the temperature was probably minus 50 degrees Fahrenheit.

The two komatics were several hundred yards apart, at times out of sight of each other. After we had been travelling a couple of hours the dogs picked up a scent and broke into a fast run, letting out excited yelps. Joanacee stood up and, balancing easily on the bucking sled, peered into the glare of the snow; but the dogs slowed down, the scent was dead.

We had another false alarm and eventually Joanacee turned to me apologetically and confessed, 'Tuctu no more,' and he waved at the hills to show that they had gone away. We got back to the igloo late that evening, finding it with unerring precision. The next morning we discovered that our fuel can had been leaking and that we had practically none left. We had no choice but to return to Pangnirtung.

Back in the settlement I felt I had seen only one aspect of Eskimo hunting; I wanted to go out again, to hunt seal, this time by Skidoo instead of dog team. I was recommended to approach an Eskimo called Owalook who was one of the best hunters in Pangnirtung and could therefore afford to run a Skidoo. He could also speak some English, having spent nine years in a mental hospital in South Canada. I could not help wondering about his background, but was reassured on meeting him. His manner inspired confidence; he was quite short but powerfully built with the battered features of a professional boxer, but in his case, the wind and cold had been his antagonist. There was a strength and kindness in his face that was offset by a twinkle of humour in his eyes. He was forty-seven years old, already a grandfather, with five children of his own.

Behind him he had a lifetime of narrow escapes; and in 1947 he had been caught on a small floe that broke away from the pack in a violent storm. He had no shelter or spare clothes, only a baby seal for food, yet he managed to survive for nineteen storm-racked days before the floe ran aground, fortunately only a day's march from his home, then at Bon Accord.

On our trip to the floe edge, I quickly saw the advantages of the modern form of transport. We raced across the ice at about thirty miles an hour; the komatic, to which I clung, yawed from side to side behind the Skidoo, bucking over every ridge in the ice. We could see the floe edge from a distance. At first it was like a solid wall, stretching across the entire horizon, but as we came closer, the wall disintegrated into a thin grey mist, rising from the open water. Ice merged imperceptibly with dark waters that seemed vicious in the cold.

Owalook stopped the Skidoo about twenty feet from the floe edge and, taking a boat-hook and his rifle, walked forward probing the ice. Close to the edge he halted and began scraping the hook from side to side with a steady rhythmic motion. A few minutes passed and a small dark blob appeared in the water and then vanished. Owalook dropped the hook, sat down on the ice, raised his rifle and waited. The blob appeared again. It was three hundred yards out, and barely discernible as the head of a seal. The rifle cracked; there was a flurry of water. 'Dead,' announced Owalook.

It had all happened so quickly and smoothly that I hardly realised what had happened, could not conceive that anyone could shoot so accurately, even with telescopic sights. Owalook had already unfastened the small, flat-bottomed dory tied on to the back of the komatic. He pushed it gingerly to the edge of the ice, rocked it once or twice to break the thin skin between him and the water, and pushed out.

Soon he was back with the seal in tow – it twitched a little and its brains flowed in a dark stream over the ice. I felt slightly sick, and walked way, but then felt ashamed and forced myself to return. I had not been watching someone killing for sport; this was Owalook's sole means of livelihood.

To me, the saddest thing of all is that Owalook is part of a dying breed. One cannot afford to be sentimental about quaint old ways involving a great deal of hardship, malnutrition and disease, but on the other hand the impact of an industrialised society on a simple, so-called primitive people can be terribly destructive. Today, the Eskimoes are fed and housed and clothed – even educated, but in a stereotyped way that has little relevance to their cultural background.

In 1965, Pangnirtung had a population of 412 Eskimoes and thirty-four whites. Today, in 1973, this will be considerably higher. Only five years before there had been just a few Eskimo families living in tents around the mission station, Hudson Bay Company store, and Mounted Police post. Forty-five years before the fjord had been empty. This gives some idea of the rate of change in the last few years.

For thousands of years the Eskimoes had succeeded in living around Cumberland Sound and along the length of the Arctic coast and its islands, in one of the harshest environments in the world, hunting with bone-tipped harpoons and arrows, living in snow-houses or tents of caribou skin, surviving without the aid of either metals or wood, dependent entirely upon the flesh, fat and bones of the animal life of the Arctic sea and land.

During these years they evolved methods of Arctic survival that have never been improved upon – with all the resources of modern technology, there is no better temporary shelter than the igloo or snow-house, the traditional garments of caribou skin are warmer than any modern-designed Polar suits. The Eskimo lived in small, self-sufficient groups of either one or several families. The Camp Boss, or Leader, was the best hunter of the group, and each person had his own role: the short-sighted or cross-eyed would be delegated menial tasks; the women did the cooking and made the clothes, but within that group everyone had a fair share of its produce.

Baffin Island was first visited by a European in 1576, when Martin Frobisher was seeking gold and the North-west Passage reached its southern coast. But the European had little influence on the Eskimo's way of life until the mid-nineteenth century when they came in increasing numbers to hunt whale, and even established whaling stations in Cumberland Sound. They also began trading with the Eskimo, giving him metal cooking-pots, guns, canvas and duffel material, in return for his skins. He acquired a taste for some southern foods, adding tea and sugar and flour to his menu of meat. Today, this is still his basic diet, although he is rapidly being introduced to other imported foods. When the whaling died down at the end of the nineteenth century, the Hudson Bay Company traders took over, establishing permanent posts throughout the Arctic.

Although the Eskimo became increasingly dependent upon these imported goods, he did not radically change his way of life. He still lived in small groups in the best hunting areas; still lived off the land. His life was undoubtedly a hard one and if he was improvident, or unlucky, his family could starve. He was also a prey to diseases, particularly those carried by the Europeans. Epidemics of polio or measles attacked complete communities. Chest troubles caused a heavy toll.

The establishment of a permanent trading post at Pangnirtung, followed by a Mission hospital and Mounted Police post, still had little effect on the life of the Eskimo. The site had been chosen for its good anchorage and position as a centre for trading to the camps scattered around Cumberland Sound. There was no reason for Eskimoes to settle there, as it was a long way from all the hunting grounds.

And then, in the late fifties, the Canadian Government suddenly became aware of the Eskimo population; before this they had been happy to leave the welfare and administration of the far North to the Mounted Police, its economy to the Hudson Bay Company, and its education to the church; but now the Department of Northern Affairs began to take an increasingly active interest in the northern coastline of Canada and developed a strong sense of responsibility towards its population of 12,000 Eskimoes, trying to bring them a standard of living and availability of opportunity comparable with that of the people living in southern Canada.

One of the most important facets of the government's programme was education. Until the Eskimo could read and write English, and eventually compete on an equal footing with other Canadians, there seemed little hope for his future development. Even today, very few adults can speak a word of English, and the children, who have been to school for some years, barely have a working command of the language.

A school was opened in Pangnirtung in 1960: in 1968 it had five teachers and over a hundred pupils. The opening of the school naturally attracted the Eskimoes to Pangnirtung from their camps around Cumberland Sound. There were other reasons, too, all of which had a cumulative effect, for as the population of Pangnirtung increased, so did the amenities: Saturday-night Bingo, the movies; a coffee bar for teenagers, complete with juke box;

an enlarged Hudson Bay Company store as well equipped as any of our own supermarkets.

The government had just launched a housing programme with the intention of renting prefabs of one to four rooms to all the Eskimoes on the basis of the individual's family size and income. The houses were undoubtedly more comfortable and convenient than the double-skinned tents in which the Eskimoes had lived up to this period, but aesthetically they were hideously ugly – little boxes littering the foreshore of Pangnirtung Sound.

There had been a wonderful peace and strange beauty in the tented camp at Bon Accord, one of the last family camps to survive. There was no Bingo or Saturday-night movie, but the family who lived there appeared to have a peace of mind which was lacking in Pangnirtung.

As I climbed into the Otter and took off on my journey back to England, I couldn't help feeling sad that a people who had survived so successfully and proudly in so harsh an environment were slipping into the role of the aimless unemployed, with full bellies, synthetic entertainment, yet with no real purpose or place in a modern technological world.

I should have liked to return home, for I was worried about Wendy, now getting close to the date when she was due to give birth, but I had another assignment in central Canada to do a story on a newly-opened oil field. My trip to Baffin Island had been the closest I had come to straight journalism, where I had to do more than just have an adventure and record it. I had been fascinated by the lives of the Eskimoes and had felt a deep sympathy with them.

The Athabaska Oil Sands were different. I was confused by the massive machinery, the economics of the operation, and felt nothing in common with the managers and operatives of the concern. At the end of a week of talking to people and taking pictures of this symbol of modern industrialisation dropped in the middle of the featureless, trackless forests of mid-Canada, I still had very little idea of what kind of story I could possibly write. In fact, I never did write one.

And then, back home to England, to write up my Eskimo story, to be with Wendy once more, now in the final stages of her pregnancy. Daniel was born by a Caesarean operation on the 25th April 1967; an agonising gap in our lives had been filled, but at Bank End Cottage, beautiful though it was, we were constantly reminded of Conrad's short life. We did not take the decision consciously, but I think we needed to make a move to break away from these reminders. We bought a house in Cockermouth early that summer, but even as we bought it I was beginning to feel restless in the Lake District. The idyllic, easy-going days of Woodland were for ever finished. I was getting more and more journalistic work, more lectures, and this meant long, awkward drives out of the Lake District to wherever I happened to be going. I began to feel isolated, both from the society of other photographers and writers and from the main climbing stream. By this time a strong climbing community had formed in Wales, based around Llanberis, but in the Lakes there was no such development. There was a fair number of local climbers, but these were scattered over a wide area.

Another factor was that although I had been climbing round the Lake District for five years and had by no means exhausted all the climbs in that area I had begun to tire of Lakeland hills and was looking farther afield.

I wanted to move to London, feeling that now my career was developing into that of a photo-journalist and since all the magazines had their offices in London, this was the place where I should also be. Wendy, on the other hand, loved the Lake District, had built a circle of close and loyal friends and had grown roots much deeper and more lasting than I ever could. With real justification she felt that since I was away from home so much, in the main doing things which I thoroughly enjoyed, she should have a strong say in where we lived.

These two, differing ambitions caused the greatest strain our relationship has had, before or since. I was determined to move; she wasn't at all sure whether it was even in my best interests to do so, but she knew she could not budge me from my view. We spent several very unhappy weekends, hunting for a possible home in London. Starting in Hampstead, where I had been brought up, we breezed into an estate office and asked for houses at around what we considered to be a reasonable figure. The receptionist raised a polite eyebrow, and assured us they had nothing at less than double that figure. Eventually we found our financial level which took us to an area where we trailed round a series of slightly grotty terrace houses, deafened by the sound of traffic, becoming suddenly aware of the smell of petrol fumes. We fled from London and headed for home.

On the way back we stayed with Nick Estcourt, who had recently moved from London to work as a computer programmer with Ferranti in Manchester. He and his wife Carolyn lived in a flat at Alderley Edge which, after London, seemed delightfully clean and quiet – the perfect compromise. Already we had plenty of friends in the Manchester area – we could get back to the Lake District comparatively easily and, living on the outskirts of Manchester, there was not the same feeling of claustrophobia which London seemed to generate in me almost as badly as in Wendy.

Less than a year after we had bought our house in Cockermouth, we started hunting for a house on the southern side of Manchester, and as we hunted the tempo of my own career seemed to grow ever faster. It was spring, 1968, and I had been asked to accompany Nicholas Monsarrat to Hunza as photographer, while he wrote a profile on this obscure little kingdom in the heart of the Himalaya. And later that summer I was due to join an expedition to attempt the first-ever descent of the Blue Nile – again as writer and photographer. But first I was to visit Hunza.

CHAPTER EIGHTEEN

The Valley of the Hunza

Hunza is an emerald in a setting of browns, greys and dazzling white, an oasis in the heart of a mountain desert of soaring ice peaks and sun-blasted rock. They say its inhabitants live to ages of anything up to 130 and that they are descended from the soldiers of Alexander the Great.

Nicholas Monsarrat and I were trying to find out how far reality lived up to legend. In London this remote Himalayan valley had seemed almost too accessible: VC10 to Karachi, a connection to Rawalpindi and the next morning a local plane to Ghilgit in the heart of the mountains. A tourist brochure assured us that there was a jeep road through spectacular scenery into Hunza itself, and it seemed we could be there within forty-eight hours of leaving London.

I should have been disappointed if this had proved true. Our first delay was in Rawalpindi where we waited for three days in the anonymous cloying luxury of the Hotel Intercontinental, while storm clouds scurried over the foothills to the immediate north. The plane could only fly to Ghilgit in perfect conditions.

Monsarrat and I must have made an unlikely looking pair. He, urbane, charming when he wanted to be, yet with a caustic wit that could lash out unexpectedly, had come equipped with dinner jacket and clothes for every social occasion. I had two rucksacks full of boots, ropes and climbing gear.

The flight from Rawalpindi to Ghilgit must be one of the most impressive in the world. The twin-engined Fokker Friendship ridge-hops over the tree-covered tentacles of the great peaks – one second the plane is barely clawing its way over a ridge and the next it is suspended over the abyss of a deep-cut valley, brown waters swirling far below. The gigantic mass of Nanga Parbat towers over the plane with its complex of ice falls, snow fields and rocky buttresses.

Approaching Ghilgit the plane dives through narrow valleys, giving the impression of driving flat out along a narrow country lane. We overshot the runway once, caught a glimpse of mud-roofed houses and upturned faces, seemed to fly straight for the rock wall of the valley, banked at the last minute and touched down at Ghilgit airport. The following day an air force plane crashed on its way out to Rawalpindi with the loss of twenty-two lives, a grim reminder of the dangers of flying among high mountains.

Ghilgit itself is a dusty garrison town, surrounded by bleak rocky hills, but the bazaar has a feeling of Kipling's North-west Frontier, of being the threshold of something more strange and exciting. Jeeps jostle with pedestrians and donkeys, bearded holy men stride through the teeming streets, and the shops, like open-ended boxes, are crammed with brightly coloured trashy goods. It is a world of men, and the few women in sight are heavily veiled by the hideous burkha. The muezzin calls the faithful to prayer over the loudspeaker, harsh and metallic. Here is an uneasy, at times ugly, marriage between progress and tradition.

We spent the night in the rest house and the next morning were ready to start the final stage of our journey by jeep to Hunza. Our party had now grown. The Pakistan Press Information Department had put at our disposal one of their officials, a Mr Mir. At times one felt he had the role of an 'Intourist' guide, deflecting us from anything that might not show Pakistan at its best. At Ghilgit we were joined by another guide from Hunza, who had with him his seven-year-old son. With the driver and his mate, six of us, with all our baggage, were crammed into the back of the jeep.

At first the road ran up a wide flat valley – weeping grey clouds clinging to its rocky flanks, the road, a dirt strip marked by cairns of stone; and then the valley began to narrow, the road crept up its side, wound in and out through tottering pinnacles of rock, clung to precarious slopes of scree. The jeep was now permanently in bottom gear; each meeting with an oncoming vehicle became a battle of wills between the drivers as to who should go back to the nearest parking place. The road was like a switchback gone mad, as it bucked from valley floor, over spurs, round re-entrants and down again. And as the rain fell, water rushed down every gully, eating away the road, carrying little avalanches of stones that built up into drifts across it. I have never known a journey like it. I was perched on the outside of the jeep and seemed to overhang the creaming torrent hundreds of feet below. The jeep snarled and skidded on the loose stones and mud, brushed the precarious outer wall, teetered past giant bites that had been eaten from the road.

After forty miles, with another twenty-five to go, we were finally brought to a halt: the entire road had been swept away. We spent the night in the rest house at the nearest village. There were no amenities and the only available food was a few hard-boiled eggs and leathery chuppaties, which we ate under the assembled gaze of the inhabitants. I could see Nicholas Monsarrat's sense of humour beginning to wear a little thin, and that night he began to mutter about returning to London to meet his publishers'

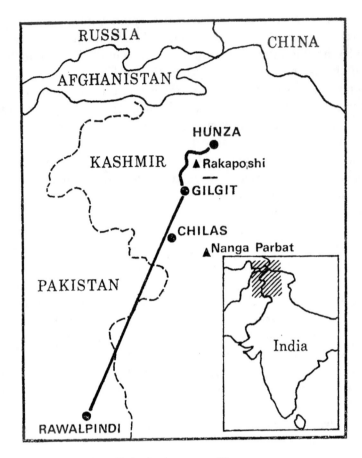

Kashmir: the route to Hunza

deadline on a new novel he had just finished. By morning, his mind was made up – he was determined to return; Mr Mir was eager to volunteer his services as escort – his winkle-picker shoes and sharp city suit were hardly suitable for a trek into the lost valley of Hunza.

I decided to walk on into Hunza. Apart from anything else, I have always preferred being on foot to being in a vehicle. In a jeep one is separated from the people of the land, not only by the speed of one's passing, but also by the barriers set up by one's relative affluence. The rain still poured down, but I had a feeling of freedom as I plodded on with my interpreter, his son and an elderly mail-runner who volunteered to carry my gear.

That night we reached the village of Hindi – we were on Hunza territory for the first time. Hindi is a tiny oasis of green clinging to the arid rocks and sand of the gorge. Houses like little mud boxes are scattered among a mosaic of terraced fields and irrigation channels. Everywhere are trees, straight rows of poplar, clumps of apricot, little jungles of lavender.

We stopped at the rest house, a mud hut with a gaping square in the roof to let the smoke out and the rain in; there was no sign of beds or food but we just sat and waited. You have got to be patient in a place like Hunza; things move slowly but eventually something happens.

One of the village elders arrived and made a courtly little speech which was translated to me:

> Just as the sun has been hidden by the clouds for over ten days, so the British have left Pakistan for many years. I am very glad to welcome you, a Briton, back to Hunza.

He then produced a rather dirty cloth full of dried apricots and apples. I had barely recovered from my last attack of dysentery, but did not see how I could refuse, so shoving my fears into the background, I tucked into the dried fruit. Another long pause and we were invited to supper.

Our host, Ali Murad Khan, was seventy but looked fifty, and lived near the edge of the cultivated area. We picked our way along narrow paths by the side of irrigation channels to his house. It was typical of a moderately prosperous Hunza home, flat roofed with two storeys; the lower one, a dark dungeon, they live in during the winter, while the upper storey is for summer. There are no windows and all the light comes from a hole in the roof.

Ali Murad Khan owns two small fields, twenty sheep, two cows and an ox. He, like all Hunza people, is almost entirely self-sufficient – has to be, for there is practically no money coming in to buy food, furniture or clothing. From his farm he gets fruit in season, apricots, grapes, apples, peaches and mulberries; he owns a few poplar trees for timber and some lavender for firewood. He also grows wheat and potatoes. His clothing comes from the wool of his sheep.

He apologised to me that this was the lean season; they were waiting for their fruit and wheat to ripen. There was little food to be purchased from the shops in the bazaar, and what there was, was expensive. The only income that Ali Murad Khan had was from selling cloth woven from the wool of his sheep and from making Hunza wine from his grapes. Although they are Muslims, the people of Hunza take a liberal view on the subject of drinking. His eldest son, who lived with him, had a pension of fifteen rupees a month from serving for fifteen years in the army. No family in Hunza could survive without sending some members down into Pakistan to earn a living either in the army or as servants or porters, thus bringing some hard cash back into the valley. In many instances men spent ten months of the year in the lowlands, leaving wives and families to look after their farms.

That night Ali Murad Khan brought out some mutton that had been hung in the cellar for the past three months; the spices barely disguised its pungent flavour. We sat on the floor round the big communal pot and, using bits of chupatti as a spoon, shovelled meat, gravy and curried vegetables into our mouths. For the first time in the week I had been in Pakistan I began to feel part of the land and people in a way that I would never have done if Monsarrat, or any other European, had been with me. The two wives sat in the background, waiting for us to finish, for they could not eat in front of a stranger.

Next morning we finished our walk into the valley of Hunza; another six miles up the gorge, and we came round a low spur that had barred our view. Suddenly the valley opened out into a great basin, about eight miles long and four wide, paved in brilliant green, yet dominated by stark rocky sides that stretched up into ramparts of snow-clad peaks.

This oasis in the midst of a mountain desert is entirely dependent on glacier melt water, which is channelled into irrigation canals by a complex system of channels and sluices, and shared out amongst the separate villages and then amongst the individual fields in strict rotation. A wide stony river splits the valley in two, dividing the State of Hunza from Nagir. At the end of it, you can just see the Mir of Hunza's palaces. His old one is a white painted eyrie, perched high on a crag, while the new, in grey granite, nestles below.

There are many theories about the origins of the people of Hunza. That afternoon, walking through the valley, I couldn't help noticing how many of the inhabitants had fair skins, blue eyes and blond hair. Hunza is on the old caravan route between the interior of Asia and the Indus Valley, one of the most important trade routes of the old world, and an area where there must have been a constant intermingling of peoples. Besides the theory that the Hunzas are descended from soldiers of Alexander the Great, there is one the Mir suggested to me: that they originally came from a place called Hunz in the Caucasus, and were driven into their present home during the reign of Tamerlane. Their language, Brushaki, bears no relation to either the Indian or Iranian language families.

The women of Hunza do not hide under the burkha, like most of the women of South Pakistan, and by Muslim standards they have a great deal of freedom. They wear an attractive embroidered pill-box hat, held in place by a scarf, brightly coloured tunic and baggy trousers. The girls are deliciously pretty, but there is one snag: under no circumstances would they allow themselves to be photographed. My guide told me that this had not always been the case, but a Brazilian film company had made a film in Hunza some years before and had then inserted into it a childbirth sequence shot somewhere else. This had so incensed the sensibilities of the ladies of Hunza that they had spurned all forms of photography ever since.

That night, and for the next ten days, I stayed at the Hunza Hotel; it was hardly four-star, except for the prices. A pot of tea cost two rupees (approximately eight pence) and a vegetable curry, the standard meal, was seven rupees. I had a bare, but clean, room furnished with a bed and a small table, with a commode next door.

Each day I explored the valley, took pictures and talked to as many people as I could. At times I could not help being painfully aware that I was in a place that was on the threshold of becoming a tourist resort, when every form of goodwill becomes a marketable commodity.

Certainly, no Alpine valley could compare with Hunza for sheer, devastating beauty – it is the contrast more than anything else, green upon arid brown all capped with white. To the south-west, Rakaposhi, a huge complex of writhing snow ridges and hanging glaciers; to the north, the soaring wall of the Passu peaks that jumps 16,000 feet to a turreted ridge of ice and rock spires. To the east, more mountains, glaciers, rock and snow.

On my first morning I attended the Court of the Mir of Hunza; it was an informal affair. At ten o'clock, the Mir, an absolute monarch with complete control over the internal affairs of his 20,000 people, walks from his palace to the Durbah, a courtyard with a verandah down two sides. The Mir sits on a small rostrum, and his Court, in strict order of precedence, squat on carpets in two lines on either side of him.

The Court consists of the headman and elders of Hunza; they are appointed by the Mir, but he is careful to choose men who are respected by the villagers. They meet every day and spend an hour or so hearing disputes, giving judgement or just gossiping. This is Parliament, High Court and Cabinet, all rolled into one. There is no civil service, taxation, army, or even police force.

Anyone can walk into the Court without appointment, and state his grievance. On this particular morning there was one case. The servant of a villager called Dadu complained that he had not been paid his wages. On the other hand, Dadu claimed that the boy had stolen a goat worth 120 rupees and had drunk his entire stock of wine. Everyone had a say in the case, sometimes everyone speaking at the same time, but eventually the Mir raised his hand and pronounced judgement.

'If Dadu makes an oath on the Koran in the presence of his headman, I am quite sure he will be telling the truth. It is therefore only fair that you lose your salary. Do you agree to this?'

The boy agreed and the case was closed.

There is little violence in Hunza. The only murder committed in recent years was two years before, when Nadir Aman, a farmer, had a dispute over the position of a poplar tree in one of his fields. By custom, trees cannot be closer than fourteen yards to another man's field. Nadir Aman was told by the village elders to cut down the tree, but he took no notice. His neighbour finally cut it down himself and, in a rage, Nadir Aman went to his house and shot him. At Court, the Mir had sentenced him to be banished from Hunza, the most serious punishment possible, for there is no death penalty or prison.

That afternoon I had tea with the Mir. A short, fairly portly man, he looks rather like an English country squire, favours tweeds and visits Europe every year.

'I always stay at the Savoy in London. I don't like those modern hotels where you do everything over the telephone; it's so impersonal and the service is so bad,' he told me. 'This is a very happy country; there are no rich or very poor. Money can bring many problems and here in Hunza there is very little. I still pay all my servants in kind, with food or cloth. People grow their own produce; if someone is building a new house, everyone gives a hand. There is no question of payment, for they all help each other and eventually it balances out.

'A few years ago the Pakistan Government started their system of basic democracy to give villagers more say in their affairs. I offered it to them here in Hunza, but the Elders turned it down. We already have a democracy.'

As I explored Hunza, I felt he was right. What other state exists without police force or prison?

It was certainly difficult to tell rich from poor. When I went to see Zafarulla Beg, who has the reputation for being the wisest man in Hunza, I found him working with a pick and shovel, alongside his servant; and yet he is headman of Hindi, a fairly big landowner and eighty years of age. As he showed me round his orchards, he was giving me a hand over walls, rather than the reverse.

He is also respected for being a skilful physician. Until comparatively recently, there were no medical facilities in Hunza, and even today there is only a small hospital run by a medical orderly without a doctor, but it is rarely used and the people prefer their own home cures. They make concoctions of herbs for illness and set simple fractures or dislocations. I saw Zafarulla Beg at work on one of his servants, a man who had dislocated his foot. He strapped it to a split piece of wood and then tapped in a wedge, which forced the dislocated joint back into place. It looked very painful, but effective.

The Hunzas have a reputation for longevity, but on this score they do not seem to be in the same class as the inhabitants of the Caucasus, who also claim they live to ages up to 130 years. The oldest man in Hunza is said to be 106 years old, and I was able to talk to the 102-year-old grandfather of my guide. He still does a little farming and showed no sign of senility. It wasn't so much the great age of the people of Hunza that impressed me, but rather the vigour and obvious happiness of the old people.

This might partly be accounted for by the balance of their diet which is frugal, yet highly nutritious. They eat meat only on special occasions, and the staple diet is wheat chuppatis with potatoes or vegetables, washed down by sour milk. In season, there is any amount of fruit, and they dry all the surplus for consumption during the remainder of the year. In addition, the family is still a strong unit, and the old are both respected and cared for. The Elders of the village have a tranquillity and pride that one seldom sees amongst old people in the West.

During the day there is always a rattle of tin drums and the squeal of whistles played by the children. At weddings, house-moving and religious festivals, the men perform their traditional dances. This is still very much part of their lives and not just a money-earner for the benefit of the tourists.

One night I was invited to a prayer evening and feast at the home of Ghullam Mohammed. There were eight of us altogether, seated round the floor of his living-room. Most of them had come straight from the fields where they had been working all day. Jan Mohammed, the priest of the Jamal Khana, their place of worship, was dressed just the same as everyone else; he received no salary, and earned his living by teaching the girls of the village and running a small farm.

That night he conducted the prayers and singing. His face was cadaverous, with a huge beak of a nose jutting from it. He needed a shave, and his bare feet were none too clean, but when he sang in a strong grating voice that pulsated with rhythm and an unbelievable happiness, it hit deep into one's emotions. They all joined in for the choruses, and I was told they were singing love songs to the prophet and ballads of their own religious experience. It made the best folk-singing in Britain sound a bit insipid.

Hunza is a place of sounds, of water hurrying through irrigation channels, a donkey braying in the night, children crying or the muezzin calling the faithful to prayer from the palace roof – there is no loudspeaker system and his voice merges with the grandeur of surrounding mountains and the peace of the evening.

That night I met my first tourists; the road from the outside world had at last been opened. They were very disappointed that I was not Nicholas Monsarrat – 'He must be such a gorgeous man.' They boiled and sterilised all their water, even when it had already been boiled once by the cook – 'You just can't trust anything out here.' They grumbled, probably with good cause, about the amount they had been charged for sight-seeing.

I couldn't help resenting their presence, and everything that tourism stands for. One has an instinctive and selfish longing to preserve places that are strange and picturesque, but beyond that, Hunza seemed a tranquil and contented island in the midst of a sea of violence, corruption and poverty. A new road has been built into the valley that links it with China. This might bring in some industry and hotels, but with it must inevitably come all the other attributes of a more sophisticated society – crime, graft, political strife, a police force and prisons.

There is no answer to the problem, and anyway there is very little anyone can do about it. Progress is a runaway monster whom no one seems able to control.

CHAPTER NINETEEN

The Blue Nile

From a distance it had seemed a harmless shimmer on the river, but now we were looking straight down a steep chute into a boiling pit of white water.

'Straighten out the boat,' shouted Chris Edwards.

But it was too late – three paddles could do nothing against such a current. We smashed on to a rock and scraped down with the water piling round us. It all happened so quickly that I cannot remember any sequence of events; there was no sense of direction or time – just an angry, foaming wall of white, towering above us. Then I was in the water. I had a glimpse of the boat only a few feet away before being dragged under.

It was like being in a washing machine. No sooner did I reach the surface than I was pulled back again. I was not particularly frightened – I had not even swallowed much water but I realised I was drowning. My body, limbs, muscles seemed to have lost their own identity and to have become an integral part of the water around me. Thoughts swam sluggishly in a brown void – a feeling of guilt at having betrayed Wendy, and then one of curiosity. 'What will it be like when I'm dead?'

Then, with equal suddenness the water released me and I found myself being swept towards some rocks just below the fall. I couldn't swim properly as the trousers of my rubber wet-suit had been dragged down round my ankles, pinioning my legs: but somehow I managed to reach a rock and drag myself out of the river.

Up to that moment, I don't think that I, or any other member of the Great Abbai Expedition, fully appreciated just how savage and powerful the Blue Nile can be. It was a turning-point in the expedition. Before the accident, it had been possible to be light-hearted and to enjoy the exhilaration of plunging through racing white water, but after it we just plugged on doggedly, trying hard to complete the job we had started.

The previous day, nine of us in three Avon Redshank inflatable boats had pushed off from the bank at the start of the Blue Nile – or Great Abbai as it is called locally – where it flows out of Lake Tana. It was difficult to believe that this was one of the most dangerous, and least known, rivers in the world, for the current was almost imperceptible, flowing in a wide stream between tossing plumes of papyrus. Heron and egret flew low across the water, and a hippo sank out of sight as the front boat glided past.

It is called the Blue Nile, but its waters are a muddy brown flood that hurtles through 500 miles of unexplored gorge to the deserts of Sudan and Egypt. It seemed incredible that at a time when almost every natural feature on earth had been conquered and explored, one so accessible and important to the history of man had succeeded in retaining its secrets.

The source of the river is easy enough to reach; it lies in a swamp in the Highlands of Ethiopia, a small spring that nurtures a stream flowing into Lake Tana. The expedition had already completed the lower and easier section of the river from the Shafartak Road Bridge to the Sudanese frontier, and was now about to attempt the first-ever descent of the completely unknown part of the Blue Nile. For its first twenty miles the river flows through gently undulating farmland, until it drops 150 feet sheer over the Tississat Falls and plunges with ever-increasing violence through twenty miles of gorge to the Portuguese Bridge. From there, the river was completely unknown as far as the Shafartak Road Bridge, 120 miles further on.

We were members of one section of the seventy-strong Great Abbai Expedition, and as we set off down-river, other groups were moving into position on the bank to give us support. Our three boats were called *Faith*, *Hope* and *Charity*: Captain Roger Chapman, leader of the 'white water' team, had made extensive modifications to the boats, having the bottoms strengthened and inserting inflated football bladders into the sides, so that they could not sink. He had decided to do without engines, since there was too great a risk of the propellers being smashed against rocks in the shallow rapids. So we were to depend on paddles for power and steerage.

I was sailing in *Charity*, with Corporal Ian McLeod and Lieutenant Chris Edwards. Edwards played rugger for the Army and was a powerful 6ft 7in. McLeod was lean, even emaciated, yet probably the toughest and most experienced member of the expedition. He had served with the crack Special Air Service regiment in jungle and desert, and was used to working in small parties under exacting conditions. *Hope* was crewed by Lieutenant Jim Masters (at forty-two years old, the oldest member of the party), Staff Sergeant John Huckstep and John Fletcher, who owned a garage at Tewkesbury and specialised in renovating vintage cars. The third boat, *Faith*, was crewed by Roger Chapman, Alastair Newman, a lecturer in physics at the Royal Military Academy, Sandhurst, and Corporal Peter O'Mahoney, who admitted to being worried by the water but volunteered to come because we needed an experienced wireless operator.

Our gentle introduction to the Blue Nile did not last long. Imperceptibly the speed of the current increased and a distant roar heralded the first cataract. We were swept round a bend and could see a cloud of spray in front. I had a sagging feeling as we were drawn towards it. It was barely possible to steer and we were spun, helpless, against the rocky bank. Somehow we straightened up before hitting the chute of racing water that led into the cataract. Walls of white water lunged above us and around us, smashed into us with a solid force. There was now no time for fear, just an intense excitement. It was like skiing and surfing and fast driving all rolled into one – a roller coaster ride down an avalanche of white water. We were all shouting as we smashed through the last wave.

That night we set up camp in a meadow near the river. We were full of confidence and talked of reaching the Tississat Falls in the following two days. Next day we started by pushing the boats through an archipelago of tree-covered islands – rather like the Everglades in Florida, with spiky palms overhead and dank undergrowth blocking the stream bed. It was midday before we reached the open channel, where the current raced wide and shallow over a series of cataracts, each one more dangerous than the last. There was no chance of making a foot reconnaissance, for the banks were covered by dense scrub and tentacles of marsh. We had to press on and hope for the best. In one of the cataracts the crew of *Hope* were flipped out of their boat by a wave. Jim Masters was dragged underwater and only got back to the surface by inflating his life jacket. As we paused on the bank to repair the bottoms of the boats, he sat very quiet and tense, slightly away from us. At that stage we could not conceive what he had experienced nor fully understand why he was so badly shaken.

As we set off again we were joking about it being '*Charity*'s turn next'. For a short distance we roped the boats down the bank, but it was a slow process and we were becoming impatient. We could hardly see the next fall – it was just a shimmer of water in the distance, but we decided to take it: Roger Chapman went first and vanished from sight with a frightening suddenness. There was a long pause and then we saw the green miniflare which was the signal to follow. We let *Hope* go a few yards in front and followed immediately. They managed to get through without tipping over, but were carried, barely in control, over several more cataracts, before pulling into the bank.

We were the unlucky ones, and capsized. I don't think there was any question of greater or less skill; it was simply a form of Russian roulette, with us and our boats helpless playthings of the river. Once I escaped the grasp of the undertow and had reached a rock, I was able to see Chris Edwards bobbing down in the main stream, a few yards from me. He had had the same treatment, but had been hurled out into faster water and was

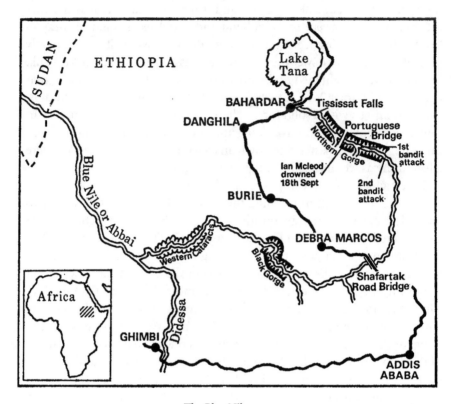

The Blue Nile area

now being dashed, helpless, over the sharp volcanic rocks. His wet-suit trousers had been dragged down over his ankles so that he could not swim, and his legs were completely unprotected. On the brink of a huge cataract he managed to hold on to a rock just below the surface.

'I'd lost all control by that time,' he said. 'It took a good five minutes just getting a grip of myself. I kept on repeating the number written on my lifejacket. It was all I could do to hold on to the rock and I knew that if I was swept over I'd almost certainly have had it.'

Meanwhile, Ian McLeod had managed to get back on to the upturned boat and was floating downstream. For a few moments the boat paused in an eddy and I even thought I might be able to reach him. I abandoned the dubious safety of my rock and dived into the river, but before I had gained more than a couple of yards the boat was clutched by the current and whipped out of sight. McLeod did his best to steer the boat into the side with a paddle, but he was helpless against the force of the water and was swept down over several cataracts, past *Faith* which had now reached the bank, to the brink of the worst fall we had yet encountered. McLeod described this as 'a smooth brown chute that went straight into a great pit of boiling water'.

He told us that he never thought he would survive. He just clung to the straps on the bottom of the boat and went right under. Fortunately, as he felt himself being torn from it, he was swept into the bushes at the side of the river. He grabbed them, but was unable to hold the boat, and had to let it go.

Roger Chapman had managed to stop *Faith* just beyond the cataract where we had capsized, and had swum out with a rope in an attempt to 'field' *Charity* as it swept past. I was now able to swim across to him and grabbed the rope, but we still had to rescue Chris Edwards. We could hear him shouting for help, a desperate, raucous quality in his voice. Knowing we could not afford to make a mistake, slowly and methodically Peter O'Mahoney and I let the boat out on a line from a tree on the bank, so that Roger and Alastair Newman could reach Edwards.

There just was not enough rope, and the boat was still twenty feet from him, so they threw a line, but it missed and the boat pivoted away. It was all we could do to pull it back against the force of the current so that they could try again.

This time they tied a paddle to the end of the line and it reached him, but he was unable to move as his leg was trapped in a crevice in the rock. Alastair Newman went over the side, fighting his way across to him: from a distance it was like a terrifying slow-motion ballet. Although the water was only around their knees, it threatened to dash both of them down the cataract with its unbelievable force. Eventually, they both got into the boat and we dragged them back to the tree. We were now presented with the problem of getting to the other side of the river in a leaking boat which was weighed down by five men.

We bottomed on every cataract, had to jump out in the swirling water to push the boats free, then on the last one I was dragged away and found myself once again swimming for my life. My nerves were so deadened that I barely noticed it, allowing myself to be swept through the turbulence till I could wait for the boat to pick me up. It was almost dark when finally we reached the bank, and then we found a thunderstorm crashing over our heads.

We had lost our boat, had nearly lost our lives, and even the next morning we were still stunned by the accident, but most of us were determined to continue. Chris Edwards was obviously going to be out of action for some time and John Huckstep decided that he had had enough.

The boat was quickly discovered by the Beaver aircraft which had been flown out from England to support the expedition, and I went out to retrieve it with several members of the shore support party. Twenty-four hours later the shock of my near-escape really hit me, and manifested itself mainly in a sense of horror at letting down my family. I had learned to accept the risks involved in mountaineering, but the risks I was taking now seemed so totally uncontrollable. I went to Roger Chapman and told him that I did not think I could go on any longer.

The entire venture was now on the brink of failure, and Roger Chapman, realising that a thorough reconnaissance was vital, decided to leave the 'white water' party for three days to make a foot reconnaissance of the river below the northern gorge while the rest of the party roped the boats down the Tississat Falls. I agreed to help in this and, working with Ian McLeod and Alastair Newman, I slowly rediscovered my confidence and peace of mind.

We edged the boats through narrow channels, often dragging them over waterlogged grass in order to avoid the worst of the falls. Even so, the river was always ready to pounce on a single mistake. John Fletcher nearly lost his life when he was dragged under as they lowered his boat down a fall.

I could not help wondering and worrying about my decision to pull out and that of the other married members of the expedition who had decided to press on. John Fletcher had a simple philosophy – 'I came out here realising that I was doing something dangerous and that I might be killed. I told my wife of the risks involved and she accepted it.' I thought of Jim Masters, happily married for twenty years, with three children; he was obviously unhappy about going on, but his sense of loyalty to the expedition was so great that he persevered.

Roger Chapman now decided to reduce his team to six men in two boats: Ian McLeod, Richard Snailham (a lecturer from Sandhurst) and himself in one; and Jim Masters, John Fletcher and Alastair Newman in the other. As a result of his reconnaissance, he decided to portage the boats from the Tississat Falls to a point about a mile beyond. I was to follow the bank on foot.

The river had now assumed a new character, racing through a single channel between tree-clad banks. Stretches of choppy, fast water alternated with boiling cataracts. As I watched the members of the 'white water' team arrive at each cataract I could not help noticing a tension which was getting close to nervous exhaustion.

'The river's alive with power,' Ian McLeod said. 'It seems to be sucking us down the whole time and you can't stop the boats filling up with water.' Once the boats were full it was impossible to manoeuvre them and it took a good 500 yards to get into the bank.

After about twelve miles the river plunges into a sheer-sided gorge.

This was one of the most frightening sights I have ever seen; the entire volume of water pouring over the Tississat Falls is compressed through a gap no more than fifteen feet wide, into a cauldron of bubbling, effervescent water. Even if they had carried the boats beyond this point, the next six miles of gorge seemed unjustifiably dangerous, for it would have been impossible to stop the boats before reaching the numerous cataracts boiling at its bottom. Roger Chapman, therefore, decided to send the boats down by themselves to be picked up by a party already in position at the Portuguese Bridge, while the two crews walked round the top.

It is one of those tragic ironies that Ian McLeod lost his life while taking the safest course. We had nearly finished our march to the Portuguese Bridge and had to cross the River Abaya, a miniature Blue Nile, at the bottom of a deep gorge. It was only thirty feet wide, but he was snatched away from us with such speed that there was nothing we could do. Alastair Newman had swum across first and McLeod followed, after tying on a safety-line. He nearly reached the other bank when he seemed to lose his strength and was swept back into the centre. As the rope came tight it pulled him under. We gave him more slack and although he came back to the surface he was now being swept rapidly downstream. The next moment the rope ran out. Someone shouted 'Free the rope' – at that split second it seemed the only way to prevent McLeod from being dragged under. At the same time Roger Chapman, with considerable heroism, dived in in an effort to save him, even managing to drag him to the side on the brink of a cataract. But McLeod was snatched out of his arms by the force of the water. We never saw him again.

We were stunned with a terrible feeling of helpless guilt that we had managed to do so little to save him. It seemed callous just to carry on with the expedition, yet there was no other course. Captain John Blashford-Snell, leader of the expedition, was waiting at the Portuguese Bridge to take command of the final phase, through the 120 miles of completely unexplored gorge, down to the Shafartak Bridge. Air reconnaissance had shown that the cataracts were not quite as savage as they had been higher up, but that there was a large number of crocodiles. He had, therefore, decided to reinforce the two Redshanks with two inflatable army recce boats, powered by $9\frac{1}{2}$ horsepower engines.

By now I had decided to return to the water for this phase, since it was impossible to cover the story from the bank, but I dreaded going back to the boats. The two Redshanks released at the start of the gorge had reached the Portuguese Bridge, only to be swept past. As a result, two new boats which had not been modified with inflated football bladders, were brought in. They were named *Deane-Drummond* and *Crookenden*, after two British generals who were supporting the expedition.

The attitude of the local villagers was a further complication. The people of the Gojjam province, particularly those living on the brink of the gorge, had a long record of warlike independence. They had been fighting with Government forces over a new tax law. Their chiefs, having taken exception to our invasion of the river, had tried to force us to withdraw, even threatening violence if we did not comply. A band of thirty local chiefs and retainers, all armed with Italian rifles captured during the war, gathered on the 300-year-old stone bridge over the Abbai, offering us a rising crescendo of threats. However, they left guards with us at night to ensure that no other band would attack us. Eventually, the police chief from the neighbouring town of Mota persuaded them to allow us to continue on our way down the river, and we set off on the final leg of our journey on the morning of the 20th September.

A belt of creaming waves stretched across the river only a few hundred yards below the bridge. The two recce boats went first, one of them helmed by Sub-Lieutenant Jo Ruston with John Blashford-Snell, and the other helmed by John Fletcher with Colin Chapman, a twenty-four-year-old zoologist, who was hoping to make a crocodile survey. Their job was to protect us against crocodiles and come to our assistance if anything went wrong. Our boat, with Alastair Newman and a newcomer to the river, Lieutenant Garth Brocksop, was the last to go. It was like waiting to go into a boxing ring for a fight which you were convinced you would lose. I had a queasy feeling in my stomach, and could not take my eyes off the tumbling waves in the distance. And then the green flare went up and it was time to start.

The water was never as bad as it had been above the Tississat Falls, but it was like going down a liquid Cresta Run, never sure what was round the next bend and barely able to stop. There was no more exhilaration, just a nagging fear and taut concentration, as we spun the boats out of the way of the boulders, or edged round the worst of the waves.

Now the river began to take on a new character, hurrying in a solid smooth stream between sheer rock walls. It was at last possible to relax and marvel at the rock architecture around us. Slender towers jutted hundreds of feet out of the river bed, while huge natural arches spanned its tributaries. We stopped that night in an idyllic camp site by the tree-covered banks of a side stream. The walls of the gorge towered 150 feet above us.

We were intrigued by two caves in the sheer cliff opposite, which had obviously been inhabited at one time. Next morning, we succeeded in climbing to them from the boat, and discovered a number of broken pots and old grain silos well covered in bat dung. We were all excited by the discovery as we packed up camp. I was drinking a cup of coffee when John ran into the camp and shouted: 'Hurry up, it's time we got out of here.' At the same time, there was a sudden, high-pitched keening from above, followed by a volley of rifle fire. We were completely taken by surprise, finding it impossible to believe that people were actually trying to kill us.

After our experience at the Portuguese Bridge, my first reaction was that perhaps they just wanted to warn us off. John Blashford-Snell ran out with the loud-hailer, shouting 'Ternasterling, Ternasterling', the conventional form of greeting, but one of the men on the cliff opposite replied by firing at him. I can remember running out myself, trying to wave to them, and then noticing a rifle pointing straight at me.

While some of us tried appeasement, others loaded the boats, racing out from cover with handfuls of gear and hurling them in. We were still arguing in the shelter of the trees about what we should do, but no one recommended firing back at this stage. One party wanted to make a break for it; the other, of which I was one, felt we should stay put and try to reason with our attackers, or call up support on the wireless. The deciding factor was a huge rock, the size of a kitchen table, that came hurtling down from above.

'Gentlemen, someone has got to make a decision,' said John Blashford-Snell, in a remarkably cool voice. 'When I say go, run for the boats.'

The next thing I remember is pushing our boats through the shallows. Glancing up, the whole sky seemed full of rocks; bullets spurted in the water around us. We were gathering speed in the main current when I suddenly felt a violent blow on my back and was hurled across the boat. I had been hit by a rock.

John Blashford-Snell and Colin Chapman had now got out their revolvers and were giving us covering fire. Fortunately, only a few of our attackers were armed with rifles. At John's third shot, one of the attackers seemed to be hurled backwards – it was almost certainly a hit. His fire might well have saved or lives, for it seemed a miracle that none of us or our boats was hit by a bullet. If an inflated side had been punctured, it would have been fatal for the entire crew.

At last out of range of their fire, we were now worried in case the entire country might have been raised against us; we watched every bluff overlooking the river with apprehension. Whenever we saw anyone on the bank we waved a friendly 'Ternasterling', but kept our weapons at the ready. Fortunately we could easily outstrip anyone following us on the bank, and that afternoon we covered about twenty miles. We even found *Charity*, snagged in some trees at the side of the river.

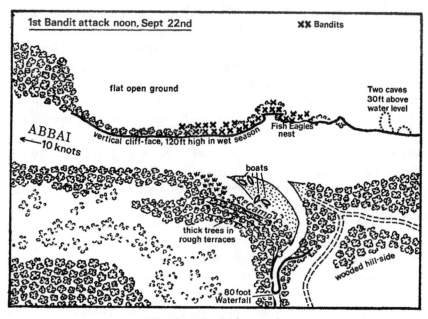

The Blue Nile: the first attack

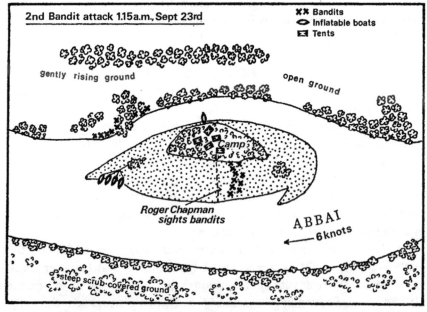

The Blue Nile: the second attack

At the end of that day we stopped on an island just off the Gojjam shore. At 1.30 a.m. Roger Chapman decided to make sure the boats were moored securely. Casually shining his torch at the water's edge, he picked out a group of men. Automatically, he called out 'Ternasterling', but they replied by firing at him; he returned their fire immediately and ran back to the camp. I remember waking to the high-pitched war-whoops of our attackers. I had been worried the previous night about the boats, thinking that if the bandits did manage to release them we should have little chance of survival.

Putting on my boots, I started down towards the boats. It was a confusion of gun flashes and shouting. John Blashford-Snell was a magnificent sight, wearing his pith helmet, firing mini-flares and taking pot-shots at a bandit.

Then, as suddenly as the noise had started, there was silence – just an occasional rustle from the bank showed that our attackers were still there. We packed up the camp in the dark and withdrew to the boats. We stayed there for a couple of hours, hoping to wait until the dawn before descending the river, but at 3.30 a.m. the bugle blared, almost certainly heralding another attack. John Blashford-Snell was worried about our shortage of ammunition and gave the order to cast off.

We drifted into the main stream in complete silence – it was an eerie experience, for we were able to see only the sheen of water and the dark silhouette of the banks. Then we heard the thunder of a cataract ahead, tried to pull into the bank, but were helpless in the current. Suddenly, we were in white water; we climbed a huge wave, came down the other side and were through, but the other two boats behind were less lucky. 'We seemed to stand on end,' Roger Chapman told me afterwards. 'I jammed my leg under the thwart and somehow managed to stay in the boat, but the other two were thrown out. I immediately realised that if I couldn't grab them we should never find them in the dark. They came to the surface just alongside the boat, and I dragged them in.'

Meanwhile, Jo Ruston's boat, which had us in tow, was sinking: the air valve had developed a fault and the front compartment was completely deflated. He had no choice but to release us and we drifted away in the dark. It was a good half-mile before we managed to pull on to a sandbank in the middle of the river. We sat there until dawn, feeling very lonely and vulnerable.

The drama never seemed to end. John Fletcher had damaged the propeller of his boat immediately after being thrown out in the cataract. As soon as they reached a sandbank he got out his tool kit to change propellers while the party waited for the dawn. A few minutes later he walked over to Roger Chapman.

'A terrible thing's happened. I've lost the nut holding the propeller,' he whispered.

The outboard motor was essential for our escape and they tried fixing it with a bent nail, but that was no good. Then, as a last resort they mixed some Araldite glue and stuck it back on the shaft, but the glue needed at least an hour to stick and by now it was beginning to get light. John Blashford-Snell waited as long as he dared before giving the order to move. John Fletcher tied a polythene bag round the propeller in an effort to keep the glue dry, and the boats were pushed off and drifted down the river.

The only noise was the gurgling of smooth, fast-flowing water. The wan light of the dawn coloured the fluted rocks and pinnacles on either side of the gorge a subtle brown. In contrast to the night's violence it was unbelievably beautiful. And we swept on down the river – it was all so peaceful, yet full of lurking threats. We began to see more crocodiles, but they seemed a small threat compared with our human attackers. The crocodiles just scrambled into the river and vanished without trace.

At nine that morning, we reached the assault boat commanded by Captain John Wilsey, which had struggled up river to meet us and escort us for the last leg of our journey. Our progress was now like a triumphal procession as the assault boat, flying the Ethiopian flag and the Union Jack, towed us for the last fifty miles down to the Shafartak Bridge.

We finished our 500-mile journey at 4.30 p.m. on 25th September. Our Beaver aircraft dived low over us and a small welcoming party waved from the bank. As we pulled the boats ashore we drank champagne, yet felt rather sad and maudlin. I think we had all come too close to death and were too aware of Ian McLeod's absence. We had succeeded in descending the Blue Nile, but no one could ever claim to have conquered it – too often we had been helpless in its grip.

CHAPTER TWENTY

Annapurna: Preparation

The Blue Nile marked a boundary in my life. We had found a house in Bowdon, Cheshire, just before I had set out for the Blue Nile and Wendy was left with all the worry and hard work entailed in the removal, together with undoubted sadness at leaving the Lake District. We had lived there for five years and she, especially, had come to love the area where we had known carefree happiness, had met day-to-day worries and in which we had experienced a total, overwhelming grief. It was she, not I, who needed the real courage while I was away on the Blue Nile.

I came back to find a sharp knife had been cut through a section of our lives. For a time we were in limbo, for the house we had bought in Bowdon was still in the hands of the builders. We had snatched it in desperation, only a few weeks before my departure. It was an ugly, old Edwardian semi-detached in a cul-de-sac on the flat top of one of the few hills in that part of Cheshire – on top of a hill, but there was no view – we were surrounded by other houses. Although it was very different from Bank End Cottage, or even our house in Cockermouth, I was glad to be living in Bowdon; there were plenty of climbing friends around; also plenty of climbing within reasonable range, of a greater variety than is available in the Lake District – the Peak District, North Wales, Bristol and the Avon Gorge just down the motorway. I could get out climbing once a week in the evening, and become again a weekend climber, going off to Wales or the Lakes.

For a period of three months, while we waited for the builders to complete alterations to our house, we stayed with Nick and Carolyn Estcourt, still in their two-bedroomed flat in Alderley Edge. We arrived intending to stay for a few days and by some miracle we did not get on each other's nerves, even though this time was extended so considerably – certainly this was a fine test of compatibility for any expedition. And it was here that the Annapurna South Face Expedition was conceived, or rather, was evolved, for it started out as something far less ambitious before it took its final shape.

Nick, Martin Boysen and I had been discussing expeditions for the past couple of years with little progress. That October we decided that come

what may we should go on an expedition in 1970, but suitable objectives
were limited. At that time all the mountains of Nepal and most of the better
ranges in Pakistan and India were closed to climbers for political reasons,
mainly the result of tension on the Tibetan border. It was possible to
climb in the Hindu Kush in Afghanistan, and in the outlying peaks of the
Karakoram in Pakistan, but I found these unattractive, for they seemed
overshadowed by the true Himalayan giants. We considered Alaska, where
there are still hundreds of unclimbed walls and the mountains are even
more empty and desolate than those in the Himalaya, though of course
very much lower.

I had known Martin for about eight years. One of Britain's finest rock-
climbers, at ground level his limbs seem unco-ordinated, but once poised
on a stretch of rock he drifts up effortlessly, a smoothly functioning climb-
ing-machine. He is like a huge intelligent sloth, conditioned to a vertical
environment. We had climbed together extensively in this country, but
never in the Alps or farther ranges. For a brilliant climber he was remarkably
uncompetitive, secure perhaps in his own natural ability and too lazy to
enter into the rat-race that can dominate some aspects of British climbing.
Even so, some of his new routes in Wales and Scotland are among the most
difficult and dangerous ever put up in this country; he went on to climb at
a very high standard in the Alps, making several first ascents and first
British ascents.

Nick, on the other hand, was not a natural climber. Wiry, yet powerfully
built, quite highly strung, very competitive, he had forced himself to a high
standard of climbing. In some ways he had the traditional middle-class
background of the pre-war climbers, and for that matter most of the Everest
expeditions right up to the successful one of 1953. He was introduced to
climbing by his father in the Alps, while still at school, and he gained a
very broad mountaineering background in Alpine climbing. Whilst at
Cambridge he became President of the University Mountaineering Club,
and also took part in an expedition to Arctic Greenland, his only experience
of climbing outside Europe. He was sufficiently devoted to climbing to try
to bend a conventional career in engineering to fit in with his sport, but
finding engineering somewhat tying abandoned it for computers. Living
in Alderley Edge, near Manchester, he was able to combine his new career
with plenty of climbing.

As the fourth member of our team we chose Dougal Haston, whom
Martin also knew well. Then, the news arrived – Nepal was allowing in
climbers for the first time in four years. Immediately we forgot about Alaska
and started to consider possible objectives. There were several unclimbed
peaks of below 24,000 feet, which to me seemed unattractive, since they

would have given me a lesser experience than I had received on my two previous expeditions to Annapurna II and Nuptse. The thought of a major face climb, however, did catch our enthusiasm – taut excitement and technical difficulty tempered with the slow snow-plodding that can turn Himalayan climbing into a featureless treadmill.

Then I remembered seeing a photograph of the South Face of Annapurna which had been sent to Jimmy Roberts.

'Let's go for that,' I suggested, with very little idea then of what 'that' entailed. The others, in their innocence, agreed. Another British expedition, to Machapuchare, immediately opposite the South Face of Annapurna, had included Jimmy Roberts and it was here that he had first seen the face. Having written to him, I telephoned two of the other members of that expedition.

'South Face?' said David Cox, a lecturer in Modern History at University College, Oxford. 'I don't remember much about it; looked huge; yes, there were a lot of avalanches coming down it, but I think they were going down the runnels.'

Roger Chorley, a London accountant, was even more discouraging. 'Going for the South Face of Annapurna?' in a voice of mild disbelief. 'It's swept by avalanches the whole time.' By this time I had begun to think of other objectives, then Jimmy Roberts' letter arrived:

'The South Face of Annapurna is an exciting prospect – more difficult than Everest, although the approach problems are easier. Certainly it will be very difficult indeed, and although I am not an oxygen fan, it seems to me that the exertion of the severe climbing at over 24,000 feet may demand oxygen.' I felt encouraged.

Then, a few days later, I received a colour slide of the face from David Cox. We projected it on to the wall of my living-room – a six-foot picture – and gazed and gazed – first excited and then frightened.

'There's a line all right,' Martin said, 'but it's bloody big.'

It was. I had never seen a mountain photograph giving such an impression of huge size and steepness. It was like four different Alpine faces piled one on top of the other – but what a line! Hard, uncompromising, positive all the way up. A squat snow ridge, like the buttress of a Gothic cathedral, leaned against the lower part of the wall. That was the start all right; perhaps it would be possible to by-pass it, sneaking along the glacier at its foot – but what about avalanche risk? The buttress led to an ice arête which was obviously a genuine knife-edge. I had climbed something like this on Nuptse – in places we had been able to look straight through holes in the ridge a hundred feet below its crest. That had been frightening, but this would be worse. The knife-edge died below a band of ice cliffs.

'I wonder how stable they are?' asked Nick. I wondered too, and, with only partial confidence, traced a line through them leading to a rock wall.

'Must be at least a thousand feet.'

'But where the hell does it start? It could be twenty-three thousand. Do you fancy hard rock-climbing at that altitude?'

'Yes, but look at that groove.' It split the crest of the ridge, a huge gash, inviting, but undoubtedly more difficult and sustained than anything previously climbed at that altitude.

The rock band ended with what seemed to be a shoulder of snow leading to the summit.

'But the picture must be foreshortened. That could be a long way below the top.'

Looking at some transparencies I had taken from Annapurna II in 1960, we saw that the top of the rock band was at around three-quarter height; there was another 3000 feet to the top of a steep snow arête, with a rocky crest on which to finish.

Sobered by what we had seen, realising that this was something bigger and more difficult than anything that had ever been tackled before, we flashed a picture of the South Face of Nuptse. It was completely dwarfed by the huge South Face of Annapurna.

In spite of everything, I felt confident that with the right team we had a good chance of climbing it; that my own mountaineering background had perhaps built up towards this attempt. In a Himalayan environment we would use the techniques developed on the ascent of the Eiger Direct; in addition I had a yardstick of comparison from climbing the South Face of Nuptse, although that had been considerably more straightforward than Annapurna's South Face. I had been to a height of 25,850 feet on Nuptse unaided by oxygen, but I had experience in the use of it from Annapurna II, and understood the tremendous difference it can make to one's climbing potential.

Although attracted to the idea of a small, compact, four-man expedition uncluttered by the paraphernalia and complications of a larger expedition, it was obvious that the South Face of Annapurna would require a larger party. Six men also seemed insufficient and we went up to eight.

The next problem was the selection of the team from the numerous leading climbers of Britain. They would have to be the men who could climb at a very high standard on rock and ice, with plenty of endurance, and an ability to subordinate their own personal ambitions to the good of the expedition as a whole. Most important of all, they would have to get on together. Many top-class climbers, having a touch of the prima donna in their make-up, are often self-centred and are essentially individualists;

in some ways the best expedition man is the steady plodder. On the South Face of Annapurna we were going to need a high proportion of hard lead climbers who would be able to take over the exacting front position as others slowed up and tired.

One can never be sure of anyone's individual performance in the Himalaya, since people acclimatise to altitude at different rates and some never acclimatise at all. The safest bet, therefore, is to take out climbers who have already proved themselves at altitude, but because of the ban on climbing in Nepal and Pakistan in the late sixties, there was a distinct shortage of top-standard Alpinists with Himalayan experience.

I approached Ian Clough first. I had done some of my best climbing with him and quite apart from being a capable mountaineer he was also the kindest and least selfish partner I had known. Certainly the perfect expedition man, he had very little personal ambition, but was always ready to do his best for the project as a whole.

Then I asked twenty-eight-year-old Mick Burke and, thirdly, Don Whillans. In some ways, Don was the most obvious choice of all, yet the one about whom I had the most doubts. Although certainly the finest all-round mountaineer that Britain had produced since the war, in the previous years he had allowed himself to slip into poor physical condition. He had lost interest in British rock-climbing, and even the Alps, preferring to go on expeditions to the farther ranges of the world. In spite of a strained relationship, which was ever-present, I had done some of my best climbing with him, each of us irritating the other, yet at the same time complementing each other's weak points.

Up to that time Don had had an unlucky streak, having been three times to the Himalaya, each time performing magnificently but never reaching the top. On his first expedition to the Karakoram in 1957 he spent eight weeks above 23,000 feet and struggled to within 150 feet of the summit of Masherbrum but was forced to retreat when his companion collapsed. On his next expedition, to Trivor, another twenty-five thousander, he worked himself into the ground getting the party into position for the final assault, and as a result was unable himself to get to the top.

On Gaurishankar once again he was unlucky. After considerable trouble in finding a route to the foot of the mountain the expedition was then forced to make its way round the peak on to the Tibetan flanks to get a feasible route to the top. Its communications were over-extended and it was finally forced to turn back.

Whilst most of the team I had invited so far were comparatively inexperienced, Don's particular qualities seemed ideally suited to the problem, but I was worried in case he had let himself slide too far into bad condition to function well on the mountain.

I suggested we had a weekend climbing together, without telling him of my plans. We were going up to Scotland one Friday night and, arriving at his house at about 10.30 p.m., I found he was out but would be back in half an hour. At 2.30 a.m. he returned, having downed eleven pints of beer, and we set off straightaway, with me in a slightly self-righteous bad temper. We arrived at Glencoe and the following day set out with Tom Patey to make the first ascent of the Great Gully of Ardgour. On the walk up to the climb Don lagged far behind, taking his time and in the gully he was happy to stay at the back, accepting a rope on all the difficult pitches. Then, on the last pitch, an evil chimney lined with ice and just too wide for comfortable bridging, he said, 'I think I'll have a try at this. It's about my turn to go out in front.'

There was an icy wind blasting straight up the chimney; it was so wide he was almost doing the splits on the way up, and its top was blocked by ice-sheathed boulders which you had to swing on. Don went up incredibly quickly and smoothly without bothering to protect himself with running belays. Both Tom and I had a struggle when it was our turn to follow. It was then that I made up my mind and that evening invited him to join the expedition. He looked at the photograph I showed him and commented, 'It'll be hard, but it should go all right. I'll come.' He was the obvious person to be Deputy Leader, and I promptly offered him this position.

So far I had selected people with whom I had climbed in difficult circumstances and knew deeply, who knew me and knew each other. This seemed the soundest basis for a tight-knit group – all with weaknesses and strengths, knowing each other well enough to accept them, and having in the past put ourselves and our relationships to the test of physical and mental stress. But now the choice of an eighth member of the team was influenced by finance.

'Couldn't you get an American? It would make my job a lot easier in the States,' asked George Greenfield, our agent, rather wistfully.

Not having any personal knowledge of any American who would be suitable, I had doubts, but we needed the money so I agreed finally. Various names came to mind, but one climber in particular interested me, and this was Tom Frost. Both Don and Dougal knew and spoke well of him.

Tom is a partner in a mountain hardware factory and is one of America's outstanding rock-climbers. The rock walls of Yosemite in California present some of the smoothest and most compact mountain faces in the world. To climb these, Tom and a few others have developed new equipment and techniques and had since adapted these ideas to tackle even bigger problems throughout the breadth of the American continents. The approach has influenced climbers everywhere. His reply to my letter of invitation was characteristic:

'I have just returned from Alaska where we succeeded in struggling up the tourist route on Mount McKinley. As a result of this experience I am somewhat confident in being able to ascend to 20,000 feet and on the basis of this credential hereby agree to come to Annapurna with you and will even attempt to climb.'

In fact, Tom had already been to the Himalaya and had climbed Kantega, a peak of 22,340 feet. He had also put up new routes in the Cordillera Blanca and the Alps. On learning that he was a practising Mormon, a faith which forbids strong drink, gambling, smoking, bad language, tea and coffee, I wondered how he would get on with us. Tom turned out be not only a good Mormon, but also a splendidly tolerant one.

The party, now numbering eight, was certainly the strongest that had ever been assembled in Britain to tackle a Himalayan peak. In addition to the hard climbers it became evident we should need some men who would be prepared to concentrate on the more mundane but essential tasks of keeping open the lower part of the mountain and supervising the flow of supplies. Mike Thompson, one of my oldest friends, was not a brilliant high-standard climber, but had an easy, equable temperament coupled with single-minded individualism. He was ideally suited to the support role I offered.

We also needed a doctor; someone capable of reaching the upper part of a mountain yet content to remain in a support role. It is no use having the doctor out in front. Dave Lambert, a thirty-year-old registrar at a hospital in Newcastle, had heard of the expedition from a friend, and telephoned me. He called to see me the following weekend and I found him bouncy, talkative, and full of enthusiasm. He was even prepared to pay his own way to come on the expedition. Having climbed in the Alps, he was a competent all-rounder without being an ace climber and I invited him on the spot.

Having the right equipment and food flowing up the mountain, in the right order, would be one of the requisites for success and some kind of Base Camp Manager would be essential. Possibly an older, experienced mountaineer would have taken on this job, but he might well have had too many preconceived ideas. A member of the 1953 Everest Expedition, Lt-Col. Charles Wylie, a serving officer in the army, at my request, recommended Kelvin Kent, a Captain in the Gurkha Signals, then stationed in Hong Kong. Not only did he speak fluent Nepali, he was a wireless expert and had a sound practical knowledge of the logistic planning required on the mountain. An assault on a Himalayan peak is comparable with fighting a war –

logistics and planning are the key to success. No matter how tough or courageous the men out in front, unless they are supplied with food and equipment they quickly come to a grinding halt.

It has been said that the ideal age for the Himalayan climber is around the mid-thirties and in this case we were slightly below, for the average age of our party was just over thirty. But at twenty-five I had acclimatised quite satisfactorily on my first trip to the Himalaya, and Don Whillans was only twenty-tree on Masherbrum where he put up an outstanding performance.

Our team now numbered eleven climbers. We planned to supplement our numbers with six Sherpas – a small figure for an expedition of this size, but with the face so steep, it seemed unlikely that we should be able to use them for more than the lower slopes.

We had succeeded in selling our story to ITN and Thames Television and hoped to get away with taking a single cameraman/director, but understandably they insisted on our taking a complete film team of cameraman, sound recordist, reporter-director from Thames and finally, since this was a joint venture, a representative from ITN to look after their interests.

I was worried about taking such a large self-contained group along, since an expedition imposes a strain on personal relationships at the best of times and a group reporting on us, yet remaining uninvolved, could have increased this danger still further. However, we needed the money and after meeting John Edwards, the Thames Television director, and Alan Hankinson, the ITN representative, I felt reassured. John was a fast-talking extrovert who would obviously fit happily into any group. Alan had a slightly whimsical, yet diffident air, not at all the kind of person you would expect to find in television. He had an unconsummated passion for mountaineering and seemed to be looking forward to our trip for its own sake.

And so the total strength of the party would number twenty-one. On top of this we should have mail-runners, cook-boys and perhaps some local porters – more people than I had ever been responsible for in the past – twelve men and three tanks having been my biggest command in the army.

We considered the ways of sending our gear, having decided that the entire team could fly out to India. We chose the sea route but found the only reliable schedules are those of passenger liners. The only liner going out to India at the right time would be sailing too early for us to have ready the enormous amount of gear we should need. The only other possibility was a cargo ship and I booked the gear on to one sailing from Liverpool on the 23rd January. We were barely ready in time and many items we had had specially designed were still not finished.

Two days before sailing date I had a phone-call from the shipping agents: 'I'm afraid your boat has gone into dry-dock with engine trouble. It won't be ready to sail for another three weeks.'

'Isn't there another boat going out?' I asked.

'I'll try,' the shipping agent said, 'but I very much doubt it.'

I was on tenterhooks for the next twenty-four hours. We had quite enough against us on the mountain without this kind of delay. Then next day there was good news; he had found another boat which was sailing from London on the 23rd, the same date as the original boat.

A frantic dash to the docks to get all the gear loaded in time; more worries that there might be a dock strike or any of the dozen delays that seem to affect cargo ships, but it sailed on time – first stop Bombay.

I felt we had overcome the biggest problem of all. Nothing very much could now go wrong. Don and Dave would meet the ship in Bombay and have an uncomfortable trip across India on the backs of lorries, and we should be ready to tackle our mountain.

CHAPTER TWENTY-ONE

Annapurna: the Climb

As it happened our troubles were far from over. The boat carrying our five tons of gear – everything from kippers to bottles of oxygen – broke down in Cape Town, eventually arriving in Bombay a full month late. Fortunately, the RAF had flown out the absolutely vital equipment – radios, medical kit, together with enough clothing, ice-axes, pitons and ropes to enable us to get started. We borrowed food from the British Army Expedition to the north side of Annapurna, and Jimmy Roberts lent us tents, ropes and sleeping-bags left over from previous expeditions.

Don and Mike left Pokhara on the 16th March; there was little point in Don waiting in Bombay for the gear to arrive, as planned. There would be a month's delay, and I wanted him on the mountain. I asked Ian, therefore, if he would undertake the grim job of shepherding the gear through Customs when it arrived, and then across India. I decided to fly out to Bombay in order to help to smooth Ian's way, before going on with the rest of the team.

The setback with our equipment was then overshadowed by reassuring news from Don, who met us in a narrow gorge leading to the foot of the South Face.

'It looks even steeper than the photographs,' he said, 'but after I sat and looked at it for a couple of hours it seemed to fall back a bit. It's going to be hard, but it will go all right.'

And so our Base Camp was established, with such a magnificent view that for days afterwards our people tended to stop what they were doing, and stare and stare at the whole gigantic wall of the South Face. Big avalanches were coming down Annapurna on either side of our chosen route, but it seemed that none was crossing the line we planned to go up; the more we studied our route, the more we liked it.

In many ways the South Face of Annapurna was super Alpine – presenting both the problems and the atmosphere I had known in 1966 during the ascent of the Eiger Direct. On Annapurna our Kleine Scheidegg was Base Camp, situated on a grassy meadow beside the lateral moraine of the South Annapurna Glacier, with the South Face a mere three miles away framed by a ridge of Annapurna South on one side and the moraine on the other. All we needed were the trippers' telescopes and a better crop of tourists to be in business; but we did have a steady stream of visitors: a stray brigadier, hippies, climbers, earnest German tourists, Peace Corps people, and so on. The trickle that might well become a flood in years to come.

And then the way we tackled the South Face; once again very similar to the methods used on the winter ascent of the Eiger Direct. A continuous line of fixed ropes, climbers dashing back to base for a rest; a Base Camp that was in a different world from the face, with its TV team, a few girl visitors who had stayed; radio communications with the outside world.

Closer up, Annapurna looked by no means simple. Our way lay across the glacier and up a rognon, a sort of island of rocks round which the glacier flowed on either side. Here we established Camp I at 16,000 feet, pushing on towards Camp II at 17,500 feet at the foot of a protective, overhanging rock cliff. To reach this point involved a couple of 'objective dangers' – risks which have to be accepted if you climb in the Himalaya. These were both fields of séracs, areas where the slowly-moving glacier passes over obstacles and breaks up into a series of ice ridges and pinnacles. From time to time the pinnacles collapse, usually without warning. The séracs, however, are passed in only a minute or two, and the risk is normally considered acceptable. It was on the higher of these two areas, weeks later, that Ian's luck ran out.

Don and Dougal reached the site of Camp III at 20,100 feet, half-way up the ice ridge, and with Base Camp growing every day and supplies flowing up the mountain, we could hardly believe the ease with which we had already climbed 6000 feet of the South Face in nine days. Our complacency was short-lived.

It took a back-breaking, lung-bursting month to climb the next thousand feet, and we all agreed that it was as hard as anything we had ever done, with very little to show for each day's trail-blazing. This entailed climbing down to Camp IV at the end of each day, it being impossible to bivouac anywhere on the ridge, then a wearying climb up the fixed ropes to begin work again the next day. With this kind of leap-frog climbing, we estimated that we climbed thirty Annapurnas before finally reaching the top!

My overall plan was to have a pair out in front at any one time, forcing the route, with the rest of the team distributed between the camps below, ferrying up the mountain. Once the front pair tired I pulled them back for a rest at Base Camp before going back to the mountain; they would do some ferrying and then go once more to the front. We were already short of manpower in the lower camps, but we were able to recruit six of the best local porters for the carry from Base Camp to Camp I which, though across

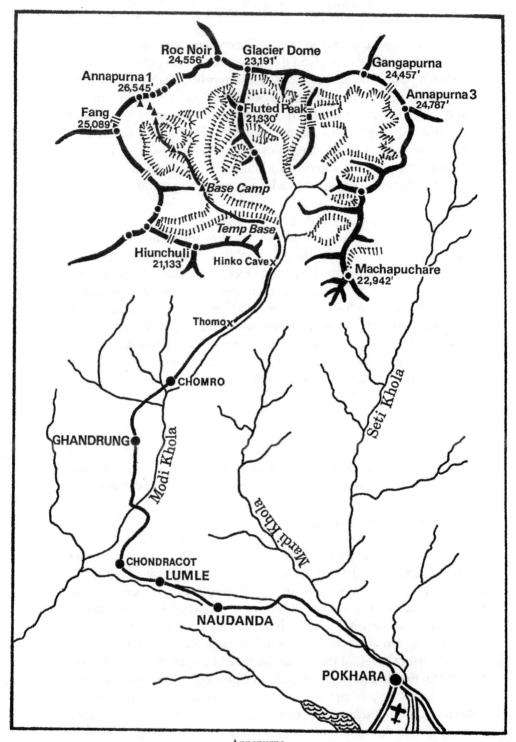

Annapurna

a glacier, was comparatively easy. These local Nepalese porters made a tremendous contribution to our eventual success.

Although frequent rests at Base Camp helped to keep members of the team climbing at a reasonable level of performance over the course of the expedition, it imposed a heavy strain on our available manpower. A pair resting at Best Camp would take three days to get back up to Camp III, four to Camp IV, and so on. These were unproductive carries, for the climbers would probably have a fair amount of their personal gear with them, and therefore would be unable to carry much food or climbing gear while shifting from one camp to another. The most efficient system is to keep changes of camp down to the minimum, but this pays little heed to the psychological factor of the monotony of carrying day after day over the same stretch on a mountain, or the fact that the climbers out in front quickly burnt themselves out, so great was the physical and mental strain of tackling high-standard climbing at altitude.

Dougal and I finished the last pitch of the ice ridge in a snowstorm. Having run out of rope we cut steps in hard snow to the top of the ridge, propelled by curiosity about what we would find on top. The angle ahead of us did not seem too bad, was certainly easier than it had seemed in the binoculars from far below, but this inviting view did not extend very far. At the limit of vision, looming out of the snowstorm, was an ice cliff, about 200 feet high which seemingly cut off all further progress.

Although it is possible to climb ice cliffs, it is a slow, laborious job, screwing in ice-screws every few feet. In addition, an ice cliff at that altitude had never before been attempted and time before the monsoon was due was running short. The seeming impassability of the ice cliff was an unpleasant discovery, since we knew that above it was the 2,000-foot vertical rock band which we had decided all along would be the most difficult of the obstacles on the South Face.

Mick Burke led this part of the climb, from the start of the Rock Band. The method he used to fix rope in place was to climb on a 500 foot reel of 9-mm perlon, running out long pitches of up to 200 feet, then pulling the rope through till it was tight back to his second man, Tom Frost, fastening it off and letting Tom jumar up the rope behind him. In this way he was running out the fixed rope and climbing at the same time.

In three days they ran out 1200 feet of rope, as much, in fact, as Boysen and Estcourt could keep ferrying to them. Eventually they took a rest from the face, when Burke dropped down to the dump at the top of the ice ridge to collect a load and Frost spent a day digging out the tent. We were now beginning to feel the strain of trying to keep open our communications. Ian Clough had been forced back for a rest but was now on his way back up the mountain. I was held down at Base Camp with an attack of pleurisy. Everyone on the face was badly run-down. We had already been using our local Gurkha porters, equipped with a variety of spare clothes and footwear, for the carry from Base Camp to Camp I. Some of these local porters were now doing the carry from Camps I to II, a fine achievement considering that they had never before been on a glacier. Various visitors to Base Camp also lent a hand. Two of them, Frank Johnson and Robin Terry, arrived on the 21st April and stayed for the rest of the expedition, ferrying loads as high as Camp IV. In doing this they gave us invaluable help. One of the TV team, Alan Hankinson, also rendered sterling service, carrying loads up to Camp III. This freed our Sherpas for work higher up the mountain and they were now keeping open the route from both Camps II to III, and III to IV; the latter run was considerably steeper than anything they had previously tackled.

On the evening of the 13th May, Tom and Mick were still at Camp V, immediately below the Rock Band at a height of 22,750 feet; Martin, Nick and Mike were in Camp IV, half-way up the ice ridge and Don and Dougal were at Camp III, on their way back up the mountain after a rest at Base Camp. Dave was with four Sherpas also at Camp III, having carried loads to Camp IV, while Ian, also on his way up, was at Camp I. From Base Camp, where I had not completely recovered from my attack of pleurisy, I opened up the wireless link.

'You're loud and clear, Chris,' replied Nick, at IV.

'How did things go today, Nick?'

'Not too bad. I was shattered from yesterday and took a rest, but Martin and Mike went up to V. Mike only reached the ice cliff, though, and was so buggered he had to turn back.'

'Don and Dougal will be moving up tomorrow,' I said.

'We're aware of that.'

'Well, I want them to move straight through to V, and go into the lead. Mick and Tom can then go down to the col at the end of the ridge to pick up loads while you three carry on up the col. Don and Dougal, being fresh, should be able to push on up the Rock Band that much more quickly! Hello, Camp V – did you hear that?'

It was Mick, at Camp V, who replied. 'I got that, Chris.' Then: 'As a matter of fact, I think you've got the wrong end of the stick, Chris. It's a lot easier going out in front than it is carrying. I don't see any point at all in Don and Dougal coming up here – it would be much better if they did some carrying first from IV to V. We've been above Base Camp for twenty-eight days. If we had to go back to carrying now we'd have to go all the way back down for a rest. We're just too knackered to carry.'

The argument went on. The crux of it was that I had originally agreed for climbers to take turns in leading out in front and in theory it was now the turn of Martin and Nick. Having been supporting Tom and Mick for a week, they had done the punishing carry from IV to V, a task so strenuous as to be almost impossible to do two days running. You needed a rest day in between, and at altitude you don't get back your reserves of strength – you are deteriorating the whole time – even when resting.

Nick admitted that he was going badly, although Martin was still climbing very strongly. On the other hand, I felt that Don and Dougal were the strongest pair and climbed superbly as a team.

'It's not that we mind Don and Dougal going through,' Nick said, 'but I don't think you have any concept of what it's like up here. Gear is piling up at IV much faster than we can shift it up the mountain. It'd be much better if we could concentrate for a few days on stockpiling Camp V before pushing Don and Dougal forward.'

I could see his point, but we were running out of time. I compromised.

'Let Don and Dougal do one carry and no more. Is that clear, Mick?'

With Mick's agreement, the argument seemed settled, but then Don came on the air with the effect of a small nuclear weapon. 'I agree with everything you've said. Dougal and I left Camp V a week ago. It isn't even consolidated and progress towards Camp VI has been so poor it's had me and Dougal depressed all the way up the mountain. I don't know what Mick thinks he's playing at, but time's short and we want to get the route pushed out. Unless they can establish VI or at least find a way, they should make way for someone else.'

It was the closest we came to acrimonious argument during the entire expedition. I did my best to smooth it out, then closed down for the evening. As always, there was something to be said for both points of view.

Tom told me later that they were both so furious that Mick suggested taking all their rope and running it out next morning – just to show Don. They did, and this resulted in the most impressive push of the entire climb, with Tom and Mick reaching the Flat Iron, a spur of rock half-way up the Rock Band and very similar to the famous landmark in the middle of the North Wall of the Eiger. In getting this far, however, the two men burnt themselves out and the following morning they insisted on coming down for a rest. Mike, the great load carrier of the expedition, was also in a bad way, having collapsed just below Camp V but having recovered sufficiently to stagger back.

This meant that we were losing people from the front faster than I could replace them so I set out from Base Camp, still feeling run down after four days' rest. Meeting Mick Burke on his way down from Camp I, I reassured him when he said, 'Don't think we've come down out of spite – we just couldn't have gone on any longer.'

Mick had done magnificently, for together with Tom Frost he had spent longer above Base Camp than anyone else. I met Tom at Camp II the same day, when he told me: 'I think you have destroyed the spirit of this expedition by pushing Don and Dougal in front, out of their turn. It was a real stab in the back for Nick and Martin.'

Although I tried to explain equably that expediency on a big climb must sometimes overrule the principle of fair shares for all, privately I was appalled at how badly the people out in front seemed to have taken my decision.

There was trouble at Camp V, a grim spot in the direct path of all the powder-snow avalanches which poured off the Rock Band whenever it snowed. Don, Dougal, Martin and Nick were all there when, during the night, one tent was crushed by the build-up of snow. Martin and Nick could have been suffocated but for a small gap left at the top of the entrance. Nick was badly shaken by this experience; Martin, suddenly becoming sick, was forced to return to Base Camp.

With our strength running out fast, I pushed straight up to Camp V, Don and Dougal moving up to Camp VI with Nick carrying some rope for them. Unfortunately Dougal dropped the rucksack containing his down clothing, sleeping-bag and food and, although Don tried to persuade him to sit out the night there with the stove going, Dougal, realising how cold it would be, returned to Camp V. It was about midday when Dougal returned and Don, who had by this time been without food for more than twenty-four hours, insisted on being fed before pushing on. Then they picked up a rope Nick had dumped about 400 feet below the Camp with the result that in the little time left they could do no more than round the corner of a buttress just above the tent, and look into a tantalising gully that seemed to lead all the way up to the top of the Rock Band.

Nick and I remained at Camp V.

At night most of us drugged ourselves with sleeping-pills. I found that two of them merely knocked me out from about 7 p.m. when we usually settled down for the night, there being nothing else to do, till two in the morning. From then on I used to doze intermittently, waiting for the dawn.

Most of our camps caught the early morning sun, but our Whillans Box at Camp V was tucked into the bergschrund below the Rock Band. A huge curl of ice, frighteningly reminiscent of the sword of Damocles, guarded us from spindrift avalanches, above – if it collapsed at least we should know nothing about it. After every snowfall it was necessary to dig the Box out;

the reason why tents were useless was that the build-up of powder snow simply crushed them.

The interior of the Box was a nightmare rectangle, 6 feet 4 inches long, 4 feet wide and 4 feet high, with green, dreary walls, no windows and a zip entrance at one end which had to be kept closed most of the time to keep out the clouds of snow. The walls and ceiling were encrusted with ice which only melted when we were cooking on our gas-stove. Drips from the roof would then soak our sleeping-bags – there was no way of drying them out.

Obviously there was no water at Camp V – just snow, which had to be melted. It takes about ten panfuls of powder snow and about an hour of cooking to produce one pan of lukewarm water. Mike Thompson, who had organised our food, had been determined to produce an interesting high-altitude diet. In the event it was a little too original. He had cut out such mundane ingredients as tea and coffee, replacing them with a variety of fruit drink cubes, all of which became equally detestable after a few weeks. We had a choice of hot Cola, orange or grapefruit for the breakfast brew, followed by a tin of mixed grill or perhaps some kippers or herrings in white sauce. If you could face it there was then Pumpernickel – thin black wafers of compressed rye bread – a cheese spread and those little containers of jam such as you get on airliners. The jam was acceptable, but the Pumpernickel had too strong a flavour for altitude and we all longed for plain biscuits. The favourite breakfast food for all of us was instant porridge.

Cooking breakfast took about three hours – a single brew required more than an hour and you needed at least two brews before starting out: you are meant to drink seven pints a day at altitude to avoid dehydration.

As the Box is only big enough to take two people lying side by side, you cook breakfast without getting out of your sleeping-bag. If you are untidy, as most of us were, the interior of the Box quickly becomes a sordid mess.

It is 5 a.m., the start of another day. Nick is still flat out, buried in his sleeping-bag, only his nose sticking out. I light the stove, fill the pan with snow from immediately outside the door, being careful to take it from the right-hand side as we relieve ourselves during the night on the left (there is no question of going out of the tent – you just open up a corner of the entrance and shoot).

By the time we have cooked breakfast it is nearly nine o'clock. I delay departure, putting off the grim moment of climbing out of a warm sleeping-bag to face another day of discomfort and hard graft. Ten o'clock – if I am to do that carry to Camp VI I cannot stall any longer. Harness on, then the struggle to fit crampons on to boots – metal so cold that it sticks to your skin; straps frozen solid like wire hawsers. It takes fifteen minutes to put them on.

I dug out a 500-foot length of rope, and, with a walky-talky radio and a few Gaz cylinders, my load was around 35 lb. This did not seem too heavy at first, but having carried it a few hundred feet I began to feel like a very weary Atlas carrying the world on my shoulders.

The route to Camp VI seemed endless. At that altitude it took an hour to cover fifty feet, slowly and laboriously. The last length of rope up on the Flat Iron was the most strenuous of all, taking two hours of lung-bursting effort to reach the top. From there, the crest of the Flat Iron curved in a sickle of snow for about 400 feet – an easy-going plod at ground level, but here, an agonising struggle. The tent was just visible at the top of the ridge – a tiny patch of blue, perched on a minute ledge.

Resting five minutes between each step, it was 5.30 that evening before I reached the top camp, and eight o'clock in the gathering dark before I returned to Camp V, where a worried Nick reheated some supper for me. That night I gulped down a concoction of powdered soup, tinned meat and sweetcorn, followed by Christmas pudding. Mike had collected our food just after Christmas and Christmas puddings were going cheap; so we had them cold, fried and even stewed!

Exhausted, the next day Nick and I stayed in the tent. It was a savage day with a bitter gusting wind and frequent snow showers. In spite of even worse weather at Camp VI Don and Dougal set out to force the route to the top of the Rock Band and managed to make 400 feet of progress.

It was the 22nd May. Nick and I hoped to make the carry to Camp VI with the tent and camp kit which Dougal and Don hoped to pitch above the Rock Band. We decided to use oxygen sets to make the journey a little easier, in spite of the heavier load we should have to carry. Nick set off first, but I caught up with him at the top of the first fixed rope – he was hanging on it like a landed fish on a line.

'Sorry, Chris,' he said, 'I just won't make it. The oxygen doesn't seem to make any difference, even at full flow. I'll just have to go down.'

There it was. Both he and Martin had burnt themselves out in support of the front pairs and in doing this they had sacrificed all hope of going to the top. It also meant we had lost another load carrier, and everything we were trying to carry up to Camp VI that day was of vital importance. I took the food bag from Nick, adding it to the length of rope I was already carrying. With the oxygen set my load weighed 40 lb.

But the oxygen certainly made a difference. On reaching the last desperate jumar pitch up on to the top of the Flat Iron, I switched to maximum flow. I could feel the extra energy coursing through my body, and managed to climb this stretch in about half an hour, compared with the two hours I had taken without oxygen.

On reaching the tent Don and Dougal told me they had reached the top of the Rock Band that day. They had run out nearly a thousand feet of rope and had reached a point 200 feet below the top of the gully. It was on steep soft snow, but they had been so keen to get that precious view of the top that they had pressed on unroped.

Don said: 'It got us out on top of the Mini Rock Band and it looks a piece of duff to the top. Have you got the tent? We'll be able to establish Camp VII tomorrow.'

I had to confess I had brought up a rope in place of the tent, which Nick had taken down with him. Dougal suggested my moving up to Camp VI the next day, when I brought up the tent – I could then go with them to Camp VII and make the bid for the summit. Ian was due to come up to Camp V that evening and would be able to help make a good carry up to VI, so I accepted immediately.

That night I returned to Camp V full of optimism but was dashed to find it empty. It had been fine on the upper part of the mountain but had not stopped snowing all day on the lower. Ian had been unable to force his way up to Camp V because of the weight of new snow. Camp V was a macabre place to be alone, and the following morning, loaded with the tent, food, ciné-camera and my own spare clothing I set off at about ten o'clock. I managed to get a hundred feet above the camp before I realised that I could never carry a load of at least 60 lb all the way to Camp VI. It seemed to weigh tons.

Returning in complete despair, I felt tired and finished. There seemed no chance now of going to the summit with Don and Dougal and I even wondered whether I had the strength left to make another carry up to Camp VI. Feeling utterly helpless, I sat down and cried, then, ashamed of my weakness, shouted at the ice walls surrounding me, 'Get a grip on yourself, you bloody idiot.'

Leaving my personal gear behind, it was midday when I left Camp V with the tent and food, and I reached the top Camp at six. Ian was waiting for me when I returned to Camp V and I don't think I have ever been so glad to see anyone. I had been dreading another night by myself.

Once again on the radio we adjusted our plans. It was agreed that the following day, Don and Dougal should establish Camp VII, stay there that night and then make a bid for the summit. Ian and I were to move up to Camp VI and Mick and Tom from Camp IV to V. In this way we should be able to make three successive bids on successive days.

It seemed in the bag, though with the weather blowing even harder than usual that morning, Don wondered whether to play it safe and stay at Camp VI for the day. Yet he, like the rest of us, was impatient to finish the climb.

He decided to leave for the top of the Rock Band, while we at Camp V also had our doubts, but set out all the same.

That morning I had bad diarrhoea, an unpleasant complaint at altitude, and felt very weak – Ian and I only got away from the camp at eleven o'clock. Clouds of spindrift were blasting across the Face, blinding us with their violence, making movement almost impossible. Half-way up I had an irrepressible urge to relieve myself – I was in the middle of a gully swept by powder-snow avalanches. This was a tricky and exceedingly unpleasant operation. I was dangling on the fixed rope, and somehow I had to remove my harness, tie a makeshift one to my chest and bare my backside to the icy blast. And at that point a powder-snow avalanche came pouring down, filling my trousers, infiltrating up my back.

Eventually Ian and I reached Camp VI at five o'clock that afternoon, to find the tent semi-collapsed by the build-up of powder snow, and barely big enough for the two of us. Five minutes later we heard a shout from above – Don and Dougal had been forced to retreat through the most appalling weather conditions we had encountered. Their clothes were encased in ice and Don was sporting a pair of magnificently drooping moustachios formed of pure ice. They had hoped to pitch their tent on what had seemed to be an easy-angled slope just beyond the top of the fixed rope but, not only was it much steeper than it looked: when they tried to dig a platform they quickly came to hard ice.

There were now four of us in a two-man tent. I have had more than a hundred bivouacs in the mountains, but that night was the most uncomfortable of all, though Ian was the worst off, spending the night uncomplainingly crouched in a corner.

Next morning the weather was even worse, leaving no choice but for Ian and me to retreat to Camp IV to keep the fitter pair, Don and Dougal, supplied with food. For the next two days it snowed non-stop and we wondered whether the monsoon had arrived and if, so close to success, we were now to be cheated. Don and Dougal had told us that morning that they hoped to establish Camp VII, but it seemed unlikely in the face of the appalling weather conditions.

I opened up the radio at five o'clock and Dougal came on.

'Hello, Dougal, this is Chris at IV. Did you manage to get out of the tent today?'

'Aye, we've got some good news for you. We reached the top.'

Don told me the story the following day. They had reached the top of the fixed ropes but unable to find a suitable place for a camp site they plodded on up through the soft snow on the ridge. They had not bothered to put the rope on, and were not using oxygen, finding that in spite of the very strong wind, the climbing was quite easy. It was twelve o'clock before they found a suitable site for Camp VII but by then they were just below the final headwall of the ridge and the summit seemed very close. As there was no point in having a top camp so high, they just kept plodding.

The climbing became more difficult, up steep snow-covered rocks, the last fifty feet vertical with big flat holds. Don said:

'Generally, I had done hardly any leading at all up to this point, but I felt completely confident, and it never occurred to me to use the rope.'

Once over the top of the ridge the wind immediately dropped and they found that the north side of the mountain was quite warm and pleasant with sun breaking through clouds. While waiting for Dougal to follow, Don looked around for the anchor point for the rope they would need to get back down.

The summit itself was a real knife-edge and there was not much to see from the top. The northern slope dropped away into the cloud, a great boulder field part-concealed by snow. The only tops visible were the other two summits of Annapurna; everything else, including the entire South Face, was blanketed in cloud.

Don said: 'We stayed there for about ten minutes. At this stage we didn't feel much in the way of elation – it was difficult to believe it was all over and anyway we still had to get back down.'

We had nearly completed our clearance of the mountain. Mick Burke and Tom Frost, forced back by the extreme cold, were now on their way down from the top Camp after their attempt to reach the summit as a second ascent of the South Face. We had been desperately worried about this attempt, since we knew that none of us had the strength to go to their help if they got into any kind of trouble. On the other hand, it seemed only fair and right that I should let them go – not only because their plea to go to the top had been so strong, but because they had their own right to taste the ultimate satisfaction of standing on top of that mountain to which they had given so much while making our successful ascent possible. Nevertheless, until the news came that they had turned back and were on their way down, I had spent twenty-four hours of sheer agony. I had a tremendous sense of relief – nothing could possibly go wrong now.

I had been waiting at Camp III for this news, with Mike Thompson, Ian Clough and Dave Lambert, and so I set off down, back to Base Camp, to start wading through the mass of paperwork which the end of the expedition, and our success, inevitably entailed. The following morning, while sitting typing out the report of the successful end of our venture, I could hear Kelvin giving out the news over the radio. Suddenly there was a pounding of footsteps and Mike Thompson, panting, hurrying, came dashing up to the tent with the cry, 'Chris – where is he – where is he? Something terrible's happened!' His voice was raucous, frightening, and immediately I knew – we all knew – that some ghastly tragedy had occurred. Rushing out of the tent I found Mike leaning over his ice-axe, having just collapsed on to the ground. I remember going down on one knee and holding his shoulders while he sobbed out the story of what had happened.

They were on the way down – Mike, Dave Lambert and Ian – and had reached the last possible dangerous section of our climb – the line of séracs which we had to pass under. It was an area which we had always known to be dangerous, but we had accepted the risk because we were only in this danger area for a few minutes. Mike described hearing a sudden, tremendous rumble from above. He looked back and saw this great tower of ice crashing down. Ian was just in front of Mike, who turned round and, with a split-second decision, ran back into the line of the avalanche. As he dived under the low wall to the sérac which was immediately above them, the ice avalanche came crashing over them. Mike just remembered lying there in complete darkness as the ice thundered down, convinced that he was going to die, and cursing the bitter futility of it. Then it all stopped and there was complete silence.

He found himself covered over in ice crystals as he pulled himself out to look for Ian. But Ian had not got back in time – he had been caught in the full force of the avalanche and had been swept down to his death. Down below, there had been a group of Sherpas coming back to pick up some loads from Camp II. Miraculously they had not been engulfed by the avalanche, and for a few minutes they all stood stunned with the shock, before starting to hunt through the debris. They finally found Ian's body – he must have been killed outright.

And so, suddenly, in that moment of joyous victory, this tragedy had struck us. We had lost a close friend and one of the kindest, least personally motivated people that I have ever known. Ian spent much of his time repairing fixed ropes or giving the Sherpas that little bit of help and instruction. I think he was genuinely loved by the Sherpas and he was certainly the one person in the team for whom no one ever had a bad word. It seemed bitterly ironic that the person in the team who was, perhaps, the most safety-conscious should have been caught out by this cruel act of fate.

We took Ian's body down to Base Camp and we buried him in sight of the mountain he had given so much to climb. It was Tukte Sherpa, our cook, who suggested the burial place. We had been looking round for a suitable place – a place which would be above any floods, and where Ian's body could rest securely and safely. Tukte pointed to a little knoll, immediately below a rocky slab where Ian had spent many of his rest periods, teaching the Sherpas the various techniques they would need for their safety on the mountain. Tukte said, 'This would be a good place for him to lie.' We dug the grave and all the Sherpas – even the porters who had come up to help carry our gear – were scattered all over the hillside, picking the short blue Alpine flowers to make wreaths. And then we carried Ian's body up to the grave. Standing there at its foot, I tried to say something that was remotely adequate, and at the same time to control my own emotion; and all I could say was, 'He was a fine mountaineer and a very safe one – but most important of all, he was the kindest, the most unselfish and, I think, the most universally-liked person that I have ever known.'

After this Tom Frost said a short Mormon prayer, while I think most of us were either crying or doing our best to hold back the tears.

Inevitably, the question arises – 'Was it worth it?' Was a successful climb worth a man's life – especially a man who was a close friend, who left a wife and a young child? But this is a question which has got to be faced and answered by all of us who climb, or base our lives round the mountains, because Ian's accident could have happened to any member of the team – could happen to any one of us, anywhere in our climbing lives – in Britain – in the Alps or the further ranges of the earth. This was brought home even more forcibly, because just before Ian's tragic death, we had received the news that Tom Patey, one of my closest friends, and certainly the richest, most wonderful personality that the mountains had produced since the war, had died in one of those inexplicable abseiling accidents – in this case on a sea-stack on the north coast of Scotland. His tragedy and that of his wife Betty, and his children, was as great as that of Ian, and all of us who go climbing must realise that we, also, could be killed by an accident over which we seem to have very little control. It is a cruel and difficult responsibility, particularly when we have wives and children whom we love. But once the mountains have bitten into us, we know, and the wives who love us know, that we could never give them up. All we can do is to try to be as careful as we possibly can, and pray that luck will remain with us.

CHAPTER TWENTY-TWO

What Next?

The grass of the lower moraines was a lush green and alpine flowers in pink, white and purple could be glimpsed from amongst their long blades. The rock was warm to the touch, the air balmy; and we were walking away from Annapurna, whose South Face had held the focus of our strength, effort and expectation for these last eight weeks. There was a strange mixture of exultation and sorrow; an exultation born from the closeness of unity that we, as an expedition, had achieved, and sorrow at the death of Ian Clough, a death which seemed the more cruel because it had occurred at the very last moment of possible danger, when he was on his way down after the final victory.

Before Annapurna, Jimmy Roberts and Norman Dyhrenfurth, joint leaders of the proposed International Everest Expedition, had invited me to join them as climbing leader of their face party. At first it had seemed too good an opportunity to miss, but on the way back from the mountain I realised, with increasing force, that I could not go through with another major expedition the following spring. Annapurna South Face had drained my reserves of nervous energy. The responsibility and the work involved in the organisation, the leading of the expedition on the mountain, and now the prospect of closing it down and writing the expedition book, had been like a long, unending marathon. I knew instinctively that I needed at least a year to recover my equilibrium and rebuild any enthusiasm for the expedition game. I do not think Ian's death affected my decision. However great the sorrow at the loss of a close friend, I realised that this is the price you must be prepared to pay if you go climbing; you minimise risk where possible, calculate the odds and turn back if the odds seem to be against you. But sometimes, however careful you are, and Ian had been the most careful of climbers, the fact that you have spent long periods exposed to risk can catch up with you.

On our return to Kathmandu, I broke the news to Jimmy Roberts of my withdrawal from the International Everest Expedition; Jimmy runs a trekking business there. He took my decision wonderfully well and was very sympathetic. He had already decided to invite Don Whillans and

Dougal Haston to join the expedition, and the three of them began planning the next year's trip, talking with the Japanese climbers who were on their way back from an unsuccessful attempt on the South-West Face of Everest. They had made a reconnaissance in the autumn of 1969, reaching a height of 26,000 feet on the face, just below the rock wall that stretches across it barring the way to the summit rocks. That spring they had failed to reach a point as high as on their autumn reconnaissance. The face had been unusually bare of snow and as a result had been swept by stone-fall. They had had difficulty in finding ledges for their camps and finally had abandoned the attempt in favour of ensuring at least a limited success, by putting the first Japanese on the summit of Everest by the South Col route.

At this point I felt no regrets about my decision to withdraw from the expedition; I just wanted to get home to Wendy, get the book written and close down our own expedition. But by the time I had reached England a few doubts began to crystallise – had I turned down the opportunity of a lifetime? These doubts came to a head when Jimmy Roberts, on a short holiday in England, came to ask my advice about equipment for the expedition. It was too much! Impulsively, I asked him if he would have me back in the team; he accepted immediately and a few days later I had a warm, friendly letter from Norman Dyhrenfurth, welcoming me aboard. But in that period I had taken yet another back flip. My change of mind had been dictated on emotional grounds, of not wanting to be left out – but now, having decided to rejoin the expedition, I began to think again of all that it implied.

The job of climbing leader could be an invidious one. I hadn't chosen the team, wondered what level of loyalty climbers from France, Austria, Germany and the United States would feel to someone they knew only by reputation. I was so involved in getting *Annapurna South Face* written that I could have done little or no work for the expedition in the preparatory stage. I found myself wondering how effectively it would be possible to take over a position of responsibility on the climb itself, having contributed nothing to the preparations, and knowing very little about the equipment which was going to be used. Another very real worry was the financial backing of the expedition. Norman Dyhrenfurth and Jimmy Roberts had taken a very courageous step in launching a massive and very expensive expedition without any kind of sponsor to back them if they failed to raise sufficient funds. On Annapurna I had had none of these worries, since we had been fully backed by the Mount Everest Foundation. As a member of the International Expedition, however, I felt that I would have a financial responsibility towards it, but very little control over whether the expedition went into the red. Obviously, I was going to become heavily involved in fund-raising for the expedition, since Dyhrenfurth, at that stage, was having considerable trouble with the finances.

Perhaps all this sounds a long way from the simple romance of climbing a mountain. I know that it was something which did not worry either Don or Dougal – they simply wanted to go and climb Everest, and were probably fortunate in that no one expected them to become involved in the organisation of the expedition. Because of the experience I had gained in the field of journalism and in expedition organisation, it was inevitable that I should become more heavily involved. The more I examined it, the more frightened I became of that involvement.

Obviously, there were going to be problems in making the team cohesive on the expedition itself. There would be problems in raising the money, in getting the equipment together for a team scattered throughout the world, and I was tired from a year of such exceedingly exacting, nerve-racking work. I rocked back and forth for three days, tossing the conflicting motives and problems from side to side, and then I finally decided – I could not face the prospect of another big, complicated expedition. I resigned yet again.

In the midst of all this indecision I was under heavy pressure, anyway, while writing *Annapurna South Face*. I have no doubt at all that, had I not gone to Annapurna, I would have stayed in the International Everest Expedition, even though I, as did many of the other members, foresaw many of the problems which were likely to arise.

But still I had not escaped from Everest. Some weeks after my withdrawal, the BBC, who had bought television and feature rights in the expedition, approached me to go out as their reporter. There is no doubt that this was a magnificent professional opportunity for me, in my role as photo-journalist, yet I felt I could not take it. My reasons, I suspect, were part egotistical, part genuine worry about the structure of the expedition and, over all, a total mental fatigue. Having just finished writing the story of one expedition – how on earth could I summon the fresh enthusiasm needed to write about another?

On the egotistical level, I had known the satisfaction of having the ultimate responsibility; it would have been difficult to have gone back to being an observer and, in the final analysis, it would have been difficult for me to have accepted the role of climbing leader, even though I respected both Jimmy Roberts and Norman Dyhrenfurth.

As the new year of 1971 came in, my own book finished, my batteries of energy recharged, I began to have many doubts about my withdrawal from the expedition. I became insufferable to live with, as I reproached myself over and over again for what seemed a failure to snatch the opportunity which had been offered.

I followed the fortunes of the expedition with mixed emotions, and have to confess I was even almost relieved that my own fears were proved justified. The South-West Face remained unclimbed. By this time I had resolved to try to organise an expedition of my own; the first problem, however, was to gain permission for the climb, and the mountain was fully booked for the next five years. Dr Karl Herrligkoffer, a German climber who had led a series of highly controversial expeditions to Nanga Parbat, had permission to attempt the Face in the spring of 1972. He had already invited Dougal Haston and Don Whillans to join his expedition. He also invited Jimmy Roberts, who declined the invitation.

It was rumoured that the Japanese had permission to try the Face next, if Herrligkoffer failed, and so that summer of 1971 it seemed very unlikely that I should ever get the chance of going for the South-West Face of Everest. Then, in the autumn of 1971, I received a letter from Dougal. He told me that Herrligkoffer wanted to increase the size of the British team, mainly as a means of tapping more funds, since he was having trouble in raising sufficient money in Germany. Dougal, having suggested my name to Herrligkoffer, asked me if I would like to join them.

At this stage I was trying to organise a small expedition with Joe Brown, Hamish McInnes, Martin Boysen, Paul Nunn and Will Barker, to the Trango Tower, a magnificent granite monolith in the Baltoro Glacier. From photographs it looked like the Old Man of Hoy, but was ten times as big. This would have been a perfect expedition, with magnificent rock-climbing and none of the problems associated with altitude (for it was only 20,000 feet high). With a small party of friends there would have been few worries about personality conflict. Our only problem was in getting permission from the Pakistan Government. When Dougal invited me to join the Herrligkoffer expedition there still seemed to be a chance that we might get permission for the Trango Tower, and so I declined his invitation with very few regrets: Herrligkoffer's expedition seemed to be fraught with even more pitfalls than those of the International Everest Expedition.

But we did not gain permission for the Trango Tower. I was in a vacuum once again and could not resist the temptation of writing to Herrligkoffer to ask whether I could accept his invitation after all. He agreed to my joining as one of the four British members. Don and Dougal were already in the team so that left one more representative from this country to be invited. I phoned Don to find out whom he thought should join us, and was gratified that, in his own mind, he had settled on the same person that I had mentally selected – Doug Scott. Doug was a climber who had always been on the outside of the mainstream British climbing scene but who, in the last few years, had completed a large number of very impressive new routes in north-west Scotland. He was essentially an innovator, having adapted himself to the American style of Big Wall climbing, being one of the Britons to have climbed successfully in Yosemite. He also had behind him a long record of small expeditions to out-of-the-way places. A school teacher by profession, he had devoted himself to climbing to a degree equalled by very few people I know. His powerful physique and big set of lungs are attributes useful for any Everest climber.

Back in the Everest stakes, the more I learned about Herrligkoffer's arrangements the less happy I became. It was now January 1972, but he did not yet appear to have any oxygen equipment at all, seemed to have made few arrangements in Nepal and, above all, was unbelievably secretive about his plans and organisation.

I had resolved that I would avoid getting involved in the preparations for the expedition and therefore went off to Chamonix to climb with Dougal. We were going to attempt a new route on the North Face of the Grandes Jorasses. We spent twelve days on the face – twelve glorious days, when the problems of life were reduced to a few feet of ice in front of our noses, trying to hack a platform for a bivouac in ice that was frozen as hard as the rocks it covered, of trying to survive the fury of a winter storm. We did not get up, but it didn't seem to matter – the experience had been well worthwhile, for we had had twelve days of real climbing, uncluttered by politics and commercial pressures. During this climb, I have a feeling that both of us, separately, without discussing it, had decided to withdraw from the Herrligkoffer expedition. And so, once again I was out of Everest!

I was, nevertheless, still trying to get permission to attempt the South-West Face. It seemed unlikely that Herrligkoffer could possibly succeed. From what I had gathered, his gear was inadequate, he had postponed engaging his Sherpas to the last minute, and there seemed to be all the risks of a bi-national expedition which could be even greater than in an international one. With two clearly divided groups, each loyal to them-selves, rather than the concept of the expedition as a whole, there seemed to be small chance of success.

And so I continued to manœuvre for a chance of going to Everest. I received an immense amount of help from Mike Cheney, Jimmy Roberts' assistant, who kept his ear close to the ground in Kathmandu, and acted as my representative.

At last, a chance began to materialise. An Italian millionaire, Signor Monzino, had permission for an autumn reconnaissance in 1972 to be followed by a spring attempt in 1973. Owing to sickness he gave up his autumn slot. Mike Cheney informed me, and I applied for it immediately. There followed months of waiting – we still did not have permission from the Nepalese authorities – Herrligkoffer might still climb the South-West Face. Even if he failed, I could not help worrying about our prospects for raising, in the seven or eight weeks before our departure, the £60,000 I estimated the expedition would cost, at the same time as assembling all the gear and food.

On top of this were the problems of the autumn season. No expedition had succeeded in climbing Everest during the post-monsoon period, although two have tried and failed, beaten by the appalling winds and the cold which is experienced during the autumn.

The entire prospect seemed too far-fetched, but then I conceived a compromise solution. Why not have a mini-expedition to Everest – just four climbers and a few Sherpas? It was an exciting, refreshing prospect. In addition, it would be comparatively easy to organise and would not demand a vast budget. I asked Dougal Haston, Mick Burke and Nick Estcourt whether they would like to come along, and they all agreed. It became obvious that we should need some support and so I asked Peter Steele, who had been a member of the International Expedition, to come along as doctor, together with Mike Thompson to be our Base Camp Manager.

The expedition was planned before we learned of the failure of Herrligkoffer's expedition. I heard the news in late May – and then the temptation built up. The South-West Face was still unclimbed!

It is not an aesthetically pleasing problem, hasn't the uncompromising yet tenuous line of ice arêtes and rock spurs that led to the summit of the South Face of Annapurna, which made that such a fascinating route. The South-West Face seemed a problem of brutal logistics – could you get all the oxygen, food and gear you needed to the foot of the Rock Band at a height of over 27,000 feet – higher than most of the other mountains in the Himalaya. Having got it there, would the climbers be able to keep going – climbing in the autumn cold, on steep ice and rock?

This was a real challenge. It was also one to which, in the last eight years, I suspect I have slowly built up – in climbing, in working as a photo-journalist and, finally, in organising and leading the Annapurna South Face Expedition.

I find a fascination in putting an expedition together, in encouraging a group of climbers, all of whom are friends and whose friendship I value, to coalesce into a single team. I am challenged by the struggle with my own personality and its shortcomings. I cannot claim to be the perfect leader; cannot claim to be unselfish; I made mistakes on Annapurna, was perhaps impulsive at times, perhaps allowed myself to be swayed by others at the wrong times. I shall probably make mistakes on Everest, because everyone is fallible. The challenge lies in learning from these mistakes.

In organising a big expedition to Annapurna or to Everest, one sometimes loses the stark simplicity and romanticism of mountaineering, becoming involved in the maze of finance, public relations, commercial exploitation. Yet there is a fascination in this – at least there is to me. This also is a game – to be played as a game. It is serious; it is exacting. There are more pitfalls than on any mountain, but surmounting these pitfalls has its own special thrill and challenge. And in the end you come back to the mountain.

I have written these last few words in the hours before flying to Everest to attempt its South-West Face. We might or might not succeed; this certainly will be the greatest challenge of my life so far. But whatever the outcome, I know that the mountains will always fill a vital part of my life; that my quest will be for the next horizon.

THE
EVEREST
YEARS

To Louise and George

CONTENTS

AUTHOR'S NOTE

In writing this book, my third autobiographical work, I have covered my main expedition years. The theme is expeditioning in every different shape and size. Of some, I have already written books, which were as full and honest as I could make them at the time. I have therefore used a different approach for the expeditions of which I have already written, looking at them in a broader perspective, showing how they related to each other and bringing them out what I felt were the highlights. Of the others I have gone into greater detail, reliving the entire experience.

The story is both my own and that of the people I have climbed with, of how a wide variety of teams have worked together to achieve a common end. In this respect expeditioning is a microcosm of life and work in general. This book certainly is the result of teamwork that has been built up over the years. Louise Wilson, my secretary from the 1975 Everest expedition, has taken on more and more, becoming a good friend and adviser, and has become my general editor of everything I write, from business letters to articles and books.

I owe a great debt to George Greenfield who has been so much more than my literary agent since 1969: he has helped steer all my expeditions through the maze of fund-raising and contractual obligations, helping to make so many of my ventures possible, as well as advising me on my writing and coming up with a host of good ideas.

Over the years I have also built up a good understanding with Hodder and Stoughton, who have published all but one of my books over this period. I am particularly indebted to Margaret Body who has edited them all and become accustomed to my foibles. I also owe a great deal to Trevor Vincent who did the design work on this book, the fourth of mine on which he has worked.

I am deeply grateful to Carolyn Estcourt and Hilary Boardman for lending me the diaries of their husbands, Nick and Pete. These gave me a valuable extra perspective on the Ogre and K2 expeditions.

And finally I should like to acknowledge the constant love and support of my wife Wendy who has backed me to the full in all my expeditioning and given so much practical help and advice both on the text and the design of this book.

C. B.

CHAPTER ONE

Beginnings

They'd reached the summit, barely a hundred metres away and a metre or so higher than me. I had to squeeze out my last bit of willpower to join them. Push one foot in front of the other, pant hard to capture what little air and oxygen there was flowing into my mask. But had I enough left to get there? And then another careful, deliberate step along the corniced snow ridge to the top of the world.

A break in the cornice and, framed down to my right was the North-East Ridge, the route we had tried in 1982. Crazy ice towers, fierce snow flutings, a knife-edged ridge that went on and on. Friends of mine on the current British Everest Expedition were somewhere down there. Perhaps also were the bodies of Peter Boardman and Joe Tasker.

Another step, and the North-East Ridge was hidden by a curl of snow. This was where Pete Boardman had last seen Mick Burke in 1975. He and Pertemba were on their way down, Mick was going for the summit on his own. He never came back. My head was filled with thoughts of lost friends, of Nick Estcourt who forced the Everest Rock Band and died on K2, of Dougal Haston who went to the summit of Everest with Doug Scott, and died skiing near his home in Switzerland.

And then suddenly I was there. Odd, Bjørn and Pertemba were beckoning to me, shouting, their voices muffled by their oxygen masks. I crouched in a foetal position and just cried and cried in great gasping sobs – tears of exhaustion, tears of sorrow for so many friends, and yet tears of fulfilment for something I had so much needed to do and had done with people who had come to mean a great deal to me. I had at last reached the summit of Everest.

It was 21 April 1985 and in the next ten days the Norwegian Everest Expedition was to place seventeen climbers on the summit – the highest number on a single expedition. We had also completed our ascents earlier in the season than any previous expedition. Judged solely as records these would be fairly empty achievements. You've got to look deeper to understand their significance. I suspect that every climber in the world dreams of standing on the highest point on earth; certainly every climber who joins an expedition to Everest does and that includes quite a few of the Sherpa high-altitude porters as well. If you judge success, therefore, in terms of the sum of individual satisfaction and fulfilment, there is a very real point in getting as many to the summit as possible. Getting there quickly both increases the chance of success and reduces the time that the team is exposed to danger.

There were five expeditions attempting Everest by different routes in the spring of 1985 and the speed with which we were able to run out the route undoubtedly contributed to the fact that we were the only successful expedition. The others were overtaken by the bad weather that occurred later in the season. We were fast because we had a superb and very strong Sherpa force and because the climbers and Sherpas became welded into a closely knit team who worked happily, and therefore effectively, together.

It was this that made the expedition such a success, not just in terms of making records, but also in terms of personal satisfaction for every member of the team. I have been on expeditions that have reached their summit and yet there has been little sense of success because the group had failed to work together and there was acrimony rather than friendship at the end of the experience.

Unless you always go alone, the essence of climbing is teamwork. You are entrusting your life to others, on a rock climb to your partner holding the other end of the rope, but on a higher mountain it becomes more complex. There you need to trust the judgement of others in choosing a route, or perhaps their ability to give support from a lower camp. There is a constant interplay of decision-making, be it between two climbers on a crag in the Lake District or amongst thirty distributed between a series of camps on Everest.

Two or possibly four people climbing together, even on a major Himalayan peak, can reach a decision through discussion. There is no need of a hierarchy or official leader, though almost always a leader does emerge – one person who has a stronger personality or who is particularly equipped to deal with a specific problem encountered. In this last respect the lead can pass around the group during the course of a climb. Mountaineering, like every other activity, is a development and learning process – about the mountains, one's personal ability and, perhaps most important of all, one's relationship with others.

This book covers the last fifteen years which, for me, have been dominated by expedition climbing. Everest has been a recurrent theme, a magnet that has drawn me again and again, not just because I wanted to reach its summit personally, but because of the scale of its challenge, the strength of its aura.

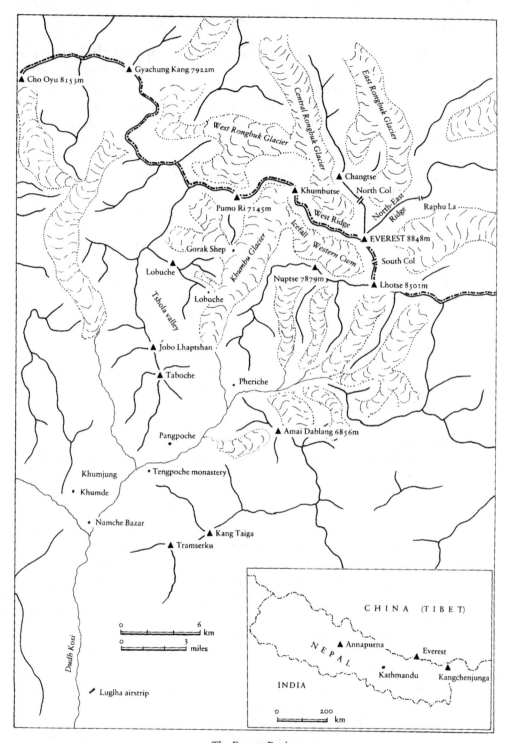

The Everest Region

I had my first glimpse of Everest in 1961, on my way to climb Nuptse. In those days you had to walk all the way from Kathmandu; there was no airstrip at Luglha and the road ended just outside the city. On the way in we saw just one other European, Peter Aufschnaiter, who had been with Heinrich Harrer in Tibet after they had escaped from a British internment camp in northern India. These were the days before trekkers and tourists. There were a few little tea shops on the pathside for the porters carrying loads and trade goods, but all you could buy were cups of tea and perhaps a few dry biscuits.

The first glimpse of the world's highest mountain comes as you climb the winding track that leads up to Namche Bazaar from the bottom of the Dudh Kosi valley. You come to a bend in the path on a small spur and suddenly, through the shrubs and small birch trees, you can see Everest framed by the precipitous sides of the Dudh Kosi's gorge, part hidden by the great wall of Nuptse that acts as its outer rampart.

The summit of Nuptse is like one of the turrets on a castle wall and to climb it we were going to have to scale that wall; up flying buttresses of sculpted ice, across steep snow fields, over sheer rock walls. It was bigger and more complex than any mountain any of us had ever climbed, though at the time we hardly realised the scale or significance of what we were attempting.

Back in 1961 we were in that first bloom of Himalayan climbing when there were still a huge number of unclimbed peaks of over 7000 metres, though all but one of the 8000-metre peaks had been climbed. Practically no mountain in the Himalaya had been climbed by more than one route and very few had had a second ascent.

With hindsight it seems almost a miracle that we got up Nuptse. The team was a small one, just eight climbers and six Sherpas, and our equipment was rudimentary by modern standards. We had no jumar clamps but pulled up the fixed ropes hand over hand. We were even reduced to buying second-hand hemp rope from the Tengpoche monastery as our own supply ran out when the climb proved so much harder and longer than we had antici-pated. It was not a happy team. We never really coalesced as a group and the expedition was rent by argument. Although we reached the summit, this failure in personal relations tainted the feeling of satisfaction that we should have had.

It was very different from my first Himalayan expedition which had been to Annapurna II the previous year. This was a British/Indian/Nepalese combined services venture with a very disparate group of people, both in terms of ability and experience, as well as race and background, and yet it had been a contented expedition which had also been a successful one. The common factor of our military background had undoubtedly helped. The leader, Jimmy Roberts, was both an experienced Himalayan climber and a colonel in the army. We therefore accepted his authority without question. In his turn, he exercised that authority well, planning in advance, communicating those plans to the team, and clearly delegating authority or responsibility to individual members.

For me, a young subaltern of twenty-five, it was all a fresh and exciting adventure. I was probably the most accomplished technical climber in the group, with a reasonable Alpine record behind me, though I lacked experience of big mountains. Dick Grant, a captain in the Royal Marines, was the most knowledgeable in this area, having been to Rakaposhi (7788 metres) in the Karakoram, although his actual technical climbing had been limited to work with the cliff assault wing of the Royal Marines. I was teamed with Dick throughout and it made a good combination. I respected his greater Himalayan experience, his age and, for that matter, his military seniority. He, on the other hand, recognised my greater climbing ability and was happy to push me out in front on steep ground. Good humoured, practical and with a no-nonsense approach to life, Dick had the perfect expedition temperament.

The other team members had very limited climbing experience but were happy to work in support roles. As a result I had the very agreeable task throughout the expedition of making the route out in front with Dick, though I think I would have accepted a more modest role with one of the support parties with reasonable grace. I was undoubtedly lucky that there were so few experienced climbers since, being my first foray to altitude, I was to have problems. The first time I went to 6700 metres was like hitting a tangible barrier. We were on the crest of the great rounded whaleback ridge that led over the intermediate summit of Annapurna IV. It was a wild gusty day and we were in cloud with the snow swirling around us. Dick was ahead setting the pace and suddenly it was as if all my strength had just oozed out of my feet, leaving me barely able to put one foot in front of the other. The rest of the day was a nightmare, with Dick out in front tugging at the rope, exhorting and encouraging me to keep going.

We went back down for a rest. Next time up was to be the summit push and, had there been anyone to take my place, Jimmy Roberts would almost certainly have given it to him. Because there was no one, I had my chance for the summit. Aided by the fact that we were using oxygen I was able to claim my first and, until 1985, highest Himalayan top.

The composition of the Nuptse expedition was very different. In terms of technical experience, the line-up was very much more impressive than our Annapurna expedition, though we were still short on Himalayan expertise. Joe Walmsley, the leader, had led an expedition to Masherbrum in the Karakoram some years before. The most experienced member of the team was undoubtedly Dennis Davis, a seasoned alpinist who also had been on Disteghil Sar, another 7000-metre peak in the Karakoram. Of the rest of the team, Les Brown, Trevor Jones, Jim Swallow and John Streetley were talented rock-climbers, while Simon Clark had led a university expedition to the Peruvian Andes to climb Alpamayo.

Climbers tend to be an individualistic lot, with powerful egos and anti-authoritarian attitudes. Our Nuptse expedition never gelled into a team but remained a group of individuals whose differences were accentuated by this failure to work together. It really came down to leadership.

We were planning to attempt Nuptse using the siege tactics that had become standard on most Himalayan climbs. This entailed establishing a series of camps up the mountain, linking them with fixed rope if the going was steep, ferrying loads up in the wake of the climbers at the front and eventually making a bid for the summit from the highest camp. This approach requires co-ordination between the different groups scattered between the camps on the mountain. The flow of supplies from Base Camp to the higher camps needs controlling, as does the manning of the camps themselves. There needs to be an overall plan in which individuals know and accept their roles. There has to be some kind of roster so that climbers take turns at the rewarding task of making the route out in front, working in the exacting support role of ferrying loads behind the leaders, or resting at Base Camp.

On Annapurna II, Jimmy Roberts had never gone above Base Camp, yet had maintained a firm grip of the expedition and, because we had been working within a plan that we all understood and accepted, the expedition had gone smoothly.

Joe Walmsley had a different approach. He had gained permission to climb on the mountain, had selected the team and had co-ordinated the preparations that got us to Base Camp. He chose a good line up the huge complex face of Nuptse, but then seemed to feel that he had fulfilled his role as leader, implying, 'I've got you here with all the gear you need, now get on with it.' And we did; the climbers out in front selecting the route and slowly pushing a line of fixed rope up a steep rock arête, to which clung a cock's comb of ice and snow. We did make progress and the supplies trickled up behind the lead climbers but in a climate of growing acrimony as each little party on the mountain made its own conflicting plans and became increasingly convinced that they were doing the lion's share of the work whilst everyone else was taking it easy.

And yet we maintained a momentum, making the route up the face until four of us were poised at the penultimate camp 750 metres below the summit. Les Brown and I carried the loads that Dennis Davis and the Sherpa Tachei were going to need for the top camp. They climbed Nuptse on 16 May and the following day Les and I, with Jim Swallow and the Sherpa Ang Pema reached the top. Our push to the top somehow summed up the expedition. It was a question of each man for himself. A long snow gully stretched towards the summit ridge. Dennis and Tachei had left a staircase of boot-holes in the hard snow, so we didn't bother to rope up and each went at his own measured pace. Ang Pema and I were going at about the same speed. He kept just behind me all the way. The others were slower and we were soon far ahead. We crossed a small snow col and, after weeks of effort with the same view of peaks stretching ever further into the distance as we gained height, now, like a great explosion, were new summit vistas. The brown and purple hills of Tibet stretched far into the distance, the deep gorge of the Western Cwm dropped away below and, on the other side of it, the summit pyramid of Everest, black rock veined with white snow and ice. It was my first view of the South-West Face but that day in 1961 there was no thought of climbing it. It had been all I could do to reach the summit of Nuptse and anything as steep and rocky as the South-West Face was beyond comprehension; we were not ready for it. I didn't even dream of reaching the top of Everest by the South Col route.

At that stage I was more interested in climbing in the Alps, was travelling back to Europe overland, and had arranged to meet up with Don Whillans in Chamonix with plans to attempt the North Wall of the Eiger. We failed on the Eiger but made the first ascent of the Central Pillar of Frêney on the south side of Mont Blanc, one of the most satisfying climbs I have ever completed. I had also changed my career, having left the army to go to Nuptse, and was due to join Unilever that September as a management trainee. I had even convinced them and myself that I was giving up expeditioning to become a weekend climber. This new resolve didn't, however, last very long.

I met Wendy, my wife to be, in 1962 and she fully backed my decision to abandon Unilever to go on an expedition to Patagonia. I vaguely thought of taking up teaching, for the long holidays, once I got back but at the end of the summer made the first British ascent of the North Wall of the Eiger with Ian Clough. I was commissioned to write my first book, *I Chose to Climb*, telling the story of those early years, and was able to make a living lecturing. But at that stage I felt very vulnerable. I had become a freelance with no real skills other than my ability as a climber. I concentrated on trying to improve my writing and photography. My first professional assignment was back on the North Wall of the Eiger in the winter of 1966.

I had met the American John Harlin in the summer of 1965. He had swept through the European climbing scene in the early sixties and had considerable influence on Alpine climbing. Amongst other projects he wanted to make a direct route up the North Face of the Eiger. I joined him, not as a climber, but as photographer for the *Daily Telegraph Magazine*. The next objective of his far-flung ambition was going to be the South-West Face of Everest. He was killed in the latter stages on the Eiger route named after him, but he had given birth to an idea.

It was on the Eiger Direct that I came to know Dougal Haston; we had met in passing on previous occasions but both of us had been reserved, no doubt regarding each other as potential competition. In climbing together those barriers had broken down. We both suffered from frostbite in the final stages of the climb, Dougal, when fighting his way out off the face in a violent storm and I, whilst waiting for him on the summit. During our stay in hospital we talked of trying the South-West Face of Everest, but neither of us felt sufficiently confident to lead an expedition. The doctor looking after us was Michael Ward, who had been a doctor on the 1953 Everest Expedition, and had remained actively interested in climbing. We invited him to lead the expedition and he expressed an interest but it never really got any further. The Nepalese Government had just placed a ban on climbing in their country because of various external political pressures and I now found myself increasingly involved in working as a photo-journalist on various adventure assignments.

I moved from the Lake District down to Manchester in 1968, to be more in the hub of things. I had wanted to move to London, Wendy wanted to stay in the Lakes, and Bowdon, on the outskirts of Manchester, was the compromise. I became more directly involved in the climbing scene and a small group of us started talking about going off on a trip. This was how the 1970 expedition to the South Face of Annapurna was born and how I became its leader, more by default than anything else. No one else seemed prepared to get it off the ground.

I had never thought of myself as a leader. My absent-mindedness had become a stock joke amongst my friends, yet the journalistic assignments I had been undertaking in the preceding years had given me a level of discipline and a need to get myself organised that was to prove invaluable on the South Face of Annapurna.

The expedition represented a huge challenge. The face was bigger and steeper than anything that had so far been attempted. Of our team of eleven, only three of us, Don Whillans, Ian Clough and I had been to the Himalaya. Inevitably I made a lot of mistakes both in planning and the way I handled my fellow team members, yet we came through and Don Whillans and Dougal Haston reached the summit. However, in the last moments of the expedition we were faced with tragedy. Ian Clough was swept away by an avalanche. It was a terrible pattern that was to be repeated on all too many expeditions in the future.

After my return from Annapurna the South-West Face of Everest began to loom much larger on the horizon as I had been invited to go there with an international expedition in the spring of 1971.

CHAPTER TWO

The Irresistible Challenge

The South-West Face was to dominate my life for the next five years and stretch the woman I love very close to her breaking point. The scale of the problem can be seen from the number of attempts that were made before the face was finally climbed. A strong Japanese expedition had made a reconnaissance in the autumn of 1969 and attempted it in the spring of 1970. They reached the foot of the Rock Band, a wall of sheer rock 300 metres high, stretching across the face at around 8300 metres. Confronted with steep and difficult climbing at an altitude higher than all but four of the world's highest summits, no expedition seemed able to find the formula for success. This was what made it such a challenge, one in which the logistics, maintaining a flow of supplies to the foot of the Rock Band, were as important as the ability and endurance of the climbers who were going to attempt it.

It was something that fascinated me. I had acquired a taste for planning and organisation on the South Face of Annapurna. The dormant interest had always been there, reflected in my study of military history and my initial choice of a military career. Everest was a natural progression from Annapurna. When I was invited to join the 1971 International Expedition as climbing leader, I accepted, but then, in the light of my experience on Annapurna, withdrew as I was worried about the structure of the expedition. It had been hard enough holding together a small group of close friends with a strong vested interest in remaining united, but the International Expedition posed an even greater problem. The idea of trying to persuade climbing stars from ten different countries, almost all of whom desperately wanted to reach the top themselves, to work unselfishly together to put someone of a different nationality on the summit, seemed an impossible task.

To withdraw was a hard decision. I was not an easy person to live with in the year leading up to the International Expedition. Part of me so wanted to be on that climb. I really felt I could solve the problem of the South-West Face, and that this would lead on to so many other things. We each have a career. Mine was a complex one of climbing, writing, lecturing, organising, planning, and the South-West Face seemed to represent such a logical step in my own life's path. I had periods of black depression, questioning my withdrawal from an enterprise that could take me to the top of the world, ignoring the very good reasons for that decision.

I could not help being unashamedly relieved when my fears were proved to be well founded. The International Expedition was split by dissension and was stopped by the Rock Band. A contributory factor to the failure of this expedition, and the 1970 Japanese attempt, was undoubtedly their choice of two objectives. The Japanese had hedged their bets with a team on the South Col route as well as one on the South-West Face, while the International Expedition initially tried the West Ridge and the South-West Face simultaneously, when they barely had sufficient Sherpas to sustain a single attempt on one route.

The face remained unclimbed, but I was no nearer to reaching it. I had already put out feelers in Kathmandu for permission to go there, but the mountain was fully booked until the mid-seventies. The next team in the lists was Dr Karl Herrligkoffer's German expedition scheduled for the spring of 1972. He had invited Don Whillans and Dougal Haston, who had reached the high point on the International Expedition. I also had an invitation, could not at first resist, but then pulled out again with the same doubts. This time it was easier; Dougal joined me. In the end Don Whillans, Doug Scott and Hamish MacInnes joined Herrligkoffer's attempt but it fared no better than any of the others.

Then at last I had my chance. An Italian expedition cancelled their booking for the autumn of 1972. We had permission but there were many imponderables. There was little more than three months in which to raise the money and organise the expedition. No one had succeeded in climbing Everest or any of the other highest Himalayan peaks in the post-monsoon season. The Swiss had tried in the autumn of 1952 and had been defeated by the cold and high winds. The same had happened to an Argentinian expedition in 1971.

I was determined to go to Everest but now, faced with the choice of route, had doubts about the South-West Face, contemplating instead a small expedition to climb Everest again by the South Col route. But the lure of the South-West Face was strong and in mid-June 1972 I committed myself to it. Once the decision was made there was no room for second thoughts and I plunged into the most taxing three months of my life. We had to organise the expedition and obtain all the equipment and food at the same time as we tried to find the funds to pay for it.

One of the most valuable things I had learnt from our Annapurna trip was the importance of delegating responsibility. Divide up the jobs, choose the right people to do them, and then, having provided a clear set of guidelines, leave them to get on with it. I followed this principle and it worked well. We arrived at Base Camp with the gear and food we were going to need and a sense of cohesion within the team that smooth if unobtrusive organisation undoubtedly promotes.

My two attempts on the South-West Face were really complementary to each other. The problems presented were so huge, so complex, that I suspect now an initial failure was almost inevitable. It was a question of learning from one's mistakes.

Our 1972 expedition was definitely on the small side with eleven climbers and twenty-four high-altitude porters. Of the eleven, I considered six of them to be lead climbers, who would go out in front to make the route, and all of whom I hoped were capable of reaching the summit. I have been accused of restricting my teams to a little group of cronies but, in many ways, this is inevitable, for the best basis of selection is shared climbing experience cemented by friendship.

Dougal Haston had been in on the climb from our Eiger Direct days with John Harlin. We had decided to pull out of Herrligkoffer's expedition whilst ensconsed in a tiny ice cave half-way up the North Wall of the Grandes Jorasses the previous winter. Self-contained yet charismatic, with a single-minded drive in the mountains, on one level Dougal was the ultimate prima donna, taking it for granted that he would be the one to go to the top, and yet he managed to do this without offending the people around him. On a mountain I felt completely attuned to him, though at ground level we saw comparatively little of each other. Living at Leysin in Switzerland, where he ran a climbing school, he was comfortably removed from the day-to-day chores of organising an expedition.

Nick Estcourt, one of my closest friends, was also an obvious choice. We had known each other since his university days and climbed together regularly. He was a computer programmer with, as one would expect, a quick analytical mind. Our attitudes and background were similar and he was an invaluable sounding board for many of my schemes. He had been very supportive of me on the South Face of Annapurna.

Mick Burke had also been with me on Annapurna. We always had quite a stormy relationship. Born in working-class Wigan, Mick had a sharp wit and, like so many climbers, automatically questioned any kind of authority. We had had plenty of arguments but had always resolved them and maintained a good friendship. After years of making a scanty living on the fringes of climbing, he had just got married and was starting a career in filming. His wife, Beth, was coming with the expedition as Base Camp nurse.

I was also building on an old friendship in asking Hamish MacInnes, with whom I had first climbed in 1953, when he took me up the first winter ascent of Raven Gully. Since then we had had many climbing adventures together in the Alps. Known affectionately as the Old Fox of Glencoe, he had made his life there, running the local mountain-rescue team, designing climbing and rescue equipment and sallying forth on a variety of adventures, ranging from yeti and treasure hunting to serious climbing. He had been on Everest that spring with Doug Scott, whom I also invited.

With shoulder-length hair and granny glasses, Doug looked like a latter-day John Lennon. Living in Nottingham, he had organised a series of adventurous expeditions to little-known places like the Tibesti mountains in the Sahara, the Hindu Kush, Turkey and Baffin Island. He had promoted lectures for me in Nottingham but at this stage I hardly knew him. Dave Bathgate, the sixth member of the lead climbing team was a newcomer to our circle. A joiner from Edinburgh, he was a good all-round climber, with an easy temperament.

But I had left out Don Whillans, the one person both the media and the climbing world expected me to take. We had done some of our best Alpine climbing together and he had reached the summit of Annapurna with Dougal Haston in 1970. He had then been my deputy leader and had contributed a great deal to our success. His forthright, abrasive style had complemented my own approach, but it had also created stress. One of the problems had been that when we had climbed together in the Alps, Don had indisputably held the initiative. He had been that bit more experienced and was also stronger than I. It would be very difficult for him to accept a reversal of those roles. He was a strong leader in his own right, had now been to Everest twice, and knew the mountain much better than I. It would not have been easy to run the expedition in the way that I wanted with Don taking part and so I decided to leave him behind.

There were also going to be four members with a support role. Jimmy Roberts who had led my first expedition to the Himalaya and now ran Mountain Travel in Kathmandu, was my deputy leader; Kelvin Kent, who had been Base Camp manager on Annapurna, was going to run Advance Base; Graham Tiso, who owned a successful climbing shop in Edinburgh and had organised our equipment, was to act in general back-up position, and Barney Rosedale was expedition doctor.

As leader I felt that I should probably stay in support, ideally running the camp just behind whoever was out in front. Base Camp leadership may have worked for Jimmy Roberts but it certainly doesn't suit my temperament. I decided to adopt the Montgomery touch. Monty always operated from a tactical headquarters in reasonably close contact with his forward commanders. I had discovered on Annapurna that it was a mistake to lead from the front, actually pushing the route out, since there one thought too exclusively of the few metres of snow or rock immediately in front of one's nose, rather than the climb as a whole.

On reaching Base Camp we supplemented our numbers with two unofficial members of the team. Tony Tighe, an Australian friend of Dougal's, was trekking in Nepal. He tagged along with the expedition and filled an invaluable role helping Jimmy Roberts to run Base Camp, while Ken Wilson, who edited a very successful British climbing magazine, called in to see us and was promptly recruited to organise Camp 1. In the event we were short of both lead climbers and people in support, for the climb developed into a long drawn out struggle of attrition against the winter cold and winds, until at last, on 14 November, we were forced to admit defeat at the foot of the Rock Band.

But it wasn't only lack of numbers that caused our defeat. There were so many unknown quantities in 1972. I was frightened of starting too early, whilst the monsoon was still at its height, because of the risk of heavy snowfall with the accompanying danger of avalanche. We set up Base Camp on 15 September after walking through the rain-soaked, leech-ridden foothills of Nepal. This was too late and meant that we had only got about half-way up the South-West Face by mid-October. It was then that the first of the post-monsoon winds hit us. They are part of the jet streams that rush round the earth's upper atmosphere and, with the autumnal cold, they drop to blast the higher peaks of the Himalaya.

When the wind arrived I was occupying our highest camp, Camp 4, three box tents, clinging precariously to a little rocky bluff in the middle of the great couloir leading to the Rock Band. The weather up to this point had been quite reasonable and our progress steady. The lead climbers had made the route first through the Icefall, laddering crevasses and ice walls, then up the Western Cwm to the site of Camp 2 which was the Advance Base. They had then moved on to the face itself, and had run up a line of fixed rope to link the camps and enable supplies to be relayed to what, eventually, would be our top camp, somewhere above the Rock Band. The Sherpas, supervised by the support climbers, were distributed between the lower camps ferrying supplies. I had moved up with four Sherpas, hoping to stock Camp 5, the site of which Dougal Haston and Hamish MacInnes had established a couple of days earlier.

But that night the wind struck out of a clear, star-studded sky. It came in gusts, first with a tremendous crash as of a solid force hitting the upper part of the face far above, followed by a roar, like a train in a tunnel, funnelling straight down the gully in which we were camped, to smash and tear into the tents, bulging in the walls and bending the thick alloy poles.

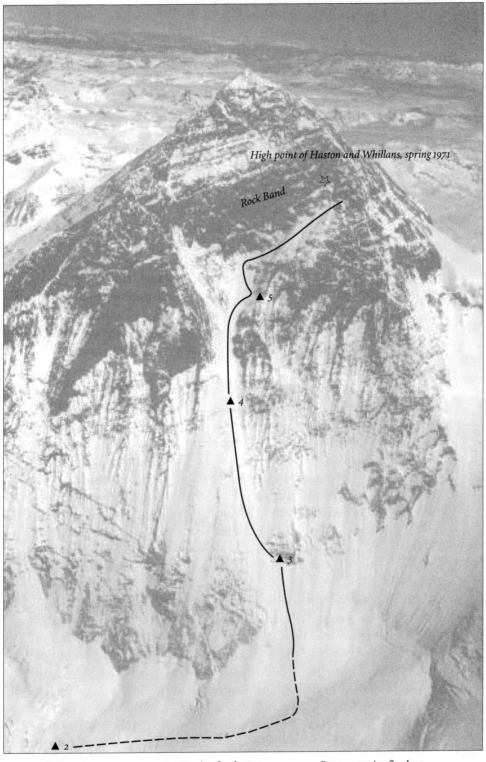

High point of Haston and Whillans, spring 1971

Rock Band

▲ 5

▲ 4

▲ 3

▲ 2

▲ Tented camp ———— *Route using fixed ropes* — — — — *Route not using fixed ropes*
Everest, South-West Face, 1972

There was no question of sleep and the next day there was little chance of movement. I was pinned at Camp 4 for a week, unable to make any real progress but loth to abandon our toe-hold on the face.

I commented in my diary on the night of 22 October:

> The wind is the appalling enemy, it is mind-destroying, physically des-troying, soul-destroying and even existing in the tents, which I think are now pretty weather tight, is still very, very hard. This will certainly be the most exacting test I have ever had to face ...
>
> Oh, the absolute lethargy of 24,600 feet. You want to pee and you lie there for a quarter of an hour making up your mind to look for your pee bottle. I've no appetite at all and it's an effort to cook anything for yourself. I suspect it is high time I did go down for a short rest – I think if you try to stay up high for the whole time, to conduct operations, you end up being ineffective in that you are just getting weaker and weaker, more and more lethargic. Part of me wants to stay up here, because this is the focus of events, but I think I really should go down.

At this first attempt we were forced to abandon all our camps on the face and were nearly wiped out in the Western Cwm. A massive storm destroyed most of our tents, burying some of them under three metres of snow. And yet we held on, though the five-day storm had taken a heavy toll, not only of gear, but of nerves and stamina as well. We returned to the face in the lull after the storm. Camp 4 had been very nearly demolished, saved only by the way the boxes had filled with spindrift that had then hardened like concrete, giving them solid cores to resist the deluge of snow and rocks that must have roared down around them. Doug Scott and Mick Burke had to work long into the dusk to make two of them habitable for themselves and their Sherpas. The next day they occupied Camp 5, tucked under an overhang of rock, safer than 4, but in the shade until late in the morning. It was a bitterly cold place for it was now early November and even in the Western Cwm the temperature at night was −30°C. At Camp 5 it was down to −40°C.

I was now faced with a serious problem of my own making. On the South Face of Annapurna I had learnt how important was the order in which I pushed my lead pairs out in front. The position of people on the mountain would determine who was best situated to make a summit bid and on the previous expedition the only serious row occurred when I pushed Don Whillans and Dougal Haston up through the other climbers, out of turn, because I thought they could make faster progress. To avoid this type of tension in 1972 I had nominated my lead climbing pairs before we had even reached Base Camp and gave them their roles, to include the summit bid. I had given Nick Estcourt and Dave Bathgate the job of making the route from Camp 5 to Camp 6 at the foot of the right-hand end of the Rock Band, partly because I knew they were the most easy-going members of the team and partly because I could trust them to carry out a less dramatic role conscientiously and without argument. Doug Scott and Mick Burke had the job of climbing the Rock Band and setting up our seventh camp to leave Hamish MacInnes and Dougal Haston to make the summit bid. Each pair had come to accept their role. Nick and Dave were at least in line to make a second summit bid just in case Dougal and Hamish failed. While Doug and Mick's task, solving the problem of the Rock Band, had its own special attraction, almost certainly offering the most interesting and challenging technical climbing of the entire route.

But we were so stretched, it wasn't working out to plan. I had had to use Doug and Mick to set up Camp 5, so that they could then move into Camp 6 immediately Dave and Nick had completed the route, but they were now so tired they needed to return to Advance Base for a rest. I therefore decided to push Dougal and Hamish straight through to tackle the Rock Band in order to keep up the momentum; they had been resting at Base Camp and were relatively fresh. This led to a colossal row. Doug and Mick had come to regard the Rock Band as their own. I had encouraged this attitude.

'Look,' Doug said, 'I've been looking forward to doing the Rock Band for two and a half months and have got it firmly fixed in my mind that I'm going to do it. I don't see why we shouldn't; I don't see that anything's changed. We could go straight up tomorrow.'

'But Doug, if you needed a rest so badly why did you come down in the first place? After only one day's rest you're going to be even more shattered when you get back up again. It just doesn't make sense.'

'You've been planning this all along,' he accused. 'In some ways you're no better than Herrligkoffer in the way you manipulate people.'

And so it went on. I finally lost my temper and suggested that if that was how he felt he could start heading for Kathmandu. But then we both calmed down, each of us temporising to find a solution to the argument. It wasn't just the outcome of the expedition. We each valued our friendship. It was this more than anything that held the team together and stopped any walk-outs such as had occurred on both the previous international expeditions.

Doug and Mick agreed to support Dougal and Hamish and there the argument ended. As so often happens, circumstances changed once again to make the entire disagreement irrelevant. Dave and Nick exhausted themselves in two long days pushing a line of fixed rope across the snow fields beneath the Rock Band. They still hadn't quite reached the site of Camp 6

but could go no further. We were almost at the end of our resources. The
Sherpas were tiring. Graham Tiso, with four Sherpas, was at Camp 4, but
we needed someone to complete the route to Camp 6 and get it stocked. I
therefore decided to do this myself, moving up to Camp 5 with the Sherpa
Ang Phurba.

It was the coldest, bleakest place I have ever been in. Even with two thick
sleeping-bags we were chilled at night. To get a gas cooker working effectively
you had to heat its cylinder with a spare stove. We made one carry, reaching
the end of the fixed rope and then running out a single rope-length to a tiny
platform on a rocky spur at the very end of the Rock Band. It was higher than
I had ever been before. At about 8300 metres I was almost level with the
summit of Lhotse and the South Col was below me. It was a perfect day but
out of that pale blue cloudless sky tore that implacable wind again, biting and
clawing at our clothes, beating the rope into the snow, and hammering at
body and mind, at the will to think, to go on.

I glanced up at the line of weakness that Dougal believed was the way
through the Rock Band. He and Don Whillans had climbed about a
hundred metres up it in 1971 to reach the high point of the International
Expedition. Dougal had assured us that there was a route up there to the
right, that if only they had had enough supplies reaching them, they could
have climbed it. I couldn't even see a gully. It faded into an open corner of
sheer rock. It would have been difficult at sea level, near impossible at 8300
metres. But I was too tired and stretched to think it through. We dumped
a tent and a couple of bottles of oxygen on the tiny ledge, turned round
and slid and stumbled down the fixed ropes back to the camp. On the way
down, I couldn't help noticing a deep-cut gully at the far left of the Rock
Band. Could this be a better route? It was the one that the Japanese had
investigated in 1970. I had never quite understood why Don and Dougal
had chosen the right-hand route, for this left-hand gully seemed to dig
deep into the band at its lowest point. Could that be the key?

Dougal, Hamish, Doug and Mick were already installed at Camp 5. There
was no room for me so, as planned, I descended the fixed ropes to Camp
4, arriving exhausted about an hour after dark. The following day the others
tried to establish Camp 6. On reaching it they also gazed up at that sheer
blank corner. The wind was so strong there was no question of pitching the
tent. They dropped back down to Camp 5 and Dougal called me on the
radio.

'Hello Chris, this is Dougal. I'm afraid it's no go. We're coming down
tomorrow.'

I didn't argue. I had half expected it. It wasn't just the steepness and
difficulty of the Rock Band. We had allowed the winds and cold of winter

to overtake us and everyone was exhausted. We could not sustain anyone camped at the foot of the Rock Band, let alone establish a camp and mount a summit bid above it. But we had taken ourselves beyond limits I had thought possible and, in doing so, had discovered a satisfaction and a respect for each other that transcended failure.

Even as we were packing up the expedition I was already beginning to think of ways we could improve our chances of success. A bigger team, stronger tentage, start earlier, and perhaps go for that gully on the far left of the Rock Band. The others, particularly Doug, were thinking along the same lines, but it all remained very academic, for we were now once again at the back of the queue and we knew that a strong Japanese expedition had permission for the following autumn.

With a sickening similarity to the final stages of our expedition to the South Face of Annapurna, we were then struck by tragedy. Tony Tighe had been at Base Camp throughout our trip, sorting out loads and manning the radio. I had allowed him to go into the Icefall a couple of times at the beginning though we had not put him on our official roster and, because of this, received a terse message from the authorities in Kathmandu that we were defying their regulations.

But I knew how much he wanted to see the South-West Face for himself and so I told him that he could go up with the Sherpas who were going to clear Advance Base. It would have been one of the last journeys through the Icefall. He was just behind the Sherpas when a huge sérac tower collapsed. The Sherpas escaped but Tony must have been immediately beneath it. We never found his body which was buried under hundreds of tons of unstable ice debris. In the short time we had known him, we had all become very fond of him. Hard-working, cheerful, and very positive, he was of that breed of young Australian nomad who wander the world. It seemed ironic that we, who had been exposed to risk throughout the expedition, had had so many near escapes and yet survived, while Tony, on only the third occasion he had entered the Icefall, should die. Although we had heard many tales of the dangers of the Khumbu Icefall, and knew eight climbers had been killed in it over the years, clad in a heavy covering of monsoon snow, its crevasses hidden and its towering unstable sérac walls banked up, it had not appeared too dangerous. We had even begun to take the route through it for granted and I can remember, only the day before Tony died, spending about twenty minutes below the sérac tower whose collapse killed him, taking photographs of the Sherpas as they passed.

We returned home saddened again by the loss of a good friend, but also with many valuable lessons to put into practice, should we get another chance at the South-West Face.

The next three years provided an enjoyable interlude, during which I made one of the most important decisions of my married life. Wendy had always hated living in Bowdon, on the south-west extremity of Manchester. It is a slightly melancholy suburb of big Edwardian houses, in walking distance of open country that still had an urban quality in its trampled paths and a river so polluted that it was barren of any form of life, never free from the background roar of traffic. Whilst I was away on Everest, Wendy, left looking after our two young sons, aged five and three, was very nearly driven to her limit.

In 1971 we had bought a small cottage at the foot of High Pike, a gentle 657-metre hill that forms the north-eastern bastion of the Lake District's Northern Fells. We had been looking for a cottage for some time and had been told of Badger Hill by a friend. We drove through Caldbeck, a sprawl of attractive stone-built cottages and farm houses, and on up towards the open fell, following a winding, single-track lane between hedgerows alternating with dry stone wall that gave way onto an open green. Two farmhouses crouched to one side and, on the far edge, part hidden by a line of young ash and an overgrown hawthorn hedge, stood a low slate-roofed cottage. The secluded little garden, engulfed in knee-high grass, was still a welcoming haven. We peered through the downstairs windows and could make out hand-painted furniture in the low-ceilinged rooms. There was an air of warmth and peace with which both Wendy and I fell in love. I had often said before that one should never become over-attached to a house and that where one lived was not really important. How wrong I was. We bought Badger Hill and used it as a weekend cottage, finding solace in the gentle beauty of those Northern Fells.

During the Easter weekend in 1973, we were both working in the garden, Wendy weeding the roses, whilst I dug over another bed. We were due to motor back to Bowdon that evening and I dreaded the hassle of packing and the drive south, but most of all I hated the anticlimax of returning to the ugly yellow brick semi. Before I had time really to consider it, an idea just crept into my mind.

'You know, love, there's no reason why we shouldn't live up here, is there?'

Wendy had not dared even dream that I would want to return permanently to the Lakes and had never applied any kind of pressure on me, even though she detested Bowdon so much. We never had any doubts or second thoughts, though we did look half-heartedly for a larger house that we could move straight into. But we had come to love the atmosphere of Badger Hill and the gentle rolling fell immediately behind. So we decided to extend it to give us the room we needed. Even though it was still going to be much smaller than our house in Bowdon, it was a price worth paying.

There were expeditions during these next three years, but they were to relatively small peaks and assumed the guise of extended holidays. In Manchester Nick Estcourt's family and mine had come to know each other well. In 1973 I went with Nick to the Kishtwar Himalaya in Kashmir with an Indian expedition, and we ended up climbing a beautiful unclimbed 6416-metre peak called Brammah. I had relied on Nick's loyalty on so many occasions on Annapurna and Everest that it was good to share the joy of reaching a high summit with him. We made a good climbing team. After sitting out a week's bad weather, we climbed Brammah from a camp at 5000 metres, going for the top as we would on an Alpine peak in a single day's dash, up a pinnacled ridge that reached to its summit cone of snow. We bivouacked on the way down on a narrow ledge where we were entertained and alarmed through the night by a light show of distant thunderstorms. The piled cumulo-nimbus glowed and pulsed, relics of the dying monsoon.

The following year I had fixed another joint Indian/British expedition to a peak called Changabang. There were to be four Britons and four Indians. Nick had not dared to ask his company for yet another extended holiday, so he stayed behind. Doug Scott, Dougal Haston and Martin Boysen, one of my oldest climbing friends, came with me. This expedition also marked our move up to the Lake District. The alterations on the house had not been completed, but Wendy was determined to escape Manchester and moved into a tiny caravan parked on the green just after I left for the mountains.

Overlooking the western extremity of the Nanda Devi Sanctuary in the Garhwal Himalaya, Changabang is a shark's tooth of granite thrusting into the skies. Amongst the most beautiful mountains in the world, it is also in one of the loveliest settings. Alpine pastures and tall fir forest are guarded by precipitous gorges and high mountain passes that resisted so many of the pre-war attempts before those greatest of all mountain explorers, Eric Shipton and Bill Tilman, finally found a way in.

The expedition was a particularly happy one. My co-leader, Balwant Sandhu, was the commanding officer of a regiment of Paras. Like so many Indian officers, on first acquaintance he was almost a caricature of a pre-war British army officer. But this was only a first impression. Well read and informed, extremely liberal in his views, Balwant had a free-ranging spirit and was a delight to climb with.

Originally we had planned to tackle the West Face, the route eventually climbed by Pete Boardman and Joe Tasker, but it had seemed too steep and technically difficult for our mixed party, and anyway the mountain was still virgin. It was only logical to climb it first by its easiest route. So we out-flanked the difficulties, climbing a steep col to escape the Rhamani Glacier and reach the inner sanctum of the Nanda Devi Sanctuary and the great hanging glacier that led across the face of Kalanka, Changabang's sister peak, to the col between the two mountains.

Six of us, the four Britons, Balwant Sandu and the Sherpa Tashi, reached the summit of Changabang (6864 metres) from a camp high on the Kalanka Face. It had been a good expedition in which the two groups had merged into a single team, forging some strong friendships that have lasted over the years. It was in Delhi, on our way to Changabang, that I learnt I had another chance at the South-West Face of Everest. A Canadian expedition had cancelled for autumn 1975. I didn't commit myself immediately. Memories of the worry of trying to raise the money and organise our 1972 trip remained very fresh. I was still attracted to the concept of a small expedition going for the South Col route. But Doug and Dougal dissuaded me.

'You couldn't just walk past the South-West Face,' Dougal pointed out. 'Anything else'd seem second best.'

I had to admit his logic, but made the proviso that this time we had to have a single sponsor who would finance the whole venture.

It was exciting getting back to England and especially to our new home at Nether Row. Wendy was more relaxed and happier than I had ever known her to be after a prolonged absence, in spite of spending seven weeks in the tiny blue caravan, and Rupert and Daniel were settled into a local primary school. The house was still not finished, but somehow it didn't really matter. We both felt that we could now gently let ourselves take root in this corner of the Lakes.

Pertemba, who had been one of our most outstanding Sherpas in 1972, was our first house guest. A Belgian trekking client had brought him over to Europe. He went climbing in the Pyrenees, visited Dougal in Leysin and then came to stay with us for a fortnight. It was a delight to have him to stay and to get to know him better than one ever could in the course of a large expedition. In his late twenties, he had the benefit of education at the school in Khumde founded by Ed Hillary. Highly intelligent, good looking, charismatic, he seemed at home in any situation in the West, and yet he hadn't lost the traditional values of Sherpa society. He had that combination of twinkling humour, dignity and warmth that is one of the enduring qualities of so many Sherpas. In the fortnight with us he joined me rock-climbing on our neighbouring crags, helped me lay a lawn in front of our part-finished cottage and showed endless patience playing with Daniel and Rupert. When he came to leave, I felt that I had built the foundations for an enduring friendship.

I was becoming even more relaxed about the daunting prospect of funding and organising another expedition to Everest.

CHAPTER THREE

Success on the South-West Face

Getting sponsorship was ridiculously easy. It took just a single letter to an acquaintance, Alan Tritton, who was on the board of Barclays Bank. They agreed to underwrite the expedition and this meant that I could concentrate solely on the organisation. Five expeditions had now tried and failed on the South-West Face. It didn't seem to matter how large the team was or how good the equipment, the chances of success were still fairly slim. This is what made it such an intriguing challenge. In 1972, when we reached the foot of the Rock Band, we were barely capable of mounting a single summit bid and this could only have had a chance of success if the ground had been comparatively easy. The team had been exhausted and the supply line to the top camp was little better than a trickle. The same was the case with all the other expeditions. It was obvious that we were going to need a team capable of sustaining a concerted push, both to climb the Rock Band and then make a summit bid from a camp above it.

Our team of six lead climbers, five support climbers and twenty-four Sherpas had not been sufficient in 1972. This time I decided on having nine lead climbers, with seven in a support role, and sixty high-altitude porters. I used the 1972 team as a base, inviting them all. Hamish MacInnes, Dougal Haston, Doug Scott, Nick Estcourt and Mick Burke were able to come. I then asked Martin Boysen who had been on both Annapurna South Face and Changabang. Newcomers were Allen Fyffe, a very talented Aberdeen climber, Paul Braithwaite from Oldham and Peter Boardman, youngest member of the team, who was our token representative of the new generation of climbers. In support were Mike Thompson, two doctors, Charlie Clarke and Jim Duff, Dave Clarke, Ronnie Richards and Mike Cheney, our contact in Kathmandu. If the route through the Rock Band proved to be very difficult or if we were overtaken by wind and cold, we should need every single climber we had.

We also improved on the equipment, particularly the tentage. Hamish MacInnes, my deputy leader, designed a range of tents that would stand up to the worst weather Everest could throw at us. The MacInnes face boxes were like fortresses and undoubtedly the strongest tents ever built.

We had a compact organisational team of Dave Clarke and Hamish coping with the equipment, Mike Thompson, one of my oldest friends who had been with me at Sandhurst before studying to become an anthropologist, working on the food, and Bob Stoodley, who ran a garage in Manchester, planning the overland transportation of all our gear. Since we were now completely funded, I had much more time than on previous expeditions to plan our tactics on the climb itself. I used a computer to calculate the logistics, or flow of supplies up the mountain. I have always enjoyed playing board war games and this was really an extension of one of these. The personal computer had not been invented then, but a climbing friend of mine, Ian McNaught-Davis, ran a computer company and he loaned me one of his bright young programmers and gave us time on his mainframe computer.

The rest of the team regarded my graphs and print-outs with a mildly amused scepticism. They did, however, prove invaluable, in that my planning was based on logic and, in the latter stages of the climb, when inevitably I had to adapt the original plan in the light of circumstances, I was able to do so because I had the overall picture in my mind and was working from a sound position. It was very different from 1972 when we were so stretched both in materials and manpower that we could only struggle through one crisis at a time, improvising as we went.

We started earlier than we had in 1972, leaving Britain on 29 July. Most of our gear was already stored in a barn in the little village of Khumde, just below Everest. We had sent it out overland before the arrival of the monsoon so that it could be flown from Kathmandu to the airstrip at Luglha. This was Mike Cheney's idea. Based in Kathmandu and working for Jimmy Roberts' trekking company, Mountain Travel, he was to be our Base Camp manager. Although Mike never went beyond Base Camp and was plagued with illness throughout the trip, he contributed as much as anyone to our eventual success.

His first contribution was the choice of Sirdar. He recommended Pertemba. He would be by far the youngest Sherpa ever to be put in charge of a major expedition, but I was confident he could handle it. Pertemba proved to be a first-class manager, supervising the entire transportation and storage of all our supplies in Khumde. We didn't lose a single item and built up a sound relationship of trust both with Pertemba and, through him, with our Sherpa team.

It also meant that our own walk in to Everest was all the more relaxed since we did not have to worry about a huge porter train. Looked after by the Sherpas, we were able to enjoy ourselves and relax. It was an intermission that I certainly needed. The lead-up to any expedition is hectic, though our

1975 trip was almost a rest cure compared to what it had been like three years earlier. The walk gave me plenty of time to think about my policy on the mountain. One lesson I had learnt was the mistake of being over-rigid in my planning. I certainly wasn't going to allot fixed roles to individuals all the way up the mountain. I was already beginning to think, however, how I was going to allocate my climbing teams for the lower part of the face itself, and how this might inevitably affect roles higher up.

My cassette diary became something of a confessional:

> I don't think there's any danger of us ever having leadership by committee. Of course, though, if there is a strong consensus against what I say, this is going to emerge in a troublesome sense later on and I think this is where I've got to be very receptive to the feelings of the team so that I can effectively sell them my ideas and make them feel and believe that these are ideas they have taken part in forming. At the same time I must draw ideas from their combined experience and not be afraid to change my own plans if other suggestions seem better. I don't think the old military style of leadership can possibly work.

This was how I saw myself, but not everyone shared this view. Doug Scott, in an interview with our television team, commented:

> It's a very strong hierarchy set-up here and he is very much the leader. However much he might say he's the co-ordinator, he is the leader. It's just something within my nature and I suspect in Mick and one or two of the rest of us, that the shop-floor mentality develops – them, the leaders, the foremen, bosses, and us. However hard you try to suppress it, it comes through.

This feeling wasn't helped by an action I had taken. The team was so large I had decided that it would be much pleasanter if we split into two groups for the approach march. Apart from anything else, it was difficult for all of us to squeeze into a single tent and eat together. But a split team in itself can foster the 'them and us' feeling, as Mike Thompson later described, in an article he wrote for *Mountain Magazine*:

> Perhaps unwisely, he labelled these the A team and the B team, and immediately there was much speculation as to the underlying basis for his selection. At first there were fears among the B team that the choice of summiters had already taken place and that they were travelling with the leader in order that they could plot the fine details of the assault in secrecy. But even the most paranoid could not sustain this belief for long and a more popular theory was that the 'chaps' were in the A team and

the 'lads' in the B team. This perhaps was nearer the truth since what had happened was that Chris had, quite understandably, taken with him all the executives: Sirdar Pertemba, Base Camp manager Mike Cheney, equipment officer Dave Clarke, senior doctor Charles Clarke, and the media in the shape of the *Sunday Times* reporter and the television team. These middle managers were, during their fortnight's walk, to have the interesting experience of, in the words of our leader, 'being let in on his thinking'.

The B team, gloriously free of logistics, planning scenarios, computer print-outs, communication set-ups and the like, immediately sank into that form of communal warmth generated by squaddies in a barrack room, that impenetrable bloody-mindedness born of the I-only-work-here mentality of the shop floor.

A series of perfectly sensible decisions led to the emphasis of a division that is always incipiently present in any large expedition. The A team represented the Overground leadership and the B team the Underground leadership.

I was barely aware of this split, even when our two teams reunited at Khumde. Things as a whole were working well and, in a way, the grumbling underground provided a useful escape valve for the inevitable frustrations of the early stages before everyone became fully involved. This was certainly the case with Doug. Once we reached Base Camp and started making the route through the Icefall, he felt very much happier:

> Before I got some definite role to play, and I think it must go for a lot of the other lads, I felt there was the leadership, then there was the rest of us that were being ordered about and I wasn't always in complete sympathy with the leadership, but as soon as we had a role to play it was fine; I felt much closer to things. There was something to go for. The underground leadership united with the actual leadership. We worked as one and were fully behind all of Chris's decisions.

We established Base Camp on 22 August, nearly a month earlier than in 1972. Because of our size and sound planning based on previous experience, we were able to push the route out very much faster. As a result we established our Advance Base at the foot of the face on 2 September and on 13 September, two days earlier than we had even arrived at Base Camp in 1972, Dougal Haston reached the site of Camp 5, our jumping-off point for the Rock Band. In running the expedition I consulted very closely with Pertemba, discussing with him how many Sherpas we needed at different camps, but leaving him to select individuals and keep track of who was due for a rest. The smooth functioning of our Sherpa team largely depended on him.

One of the most important decisions affecting our eventual success was to change the route from the right-hand side of the Rock Band to the gully splitting its left-hand end. We were now venturing on to new ground and I used this fact as a justification for me to go out in front. I felt I needed to get at first-hand the feel of what the route was like up into the Rock Band. I could also see that Camp 5 was going to be the crucial point in the forcing of the Rock Band and then stocking the top camp. I could therefore use this as my command post.

I moved up with Ronnie Richards on 17 September. Ronnie was a late addition to the team. Living in Keswick, just a few miles from my home, he had been recommended by Graham Tiso as a good all-rounder. Quiet, and not over-ambitious, he was happy to act in support and yet was a thoroughly competent mountaineer. It was immensely satisfying to get out in front and to escape from the day-to-day organisation. The site that Dougal had chosen for Camp 5 was tucked into a little chute that abutted the Great Central Gully just below the point where we would have to cross it to get to the left-hand gully.

We had dug out a ledge, no easy matter at nearly 8000 metres, and had erected one of the super-Boxes. It was time for the evening radio call. Everyone came on the air, Camp 2 talking to Camp 4, Base calling Camp 2. I tried to butt in, to take control, but nobody took any notice. The awful realisation crept upon me that our set was receiving but not sending. I had lost control of the expedition. I was like a frustrated general in charge of a battle, whose communications have collapsed. Ronnie watched with quiet amusement as I shook the recalcitrant set, yelling into the mouthpiece as if sheer volume of sound would get through to the others.

Once the radio call was over he offered to try to fix it, spending the rest of the evening taking it apart and putting it back together after repairing the sender switch. I was back in command once again.

I stayed at Camp 5 for eight days, helping to make the route up to the foot of the Rock Band, bringing up other climbers and Sherpas until it had become a tiny hanging village of four box tents perched one above the other. Doug and I, working in complete accord, pushed the route through to the foot of the Rock Band. I had already decided on the final order of play, with Doug and Dougal, as I and, I suspect, the rest of the team had assumed all along, making the first summit bid, and Nick and Paul Braithwaite forcing the route through the Rock Band. Paul – Tut to the climbing world – was a friend of Doug's and had been with Hamish to the Caucasus. A decorator by trade, he was a brilliant climber on both rock

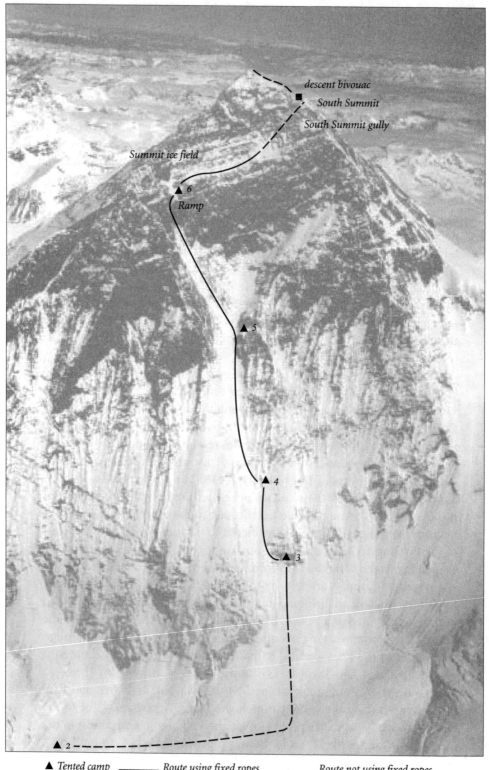

descent bivouac
South Summit
South Summit gully

Summit ice field

▲ 6
Ramp

▲ 5

▲ 4

▲ 3

▲ 2

▲ Tented camp ——————— Route using fixed ropes _ _ _ _ _ Route not using fixed ropes
Everest, South-West Face, 1975

and ice. He had a whimsical sense of humour and had settled comfortably into the team, getting on with everyone.

Mick Burke and I followed behind Nick and Tut, carrying loads of rope for them to fix through the gully. This was one of the crucial days of the climb. We were the first expedition with the capacity to lay effective siege to the Rock Band. We had both the climbers and the carrying power to sustain successive attempts on the wall.

The previous day I had stopped on the edge of a steep snow-plastered arête that barred our way into the gully. Tut took the first lead, floundering cautiously over near-vertical snow-covered rock, to reach the other side. Nick led through, up the easy snow tongue penetrating into the gully, but his pace got progressively slower, until he finally sank into the snow to anchor the rope, so that we could follow up. When we reached him, we learnt that he had run out of oxygen. Either his regulator was faulty, or perhaps by mistake he had picked up a bottle that had already been part-used. It never occurred to him to turn back. I suspect that he had already made the Rock Band his own personal summit and was determined to attain it.

It was like a Scottish gully in winter, snow-based, curving up between sheer walls of black rock. A spume of spindrift cascaded down the walls, a grim portent of our fate if the gully was swept by a major avalanche. It was Tut's turn to lead; the first obstacle was a huge chock-stone encased in snow that blocked the bed of the gully. It would have been easy at sea level, but at 8300 metres, encumbered with the paraphernalia of high-altitude climbing, it was a laborious struggle. Beyond this the gully opened out for a short section but then steepened. Tut was poised on a precarious rocky gangway when his oxygen ran out.

> I don't think I shall ever forget the feeling of suffocation as I ripped the mask away from my face. I was on the brink of falling, beginning to panic, felt a warm trickle run down my leg. God, what's happening? Scrabbled up the rock arête until at last I reached some firm snow. I collapsed exhausted. I had no runners out and was over a hundred feet above Nick; I'd have had it if I'd fallen.

Tut had reached a spot where the gully widened into a small amphitheatre. The main arm of the gully continued up to the left, but a ramp forked out to the right, beneath an impending wall of yellow rock. It was Nick's turn to lead. Now neither of them had any oxygen. Mick and I had been following up the ropes they had fixed and still had oxygen in our bottles, but neither of us thought to offer the other pair our supply or to take over the lead.

Exhausted, with oxygen-starved minds, it was as if each one of us was in a narrow tunnel, his role predetermined, unchangeable.

Nick started up the ramp, moving slowly, awkwardly, his body thrust out of balance by the overhanging wall above.

> I was getting desperate; goggles all misted up, panting helplessly. I somehow managed to clear some of the snow behind the boss, using my fingers while my arm, hooked round it, held my weight. I was losing strength fast. I think the others thought I was about to fall off, but whatever happened I wasn't going to give up. If I had and let Tut do it, I'd have kicked myself for years.

He didn't give up, and slowly, precariously, picked his way over the bulging snow-encrusted rock, from out of the shadows of the gully on to the sun-blessed snows of the upper reaches of the mountain. Nick and Tut between them had solved the problem of the Rock Band and discovered the key to the South-West Face. The climbing, even to this day, was probably the hardest that had ever been done at that altitude, and they did it without supplementary oxygen. They had shown they were capable of getting to the summit of Everest, and yet were paving the way for Doug and Dougal. It was teamwork at its best.

The following day was a rest day. Doug and Dougal were now at Camp 5 ready to establish our top camp. We had all the gear they were going to need for their bid for the summit and the people to carry it – Mike Thompson, Mick Burke and myself, with three of our best Sherpas, Pertemba, young Tenzing and Ang Phurba, who had shared a vigil with me at Camp 5 in 1972.

I had already asked Doug and Dougal to spend a day running a line of fixed rope out across the summit ice field. This would ensure they had a sound line of retreat on their return, and make it easier for a second attempt. I used that rest day to plan the subsequent summit bids.

The strength of our supply line could enable us to sustain four-man teams for these. However, as I juggled logistics and summit aspirations I knew one of my problems was that there were too many lead climbers who wanted to get to the top. So far I had been dividing them into teams of two, three or four and giving each group turns out in front with a defined objective. But they still had a lot of time on their hands, especially in the latter stages of the expedition. This inevitably led to tension, particularly when it came to allocating climbers to the summit bids. I would have made life easier for myself if I had had more support climbers whose main task was to supervise the Sherpas and check out the supplies being carried up the mountain. This role called for competent mountaineers who accepted the fact that they hadn't the skill of the potential summiters. In some ways they had a more relaxed time, as Mike Thompson described:

As a 'support climber' I was aware that I was fortunate to have got as far as becoming Camp 4 commandant, responsible, in theory, for five face boxes, an equipment dump, nine Sherpas and a variable number of 'lead climbers' in transit. I became obsessed with becoming a Sherpa and increasingly resented the lead climbers who passed through on oxygen, carrying just their personal equipment. I was quite ridiculously touched when, having managed to drag myself and my load up to Camp 5 without oxygen, Pertemba said, with what I now suspect was heavy sarcasm, 'You are a real Sherpa now.'

It was much easier for the support climbers to fulfill, or even exceed their ambitions. Mike ended up making the vital carry to Camp 6, reaching an altitude higher than he had ever thought possible. A lead climber, on the other hand, would almost inevitably have a sense of disappointment if he failed to reach the summit. Those that were not acclimatising quickly found it very difficult, indeed impossible, to adapt to a support role, even though they could have been very useful to the expedition in that capacity.

Bearing all this in mind, I decided that we could put in two subsequent bids – eight tickets to the summit of Everest. I had promised Pertemba at the beginning of the expedition that at least one Sherpa should have a chance of going to the top and now gave him the choice. He had no hesitation in choosing himself and he was probably the most suitable. I decided that I should have a Sherpa on each bid and so Pertemba nominated Ang Phurba for the third team. That left six places.

Nick and Tut surely deserved a chance of going for the summit, but I also had to think of the others who in the last exciting days had been waiting in frustrated inaction back at Advance Base. Of the lead climbers, there were Hamish MacInnes, Peter Boardman, Martin Boysen and Allen Fyffe. Hamish had been caught in an avalanche whilst we had been forcing the route to Camp 4 and his lungs had been filled with powder snow. I knew that he had been badly affected, so I ruled him out, along with Allen who had been acclimatising too slowly and had only been on the lower part of the face. I decided, therefore, that it would be best to bring Pete and Martin up to Camp 5 to join Mick Burke for the second summit bid and they could be followed by Nick and Tut, after they had had a brief rest back at Advance Base, for the third push.

That left one place for the third summit bid. I could not resist putting myself into it, even though this would mean spending another week up at my Camp 5 command post. From there I could control the movement of the summit teams and react to any crisis.

I announced the results of my morning's work at the two o'clock radio call. Martin Boysen described the impact down at Camp 2:

> We waited tensed with expectation and ambition. Hamish took the call and Chris came over loud and clear in the warm air of the afternoon.
>
> 'I've decided after a lot of thought ...' Wait for it. I listened only for the names not the justifications. 'Mick, Martin, Pete and Pertemba ...' Thank God for that. 'Tut, Nick, Ang Phurba ...' I had no further interest in listening; I had been given my chance and now I looked at the others. Poor Allen, his face hardened with disappointment as the names poured out, but not his own. The radio stopped and everyone departed quietly with their own hopes, ambitions and disappointments.

I spent the rest of the afternoon dozing. The decisions were made and next morning we were going to help Doug and Dougal move into the top camp. The evening radio call was filled with routine matters. Once we climbers had finished our business, the Sherpas took over, filling the air waves with their staccato language. After half an hour Pertemba had finished deploying his Sherpa force and turned to me.

'Charlie wants to talk to you. He'll come up on the radio at seven o'clock.'

I was both disturbed and intrigued. He obviously wanted to talk to me privately, for no one else would be listening in.

I switched on the radio at seven.

'Hello Chris, this is Charlie. Can you hear me OK? Over.'

'Yes. Over.'

Charlie has a wonderful bedside manner, his voice both reassuring and confident. He asked me to reconsider my decision to stay on at Camp 5 and take part in the third summit bid. He pointed out the length of time I had been living at around 8000 metres, the fact that my voice was often slurred over the radio and that my calls that day had sometimes been muddled. He also made the point that I was getting out of contact with the situation on the rest of the mountain, my eyes just focused on establishing the top camp and making the summit. He then told me that Hamish wanted to have a word with me.

Hamish stated that he had decided to go home. There was no longer any need for him on the expedition. He assured me that he was not going to talk to the press but that, if he was cornered, he'd say he was going home because of the after-effects of the avalanche.

When the call came to an end I had a lot to think about. The euphoria of the last few days had evaporated. I had no illusions why Hamish was going home and could sympathise with his disappointment. This more than anything made me realise that Charlie was right. I had been at Camp 5 for too long, had inevitably, and perhaps essentially, been single-minded about mounting the first summit bid, but now my place was definitely back at Camp 2. Once Doug and Dougal were in their top camp, I could do no more to help them. I had to start thinking of the expedition as a whole and particularly of the feelings of my team members. I resolved to return to Advance Base once I had made my carry to Camp 6 and give Ronnie Richards my place in the third summit bid, though natural optimism reasserted itself with thoughts of yet another bid in which perhaps Mike Thompson, Allen Fyffe, Hamish, if I could tempt him back, and I could go for the top.

We made our big carry on 22 September. I knew that we had done everything we could to help the first bid for the summit. For me it was a moment of intense fulfilment, perhaps as great as anything I have ever experienced. All I could do now was to sit it out and wait ... and wait.

I dropped back to Advance Base on the 23rd, the day that Doug and Dougal ran a line of fixed rope across the summit ice-field. I took turns with the others the following day to gaze through the long-focus lenses as they went for the summit, picking their way, tiny dots on the snow field, which vanished into the South Summit gully. And then the long dragging hours as the afternoon slipped away without a sign of them.

It was Nick who spotted them next.

'I can see something moving. They're at the top of the gully. Look, you can see something flash. They're still going up hill.'

It was four thirty in the afternoon, only another two hours of daylight and they were obviously going for the summit. We saw nothing more that night. Everyone was subdued, tense. I hardly slept at all and was back at the telescope first thing in the morning when I saw, to my vast relief, two tiny figures moving slowly back towards the haven of the top camp.

The radio that we had left on all night crackled into life. They were back. They had reached the top just before dark, had survived the highest ever bivouac, just below the South Summit of Everest, by digging a snow cave, and had come back unharmed except for a single frostbitten finger. I cried with relief and joy at their success. It had been a magnificent effort, one that I suspect very few other climbers could have equalled.

But that untrammelled joy was short-lived, for the expedition wasn't over. I should have dearly loved to have ordered everyone off the mountain, to have escaped while we were all still safe. But I knew I couldn't, for I owed it to the others to give them their chance of the summit. Worries were already crowding in. The second team was moving up to Camp 6 that day. I waited tensely for the two o'clock call.

Martin Boysen came up on the air, telling me that Pete Boardman and Pertemba were with him at Camp 6, but Mick Burke hadn't arrived yet. He was obviously worried about the time that Mick was taking. One of the Sherpas making the carry had also failed to turn up, so they were short of oxygen and only had enough for the three of them. I had been worried about Mick all along. He had stayed at Camp 5 for almost as long as I had and certainly hadn't been going as fast as I on the two occasions we had climbed together above Camp 5. I had tried to persuade him to come down with me when I pulled out of the third summit team, but he had been adamant. He said he was feeling fine and was determined to go for the summit. It was not just to reach the summit for its own sake. Mick was working for the BBC as an assistant cameraman with the job of filming on the face. Getting film on the summit was of immense importance to him and for the team as a whole. So I had agreed to his staying.

But now my anxiety, triggered by Martin's, burst out with all the violence of suppressed tension. I told Martin that in no circumstances did I want Mick to go for the summit the next day. Martin was shaken by the violence of my reaction and after he went off the air I realised I was perhaps ordering the impossible. Once climbers have got to the top camp on Everest they are very much on their own. Up to that point they are members of a team dependent on each other and the overall control of a leader but the summit bid was different. This was a climbing situation that you might get on a smaller expedition or in the Alps. It was their lives in their own hands and only they could decide upon their course of action.

I kept the radio open and was working in my tent when Mick called me about an hour later. He sounded guarded, potentially aggressive, explained that he had been delayed because he'd had to sort out some of the fixed ropes on the way up and that anyway his sack, filled with camera equipment as well as his personal gear, was a lot heavier than everyone else's. Lhakpa Dorje had also arrived and they had found another two bottles of oxygen buried in the snow. I was still worried about him, but there was no point in trying to order him down when I had no means of implementing the order, and, anyway, I wondered whether I had the right to do so. As an experienced mountaineer who had contributed so much to the expedition, surely it was up to him and his partners to decide how much farther they could go.

Nonetheless, I didn't sleep much that night. The following morning was hazy with high cloud coming in from the west and great spirals of spindrift blowing from the summit ridge, meaning you could only get odd glimpses of the upper snow field. At about nine that morning Mike Thompson reported seeing four figures, but they were scattered; two close together, far ahead, nearly at the foot of the South Summit gully, one about half-way across and the other far behind. At the two o'clock call Martin Boysen came on the air. His crampon had fallen off, his oxygen hadn't been working and so he had had no choice but to return to the camp. Mick, though far behind Pertemba and Pete, had decided to go on alone. The afternoon dragged by. Was the achievement of a successful ascent in danger of being destroyed by a stupid accident? I recorded in my diary:

> I've just got to sit it out. I must say it's going to be hell for the next three days until I get all my climbers down. I just pray I get them down safe.

As the afternoon crept on, the weather deteriorated steadily. The upper part of the mountain was now in cloud and the wind was snatching at our tents. We were keeping the wireless open the whole time. Dusk fell and still there was no sign of the other three. Then just after seven, Martin came on the air.

He spoke in a flat, toneless voice that indicated that something was desperately wrong, just saying he had some news and he'd put Pete on. You could feel the exhaustion and anguish in Pete's voice as he told us what had happened. He and Pertemba had reached the top at one that afternoon. Because of the tracks left by Doug and Dougal, they had made good progress in spite of a fault in Pertemba's oxygen system. They had assumed that Mick had returned with Martin and were therefore amazed to meet him on their way back down, about a hundred metres below the summit, just above the Hillary Step.

Mick was determined to make it to the top and even tried to persuade them to go back with him so that he could film them, but they were moving slowly, one at a time, belaying each other. Pete said that if Mick hadn't caught them up by the time they reached the South Summit, they'd wait for him there. I'm sure that Mick made it the top. He was so close. They waited for an hour and forty minutes with the storm getting progressively more fierce and then decided they must start down. It was four thirty in the afternoon and they had all too little daylight left for the their descent of the gully and the long traverse back over the summit snow field. It was an appalling decision to have to make, but if they had waited any longer they would almost certainly have perished. The most probable explanation of Mick's failure to catch them up was that he had walked through a cornice on the narrow ridge on his way back from the summit of Everest. This would have been all too easy in the maelstrom of snow that was now hurtling across the upper reaches of the mountain.

Even so we couldn't give up hope. Mick was so very much alive, cocky, funny, and at times downright exasperating, I convinced myself that he'd get back during the night and call up on the radio the following morning with his special brand of humour. But, of course, he didn't and, as the storm raged through the day, pinning everyone down in their camps on the face, we had finally to admit to ourselves that there was no hope. It dawned fine on the morning of 28 September, but the mountain was plastered, with powder snow avalanches careering down the face. My third summit team was at Camp 5, but there seemed no hope of their being able to find Mick alive, no justification for a further bid for the top and I was prepared to take no more risks. I ordered the evacuation of the mountain.

Once again we had had tragedy and triumph, that painful mixture of grief at the death of a friend and yet real satisfaction at a climb that had not only been successful in reaching the top, but in human terms as well. This very diverse group of nearly a hundred people had merged as a single team. Mike's 'underground and overground' had become one. From my point of view, leading the South-West Face Expedition was the most complex, demanding and rewarding organisational challenge I have faced.

But where did I go from there? Success on the South-West Face opened up many possibilities. When I had started to make a living around mountaineering, lecturing, writing and appearing on television, in the early 'sixties after my ascent of the North Wall of the Eiger with Ian Clough, I had faced a fair amount of criticism from my peers. My sin was not only that of making money out of climbing, with all the accompanying controversy of amateur versus professional, but also in trying to describe the mysteries of the sport to a much wider public. I suppose I was the first climber in the post-war era to do this in a big way, though there was nothing new about it. Albert Smith, one of the Alpine pioneers, had drawn huge crowds to his magic lantern spectaculars in the 1850s and Frank Smythe had earned his living by writing and lecturing in the thirties in a very similar way to what I was doing in the sixties.

But the 1975 expedition, perhaps helped by the fact that an increasing number of climbers were making their livings in this way now, changed many attitudes. I almost seemed to be becoming an establishment figure, was honoured with the CBE, made a vice-president of the British Mountaineering Council, appointed to the Northern Sports Council and asked to take part in an increasing number of charitable activities. I suppose I could have followed a path into public service similar to that of John Hunt, leader of the 1953 expedition, but I am not a natural committee man, and enjoyed the freedom of being a freelance writer and photographer, based on our Lakeland home.

My lifestyle therefore didn't really change. The lecture tours were more hectic; I found myself taking part in business conferences in exotic parts of the world and the pressures of work were to increase steadily over the years. I do enjoy this side of my life, as I do the wheeling and dealing associated with organising expeditions. In contrast my climbing remains a relaxing, if physically exacting, recreation, something to be grabbed at the end of a day's work at home or in the middle of a promotional tour in the United States.

My love of mountaineering was, if anything, stronger than ever, but I wanted to return to the mountains now with a more tight-knit team, without the heavy responsibility for other people's lives that command of a large expedition inevitably entails.

CHAPTER FOUR

Laissez-Faire on the Ogre

'Fancy a trip to the Karakoram next summer? I've got the Ogre. I've asked Tut, Dougal, Mo and Clive. I'll send you some pictures. Tut and I are going for the big rock nose but Clive prefers a route to the left. If you want to come you can decide which route you want.'

It was Doug Scott on the phone in the summer of 1976. I accepted without hesitation. What a contrast to Everest. A small team, no responsibility, a trip that would be like an Alpine holiday. The photograph arrived a couple of days later. The Ogre is well named; this was no shapely summit of soaring ridges to an airy peak. It *is* an ogre, solid, chunky, a complex of granite buttresses and walls, of icy slopes and gullies; a three-headed giant towering 7285 metres above the Baintha Brakk Glacier. Doug had marked his line up a sheer nose of rock that resembled El Capitan in Yosemite. But this only went a third of the way up the peak to a band of snow ledges that wrapped their way like a big cummerbund around the Ogre's middle. Doug's line went on up a ridge of serried rock walls to the left, or western, summit.

I didn't like the look of it. The mountain appeared big and hard enough by its easiest route. You could climb a wall to its left by a series of snow and rock arêtes, traverse right over the cummerbund to cross Doug's line, and reach a big snow slope that comprised the Ogre's South Face. That would lead to its three heads. The middle one seemed the highest.

I phoned Dougal, who had also received the picture. He felt the same as I did, preferring the most reasonable way up what looked an extremely difficult mountain. Without saying so specifically, we both took it for granted we'd be climbing together.

In January of 1977 I drove out to Chamonix to join him for some winter climbing and to discuss Doug's plans for the Ogre. I gave a lift to Mo Anthoine whom I had known for years, but only on a bumping-into-in-the-pub level. He is one of the great characters of the British climbing scene; an exuberant extrovert who dominates most conversations with his wit, capacity as a raconteur and, at times, downright vulgarity. His sense of humour has a Rabelaisian quality that can offend some people, particularly his targets.

He is a complete individualist, little influenced by trends or the need to keep up with his peers. His adventures reflect this approach. In the early sixties he and another climbing friend, Foxy, hitched to Australia before the hippy trail had become well-worn, various adventures later making their way back towards Europe as crew on a yacht, little worried that they knew practically nothing about sailing.

On his return he and Joe Brown had started up a business in Llanberis making climbing helmets. Mo built it up over the years but was always careful not to over-expand so that he could maintain his freedom to go climbing and adventuring for several months each year. In 1973, with Hamish MacInnes, Joe Brown and Don Whillans, he climbed the Great Prow of Roraima, a huge sandstone wall in Guyana, festooned with creepers and infested by snakes, spiders and other creepy-crawlies. In 1976, with Martin Boysen, he reached the summit of the Trango Tower, one of the most spectacular rock spires in the world on the side of the Baltoro Glacier.

I was looking forward to climbing with Mo and certainly our first few days in Chamonix below Mont Blanc were a lot of fun. With us was Will Barker whose wit was even drier than Mo's. The weather was bad when we arrived and there was a surfeit of fresh snow. Dougal was polishing the first draft of a novel he had just completed, and therefore urged me to stay in Chamonix and ski so that he could get some work done while the weather was still unsettled. The three of us were about the same standard on skis, self-taught, with appalling technique, but quite bold. Mo and I had a great time and a lot of laughs, though the weather showed little signs of improving. On the third evening, I phoned Dougal and he decided that he'd come over a couple of days later to join us.

It was on the evening of 17 January, when we were drinking in Le Chamoniard, that Titi Tresamini, the proprietor, called me over. There was a phone call for me from England. Slightly apprehensive – could it be some kind of emergency at home? – I took the call. It was Wendy.

'Have you heard about Dougal?'

'No.'

She was crying. 'He's dead. He was killed in an avalanche while skiing this afternoon.'

When she heard the news that Dougal had been killed in an avalanche, she had assumed I was with him and inevitably feared that I might have been caught in it too and that my body had not yet been found. She had gone through hell all that day until at last she traced me to Titi's chalet. She didn't know any of the details but I told her that I'd get over to Leysin the next day. There was that mixture of shock and grief, all the more acute for being totally unexpected. Dougal, like all of us, had had plenty of near-misses, a fall on the Jorasses just one of them, but to die skiing a few minutes from his home. I went back and told the others; we drank through the night, talked about Dougal, becoming maudlin as one tends to in the aftermath of tragedy. Next morning I drove over to Leysin to learn what had happened and to try to help console the bereaved. He and his wife, Annie, had split up quite recently and Dougal was living with Ariane, a local girl who was also a very good skier. I found Annie with Dave, Dougal's partner in the International School of Mountaineering, and learnt what had happened.

Dougal had had his eye on a gully for some time. It needed plenty of snow in it to make it feasible. The heavy falls of the past few days were certainly sufficient. He had gone off that morning on his own, mentioning to Ariane that he might try to ski it if it was in condition. When he didn't return she sounded the alarm and they went straight to the foot of the gully. There was fresh avalanche debris and only a metre or so under the snow they found Dougal's body.

And so died one of the most charismatic British climbers of the post-war era. I felt his loss acutely, both as a good friend and as a climbing partner. I don't think I ever got really close to him. I'm not sure that anyone did. We didn't talk much, either on a climb or back on the ground, and yet we had a very real understanding and a similar approach to climbing.

Dougal had a first-class mind and was always a realist, be it about the immediate problem or the planning of an expedition as a whole. He had always given me his quiet support on the expeditions I had led and organised. In a way, he was getting it all on a plate, having little to do with the organisation and then, on the climb, fitting in with my plans, confident that I would use him as my trump card in making the final summit bid. At the same time he was accepted by his fellow team members, partly for his combination of drive and competence out in front, but also because of his personality and his capacity to avoid confrontation. At the end of the International Expedition in 1971 he was one of the few members of the team who had made no enemies. He had pursued the same policy as Don Whillans, had favoured concentration on the South-West Face and had stayed out in front throughout the expedition, as indeed he had done on the South Face of Annapurna, and yet he received none of the criticism that had been directed at Don who had done most of the talking.

Quite apart from my sorrow, I had also lost my climbing partner for the Ogre. I had to find someone whom I was totally happy to climb with and who would fit into the expedition. I didn't have to think hard, for Nick

Estcourt was an obvious choice. Doug also was quick to utilise Nick's organisational ability, handing him the job of getting together all our food. Tut Braithwaite, who had recently opened a climbing shop in Oldham, got together what gear we needed. He combined a forceful drive whilst actually climbing with an easy-going disposition and was adept at avoiding confrontation or argument.

I had practically nothing to do, a delightful change from the expeditions of the last few years. It was just a question of getting together my personal gear before catching the sleeper down to London and meeting the others at Heathrow. Clive Rowland met us in Islamabad on 23 May, having driven most of our gear out overland in Mo's Ford Transit.

We were staying with Caroline Weaver, one of the secretaries from the British Embassy. Mo had made the contact the previous year on the Trango Tower expedition. They had been rescued from a hot, flea-ridden, and, of course, 'dry' guest house in Rawalpindi by a member of the British Embassy and had been brought over to this oasis of cleanliness, comfort, and air conditioning. This generous tradition of expedition hospitality by Embassy personnel has continued ever since.

The next few days alternated between visits to the Ministry of Tourism, the hot dusty colourful bazaar in Rawalpindi to buy sacks of flour, rice and dahl to feed our porters, and the British Club, which had a swimming pool, badminton courts and a well-stocked bar. The Karakoram Highway, the road from Islamabad through to Gilgit and then into China, had not yet been completed and so the only way to Skardu was by plane. The flight was notorious for its unreliability. There were tales of people being stuck in Skardu for weeks at a time, fighting to board planes when they eventually arrived, but we were lucky and were only delayed for a day.

The Fokker Friendship aircraft lifted over the foothills that crowd on to the wide plain of Islamabad and headed up the Indus valley. Distant snow peaks appeared through the cloud. Doug and I beat Tut to the windows and blazed away with our cameras, ignoring the hesitant remonstrances of Captain Aleem, our Liaison Officer. You are not allowed to take pictures from the air. We dodged through the clouds, banked down over a rocky ridge and dropped into the Skardu valley, a wide flat expanse of desert with the river Indus, as brown as the sands, winding through it. The airport was no more than a dirt strip and a shed. Nick and Clive had flown in a couple of days earlier but there was no sign of them, so we took a jeep for the drive down an incongruously broad and metalled dual carriageway into Skardu.

For me, it was all a fresh experience. I had not been to Pakistan before. Mo had been there the two previous years and Doug had been up the Biafo Glacier with Clive to attempt some of the Ogre's sister peaks in 1975, so

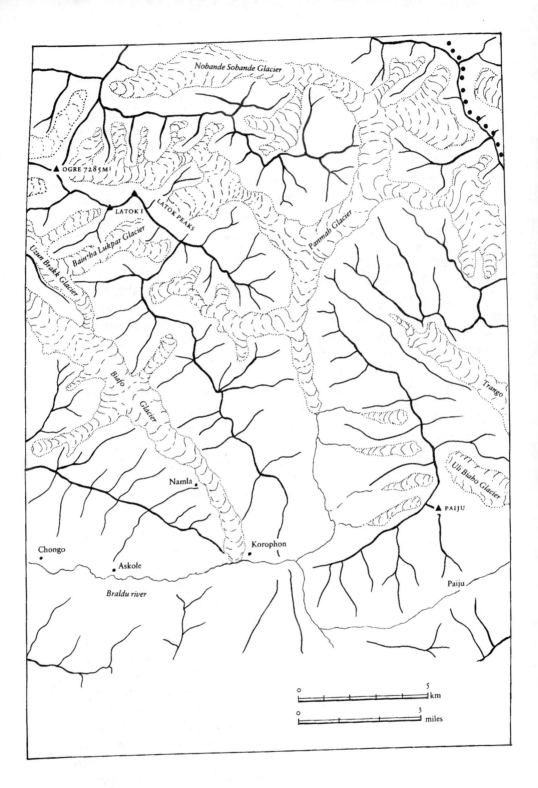

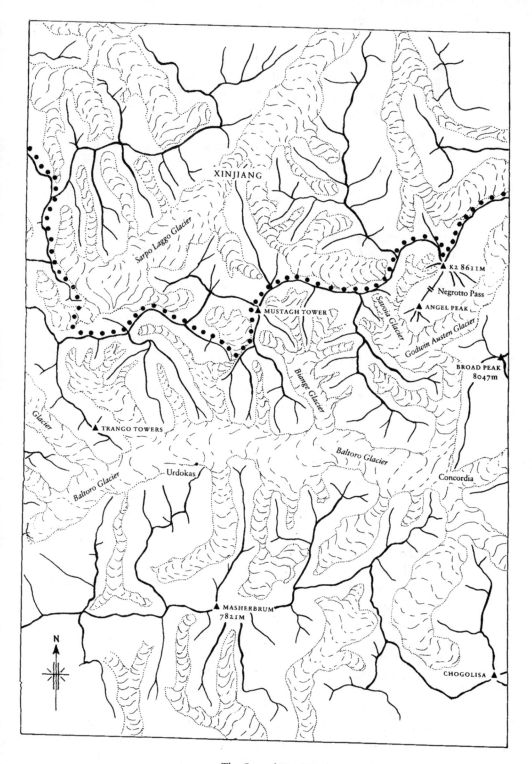

The Central Karakoram

they were making the decisions. Up to this moment I had enjoyed my non-role, just absorbing the sights and sounds around me. A rocky hill crowned with a ruined fortress dominated the town of Skardu. Jeeps and trucks, dressed with chrome and ornate paintwork, honked and spluttered up the wide street, flanked by the shops of the bazaar, open-ended boxes bright with bales of cloth, vegetables and dried chillies or high-piled billies and kitchen utensils. It felt good to be in this small mountain town away from the comfortable diplomatic suburbs of Islamabad.

We stopped at the government rest house, a bungalow with a verandah and stark but clean rooms opening onto it. There was a note from Nick and Clive warning us that the road bridge was about to be closed for repairs and that they had seized the opportunity to cross with all our supplies, so that they could get them by jeep to the roadhead at Dasso, about forty miles up the valley. They had left us the job of selecting and bringing along the porters who would carry the loads to Base Camp.

Doug and Mo were impatient to be off, discovered that there was a ferry over the Indus and wanted to catch it that same afternoon. This would mean leaving the selection of our porters to Captain Aleem who would have had to catch us up the following day. I couldn't see the need for the hurry. Surely it would be better to ensure we had a really good team of porters and all stick together. But I didn't push the point; I was the new boy this time, no longer the leader, and felt Doug and Mo particularly might resent anything that had looked like a takeover bid by me.

So we packed our sacks, left the gear that would have to follow with the porters, and walked down to the banks of the Indus. The river is about a hundred metres wide at Skardu, an opaque soup of fast smooth-flowing, glacier dust-laden water. The ferry was beached on the other side, a lonely white blob on a desert sandbank, with no sign of boatman, habitation or any kind of life. We shouted and waved but to no avail. There was no choice, we would have to wait for the following day. At least we could now choose our own porters and travel with all our baggage. I was secretly pleased, but was careful to hide my satisfaction.

The Baltis had come in from the surrounding hill villages, some of them several days' walk away. Physically they reflected the harsh mountain desert they came from with sun and wind-beaten faces, fierce hooked noses and deep-set eyes hidden by bushy brows. They are lean and stunted by toil and the harshness of their lives. This even seems reflected in the language, which is sharp, staccato and insistent. They are very different from the Nepali people who are so much quieter and more gentle, who have a tranquillity which is mirrored in the carefully terraced green lines of their foothills.

Half a dozen policemen, who towered over the porters wielding batons, pushed and shouted them into some kind of order. Mo, as the oldest hand, appointed himself the chief porter selector, walking down the straggling rows, picking ones that seemed strong and then asking through Aleem, which village they came from.

'The ones from Kaphelu are by far the best,' he told us.

The lucky few would be paid the equivalent of five pounds a day for carrying a load of twenty kilos a distance little more than eight miles. This was very good pay by Pakistani standards, considerably better than a teacher or even a police inspector would receive. It was one of the few means by which villagers could earn cash since their farming was still at subsistence level. The Pakistan Government had introduced the pay scale and regulations in 1976, the year after they reopened the Karakoram to climbing. In 1975 it had been a question of free-market bargaining with a series of strikes and constant trouble between porters and expeditions. This had now settled down to a degree but, even so, there is an excitable volatile quality in the Balti and trouble can erupt at any time.

We set out early the next morning. The boat was waiting for us and we piled in, loads and all, until the gunwales were almost level with the water. Our porters helped paddle the boat across and as they rowed they began to sing. It was curiously melodious, enhancing the sense of romantic adventure, the beauty of the water lit by the early morning sun and the arid grandeur of the desert valley through which lay the start of our journey.

We walked through the day, each at his own pace, sometimes joining up to talk, or to climb the big mulberry trees to pick succulent little bunches of white berries. The occasional oasis of cultivated land, irrigated from the river, was like a brilliant emerald set in the drab brown of the desert. We rejoined the road at Shigar and assembled at the K2 Café, the only transport café in the entire valley. You could get cups of tea and chupatties but not much else. Nick and Clive had sent a jeep back from the roadhead at Dasso to pick us up and that evening the expedition was together once again.

The porters straggled in the following morning, having walked all the way. Nick and Clive had brought in most of the gear by road so the next morning was spent allocating loads to porters. Mo once again emerged as the driving force. He has a practical dynamism and a quick wit that makes him a natural leader.

This expedition couldn't have been more different from Everest, just seven of us, including Aleem. We were doing our own cooking, but Doug didn't believe in any kind of duty roster for the chores. The jobs just got done. Tut and Nick had cooked supper the previous evening and Doug made breakfast that morning. Loads were packed, allocated with a lot of shouting, and by midday we were ready to start walking up the valley.

The route into the mountains follows the Braldu river, which drains some of the greatest glaciers of the Karakoram, along a tenuous footpath that takes a switchback ride over high rocky bluffs and clings to the very edge of the swirling brown waters. It is a landscape of reds, browns and greys, of crumbling sun-baked rocks in jagged towers and great scree slopes. Lizards skitter off the path and the occasional dog rose with its clusters of delicate pink flowers gives some relief to the harshness of this land. There are glimpses of brilliant cultivated green where the irrigation ditches from the glacier torrents form a necklace, strung across cliffs and steep scree slopes, to the shelf of flattish land nestling in a curve of the river valley or high on the sides of the gorge. Poplars with long fingers reach up to the sun while the apricot trees spread their boughs untidily in bushy clusters. The green is the more welcoming and intense for the aridness of the desert rock that dominates the landscape.

Most improbable of all, deep in the gorge, close by the icy brown torrent of glacier waters, there was a pool of steaming water. The rock around the spring was encrusted with sulphurous yellow deposits and the algae streaming from the pool were a particularly brilliant green. It provided the most luxurious of hot tubs.

It was three days' walk to Askole, the last village in the valley, at an altitude of 3048 metres. It is typical of all the Balti villages, a collection of flat-roofed, single-storeyed, windowless houses of stone rendered in mud. Entry is through a small wooden door, opening on to a tiny courtyard, from which open the store-rooms, byres and living quarters. These are usually windowless, but lit by a big square gap in the ceiling which serves both as a flue and a stairwell to the roof. On the roof are piled stocks of firewood and often there is a small wooden penthouse in which to sleep during the summer. Chillies or apricots must be spread out on an old blanket to dry in the sun. The women don't wear the bhurka, the shapeless garment that totally covers the women of the lowlands, but have an attract-ive decorated cap-like headdress over their plaited dark hair, which is often interwoven with beads and ribbon. You can see them working in the fields or sitting chatting outside their homes. They object to being photographed and who can blame them? There are no shops in the hill villages, none of the tea shops that have sprung up throughout Nepal.

Hadji Medi was the headman of Askole, a small plump man with shrewd eyes, in a homespun jacket and woollen cap. You could tell his status by looking at his hands, which were soft and clean, unused to any kind of manual work. He owned much of the land, had a surplus of flour and made money by selling it to expeditions at a handsome profit. We bought several loads from him, both to feed our porters now that we were going beyond the last village, and to supplement our own supplies at Base Camp.

Next morning heavy clouds clung to the rocky flanks of the Braldu valley, concealing the snow peaks beyond and weeping with a thin cold rain that formed muddy puddles on the sandy path. We reached the snout of the Biafo Glacier after a couple of hours' walk from Askole.

Doug had already gone striding ahead into the glacier maze, but Mo suggested the rest of us wait for the porters to ensure that we all ended up at the same campsite that night. It was late afternoon before we started up the glacier, first stumbling over an assault course of crazily piled rocks, but then finding a motorway of smooth ice that stretched up into the distance. At last we had a feeling of being on the threshold of the real mountains, with snow peaks on either side and the hint of bigger mountains ahead. It gave a sense of boundless space, a sensation I had never had in the more crowded piled-up peaks of Nepal, where the glaciers tumble into deep forest-clad valleys.

That night we camped in a grassy hollow sprinkled with delicate alpine flowers beneath the lateral moraine of the glacier. Doug roamed off to search for wild rhubarb, while Mo supervised the issue of rations to our porters. I looked for wood for our cooking fire and ended up sitting on a boulder high on the slope above the camp gazing over the great sweep of the glacier, its wrinkled surface accentuated by the evening shadows, content that I was amongst the mountains.

The person I knew least, and with whom I had never really felt at ease, was Clive Rowland. An old friend of Doug's, he had worked in a steel foundry before moving up to the Black Isle, north of Inverness, to make a living as a builder. A good rock-climber, he had been on several of Doug's expeditions, including the trip up the Biafo Glacier in 1975. He has a sharp tongue and I had sensed an underlying resentment perhaps of my background and reputation as the big expedition organiser. The following day he, Aleem and I got too far ahead of the others, missed the camp-site and shared an emergency bivvie huddled under a wet boulder. It was exactly the right sort of little misadventure to bring us closer together.

The next morning we made our way back about three miles to where Clive thought he remembered camping the previous time in 1975. The others had indeed been there. The ashes of several cooking fires were still warm, but they had already left. Even though we had kept our eyes open we must have passed each other on the glacier. We only caught up again six hours later at the next stopping place at the foot of the Baintha Brakk Glacier, where we had a fairly caustic greeting from Mo.

Didn't you see Doug?'

'No.'

'You're going to get an earful when he gets back. He'll be really fed up. He and Nick have gone all the way back to Namla to try to find you.'

'What the hell's he fussing about for goodness' sake? There are three of us. We couldn't possibly have come to any harm, and even if someone had broken a leg, there would have been one of us to stay with whoever was injured and the other could have come here.'

'That's as maybe, but he was still dead worried about you.'

Nick and Doug got back a couple of hours later, just as it was getting dark. They were very annoyed.

'Why the hell didn't you get back to our camp-site really early? We only left it at about nine. Surely you realised we'd be worried?'

We were defensive in our reply, because we realised that we were in the wrong. But I was touched by Doug's concern, his essential warmth of character masked by sharp words.

I was happy that night as I settled down under the stars, using my new Gore-tex sleeping-bag cover for the first time. This was the material that had just come out and was to help revolutionise lightweight climbing in the Himalaya. It is a porous membrane, laminated between protective fabrics, that allows the water molecules from condensation to escape, while keeping out external drops of water from rain or wet snow. I had bought some of the material in Colorado and had had it made up into a windproof suit and sleeping-bag cover. That night was hardly a test but at least I confirmed that it allowed condensation to escape. My sleeping-bag and the inside of the Gore-tex cover were bone dry.

The next day we walked up to Base Camp, following the lateral moraines of the Baintha Brakk Glacier to a shoulder from where we had our first close-up view of the Ogre. Its bulk was hidden by intervening peaks, but its triple heads peered at us over their tops, even more impressively than the pictures had indicated. We were on the western edge of the confluence of two glaciers, the Baintha Lukpar that led up to the south side of the Latok range, and the Uzun Brakk Glacier, which pointed to the Ogre. We scrambled across the tumbled rocks, climbed a high moraine and suddenly we were on the brink of a gentle haven, cradled in the arms of the lateral moraines of the two glaciers. The hollow held a shallow lake, was carpeted with lush grass, sprinkled with alpine flowers, and was dotted with big boulders, as if designed to be shelters for itinerant climbers. A few tents were already clustered round one of the boulders. We knew we would have neighbours for another small British expedition was attempting Latok I, a peak slightly smaller but no less challenging than the Ogre.

It was a little like arriving at the Chamonix camp-site. They gave us a wave and carried on with what they were doing while we pitched our tents.

Later on Paul Nunn and Tony Riley wandered over to chat, and Nick picked up a conversation with Paul that had begun a fortnight before in the Moon, the Peak District pub much used by climbers. Their team was very similar to our own, six in number and all of them from the Sheffield area. They had arrived a week earlier, but had been delayed by the bad weather we had experienced on the walk in. For us the rain had merely been an inconvenience but they had had snowfalls of up to half a metre. They had established an Advance Base Camp but only had food and fuel for three weeks which put a strict limit on the time they could spend in the area.

That afternoon Clive and I set off across the glacier to try to find a dump left by their expedition in 1975. Doug has little caches of gear scattered all over the Himalaya, in friends' houses in Delhi and Kathmandu, in porters' huts in the Karakoram and under boulders at the head of obscure valleys like the Uzun Brakk Glacier. We went from one pile of boulders to the next, all of them looking alike, as Clive tried to remember where they had left the dump. After an hour's search, to my amazement, we found the remains of the gear, but unfortunately a crevasse had opened up immediately beneath it. We managed to salvage a tunnel tent, some rope, gas canisters and a pair of tweezers, before wandering back to Base Camp under the late afternoon sun.

We talked long into the night – gossiping about the climbing scene back in Britain, laughing at outrageous stories from Mo, and getting into hand-hold by hand-hold discussions of gritstone problems under a star-studded sky with the peaks flanking the Ogre silhouetted like stark black fingers against the night.

CHAPTER FIVE

Nearly, But Not Quite

The Ogre, foreshortened by proximity, towered above us. Its first defence was the sheer granite nose which Doug and Tut were planning to climb, but the rest of us were going to outflank its obvious difficulties by tackling the broken wall of rocky buttresses and snow gullies that led to a broad col to the west of the mountain. Nick and I had come up the previous day (15 June) to what was to be our Advance Base and were now its sole occupants.

It was a good feeling to be in the heart of the mountains immediately below our objective and an even better one now to be out in front as a pair. We had spent the last four days ferrying up supplies. To do this we had kept on six of the better equipped and more determined porters and had carried heavy loads ourselves. We were working well together, and Nick had made up a selection of foods to last a month up at Advance Base. At this stage we were all in accord over what we were doing, though on our western route we would be operating as two pairs with separate approach tactics.

The wives of Mo and Clive were due to arrive at Base Camp around this time. Steph Rowland and Jackie Anthoine both climbed and were hoping to attempt some of the neighbouring smaller peaks whilst their menfolk climbed the Ogre. This was one reason why Mo and Clive had stayed behind while Nick and I had been keen to get up to Advance Base.

Sitting outside our tent in the setting sun, I could savour the quiet of the early evening. Down the glacier a wall of jagged minor peaks separated us from the Biafo Glacier. Base Camp was a thousand metres below and about three miles away round the corner. It was as if we had the mountain to ourselves and we both relished the prospect of being the first of our team to set foot on it. The previous year a Japanese expedition had attempted the Ogre by the same line that we were trying but they had only got a short way above the col to the west of it.

It was a glorious morning without a cloud in the sky as Nick and I, roped together, picked our way across the snow-covered glacier. He was breaking trail, whilst I carried a heavy load of rope and pitons so that we could start fixing the route. About half-way across he suddenly sank down to his shoulders in the snow; he had stepped into a hidden crevasse. I heaved back on the rope and he was able to struggle out unaided. Gazing into the dark hole he had left I could see a rope stretched across the void about three metres below, the first evidence of our predecessors.

We reached the foot of the face and kicked up a snow gully until we could escape from it by a horizontal break. This led towards a rocky spur that would give us some protection from the threat of avalanche. It was still in shadow as Nick started climbing a steep slab, his head haloed by the sun as he breasted the top. This was real climbing. He fixed the rope and I jumared up into the sun. It was only ten in the morning but already it was getting oppressively hot – time to return. We could see two tiny figures slogging up towards Advance Base, Doug and Tut probably. But where were Clive and Mo? Could they still be lolling about at Base waiting for their wives? Later we learnt Steph and Jackie had in fact reached Base Camp that morning but, assuming they were part of the expedition, had not bothered to get trekking permits and consequently had had to talk their way through the police posts at Dasso and Askole. An armed police posse had caught them up as they reached Base Camp and it was only through the good offices of Aleem, who insisted that they should stay until he sorted it out by letter, that they weren't hauled off back down the mountain. Their late arrival had triggered two all too human responses: the way individual groups on a mountain automatically assume that they alone are doing all the work, and the problems that almost inevitably arise when some, but not all, team members have their wives or girlfriends at Base Camp.

But our group was now complete with everyone keen to start climbing. In the next few days both teams began pushing the routes up their respective lines. Then on 18 June we had a near disaster. Doug and Tut were ferrying gear up the gully leading to the foot of the Nose when a rock the size of a football came hurtling down. Tut tried to dodge but it hit his thigh a glancing blow. If it had hit him on the head he would probably have been killed. As it was, he was badly bruised and had difficulty in limping back to Base Camp. He was certainly going to be out of action for at least a few days. I was very impressed by Doug's acceptance of what had happened. He was full of concern for Tut and showed no signs of impatience, though he must have realised that the accident had seriously prejudiced his chance of completing their route.

On 20 June, Nick and I moved up to a camp we had sited about half-way up the face. It was a magnificent eyrie on the crest of a little rock spur, making it safe from avalanche. The previous day we had carried up about forty kilos of food while Mo and Clive had pushed the route on up towards the col. We were making good progress but some rifts in our team were beginning to show. Mo and Clive were altogether more relaxed in their

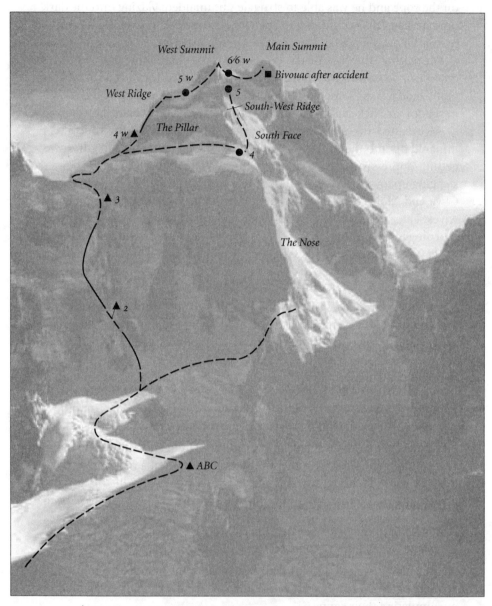

West Summit   Main Summit

6/6 w

■ Bivouac after accident

5 w

West Ridge   5

South-West Ridge

4 w ▲   The Pillar   South Face

▲ 3

The Nose

▲ 2

4

▲ ABC

▲ Tented camp   ● Snow cave   W West Ridge   ABC Avance Base Camp
_____ Route using fixed ropes   _ _ _ _ Route not using fixed ropes
The Ogre

approach and did not have the same sense of urgency that Nick and I shared. We believed that we should grab the good weather and make as much progress as possible, get ourselves established on the col, and then go Alpine-style for the summit. Mo and Clive, on the other hand, seemed to favour a more deliberate approach and preferred the idea of going for the West Ridge of the mountain.

Next day while pushing the route out ourselves, Nick and I saw three figures carrying loads to our camp and on returning we were indignant to find only a few gas cylinders, three ropes and a few pegs. We assumed that the third man had been Doug. Surely, if they were serious about the climb, they would have carried more up. It was around this time that we began discussing the option of going for the summit by ourselves as a twosome. We were already operating as two self-contained pairs, each party responsible for its own food and fuel.

The following afternoon we found Mo and Clive ensconced in a Denali tent on the very tip of the rock arête. It was good seeing them, and, as so often happens, all our resentment evaporated with explanations. They told us that Jackie had been with them the previous day and that this was why they didn't carry more up. She had now returned to Base Camp to attempt a rock peak on the other side of the valley with Doug. Tut's leg was still giving him trouble and he was resting at Base. Mo and Clive agreed to go out the next day to complete the route to the col, while Nick and I had what we felt was a well-earned rest. They got back just after midday to tell us they had run out of rope a metre or so below the crest. Nick and I therefore planned to move up to the col the following morning. With the dump of food we had over half-way up we reckoned we had around a week's food and fuel, just enough to go for the summit.

We both slept badly that night. I had a cough and was restless, partly from discomfort, partly excitement. I tossed and turned, keeping Nick awake. But it was worse for him when I did drop off as I snore. I think I actually slept for most of the night while he was convinced he hadn't had a minute's sleep and was justifiably exasperated in the early hours of the morning when he woke me to make breakfast. We had a good working agreement that I cooked breakfast, as I am at my best in the mornings, while he coped with supper.

We were ready to leave at five thirty with twenty kilos of gear each to carry up. Mo and Clive were still in their sleeping bags with the tent door firmly closed. They seemed evasive about their plans saying they were too far behind us in their food build-up and anyway that Doug might want to join us if Tut didn't recover. Nick and I were determined to go for the summit.

There was approximately 500 metres of fixed rope to the crest of the arête leading to the final head wall. We hadn't enough rope to fix the arête itself, a knife-edge of fragile snow, with the route winding from side to side and dizzy drops whichever way one went. The rope started again at the head wall, a steep slope of softish snow on very hard ice. We jumared up to where it ended below a cornice which curled over above us. I dumped my heavy sack and led off round the corner, crampons barely penetrating the steel-hard ice beneath the snow. A narrow runnel led through the overhangs to the crest of the col. Suddenly it all flattened out on to a snow-covered shelf with a gentle crevassed rise restricting our view to the ground beyond. But it didn't matter. We had climbed the wall. I anchored the rope to a couple of ice pitons and Nick jumared up behind me. Our bad temper of the early morning was forgotten in our excitement. I agreed to drop back to the dump and bring up all the food and fuel we had left there while Nick prepared a camp-site.

It was easy going down unladen, but desperate returning. The altitude was around 6100 metres and I was carrying about twenty-five kilos of food and gas cans back up to the col. It took me nearly three hours to cross the snow arête and climb the fixed rope but there I found the tent pitched and heard the welcome purr of the stove. Nick had a brew of tea ready for me. During the day, the clouds had begun to build up threateningly but in the late afternoon they rolled away and it turned into a still cloudless evening. We could see over the minor peaks of the Ogre and across the mountains on the other side of the Biafo Glacier to the distant mass of Nanga Parbat jutting over the far horizon.

We were now on our own, committed to the climb and content with that commitment. Our decision-making was easy since we were agreed on the basic principles, even if we differed at times on the best tactics to achieve the immediate aim. We had almost a week's food and just about a thousand metres to climb. That night we slept well, with Nick so tired that he could sleep through my snores. We had set the alarm for two in the morning, but by unspoken consent, ignored it and had another hour's sleep before beginning to cook. We set out at five, picking our way round the heavily crevassed slope that led up to a wide plateau that formed the col between the Ogre and its western neighbour. We were still in shadow when we reached the foot of the slope that led up to the long shelf (the Ogre's cummerbund), leading back to its South-West Ridge. A layer of insubstantial snow lay over hard ice. Nick was out in front and suddenly let out a whoop of relief. He had stumbled on a fixed rope left by the Japanese. Handling it cautiously, for he didn't know how it was anchored, he pulled it out of the snow as he climbed the slope. At its top we found another two coils of unused rope. It was still only ten thirty in the morning. The shelf stretched away to our right beneath a sheer wall of granite but we were tired and decided to have a short day. We were back in camp by eleven.

We spent the rest of the day dozing and checking our supplies. Next morning we resolved to make a carry to the end of the shelf and find a good launching point for our bid on the summit. We were both tense, overpowered perhaps by the scale of the climb and our own isolation. On the way across the traverse I took a line that Nick thought was too high. He said so, and I blazed back:

'You can't see where the hell to go from back there. Can't you trust me to pick the best line? I haven't interfered when you've been out in front. Just bloody well shut up and leave me to get on with it.'

I was all the more resentful for the sneaking feeling that Nick could be right. But Nick apologised for interfering.

'I was just trying to help.'

I also apologised for losing my temper. We continued, edging across the unconsolidated snow lying on hard ice. It all felt very insecure and went on so much further than we had expected. At last we reached the end of the shelf and could peer excitedly around the corner. A band of smooth granite slabs separated us from the steep snow field of the South Face. Gazing up the corridor between the soaring wall of the Ogre and the jagged rock and snow peak on the other side, we could see in the distance a triangular pyramid-shaped peak that surely must be K2, our objective next year, for I already had permission for the mountain.

On the way back down we could see two tents at our first camp half-way up the face to the col, just tiny blobs, dark against the snow. There had only been one when we had crossed the traverse early that morning.

'Looks as if they're moving up,' Nick remarked.

We wondered who was there.

Back on the col we were shaken to find we only had four gas cylinders left, barely enough for three days. But we were loth to drop down to rejoin the others and get some more. There was an unspoken desire to stay out in front, to remain independent, uninvolved with whatever the others were doing.

'Let's leave the tent,' I suggested next morning as we left to establish our final camp. 'We'll be able to dig a snow hole on that spur at the end of the shelf.'

'What if there's ice underneath? We really will be in trouble if we can't snow-hole. Anyway, you agreed yesterday that we should take it just in case.'

'I'm sure we'll find something. It's a hell of an extra weight. I think we've got as much as we can manage already. We snow-holed all the way up the North Wall of the Eiger and there wasn't anything like as much snow there.'

We never resolved the discussion, but neither of us picked up the tent. Our loads already felt too heavy. It was another perfect morning. From the top of the Japanese fixed rope at the start of the shelf we could gaze on to the great white expanse of Snow Lake which marked the confluence of several glaciers. The Hispar Glacier, like a gigantic motorway, stretched to the west, while to the north of it towered the mighty snow peaks of Kanjut Sar, Kunyang Kish and Disteghil Sar. It was just eight thirty when we reached the end of the shelf. We had taken only an hour and a half, compared to the five hours of the previous day. We were slightly better acclimatised and our tracks had consolidated, making it all feel much safer. Since it was so early we decided to fix our two ropes across the rock slabs barring the way to the snow field of the South Face.

Nick led off, front-pointing delicately up hard ice leading to the base of the slabs. The ice became progressively thinner until he was tiptoeing on his crampon points up the smooth granite slab. He managed to place a rock piton belay and anchored our first rope to it. I followed up and looked across the slabs nervously. A belt of about fifteen metres of smooth, polished granite separated us from the snow slope.

I removed my crampons and started off. It resembled the Etive Slabs in Scotland. There were no positive holds for fingers to curl round and it was a matter of padding, frightened, up and across the slabs. I was soon ten metres or so above Nick. What if I fell? Any injury would be desperately serious in our present position. I reached a hairline crack, tapped a knife blade piton in about a centimetre, tied it off with a tape sling, clipped in the rope and tensioned off on it, edging my way across the slab, using just enough tension to keep me on the rock but not enough to pull the piton out. The slab was now covered with an inch of fresh snow that I had to clear away in order to find rugosities of rock to stand on. I managed to tap in another two pitons behind rotten flakes but I doubt whether they would have held a fall. It was nerve-racking yet enthralling. A further three moves and I reached another crack, hammered in a piton, and tensioned across a few more paces. It took me an hour and a half to traverse the slab, an hour and a half of total concentration and controlled fear, culminating in heady elation as I reached the snow on the other side and placed an ice screw in the ice underneath. We had at least turned the key that gave entry to the huge snow slope of the South Face – but close up it seemed so long and steep. There was a rock band barring our way near the top and the snow did not look, or feel, well consolidated.

We returned to the relative safety of the snow shelf where we had left our rucksacks. It was time to make ourselves a secure base on the edge of a very uncertain unknown. We started digging into a prow of snow that gave promise of having sufficient depth for a cave. We were now at 6650 metres and feeling the altitude. We had been above Advance Base for a week and had had just one rest day during that period. After three hours' hard work we had a snug avalanche-proof cave that was just large enough for us to lie in. We set the alarm for two a.m.

I was restless again that night and started cooking at one thirty, waking Nick with a cup of tea, followed by reconstituted plums and sugar puffs. Nick just groaned and said he felt terrible. He could barely stay awake to drink the tea. I was worried by how tired he was but keen to get going. We had now very nearly run out of gas though, ironically, we had plenty of food. Since most of it was dehydrated, gas was essential to melt the snow to reconstitute it. A day's rest would mean one cylinder less for our summit push. I noted in my diary:

> It's a perfect day and I want to get the climb over. Was not over gracious and Nick agreed to have a go but he was obviously in such a terrible state that I had to let him off. It's now 7 a.m. and he's lying comatose beside me in the snow hole. I only hope the one day's rest will do the trick. He blew himself up on Annapurna. The trouble is in the last year he has been working too hard and not done enough climbing. I wonder if this has caught up with him? I am tempted to try to solo the last part of the climb if he is not fit tomorrow – have I the nerve?

Later that day, Nick entered in his diary:

> Woke up at 10 a.m. feeling much better. The problem was probably accumulated lack of sleep aggravated by Chris's snoring and thrashing about – how does Wendy stand it? Still wondering what the others are doing. Chris keen on the two man push but I would like the others to be around. Chris spent most of the day planning the K2 expedition for next year. Me, day dreaming about comforts of home or even Base Camp – or even Advance Base Camp!

That afternoon I wrote:

> Fortunately Nick feeling a lot better – we should be able to make our push tomorrow. In retrospect I suspect this rest day will have been good for me as well as Nick. I feel a bit ashamed at having got worked up about it.

We woke up at three thirty the following morning and I made breakfast. Nick was feeling much better but when I crawled out of the cave I was appalled to see a dark bank of cloud stretching across the western horizon.

It had already covered Nanga Parbat and would soon reach us. In my worry, I lashed out at Nick, bemoaning the fact that we hadn't gone to the summit the previous day, though immediately apologised for the injustice of my attack. We decided to start out anyway, since we now only had one can of gas left for cooking.

By the time we had climbed the ropes we had left in place two days before and had reached the snow of the South Face, ragged clouds were forming round the Latok peaks and a cold wind, blowing plumes of spindrift, was blasting the face. There was about half a metre of unconsolidated snow lying on hard ice. It felt quite incredibly precarious. We had to pull the ropes up behind us since we needed them for the climb. We moved one at a time, the second man belayed to an ice piton, and the leader running out the full length of the rope, kicking into the snow, crampon points barely biting into the ice, the snow barely supporting the weight of the foot. We took it in turns to lead. I'm not sure which was worst, going out in front, trying to distribute one's weight as evenly as possible, never feeling secure, or paying the rope out as second, all too conscious of the results of a fall. It was most unlikely that the ice piton belay would have taken a violent pull and, whilst stationary, the cold crept into one's very core. Spindrift avalanches swirled down the slope, plucking at our cringing limbs, the icy powder finding chinks in our anoraks and penetrating to the chilled skin underneath.

Pitch followed pitch, as we headed towards a band of rock that stretched the full width of the face. It was late afternoon when we reached it. The entire sky was now overcast with a scum of high grey cloud. Nick suggested going down but I was convinced we could make it to the top, a conviction that had taken me through threatening situations in the past. Even though the weather looked ominous I had a feeling that it wouldn't break. Nick later commented in his diary:

> Chris would not take the hint that I wanted to turn back; became convinced that he was leading me to my doom.

But he kept climbing and now led the most frightening pitch of the route. I was belayed to an ice screw that only bit into the ice for a few centimetres before being stopped by the rock underneath. It would never have held a fall. A rock rib barred our way to an ice runnel. Nick climbed above me to fix a high running belay and then, protected by this, descended the ice at the side of the rib until he was able to cross it with some tension from the rope. He then climbed up ice that was a bare centimetre thick lying on the steep slab. As he got higher, he was going further and further from his running belay, with the threat of a fatal fall for both of us if the ice shattered under his weight.

I huddled over my piton, passing the rope inch by inch through my hands as he edged his way up the runnel. It was now beginning to get dark and I had time to question my single-minded drive. But suddenly there was a shout from above. The ice was thick enough to place an ice screw. He could bring me up.

It was very nearly dark by the time I reached him. I led out two more rope-lengths in the gathering gloom, desperately looking for somewhere to bivouac. We could go no further. I dug into the snow but after a metre hit rock. There was not enough depth for a proper hole but at least we could have a bit of a roof over our heads. We spent the night in a sitting position, leaning back against the rock.

Nick wrote:

> Had a brew, felt miserable and Chris snored all night. I sat and watched the swirling mist and wondered what it was going to be like to freeze to death. Didn't exactly wake up early (never slept) but weather still very threatening. I wanted to go down, Chris to sit it out. He won. However a bit later (sixish) it improved and we decided to set off for the col below the final tower.

Nick was out in front, with me following, at the full extension of the rope, when doubt at last began to set in. The cloud was swirling around us, whipped by a cold, insistent wind. We were now nearly level with the base of the Ogre's head. From Advance Base it had seemed little more than a knobble of snow-veined rock. I had convinced myself that there would be an easy gully or ramp but now, at close range, it seemed to have no weaknesses; it was compact, massive, invulnerable. I suddenly became aware of the reality of our situation. We had only eight rock pitons, one day's food, and just one gas cylinder.

I caught Nick up.

'We'll never make it, we haven't enough stuff. How about going for the West Summit? It looks a hell of a sight easier.'

'Suits me.'

And so we veered up towards the crest of the ridge between the West and the main summits. By the time we reached it, the cloud had rolled away. The dark threatening weather had vanished as if by magic. We could peer cautiously over a cornice down the dizzy North Face of the Ogre. Range upon range of peaks stretched to the north, and with the sun and the expansive view, my own spirits soared.

'You know, we could still have a go at the main summit.'

'For pity's sake, Chris, can't you keep to a decision for ten minutes? We decided to go for the West Summit for a completely logical set of reasons that haven't changed with a bit of bloody sun. *You* said that we didn't have the gear or the fuel, not me. At least try to be consistent for once.'

I was shaken by his vehemence and didn't press the point. He was right. We dropped back down the slope about forty metres and started digging a snow hole. We had left the shovel behind so had to use our axes to carve out a broad verandah, this time big enough to lie on. We spent the rest of the day lazing in the sun.

Nick commented in his diary:

Chris havering – if he had his way he'd spend the rest of his days up here.

It was a perfect dawn the following morning (1 July) and we set out for the West Summit, following the knife-edged snow arête. I led all the way. Nick had an appalling throat and was coughing up blood, while I was going quite strongly. Although the slope steepened just below the summit, it was comparatively straightforward, and suddenly everything dropped away below us. We were on top. The view was magnificent, with the Biafo Glacier stretched beneath us in its entirety, the great white expanse of Snow Lake and, beyond it, range upon range of peaks reaching to the far horizon on all sides but one. The main summit, a couple of hundred metres away, could only have been fifty or so metres higher than we were, but it blocked the view to the east, and its immense solid rock tower seemed to be mocking us. We had done the only sensible thing, but we turned and dropped back to our bivvie spot with a nagging sense of anticlimax that we had backed down from the real challenge.

We ate all the food we had left, had a couple of brews and then started the long descent. We abseiled down the desperate stretch that Nick had led on the way up and went seemingly endlessly on down the slopes beneath it, until at last we were approaching the smooth slabs near the bottom of the face. I had been worried about how we were going to get across these. I'd had visions of the fate of Hinterstoisser and his party on the North Wall of the Eiger in 1936, when they had crossed the slab which became known as the Hinterstoisser Traverse, had not left a rope across it and then on their return had been unable to get back. They all perished as a result. Fortunately we were able to find a high anchor point from which to make a long diagonal abseil to the crest of the spur, reaching the relative safety and luxury of our snow hole at six that night.

'It seemed like the Carlton Tower after the last two nights,' Nick commented in his diary. But there was no sign of the others.

Both of us quite worried about them – Bumbling? Accident? Bureaucratic hassle over the girls? Chris almost in tears at the thought of an accident to Doug (and Jackie).

We hadn't set the alarm but both of us woke at two anyway. We had got so used to our early starts and were also quietly anxious about the others. We set off shortly after dawn and as we came round a corner on the traverse back towards the West Ridge we saw, far below us in the middle of the plateau, two little tents with figures around them. The others were obviously all right, but what had delayed them? What were their plans? Already I was beginning to wonder about our chances of getting a second try at the Ogre's main summit.

CHAPTER SIX

A Second Chance

The others had been as worried about us as we had about them. They had not seen us for ten days but they said nothing as we approached the tents. Mo was crouched over a stove, cooking. Doug and Tut were packing rucksacks, Clive taking down one of their tents. They were obviously on the move.

'Don Morrison's dead,' Doug stated flatly.

An accident to the team on Latok had been one of our hypotheses for their delay. I found that I accepted it factually. I hardly knew Don and had only talked with him a couple of times at Base Camp. Our own isolation and the constant stress of risk we had been under in the last few days deadened my reaction still further. It wasn't callousness, rather the acceptance of the inherent risk we constantly lived under, a reaction similar, I suspect, to that of the soldier in the front line.

'What happened?'

'He fell down a crevasse.'

Tony Riley and he had been walking up to their first camp in the late afternoon. It was a route they had followed dozens of times, so they had stopped roping up. The snow had hidden a deep crevasse. Don must have stood on the critical weak point and had fallen in. It was so deep and narrow that they had been unable to reach him. They could hear nothing so it seemed he had been killed by the fall.

But there was more than the shock of Don's death that seemed to divide us. I felt uncomfortable, disappointed at not having reached the main summit and, at the same time, guilty now that we had attempted it and allowed ourselves to be drawn into unspoken competition with the others. I also sensed their relief, not only that we were alive and well, but that the Ogre was still unclimbed. Casualness concealed tension.

'Did you make it?' Doug asked.

I told him. 'But what are you doing? Are you going to try our route? It's not too bad.'

'No, we're going for the West Ridge.'

They had reached the crest of the ridge at the foot of a steep rock spur that eventually led to the West Summit and were planning to establish a camp at its foot. Already I longed to be with them but I was too tired and too much in need of a rest. I looked at the pile of food and gas cylinders they were about to pack.

'Is that all you've got?'

'Yeh. Should be enough,' said Mo.

'I just don't think it is. You've no idea how hard the final bit is and surely the West Ridge is going to take you a few more days. If you're not careful, you'll end up doing what we did, getting below that final summit block and not having enough fuel or food to go for it.'

My reasoning was sound but my motivation was not entirely unselfish. If I could persuade them to return to Base Camp to get more supplies, Nick and I could grab our much needed rest and then go for the summit with them.

Nick had other feelings which he confided to his diary:

Regrettably I kept quiet – also most other people, as it seems Chris got his way. Their route was only leading to the W. Summit and they had insufficient food and gas to continue to the main top. So Chris persuaded everyone to go back to Base Camp for more of same and to come back up. So, suddenly, just when I thought the trip was over, I was feeling satisfied and had survived, I have got another fortnight to contend with.

Quite apart from his terrible throat – Nick could only talk in a harsh whisper – he was already nearly two weeks overdue for work, but now it could be a month or more before he was going to get back.

We dropped down to Base that same day. Nick and I had been above the snow line for over two weeks and in that time had only taken two days' rest. We had all but climbed a difficult and certainly very taxing mountain of over 7000 metres, yet on the way down I felt quite fresh, stimulated by the fact that I still had a chance of sharing in the first ascent. Base Camp was an oasis of green. You could smell the grass, lie in it, feel it, revel in it. The harsh world of glaring snow, steep rocks and constant danger had ceased to exist.

Paul Nunn and Tony Riley, quiet and subdued, were packing up their camp. They had built a cairn and memorial to Don Morrison on a little knoll above the lake. That night Doug and the others talked long into the night but I slid off to bed and collapsed into sleep. It was only the next day that I realised just how tired I was. Nick and I spent it sleeping, only getting up for meals. The others were in a hurry to get back on to the mountain. Doug, Mo and Clive were going back up the following day, giving Nick, Tut and myself just one more day at Base, after which we also would go back up the hill. But we were to spend a day clearing the gear that Tut and Doug had left at the foot of the Nose on their earlier attempt, before going on to join the others. Doug sent a message with Paul Nunn for Hadji Medi, the headman of Askole, to send us twenty porters on 12 July. We hoped to reach the top and get back down again by then.

The decision-makers now were Doug and Mo; Clive tended to go along with what they said and Tut was at a disadvantage because of his leg. Nick was still almost speechless with his sore throat and I was very aware that having got the chance of a short rest, it was now a matter of fitting into their plans. I was so tired, there was little else I could have done anyway.

The two days at Base Camp went all too quickly and on the third morning, 5 July, the three of us walked back up to Advance Base. It had that messy, neglected feel that comes to any transit camp on a mountain. Rubbish was scattered over the snow and the remains of spilt food littered the communal tent.

We felt very much the B team the following morning as we slogged up the gully to the col where Tut and Doug had left their gear, with the great granite wall soaring above us. Tut's leg was giving him trouble and he pointed out where the boulder had come hurtling down. We were due to rejoin the others the following morning. But that afternoon in camp Tut and Nick decided that they had had enough, what with Tut's leg and Nick's sore throat. If Nick and I had been on our own I am sure I would have returned home quite happily, having reached the West Summit. But although I was tired, I still had a driving urge to reach the top of the Ogre. It was a combination of a feeling of failure that I hadn't at least had a try at the summit block, and the very human, if somewhat childish, fear of being left out of a successful party.

My resolution was not quite as strong at three the following morning. It had only just begun to freeze and the snow was still soft. I would have to cross the snow-covered glacier on my own. It would have been fairly safe if the snow had been hard frozen but in its present condition it would be all too easy to step through the snow cover into a hidden crevasse. Don Morrison's death made the danger all too obvious. I decided to delay my departure a couple of hours to give the snow a chance to harden but even at five it was still soft. I set out all the same. I was carrying about fifteen kilos of food and gas cylinders. It felt too heavy even at the start.

As I plodded in the glimmer of the dawn back towards the Ogre, each step was filled with trepidation. I constantly glanced around me, trying to glimpse hints of hidden crevasses indicated by slight creases in the dim grey snow. At times the crust would give, my foot would plunge, I'd experience a stab of terror, but each time it reached a solid base.

At last I was off the glacier and on the wall leading to the col. This was safer. There was a fixed rope to clip into and follow but the face had changed. Most of the snow had melted, leaving steep stone-swept ice. No longer was it a question of walking up steps in the snow; each step had to be worked for, kicking the front points of my crampons into the ice and heaving up on the jumar. My progress was painfully slow. It took me ten hours through the heat of the day just to climb the thousand metres of wall. After that was the easy but weary plod over the plateau to the camp-site by the col.

One lonely tent was pitched. The others had obviously moved up to the foot of the ridge. That night I was too tired to cook a meal, just made a brew of tea and crawled into my sleeping-bag. I joined them the following day, climbing a snow gully that stretched up towards the red tunnel tent at its top. I still felt tired and was going painfully slowly. I needed more rest. What was this driving ambition and ego that made me return to the Ogre? More to the point, had I enough strength to reach the West Summit a second time and then go on to the main top? Maybe we'd have some bad weather. I could do with the rest that it would impose.

I could see three tiny figures at work on the steep sunlit rock of a pillar that barred the way up the ridge. They got back down that afternoon, pleased with their progress, enthusing about the quality of the climbing. In the past two days they had run out 150 metres of fixed rope, most of it salvaged from the dump left by the Japanese.

I had been worried about my reception but they seemed glad to see me and I almost immediately felt a part of the team. That night, as there was only one tent, I slept outside, using the Gore-tex cover over my sleeping-bag. It was chilly but also satisfying, the sky a brilliant black, studded with stars that had that clarity only altitude can give. I decided it wasn't just ego that brought me back. It was good to be part of this mountain, part of a team with the simple all-consuming objective of reaching the top of that great citadel of rock that had defeated Nick and me only a few days before.

The following morning Mo and Clive returned to the Pillar to try to reach its top, while Doug and I dropped back to the camp on the plateau to pick up a tent and the rest of the food and fuel. I was worried by the ease with which Doug pulled away from me on the way back up. That evening a bank of high cloud rolled in from the west. Could it be the break in the weather I had been secretly hoping for? My prayers were granted. The others debated whether to go for the top but finally decided to give it another day, even though this meant that our food reserves, once again, were getting low.

It dawned fine on 11 July. We only took one bivvie tent on my assurance

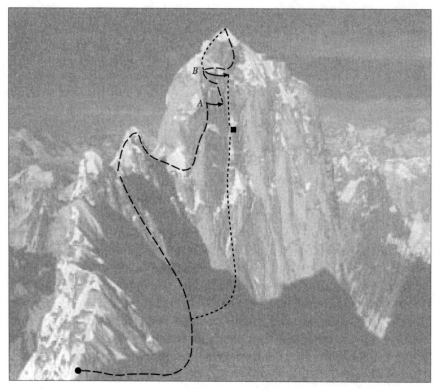

● Snow cave ■ Bivouac in open A: pendulum on ascent B: Doug's involuntary pendulum on descent
— — — — Route not using fixed ropes   ▪ ▪ ▪ ▪ ▪ ▪ Descent
The Upper Reaches of the Ogre

that we could snow-hole on the col between the two summits. Even so our
sacks were heavy with climbing equipment, food, fuel and bivouac gear. I
was impressed by the steepness of the Pillar as I jumared up the line of fixed
rope laid by the others. It worked a serpentine line up the Pillar, starting
on its left, working round on to its nose and then creeping on to its right-
hand side across the base of an open ice gully. Mo and Clive had reached
the top of the gully but had used the ropes we would need to climb with to
reach the crest of the Pillar. This meant we had to take them up with us,
removing the umbilical cord that linked us to the security of our camp at
the foot of the Pillar.

A band of snow stretched away towards the South-West Ridge, but the
route up the ridge was barred by another rock wall much lower than the
one we had just climbed. Doug surged out in front, traversing a horizontal
line of broken rock interrupted by ice bulges. It didn't look too hard until
I came to follow him. We were carrying our sacks and the weight pushed
me out of balance. In some ways on a traverse it is more unnerving to be

the second man than the first. You've got just as far to swing if you slip but you can actually see how far you would go, for the rope snakes out in front of you. About half-way across Doug had stepped down on to a steep little slab. Here he had had the benefit of a back rope through a piton just above him. I didn't. The next runner was about three metres away at the same level. I dithered; stepped down, made a lunge, missed and slipped, skating down and across the slab until I hung from Doug's runner. I'd banged my elbow on the way across and the pain, merged with the adrenalin surge, left me shaky and trembling. I scrabbled up to Doug, panting, but then led through up easier snow lying on ice towards the crest of the ridge. We were able to drop the rope down the other side so that Mo and Clive could jumar straight up.

But it was getting late. The sun was already low in the sky, yet there was another rock tower to climb before we could cross the West Summit. We'd certainly never make it that night and so bivouacked where we were, Mo and I digging a small snow cave that was just big enough for the two of us, Doug and Clive setting up their bivvie tent outside.

Next day the weather was perfect, with the sun shining from a clear sky as we started up a long steep snow rake leading to a ridge that dropped southward from the West Summit. Today it was Mo and Clive's turn to be out in front. The snow rake was nerve-racking, for a couple of centimetres of powder snow covered hard ice at an angle of sixty degrees. Inevitably Mo slowed up as he crossed this section and I could sense Doug's impatience. I tiptoed my way across immediately behind Clive, the points of crampons and ice tools barely making any impression on the ice. Doug followed. There was now more snow over the ice and the climbing became more relaxed. I was content to wander up the steps left by the front pair. There was time to enjoy the unfolding view, to absorb the heat of the sun, but Doug couldn't relax. He climbed on up past Clive, who was belaying Mo, and was soon following in Mo's footsteps. As Mo paused for breath, Doug surged past leading the last few metres to the crest of the South-West Ridge.

Doug was now firmly in the lead once more and worked his way up the snow-plastered crest of the ridge towards the West Summit. I followed on behind him. He hadn't bothered to belay, since the rope running over the top gave us a degree of security. I hardly had time to savour my return or gaze across at our objective before the rope tugged insistently and I followed down the steps Doug had left. You could still see traces of the route Nick and I had taken. Our little balcony was still there. That afternoon we expanded it into a commodious snow hole, but the others were not too happy about the safety of the snow; it was lying on quite steep ice, even though it seemed consolidated.

Doug and I set out at five the next morning. Mo and Clive were going to come on later. We followed the snow slope skirting below the rocky crest of the ridge, at first moving together and then, as the slope steepened, one at a time. Several rope-lengths brought us to the foot of the summit rocks that soared steep and massive above us. Snow-covered rocks led back up to the crest of the ridge and I moved to the foot of these to let Doug lead the first pitch. He climbed it powerfully up a series of awkward icy grooves. When I came to follow I was breathless by the time I reached him.

'You might as well keep the lead, while I get my breath back,' I muttered.

He pushed on straightaway, heaving over a rock bulge, running out the full length of the rope and anchoring it at the top so that I could jumar up it while he reconnoitred the way to the final pyramid. By the time I reached the top he was already out of sight. I coiled the rope and followed the line of tracks round the snow-clad crest of the ridge down a steep little gully to find myself on the col that immediately abutted the final tower. An open groove, capped by a small overhang, presented a possible line of weakness. Doug was already festooned with a variety of nuts and pegs and had one rope uncoiled at his feet.

'I think it's about time I did some leading,' I commented.

'Not here, youth,' Doug replied. 'It's going to be hard technical climbing up that. It's getting late already. Give me that rope.'

I felt overwhelmed by the sheer force of Doug's drive. In surrendering one lead, I seemed also to have surrendered any share of the initiative. I was too tired and lacked the self-confidence to argue. Perhaps he was right. Doug grabbed the rope, tied on to one end, threw down the coils and started climbing, swinging up a corner crack on a hand-jam. He was only a metre or so above me when the slack in the rope formed into an inextricable knot.

'Hold it, Doug. You've got the rope into a bloody tangle.'

I resented the rush that had caused this to happen, resented being relegated to the mere status of rope holder, and was even more resentful of the fact that Doug was going so much more powerfully than I.

'Hurry up, it's bloody tiring hanging on here.'

'It's your fault the rope's tangled anyway. I can't do it any quicker. You'd better come back down.'

It was one of those tangles that you couldn't believe were possible. I ended up having to untie from both ropes and painstakingly unravel them until at last they were clear. Doug returned to the fray and climbed the groove quickly and elegantly. I followed, jumaring up the rope; it was a pitch that I could have led. Why the hell had I let myself be steamrollered?

Doug was on a small ledge at the foot of a sheer rock wall split by a thin crack.

'Can't we get round the corner?' I asked.

'Don't think so. I've had a look. It's just as steep round there. The crack should go.'

I didn't volunteer to lead it. This was obviously going to be hard. I started pulling in the rope I had just jumared up. It jammed almost immediately. I cursed my inefficiency. Doug said nothing. I had no choice but to abseil down to the bottom, find the knot that had somehow formed in the rope and then jammed in a crack, clear it and jumar up again, all of which wasted a precious half hour.

Doug took off his crampons and started climbing the crack, making some moves free, using the rock holds, and on others stepping in slings attached either to pitons or nuts. I sat in the sun and watched the progress of Mo and Clive. They were now climbing the snow-covered rocks leading up to the crest of the ridge. Looking along the corniced rim I could just see the little hole that was the entrance to our snow cave and the tracks leading down from the West Summit. The rope stopped sliding through my hands.

'The crack's blind. Can't get a peg in.' Doug was scraping snow from a little scoop in the rock, but it concealed no hidden cracks or holds. 'Let me down.'

He lowered himself about fifteen metres on his top runner, a wired nut.

'Hold me there, I think I might be able to pendulum to that crack over on the right.'

He started running from side to side to gain some momentum on the sheer wall and at the end of each swing tried to reach the crack to the right with a sky hook. It took several tries but at last he managed to lodge the sky hook, haul himself across, and jam his fingers into the crack. He tried to get a foot-hold but his boot, big and clumsy against the finger-width crack, slipped and suddenly he was swinging back away from his objective. He rested on the rope and then tried again. This time he found a toe-hold, was able to consolidate his position and began finger-jamming up the crack until he was level with, and then above, his wire runner. It would have been strenuous at sea level. Here, at over 7000 metres, it was incredible. I lost all sense of resentment in wonder at what Doug had managed to do, at his strength, ingenuity and determination.

It was now my turn – a simple matter of jumaring up the rope, though extracting the nuts Doug had dangled and pulled on was slow, hard work. By the time I joined him the sun was already low on the western horizon. The day had slid away from us and we still had another thirty metres or so to climb. Mo and Clive had been watching Doug's acrobatics from the col and now decided to return to the snow cave. It didn't look as if we had much chance of reaching the top before dark – they had none at all.

I was determined to have a lead. A short snow crest led to the final summit block, a smooth boulder of brown granite. It was steep and holdless. I tried to work my way round the corner along a narrow snow ledge, and came to a little overhanging scoop that led into a snow bay that in turn seemed to lead up to the top. I hammered in a piton but still couldn't muscle my way up the scoop.

'You'd better come and have a try,' I shouted to Doug.

He hadn't put his crampons back on so was able to stand on my shoulder to reach holds above the overhang. He heaved himself up and a metre or so higher managed to get a belay. Without the shoulder it was all I could do, on a very tight rope, to fight my way over the bulge. I landed at Doug's feet like a stranded fish, panting my heart out. Before I could get my breath back to talk, Doug had undone his belay and already started up the snow gully. I was left to put on a belay and hold the rope.

It would have been logical for me to have led through, since I was wearing crampons, which was one reason why I had been unable to lead the rock scoop behind me. As Doug slowed down above me, I regretted not being more assertive but his energy was that of an erupting volcano, in which his own driving force swept everything else aside. As I shivered in the growing cold of the gully I had time to reflect. Doug was going more strongly, but in the past I had experienced similar imbalances with Don Whillans and Dougal Haston, both of whom were stronger and more forceful climbers than I, but the climbing had always been harmonious with a sense of shared decision and participation.

He had disappeared from view. Slides of snow came tumbling down as the rope slipped slowly through my hands. The light dimmed to a uniform grey as the shadows of the valley crept up the peaks bordering the Biafo Glacier. We hadn't much time left before dark.

At last there was a shout. He was up. Another pause and he called for me to start climbing. I kicked up the snow of the gully. With crampons on it felt fairly secure. At its top I pulled out onto a small block of rock with Doug crouched upon it. There was too little time for jubilation. Doug had been there for about twenty minutes and was anxious to start down in the little daylight that was left. I quickly took a photograph of him and then of the four quarters of the horizon. The mountains were silhouetted against the purple of the gathering dusk.

We had climbed the Ogre – all we now had to do was to get back down.

CHAPTER SEVEN

Getting Down the Ogre

Doug was already sorting out the ropes, pulling them down to a small rock outcrop a couple of metres below the summit. I followed and helped set up the abseil.

'Do you want me to go down first?' I asked.

'I'm off now, youth.'

He set off down into the gloom. Waiting, I could just pick out the pyramid of K2, etched black against the eastern horizon, dominating the peaks around it. That surely must be the Mustagh Tower and closer were the fierce upthrusts of the Latok peaks, black teeth against the sky. To the south-west the afterglow of the setting sun threw the great mass of Nanga Parbat into clear relief. I felt a sense of contentment at being on this high summit, a satisfaction that washed away all my earlier frustration. I loved the beauty of the still cold clear evening.

And then from below came a moan that built up into a penetrating scream. Then suddenly was cut off and it was as silent as it had been before. I was sure Doug had gone off the end of the rope. I tugged at it for confirmation. It was taut. He was still on the rope. I shouted down but there was no reply. Was he unconscious? If he didn't get his weight off the end of the rope I couldn't abseil down to join him but I could jumar. It's a slow painstaking process in reverse but perfectly possible. I felt very very lonely standing on the Ogre's summit in the gloom of the night. 'You might not get out of this one, Bonington,' I thought.

And then there was a distant shout from below: 'I've broken my leg.'

I felt a flood of relief. He was alive and conscious and I was no longer alone. I had a role to play.

'Can you get your weight off the rope?'

'I'll try. There's a ledge just below me.

Another pause, and the rope went slack in my hand. I could abseil down to join him but how on earth were we going to get a man with a broken leg back across the West Summit and all the way down that long and complex route? Even the three of us couldn't possibly carry him. As I came in sight of Doug, I assumed a confidence I didn't feel.

'What ho, mate.'

He was sitting on a tiny ledge, belayed to a piton he had just hammered in. 'I slipped on some ice,' he told me.

Later I gathered he had just finished traversing the snow ridge leading to the top of the long rock pitch that had provided the crux of the climb. He was stepping down to clip into the piton we had left in place and had braced his foot against the rock. In the gathering dark he hadn't seen the thin film of ice and, because he wasn't wearing crampons, his boot skidded off, sending him swinging like the weight on the end of a pendulum into space across the rock wall. He must have been a good forty metres out horizontally from the anchor point, yet only twenty metres or so below it. As he swung through the dark he instinctively raised his feet to act as buffers as he came crashing into a rock corner. The impact had in fact broken both his legs though neither of us realised this immediately. But perhaps this saved him from more complex injuries.

'We'll just work at getting you down,' I said cheerfully. 'Don't worry, you're a long way from being dead.'

Probably not the most tactful thing to say, but it was the thought uppermost in my mind. It hadn't remotely occurred to Doug, who felt extremely rational and remarkably clear about what to do. I pulled down the doubled rope and fixed another abseil. It was now very nearly pitch dark. We did not have head-torches and I didn't fancy the prospect of trying to get all the way down in the dark. I could just see through the gloom a wider snow ledge about fifteen metres below. It might be suitable for a bivouac. On arriving, I hacked away at the snow. There was enough to clear a comfortable ledge that we could at least sit on.

'It's OK, Doug, you might as well come on down.'

He slid down the rope, keeping his legs behind him, but once on the snow he had to traverse a metre or two to reach the ledge I had started to dig. He tried to stand. There was a distinct sound of bone scraping on bone. He let out a cry of pain and keeled over onto his knees where he paused slumped, then crawled over, his legs stuck out behind him clear of the snow, to join me on the ledge. Kneeling, he helped enlarge the ledge for the night. We might get out of this after all, I began to think.

We had nothing with us, no food or drink, no down clothing, just what we had climbed in during the day and the gear we had used. We took off our boots, though it was too dark to examine Doug's legs. Fortunately they did not hurt too much, provided he didn't put any weight on them and I didn't inadvertently lean on them. We tucked out stockinged feet into each others crutches, massaged them from time to time through the night, occasionally talked. At one point Doug said, 'If you've got to get into this kind of predicament, I can't think of a better person to be with.' Most of the time we were wrapped in our own thoughts. The penetrating cold soon dominated everything. I rationalised it by telling myself that the discomfort was ephemeral, that it was just a few hours, a tiny fraction of my life span, and then the sun would rise and we would be warm once again. I limited my thoughts to the prospects of the haven of the snow cave just a hundred or so metres away, of hot drinks and a warm sleeping-bag and the support of Mo and Clive.

I became aware of Doug rubbing my feet, a strong hint that he wanted his toes massaging. I did so with care, to avoid hurting him. He was particularly worried about the dangers of frostbite which would inevitably be increased by the injuries he had sustained. The night slowly dragged by until at last the sky began to lighten. We were on the western side of the Ogre and so couldn't expect the sun until late in the morning. We didn't wait. Doug managed to get his boots back on; another relief.

I set up the abseil and plunged down to a ledge nearly fifty metres below. Doug followed more slowly but very steadily. Three more abseils and we were on the snow at the foot of the summit block. With action and with Doug's absolute steadiness and quiet competence, I was becoming more optimistic about our chances. We now had our next test. The snow cave was about thirty metres higher and a hundred metres from us in a horizontal direction. Would Doug be able to crawl across fairly steep snow?

I left him at the foot of the abseil and set out to warn the other two whom I met just short of the snow cave. They had seen the fall the previous night and were coming over to see what they could do to help. I carried on into the welcome shelter of the cave, leaving them to collect Doug. They met him about a third of the way up the tracks I had left. Doug is not the kind of person to wait around. He had already started crawling. Clive picked up his sack while Mo started digging out great bucket steps for Doug to crawl in. Mercifully he did not have compound fractures or he would not have been able to crawl without acute pain, and we had no painkillers.

They got back to the snow cave two hours later. We all now felt confident that Doug would be able to cope with the descent, in spite of its length and complex nature. It was wonderful just to lie in the warmth of one's sleeping-bag cocooned in the confines of the snow cave, brewing endless cups of tea. That day we ate and drank our fill but in the evening we finished our last freeze-dried meal. All we had left was some soup and a few tea bags. This didn't seem too serious, however, as surely we should get back down to Advance Base in a couple of days.

Mo had brought a pack of cards with him and we spent the rest of the day playing Min, or Black Bitch as it is called in some circles, a delightful trick-taking game that had had us entertained throughout the expedition. A bank of high cloud stretched across the western horizon but we had seen plenty of threats of a storm in the last few weeks and none of them had materialised. We settled down for the night confident that we would be able to get most of the way down the following morning.

When I woke I thought it was too early, the light was so dim. I glanced at my watch to see that it was six o'clock. It should have been broad daylight outside. I looked across the cave to see that Mo, who was on the outside nearest the door, was covered in spindrift. The entrance was completely blocked with fresh snow. It looked as if the weather had at last broken. We slowly crept into consciousness. Clive, who was next to the stove, scooped some snow from the wall and started brewing the first drink of the day. We had plenty of gas, which was a blessing. You can go for some days without food, but the effects of dehydration are much more serious. Without liquid we would deteriorate very quickly and to get liquid we needed fuel.

It was only after having a cup of tea, each using the last of our few cubes of sugar, that we dug out the entrance. A cloud of spindrift immediately blew in. Within the cave it was sepulchrally quiet; outside was an inferno of screaming wind and driving snow. But we had to move; Clive and I ventured out to see how bad it was and I belayed him while he ploughed up to his thighs using a swimming action to make any progress at all. He turned back after running out twenty metres of rope in a struggle that took over an hour. The furrow he ploughed on his return journey was covered almost instantly. Cold and wet, we crawled back into the snow cave. Our situation was now very much more serious but, whatever anyone thought privately, there was no sense of despondency within the party. Mo's humour was as sharp as ever and Doug only complained if someone sat on one of his damaged legs. We snuggled down in our sleeping-bags and waited out the day.

Next morning the storm still raged. It had the feeling that a spell of extreme weather, either good or bad, brings, that it will last for ever. This was our second day without food; we couldn't wait any longer. However bad the storm and the snow, we had to fight our way out. To assert our determination, we all packed our rucksacks, dividing Doug's gear between the three of us, and set out into the storm. Clive and Mo took turns forcing the route up towards the West Summit, leaving a rope behind them. Doug needed all his strength to crawl up through the deep snow, hauling himself bodily on the jumar. I stamped and shivered in the rear collecting the ropes. It took four hours for me to reach the top. I crouched on the West Summit while Doug painstakingly part-crawled, part-abseiled down the snow-plastered rocky ridge. It was so different from the two previous occasions when there had been a cloudless sky and brilliant sun. Visibility was down to a metre. There were glimpses of rock walls dropping darkly into the white of driving snow. Mo was out in front, setting up abseils, picking a route through this maze of snow and cloud and rock. All I had to do was follow the line of rope, the thread through the Minator's labyrinth. I could hear the great bull roar.

There was no question of abseiling down the ridge line. The rope would have caught in the rocks when I tried to pull it down. I therefore climbed down, coiling it as I went. The others were waiting below, having run out all the rope. They were like snowmen, faces rimed with ice, clothing plastered. Mo plunged on down with the ropes I had given him, while I squatted ready for another long cold wait. We were now descending the steep snow rake below the West Summit rocks. This in turn led to the ice slope that had been precarious even in perfect conditions. I couldn't help wondering how Doug would manage to crawl across it and the consequences of a fall.

But so much snow had fallen, even though it was still precarious, the snow just held Doug's weight as he edged across. Once again I brought up the rear, uncomfortably aware that no one was belaying me. I couldn't afford to fall. By the time I reached the site of our previous bivouac it was very nearly dark. Mo had already vanished into the snow cave he and I had excavated on the way up.

It had been only just big enough for the two of us. Now it was part filled with snow and was much too small for four. Only one person could work in it at a time. Another could shovel the excavated snow out, but the other two just stood and shivered in the dark and cold. Consequently we piled into the cave before it was big enough. Doug urged us to do some work on it, but we were all too tired. We just wanted to slide into our sleeping-bags and have something to drink, though it could only be milkless, sugarless tea with one tea bag between the four of us.

Just taking off our outer, snow-plastered clothes was a struggle. It was impossible to keep the snow off the sleeping-bags. I was on the outside and tried to block the entrance with rucksacks and climbing gear but the spindrift sought out every chink. It blew into our little cave, covering everything in a cold white film that, as we tossed and turned to avoid it, melted on our sleeping-bags, turning the down into a useless congealed mess, then penetrating our clothes until by morning everything was wet and soggy. We weren't cold in the night. There was a warmth in our very proximity but that morning, 17 July, four days after the accident and two days since we'd had any solid food, the cold penetrated as soon as we crawled out of the shelter of the cave into the storm that still screamed around the Ogre.

A knife-edged ridge led down to the top of the Pillar. Mo went on ahead to fix the first abseil, while Clive and I put Doug between us, as we slowly made our way down. We could do nothing to help Doug, other than carry his gear, dig big bucket steps for him where possible, and be ready to hold him on the rope should he slip. He went carefully, steadily, never complaining, never showing the pain and stress that he must have felt. At last we reached the top of the Pillar. Mo had fixed the doubled ropes of the abseil and had already vanished. At least we were going straight down – the steeper the better.

Doug went first. We peered down, his shape blurred into the driving snow and then vanished. There was a shout from below but we couldn't make out any words. The rope was slack and so Clive went down. Another long pause. Then I clipped in and slid down the doubled rope, blinded by the driving snow that seemed to be blown from every direction. My frozen clothing was like a suit of armour, restricting movement. But it was good to be on the rope. All I had to do was slide; I could relax my concentration for just a few minutes. I was nearly down and could see Clive's shape, opposite and just below me. That surely must be the top of the fixed rope. We were very nearly out of trouble.

And then I was falling, plummeting head downwards. Had the anchor come away? A stab of absolute horror surged through me; this was it. Then came a jarring, smashing pain in my chest. I was hanging suspended on the rope. I just hung there, shocked and frightened for a minute. Then my mind took over once again with an instinctive analysis of what had happened.

I was attached to a single rope by my abseil brake. The ends of the rope must have been uneven and I had come off one end, pulling the rope I was still on down, until I was brought to a halt after a fall of some seven metres or so by the loop on the longer end of the rope that had been placed over a spike of rock. I swung across and clipped in to the start of the fixed rope. My ribs ached but I had no idea that I had done anything more than hit something on the way down and would probably be badly bruised as a result. There was no time for worry. We had to get back to the tents that day. I could see Doug over to the left, secured to the fixed rope, working his way painstakingly over an awkward rock traverse. It wasn't too bad in cramponed boots but he had to crawl.

It was only that evening that I learnt that Doug had had an even narrower escape than I. When he abseiled neither of the ropes at the bottom had been anchored. He went straight off the ends and was plummeting down the gully. Fortunately the fixed rope we had left in place went across the gully about five metres below. As he shot passed it, he managed to grab it and arrest his fall. Otherwise he could have gone another 1300 metres to the glacier far below.

There was no time to linger over near-misses. Slowly we worked our way back along the fixed ropes, abseiling and traversing, until at last we were just above the snow spur leading down to the tents. Mo had already got down and we could see him begin to dig them out. The fixed rope ended just above a bergschrund. It had been easy enough to climb up uninjured, in perfect conditions. Getting down in a storm with an injured man was very different. I had brought with me a short length of rope for this contingency. We tied Doug to the end of it and began to lower him. It wasn't quite long enough. The storm suddenly rose to a crescendo. Spindrift avalanched down the spur engulfing and blinding us; it was as if the Ogre didn't want to let us go. Could we die now, so very close to relative safety? And then the storm relented. Doug managed to establish himself on easier angled snow so that he could untie the rope. Clive and I followed and soon we were digging out our buried tents. At least we had some kind of shelter now, though our sleeping-bags and clothing were soaked and we had only a few tea bags supplemented by a few cubes of curried Oxo and a packet of sugar. There was no solid food.

It was when I undressed that I realised my injuries were more serious than a few bruises. I could feel an uneven indentation on the right-hand side of my rib cage. I had probably broken some ribs. My left hand was also part-paralysed and the wrist was swollen. Had I broken it? I crawled into my wet sleeping-bag. Mo, who was sharing the tent with me, brought me a mug of tea. Hot and sweet, it tasted like nectar. I just curled up in the bag, trying to hold on to the little glimmer of warmth it had kindled, and wondered what the next day would bring.

I slept intermittently, listened to the wind screaming around the tent, and prayed for the weather to clear. But the storm was as fierce as ever in the morning. I dragged myself out to relieve myself and realised how weak I had become; I felt terrible and returned to my sleeping-bag. It was beginning to dry out but was stealing my body heat to do so. I curled up and let the rest of the day slip away in a semi-coma. My chest didn't hurt as long as I didn't move or cough but every cough was like a fierce stab and my throat, raw from our ordeal, built up into a sore tickle until I broke out into a paroxysm of uncontrollable coughing. I crouched, hugging my ribs, trying to alleviate the pain.

I was coughing up a bubbly froth. Was this pulmonary, or perhaps pulmonary oedema caused by the trauma? As the day dragged on I became

convinced that I could die if we didn't get down soon. In the dark blue
gloom of the tent my fears built up. I staggered next door and expressed
my worry about pulmonary oedema, urging that I needed to get down
before it took a grip, yet feeling ashamed of the fuss I was making.

Mo pointed out that we would never be able to find our way across the
plateau in a white-out. We had to wait for a clear day. He was right and I
crawled back to the tent to wait out the rest of the day and the long night.
Waiting was much worse than the struggle of the descent.

And then came dawn. The wind still hammered the tent but suddenly a
finger of light touched its walls. It was the sun. The sky had cleared; we
could see the plateau stretched out below us and escape from our trap.

Mo and Clive were now carrying colossal loads as we slowly abseiled
down the steep slopes leading back to the plateau. One of the tents, secured
under the straps of Clive's rucksack, slipped out and went bounding down
the slope. Clive cursed but resigned himself to making the long detour to
get it. At last we had reached the relative safety of the plateau. Under a clear
blue sky we felt almost out of danger. Doug volunteered to take Clive's pack
while Clive went for the tent. He set out on all fours, weighed down by the
huge sack. I followed and was appalled to find I couldn't keep up with him.
My strength had oozed away. I took a few steps, sat down and rested, then
took a few more.

We had now been five days without solid food, but we just had the last
thousand metres of descent, all safeguarded by fixed rope, and we would
be back on the glacier. The others surely would have come to Advance Base
to meet and help us, as they would be worried by now. Soon it would be
their responsibility. The ordeal was nearly over.

On the morning of 20 July, Mo and I got away first. I had dumped every
piece of gear that wasn't absolutely essential to lighten my rucksack. I even
left my camera behind. Mo fix-roped the upper part of the ridge and I
followed trying to cut bigger steps for Doug to crawl down. It was awkward
work because I couldn't use my left hand at all. This made the descent
difficult as well, particularly as the fixed ropes had deteriorated in the time
we had been on the mountain, becoming stretched in places and tangled
in others. The descent seemed interminable. I kept gazing down at the
glacier trying to see a welcoming committee. There were no tents at Advance
Base and no sign of any kind of life.

The fixed ropes ended on the last of the rock. Below that was a snow
slope which in the intervening time had turned to ice. It was just a matter
of cramponing down it but each kick of the crampons sent an agonising
stab of pain into my chest. I couldn't bear it. To hell with it, I'd slide. I
threw my rucksack down the slope and then followed, sliding on my

backside, the classic sitting glissade. But I could only hold my ice axe with one hand and was unable to use it as an effective brake. I rapidly gained speed and was soon hurtling down towards the bottom, doing what I could to protect my ribs. I arrived with a crunch and just lay in the snow, exhausted and relieved that the worst of the descent was over.

Mo was waiting. 'We'd better rope up for the glacier,' he said. 'After all that I'd hate to end up in the bottom of a crevasse.'

I took the proffered rope and Mo set off, ploughing through deep soft snow. He was like a tug boat towing a derelict ship. I could feel the pull of the rope at my waist and wearily put one foot in front of the other in the tracks that Mo had made. At last we reached the rocky moraine at the end of the glacier.

'You should be all right from here,' Mo said. 'I'd better get down and see what the others are up to.'

He quickly disappeared from view, leaving me to wander down the moraine. I staggered a few paces at a time then sank down to revel in the heat of the sun as it slowly penetrated the chill of my body.

The terrain changed from barren piled rock to the beginnings of vegetation, a pink cluster of primula almost hidden in a crevice, and then, round a corner, the little oasis formed by the meadow and lake of our Base Camp – emerald green grass embraced by the arms of the glacier moraine. But there were no tents, no sign of humanity. I reached the boulder where we had our cooking shelter. There were pots and pans and boxes of food stored under the overhang. There was also a note. It was in Nick's hand, dated 20 July, that very day, and started:

Dear All,
In the unlikely event of your ever reading this, I've gone down to try to catch up with Tut and the porters so that we can come back and look for you. We saw you come down off the summit on the 14th and assumed you'd be back down next morning. The porters had already arrived and we had neither the food nor the money to keep them. Tut and Aleem therefore went down with the porters and all the gear while I waited with six of them to help carry your stuff.

I can only assume something has gone badly wrong but I couldn't come up to see for myself as I've sent away all my hill gear. Tut and I will get back up as quick as we can.

Nick

There was another note in Mo's handwriting at the bottom:

I've pushed straight on to try to catch up with Nick. I'll go down with him to get the porters back up here as soon as possible to help you all down.

Mo

We were still on our own. Would Doug be able to crawl all the way to Base? It was a good four miles. I should go back to help Clive but I was too tired, too tired even to eat. I had had no solid food for five days yet did not feel particularly hungry. I just lay down and felt the soft warm blades of grass against my face, could smell it, pungent with the scent of life; I could hear the buzz of flies and rustle of the wind in the reeds of the lake. I was alive and knew that I could hang on to life. I just had to be patient and soon I'd be home.

I summoned the energy to fetch some water from the stream and lit the stove. Soon I was sipping soup and nibbling at some biscuits. But I really should go back for the others. Just a little rest first. I pulled out my sleeping-bag, crawled into it and dropped off to sleep. It was dark when I woke. Nine o'clock. I had been asleep for several hours. Still no sign of Doug and Clive. Full of foreboding, I pulled on my boots and, taking a head torch, slowly retraced my steps back up the glacier. To my immense relief I saw a little pool of light in the distance. It was Clive. Just behind him was Doug, slowly but steadily crawling on his hands and knees over the sharp and broken rocks of the moraine. Clive pushed on to the camp to start a brew while I walked with Doug the last few yards back to the boulder. We'd made it. We were alive and now, whatever the delays, whatever the discomfort, it was just a matter of time.

I might not have waxed so philosophical had I known just how long this would take in my case. It was four days before Nick arrived back with porters who carried Doug on a makeshift stretcher down to the Biafo Glacier where he was collected by a helicopter. Nick had had an appalling time waiting for us at Base Camp, seeing us intermittently near the West Summit, trying to guess what had gone wrong, and then not seeing us at all and having to decide what to do next. I had experienced the same emotion on Everest, waiting for Pete Boardman, Pertemba and Mick Burke to return, but I had only a matter of hours to wait, sharing my anxiety with friends, while Nick had suffered seven days in effective solitude. For he could barely communicate with the few porters who had stayed behind with him. His diary recorded his growing despair:

19 July: Fine morning. They *must* come down today.

Still no sign of them at 5.30 in spite of fine weather all day. Preparing to go down to Askole tomorrow to collect Tut and form a search party.

Beginning to give up – thinking of Wendy and other wives and how to get news to them. Spent whole day looking through binocs. Every stone on the glacier seems to move until you examine it. Also if you listen hard enough you can hear human voices in the sound of running water or falling stones.

Summit appeared for half an hour in early afternoon – snow cave now invisible and no sign of tracks.

20 July

Hardly slept a wink – in the early morning I have hallucinations, or were they dreams? In the middle of the night I thought I saw a green flare up the glacier – also a distinct shout of 'Nick'. No further signs, though.

After the evacuation of Doug the rest of us plodded on down to Askole where Mo and Tut were waiting. That night had a good party atmosphere. An American expedition, on their way back from climbing the Trango Tower were also in the village. We had a camp fire, chupatties, apricots and endless cups of tea. But the following morning they were all anxious to get on their way, unhindered by me.

'Don't worry, Chris, the helicopter pilot promised to come back for you today.'

They wanted to get out quickly, walking long days. They reminded me how painful the jeep journey would be with my broken ribs. I had no choice but to resign myself to waiting for the helicopter.

The Americans had a doctor. He dug his hand into his pocket and produced a handful of multi-coloured pills, giving me half-a-dozen striped ones as antibiotics, some little white ones for sleeping and red ones for pain. He also gave me a paperback to help pass the time while I waited to be evacuated.

I couldn't help feeling desperately lonely as they shouldered their ruck-sacks and all strode away down the path, leaving me propped against a tree just outside the village. Still, I was only going to have to wait an hour or so and I would be picked up and whisked into Skardu while they were still plodding down the Braldu Gorge.

I waited through the day but there was no sign of the helicopter. A few youngsters played in the dust around me but the rest of the village seemed to have forgotten my existence. As dusk fell and it became obvious that the helicopter was not coming back that day, I went in search of shelter, knock-ing on the door of one of our porters' houses and trying, with sign language, to show that I had nowhere to sleep. Hadji Fezil, a middle-aged Balti, with a thin face and large very dirty, gap-teeth, took me in and let me lay my sleeping mat under an awning on the flat roof of his house.

The helicopter didn't come the next day. Nor did it come in the next five.

I was weak and still felt very ill. I just lay in my sleeping-bag, dragging myself once a day down through the house and along the path in search of a quiet spot to relieve myself. The village youngsters would follow me, whistling a whirring noise, grinning and calling, 'Helicopter no coming, helicopter no coming.' The cry reverberated round my brain, accompanied me back to my rooftop and crept round my head at night.

I became quite paranoid. 'They've left me. The whole bloody lot of them have just pushed off home.' It was just as well that the American doctor had given me a thick book. It was *Centennial* by Michener, one of those bumper chronicles about a patch of Colorado from the beginning of time to the present day – a good easy read for an invalid marooned on a flat mud roof in the middle of the Karakoram. The only other events of the day were meal times. These consisted of chupatties, a spinach-like vegetable and boiled eggs. I had to brush the flies away as I took each mouthful. Hadji Fezil and his family were very kind. I had no money, was unable to communicate, except by signs, and seemed to have been abandoned.

On the sixth day, I was so desperate I set out to walk accompanied by the faithful Hadji Fezil. If anything I had become even weaker in the intervening days. Walking was purgatory. That day we reached Chongo and stayed in the house of one of his relatives. We had now to get through the steep section of the Braldu Gorge. The river was in full spate, tearing at the boulders of the path. In places we had to wade through it or its subsidiary streams. I just hugged my ribs, terrified of the pain that the slightest stumble or sudden movement created. That night we reached the village of Kunul. The following day we should be at Dasso where we could get a jeep but I dreaded the thought of the jeep ride.

We had just started breakfast when the distant whine of an engine alerted us. It could only be a helicopter. I rushed out of the hut, followed by Hadji Fezil. We were in a grove of apricot trees at the side of the valley. The helicopter could not possibly see us. I dashed down into the flat valley bottom, the pain of my ribs ignored. The helicopter was already overhead, flying purposefully up to Askole. Would it see us on the way back? We lit a fire, made a marker of yellow foam mats and waited, full of a desperate uncertainty. An hour went by. And then the distant roar. It was flying down the valley floor. It dropped down beside us, and the smiling pilot flung open the door. My ordeal was over.

The pilot, a major in the Pakistan army, explained that the helicopter which had evacuated Doug had had a crash landing in Skardu that could easily have proved fatal, and there had been a delay in getting a replacement. He had flown up that morning from Islamabad.

Above: Changabang, in the Garhwal range.

Left: Nick Estcourt on the first ascent of Brammah.

Chris, aged twenty-six, on the south side of Mount Blanc in 1961.

Below: View from high on the South-West face of Everest.

Top left: Doug belaying me near the foot of the Rock Band on Everest, 1975.

Top right: Dougal and Doug at the site of Camp 6, Everest, 1975.

Above: The Ogre Expedition – Clive Rowland, myself, Nick Estcourt, Doug Scott, Tut Braithwaite and Mo Anthoine, with the Ogre in the background.

Left: Bath in a hot spring by the Braldu river on the Ogre expedition.

Nick crossing the difficult slabs at the
foot of the South Face of the Ogre.

Clive on the fixed rope on the
lower slopes of the Ogre.

Nick on the South Face of the Ogre.

Going for the
West Summit
of the Ogre.

Return to the Ogre;
Camp 4 at the foot
of the West Ridge.

Below: Chris back at base camp
on the Ogre after five days without solid food with broken ribs
and pneumonia.

Right: Doug crawling down the
Ogre after breaking both his legs.

K2 Expedition: Nick paying off the porters whilst I fill in their conduct books.

Joe on the way up to Camp 2 on K2. The highest peak in the background is Masherbrum.

Climbing the lower slopes of the South-East Ridge of Kongur in our first bid for the summit.

The Kongur massif from near the Karakol Lakes.

Looking up the North-East Ridge of Everest from the Raphu La.

Pete and Joe at work on the second snow cave on the North-East Ridge of Everest, 1983.

Above: Bunk accommodation on our first bivouac on Shivling.

Above right: The expedition group just above Namche Bazar.

Right: Chris going for the fairytale summit of Shivling with Everest in the background. Norweigan expedition, 1985.

Summer rock climbing on Black Crag in the Lake District, Borrowdale.

Approaching the Hillary Step, Everest.

Fulfilment. Chris (left) and Ang Lhakpa on the summit of Everest.

'I might as well take you straight there if you want. I'm going back anyway.'

And so we flew all the way to Islamabad, down the great gorge of the Indus and across the foothills to Pakistan's capital.

'Where are you staying? Might as well get you as close as I can.'

'At the British Embassy.'

'I can't land there. The closest I can get is the golf course.'

We landed on the eighteenth green. A group of golfers eyed the helicopter respectfully, no doubt expecting to see a general descend. They must have been surprised to see the filthy, skeletal apparition that I had become climb out. My hair and beard were unkempt and tangled. I was wearing dirty red Lifa long-johns and vest and had one arm in a sling.

The helicopter took off and I walked over to the clubhouse. People shrank away from me as I approached the desk and asked if I could phone the British Embassy. Half an hour later Caroline, with whom we had stayed on our way out, came to pick me up.

It's easy to talk of heroism in describing a near-catastrophe. Doug had shown extraordinary fortitude and endurance in crawling back down the mountain but that was a matter of survival. Mo and Clive, who had lost their chance to go for the summit, had risked their lives in helping Doug and me to get down, though they couldn't very well have left us and certainly the thought would have never entered their minds. But if one wants to talks of heroes, I believe that Nick came the closest to that role. He was landed with the grim task of sitting it out, of taking desperately difficult decisions armed with inadequate information, of organising first Doug's evacuation and then mine. This kind of role demands greater moral courage and fortitude than direct involvement in a crisis where the struggle for personal survival has a stimulus of its own.

As for the villain, that was the Ogre himself. He was to leave us all with wounds that were going to take a long time to heal. He had played cat and mouse with us. He had had his fun and then, having battered and mauled us, had let us go.

CHAPTER EIGHT

K2

'Going to hang up your boots now, are you?' had been a recurrent question in 1976. The layman tended to assume that having led a successful expedition to Everest there were no other challenges left. This, of course, was far from the truth. The Ogre was to prove able to provide enough alternative challenges for a lifetime, but even before Doug's invitation, I had been looking for another big long-term challenge and had put in my application for K2, second highest mountain in the world. Only 237 metres lower than Everest, steeper and more dramatic, towering in splendid isolation over the other peaks of the upper Baltoro Glacier, it is one of the most magnificent mountains in the world and, in 1976, had only had one ascent – by an Italian expedition in 1954.

I wanted to tackle a new route, but to do it with a small expedition. My original invitation to five members of the 1975 Everest expedition had been reduced by the tragic death of Dougal the previous year. I was left with Doug, Nick and Tut, Pete Boardman, and Jim Duff as a high-altitude climbing doctor. But then came the question of the route. I certainly didn't want to repeat the Abruzzi Spur, the route of the only ascent. An American expedition, led by Jim Whittaker, had attempted the formidable North-West Ridge in 1975 but had barely gained a footing on the bottom of it. The entire western aspect of the mountain seemed very testing, being both steeper and more rocky than the South-West Face of Everest. More attractive to me was a nearly-successful Polish route on the North-East Ridge. For this was mainly on snow and seemed more suited to a small expedition than any of the western routes.

But I came under the same pressure that had occurred in 1972 and 1975. I had originally preferred the concept of a small Everest expedition going for the technically easier and better known South Col route but then it had been Doug and Dougal who had persuaded me to go for broke on the South-West Face. This time it was Pete, his confidence boosted by Everest and even more by his impressive ascent of the West Face of Changabang with Joe Tasker in the autumn of 1976. We were having a K2 expedition meeting at the Clachaig Hotel in Glencoe in February 1977. Pete put up a strong case for an attempt on the West Face. Inevitably he was backed by Doug. My own imagination was caught, and so I agreed, but on the proviso that the team was increased to eight and that we would plan on sieging it. But which route to go for? Discarding the ridges attempted by the Americans and the Poles, we turned our attention to the West Ridge.

On the Ogre my eyes had frequently strayed over to K2, a perfect pyramid shape that cut the eastern horizon, dominating the jumble of peaks around it, but now in the summer of 1977, I was nursing my wounds. I had lost over ten kilos, my ribs still ached and my left hand was part-paralysed. I couldn't walk more than a few hundred metres without needing to take a rest. It was the end of August before I felt up to working on the K2 expedition. Time was slipping by and we hadn't even started looking for a sponsor or getting together the gear and food we were going to need.

At first I was quite relaxed, confident that after the single letter I had had to write to Alan Tritton of Barclays to get sponsorship for Everest, companies would now be queuing up to give us their support. I was soon disillusioned. It is much harder getting sponsorship for the second highest mountain in the world. It was no good describing it as more beautiful and the most challenging. The public relations industry likes only the biggest and best.

Eventually support came from perhaps a surprising quarter when my literary agent George Greenfield happened to meet the financial director of the London Rubber Company's wife at a cocktail party. Best known for the manufacture of Durex, they were seeking a fresh image, and while they were not prepared to underwrite the entire cost of the expedition, which I had budgeted at around £60,000, they would give us £20,000 which took us a good way along the road to solvency.

I was now fully embarked on the organisation. We invited Joe Tasker, Pete's partner on Changabang, to join us, and Tony Riley who had been on the Latok expedition and was a film-maker. With no single sponsor taking over the complete financial responsibility of the expedition, George advised us to form ourselves into a limited company to give individual members some protection just in case things went wrong. It also had the useful effect of formalising our relationship and making it clear that each one of us had an equal stake in the enterprise.

We had a series of planning meetings at Nick's house in Bowdon, since it was the most centrally placed for all of us. Some of the others found it all a little too formal with its agenda and minutes, yet it was this very formality that ensured that everyone had a say and that the decisions of the group were acted upon. Tut, helped by Joe Tasker, was looking after the equipment – they were both now running climbing shops; Pete was getting all the food, while Nick acted as treasurer.

Most of the team who had been with me before knew the form, knew too that they could bend things to suit their own purposes as the climb unfolded. Joe, being new to it all, found this less easy. He had an inquisitive mind, sharpened, perhaps, by the time he had spent in a seminary training to become a priest. He took nothing for granted and frequently questioned my proposals. The expedition contract was a case in point. We obviously needed a contract since we were obligated to a newspaper and a publisher for articles and a book. For my last three expeditions I had used a contract form produced by George Greenfield that originated from a 1960s services expedition to Greenland. In it the members of the team promised to obey their leader at all times. I don't think any of us had taken much notice of this, knowing that on the mountain my authority would depend on the team's respect for the way I was running the expedition at the time and that any signatures back in Britain would be irrelevant.

But Joe did question this part of the contract. I remember feeling defensive at the time, the more so because I could see his point and yet resented my authority being threatened. In the end he signed simply because everyone else had done, but it left me feeling that Joe was a bit of a barrack-room lawyer – the classic reaction of any bureaucrat who has a comfortable system working and feels annoyed with anyone who questions it.

I was working as general co-ordinator and chief fund-raiser. I also spent a lot of time on logistic planning, once again using a computer, though this time I was able to bring it back home, a reflection of how much smaller computers were becoming.

We were trying to lay siege to a mountain wall that was almost as high and probably steeper than the South-West Face of Everest, with a team of eight as opposed to the sixty we had had on Everest in 1975. As I started playing through the logistics it very quickly became apparent that our team was too small. We simply couldn't ferry all the supplies, fixed rope and oxygen we were planning to use for the summit bid without using up too much time and exhausting ourselves in the process.

It could be argued that we would have been better off trying to climb it in pure Alpine-style – packing our sacks at the bottom and moving continuously until we reached the top, but the scale of the face and level of difficulty seemed too great. You can't really carry more than ten days' food for a single push and it looked as if we could easily take more than ten days to reach the summit.

Another possible compromise would be to establish a line of fixed rope linked by camps on to the middle reaches of the mountain and then go for the top Alpine-style. This would mean doing without oxygen, since we couldn't possibly carry the bottles even in a partial Alpine-style push. I was worried by this prospect, since I had no illusions about my own high-altitude performance. I had serious doubts whether I would be able to get to the top of K2 without oxygen and I very much wanted to get there. On Everest I had been resigned to sublimating my own summit ambitions in the overall running of the expedition, but I didn't want to do this again.

In the end I abandoned trying to climb the mountain by computer with the thought that we would have to rise above the logistic barriers – one usually did! With that thought I plunged into the mass of work that inevitably accompanies the organisation of a major expedition and also my own work to earn a living, lecturing about how Doug and I had struggled up and down the Ogre. On top of this we had agreed with LRC that each member of the team would visit at least one of the LRC factories. I drew the Durex factory in the East End of London.

I can still visualise the assembly line – long baths of liquid latex rubber, with hundreds of giant phalluses, going round and round on a long spindle, dipping into the baths. On either side of the baths were seated lines of women whose job was to peel off the contraceptives once they were completed. I could sympathise with royalty who always seem to be visiting factories, though I am sure they have never been to one like this, as I walked down the line surrounded by a little cluster of managers, trying to think of intelligent questions.

'Do you find this job interesting? – How do you maintain quality control?'

I got an answer to that – and was shown another phallus, on which were placed randomly selected sheaths and into which was blasted a jet of compressed air that would seek out any leaks. I watched bemused.

But things were going well. We had now got enough newspaper, film and book contracts to cover the cost of the expedition. British Leyland were lending us two Sherpa vans to carry all our gear out overland and the equipment was coming together. It was just before Christmas 1977 when I noticed a big septic pustule on the side of my chest where I had broken my ribs. I went down to our family doctor and he sent me into the local hospital. Hugh Barber, the orthopaedic consultant, told me that it was almost certainly caused by osteomyelitis, a bone infection resulting from my broken ribs.

They put me under an anaesthetic, opened up the pustule and scraped it out, down to the bone, hoping to remove the infection. But in February, only a few months before we were due to set out for K2, the boil reappeared. I was in the middle of a lecture period and was meant to be giving a lecture and opening a climbing wall in Sunderland a couple of days later. This time Hugh cut an even wider hole, gave my ribs another good scrape and then despatched me, stitched up, sore and aching in time to give my lecture. It was another fortnight before I could start running again to train for K2.

I had only been jogging as a regular training schedule for a couple of years. Before Everest in 1975 I had thought that a brisk walk up High Pike was quite sufficient. It was Louise, my secretary, who started running some time in 1976. She joined me shortly after we moved permanently to Cumbria in 1974 to assist with the organisation of the Everest expedition and has been with us ever since, looking after my affairs when I'm away, helping Wendy, becoming a close friend and adviser to both of us and doing much of the basic administrative work on all my expeditions, as well as helping me write my books. The first tentative jog we both made was around our block, about a mile of tracks to Pott's Ghyll, a house tucked away to the west at the bottom of the fell. A quick lunchtime run became a regular feature. We slowly expanded its length, first adding a leg up to the spoil tip of the old barytes mine about 120 metres above the house, then going for the summit of High Pike itself. This gave around four hundred metres of climbing and a run of five miles. I then started going further afield, south-east across to Carrock Fell, whose summit is girdled with the remains of an iron-age fort, and south-west to Knott, a round hump with a sprawl of grassy ridges embracing secret valleys in this least trodden of all the North-ern Fells.

My companion was Bess, our Staffordshire bull terrier, and then Bodie (short for Boadicea), an indeterminate mix of sheepdog, setter, perhaps a bit of lurcher and heaven knows what else. She is a fine-boned dog, nervous and affectionate, with a good head for heights and real ability as a climber. My running has brought me a deeper and more intimate knowledge and love for the hills that border our home. Running amongst them has become a very important part of my life.

By the beginning of May I had built up my running fitness once again. We had packed all the expedition gear, squeezed it into our two Sherpa vans and they were on their way, overland to Pakistan, supervised by Tony Riley.

The rest of us were going to fly out to Pakistan in early May. I had decided to go out three days early with Pete Boardman so that we could shop for local food and get through a lot of basic administration before the rest of the team arrived.

Tony was at the airport to greet us. He had had an eventful trip having been nearly caught up in the Russian invasion of Afghanistan. There were tanks in the streets of Kabul and the two vans had only just got through the Khyber Pass before the frontier closed. I don't think any of us gave him full credit for the way he had got the gear to Pakistan under very trying conditions.

I enjoyed the next few days. I spent more time with Pete than I had done on the entire 1975 Everest expedition. We called round to the Ministry of Tourism, had our initial briefing and met Captain Shafiq, our Liaison Officer. He was short, well-built and immensely enthusiastic. I took an immediate liking to him. Everything was 'no problem'.

The three days were filled with visits to the air cargo hangar to try and find the boxes we had air-freighted out at the last minute, trips to the bank to draw money and excursions into Rawalpindi to buy local food from the bazaar – sacks of lentils, flour, dried tomato and chillies to the accompaniment of cups of black tea, bargaining and chatter. It brought us closer both to the country itself and the reality of the expedition. At the same time I got to know Pete better, found that we were very much on the same wavelength in that we liked to be soundly organised, and I felt that we probably had a similar approach to mountaineering, a combination of romanticism and ambition, allied to a methodical approach to climbing. I felt at ease in his company and enjoyed working with him.

With the arrival of the complete team, the tempo hotted up. We had a series of social engagements and a lecture on the Ogre expedition to give at the British Club. I had already given one for the British Council and was very happy to leave Doug to do this one. Climbers rarely enjoy listening to each other's lectures or, for that matter, giving them, knowing that friends and colleagues are in the audience. The rest of us sat by the swimming pool swilling down beer while Doug gave an alfresco lecture to a packed audience. There was a reception in Rawalpindi, laid on by LRC for Pakistan dignatories – it was at this that we learnt that one of the factors that had influenced them in sponsoring us was that they had been trying to open a contraceptive factory at Karachi – and then an all-night party at Caroline Weaver's, the Embassy secretary with whom most of us were staying again.

We were due to fly out to Skardu the next day. I felt like a harassed sheepdog as I chivvied my hung-over team to the airport to catch the plane. It was a repeat of the previous year – the same spectacular flight to Skardu, the hectic selection of porters, the jeep and tractor journey to Dasso. It was good to be walking once again, to recognise a cluster of houses, a multiveined rocky crag or a solitary briar bush by the path. We also recognised some of the Balti porters who had been with us the previous year.

But this time it was more luxurious. We had with us two Hunzas. Sher Khan was to be our cook, though we found that he needed constant supervision and had no experience of European processed foods. The other one was very different. Quamajan was going to act as a high-altitude porter and generally liaise with the other porters. He had been on several expeditions, spoke good English and was immensely helpful. He quickly became a good friend and was very much a member of the team. The Hunzas are the Karakoram's version of the Sherpa and are very different in both physique and personality from the Balti who live in the valleys bordering the Baltoro massif. Quamajan's hair was almost ginger and his features European, as are those of many Hunzas. Occupying the valley north of Gilgit leading to one of the political and geographical cross-roads of the great mountain chain dividing Asia and India, the Hunzas are reputed to be descendants of one of Alexander's armies and certainly an amazing number of them are blue-eyed and fair-skinned.

The journey to Paiju, the camp-site just short of the snout of the Baltoro Glacier, was uneventful and relaxed. We were now on fresh ground and had just crossed the Panmah river which, since it was early in the season, was still fordable, though it was a chilling and frightening experience, with the waters coming over our knees, pulling at our legs and undermining the rounded stones underfoot. We crossed it in groups, clinging on to each other for support.

At Paiju our porters were due a regulation day's rest. It was a delightful spot, the last glade of trees before the Baltoro Glacier. After seven days' continuous walking it was good to have a day to catch up with letter writing. It was late afternoon. The porters were encamped in small groups under the trees across the stream. I was aware of the murmur of talk mingled with the babble of the water. Shafiq, sitting in the entrance of his tent, was arguing with one of the porters. As their voices began to rise in anger more and more porters gathered round. Suddenly, Shafiq leapt from the tent and began hurling stones at the audience to disperse them.

I was just hurrying over to try to cool things when he rushed after one of the porters with a rock in his hand and next moment had the man on the ground as if he was about to smash out the unfortunate porter's brains. Doug, Nick and I rushed up, seized the stone from Shafiq's hand, and tried to find out what on earth was going on. By this time all the porters were on their feet, crowding around us, shouting, screaming and gesticulating. Shafiq, in a rage, was shouting, 'He insulted me. He assaulted me. I'm going to put him in prison.'

As far as I could see it had been Shafiq that had done all the assaulting but I was more worried about calming everyone down – the porters were building themselves up into a state of hysteria and, if we weren't careful, they might all take off, leaving us in the lurch.

'But Shafiq, what was the cause of the trouble in the first place?'

At this Shafiq plunged into another torrent of Urdu with everyone shouting and screaming at once. I grabbed Shafiq and pulled him away from the crowd.

'I think Shafiq should apologise,' suggested Doug. 'It was he that started all the agro.'

'You can't undermine his authority too much. We've got to try to help him out of this.'

It took about half an hour to discover that the porters wanted to be paid in advance before they set foot on the Baltoro Glacier, that they weren't happy with the gear we had given them and that they thought they were owed another rest day. Checking with Nick, I conceded that we would pay them half their wages that same day, that we would also pay for the extra day's rest, which we owed them anyway, but that we couldn't improve on the shoes we had already issued, since we did not have any others.

The background shouting had died down to a mutter. The audience were beginning to drift away; that particular crisis was over. I walked back to my tent and slumped on to my sleeping-bag. Later that afternoon it began to rain. I knew we didn't have enough tarpaulins to cover all the loads and lay listening to the rain patter on the tent roof for half an hour before summoning the energy to crawl out of the tent and look for some plastic sheets. The porters, crouched round their cooking fires, were singing quietly – it sounded like a ballad – a mournful dirge in keeping with the heavy grey sky, the dripping branches of the trees and the barren rocky slopes stretching up into the clouds.

Next morning it was still raining. We delayed our departure for a couple of hours and then, as it began to clear, set out for the Baltoro Glacier. Powder snow avalanches were tumbling down the snow-veined ridges and gullies of Paiju, the rocky spires flanking the Baltoro Glacier were wreathed in shifting clouds – it was a confusion of greys and blacks – even the freshly fallen snow had a grey quality that rendered the scene unutterably grim. The Braldu river swirled brown and turgid from the snout of the glacier as I scrambled up the initial rocky slopes of the moraines. From the top we gazed over the tossing waves of piled rocks that we knew stretched some thirty miles up the glacier to Concordia near its head. There was an ominous, yet immensely exciting quality about it.

It was two days' walk to Urdokas, the last grassy camp-site on a terraced hill littered with gigantic boulders. There was an awe-inspiring panorama of granite peaks – Uli Biaho, slender and thrusting, the Trango group with gigantic walls and the slender finger of the Nameless Tower, almost dwarfed by the mass of its neighbours. We were going to have a day's rest in hope of an improvement in the weather. From Urdokas onwards we would be very vulnerable, since we barely had enough tarpaulins to go round for makeshift tents for the porters.

There were other problems as well. We were now responsible for feeding all our porters who had divided into little groups of different sizes, based on friendship, family or because they came from the same village. Issuing the rations each day was quite a task. They were entitled to a box of matches per day for each group and they got through them as well, for lighting fires, particularly in the rain, was never easy and they all smoked prodigiously. Unfortunately Pete and I had forgotten to stock up in Rawalpindi. We searched through all the boxes to dig out our spare lighters, but we were still short. The thought of the expedition failing for the want of a match haunted me.

I was more worried about the weather. There were two inches of fresh snow at Urdokas and I wondered what was it going to be like at Concordia. I therefore decided to push out an advance party to recce the ground ahead and find out if it was going to be possible to get the porters all the way to our proposed Base Camp on the Savoia Glacier. Doug and Joe were the obvious choices, since they were the only ones without any specific responsibility for the day-to-day running of the expedition. They took Quamajan with them and eight porters. By now Joe had had a chance to size up my leadership profile. His judgement of my decision-making was perceptive and not exactly flattering:

> On this trip, with Chris in overall command, there was a tendency to analyse his every statement or action, to sift out his train of thought and underlying intentions. On other expeditions he had engineered the pairing of people and subsequently the ordering of the movements on the mountain which would dictate the role of anyone in an attempt on the summit.
>
> Chris was changeable in his opinion and his great failing or strength was that he usually thought aloud. This gave the impression of uncertainty but was simply a process which most people conduct within themselves and then produce a considered final decision. An interpretation of Chris's overt mental process as uncertainty, and any subsequent attempts to impose a decision on him, was a mistake. No one succeeded in changing Chris's mind by any outright statement and each of us guarded the conceit that we had worked out the way to get Chris to adopt our own point of view, whatever premise he had started from, as if it were his own.

My version of this would be that I believed in talking through problems informally with other members of the team and was always ready to adapt my own views if their ideas seemed better. However, I didn't believe in doing this in the frame of a formal meeting, since it is all too easy to slip into the trap of running the expedition by committee when every decision has to be reached by a vote. This is an unwieldy way of making decisions and doesn't necessarily lead to the best choice. Tacitly it was accepted that I had the final say, though inevitably this led to lobbying, as Joe described:

> We all conspired to see whether we could each manage to win Chris over to doing what we wanted him to do, given that we knew his initial reaction had been negative.

Of the 300 porters we had had at Askole, 233 were left; they had consumed nearly seventy loads of food in the last four days. Nick had paid out £1500-worth of rupees in wages but still had over £20,000, all packed in an aluminium box that was carried by one of the porters. To them it was worth several fortunes – the equivalent of £1,000,000 in a London security van. And yet there were no special precautions. The porter allotted to carry it picked up the box in the morning and delivered it to Nick's tent at the end of the day. Everyone knew its contents but, perhaps because it belonged to all of us, it was totally safe.

The porters spent the day preparing chupatties over their wood fires, for this was the last of the wood. Beyond Urdokas they would be dependent on oil stoves. The rest of us lazed in the sun, read books and played on the boulders. We were told that a narrow chimney that cleaved a huge boulder had been climbed by Walter Bonatti back in 1954. We all had to climb it, watched by a group of Baltis. Another route was then pointed out up a thin crack in a bulging fifteen-metre wall. Galen Rowell had climbed this, we were told. Pete couldn't resist the challenge. He got about three-quarters of the way, became aware that he would injure, or perhaps even kill himself if he fell off, and called for a top rope. The Baltis were content to watch, except for Sher Khan, our cook, who was a natural climber and in his bare feet eased up boulder problems on which we were struggling in our specialised rock-climbing boots.

I felt happy and relaxed, even though there was an immense amount of work to do, so much more than in Nepal where one tended to leave everything to the Sherpas. Here we not only had to sort out the issue of the porters' food but also had to supervise closely the cooking of meals. The very pressure of work, the vast scale of the mountains and the threat of bad weather helped unite the team. We set out for Concordia on the 28th.

The Baltoro has some of the most exciting mountain scenery in the world. At the far end of the glacier is Gasherbrum IV, a shapely wedge of ice-veined granite; first to our right came Masherbrum – from this side fierce and inhospitable, bristling with icefalls and sheer rock walls. Next day we sighted the Mustagh Tower, improbably sheer and bulging, dominating the Biange Glacier. We arrived at Concordia late in the evening. It was snowing hard, causing almost white-out conditions. In an impassioned speech Shafiq had persuaded the porters that they were not fit to be considered Muslims but were just dirt, unless they made this one great effort to cover the last two stages in a single day. In the prevailing weather it had proved to be nearly disastrous. The porters were tired and cold, huddled under their tarpaulins. Some were still missing at dusk and came straggling in during the night.

But it dawned fine, the freshly fallen snow glistening in the early morning sun. K2, massive and snow-plastered, towered over the end of the Baltoro Glacier, framed by the shapely mass of Broad Peak and the fairytale pointed peaks of the Savoia group. Gasherbrum IV was even closer, rivalling K2 for threat and beauty, while across the glacier to the south-east was Chogolisa with its soaring snow ridges.

The sun warmed the porters' limbs and spirits. They were anxious to get started across the wide snowy basin at the confluence of the Savoia Glacier, that led up the western side of the mountain, and the Godwin Austen Glacier, that stretched round its eastern flank. For once the Baltis were hurrying, even ahead of us, in their haste to reach the site of the Base Camp of the Japanese expedition that had been on the mountain the previous year. There would be some good loot lying scattered in the snows. We saw a couple of tents snuggled against a rocky spur. Doug crawled out of one of them.

'What's it like up the Savoia?' I asked.

'Don't know. We only got here a couple of hours ago. Trouble with the porters.'

'What happened?'

'Two of them didn't wear their goggles. Got snow blind. Had a hell of a job getting them along. We'll go up the Savoia today.'

Our porters had now had enough. There was too much snow; the gear we had given them wasn't good enough; they were wet and cold; they wanted to go back. I couldn't blame them and was almost glad to see them go. There were too many to look after. We had brought enough clothing and footwear to equip twenty-five of the best of them to carry on to Base Camp. Nick started paying off the rest – the equivalent of £15,000 in a couple of hours. Each of them had a newly issued reference book, which I had to fill in and sign. It was late afternoon before we had finished. Doug and Joe got back just before dark. Doug wasn't pleased that I had let the porters go because he was enthusiastic about the route and keen to get started.

'I think as many of us as possible should get up there tomorrow. I want to have a look at the route up on to the ridge.'

I could feel myself being taken over by Doug's forceful drive to get on to the mountain, to get climbing, to be out in front. But all my instincts were against it. We needed to get ourselves organised, sort the loads and keep together as a team. It would be all too easy to let Doug and Joe shoot out ahead, get the initiative, and for the rest of the team to trail behind like an elongated tail.

I decided, therefore, that we should just make a carry and a reconnaissance the following day so I, and the rest of the team, could also see what was involved and, from that knowledge, decide on our future course of action. Doug accepted my decision.

It was another frustrating slog to get our remaining porters up to Base Camp next day. One old man, who was one of their main spokesmen and whom I had kept on against my better judgement, announced he was going back. We split his load between Pete and myself. Another younger man also wanted to return but I drove him on, threatening to sack him and take all his newly issued gear from him if he let us down.

The walk dragged on, clinging to the side of Angel Peak, up a sérac-threatened icefall, across avalanche-prone slopes just above the glacier, then at last we too reached the little pile of loads under a tarpaulin in the big emptiness of the Savoia Glacier. The West Ridge, like the corner of a gigantic pyramid, stretched above in a complex mesh of snow fields, rock walls, runnels, and gullies. It looked so much bigger and more difficult than the South-West Face of Everest, but it also looked safe, freer from objective danger.

As soon as the porters got back I could hear them grumbling and Shafiq's voice rising once more in anger. The walk was too far, they wanted more gear, more money. The Japanese had paid them twice as much last year. Quamajan, who had been with the Japanese, was able to tell us that this was not true.

In the end I compromised and promised them more pay on condition they carried the next day and didn't demand any more. At last the arguments were over. The others had sat on the side-lines listening, worried at the threat to the continuance of the expedition. Tut now produced a bottle of whisky, Nick, a splendidly obscene inflatable rubber doll that his workmates had presented him with at his going-away party. We laughed and drank and talked into the night.

The following morning I decided to accompany the porters again, just to make sure they made it to Base Camp. As so often happened with these volatile people, there were no problems at all. They went further without a rest, were laughing and singing and made the round journey in three and a half hours. The weather seemed to have improved and the next day, 2 June, five of us moved up to establish Base Camp. Doug, Joe and I arrived first and walked on a short distance up the Savoia Glacier to get a better view of the route. It looked huge and difficult, yet just feasible. We discussed how to reach the crest of the subsidiary ridge that led up to the West Ridge and then returned to camp both relaxed and excited.

Pete, who had set out for Base Camp later than the rest of us, had meanwhile been having a drama of his own. He was about two-thirds of the way across the snow field around the base of Angel Peak, when he saw the big sérac far above him collapse and a great wave of snow dust tumbling down towards him. He threw away his rucksack, turned and tried to run before he collapsed into the snow, pulled his hat over his face and crouched, huddled, as the wave of snow swept over him, penetrating his clothing and clutching at his face. Suddenly it was over. He was alive. It was as if the avalanche had never happened. The cloud of snow had settled, the freshly avalanched blocks merged with the snow that was already there. The sun shone out of a cloudless sky. There was no sound; nothing seemed to have changed. The only evidence of what had happened was his snow-covered clothes, his face wet and stinging from the melted powder and his heaving aching lungs.

He retrieved his sack which was partly buried and hurried, panting, across the avalanche slope to the other side. Once out of danger he sank into the snow, wheezing and coughing to rest for an hour before continuing the walk, until he met Nick and Quamajan who had come down to look for him. That evening Pete wrote in his diary:

> One of those magic moments, sat on the Savoia Glacier listening to Carole King singing 'Tapestry'. The sun has moved off us, but wind is pluming cold powder snow off the summits behind us. K2 is catching the evening sun. The tents and Base tent are up and soup is on the stove.
>
> I am happy to be up here. I think we all are. I can't imagine any other nationality having this sort of atmosphere to enjoy ourselves so much. K2 is a great squat pyramid, a sobering thought that its summit is 11,000 feet above us ... Also I'm glad to be alive.

CHAPTER NINE

Avalanche

'I've peed into China!'

That was Nick with his broad gap-tooth grin, returning to camp the following afternoon after he and Pete had climbed up to the Savoia Saddle at 6600 metres, confirming on the way that the northern flank of the ridge was much too steep and icy an approach to the West Ridge. However Doug and Joe had more success, finding a good route to the crest through the glacier to the south, and the following day Doug, Pete, Nick and I made our first serious foray onto the mountain hoping to find a good site for Camp I. The way through the small icefall at the confluence of the glacier was straightforward but there were some huge hidden crevasses, vast black bell-like chambers with barely perceptible mouths all too ready to suck down the unwary. Beyond, it opened out into a wide basin with a snow slope broken by little buttresses reaching up towards the crest of the ridge. It was steep enough to need a fixed rope and we got out the first drum, taking it in turns to run out a hundred metres each.

It was nearly midday and we had reached the first rock buttress. Doug typically wanted to press on to the foot of a big gendarme on the crest of the ridge. Nick was for stopping where we were.

Doug flared at him, saying, 'You're disagreeing with everything I say.'

Conciliatorily, I thought we should get somewhere in between, where there was a second bluff, and I ran out another reel of rope, took the wrong line and was shouted at by Doug, Pete and Nick. As Nick came up to join me he pointed out that I was unreeling the cable cylinder incorrectly, but he did so jokingly, hesitantly, having already been put down by Doug.

I noted in my diary:

As Nick said, in his job back at Ferranti's they are constantly making suggestions, criticising, to get the right solution in the end. It is unfortunate that Doug and Nick over-react to each other; yet I feel a real affection for Doug. He has a good sized ego which he doesn't really acknowledge, but he has a tremendous warmth of heart and a great climbing drive which will stand us all in good stead.

The following day Doug, Pete and Joe moved up to the site of Camp I, which, in the end, was placed at the compromise half-way spot at a height of around 6000 metres. Tut seemed to be acclimatising slowly, was wheezing a lot and had pains in his chest. Jim Duff was staying behind with him, while Nick, intensely frustrated, was also going to have to wait at Base until he had paid off all but eight of our porters.

I went up to our first camp on the following day, 6 June. It already had that well-established look, gear and food boxes scattered over the ledges we had dug, yellow stains in the snow and traces of discarded food. The others were still on the hill as I shoved my gear into Doug's tent – Joe and Pete were sharing the second one. They got back down in the late afternoon, well pleased with themselves, having nearly reached the crest of the ridge. Pete described the day in his diary:

> We got away much too late, in a sort of staggered manner. Doug went first and even then the snowfall of the night was melting in the morning sunshine and the first porters were arriving. The sun wastes me away, enervates, dissolves me. I had to sort out a 600-foot rope that had fallen off its reel and tangled itself. Then I tried hauling it behind me but couldn't move in the collapsing snow.
>
> Bloody 9mm fixed ropes aren't non-stretch and so its impossible to use them to pull yourself over collapsing steps. Doug leading without a sack on – all right for him! One compensation – expanding views of Broad Peak through Negrotto Pass and over Angel Peak's flanks.
>
> 600-feet ropes – Doug led two; then Joe relinquished his rope, went back down and I ran that out. Easy-angled stuff, but traverses and an unstable feel to it, soggy, on top of hard ice. We then made a route-finding error that cost us two hours, missing a gully. Deceptive from below.
>
> I hope we can use porters to Camp 2 and site it at the 22,000-foot mark. We're using so much fixed rope that when we get higher we'll have to pull a lot of it up to use again. Climbing, staggering, only managing five paces at a time, thoughts completely elsewhere, body a tortured cell in a hostile environment.
>
> Just stopped writing as an enormous sérac collapsed up the valley, spreading a cloud of dust and a rumble.

Doug squeezed into the little Denali tent that I was sharing with him – we both seemed too big for it. Pete wryly commented:

> 'Not much room' says Chris, at least he hasn't got his typewriter with him! – 5°C – cold evening light outside – one can adapt to almost anything. Doug reading *Healing Ourselves* now. Chris refreshed after a day's 'rest' –

twelve hours of writing reports, including a long *Sunday Times* article. Tony Riley doing chatty ITV interviews – a real lads' trip!

The following morning Joe and I were to go off in front to push the route out. We climbed the fixed ropes to the previous day's high point. I felt all the weight of organising and planning fall away from me. Joe also noticed, commenting:

> He seemed to relax from his assertive role once free of his paperwork, calculations and the onerous duty of presenting reports on progress for TV News, radio and newspaper. It was only the second time that I had climbed with him and he was eager to do as much as anyone. He took pleasure in the progress so far and enthused simply and directly about how well everything was going.

For my part, my image of Joe the barrack-room lawyer who was frequently provokingly right slid away. We were happily attuned choosing the route, delighted to be out in front and climbing. I led up a shallow icy gully and escaped from it on to the crest of a rocky arête that bordered the broad snow basin leading across to the pyramid of K2 itself.

Back home I had spent hours examining a big blow-up picture of K2 and had always assumed that we would skirt the top of this basin. It looked easy-angled and I thought secure. Joe murmured about Doug thinking that we should follow the gully to the crest of the ridge, but this seemed a long way round. I urged for the basin and Joe agreed without further demur, climbing down into it. The angle was so easy we didn't even bother to rope up. We just plodded steadily across. I took the lead at first, then feeling the altitude, handed over to Joe who finished the trail-breaking to the foot of a bergschrund which seemed to give some shelter from the slope above. At 6400 metres this was to be our second camp.

Pete and Doug had been in support that day and reached our high point with loads of rope and hardware just as we set off down. Back at Camp I, Nick and Quamajan had arrived and had a brew ready for us. Sitting in the afternoon sun, gazing over the vista of peaks to the south and west, we began discussing plans for the next day. I wanted a rest day, Pete wanted a go in front.

Doug said, 'Well, shall you and I go up tomorrow?'

I could feel my control of the expedition slipping away from me so quickly chipped in, 'Let's draw lots for it.' Nick also wanted to be included. I must confess I was quite relieved I didn't pick a short match. Joe and Pete were the lucky ones and Doug was obviously disappointed, coming out with a heavy, 'It's a big responsibility. You could waste days if you made a mistake.'

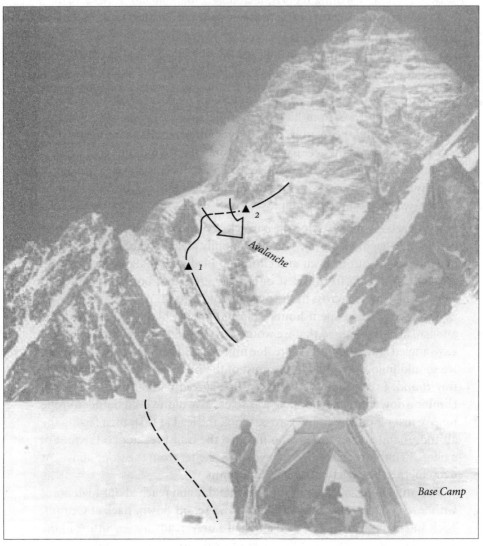

▲ *Tented camp* ——— *Route using fixed ropes* — — — *Route not using fixed ropes*
West Ridge of K2

Doug's attitude underlined once more the fundamental difference in our approach to expeditioning. Doug prefers a spontaneous approach to climbing in which you climb, or eat, or come to decisions as the moment dictates in a structure-free situation. But through the sheer force of his personality, he ends up decision-maker and leader of that group. I am happier with quite a structured plan, a plan everyone has discussed, and see my role as leader to make decisions within that plan.

As for Doug, he had agonised during the Everest trip in 1975 but then, as the climb unfolded and he found himself out in front, had become more resigned to the structured nature of the expedition. I hoped that the same thing would occur this time, but it was more difficult to contain, because we were so much smaller a group and therefore very much more on top of each other.

Before we turned in Doug asked if I'd mind him changing tents.

'I was awake for at least three hours last night, what with your breathing and snoring and thrashing about.'

Long-suffering Nick said he was used to putting up with my snores, so Doug moved in with Quamajan. It was a petty matter but it showed how little things irritate out of all proportion at altitude, where an easily identifiable complaint can hide other stresses.

Joe and Pete moved up to Camp 2 the following day. Nick, Quamajan and I went with them carrying loads of food and tentage. The round trip only took three and a half hours and on getting back we found that Doug had tidied up the campsite and had a brew ready. After a successful day, enriched by a bright sun and cloudless sky, the tensions of the previous evening slipped away.

During the night a thick layer of cloud crept in from the west and we woke to a still, heavy gloom in the frosted dimness of the tent. Everything was silent until I pushed at the sagging walls to hear the swish of sliding snow on the outside and a flurry of ice crystals fell on our sleeping-bags. Peering outside, the air was full of snow. The ledges, and the gear piled on them, had vanished and the tops of the tents jutted out like shipwrecked boats. We debated whether to try a carry but eventually resigned ourselves to sitting out the storm. Pete and Joe were doing the same in relatively less comfort at Camp 2.

We were trapped in our tents for two days, but the third dawned clear and windy. We dug ourselves out, searched for gear under the uniform slope of fresh snow and at last were ready to set out for a carry to Camp 2. I could barely keep up with Nick and Doug who were sharing the trail-breaking.

Pete and Joe were also moving up:

Joe takes over and runs out 450 feet of 8mm rope, then another 150-foot pitch diagonally. The distances on this mountain are enormous, but it is important to maintain a springboard sense of urgency. Then I lead a couple of hundred feet, but still not able to see up the gully, the state of which is critical to the next big route-finding decision. Fantastic views – new peaks appear with every rope-length.

It dawned fine again the next morning. Up at Camp 2 Pete and Joe climbed the fixed ropes they had put out the previous day and began on new ground. Back at Camp 1 I had decided to take the day off. That night a head-cold had overwhelmed me, blocking my nostrils and making my head feel like a giant over-ripe melon. I had snuffled and snored all night, keeping Nick awake and not sleeping much myself either. I felt lousy but it was good to lie in the tent until the sun crept round to our flank of the ridge and we could feel its heat on the tent walls.

I heard a shout from below. It was the porters on their way up. Jim Duff was with them and I dropped down a length of rope to give him a hand with his sack. It was good to see him, suave, relaxed Jim, with his ready smile through his dark beard. His sack was heavy but I felt that my strength had returned and I carried it easily up the fixed ropes. I made the Balti porters some tea and listened to the news from Base Camp. It was only after the porters had left that Jim told me, 'Tut didn't want me to tell you. He was going to leave a note. He's going home. His chest hasn't cleared up. He's certainly under the weather.'

It didn't surprise me, somehow. Quite apart from his chest, Tut had been thinking of home throughout the expedition and particularly of his girl-friend, Jane, whom he was planning to marry when we got back. I was sorry that he hadn't felt able to tell me what he was doing, for I would not have tried to dissuade him and certainly wasn't angry. We weren't fighting a war. We were playing a game, admittedly a very serious one, and it must be up to the individual to decide whether he wants to go on or not and the level of risk that he wants to accept. Tut's departure would leave us short-handed, but that was something we would have to cope with.

Jim and I were sitting in the sun, talking about Tut's decision and expedition prospects. It was a wonderful cloudless, windless day. We felt relaxed, happy to be ensconced on this high perch surrounded by some of the most magnificent peaks in the world when suddenly, with little more than a muffled rumble, a huge avalanche billowed down the icefall between us and the main mass of K2. Instinctively I dived for my camera and started taking pictures. Jim shouted:

'For God's sake stop. The lads could be in that.'

'They can't. I'm sure they can't. That's just broken away from the icefall. They'll be above it.'

But I stopped taking pictures. The avalanche poured down to the glacier over 400 metres below, forming a great boiling cloud of white that thinned, dissipated and then vanished. There were no signs of debris on the avalanche cone that had already been formed by repeated sérac falls. It was as still as it had been before. The sun blazed out of the blank sky, the mountains were changeless in the flat glare of midday, but we didn't chat any more, just sat and waited. I tried to pretend there was nothing to worry about but switched on the walky-talky radio. Ten minutes dragged by, the crackle and hum of the radio the only sound.

'Please, please, God, don't let them have been in it.'

'Hello, is anyone on the air? Over.' It was Doug's voice, distorted by static.

'This is Chris. Are you all right? Over.'

'Nick's copped it. The whole bloody slope went and he was in the middle of it. Didn't have a hope.'

'Roger. Can you get back down? Over.' Keep a tight grip. Hold back emotion. Get them back, find out what's happened.

'Yes, we're on our way back now.'

'Be careful. Take it steady. See you soon. Out.'

I switched off the set and crouched and cried. Nick, my closest friend, was gone, and the pain deep inside welled up, with the confusion of shock and a terrible growing sense of guilt. I had chosen that route. I had been so convinced it was safe. A figure came round the corner, tumbled and half-ran down the fixed rope into the camp. It was Doug. He slumped down beside the tent, his face in his hands. He was crying, too. I held his shoulder, felt very close to him and he started telling us what had happened.

On reaching the basin, Doug and Nick had decided to put a fixed line across it for greater security. The basin was full of fresh snow and if there were any small slides the rope would act as a handrail. Doug tied one end of a big reel of 5mm nylon cord round his waist, handed the reel to Quamajan to wind out, and set off, plodding through the snow. Nick set off after him. He was about seventy metres behind.

Doug had reached the other side and was just beneath the tent of Camp 2. Nick was in the middle of the basin. He hadn't clipped into the rope and was just walking along in Doug's footsteps when suddenly the entire slope above him and around him began to shift, breaking up into huge floes, jostling with each other, moving down inexorably, faster, breaking into small bits. And Nick was in the middle of it, struggling to stay on the surface until he was swept from sight over the séracs.

Doug sensed the avalanche but before he could do anything the rope round his waist, trailing back into the fast-shifting snows, plucked him from his steps and heaved him down the slope. He was tumbling head-over-heels, helpless, ever closer to the rushing torrent of snow, and then suddenly the momentum stopped, the cord had broken. Upside down, half buried in the snow, he was alive. On the other side of the basin, Quamajan, his hands burnt from the rope, was also on the edge of the avalanche. Pete and Joe had seen the avalanche and climbed back down their fixed rope to find Doug by the tent, still covered in snow.

'I'd written myself off there,' Doug said. And they talked of Nick. Just before setting out over the basin Doug had remarked to Nick: 'It looks like me and you going together for the top, youth.'

Pete and Joe packed a few items and they all started back across the firm avalanche-polished snow down to Camp 1. Doug joined Jim in his tent. They were close friends and had much in common. Pete joined me and Joe was sharing with Quamajan but joined Pete and myself to cook a meal and sit and talk. We avoided the accident or even the expedition, reminisced about Nick, telling outrageous stories about climbing weekends in Wales and booze-ups in the Peak District. I still half expected him to poke his head through the tent door; I hadn't accepted that the avalanche had occurred.

That night neither Pete nor I could sleep. We talked occasionally or just lay wrapped in our own thoughts, waiting for the dawn. I thought out the future of the expedition. I felt we should go on. We had always known that an accident could happen and I felt that, however deep my grief, we should continue. Pete felt the same.

It was snowing in the morning, the sky a grey gloom. Dark buttresses on the slopes below loomed through the cloud. The mountains of yesterday had vanished. Doug and Jim had already packed as if this was the end of the expedition. I contented myself with saying, 'Let's talk it over when we get back down to Base and all of us are together.'

On the way down we each went over to search the huge avalanche cone at the foot of the sérac wall but there was no sign of Nick. Thousands of tons of snow had fallen but though, high above, a great sickle-shaped scar marked where the wind slab had broken away, the cone didn't look any different from when we had seen it a few days before. Back at Base Camp we trickled in to the big mess tent. Sher Khan was brewing tea in one corner. There was a tense subdued atmosphere, born from shock and exacerbated by the knowledge that only we knew what had happened, that to Carolyn and the children, Matthew, Tom and Martha, Nick was still alive. They remained to be told.

Pete was the last to come in. Then we began to talk about what we should do next. I still felt that we should continue with the climb, not as a means of justifying Nick's death, you couldn't do that, but simply that this was part of what we had undertaken and somehow we had to come to terms with it. I had to fight hard to control my feelings, but I had thought it out many times in theory and now I was confronted with reality.

Doug had no doubts at all. He wanted to end the expedition, could see no point in going on and pointed out the agony that all our wives would have to go through if we prolonged our stay. Jim agreed with him and then, to my surprise, Joe also said he didn't see much point in going on. Tut had already stated that he was going home. Tony, though, was keen to carry on, quietly saying that he had come out to make a film and that he wanted to complete it. So that left Pete, Tony and myself, wanting to continue.

Pete wrote:

Only Chris, with me, wants to go on. Nick would certainly have gone on, would have been consistent. I say, I just love being in the mountains, seeing more peaks emerge, that I am enjoying myself and that is what I am here to do. But a host of outside influences and problems are affecting Tut, Doug and Jim. Doug swings like an emotional, powerful pendulum, and he and Joe presumably have Nuptse this year to look forward to.

I want to give the mountain everything I have, to have a struggle amongst overwhelming beauty above 25,000 feet.

But it was no good with just three of us. Doug, Jim and Tut had certainly made up their minds. With the expedition so divided there seemed no other prospect but retreat. So we turned to the business of breaking the news to Carolyn and the rest of Nick's family before the story got into the papers. We eventually agreed that Doug and I should go out together. I was split between my responsibility to the expedition as a whole and the fact that Nick was my closest friend. So Doug and I set out the next morning with Quamajan. There was a solace in action as we picked our way down the Savoia Glacier and then on down the Baltoro, glancing back at K2, towering, massive and now peaceful, at the end of the glacier. We walked till dusk and camped on a moraine about half-way down the Baltoro Glacier.

I now accepted our decision to call off the expedition and was even relieved. I was longing to get back to Islamabad to be able to phone Wendy and, at the same time, dreaded having to carry our news. In our own tiny microcosm of a world we had come to terms with the tragedy. It didn't reduce my grief, but it was something that I could control, store away while I coped with our daily functions. Each day's walk, the need to place feet carefully on the rocky moraines, the heavy fatigue all helped to alleviate the aching pain. But once we were back in Islamabad we would have to tell others what had happened.

It took us five days to get back to the roadhead, long hard walks, a frightening fording of the Korophon river, succulent apricots and mulberries at Dasso. With just Doug and myself together there was no conflict. The friendship, the mutual affection and respect that had grown over the years we had climbed and expeditioned together could flourish without the external pressures of group politics, different ethical stances on how to climb a mountain or raise funds. We found support in each other and although we knew that our climbing plans for the immediate future were almost certainly going to take different paths, in accepting this, we could also sustain our friendship.

And then we were at the roadhead, an afternoon's bone-shaking in the jeep back to Skardu, and our peaceful limbo was over. We made our report to the District Commissioner. He was kind and sympathetic, promising to embargo the news until we had contacted the next of kin. We got a flight out the following morning. At the embassy our way was smoothed and I was able to phone home, giving Wendy the grim task of letting Carolyn know what had happened. As so often, it was our wives back home who had the toughest task, who had to sit it out whilst we played our dangerous game, and who, now, had to cope with the cruellest part of all.

I had already lost too many friends from climbing but this hit me the hardest of all. Nick was not only a superb mountaineer, but had given me vital support on all my major expeditions. Loyal, yet logical, he was consistent and totally fair, not just to me but to the concept of the expedition as a whole and to the interests of its members. Within an expedition he combined humour, a capacity for discussion and analysis and a selfless willingness to work for the group as a whole.

But most of all I had lost a friend whom I was always glad to see, whom I could drop in on at any time and with whom I had done some of my most enjoyable climbing. Mike Thompson had commented after the 1975 expedition on how, at this level of mountaineering, it was like being prematurely aged with so many of one's friends and contemporaries dying around one.

I felt this acutely as I flew back to Britain with the responsibility of telling Carolyn exactly what had happened on K2.

CHAPTER TEN

Chinese Overtures

Two nights after I got back to Britain, a septic pustule over my old rib wound erupted and burst. It was as if my body had suppressed the poison until that moment but, now that my journey was over and I had talked to Carolyn, sharing her grief and reliving those final days of the expedition, my defences collapsed and the dormant bacteria hidden in my ribs burst forth. A week later a section of my lower rib was removed, leaving a gaping cavity that had to be allowed to heal from the inside, to ensure that no further pockets of infection remained. I had at least been lucky that I had osteomyelitis in a bone that I could do without.

I spent the summer convalescing and was beginning to look into the future. George Greenfield had suggested that I should write a book on the broader spectrum of adventure. I had thought little about it before the expedition but now welcomed it, almost as a therapy. It took me out of my own climbing experience to look at the whole field of adventure. In the next two years I was to go round the world interviewing the subjects for my book, *Quest For Adventure*, becoming immersed in the mystery of long-distance sailing, of polar exploration, flying the Atlantic by balloon and reaching the moon. It was intriguing to meet so many people from widely differing backgrounds with the common factors of a taste for risk and the passionate curiosity for the unknown that marks the adventurer.

The one who impressed the most of all was Geoff Yeadon the cave diver. I could not contemplate swimming and wriggling down passages far beneath the earth, visibility in the muddy water down to little more than centimetres, with the knowledge that if anything went wrong with the equipment, drowning would be inevitable. He found it equally difficult to contemplate rock-climbing and was just as appalled at the prospect of making difficult moves above a long drop. I suspect though that our motivation for our different ventures was very similar, with the stimulus of risk, the fascination of the unknown and, in his case, the wonder of stalactite-filled caverns far beneath the earth. His ventures into the cave system of Keld Head, beneath the gentle limestone hills of Yorkshire, came closer to true exploration than any form of adventure on the surface of the earth today. The remotest spots can be reached by helicopter, or scanned from planes or satellites, but the only way of tracing the passage of a cave is physically to follow it.

I did, in a very modest way, share the adventure of sailing with Robin Knox-Johnston, joining him in *Suhaili*, the boat he had sailed single-handed non-stop round the world to win the Golden Globe race. He was enjoying a family sailing holiday with his wife and daughter and I sailed with them from Oban to the Isle of Skye. The deal was that I should show him climbing in return for learning something about sailing. Mildly sea-sick, I clutched the tiller as we approached Loch Scavaig in a choppy sea. Then it was my turn. I took him up the ridge of the Dubhs, several hundred metres of rounded boiler-plate slabs of gabbro. Half-way up the route was barred by a sheer drop and it was necessary to abseil. Robin didn't like the look of the standard climbing method and insisted on using a complicated system he had devised for going up and down his mast. I learnt a great deal in those few days at sea, both about sailing and sailors.

A few weeks later I was near Houston, Texas at the NASA Manned Spacecraft Center. Reaching the moon might have been man's great adventure of the twentieth century, but I felt little in common with the astronauts I met there. It wasn't just their dependence on technology, it was also the way they had been selected, almost programmed, for their roles. But some days later in a small town called Lebanon, in his home state of Ohio, I met Neil Armstrong, then chairman of an engineering company. As we started talking I couldn't help wondering what we would find in common and yet, as he described his work as a test pilot flying the X15 rocket plane that reached a height of 63,000 metres and a speed five times the speed of sound, I could see that the way he was exploring the limits of what the aircraft could do was very similar to the climber taking himself to his own limits on a stretch of rock.

In choosing my adventures I had set myself the guidelines that each adventure should represent a major innovative step into the unknown in that particular field – the first men on the moon, the first to row the Atlantic, cross deserts, explore the Poles or push forward the bounds of climbing. As a result of my self-imposed rules I found my book populated by men. Women, whilst being increasingly involved in almost every type of adventure, were still following, albeit very closely, in their footsteps.

The one area, however, where they seemed on an equal footing was in the realm of adventurous travelling. There is a long tradition of great women travellers like Gertrude Bell, Annie Taylor, and Freya Stark, who ventured into places few, male or female, had ever reached. One great modern-day traveller came to stay with us. Christina Dodwell had been wandering across Africa, using horses, camels and dug-out canoes for transport. In the course of her travels she was threatened on several occasions, sometimes with amorous advances, sometimes because she was a lone white, but by keeping cool and taking a positive stance, she managed to talk her way out of each situation. In some ways her sex might have been a positive advantage, since a woman does not offer the same potential threat as a man and is also better at avoiding confrontation.

I took her off climbing one afternoon and in spite of being caught by a rain storm that turned the rock into a vertical skating rink, she quietly worked her way up it without a trace of fluster. My research for *Quest For Adventure* certainly broadened my own outlook and brought me new friends scattered across the world but my love of climbing was undiminished. I used the excuse of a lecture tour on the west coast of the United States to visit Yosemite, climb some obscure rock towers called the City of Rocks in Idaho, and crumbling old granite near Mount Shasta in North California. But I was not planning any other expedition and had even withdrawn from a venture that Nick and I had planned together to climb Kang Taiga in Nepal in the autumn of 1979.

There was also more time to enjoy my family. Daniel and Rupert were growing up fast and were now twelve and ten years of age. Although they had the inevitable sibling rows, they basically got on well together, playing endless games of soldiers, as I also had done as a youngster. I suppose it is inevitable that parents enjoy trying to pass on their own pursuits to their children and equally probable that their children will want to find other outlets, if only to establish their own identities. Daniel quite enjoyed climbing and occasionally came out with me. He wasn't a natural gymnast but had a good head for heights and remained cool under stress. Rupert, on the other hand, though small, had a superb athletic build and was already able to outrun me without much trouble. He has no head for heights, however, and consequently did not enjoy climbing. It was in skiing that we could share the most. We had our first ski holiday together in the spring of 1979 in Verbier. It was a delight to see how quickly the lads caught up with my own fairly timid performance and then began to outstrip me.

At first glance Wendy and I have little in common. She does not climb, nor is she particularly interested in the climbing fraternity. But she has always supported my projects in so many direct and practical ways over the years, in the selection of pictures and the design of my books, in the creation of audio-visual sequences for my lectures and a critical appraisal of my writing. The most important thing for me is that she is always there, quietly supportive of all my ventures.

Her adventures are of the mind, exploring her own creative ideas. She went to art school and when we met was working as an illustrator of children's books. Since then, whilst rearing our children, she has pursued folk-singing and become interested in pottery. Whilst I was working on *Quest for Adventure*, Wendy had an equally challenging project, building a large wood-fired kiln for her pottery at the bottom of the garden. Yet we do enjoy doing things together. It was Wendy who introduced me to orienteering. Although we chase off on our different courses, it's deeply satisfying at the end of the day to return home together swapping tales of our tribulations in trying to find the elusive markers hidden away in clumps of trees or in sneaky little dips in the ground. We also have fiercely competitive yet light-hearted games of squash, Wendy offsetting my greater strength with skilful ball placement. It is in our tempo of living, a similar level of social stamina (not very high in either of us), and basic values that we are very close. Wendy has a quality that is both tender and very gentle, and yet within this there is a great strength. Not only I, but also many of our friends, especially in moments of crisis or tragedy, have found solace from it. Our love and enjoyment of each other has grown stronger and stronger over the years.

In 1979 an opportunity that I couldn't resist came my way – the chance of going to China. It had been closed to foreign climbers since the communist take-over but the Chinese Government had now decided to open up eight mountains, including Everest from the north. The Mount Everest Foundation, which had been established with the profits from the 1953 Everest Expedition to support British mountaineering ventures, had decided to promote one of the first trips into China. Michael Ward, the chairman, and I were sent to Peking to negotiate with the authorities in early 1980.

From the eight peaks available we chose Mount Kongur, in Western Xinjiang, as our objective. It was the only unclimbed peak on the list and the combination of its height at 7719 metres, and the fact that so little was known about it, made it particularly attractive. We quickly discovered that mountaineering in China was going to be extremely expensive. However, we were very fortunate on our way back through Hong Kong to get the promise of sponsorship from Jardine, Matheson, the celebrated trading house.

So little was known about the Kongur region that a reconnaissance seemed essential and so it was decided that Michael Ward, Al Rouse and I should set out that summer to take a closer look at the area. It was a delightful experience, a little adventure in mountain exploration with none of the concentration of vision that accompanies the siege of a single mountain objective. As the three of us travelled through Xinjiang, we were invited

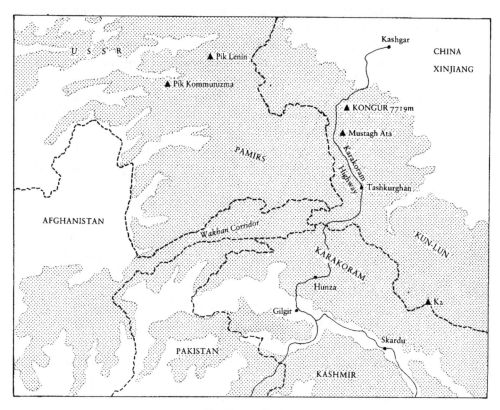

The Kongur Region

into the domed tents, or yurts, of the Khirghiz tribesmen who were leading the same nomadic life that they always had, travelling with their herds of sheep and goats from one desert pasture to the next. They were now members of a collective rather than a tribe, with a chairman rather than a chief in charge, but I suspect the pattern of family life was much the same as it had always been. They were a jolly, friendly people, with the natural hospitality and courtesy of all nomads. We were offered bowls of delicious yoghurt drink accompanied by a plate of cake-like bread whenever we visited one of their encampments.

The reconnaissance also enabled me to get to know my two new climbing partners. Michael Ward, a doctor on the 1953 Everest Expedition, was a general surgeon at a London teaching hospital but was also very interested in mountain medicine. It was he who had treated Dougal and me for frostbite after the Eiger. Our main expedition was going to combine medical research with climbing. Michael had been an outstanding rock-climber in the late thirties and early forties but in recent years he had done comparatively little climbing.

Our small team certainly covered a broad age range, with Michael in his late fifties, me in my late forties and Al Rouse in his early thirties. He was a brilliant rock-climber who had progressed from British rock, first to the Alps and then to the Himalaya. A Cambridge mathematics graduate, he had played chess to county standard, but his commitment to climbing had stopped him following a conventional career and, like me, he was making a living from a combination of lecturing, writing and working with equipment manufacturers. I enjoyed his company. He had a buoyant enthusiasm and a range of interests that went well beyond climbing.

At the end of a month's exploration we had viewed the mountain from several different aspects and had decided that an approach from the west gave us the best chance of success, though the summit of Kongur remained a mystery. From the west, the view of it is barred by a high shoulder. It was a massive sprawling mountain that I had a feeling might have some unpleasant surprises awaiting us.

On the main expedition the following year there were to be ten in the team but, of that number, only four of us were to attempt the mountain. Pete Boardman and Joe Tasker were to join Al and me. The rest of the team were mountain scientists and helpers, with Michael Ward in overall command, though I had the title of climbing leader.

We set up Base Camp on a grassy alp at the side of the Koksel Glacier at the end of May 1981.

I was nearly knocked out of the expedition at its very start. An influenza virus struck several members of the team and I went down with pneumonia, my chest weakened, perhaps, from my injury on the Ogre. I could not have had a more powerful medical team to care for me. As well as our leader, Michael Ward, there was Jim Milledge, a consultant physician specialising in lung complaints, Charlie Clarke, our doctor on the 1975 Everest expedition and a consultant neurologist, and Edward Williams, a professor of nuclear medicine. It was Charlie who put me on a powerful course of antibiotics, and whilst the others set off for a training climb on a neighbouring peak I tried to concentrate my entire being into recovery. I think it is a question of accepting the ailment for what it is, and then just trying to relax, to enable one's body to recuperate from the illness. I have always been a great reader on expeditions and in the next few days lost myself in my books and went for gentle convalescent walks on the hillside above the camp.

The weather was unsettled and, as a result, I missed very little. The others had not managed to climb their peak. Once they returned we took stock. We decided to have a closer look at the mountain, since there were two

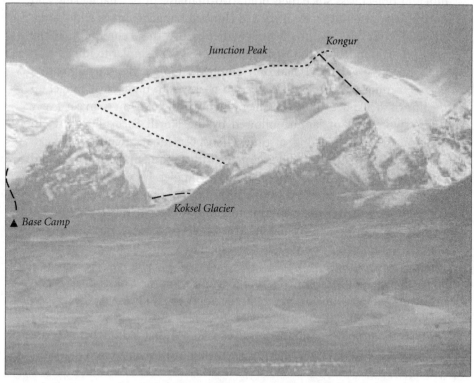

—————— *Route of first attempt* ········· *Route of second attempt*
The Kongur Massif

possible approaches to the high shoulder that barred our view of the summit. This would also give me a chance of building up my fitness and discovering if I was strong enough to accompany the others on the final push.

Although I had the title of climbing leader, my role was more chairman of the discussion group that naturally formed whenever we had to come to a decision. In a four-man team there is neither the need nor the place for a leader as such. We were a group of peers who could share in the decision-making. Nonetheless, it can still be useful to have some kind of chairman to help direct the discussion and sum up what the group has decided. There were differences of opinion that arose in part from the way Pete and Joe as a pair and Al separately had evolved their mountaineering careers. All of us had started from the same base of rock-climbing in Britain, followed by mountaineering in the Alps, but our expedition experience had been different. Pete and Joe, like me, had used both siege and Alpine tactics on different objectives. Since their bold, two-man ascent of Changabang and our abortive attempt on K2, they had climbed Kangchenjunga with Doug. Their attitude was essentially pragmatic; to use the technique that the occasion demanded. In this their approach was very similar to mine.

Al, on the other hand, had only climbed Alpine-style, starting with a barn-storming tour of South American peaks from the Fitzroy range, up the line of the Andes to the Cordillera Blanca and going on to make a very impressive ascent of Jannu, followed by the North Face of Nuptse. In addition Al enjoys arguing, at times, I suspect, for its own sake. He can seize on any ambiguities in an argument with a mathematician's logic and pursues it with the enthusiasm of a senior wrangler. He was quick to point out that we had announced in our promotional brochures, and at press conferences, that we were planning to climb Kongur Alpine-style and we were now compromising by making a reconnaissance foray. He was shouted down, but took it amicably, saying that he just wanted us to be clear about what we were doing.

We had already established an Advance Base on the Koksel Glacier and now climbed to around 6000 metres, deciding to go for the steeper of two ridges that rose from the Koksel Col. It gave a shorter, if more difficult, route to the subsidiary summit. I was reassured that although I was still going quite slowly, I could keep up with the others and I seemed to be gaining strength daily.

After a couple of days' rest we set out for our Alpine-style summit push, carrying about fifteen kilos each, to include food and fuel for a week, two tents, personal gear and some climbing equipment. The ridge above the Koksel Col rose steeply, an elegant staircase into the sky. It took us all day to reach its crest and we were still a long way from the summit of the intermediate peak.

One of the snags of climbing in the Kongur region was proving to be the weather pattern. It was much worse than we had anticipated, with only two or three days of fine weather before a fresh storm rolled in. We were pinned down half-way along the ridge, unable to see where to go or exactly where we were. Living in a tent in high winds is always a nerve-racking business. The constant rattle and flap of the nylon fabric emphasises one's vulnerability.

I was sharing a tent with Joe Tasker. We paired up throughout the expedition and, consequently, were able to build on the understanding that had only just started on K2 after we had climbed together for a day. We settled into an easy role allotment in which I did most of the cooking, while Joe did more than his share of trail-breaking, particularly towards the end of the day when I was beginning to tire. We didn't talk that much, but our silences were companionable, and I was beginning to discover that underneath a hard protective shell there was a warm, concerned heart.

None of us got much sleep that night, though it was worse for Al and Pete. They hadn't tied down their tent as securely as we had and spent the early hours of the morning sitting fully dressed, with rucksacks packed, ready to abandon the wreck if necessary. That morning, through driving clouds of spindrift, we had our first glimpse of the summit pyramid at relatively close range. It looked frighteningly formidable, and it was only at this instant that we began to realise just how serious and committing our climb was going to be.

At least we could see where we were going and soon reached the top of the subsidiary peak, a rounded snow dome from which we had a magnificent view. To the south-west was Mustagh Ata, massive and rounded like a huge extinct volcano, whilst to the south the snowy crest of the ridge we had just followed pointed to a myriad snow peaks stretching to the far horizon and the distant summits of the Karakoram. To the north-west, across the brown desert hills of Central Asia, was Russia and, in the distance, little more than a white blur, the peaks of the Pamirs and the Tian-shan. But most commanding was the summit pyramid of Kongur.

To reach it we were going to have to lose height and cross a precarious bridge formed by a knife-edge ridge linking the col with the summit mass. We had had enough of tents after the previous night so dug a snow cave on the col. It took us four hours to make but, once complete, we had a secure and relatively comfortable base in which all four of us could fit and plan our next move together. Separate tents can be divisive even on the happiest expeditions.

Pete was undoubtedly emerging as the most forceful of us, largely because he was the most physically powerful with a great reservoir of stamina. I noticed how much more self-confident he was than he had been in 1978 on K2. I suspect Joe, with his leaner build, had always operated more on will-power than sheer stamina. I don't think he was any stronger than I was, in spite of our age difference. He just had a greater capacity to endure fatigue, but our perceptions of risk and strategy were very similar. I had already noticed a competitive tension between Pete and Joe, which had been present on their ascent of the West Face of Changabang and to which they both alluded in their books describing the climb. It was combined with a very real friendship and mutual respect but it led to neither of them ever wanting to be the first to counsel retreat. But I was not in their peer group. I didn't compete with them physically and I felt that Joe welcomed my presence and was happy to let me be the advocate of caution in our discussions.

The following morning we were late in waking. Nonetheless, Pete took it for granted we were continuing the push for the summit, but both Joe and I were concerned about our position, for we were now out on a limb, with a 150-metre climb to the top of what we had called Junction Peak and a long complex descent back to safety. Four days out from Advance Base, we were beginning to run low on food and fuel. We finally agreed to make a bid for the summit from the secure base of the snow cave, though I suspect that none of us was under any illusion that this would be little more than a reconnaissance. It took us most of the day to reach the base of the summit pyramid – sensational, exciting climbing with giddy drops. There was no question of going for the top, but at least we had spotted a gully running down into the North Face that looked as if it might contain enough snow in which to dig a cave.

The following morning the argument resumed, but this time more heatedly. Pete wanted to press on, even though it was now obvious that it would take at least two days to reach the top and that our supplies were even lower. I was in favour of retreat, so that we could replenish our supplies, and Joe came in on my side. Al didn't seem to want to commit himself to either view but, after an hour's fierce discussion, the forces of caution won and we started back with the long hard haul over Junction Peak.

The weather broke the following day. If we had gone for the summit we would have been defeated by the storm and had to sit it out provisionless in a white-out. Our four days' rest went all too quickly. Sleeping, lazing and reading filled in the gaps between huge meals of well-cooked Chinese food. Our scientists also got their hands on us, taking our blood and putting us through an exhausting treadmill exercise with a mask clamped over our mouths to capture our exhaled breath. They could thus trace our levels of acclimatisation.

The two themes of the expedition had combined well and the four scientists, with David Wilson, the Political Adviser to the Governor of Hong Kong who had come with us as our interpreter, and Jim Curran, our film-maker, gave life at Base Camp a pleasant variety. Michael Ward, as overall leader, chose the very sensible course of leaving the various components of the expedition to function naturally. Because everyone knew what needed to be done, and had their own clear set role and responsibility, the entire enterprise worked harmoniously.

But we were running out of time. It was 4 July when we started back up the mountain, taking three exhausting days to reach the snow cave on the other side of Junction Peak. After a day's rest, we set out along the ridge with sacks loaded with four days' food, our sleeping-bags and some climbing gear. It was very different from when we had last been there for there was a metre of fresh snow covering ice and rock. Nonetheless, we made faster progress than we had on our first crossing – familiarity always breeds confidence. But we were being chased by a great wall of cloud that was already lapping around the summit of Kongur Tiube, the second peak of the Kongur range. I just prayed there was going to be enough snow in the gully to dig a snow cave.

There wasn't. After digging for a metre we hit hard ice and, not far beneath that, rock. By this time it was six in the evening and the cloud had swept over us. There was no other place to find shelter and we ended up burrowing in narrow slots parallel to the gully sides that were little larger than coffins. The outer walls were only centimetres thick and there was barely room to sit up. We were trapped in the 'coffins' for three days and four nights. It was a strange experience. The only incident was when my cave collapsed when Pete trod through the roof. It was as if the world was falling in and triggered in me a furious rage which, fortunately, quickly evaporated. We had no books and there was nothing to do for most of the day. We could only cook or brew up very occasionally, for we were short of food. I committed the unforgivable crime of upsetting a complete panful of boeuf stroganoff over Joe. We scraped what we could off his sleeping-bag and forced ourselves to eat it. Our sleeping-bags got progressively damper, the chill enveloping our undernourished, under-exercised bodies.

We were sealed within our coffins and relieved ourselves against the walls or into little holes dug under our sleeping mats. It was just as well the temperature was well below freezing. And yet I don't think any of us even considered retreat. We knew that we would never have the strength or the time to return for another try. We had committed so much that we were now prepared to accept a very high level of risk to complete the climb. This had nothing to do with obligation to sponsors or the reaction of the rest of the world. Another group, with a different chemistry between them, might well have retreated in similar circumstances. The decision to retreat or go on is intuitive rather than one of logical analysis, though of course that intuitive feel is born from one's years of experience in the mountains. We shared complete unity as a team and confidence in each other which gave us our upward drive.

Enclosed in a soundless snow-walled capsule, the rest of the world seemed so remote that it barely existed. I gazed up at the whorls in the roof and picked out pictures and images described by the dappled variations in light and shade. I dreamt of food, of lavish fry-up breakfasts, of home and Wendy, of the climb ahead, until they all became scrambled into a kaleidoscope of hallucinatory thought.

But on our fourth evening my altimeter showed that the pressure was rising. The storm, surely, must be drawing to an end. The following morning I cautiously drilled a hole through the external wall, but could only see swirling snow. With a blank disappointment I thought the storm was raging as fiercely as ever but, even so, I enlarged the hole. Snow poured through, but then I saw beyond this that the sky was blue. This was just surface spindrift whipped up by the wind. I pushed and dug, shouting with joy to the others that it was a perfect day. We could go to the top.

But it was bitterly cold. We were in the shade, the wind blowing from the north with all the chill cold of the Siberian wastes. Pete and Al were away first, crossing rock and snow that was as steep and inhospitable as the North Face of the Matterhorn. Pete led one pitch and Al the next. By this time Pete had lost all feeling in his hands and feet. He took off a mitt to investigate and found that the tips of his fingers were black with frostbite.

Joe and I took over the lead and he set off first, reaching a little edge about twenty metres below the ridge. It was now my turn and I moved up towards the sun, whose fingers were already beginning to claw over the crest to reach down towards me, pulling me up through spiky rocks and steep snow. Suddenly I was there in a different world where the sun caressed with its heat. The others joined me. We still had a long way to go but would now be following the crest of the ridge and could walk rather than climb. The other mountains were beginning to fall away. Even Kongur Tiube was now below us.

Joe was out in front; he pulled over a step in the ridge and let out a yell. Once I caught up with him I saw why. Just a swell of snow away was the summit of Kongur. We waited for the others and went to the top together. It had been a wonderful climb and one of the most committing I have ever made. Nothing to the north, west or east on the whole surface of the earth, was as high as us. Our nearest rival, K2, was lost in cloud two hundred miles to the south.

We bivouacked that night in a snow cave only fifteen or so metres below the top. Next morning I had to raise a doubt. Kongur has twin summits and the rounded cone about half a mile to the east, which had definitely seemed lower the previous evening, had grown by some trick of early morning light. Could it be higher? We gazed across at it, tried to talk it down, but the doubt remained, and so we laboriously trailed our way across to it, to find that our own first summit was, in fact, the true top.

Fortune was kind to us on Kongur. We took as many liberties as I have ever taken on any mountain I have attempted. I don't think I have ever been so isolated as we were on that summit, with its steep final pyramid, the fragile bridge of the linking ridge, the climb over Junction Peak and that long ridge back down. There was no room for error. This was brought home on the descent of the last steep step of the pyramid. Pete was abseiling and dislodged a rock the size of a football with the rope. We saw it spin down and strike his head a glancing blow. He was knocked out, hurtled down the rope out of control and was only saved by his fingers becoming jammed in the karabiner brake. The agonising pain brought him back to consciousness.

Success and tragedy are divided by such a hair's breadth. We avoided tragedy not by skill but by luck alone and, because we had avoided it, we quickly forgot the narrowness of our escape in the enjoyment of success. The following year we were to be less lucky.

CHAPTER ELEVEN

Pushing the Limits

I was down to ten paces, then a rest. It was all I could do to force out the eighth ... then the ninth ... I just slumped into the snow, panting, exhausted. I couldn't even make that target. Joe had drawn ahead long ago and I was on my own on this huge, endless ridge that had so sapped our strength in the preceding weeks. The North-East Ridge of Everest soars like a vast flying buttress up from the Raphu La, the col to the north-east of the mountain. I had dreamt of climbing it with a small team, a repeat of what we had done on Kongur, but the reality of scale and altitude were beginning to weigh heavily upon me.

Sitting crouched in the snow, I was already higher than Kongur. The North Col was far below and even the summit of Changtse now seemed dwarfed. I could gaze out over the peaks to the north-east to see the rolling hills of the high plateau of Tibet stretch in a perfect arc and yet we had another thousand metres to gain, to reach the summit of Everest. More than that, we had to cross the serrated teeth of the rocky pinnacles that guarded the final stages of the unclimbed section of the ridge. It was joined at 8400 metres by the North Buttress, the route from the North Col, attempted by all those pre-war British expeditions and finally climbed by the Chinese in 1960. From there it would be comparatively straightforward, but it was also a long way.

We had started out that early March so full of hope, just four of us, myself, Peter Boardman, Joe Tasker and Dick Renshaw, a newcomer to my expeditions. Four pitted against the North-East Ridge. Charlie Clarke and Adrian Gordon, who had been with us on Everest in 1975 as our Advance Base Manager, were coming in a purely support role, but we didn't envisage them going beyond Advance Base at the head of the East Rongbuk Glacier.

We had never considered attempting the entire climb Alpine-style. The route was too long and the Pinnacles were obviously going to be time-consuming. To climb successfully with Alpine techniques at extreme altitude, you need to move quickly, particularly above 8000 metres. You can't afford to spend more than a night or so above that altitude, because of physical deterioration. We therefore decided to make several forays on to the ridge, to gain a jumping off point at about 8000 metres from where we could make a continuous push for the summit, carrying bivouac gear.

It had seemed a sound strategy back in Britain but, faced with the colossal scale of the ridge, the effects of altitude and the debilitating wind and cold, we were all beginning to have our doubts. At night, even on the glacier, it was down to −20°C, and during the day the temperature never crept above freezing. Only the day before, Pete had commented that we could have done with another three or four climbers to share the burden of making the route and ferrying loads. Because our team was so small there was no question of having a continuous line of fixed rope − we couldn't have carried it. We used fixed rope only on the very steep sections and so far had run out only 200 metres over a stretch of a mile in horizontal distance with a height gain of 1400 metres. It wasn't desperately hard climbing, but it was sufficiently steep for it to have been difficult to arrest a slip. Consequently it was essential to concentrate the whole time. There could be no let-up, no relaxation. On the whole we climbed without a rope. Unless you are moving one at a time, belaying each other, it is probably safer. But it all added to the stress.

This was our third foray on to the ridge. We had been at work on it for a total of seventeen days, interspersed with two rests, one at Advance Base and one of nine days at Base. Because of the wind we had not even tried to pitch tents, instead had dug three snugly effective snow caves, one at 6850 metres, the next at 7256 metres and the top one, in which Dick and Pete were already installed, at 7850 metres. Digging them had been an exhausting affair as the snow of the North-East Ridge was wind-blasted into an iron-hard surface, there were few drifts and our second snow cave had taken us fourteen hours, spread over three days, to carve out of ice and crumbling rock.

I crawled to my feet; another ten paces without a rest; a steepening of snow, broken by rock; its very difficulty took my mind off my fatigue. I even forgot to count and exceeded my target before pausing once again. But I was nearing the crest of the ridge. Soon I'd be able to crawl into the snow hole that the others had dug and just lie down and rest. I suddenly became aware of someone below me, couldn't understand it, because Joe had pulled ahead a long time before. Pete and Dick were already at the snow cave. But as the figure caught up with me, I saw that it was Joe. He had come back to see if I was all right, had missed me on the way down and had therefore lost even more precious height. I was tremendously touched by his gesture. Going back to help someone at that altitude shows a very real concern.

He offered to take my sack but I felt I could manage. It was just a matter

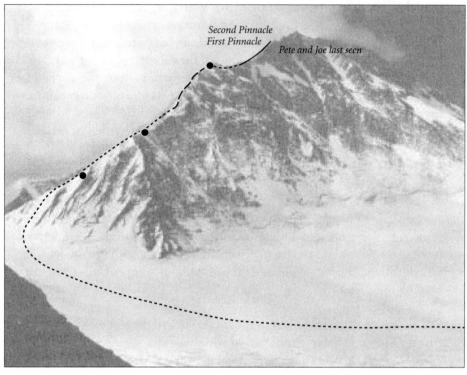

Second Pinnacle
First Pinnacle
Pete and Joe last seen

● *Snow cave* — — — — *Route not using fixed ropes* ———— *Route using fixed ropes*
The North-East Ridge of Everest

of taking my time. We plodded together those last few metres to the top of
the snow dome, where suddenly the view opened out; the great snow sweep
of the Kangshung Face, Makalu towering over the Kangshung Glacier, the
huge sérac-infested wall of Lhotse, the South Col of Everest looking so
different from the view I had seen so often from the Western Cwm, and
Everest itself, the highest point of this crenellated ridge, looking so very
distant and unattainable. And at last I could see the Pinnacles, the jagged
rock teeth, piled one on top of the other, that barred our way to the easier
upper reaches. But the sight was alluring.

What a strange mixture of suffering, apprehension, elation and friendship this climb had brought us. Crawling through the narrow entrance of
the snow hole it was good to see Pete and Dick once again. Until this climb
Dick had been just a name Joe had often spoken of, for they had done some
of their best climbing together – in the Alps, on the North Wall of the Eiger
in winter and on a desperate ascent of an unclimbed ridge of Dunagiri, just
opposite Changabang, in the autumn of 1975. I had come to like and respect
Dick in the past weeks. Always ready to help others, quiet, yet immensely

determined, Dick simply had a quiet love of the mountains, combined with a need to push himself to the limit that had nothing to do with competing with others.

The warmth of friendship, strengthened perhaps by adversity, was one of the factors that made the struggle worthwhile. Of all the expeditions I have been on, this was the most closely united, one in which I don't think there was a serious spark of anger throughout its course. We did have differences of opinion on tactics, discussions that became heated, but there was a holding-back born from a mutual respect and liking.

There were some great moments on the climb; the exhilarating moments when you were out in front. I had led a steep snow gully on the way up to our third snow cave. For an hour or more, I had forgotten the altitude and cold, the deadening fatigue in the elation and concentration of hard climbing. I had run out a full fifty metres of rope and regained the crest of the ridge with a sense of pride in what I achieved. And there were moments, too, of sheer wonder at the austere beauty of our surroundings.

The following morning, 4 May, Pete, Joe and I set out for the Pinnacles. Dick was dropping back down the ridge a hundred metres or so to pick up some rope we had left there. Stimulated by a sense of exploration, I found that the strength-sapping tiredness I had experienced the previous day had vanished, but even so, I was unable to keep up with Pete who strode ahead, seemingly effortlessly, picking his way across the airy crest that joined the snow dome to the foot of the First Pinnacle. From there the ridge soared in an upthrust that led to a mini-peak which, as we came closer, masked the continuation of the ridge. It was as if that First Pinnacle was the summit we were trying to attain.

Pete, who had reached the bottom of the Pinnacle three-quarters of an hour or so in front of Joe and me, had already uncoiled the rope and was about to start climbing. There was no discussion about who should take the lead. He was going so strongly, with such confidence. I was all too glad to belay myself and sit crouched on a rock, whilst he cramponed up the steepening slope leading to the base of a rocky buttress split by an icy groove. He could not find any cracks in which to place a piton anchor for a belay, and so carried on, bridging precariously on smooth, slaty shelves on either side of the groove. The rope ran out slowly through my fingers, came to an end and I knotted another rope on to it. If he fell there was nothing that could save him and he'd probably pull me off as well.

At last he reached the top, managed to hammer in a good piton anchor and I followed him up the rope. He had set out on the next pitch, trailing a rope behind him, before I had reached the top. I followed on. The afternoon slipped by, with cloud swirling around the crest of the Pinnacles,

engulfing us in a close grey-white world. But he was determined to reach
the crest and was running out yet another length of rope, as I, the portable
belay, stamped and shivered and wished he'd come down.

Next day it was the turn of Dick and Joe to lead. Pete and I were to carry
loads of rope and tentage behind them. My own strength had oozed away
once again. Pete just walked away from me. Dick and Joe were already at
our high point of the previous day. By the time I had reached the foot of
the rope we had fixed, Pete had caught them up. Hardly thinking, I dumped
the tent and ropes on the boulder at its foot and fled back down the ridge
to our snow cave. I watched their progress through the rest of the afternoon.
And it was so slow. That day they only pushed the route out for two more
rope-lengths, but at what a cost.

On their return that evening I learnt that Dick, who had climbed the
penultimate pitch up the corniced ridge in frightening bottomless unstable
snow, had experienced a strange sensation of numbness spreading down
one side of his body. By morning the sensation had worn off, but we were
all worried by its implications, though we didn't know the cause. We talked
it out. Pete, as always, wanted to press on but, quite apart from Dick's
mysterious ailment, I was worried about the time we were spending at very
nearly 8000 metres – Dick and Pete had been at this altitude for four nights.
We were making so little progress for so much effort, it seemed much better
to get back down for a rest, and then go for the summit Alpine-style,
without any more of this exhausting to and fro. We finally decided to drop
back.

I had been having increasing doubts about my ability to go much further,
and yet, as if to commit, perhaps con, myself, I left not only my sleeping-
bag but also my camera equipment in the snow cave when we started down.
It was a slow, nerve-stretching descent, for the weather had broken and half
a metre of fresh snow covered a hard base. It took all day to get back down
to Advance Base. Charlie commented that we looked like four very old
infirm men as we plodded back across the glacier. He didn't give Dick an
examination that night, telling him it would be better to do it at Base the
following day, but as we walked down he told me of his fears that Dick had
suffered a stroke and would almost certainly have to head for a lower
altitude and probably go all the way home.

I, also, was coming to a decision. The doubt had been present throughout
the expedition, indeed from the earliest stages of planning. I knew, both
from my age and performance at altitude, that my chances of getting to the
top of Everest without oxygen were slim. Yet I hadn't been able to resist the
lure of the North-East Ridge. I don't think it was egotistical ambition, since
I knew all too well that our chances of success were scant, particularly for

a small team who would not be able to use oxygen, even if we wanted to, since we could never have ferried it to where it was needed. I should have been as happy to go for the original North Col route, which would have given a much higher chance of success, but I knew that the others wanted to try the great unknown of the North-East Ridge. I enjoyed climbing with them, for their company and ability as mountaineers. Because of this I was happy to accept the possibility that I couldn't keep up.

Now I was faced with the reality. I could never keep up with Pete and Joe and so would either have to force their retreat, or descend by myself. I doubted if I any longer had the strength or the will even to reach our high point.

Back at Base we confronted our change in circumstance. Charlie diagnosed that Dick had had a stroke and felt that he would have to escort him all the way back to Chengdu. I told the others of my decision not to return to the ridge but that I wanted to give them all the support I could. I suggested that Adrian and I should climb up to the North Col, so that we could meet Pete and Joe there, giving them a safer line of retreat once they had crossed the Pinnacles and reached the line of the old route.

We returned to Advance Base on 13 May. I felt no regret or disappointment about my decision, for now I had a role that I could fill effectively. Adrian and I were a little expedition of our own with an objective that we could realistically attain.

Pete and Joe were undoubtedly subdued by the scale of the challenge but, all the same, their plan was realistic. There remained less than 300 metres of height gain, but very nearly a mile in horizontal distance, most of it above 8200 metres, to where the North-East Ridge joined the original route. I thought they had a reasonable chance of making this and then, if they were exhausted, as I suspected they probably would be, they could just drop down to the North Col where we would be awaiting them. We could see that the route back down to the North Col looked comparatively straightforward. If they managed to do this, they would have achieved an amazing amount, even if they didn't reach the summit, which once again, I felt, would be beyond their reach – it was another 500 metres in height, a mile in distance. You can only spend a very limited time above 8000 metres without using oxygen, at least for sleeping. Reinhold Messner's formula for success in his solo ascent of Everest had been to spend only two nights above 8000 metres on his way to the top. But he had chosen a very much easier route in 1980. It would all depend on how quickly Pete and Joe could cross those Pinnacles.

15 May dawned clear though windy. Pete and Joe fussed around with final preparations, packing their rucksacks and putting in a few last minute

goodies. Then suddenly they were ready. I think we were all trying to underplay the moment.

'See you in a few days.'

'We'll catch you tonight at six.'

'Good luck.'

Then they were off, plodding up the little slope beyond the camp through flurries of wind-driven snow. They were planning to move straight through to the second snow cave. Adrian and I set out shortly afterwards for the North Col, though that day we barely got started on the bottom slopes. It was all much steeper and more complex than I had anticipated. We returned the following day and by six that evening were about a hundred metres below the col, our way barred by a huge crevasse. Pete and Joe had reached the third snow cave and came up on the radio. They sounded cheerful and confident, were going for the Pinnacles the next day. We arranged our next radio call at three o'clock the following afternoon and then again at six.

It was after dark when we got back to Advance Base. We had been on the go for twelve hours and were very tired. Adrian had never been on snow slopes that were so steep and consequently it had taken even more out of him. We were too tired to cook and just crawled into our sleeping-bags.

It was always difficult getting up before the sun warmed the tent, which happened at about nine. Even then I lay for a long time in a stupor before thirst and hunger drove me from out of the warmth of my sleeping-bag. It was a perfect day without a breath of wind. I immediately went over to the telescope and started scanning the ridge. I looked at the snow shoulder, behind which hid the third snow cave. No sign of them there. I swung the telescope along the crest of the ridge leading to the First Pinnacle. Still no sign. Could they have overslept? And then I saw them, two small distinct figures at the high point they had previously reached on the First Pinnacle. They had certainly made good progress. They must have set out before dawn and were still moving quickly. But now they were on fresh ground and their pace slowed.

We spent the rest of the day taking turns at watching them work their way gradually across the First Pinnacle, but now their progress was almost imperceptible. They were moving one at a time and the going must have been difficult. Three o'clock came and I tried to reach them on the radio, but there was no reply. Perhaps they were so engrossed in their climbing, they had no time to respond to our call. Six o'clock. Still no reply. Could there be a fault in the radio? We kept calling them every half hour.

At nine that evening, when the sun was already hidden behind Everest, we looked up at them for the last time and called them yet again on the radio. One figure was silhouetted against the fading light on the small col immediately below the Second Pinnacle, whilst the other figure was still moving to join him. They had been on the go for fourteen hours, still had to dig out a ledge for their tent and would then have a night out at over 8250 metres. I couldn't help wondering what shape they would be in the following morning.

There was no sign of them next day. They had presumably bivouacked on the other side of the ridge and, because of the steepness of the flank that we could see, it seemed likely they would be climbing for some distance out of sight. That morning, Adrian and I set out for the North Col, reaching it the following day. We spent the next three days gazing across at the ridge, waiting, hoping, willing Pete and Joe to reappear. But they never did. We were sure that they could not get beyond the point where the unclimbed section of the ridge joined the original route without us seeing them and, as the days went by, our hopes faded. Unless something had gone catastrophically wrong, they would have either retreated or have come into sight. They couldn't possibly spend four nights above 8200 metres without supplementary oxygen and keep going.

Meanwhile Charlie had returned and was at Advance Base. On 21 May Adrian and I abandoned the North Col and joined him. We could come to only one conclusion, that either they had had a fall or had collapsed from exhaustion. My first impulse was to try to climb the ridge to see for myself, but I had to abandon that idea immediately. Neither Charlie nor Adrian had the experience even to reach our previous high point. And if we did get to the third snow cave, it is very unlikely we could have seen anything.

Then Charlie suggested that we should go right round the mountain into the Kangshung valley to examine the other side of the ridge through the telescope. The chances of seeing anything seemed slight but at least we would have done everything we possibly could. But someone had to keep the north side under observation as well. It was just possible that they were still alive and could be on their way back. We decided that Adrian should stay in lonely vigil at Advance Base while Charlie and I went round to the Kangshung valley.

A week later we were at the head of the Kangshung Glacier gazing up at the huge face, the biggest and highest in the world, a gigantic hanging glacier clad in snow, contained on its right-hand side by the North-East Ridge. The ridge looked even longer, even more inhospitable than it had from the East Rongbuk Glacier, with steep fluted snow dropping down from bulging cornices, and the only glimpses of rock high up near the crest. We gazed at each tiny black patch but came to the conclusion that these were rocks, sticking out of the snow. There was no sign of life, no tracks, nothing that could be a human body. It was silent in the early morning sun at the head of the Kangshung Glacier but cloud was beginning to form below the summit of Everest and was slowly drawn like a gossamer veil across the face, hiding features but leaving the shape of the mountain just discernible.

We turned away, still no wiser as to what had happened to Pete and Joe, and started back down the long valley. I still couldn't believe that they were dead and, as the truck took us on the final stage of our journey back round to Base Camp, fantasised that Pete and Joe would be waiting for us, laughing at all the fuss we had made, keen to go back up and finish off the climb.

But I knew that that couldn't be. Adrian, as arranged, had now evacuated Advance Base with the help of some Tibetans with their yaks, and was waiting for us at Base. We had to accept that Pete and Joe were dead, lost somewhere high on that North-East Ridge of Everest. Charlie, perhaps more realistic than me, had each evening been quietly chipping out a memorial plaque. We placed it on a plinth of stone just above our camp, alongside several memorials to others who had died on the north side of Everest.

Once again I set off by myself to bring out the ill tidings to those who loved Pete and Joe. Back at home, Wendy, Pete's Hilary, Joe's Maria, Charlie's Ruth and Adrian's Frenda, all of them experienced in interpreting implications in those final dangerous days of an expedition, were becoming anxious. There had been a long inexplicable delay in receiving any letters or news while Charlie and I had made our journey around the eastern side of the mountain. They knew all too well that this could mean some kind of crisis, but just what and to whom they could not know. They waited, phoning each other, trying to read what little clues there were, whilst I rattled and bumped in a jeep the 200-mile journey to Lhasa, and then flew into Chengdu, the first place from which I could telephone England.

Once again it was Wendy and Louise who had the dreadful task of organising the breaking of the news to their families, of giving what support and help they could. I was shattered with grief by the deaths of Pete and Joe, both as friends and climbing partners, as people who had so much to offer in their creative ability as writers, and in Joe's case as a film-maker but, most of all, for the cruelty of bereavement to their loved ones. It also showed me what it would do to Wendy if I lost my life, and yet, even in that initial shock of grief I knew that I could never give up climbing. It was too much part of my life, the fun, the challenge, the thrill of risk, of exploration and beauty of the hills – all the many facets that make it so addictive.

But immediately after getting home, I did make one promise – that I would never go back to Everest.

CHAPTER TWELVE

Small is Beautiful

It was spring of 1980 and I was wandering along the bottom of Shepherd's Crag in Borrowdale. It was a Carlisle Mountaineering Club evening meet which are very informal affairs. A different wayside crag is advertised for each Tuesday night and it simply acts as a focus for people to meet and climb and then drink together at a neighbouring pub. It was the first such meet that I had attended. I hadn't yet seen anyone I knew, so had just soloed up Ardus, a fairly straightforward Severe which follows a clean-cut groove. I was trying to summon up the courage to try Adam, a steeper and harder route just round the corner, when another climber came along. He also seemed to be looking for someone to climb with.

It saved me from having to solo Adam and we tossed over who should have the lead. That was how I met Jim Fotheringham. He didn't really look like a hard climber. Slightly taller than me, he has a gangling build that makes him appear almost awkward, yet once on the rock, he is both sound and forceful. We did two climbs that evening and in the pub afterwards I learnt more of his background. He was in his late twenties, had recently qualified as a dentist and was working as a schools' dental officer. He was certainly a widely experienced mountaineer, having climbed in Scotland, the Alps and, further afield, in Kenya and Baffin Island.

We arranged to climb together again and in the next three years rock-climbed regularly around the Lakes. Whilst I was on Kongur and then on the north side of Everest, Jim had his first Himalayan expedition when he and a friend, Ian Tattersall, climbed a 6000-metre peak in the Karakoram. Then in the spring of 1982 he made a very fast ascent of the Cassin route on Mount McKinley. On British rock we climbed at around the same standard, though he definitely had a little bit more push than I had, and would make long bold leads with poor protection. However, on the whole we led through, taking the lead on pitches as they came.

In January 1983 I was working on my book *Everest the Unclimbed Ridge* and escaping up to Scotland at weekends. We had a booking for the CIC hut in the Allt a Mhuilinn, just below the North Face of Ben Nevis. It is a single-roomed bothy, built like a fortress with heavy iron shutters on the windows, a steel-plated door and instructions prominently displayed inside that under no circumstances are any unauthorised passers-by to be allowed in. There are tales of climbers, almost dying from hypothermia, being turned away from its doors for fear it will become engulfed by the growing hordes who flock to the Ben in winter. The Scottish Mountaineering Club guards it fiercely.

But we were going up with a member, Alan Petit, Jim's regular Scottish winter climbing partner and a fellow dentist. With us were two young climbers at Stirling University. The forecast was bad. It predicted rain, high winds and a freezing level at 1500 metres, but a hut booking is not something to throw away, and so we decided to go in the hope that the forecast could be wrong.

Jim had initially decided to stay at home for a family weekend, so I had driven up by myself to Alan's house just outside Stirling, reaching it at about eight on the Friday evening. We had just finished a large spaghetti bolognese when there was a ring at the door – it was Jim. He hadn't been able to resist the lure of the Ben, weather forecast and all.

It was midnight before we reached Fort William and, rather than leave the cars low down by the golf course, we decided to find our way through the forest roads to the foot of the Allt a Mhuilinn. This gives a height advantage of around 450 metres but the gate to the forest is not always left open. This time we were lucky. I followed Jim's car. He and Alan were the experts. The forest is huge, stretching around the northern flanks of the massif with a maze of tracks through the dark conifers. Jim and Alan missed the turning and we spent two hours exploring the Leanachan Forest before we finally hit on the right track leading up to the dam.

It was snowing wetly and the ground had thawed. We plodded through the dark up to the hut, boots sinking into the peaty morass, weighed down by sacks heavy with food, sleeping-bags and spare gear. It was 3 a.m. when at last we arrived. The following morning I was relieved when Jim, ever-enthusiastic, looked outside the hut and reported that it was raining. Nonetheless it was difficult to halt the upward momentum. Over a breakfast of bacon and eggs, cooked on the grease-encrusted calor gas stove, we discussed what to do, expanding the conversation to delay making a decision.

It was in the course of this conversation that we conceived my next expedition. Pete Boardman and I had obtained permission to attempt a mountain called Karun Koh in the Northern Karakoram near the Chinese border. We had been intrigued by an impressive pyramid-shaped peak we had seen from the summit of Kongur. At first we had thought it was K2, but Pete, the geographer, had taken a bearing on it and looking through his maps, had calculated that it must be this interesting unclimbed peak of 7350 metres. We had applied for permission to climb it as a joint Pakistan/British expedition and had received the go-ahead whilst on Everest.

In the immediate aftermath of the tragedy on Everest, I hadn't the heart to go to Karun Koh in 1983 and had therefore asked for our expedition to be postponed until 1984. I also invited Jim Fotheringham to take Pete's place. But now, nearly a year later, the old restlessness was reasserting itself. I had been invited to attend a mountaineering and tourism conference organised by the Indian Mountaineering Foundation in Delhi that coming September. It seemed too good an opportunity to miss – free flights to Delhi, a quick trip to the nearest mountains, grab a peak and home. Not so much an expedition as a super Alpine holiday in the same kind of time-scale. Neither of us could spare any more time anyway. *Everest the Unclimbed Ridge* was being published at the end of September, while Jim had recently changed jobs and was planning to buy a new house. We both wanted a short exciting climbing holiday.

Having decided on this, we set off for Observatory Ridge, a route which should be climbable in any condition. We were soaked before we got anywhere near the base. The snow was wet and glutinous and the ice was running with water but no one wanted to be the first to cry chicken. Eventually it was Alan, the resident Scot, who called for retreat and the rest of us turned back, relieved. Over morning coffee in a Fort William hotel, Jim and I considered our summer holidays a little further. The Gangotri region could be a good objective. It was a two-day bus ride from Delhi, and had an array of steep and exciting mountains in the 6000-metre range. It should be ideal for our purpose.

In the following weeks Jim and I began to collect photographs of the area. Doug Scott had been there two years earlier when he had made a fine new route up the North-East Ridge of Shivling, and the previous year Allen Fyffe had done a route on the West Ridge of Bhagirathi III – a ten days' climb with an epic descent down the other side and a long walk back to their Base Camp. There was a prominent rock buttress to the left of Allen's route which reminded me of the Bonatti Pillar on the Aiguille du Dru. It was very steep, looked as if it was on good granite for the first two thirds, but was capped by a different type of rock that was obviously very shaly. This, however, laid back in a big ice-field above our pillar. We decided that this would be our primary objective.

I did more climbs on Ben Nevis that winter than I had done in the past thirty years. Most of them were accomplished in lightning forays, driving up from home one evening, sleeping in the car at the car park, doing the climb the following day and returning that night for another day's work on the book. In this way I climbed Zero Gully, Point Five, Orion Face and Minus Two Gully, all of them classic routes which, when they were first climbed, had been extremely difficult but, with the development of modern ice tools, were now within the reach of the average competent winter climber.

The change has been dramatic. It is all in the shape of the pick on the axe. Until the late sixties the pick was straight, set at ninety degrees to the shaft. It was purely a cutting tool for making steps and, on steep ice, hand-holds as well. The art was to chop the holds in just the right sequence, clinging with one hand to the slippery ice slot you had cut, while smashing away with the other to cut out the next step. It made ice climbing a very committing, strenuous and frightening affair. It also took a long time. The modern climber can have little concept of just how serious routes like Zero Gully and Point Five were when they were first climbed. A whole series of English parties, one of which included Joe Brown, came to grief on the steep ice near the foot of the gullies, experiencing spec-tacular falls down the snow slopes below, before it finally yielded to the formidable all-Scottish team of Tom Patey, Hamish MacInnes and Graeme Nicol.

It was Yvon Chouinard, the brilliant American rock climber, who had been a leading light in the development of big wall climbing in Yosemite in the early sixties and designed some of the best technical rock-climbing gear of that time, who then became interested in ice-climbing and brought a completely fresh approach to it. He improved crampon design, introducing a rigid crampon which gave greater stability. The basic design of twelve-point crampons had not really changed for some fifty years until, once again in the States, Geoff Lowe designed the Foot Fang. This clamps on to the boot like a ski-binding and looks almost like a super-short ski, bristling with points that go forward and down.

Chouinard's most famous and revolutionary concept was in ice-axe design. He produced a gently curved axe pick that hooks into ice and remains in place, enabling the climber to pull his full weight on it and use it as a hand-hold. Using two picks, one on the axe and the other on the hammer, the climber can ascend vertical ice without cutting any laborious steps.

A significant development was made by Hamish MacInnes. Working independently in the same field, he came up with the concept of the dropped pick. This was a straight pick set at an angle of forty-five degrees, with an adze that was very broad and set at a similar angle. He called it the Terrordactyl. It wasn't as aesthetically pleasing in design as the Chouinard axe, but it was more effective, hooking in steep ice to give a much greater sense of security.

The most important development of all was the banana, or reverse-curve, pick by Simond in France. The straight-drop pick is awkward to use and you end bruising your knuckles. The reverse-curve can be flicked in with a neat wrist action, and is also much more secure, for the pick slices into the ice and then one's weight on the shaft causes the serrations to bite without breaking the ice away.

Armed with my Foot Fangs and reverse-pick axes, I could enjoy modern climbing to the full. There is a beauty and adventure in winter climbing that can never be matched by summer rock-climbing. It's not a poor man's alpinism, nor training for the Himalaya, for it is an end in itself, a joyous commitment to steep ice and snow-covered rocks, to swirling spindrift and cold fingers, to rolling snow-clad mountains, whose shades and tones of white and grey or warm rich yellow change through the day with the shift of clouds and the angle of the sun.

With the spring and summer came rock-climbing. As with ice-climbing, I have embraced all the modern gear; elaborately cammed devices called Friends that will slot into any crack, specially curved wedges called Rocks, sticky-soled climbing shoes called Super Ratz and chalk to give the hands a better grip. These are the aids of the modern rock-climber and, combined with intense training on climbing walls and multi-gyms, they have pushed the standard of modern climbing to new heights which have far outstripped my personal climbing ability. Nonetheless I have steadily improved my own skill over the years. To understand how the standard of climbing has increased in the post-war period one can examine the Extreme grade which is the top grade in British climbing. It was introduced in the late forties by the very talented English rock-climber, Peter Harding, in the climbing guide-book to the Llanberis Pass. In the Lake District the Fell and Rock Climbing Club, who have traditionally produced the area's guide-books and always been fairly conservative, clung to a top standard of Very Severe, even though this was having to embrace a progressively wider spectrum of difficulty as standards improved.

Eventually the Extreme grade was accepted throughout Britain, then with the advent of steeper, thinner, more strenuous and more necky climbing, this grade, too, became over-full. A numerical grade was then introduced which, in 1983, ranged from E1 to E5. The hardest climbs put up in the fifties – the most significant ones being by Joe Brown and Don Whillans – are classed as E1 today, though one, a ferocious overhanging groove called Goliath on Burbage Edge in Derbyshire, even today is considered E4. This is a tribute to the quite extraordinary strength and determination of

Don Whillans. E2 was the grade of the sixties, produced in part by a radical improvement in protection techniques with the introduction of nuts. Metal nuts of various sizes with their threads drilled out, strung on a loop of nylon line, are jammed in cracks for use as running belays. These were the predecessors of the more sophisticated tailored metal wedges and the cammed devices that have since been introduced.

I suppose my own rock-climbing zenith was in the late fifties and early sixties when I was climbing the hardest routes of the time and even making a few new routes of my own, but the seventies brought an explosion in climbing standards equivalent to the jump forward pioneered by Whillans and Brown in the early fifties. Pete Livesey, a Yorkshire climber who came to the sport comparatively late at the age of thirty, was in the forefront of this new development. He came from a background of competitive sport and had run middle distances as a junior at national level. He had then taken up white-water canoeing and caving before being attracted to climbing. He immediately saw the potential for systematic training as a means of improving his climbing standard and began to put up a series of very hard new routes, at first in his native Yorkshire, then branching out into Wales and the Lake District. Quite a few of them were routes that had originally been climbed using a lot of aid. The most outstanding route he put up in this period in the Lakes was Footless Crow, a bold line that weaved its way through a series of overhangs on Goat Crag in Borrowdale.

These new Extreme climbs are way beyond my powers, but each year I have enjoyed pushing up my standard that tiny bit, trying to do the odd E3. There is a level of ego-gratification in chasing the grades. I get satisfaction in knowing that I can climb something that is harder than anything I have done before and I must confess to thoroughly enjoying happening to mention, 'Oh, did Prana the other day, my E3 for the season.' But there's more to it than that. The harder routes take you onto lines that are so much more committing, aesthetically pleasing, cleaner and bolder. There is an immense sense of achievement in pushing one's own boundaries, in over-coming both one's fear and also one's physical limitations. I know a heady joy when I push my limits climbing on our own small British crags. There is also the excitement of climbing hard, an adrenalin rush that I suspect becomes addictive. I certainly need this surge of excitement on a regular basis and become irritable and sluggish if I'm denied a fix of my own special climbing drug.

There is never any shortage of climbing partners. Living around the flanks of the Northern Fells are a dozen climbers who have settled here over the years. Doug Scott moved in just a few fields from us in 1983. Since both of us freelance, we can steal fine sunny days in the middle of the week, when the rest of the world is at work, to go out climbing. In doing this we have rebuilt a friendship tested by the pressures of expeditioning. My half-brother, Gerald, whom I introduced to climbing in the Avon Gorge when he was five, moved into the village a few years ago, and has become a close friend and a keen climber. These, then, are my afternoon and evening climbing partners and in a good season I go climbing three or four times a week.

The summer of 1983 was a good one and I ticked off a whole series of routes I had long dreamt of climbing: The Lord of the Rings, a complete girdle of the East Buttress of Scafell, over 300 metres of hard climbing; Saxon, a tenuous crack line that cuts the smooth wall of the upper part of Scafell's Central Buttress, the most spectacular stretch of rock in the Lake District; and Prana, my statutory E3.

Jim and I climbed together at weekends, building up a partnership that was to stand us in good stead later on that summer. Our most enjoyable foray was to Scotland, when we drove up to Aviemore one Friday night, slept out on the shores of Loch Morlich and then walked over Cairngorm in the early morning to Shelterstone Crag at the head of Glen Avon. It is one of the finest crags in the Cairngorm, 300 metres of steep dark granite in a stark lonely setting above Loch Avon. We climbed a route called Steeple. Smooth compact slabs alternate with overhanging rock, culminating in a sheer corner leading to the top. It has an Alpine scale, pitch after pitch of exhilarating climbing. Three tiny figures walking along the shore of Loch Avon were the only signs of life we saw that day.

On the way back we soloed up one of the easier climbs on Hell's Lum Crag, tiptoeing insecurely in our climbing shoes up the steep drift of hard compact snow left from the winter. We dropped down Coire an t-Sneachda in the golden light of the early evening, passing the empty skeletons of the ski lifts, ugly against the heather.

That evening we drove over to Fort William, slept in the car park by the Golf Club, and set out once again in the early dawn for the north side of Ben Nevis. We were bound for Carn Dearg, a great buttress of rock that acts as a portal to the cliffs of the Ben. That day we completed a climb called Toro, another 300-metre job, pitch after pitch of stimulating climbing. Neither of these routes was hard by modern standards but that didn't matter. It was the quality and length of the climbs, combined with their situations that made them so rewarding.

Jim and I were building up as a team. We understood each other's style of climbing, thought processes, strong points and faults. There was an element of competition to get the best pitch, but even this was muted, since we both tacitly recognised that Jim had the edge on me when it came to hard and particularly necky rock climbing. The difference in age probably helped.

One wet weekend we went high on to Ill Crag above Eskdale to scramble on easy rocks and find new routes on little moss-clad outcrops which had avoided attention because of their height and isolation. We continued discussing our plans for the summer and examined alternative objectives. A friend of Jim's had climbed in the Gangotri the previous summer and provided some more pictures and a report on the size and challenge of the East Face of Kedarnath Dome. It looked attractive – a 3000-metre face that in the picture seemed as sheer and blank as the walls of Yosemite. The other side, its west flank, was a huge easy-angled snow face providing a straightforward descent. It had everything, hard challenging climbing, size, easy descent and, because it faced east, it got the early morning sun, more than a luxury after cold bivouacs. We decided to change our objective.

It was the end of August 1983, time to go. Putting together a two-man mini-expedition is delightfully easy. We already had most of the gear we were going to need. Jim spent a morning in his local supermarket buying expedition food. We had grain bars, dried fruit and nuts from the health food co-op that Jim's wife Penny had helped to found, and I had written off to White Horse for whisky, Dolamore for some boxed wines and Olympus for their latest miniature cassette stereo system. I have always believed in living well on an expedition.

We packed the expedition gear one sunny afternoon in my garden. We had to sample the wine and so broached one of the boxes. It was disorganised, fun, and by the time we had finished we were both tipsy – a long call from fraught days spent in an icy, dusty warehouse before the 1975 Everest expedition. Jim was suffering from house moving teething troubles so flew out a few days later than me.

Three days of speeches, elaborately exquisite Indian buffets and meetings with many old climbing friends gathered from around the world was an unlikely prelude to an expedition and yet a great deal of fun. The Indians have a capacity for hospitality and a love of conferences. The money for it all comes from government sources. Indira Ghandi opened the conference amid great pomp. I was frequently asked by the Indians when a European country would host a similar get-together, and, of course, we do, but without the same scale of government funding these affairs are inevitably more parochial, with only a small number of foreign guest speakers.

This was both a mountaineering and tourism conference and the organisers had planned to link it with a series of treks going into the foothills of the Himalaya, led by some of the eminent mountaineers attending the conference. I had agreed to do the honours in the Gangotri, taking a group of tourists as far as our Base Camp. In return for this Jim and I were to get free transport. The Indian Tourist Board had prepared an elaborate brochure advertising the trek but, unfortunately, had published it only a few weeks before the conference, which was too late to get many customers. They ended up with just one taker, an Australian girl called Jean who came from Sydney. The numbers were to be made up by some of our fellow guests. There were three Everesters, Barry Bishop, who had been to the summit of Everest in 1963 as part of the American Everest Expedition, Wanda Rutkiewitz from Poland, one of the most talented women climbers in the world and the third woman to reach the summit of Everest when she climbed it in 1979, and Laurie Skreslet, the first Canadian to reach the top. We also had with us Adams Carter, editor of the *American Alpine Journal*, arguably the finest and most comprehensive compendium of mountain information in the world, John Cleare, mountain photographer and all-round expeditioner from Britain, and Warwick Deacock, an old friend from my army days who had emigrated to found the first Outward Bound school in Australia. We also had an Australian film crew who were going to make a promotional film of the trek.

Jim had arrived the previous evening and, on the morning of 30th August, our little expedition, accompanied by its prestigious trekkers and our Liaison Officer, Captain Vijay Singh, set out in a tourist coach from the portals of the Janpat Hotel. Adams Carter, as senior member of the team, cut the ribbon across the doors of the coach. Garlanded with flowers we piled in. Jean looked slightly bemused.

That night we stopped at Rishikesh in a government rest house near forested hills. Wanda and I went for a walk in the early morning following a path through creeper-covered trees that wound up the steep hillside. Monkeys chattered in the mist. We were on the verge of an adventure. It was slightly incongruous through the sheer luxury of our approach; a conducted tour viewed through the naive eyes of our ebullient film crew and the dazed eyes of our solitary free-paying customer, but it was fun and it was India, a country that I have come to love.

The road wound in a series of wild corkscrews up and over the foothills of the Himalaya. We were still in the dying stages of the monsoon and rain fell from heavy grey clouds. We caught glimpses of pylons carrying electricity cables, marching over the forested hills and we stopped at a village perched high on the top of a hill for a tea-break and the chance to buy fresh vegetables in the market. Vijay, determined to look after his little flock, bargained hard over the price of bananas and garlic.

We crossed a hill system and dropped down into the valley of the Bhagirathi river, a tributary of the Ganges, and consequently also one of India's holy rivers. Our destination that night was the town of Uttarkashi. It was also to be a reunion for me, since Balwant Sandhu, my co-leader on the Changabang expedition, now ran the Nehru Mountain Institute, situated in a fine pine forest above the town. Balwant had hardly changed, apart from his hair being slightly more grizzled, and he was as warmly enthusiastic as ever. Since Changabang he had married a German girl called Helga and they had a six-year-old son. He was still an active climber and was organising and leading a training meet for the first Indian mixed-sex expedition to Everest. He would be climbing in the Garhwal mountains whilst we were in the Gangotri. We reminisced that night over a good German dinner and Balwant told us that he would trek into his expedition via the Gangotri so that he could come and see us.

We set out on the final leg of our journey the next morning. We were now on the pilgrim trail, joining queues of buses heading for the holy town of Gangotri. The monsoon rain was falling in a steady deluge from heavy clouds. Every stream was a muddy, swirling cataract and the hillside was a sheet of tumbling water carrying rocks and earth down onto the road. The convoy of buses frequently stopped for minor earth slides and rock falls which the passengers cleared by hand, but then we reached a major fall that completely blocked the road. Engineers were laying charges of dynamite to shift a huge boulder. A dull thud, a puff of yellow smoke and the rock had disintegrated, but there remained tons of rubble to clear away. It looked a good moment to start walking. People materialised out of the gloom eager to carry our gear, and we all set off, umbrellas raised, through the deluge. It was good to be walking.

That night we stopped at a rest house by a spring so hot that it took five minutes of gradual immersion to adjust to the temperature. Next morning we began getting tantalising glimpses of high snow-clad peaks at the ends of the deep-cut side valleys that fed the Bhagirathi river.

Gangotri lies in the base of the valley, a collection of shingle-covered lodges and ashrams around a garish little temple. Jim and I joined the pilgrims to wash our feet in the icy holy river, and went up to the temple for a puja. We made an offering of a few rupees, had a blob of red paint daubed on our foreheads and a blessing muttered over us.

Vijay, meanwhile, had hired the porters. We were to take three short days to reach Tapoban, the grassy alp which is the accepted base for most Gangotri expeditions. It was as well to take it slowly for we had made such fast easy progress by bus that we had hardly had time to start acclimatising. We were already at 3000 metres and in the next few days would reach over 4000.

It is a beautiful approach along a path well crafted for the more energetic

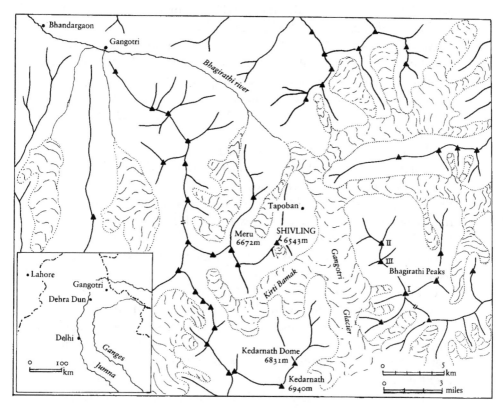

Shivling and Kedarnath

pilgrims who want to bathe in the Bhagirathi river where it emerges from
the snout of the Gangotri Glacier. The rock scenery is magnificent. Great
buttresses of weathered granite tower on either side of the valley. If they
had been in Europe or North America they would have been meccas for
climbers, but here, on the way to the greater peaks of the Himalaya, they
are just passed by.

On the third morning we crossed the rocky debris of the bottom of the
glacier and climbed a long broken spur to the pastures of Tapoban. It was
as lovely a spot as I have ever seen in the Himalaya. Wild flowers nestled
amongst the rocks and lush grass, and clear streams trickled amongst the
boulders. The entrance to the Gangotri Glacier is flanked on its western
side by Shivling, a magnificent phallus of ice and granite, aptly named,
Shiva's penis. On the other side of the glacier, its eastern gatepost was
Bhagirathi III, our original objective. It looked steep and hard, and didn't

get any sun until late in the morning. We didn't regret changing our objective to the East Face of Kedarnath Dome.

We were not the only ones to have chosen Tapoban. A big blue tent sat in the middle of the field. It belonged to a Polish women's expedition who were attempting a route on Meru, a massive complex peak to the west of Shivling. The team were on the mountain and the only occupants were one of the Poles who was feeling sick and Mala, their Liaison Officer, a young student from Calcutta who was very glad to have some one with whom to speak English. We invited them to dinner. Sitting round a fire in the light of a full moon, we washed down our boeuf bourgignon with red wine. The grass was soft beneath us and the mountains black jagged silhouettes against the starlit sky. It didn't feel like a Himalayan expedition – it was too much fun. Balwant arrived in time for the dessert. He had walked all the way from Gangotri in a single day. We broached the whisky in his honour and talked and laughed long into the night, waking the next morning with terrible hangovers to a perfect dawn.

I was keen to explore the Gangotri Glacier and establish our base at the foot of the East Face of Kedarnath Dome. Jim had picked up a bad cold on the way in and was acclimatising slowly. I must have seemed unbearably enthusiastic and at the same time edgy. I was worried whether Jim was going to be fit for the climb – always the risk on a two-man expedition. We decided that I should push ahead with the porters to establish a camp as far as possible up the Gangotri Glacier. Laurie Skreslet, Wanda Rutkiewitz and John Cleare had moved up with us to Tapoban and were also going to come as far as the foot of our climb. I was already viewing them as potential porter-power.

I got away first with the four porters we had kept on to make the initial carry. As porters always do, they stopped every few hundred metres for a rest. I kept with them, partly because they knew the way and also to chivvy them on. They had carried for a Japanese expedition that had made a new route on the South-East Face of Shivling and so thought they knew where our Base Camp should be, just round the corner of the mountain on the northern bank of the Kirti Bamak. It took some persuasion to coax them to the other side of the glacier and around the eastern flanks of Kedarnath Dome. I was reminded of walking with my own children when they were young, jollying them on to the next bend, and then the one after that. At last, at five that afternoon, we reached a sandy moraine flat on the end of the East Ridge of Kedarnath Dome.

The porters dumped their loads leaving me on my own. There was no sign of the others. Had they stopped further back? I rather hoped they had, as I basked in the silent beauty of the mountains. On the other side of the

Gangotri Glacier ranks of rock and snow peaks, most of them unclimbed, were lit by the late afternoon sun. I erected our small bivouac tent, collected water and started preparing supper. I am not a solitary person, yet I find that I do need periods on my own. Just before dark, I noticed a figure plodding over the flat ground towards the camp. It was Laurie Skreslet. He told me that Wanda and John had left in front of him, so it looked as if they had got lost on the way and must be bivouacking.

The following morning we got away early to make our first recce of our objective. The East Face of Kedarnath Dome hides itself well, tucked into the back of the Ghanohim Bamak, a side glacier reaching up to Kedarnath itself. A subsidiary spur masked the face as we picked our way through a maze of rocky moraines and hills of ice at the foot of the glacier. Then it appeared round a bluff, a soaring wall of grey granite, so much bigger than on any of the pictures we had looked at – 2000 metres of continuous rock wall, with the occasional snow ledge linked by crack lines. We lay back on a boulder and gazed through binoculars, trying to pick out lines on this huge upthrust of rock. It was the closest thing to Yosemite I had ever seen in the Himalaya. At least though, over on the left, there seemed a soft option. You could gain height on a subsidiary glacier, reach the crest of a buttress and then climb the left retaining buttress of the face. This would probably give a mere thousand metres of serious climbing.

The others, including Jim, had reached our camp by the time we got back. Jim, still feeling off-colour so tending to be cautious, preferred the softer option. The following day we employed our volunteer labour to carry in all the gear and food we were going to need for our climb. It took only three hours to reach our Advance Base on a little pile of moraine rocks set back from the face.

Two days later, Jim and I were ensconced in our camp. Our gallant helpers were on their way back to Delhi. Their assistance had been invaluable, their company pleasurable and yet it was only now that the expedition became real, in some ways, all too real. We decided to have a look at the easier left-hand option and climbed the hanging glacier that led round the buttress on the left of the face. The scale was all so much greater than it had seemed at first glance; crevasses that were invisible from below materialised as huge caverns once we started picking our way up the icefall.

At the top of the buttress we peered up at the route. There certainly was a line going all the way to the top but it looked by no means easy and escape was barred by a bristling line of corniced rock. We could only carry a limited amount with us. If we had more than two loads it would mean relaying sacks up the face and climbing it several times over. We certainly wouldn't be able to do much sack hauling for the rock wasn't steep enough.

More basically, the psychological barrier was too great for the two of us. Had there been four, our numbers would have given us both an impetus and a forum for discussion which would probably have led us on to the face at least to have a try. With only two, the negative elements seemed all too dominant. Jim was worried about getting back to his practice on time; I was just plain worried by the sheer gigantic scale of the face, frightened that we might get part-way up, run out of steam, retreat, and then have neither the strength nor the time to try anything else.

We discussed alternative objectives; a traverse of Kedarnath and Kedarnath Dome, but that seemed even more committing than the face; or an ascent of a rocky buttress to the right of the face that resembled the North Face of the Piz Badile. But this seemed too limited an objective when we were surrounded by such magnificent unclimbed peaks, ridges and walls. We found a large boulder, climbed up on to it and looked at the route. It was uninspiring, a great whaleback of snow with the occasional rock step, undramatic, a nothing. I turned my frustration on to Jim.

'There's no way I'm going on that. It's a lousy line. It's just a bloody slog.'

'It's probably harder than it looks,' Jim temporised, mildly.

'But it looks so boring. How about the South-West summit of Shivling? At least it looks good and it's unclimbed.' We talked around it and Jim agreed. Shivling it was. The days of indecision were over.

It was the evening of 12 September. Jim was due back home in a week's time. We had achieved little, had just changed our objective to a peak we knew practically nothing about, except that it was steep and obviously difficult, and yet I felt a sense of excited anticipation, a confidence that had no basis of logic. We cooked a lavish meal, washed it down with the last of the wine, set the alarm for three in the morning and crawled into our sleeping-bags. We hadn't bothered to erect the tent and I lay on my back staring at the blue-black vault of the sky glittering with a myriad stars.

CHAPTER THIRTEEN

A Fairytale Summit

It had cleared during the night and after a quick breakfast we set out in the dark of the pre-dawn, plodding up the slopes above the camp. The beam of my torch picked out the purple gentians peeping through the lush grass. I felt a delicious sense of joy at the prospect of our adventure and the beauty of our surroundings, about the fact that there were just the two of us, that as far as we knew, there was no one else in the entire valley at that moment, that no one even knew where we were, though we had left a note of our change of plan among the boxes at our previous night's campsite.

We were skirting the southern slopes of Kedarnath Dome above the Kirti Bamak and as the sky lightened with the dawn we could start picking out features on the black mass of Shivling. The mountain was like a gigantic fish-tail jutting into the sky, the two fins being the two summits. The main one to the north-east, higher by around a hundred metres or so, had first been climbed in 1974 by an Indian para-military expedition. They had climbed from the north, using a large quantity of fixed rope. Since then Doug Scott, with Rick White, Greg Child and Georges Bettembourg had climbed the spectacular North-East Ridge. Nick Kekus and Richard Cox had nearly achieved the North Face, when Cox was killed by a falling stone. Earlier that summer a Japanese team had made a route up the East Face, reaching the summit ridge of Shivling just above the col between the two summits.

The South-West Summit remained unclimbed. The Japanese had also tried the South-West Summit from the north but had turned back. The route that attracted us was its unclimbed South-East Ridge, an airy rock spur that ran up to the South-West Summit. It looked feasible. The problem was how to reach it, for the mountain was guarded on its south-eastern flank by a series of huge bastions of crumbling granite, split by gullies leading into blind alleys of overhanging, probably rotten, rock.

Jim and I walked across the hoar-frosted grass in the early dawn, seeking the castle gate. We found it after about an hour. A broad gully swept down from a high basin cradled by the arms of the South-East and South-West Ridges of our summit. The basin obviously held a glacier that spewed in a sheer tumbling icefall down the head wall of the gully. It would be suicidal to try to climb this, but a gully or rake seemed to slip across to the right and would perhaps bypass the barrier. At least it gave us a chance.

We crossed the Kirti Bamak, a wide expanse of smooth bare ice, and climbed the moraine wall on the other side. There was a little grassy nook with a small stream running through it, tucked amongst some boulders. The sun had now risen above the Bhagirathi peaks and it was agreeably warm. We got out the stove, made a brew and a second breakfast. But what to do? The icefall at the head of the gully was already in the sun. It was obviously an avalanche trap and caution dictated that we should laze away the rest of the day in this idyllic spot, then in the cold of the night, when stones would be frozen in position and the snow would be firm and hard, we could try to get round the danger area. It made good sense but we were impatient, felt we had already wasted too much time and, therefore with hardly any discussion, because both of us instinctively wanted to get moving, decided to climb the gully that morning.

We repacked our sacks taking food and fuel for six days, a light tent, sleeping-bags, cooking gear, ropes and climbing hardwear. The loads felt heavy and must have weighed about fifteen kilos each. We climbed a talus slope beside the long tongue of avalanche debris. At the base of the cleft we put on our crampons. The snow was packed hard, worn smooth by the passage of avalanches and stone-fall. The walls on either side were sheer, scored by more falling rocks and stones. The gully was about twenty metres wide, but we hugged the right-hand side, getting an illusory sense of cover from the solid wall beside us.

Jim drew ahead. I was feeling the altitude and the weight of my sack, was becoming increasingly aware of the threat posed by the icefall that now seemed to hang over us. There was no sound except the crunch of our crampons. We were about half-way up when a huge boulder, the size of a car, broke away high above us. It came bouncing down the gully, ricocheting from wall to wall. There was no cover, no point in moving, because you couldn't tell where it would bounce next. I just stood there and tried to shrink into myself as it hurtled down. It passed about two metres from my side and then vanished below. Everything was silent once more.

Until this moment I had plodded slowly, regulating my breathing and saving my energy, but I now abandoned all economy of effort, kicked fiercely up the slope, lungs aching, sweat pouring down me, to escape the gun barrel as quickly as I could. As always happens, the point at which the gully forked, foreshortened from below, never seemed to get any closer. But at last we were on a slight spur to the side, the gully had opened out and we could see up the right-hand fork. It was more a rake than a gully, leading up to an overhanging head wall, but this in turn looked as if it could be bypassed by a traverse to the crest of the ridge on the right.

But the quality of the snow had now deteriorated. We waded through soft snow lying on shaly, slabby rock. I caught Jim up. He had decided it was time for a rope. A steep corner running with water blocked our way. I had no belay, so the rope simply meant that both of us would fall should Jim come off, but it somehow gave a psychological feeling of security as Jim straddled up the rock and continued above more easily. I led through another pitch, reaching a bunk-like ledge tucked beneath a huge roof overhang. Beyond, the angle became steeper, with wet snow lying thinly on smooth slabs. Jim flirted with them half-heartedly before retreating.

It was only midday, but the ledge provided a perfect bivouac spot and we could hope that after a night's frost the snow on the slabs would have frozen, making the route out of the top of the gully both easier and safer. We settled down for the afternoon, clearing rocks and snow to give us two bunk berths, each about half a metre wide. We couldn't do much cooking, for we had kept our fuel to the minimum, and had designed our diet so that the only thing we needed to heat was snow for our tea. All our food was to be eaten cold, a combination of biscuits, cheese, nuts, dried fruit, canned tuna fish, a Parma-type ham and Calthwaite Fudge prepared in Cumbria, and dried fruit. We nibbled through the afternoon, snuggled into our sleeping-bags, dozed and chatted.

But it didn't freeze that night. The water dripped steadily from the overhang. In the cold light of dawn we assessed the situation. Jim, always realistic, questioned whether we should go on. But apart from hating the thought of venturing beneath the icefall once again, I had a gut feeling that we could do the climb.

'I'll just have a look,' I said.

The snow over the slabs hadn't frozen, but it was firmer than it had been the previous afternoon. About eight centimetres deep, it just took my weight. I tiptoed up to the base of the head wall; the angle eased slightly and the snow became deeper. I hammered in a piton and carried on for the full length of the rope. As Jim came up to join me, I was able to gaze down into the gully we had climbed the previous day. The hanging glacier looked not only nearly vertical but was eaten away by giant bites as if the entire tumbled mass of ice was ready to collapse. Our route was even more dangerous than we had judged from the bottom.

We picked our way over crumbling rocks and insubstantial snow, surmounted a small rocky peak and, almost two hours later, reached a col only twenty metres above where we had spent the night. This was a magical mystery tour indeed. A long traverse over snow-clad scree ledges and we were at last in the upper basin, a high cwm held in Shivling's arms. But the sun once again had softened the snow that now clung to the steep icy slopes barring our way to the crest of the ridge. Another good reason for an early halt. We dug out a platform for the tent and settled down to a lazy afternoon.

We had gained about 300 metres and crept up into the freezing zone. The following morning the snow was iron hard. Crampons bit reassuringly and we were able to make fast easy progress across the bottom snow slope, choosing runnels of snow between the fingers of granite and hard black ice that ran down from the rocky cock's comb above.

The sun had already tipped Shivling's summit, lighting it with a golden sheen that now dropped quickly down its flanks. It was a race, for that sun with its rich strength-giving warmth would also soften the snow that provided our path to the ridge. It touched the crest of an arête just beside us, racing its thawing, melting fingers down the slope, but we had been cunning and had chosen a runnel that was protected from its rays for just a little longer. Jim was out in front, picking his way up the still hard snow, reaching for the start of the rocks that would give us safe passage to the ridge.

The sun had now reached us but we were nearly there. The rock was already warm to the touch. It was grey granite, rough under hand, revealing cracks and holds as I clambered those last few feet to the crest. The view opened out. We could now gaze across the Gangotri Glacier to the Bhagirathi peaks and could see beyond them an endless vista of shapely jagged mountains. Time for a brew. We lay back on a rocky ledge absorbing the morning sun while the stove roared beneath a panful of snow. Soaring upwards, the ridges swept in a crescent towards the summit some 700 metres above. It was all rock, yet such a light grey that it was almost indistinguishable from the snow. The concave curve meant that we could see all the way to the top. The start looked comparatively easy-angled, comprising great blocks, dovetailed together, piled like gigantic building bricks in a crazy staircase towards the summit.

We climbed carrying our sacks, running out pitch after pitch under a cloudless sky, until in the late afternoon we reached the crest of a huge boulder. It was like a flying buttress leaning against the main structure of the mountain. Ahead the angle steepened; the rock appeared to be more compact and the way less obvious. It was a good place to stop for our third night. There was some ice down behind the boulder and I dug this out for our evening drink. We didn't bother to put up the tent but found two level areas on to which we would curl in our sleeping-bags, tied ourselves on and dropped off to sleep in the dusk.

I was woken by the wind. A great cloud was blanking out the starlit sky.

Suddenly our situation seemed threatening. I woke Jim and we decided we had better erect the tent. In the confusion of doing this in the dark I dropped my head-torch. It slithered crazily down a wide crack at the back of the chimney. But the storm didn't materialise. The following morning there was no trace of cloud. We waited for the sun to warm the tent before starting to cook, made a leisured breakfast and got away from our bivouac spot by eight o'clock.

Now the rock was steeper, the holds smaller. The sack was too serious an encumbrance for the leader, so whoever was out in front left his behind. We tried hauling the sack but the angle was too easy. So it kept jamming and was being torn to bits by the sharp rock. We therefore devised a system by which the leader anchored the rope on completing each pitch, abseiled back down to pick up his sack and then jumared back up to his high point, followed by the second who would also remove any nuts or pitons. It was a slow and tiring process.

The ridge was flattening out into little more than a rounded buttress, losing itself in the upper part of the South-East Face. The rock was becoming more compact, there were few cracks and the holds were becoming increasingly rounded. It was my turn to lead. I couldn't get in any runners and was faced with a move that would have been very difficult to reverse. I couldn't afford a fall.

I retreated, picked out the line of least resistance, and made a long traverse on to the face, over easy-angled but smooth slabs, for a full rope-length. Jim followed, leaving his rucksack behind. We planned to abseil back down to rescue them both once we had completed our dog-leg. It took us two hours to get back on to the crest of the ridge about thirty metres above our starting point. The morning had slipped away. The rock was now more broken but pitch followed pitch towards the crown of a small spur. We were becoming worried about a water supply. We needed snow but the rock had been bare for some time. We found some ice in the back of a crack on the crest of the spur, enough for a few brews, but it was hardly a luxury bivouac spot. There was barely room for both of us to sit down, yet it would have to do, for there seemed neither ledges nor snow above us.

It was only three in the afternoon, so we resolved to run out our two rope-lengths before trying to construct a bivouac site. It was my turn to lead up a rocky prow that was rich in holds, but above the ridge merged once again with the face in a steepening of slabs. Jim set off following a series of grooves. The cracks were blind, the holds sparse and his progress slow and hesitant. All I could do was watch the rope and gaze at the clouds boiling over the high walls of Meru and Kedarnath. Big thunderheads were forming to the west. Could this be a break in the weather, and, if there were

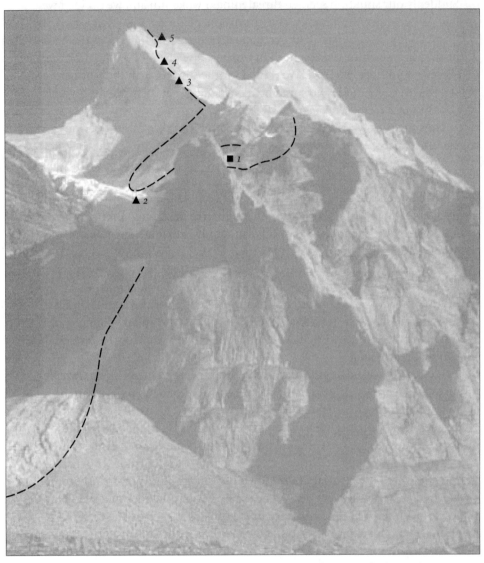

▲ *Tented camp*   ■ *Bivouac in open*   _ _ _ _ *Route not using fixed ropes*
Shivling From the South

a storm, how would we fare on the last of our rations, with the choice of a desperate retreat or smooth difficult rock above, leading to unknown ground on the other side of the mountain? I glanced across the face to the east. We were below the level of the col between the two summits and must be at least 200 metres from the top.

'I don't think this is going to go,' shouted Jim. 'I'll abseil down and try out to the right.'

He fiddled with his pegs, trying to get a good placement. The hammering sounded flat and dull with none of the resonant ring that is the sign of a peg well in. We were uncomfortably aware of the dangers of abseiling. We had met three young British climbers in Delhi at the headquarters of the Indian Mountaineering Foundation. They had made an impressive new route up the West Ridge of Bhagirathi I, the fine pointed peak we could see dominating the other side of the Gangotri Glacier, but one of them had fallen to his death on the way down while abseiling from a nut anchor. Jim was now abseiling from the piton he had finally managed to place to his satisfaction, stepping down carefully, putting as little weight on the rope as possible.

He pulled the ropes down and picked a way to his right in a long diagonally rising traverse towards what appeared to be a break in the smooth band of rock. In the meantime the clouds had rolled in to cover the sky. Our friendly ridge was looking bleak and threatening and I had now had over an hour to savour the isolation and commitment of our position. The rope had nearly run out.

'Only ten more feet.'

'I'm nearly there.'

There was a whoop of success.

'It'll go all right. Looks great.'

I shivered. 'Come on Jim, we've still got to build a bivvie site.'

He anchored the rope, and picked his way back to join me. The ledge where we had left our sacks looked even smaller than it had been three hours earlier. Jim set to with a will, heaving rocks from the ridge to build a delicately balanced platform projecting out from the original tiny plinth. After an hour's work we had quite a respectable platform, though the tent, once erected, was overhanging it at both ends and on the outer side. From outside it looked incredibly precarious but inside, though we could barely sit up it had a reassuring enclosed feel. We had chipped away at some ice and collected it in a pile by the entrance. The stove was purring and our first brew was almost ready. In our effort to save weight we had just the one pan and a single spoon.

It had begun to snow, pattering lightly on the tent. I suspect that Jim was wondering, in much the same way that I was, just how we would manage to get off the climb in bad weather, but we didn't discuss it. There was no point. We chatted lightly and easily. Our climbing judgement and attitudes seemed so close that there was very little need to talk over plans or intentions. Whoever happened to be out in front took the tactical decision; it was as good and as easy a level of teamwork as I have experienced in the mountains.

It was now dark. Just one more brew before settling in for the night. Jim opened the tent door to get some ice, there was a rattle and our only remaining torch, which had been propped in the entrance, went hurtling down the slope, casting its beam erratically over the snow-plastered slabs.

'That'd give someone a shock, if there was anyone down there to see it,' commented Jim cheerfully.

We had now lost both head-torches but we could do without them. At least it gave us an excuse to lie-in until it was light in the morning.

About an inch of snow had fallen in the night, but this was quickly burnt away once the sun crept above the cloudless peaks to the east. We were away by eight thirty, jumaring up to the high point. I had the first lead of the day up a steep crack line that yielded both holds and placements for protection. This led to an overhanging corner. It looked as if Jim had captured the crux. He bridged out widely, managed to get a running belay above him, swung out onto the overhanging wall and let out a yell.

It looked spectacular. He was moving steadily out over the bulge until he vanished from sight. Slowly the rope ran through my hands. There was a shout from above; he'd made it. Another pause and he zoomed back down the rope to pick up his sack. As I followed, jumaring up the rope, I was part envious that he had probably got the best pitch of the climb, and part relieved that it hadn't been my turn. It looked hard and committing with widely spaced holds over a giddy drop.

The angle now relented but every ledge was piled with rocky debris which the rope dislodged on to the man below. Pitch followed nerve-racking pitch. We were now above the col but the top seemed as far away as ever. The higher we got, the more insecure the rock became, with great flakes piled precariously one on top of the other. We weaved from side to side, trying to take the safest line. There was no point in putting in any runners, for nothing was solid. Then, suddenly, I was nearly there. I pulled carefully over a huge block and found myself on steep snow just below the crest of the ridge. But I'd run out of rope. There was no alternative, I'd have to stop and bring Jim up. We were now both carrying our sacks and he hardly paused as he came alongside, excited to reach the crest and see the view from it. He kicked up it, feeling the lack of crampons, and peered over the top, a precarious knife-edge of snow. The other side fell away in a precipitous slope that swept in a single plunge of some 300 metres to a snow basin far below.

The summit seemed barely a rope-length away. It was a slender tapering tower, sheer rock on the southern side, near vertical snow on the northern; a mythical peak from one of those eighteenth-century pictures or perhaps a Chinese watercolour. It was now five in the afternoon. The snow of the final ridge would be safer after a night's frost, so we decided to stop where we were. We cut away the crest of the ridge until we had a platform just big enough for the tent with crazy drops on either side.

That evening we finished most of the small quantity of food we still had. We were just thirty metres or so below the South-West Summit of Shivling but, having got up, we now had to get down again. Descending the way we had come would be a nightmare. The rope would almost certainly jam on all those loose rocks and, even if we got down the ridge, we would still have to negotiate the crumbling walls near the base and the bottom gully with the threat of the icefall. Yet descent on the other side didn't seem much better. The snow slope was ferociously steep, the crest of the ridge knife-edged and it was a long way back to the col. We couldn't have been much further out on a limb.

'You know, we're just about on top. We've climbed the route. Don't you think we should start getting down? It looks bloody desperate to me,' Jim suggested tentatively next morning.

'Oh, come on Jim, we've got to finish it off. Don't you want a picture of yourself standing there on top? Where's your sense of glory?'

'I'm more interested in getting down in one piece.'

'It'll only be twenty minutes or so. You'll regret it for ever if you don't go to the top.'

It took more than twenty minutes. It was my turn for the first lead and I set out, kicking carefully into the snow that was still soft even after a night's hard frost. I ran out a rope-length and started bringing Jim up. I was barely half-way to the summit. As he came towards me, using the steps I had kicked carefully, my eyes were drawn beyond him to the line of descent. It looked quite incredibly frightening. The top of the ridge curled over in a cornice, making the crest itself dangerous to follow. That left the steep snow slope on the left, but was it secure?

Jim was now kicking into the snow above me, moving steadily. He reached a little rock outcrop, pulled up it and then he was there, perched on a tiny platform just below the top. He brought me up and offered me the summit with a sweep of his hand. It was just a single clamber to the perfect point of Shivling. I have never been on a summit like it. There was

barely room for a single person to balance on its tip. I stood there and
waved my ice tools in a gesture of victory, not over our mountain, but of
joy in the climb we had completed, the beauty of the peaks and sky around
us and the complete accord with which we had reached our summit. But
then reality returned. We had to descend an unknown route that, from
what little we could see of it, was going to be frighteningly difficult. We
returned to the tent and packed up, leaving behind anything that we felt
we definitely would not need again.

'We might just as well solo down,' I suggested. 'I don't think we'll get any
decent belays. If we're far enough apart and unroped, if the slope does go,
at least one of us might survive.'

'Oh!' said Jim. 'It's like that is it? OK.'

He admitted afterwards to being horrified by the prospect. He was
less used than I to Himalayan snow slopes and hadn't experienced an
apprenticeship with Tom Patey, the legendary Scottish climber who rarely
agreed to use a rope on anything but the most difficult ground.

I started down, kicking hard into the snow, trying to get the tips of my
crampons into the solid ice beneath, hoping that the snow was just firm
enough to take my weight and that the whole lot wouldn't slide away. It
was as frightening ground as any I have been on, steep, insecure and going
on for a long way. I moved as fast as I could, concentrating on each separate
step, trying to insulate my mind from the drop below and the scale of the
danger. Just kick, step, kick, step, place the ice tools, balance the weight
evenly, delicately yet firmly, and hold the fear in tight control. The knife-
edge went in a great curve and I kept just below the crest, slowly getting
closer to the col, gradually lessening that terrifying drop. At last I was above
the col and, if I fell now, I'd stop where it levelled out. It was broad and
inviting. I turned outwards, started walking down with greater confidence,
negotiated a filled-in bergschrund with care and then at last was on the
level. I could relax.

I pulled off my sack, slumped onto it and looked for Jim. There was no
sign of him. After twenty minutes I began to worry. I was just starting to
retrace my steps when to my immense relief I saw him come round the
crest of the ridge.

'That's the worst bit of ground I've ever crossed,' he announced.

We were now on the col and had joined the route by which the mountain
had first been climbed. There was a snow bowl just below which dropped
away in what we presumed was a hanging glacier. We certainly didn't want
to go down that. We could see the ridge that formed the boundary of the
North Face of the main peak. It didn't seem too steep.

'That must be the way, surely,' I suggested.

'Looks as good as any other,' Jim agreed.

So we roped up, for fear of crevasses, and started down, at first traversing across the ice slope at the foot of the West Face of the summit pyramid, then dropping down over the bergschrund with a two-metre jump into the snow basin. Getting across to the North Ridge was less easy than it had looked from above. We were soon on steep bare ice, traversing fearfully on the tips of crampons for three rope-lengths, until at last we gained the ridge. Down the sheer slope of the North Face we could see the gem-green oasis of Tapoban far below. But it was going to be a long time before we reached it.

I felt a constant nagging fear that is never present on the ascent. Then all one's energy and thoughts are directed to reaching the top, whilst on the way back down, survival dominates the mind. But it is this very fear, the banishment of all euphoria, that helps one avoid careless mistakes which are the bane of so many descents and the cause of so many accidents to good climbers. The ridge seemed endless. We soloed some sections and roped up on others. Most of it was easy-angled, but it was slabby and smooth, the ledges piled with scree and the snow soft. There were no signs of our predecessors; none of the old fixed ropes that we had expected to find. We reached the top of a vertical step – time to abseil. We completed one rope-length but were still only part-way down, made another over a steep void, swinging awkwardly back on to the ridge.

We tugged one end of the doubled rope. The rock was broken and spiky, full of traps for the unwary abseiler. We had been careful and the rope was coming free but, as we pulled the end through the sling at the top, it fell in a wild arc over a rocky spike some thirty metres above us, looping round it in a knot that got tighter the harder we pulled. We had lost a rope which meant that we could now abseil only twenty metres at a time.

But the angle had eased once again and we climbed down unroped to a glacier that dropped down from the West Face in a great convex sweep. At first it was easy walking on ancient iron-hard ice, then it steepened alarmingly. We were still a couple of hundred metres above the valley floor. To escape the glacier we climbed up on to a broken ridge and were just wondering where to go next when Jim noticed a line of fixed rope across to the left. We had not only made a first ascent but we had found, inadvertently, a new way down. The original route went up a rocky spur in the centre of the West Face.

We were glad of the ropes, for the last hundred metres or so were on smooth water-worn slabs which would have been difficult. A last snow slope and we were on grass once more. It was five in the afternoon. We had just made a 1500-metre descent, but were determined to get back to Base that evening. We were four miles from Tapoban, night was falling and we had lost our head-torches. But it didn't seem to matter. We were alive and we'd just completed one of the most wonderful climbs that either of us had ever undertaken. All we now had to do was put one foot in front of the other as we dropped down the side of the Meru Glacier.

It was ten that night before we stumbled into Tapoban, first passing the camp of a group of young Indian climbers from Calcutta. They were delightfully naïve and ill-equipped but full of enthusiasm and warmly hospitable. After having a cup of tea with them we walked another half mile to our own little camp site, to find Vijay pitched alongside the Poles and very relieved to see us. We had gone beyond fatigue and were in a state of excitement, needing to communicate everything that had befallen us in those five intense days. The Polish girls had climbed Meru and were also about to return.

The following day we all had breakfast together and started back for Delhi. We no longer had the red carpet of the tourist organisation and, squeezing on to a bus packed with pilgrims, were rattled for twelve hours to Uttarkashi and then for another eighteen dusty hours all the way back to Delhi, talking, laughing and swigging Polish vodka until we reached the bus terminal in the early hours of the morning.

Shivling had been a delight. It was an intense, fast-paced experience on a challenging and very committing climb in a tight timespan. It really was Alpine-style, not just in the way we made the climb, but in its entire spirit. Tapoban, with its little groups of climbers, had the feel of an obscure Alpine camp-site and the mountains themselves were Alpine in scale. While the way we had been able to change our plans and react to circumstances had created a sense of freedom you can never feel on a larger expedition. It all added up to one of the best mountain experiences I have ever had.

CHAPTER FOURTEEN

One in Seven

The breaking seas 3000 metres below were little more than hazy white hachures on the dark shifting grey of the Southern Ocean. We were flying over Cape Horn, heading for Antarctica with 600 miles of storm-racked ocean to cross in the strangest aircraft I had ever seen. It was a converted DC3, the old Dakota, work-horse of the Second World War and of Third World airlines ever since. The plane had first flown in 1942 but since then it had undergone a transformation. The engines had been changed to modern turbo-props in elongated, thrusting nacelles and, even more improbably, a third had been added to the nose. Skis had been fitted to the undercarriage and a big alloy box in the cargo bay held a giro whose spin gave our exact position above the surface of the earth at all times.

I glanced out of the window in the cramped passenger area and could see ice beginning to form on the wing by the engine cowling.

'Nothing to worry about,' said Rick Mason, the engineer. 'It's got to be several inches thick before it'll affect our performance and even then it wouldn't take us down.'

'What would?' someone asked.

'If the engine ices up,' was the reply.

'How do you know if that's happening?'

'You don't. The engine just stops.'

Thick-set and bearded, fur hat hugging his head, Rick looked the polar hand that he was. When he wasn't caring for this unique plane he lived in Alaska. It was his job to keep it flying in the coming weeks when we would be far from any kind of maintenance support. We were heading for Mount Vinson, the highest peak in Antarctica and probably the most inaccessible summit in the world.

I was immensely lucky to be in that plane. I can't think of a single mountaineer who would have turned down the chance of a seat in the modified DC3. My own good fortune dated back to a chance meeting at the foot of the north side of Everest in 1982. The Seattle-based American expedition that was attempting the North Face, whilst we were going for the North-East Ridge, had been underwritten by two wealthy Americans,

Dick Bass and Frank Wells. Although they were not climbers, they had conceived the ambition of reaching the highest point of all seven continents.

I first met them carrying colossal loads on pack-frames up to their Advance Camp at the foot of the face and was impressed by the way they were mucking in, portering for the team that they had funded. I took an immediate liking to them. They seemed to complement each other. Frank Wells, then President of Warner Brothers, was very tall and ungainly with a thrusting abrasive manner. He was a highly successful super-executive who had worked his way up the corporate tree. Dick had inherited wealth and was more relaxed. At five foot ten and compactly built, he looked a more likely mountaineer. A Texan, he came from an oil and mining background, but the love of his life was Snowbird, a ski resort in Utah that he had built from nothing. He was a great talker with a fresh enthusiasm that verged on the naïve, happy to tell stories at his own expense, cheerfully confessing that he was known as Bass the Mouth.

I barely gave them a second thought then, as my horizon was filled with our own climb and later with the loss of Pete and Joe. The Americans, too, lost one of their team on the north side of the mountain and it was while I travelled out to Chengdu with them after the sad end of our two expeditions that Dick and Frank told me of their plans and invited me to join them the following year, particularly on the Antarctic venture but, with typical generosity, they also extended it to all seven summits which they ambitiously intended climbing all within one calendar year. At that moment I could not contemplate going back to Everest and could not commit myself to any venture, though my imagination was immediately caught by the prospect of visiting Antarctica. Even so, I temporised. The shock of grief was too great to make an immediate decision.

On getting home, however, I had quickly realised that my love of climbing was as great as it had ever been and that I could never give it up so I wrote to Frank asking him to count me in on the trip to Mount Vinson. With 1983 came their onslaught on the seven peaks. Aconcagua was the first in January, the southern summer. Frank had had a hard struggle but he made it to the top. The odyssey had got off to a good start. Their next objective was Everest, the toughest of them all. They had bought their way into an expedition organised by Gerhard Lenser, a German climber who had permission for the South Col route for spring 1983. Frank managed to get up to the South Col, while Dick very nearly made it, reaching a height of almost 8400 metres on the South-East Ridge before being turned back by the weather.

But they didn't give up. That summer, they climbed McKinley, Elbrus and Kilimanjaro. By far the biggest challenge, however, was Antarctica –

just getting there was the problem. It wasn't a matter of obtaining permission. Since no one nation owns Antarctica, no one can actually stop you going there. The problem is getting the logistic support.

Antarctica today is very different from the empty continent that Amundsen, Scott and Shackleton first explored in the early twentieth century. With modern aircraft and satellite observation and communication it is difficult to conceive the mystery and appeal that the totally unknown immensity of Antarctica must have held for the early pioneers. Now bases are scattered over the continent and the South Pole itself is encapsulated in American suburbia, with deep-freezes full of steak and hamburgers, video, hi-fi and exercise machines, all buried under the snows in windowless huts at the temperature of an overheated hotel.

If you are in the system you can be whisked to the Pole within a couple of days of leaving Washington or London but, if you are an adventurer, without official approval, the barriers are considerable. If you have plenty of time, it is easier. Nobody can stop you sailing down to Antarctica and a growing number of intrepid mariners are penetrating the fjords and sounds of Graham Land. But Vinson, the highest point of Antarctica, is more remote. It is in the Sentinel Range which in turn is part of the Ellsworth Mountains, on the ice cap near the base of Graham Land, the peninsula that reaches out from the solid mass of Antarctica towards the southern tip of America. The range is less than a hundred miles from the southern coast of the Weddell Sea but that part of the sea is permanently frozen. It would be a long trek from where a party had to leave its boat and would mean having to winter in Antarctica before setting out for the mountain.

Frank and Dick certainly didn't have the time to do this, and that meant flying in to Vinson. This was perfectly practicable, provided they could find a way of refuelling their aircraft. The only other major expedition that had climbed in the massif was an American one in 1966. This had had the blessing of the establishment and was flown in by C130, the four-engined work-horse of Antarctica. With a large team, Skidoos for transport and plenty of time, they climbed all but one of the major peaks of the Ellsworth Range. But having seen the stars and stripes on the highest peaks of Antarctica, the National Science Foundation, who control American Antarctic operations, felt they had done their bit for frivolous adventure and since then have refused all requests for help.

They also actively discouraged any alternative sources. It was at this stage that Frank discovered the Japanese skier, Yuichiro Miura, the man who had skied down from the South Col of Everest in 1970, was anxious to ski down the seven summits and had done them all except Vinson. He had plenty of backing from Japanese television as well as some useful contacts with the

Chilean Air Force. The Chileans had bases in Graham Land and would probably be willing to charter one of their C130s. The problem, though, was that they did not have ski landing gear to land on unprepared snow runways. This didn't seem insuperable. Frank, who was the main organiser of this trip, even contemplated buying the ski fittings for the C130, only to find that they were classified as strategic weapons and that under no circumstances would they be released to a foreign air force.

He then heard about the existence of the modified DC3. It had the capacity and range to get the team down to Vinson with one refuelling stop each way from Punta Arenas on the southern tip of South America. This is where I came in, for the British Antarctic Survey had a base with an airstrip at Rothera, half way down the Graham Land peninsula. If we could purchase fuel from them or even have some carried in by their supply ship, the trip was on. But the attitude of the British Antarctic Survey was much the same as that of the National Science Foundation. A lengthy correspondence brought little more than sympathetic letters full of regrets.

But Frank never gave up. Each rebuff was a further challenge, and in between all the expeditions of 1983, he was working away to find new avenues. It was on and off and on again to within a week of our departure. There were problems with insurance; the Chileans threatened to abandon their entire Antarctic programme and therefore would not be able to make the essential airdrop of fuel on to Rothera. The pilot the owners insisted on us using for the venture was forced to drop out at the last minute. But Frank found solutions and at the beginning of November I had a phone call that the trip was definitely taking place.

Frank and Dick had invited two climbers to take part in this venture, the American, Rick Ridgeway, and myself. I had met Rick once before when I had gone climbing near Santa Barbara with him and Yvon Chouinard. Short and thick-set, full of warmth and fun, he wasn't a super-hard climber, either on rock or in the big mountains, and yet had achieved a great deal, reaching the South Col of Everest and, in 1978, getting to the top of K2 with John Roskelley as a member of Jim Whittaker's expedition. I liked him and was delighted when I heard he was to be my climbing partner on Mount Vinson.

We had both had busy years in 1983. In the tradition of Shipton and Tilman we planned the food and gear we were going to take on the back of a menu over a boozey meal in an East Side restaurant when our paths crossed in New York. The trip was by no means certain at that stage and consequently seemed unreal.

I arrived in Santiago the day before Rick and Dick Bass flew in from California and it was only in the taxi on the way from the airport that we really began to co-ordinate our detailed organisation. Frank had done a magnificent job in getting the logistics of our flight down to Antarctica organised. It had cost around a quarter of a million dollars. The pilot was to be Giles Kershaw, an Englishman who is undoubtedly the most experienced Antarctic pilot in the world today. But the mountaineers' forward planning was a shambles.

'Have you got enough rope?' I asked Rick, who had barely caught up with himself after the long flight.

'I thought we agreed that people were responsible for bringing their own. I've got enough for us, but Frank and Dick should have some. Say, Dick, have you got the rope?'

'Gee, no, I thought you were getting all that stuff. I'm not sure I've even got my boots.'

'What about hardwear?' I was remorseless.

'I've got a few ice-screws. We shouldn't need that much.'

'A first aid kit?'

'I haven't done anything. Maybe Frank's got it. Must be one on the plane.'

Back at the hotel we sat down and made out a list. There was a lot we hadn't got, including medical supplies. The plane carried a few plasters and the odd burn dressing. Within twenty-four hours we had bought a comprehensive medical kit and had borrowed ropes and other equipment from some helpful Chilean mountaineers whom Frank and Dick had got to know in January on their way into Aconcagua.

We were now on course for Antarctica; the plane's freight hold was filled with food for three weeks, sledges, tentage, film equipment and climbing gear. Besides the crew of three, there were eight of us, Frank, Dick, Rick and myself, Steve Marts, who was the cameraman and film-maker who had accompanied them on all the summits, Miura and his cameraman, and finally Captain Frias, a lugubrious Chilean C130 pilot, who had been appointed our Liaison Officer.

We were crammed into the little heated passenger compartment, looking out of the small windows for the occasional glimpse, through the clouds, of the stormy ocean below. We gazed forward, peering over the pilot's shoulders, for a first sight of Antarctica. It was difficult to discern distant snow peaks from the boiling clouds that filled the horizon. Then, suddenly, we were over real mountains with glaciers sweeping down into the dark waters of deep fjords, their broken ice forming an untidy jigsaw of white on black.

We flew down the peninsula with Giles pointing out landmarks, until we swept over a big mountainous island to land on a snow field with a strip marked out by empty fuel drums. Three twin-engined Otters, painted a

Antarctica and the Vinson Massif

cheerful orange, were tied down into the snow at the side of the strip. A few huts and a little camp of tents formed the Chilean base and the British base was nearby. Rothera didn't have many visitors and they had never seen an aircraft like ours, so we had an enthusiastic reception committee. Giles knew several of the British Antarctic Survey team and it was a pleasant surprise to find that I knew the base commander, John Hall, who had been married to the daughter of our local doctor back in Caldbeck.

Our fuel had already been dropped by parachute from a C130 of the

Chilean Air Force. Whilst the aircrew were refuelling, Giles got in radio contact with Siple, an American base 180 miles from the point in the Sentinel Range where we planned to land. Siple was clouded in and it looked as if Vinson was affected by the same weather. Giles had a huge responsibility, for we only had sufficient fuel at Rothera to get us to Vinson and back, and then return to Punta Arenas. Should he arrive at Vinson 700 miles to the south but be unable to land because of the weather and then have to return to Rothera, we wouldn't have enough fuel for a second try. But Giles was perfectly calm about things.

'We'll stop here for a few hours and see what the weather's going to do. It'll give you a chance to see the base and get some sleep,' he told us.

We all piled aboard a Snowcat which carried us the three-mile journey down to the shore where the British base was situated. It was much bigger than I had imagined, a collection of single and two-storey buildings, with big workshops, laboratories and comfortable, though quite spartan, living quarters. We were given a wholesome meal of stew, mashed potatoes and vegetables, followed by sponge pudding and custard. After dinner, though it could easily have been lunch, since the sun never sets in the summer at these latitudes, we were shown the base which was an intriguing combination of modern and traditional. They were getting ready for the summer scientific work, most of which would be done from outlying camps under canvas.

Rothera is one of the very few Antarctic bases that still have some dog teams, who stay outside throughout the year, tethered in their teams to a steel cable. They were in beautiful condition and friendly, very different from the dogs I had travelled with in Baffin Island some years earlier. These animals, though, are used more for recreation than serious work. The Skidoo, with its greater speed and pulling power, has taken their place for the long scientific trips, so the huskies are kept mainly out of sentiment and to give the people over-wintering at the base an interest.

Talking over a beer in the bar, I could easily see how addictive life in Antarctica must become. In some ways it is like a long drawn out expedition with the simplicity and clarity of purpose that goes with it. There were the scientists who undertook the research, and a support staff whose primary job was to look after the scientists, getting them to their camps, maintaining all the gear and running the operation. A proportion of these stayed on over the Antarctic winter getting everything ready for the summer work. They did have some leisure during this period and it was then that they could set off on their own exploratory journeys with the dog teams.

They weren't meant to do any climbing because of the accident risk but there was no one to check what they got up to once they were away from base and a tolerantly blind eye was turned.

The weather was still unsettled to the south, so back at the airstrip we bedded down for our first Antarctic night. It was nearly as bright as it had been at midday, though just a little colder, with the sun slightly lower on the horizon. We were woken by a call from the Chileans, an invitation to breakfast in their little officers' mess, a deep snow hole, reached by ladder. It was cramped and dark, lined with plywood, with a wobbly oil cloth-covered table filling most of the space, but it was warm and the atmosphere was friendly. We had hardly finished eating when Giles arrived.

'Time to go, folks. It's all clear down at Vinson.'

This was the most critical take-off on the trip. The plane was loaded to full capacity with fuel and the snow on the runway was wet and heavy. There wasn't much joking as we fastened our seat belts and sat listening to the whine of the engines. Giles slowly taxied to the end of the runway, swung round to face towards Alexander Sound, opened the throttle, and we surged forward sluggishly, as if the skis were fighting their way through syrup. We gathered momentum, the tethered Otters flashed past the window, Giles eased back on the stick and the plane pulled tentatively into the air, then flopped back on to the snow. We were approaching the end of the runway and the sheer ice cliff that dropped away to the sea. Just before we reached it the plane nosed up once again and this time stayed airborne. There was a relieved cheer from the passengers.

We gained height slowly, climbing to an altitude of around 3000 metres over the open waters of Alexander Sound. There were peaks and islands, walls of ice-veined rocks, icebergs glinting with a greenish sheen and the pack ice broken up by a mosaic of thin dark lines delineating the convoluted channels of open water. There was an empty desolation and beauty, the like of which I have never seen before.

It went on for hour after hour – unclimbed, unnamed peaks, walls as challenging and big as the North Wall of the Eiger. The channels and the sea itself were now frozen, an unrelieved carpet of white and then, on the far horizon, difficult to distinguish from an upthrust of clouds, was a mountain mass, much higher than anything we had yet flown past.

These were the Ellsworth Mountains which soon stretched across the horizon with great glaciers coiling down from their spine towards the flat frozen expanse of the Weddell Sea. We were heading straight for the high point of the Sentinel Range, and the rounded complex of peaks that was Mount Vinson, but it was difficult to tell which was the highest bump. To the west of Vinson the peaks became more defined, a bristling spine of mountains, Shinn, Epperly, Tyree and Gardner. We were heading for the col between Vinson and Shinn. Beyond you could see an ocean of ice stretching to the far horizon. This was the ice cap, over 2000 metres of solid ice at an altitude of between 2500 and 3000 metres, stretching across the continent. Giles swung the plane to the right and followed the line of peaks, contouring from cirque to cirque. At times the wings almost seemed to touch the ice-shattered rock.

I had seen photographs of the West Face of Mount Tyree. It was even more impressive close to – a 2000-metre face of rocky spurs and steep ice fields leading to a dramatically steep summit. Rick and I had talked of tackling this big unclimbed face once we had climbed Vinson. The highest point in Antarctica looked little more than a long walk, whilst the face was as exciting a climbing challenge as any I have seen.

Then Giles turned the plane away from the mountain wall and out over the ice cap to look for a place to land. This time it would be an unprepared site. As we skimmed down close to the surface it looked far from smooth with sastrugi, furrows of snow carved by wind like sand dunes, spread in haphazard patterns. There were troughs and mounds, long ridges and gullies over what had seemed a smooth surface from altitude.

He made a tight circuit of a valley leading up towards the col we would have to cross to reach our objective, but dismissed it as a landing ground. It was too close in to the mountains and could be subject to gusts and eddies coming from different directions. Flying out into the ice cap, the wind direction would be more consistent. He coursed over the surface seeking out a smooth stretch on which to land, while Rick Mason, the engineer, threw out a smoke bomb. The smoke rose almost vertically, a sign that there was little wind. We swung round in another circuit, swooped in low, touched the ground, bounced violently and, with an open throttle, took off once again.

'Just to check it out,' Giles reassured us.

We came in again and this time landed smoothly, the tail ski easing down onto the snow. We were on mainland Antarctica some 2500 metres above sea level. The sun glared from a pale blue sky but there was no heat from it. The contrast after the warmth of the cabin was fierce. We gathered in a little group, gazing across at the Vinson Massif. You couldn't see the summit but it all seemed very close and the angle so easy. Ever optimistic, I was convinced we could climb it in two or three days and then, once Rick and I had fulfilled our duty to Dick and Frank, we could go and grab a new route, the West Face of Mount Tyree or perhaps climb Mount Epperly, the only major unclimbed peak in the range.

First, however, we had to make ourselves secure on the ice cap. Both Rick, who had climbed in the peninsula of Graham Land, and Giles had regaled us with tales of sudden changes of weather, of windstorms that gouged out the hard snow, carrying splinters of ice that could tear all but the strongest tents to bits. I was uncomfortably aware of how flimsy were our standard lightweight mountain tents and wondered how well they would stand up to a fully-fledged Antarctic storm. At Rothera I had seen some of the pyramid tents used by the British Antarctic Survey. They were made from heavy nylon and had solid tubular poles – fine for sledging but much too heavy to carry up a mountain.

We dug our tents into the snow, building round them a low wall of snow blocks. The plane crew were securing the tri-turbo, digging deep holes beneath each wing in which to bury an anchor attached to a rope that was tethered to rings on the underside of the wing. It looked secure enough but I wondered if it would hold against a violent gusting wind. This was Giles' greatest fear, for if the plane was damaged we would have no choice but to call for help. We could always do this, for we were in radio touch with both Siple, 180 miles away and also the South Pole base. Within hours a rescue aircraft could reach us, but the disgrace, particularly to Giles, would be immense. It would confirm all the criticism our venture had already excited in official circles and would place a serious blemish on his record for working in polar regions in the future.

You quickly lose track of time in this land of constant sun. There is a temptation to work until a job is finished, but over a period of days this would lead to total exhaustion. It is necessary, therefore, to impose a discipline of artificial day and night to get sufficient rest and sleep. Once the camp was weather-tight, we settled down for a rest. Rick and I were sharing the same little tent that I had taken with me to Shivling. We were also cooking together. I could see that we were going to get on well together. Sharing the various minor chores just seemed to fall into place and it was quickly apparent that we had a very similar approach to climbing and our role on the expedition.

I buried my head in my sleeping bag and covered my eyes with my balaclava. I woke at five, after sleeping for about six hours. The camp was silent, everyone still sleeping. I clipped on the cross-country skis that Rick had obtained for both of us and set out for a little exploration. The mountain wall looked so close, the rise above the camp little more than ten minutes away. I skied towards it. The snow was iron hard, blasted by the winds and the skins on the soles of the skis barely gave any traction. I picked my way between sastrugi, finding paths of smooth snow leading towards the crest. Twenty minutes went by and, although the yellow and black plane, beside its little brood of tents, had receded to toy size, the crest of the ridge seemed no closer. It took me nearly an hour to reach it. It was only then that I began to comprehend the scale of the mountains and to realise that, in the clarity of the atmosphere of this polar desert, all distances were distorted and the way to our summit might be much longer than it seemed.

I had reached the crest of a low ridge that barred our way into the valley that led towards Mount Vinson. It wound in a broad sweep of snow behind an outlying peak that concealed the head wall at its end, but it looked easy going and there didn't seem to be any crevasses. At the moment the weather was settled and the wind, little more than a breeze, sighed over the plateau that stretched in a perfect arc of 180 degrees to the south, broken only by the distant wave-forms of high snow dunes or nunataks which Giles told us were some thirty miles away. Apparently a dump of food and fuel had been left there by the British Antarctic Survey. To the east I could see the start of the gigantic trench carved by the Nimitz Glacier in its course through the Ellsworth Mountains down to the ice of the Weddell Sea, whilst to the north the view was barred by the serrated wall of the mountain range that now seemed to hang over me.

I was alone for the first time for several days in this vast empty land. I revelled in its emptiness, the purity of the air, the absolute silence, the still grandeur of the mountain forms and the immense space of the polar ice cap. I peeled the skins from my skis and skittered down the ice-hard slope back to camp.

CHAPTER FIFTEEN

Alone on Top of Antarctica

The three of us heaved at the heavily laden sledge, dragging it across the sastrugi. To think that Scott and his doomed team did this for over a thousand miles and we were tired after only three. The temperature was −25°C, yet we were sweating, stripped down to our underwear in the still bright air. Rick, Giles and I were pulling 250 kilos of tentage, food, climbing gear and film equipment to the head of the valley reaching into the Vinson massif. The others were a few hundred metres behind, struggling with an equally heavily laden sledge.

The terrain was unlike anything I had ever experienced. The snow under-foot was rock hard and sculpted, presumably resting on the ice of a glacier, but there were no signs of crevasses, perhaps because there was no move-ment of the ice. This was not so much a frozen river as an inlet thrusting into a mountain fjord from the ocean of the polar ice cap.

On our right the valley we were following was bounded by a graceful little peak, a pyramid of rubble and ice, rising just several hundred metres above us. On the left was the huge wall of the Sentinel Range, a sharply serrated ridge leading up to the unclimbed summit of Mount Epperly. A side valley holding a chaotic icefall reached up to the col between Epperly and Shinn, but my eyes were drawn to a gully, a ribbon of snow, edged with steep black rocks, that cut the precipitous wall of Epperly, going all the way to the shoulder just below the summit pyramid. I paused, leaning on the rope harness. This was as good excuse as any for a rest.

'You know, Rick, we could have a go at that once we've climbed Vinson. Doesn't look too bad, does it?'

'Looks OK, but we'd better get Vinson climbed first and see how much time we've got. I've a feeling this is all going to take longer than we thought.'

It took us more than three hours to reach the end of the valley which terminated below a steep head wall of snow and ice. We knew that this led up to a col on a subsidiary ridge which we would have to cross to reach the glacier leading to the main col between Vinson and Shinn. Although quite steep, it did not look far to the top.

'Shouldn't take us more than an hour,' I commented cheerfully as we unharnessed ourselves and started preparing our campsite.

It was good to snuggle into my sleeping-bag while Rick made supper, a concoction of dehydrated stew fortified by over a pound of butter. Eating needs in the polar regions are so different from those in the Himalaya. There is none of the queasiness of high altitude, just a huge appetite and an instinctive desire for fat. At altitude, on the other hand, the human body is unable to absorb fats and probably the best diet is one high in carbohydrate, based on grain foods like tsampa, the roast barley flour which is the staple food of the Sherpas. We did, however, have the same need for large quantities of hot liquid since in the cold dry air you quickly become dehydrated.

Night was marked by the sun slipping behind the ridge, plunging us into shade which meant that the temperature dropped abruptly to about −30°C, bringing with it a fierce cold that penetrated clothing and even frozen fingers clad in thick mitts. Next day we roped up for the first time to help Dick and Frank jumar up a steepening concave slope. Miura and his cameraman, Tae Maeda, carrying very heavy loads which included Miura's skis, were quietly climbing together. They exuded a modest confidence. Frank was very careful to draw them into any planning discussion but Miura always courteously concurred with whatever was being decided.

We were now moving very slowly, with long pauses whilst one person at a time climbed the ropes Rick and I had fixed. It took us six and a half hours to reach the top of the slope where we were rewarded with a view of the glacier some hundred metres below us which stretched easily up towards the broad col between our objective and Mount Shinn. The summit, though, was still concealed by a subsidiary peak. I was beginning to appreciate the scale of everything, in addition to which we were starting to feel the effects of the altitude. The previous night we had been at just under 2500 metres and we were now at nearly 4000. We stopped for lunch and enjoyed the magnificent mountain vista around us. Dick treated us to an impromptu recitation; he had a huge well of poems he had memorised as a child, and had continued to learn as an adult, ranging from the romantic to the bawdy. His favourite poet was Kipling and the lines that were his motto came from 'If':

> If you can force your heart and nerve and sinew
> To serve your turn long after they are gone,
> And so hold on when there is nothing in you
> Except the will which says to them: Hold on!

I couldn't help thinking what an improbable group we were, picnicking in the Antarctic sunshine to the strains of Kipling. The main col immediately below the Vinson massif seemed quite close, but once again this was deceptive. It was about three miles away. We didn't reach it that day but finally dumped our gear at the side of a partly covered crevasse.

I was very concerned that we should be able to build a snow cave which we could use should a sudden violent storm destroy our tents. The Bonington bolt-hole became something of an expedition joke and I suspect that Frank and Dick felt I was being over-cautious. Even so, we took turns in digging away at a bank of snow only to hit hard ice after three metres. However, on inspecting the crevasse, I found a broad shelf just inside. It was easy to widen this into a chamber that all seven of us could squeeze into in an emergency. Blocking off the hole at the top, and then tunnelling out horizontally to make a new covered entrance, we had the perfect emergency shelter.

Giles now left us to return to the plane. We hoped to climb Vinson within three days and it was therefore decided that, if he hadn't heard from us after six days, he should fly in to look for us.

I couldn't help sympathising with Steve Marts. Not only was he carrying the heaviest load and doing the filming, he also did all the cooking for Frank and Dick. It was the one thing they refused to do. Both had domesticated wives who took total responsibility on the home front. Frank had never even packed a case for himself before setting out on his many business trips.

'You know, if you two want to feel you really are part of the team and are not just clients being guided up a mountain, how about sharing in some of the chores? You could start by doing a bit of cooking,' I pointed out, jokingly.

'Hell, no. I've spent a hundred thousand dollars on this trip. I'll carry loads, dig snow holes, do anything, but I'm damned if I'm going to start cooking. Apart from anything else, I'd poison you all if I did,' was Dick's reply.

Steve cooked the evening meal and washed the pans. He didn't really seem to mind. Prematurely grey haired and bearded, he had a very young, easy smile that seemed to guard his inner thoughts. He had been with Frank and Dick on all the seven summits so far and had become a butt for both their displeasure and humour. He had the status of an old family retainer who was both part of the family and yet an employee.

We planned to make one more camp before going for the top and the next afternoon found us plodding steadily upwards, bathed in the warm mellow light of the late afternoon sun. I stripped off down to my Damart underwear, it was so warm. Above us, like the walls of a mythical city, gleaming ramparts and towers of ice guarded the col; cavernous crevasses

▲ *Tented camp*   _ _ _ _ *Route not using fixed ropes*
.... *Continuation of route on other side of ridge*
Mount Vinson

with fragile airy snow bridges formed deep moats. But, as we entered the frozen inanimate city, we walked into the shade. Its effect was immediate. We put on our overtrousers and down gear, but even so, the cold penetrated remorselessly. Without the brightness of the sun the icy towers and walls around us appeared grim and threatening. There was no more laughter. We were like a band of hobbits entering the stern confines of the Misty Mountains.

Above the col the glacier running down from the summit mass of Vinson opened out. We were heading for the crest of the ridge over to our right but had to make a series of diversions to weave our way through a maze of crevasses, some of which were partly covered. We were now exposed to what was little more than a gentle breeze, but it insinuated its way into every chink of our clothing, bit at our unprotected faces, first stinging and then numbing cheeks and noses. I glanced at Frank. A tell-tale patch of white had appeared on the tip of his nose; a sure sign of frostbite. I pulled my hand out of my mitt and placed it on his nose. It was ice cold but my hand quickly warmed it and the patch vanished.

Rick was out in front with Steve Marts, picking the route. I had Dick and Frank on my rope. The snow was so hard that our crampons barely made any impression, sinking in little more than a few millimetres, making the faintest of traces in the snow.

'Put your feet exactly where I do,' I called back. It was like walking through a mine-field and I was uncomfortably aware of just how serious it would be if we had to stop to pull anyone out of a crevasse. If you stopped even for a minute the icy cold started to bite into your inner core. I concentrated on the faint pattern of point marks in front of me. 'Dick, Frank, keep that rope tight. Watch where you're going.'

There was a sudden heave backwards. I lunged forward, swung my axe pick into ice, ready to take Dick's full weight, simultaneously glancing behind me. He had stepped off the ill-defined path and straight into a crevasse, stopping himself with one leg buried up to the thigh.

I yelled at him. 'You must bloody well concentrate on every single step. Shove your feet exactly where I've put mine. You could kill us all if you're not careful.'

Dick grinned and apologised and I immediately felt bad at having shouted at him, but it did mean that both he and Frank concentrated even harder on following the trail. At last it took us onto the retaining ridge. We were off the glacier and could begin to relax. It opened out onto a wide shoulder, ideal for a camp-site but very exposed and with snow so hard that there was no question of being able to dig in the tents.

I scrambled up to a rocky pinnacle on the crest of the ridge. It just caught the sun and from this perch you could capture the magic of the Antarctic, the endless white of the ice cap, the huge trench of the Nimitz Glacier curving round out of sight towards the Weddell Sea and, to the west, the rest of the Sentinel Range, a rocky spine jutting out of the snow and ice. Our own objective was hidden by the swell of the ridge immediately above, but we had seen the summit of Vinson from the glacier and knew that we were within striking distance, probably just a few hours from the top.

We got four hours' sleep before brewing up and getting ready for our summit bid. It was 23 November. We took the tents down, for fear of the wind building up during the day, and left them safely secured under a pile of boulders. It was good to climb without the weight of a rucksack. Rick and I tossed up as to who should find the route and who should look after Dick and Frank. He won and set out, roped to Steve Marts. I followed with my charges while Miura, carrying his skis, brought up the rear. At first we took the line of ridge. It was no more than steady walking, yet the vast emptiness around us gave it both a beauty and seriousness that were unique. Glancing up I could see clouds of snow, like dancing dervishes, swirl around Rick and Steve. It was the wind, just beginning to catch the ridge.

They began to traverse round the slope on to the side of the valley that led up towards Vinson itself. The bed of it seemed quite flat but was probably crevassed, so we avoided it. At first the wind came in gusts but, slowly, as we progressed, it built into a steady savage blast until it was almost impossible to face into it. Rick had stopped to put on extra clothing and had to ask me to do up the hood of his down jacket. The others had now caught up. Frank, at the end of our rope, had been going quite slowly. I had been conscious of the steady drag from behind. He was wearing a face mask but it only gave him partial protection and, as he reached me, I saw that once again his nose had been nipped by the cold but this time, when I tried to warm it with my hand, I could feel a long, solid lump of frozen tissue down one side. Even if I thawed it out, it would still be vulnerable and the capillaries carrying the vital blood supply would almost certainly have been damaged. It would freeze up again and in the hours it would take us to reach the top the injury could be serious.

'There's nothing for it, Frank. With your nose like that you'll have to go down. I'll take you back.'

As I said it, I felt a sense of vast disappointment. I was going well and had the summit of Vinson in my sights but there seemed no other sensible course. But then Frank said, 'It's all right, you go on. Steve can always come back with me.'

It was like a condemned man's reprieve, but it didn't last long.

'Hell, Steve can't go back,' Dick butted in. 'We need him for filming the top.'

At that I couldn't stop myself and just burst out, 'I'm sorry. I don't mind taking Frank back down and missing the summit if it's a question of safety, but I'm not going to sacrifice the top for a bloody film.'

By this time we were all shouting against the roar of the wind, and then Rick, who had been standing quietly to one side, interjected, 'Hey fellas, can I say something? I guess I owe you guys a hell of a lot. You've taken me on your trips, given me some of the greatest times I've ever had. It's O.K. I'll take Frank down.'

I felt a surge of guilt for my own single-minded need for the top, but then Miura spoke quietly. 'It's too windy to ski. We're going down anyway.'

That solved the dilemma but it still wasn't over.

Dick yelled, 'Hell, Frank, I'm not going to the top without you. We've been in this together and we're going to the top together. I'll go down with you.'

'You don't seem to realise,' I said, 'you don't get second chances in the mountains. This might be the only bloody one you get. You just can't afford to give up an opportunity if it's there, can't you see that?'

But Dick's mind was made up.

'He who fights and runs away, lives to fight another day, but he who is in battle slain, will never rise to fight again.'

'Don't be so flippant,' Frank shouted at him.

'Hell's bells!' Dick replied. 'You're the one always saying you have more than one chance on these climbs. I want that picture of us together on the summit.'

'O.K. I really appreciate how you feel, old buddy, but I think Chris and Rick had better go for the summit. At least we'll be sure of getting someone there. Let's hope we get our chance when this wind drops.'

I promised that Rick and I would go with them in a second attempt even if we did manage to make it that day, and then we separated, Rick and I heading into the wind, the others dropping back down that high cold valley towards the camp.

I couldn't help a sense of relief that there was no one to look after and that we were now two peers, each capable of looking after himself. We reached the head of the valley and were on a broad col with a subsidiary peak on our right barring any view of the ice cap. On our left an easy-angled ridge curved up towards the summit of Vinson which was now in sight. It must have been about 500 metres above us, not much more in scale than from Red Tarn to the top of Helvellyn in the Lake District, and we were approaching the equivalent of Striding Edge. We had dispensed with a rope, since we were now off the glacier and there was no danger of crevasses. The snow was firm under foot and it was just a question of steadily plodding, head bent in an effort to protect one's face from the wind. I was just wearing sun glasses since my goggles had broken on the previous day. I didn't try to cover my mouth and nose since I found that the glasses misted up. I would just have to put up with the agony of ice particles being driven into my face and the accompanying risk of frostbite.

I had drawn ahead of Rick but waited for him just below the crest of the ridge. The wind was so fierce that I had to cling to my axe, driven firmly into the snow, for fear of being blown over. When Rick caught up, he was having trouble with his goggles. He had masked the lower part of his face with a scarf and, consequently, was having problems from frozen condensation. He could hardly see where he was going.

We set off once more. The wind drove you into a small world all of your own. I kept one mitt over my face, leant on my axe, took each step very carefully, braced against the force of the wind, looking only the few metres in front of me. Step followed painstaking step until I reached a rocky gendarme on the crest of the ridge. I tried to find shelter in a small niche to wait for Rick. There was no sign of him. And then I became so cold, I could wait no longer. I picked my way over the rocks, clinging to them to avoid being blown off balance, and followed a series of snow-covered ledges with awkward strides in between. I was uncomfortably aware of the steep drop into the high cwm below but soon I was on the other side of the rocks and the ridge broadened out once again into a snow slope. It stretched up to a head wall of snow and there, beyond that, perhaps 200 metres above me, was the summit of Vinson.

I waited, worried about Rick. Should I go back for him? But surely he couldn't have got into trouble? It was little more than a walk as far as the gendarme. Had he turned back? I couldn't tell. But the summit was there, a siren that for me was irresistible. It would only take an hour to get there. Go up and then look for Rick on the way down. I set out once again, but I kept glancing back and then, to my immense relief, I saw a tiny figure near the end of the ridge. Rick had turned back, maybe because his goggles had been misting up so badly. The head wall was now in front of me, looking steep and daunting. I plunged my axe into the snow, kicked into it and slowly worked my way up. Each step had become an effort. It was as if I was on a Himalayan peak at over 6000 metres, rather than the 4897 metres of Mount Vinson; perhaps the speed of our ascent had not allowed enough time for acclimatisation. But the remorseless wind was the greatest impediment, tearing out of the clear emptiness of the pale blue sky. I have never felt so alone.

I had reached the top of the head wall and the snow fell away gently on the other side. I pulled myself to my feet, pushed one foot in front of the other against the wind as I stumbled those last few steps to the highest point in Antarctica. Part of me wanted to share the joy of being on this summit with the others, and yet I found myself revelling in the absolute isolation. I was the only person left on the surface of the earth. There was no life, just a sky that was almost unbearably clear and the great sweep of the polar ice cap on one side, with the Welcome Nunatak, like the fins of a school of dolphins cutting its smooth surface in the middle distance. The view had now opened up for beyond the dividing line of the range I could gaze northwards towards snow-clad peaks stretching into the distance. Above them, very high in the pale sky, in a light feathered fantail, was a wedge of cloud. Could it be the vanguard of a storm? I prayed, prompted by my mixed emotions of supreme elation and guilt. I prayed to God to help me be less selfish, less single-minded in my drive for my own gratification.

Then I noticed a token of man's former presence. An up-ended ski pole was stuck into the snow close to the summit. I had brought with me a little Union Jack given me by John Hall at Rothera. I tied it to the pole and photographed it with Vinson in the background. I then photographed my own long-flung shadow to prove I had been on top of Antarctica. It was time to turn back. I scrambled down from the summit, finding an easier route to avoid the steep head wall, treading carefully, for the drop on either side was steep and long, then over the gendarme, and it was easy snow all the way after that. Just a matter of putting one cramponed boot in front of the other.

As I came closer to the camp, I couldn't help feeling a reticence. What was their reaction going to be? They must have mixed feelings about my having gone for the top. I let out a whoop. Dick poked his head out of the tent.

'Hey man, you made it. Well done!'

The others added their congratulations. They were warm and kind. Rick got the stove going and soon pushed a mug of tea into my hand. But I couldn't drink it. My beard and moustache had built up so much ice that it had frozen them on to my balaclava. It was as if I had an armoured visor guarding my face, and it took half an hour's painful pulling and cutting to free it so that I could get the cup to my lips. Meanwhile Rick told me that he had begun to feel dizzy with weakness at the base of the rocky gendarme. It was this, combined with the fact that his goggles had completely frozen over, that had forced him to turn back. He had nearly died from typhus whilst crossing New Guinea only a few months earlier and he probably still hadn't fully recovered his stamina.

I longed to crawl into my sleeping-bag but I was desperately worried about the high cloud I had seen from the summit. Our camp was so exposed that it would have had little chance of resisting a wind storm. I could remember all too vividly how slow and precarious our walk through the crevassed glacier had been the previous evening.

'I hate to say this, fellas, but I think we must get the hell out of here back to the lower camp. The weather looks as if it's going to break and if it does we need my bolt-hole.'

'But what about our next attempt?' Frank protested. 'We'd have to come all the way back up.'

'It's a hell of a sight better having to do that than risk being caught here by a wind storm. You wouldn't have a bloody hope. This mountaineering is a serious game. Believe me, Frank, I know.'

'I think Chris is right,' Rick said. 'We shouldn't risk it.'

'I don't agree, but I suppose I'll have to defer,' was Frank's response.

'Well, I'll just go along with our leaders,' said Dick, easy-going and relaxed as always.

So we packed and started back down the glacier. I didn't relax until we had passed the col and were descending the easy slope leading to our bolt-hole. I then knew that whatever the weather did, we would survive. It was only later that I learnt just how deeply depressed Frank had felt at this moment. He had to put so much effort into every step he made on the mountain and was pushing himself in a way that I could never fully appreciate. He had known so many disappointments and through sheer dogged determination had kept going.

It wasn't just the cost of getting to Antarctica, it was the effort he had made as well. He knew that he could make it to the summit if he was given the chance and was certainly prepared to risk losing his nose in the process. The dangers I had pointed out were all nebulous. My judgement and caution were born from experience, influenced by the cruel toll the mountains had taken on friends. In addition I was having to take responsibility for others. It is much easier to take a finely calculated risk for yourself.

It was midday before I woke. The others were beginning to stir.

'Can you guys come over in half an hour or so for a chat?' called Frank.

It was only when I crawled out of the sleeping-bag that I realised just how tired I was. In terms of distance and height gain the previous day's climb had been little more than the equivalent of a walk up a Lakeland peak, but it had meant reaching 4897 metres, and I had certainly felt the altitude. On top of that had been the Antarctic cold and wind.

There was plenty of room for the seven of us to sit around in the big tent on foam mats and sleeping-bags. Frank, as usual, presided over the meeting. He did it well, a sign of his effectiveness as a senior executive. Dick, his equal partner and undoubtedly the stronger and physically the more competent of the pair, seemed happy to let Frank take the chair, recognising his expertise in this particular field. It was in part the secret of their success as a team, each valuing the other's strengths.

Frank started by asking me for my views on what we should now do.

I replied: 'I know you were unhappy about coming back down here but I think we're now in a really good position. We've got about three days' food and fuel and you've got the snow cave if the weather breaks and your tents are destroyed. You can sit it out here until the wind drops and you think you can make it to the top. In the meantime I'm happy to act in support. Someone is going to have to go down to the plane, anyway, to tell Giles what's happening. Otherwise he's going to have to come looking for us.'

Down with the plane crew I slept for twenty-four hours and still felt tired when Giles and I set out to make the food carry up to the others. Although he was a comparative novice on crampons, he moved naturally and easily, far outstripping me. Back at the plane again time dragged. It was impossible for us to judge conditions high on the mountain, but we were convinced that the weather must be suitable for a summit bid and couldn't understand why they hadn't completed the climb and returned.

After three days Giles and I made another carry. As we approached the tents, we saw two little figures coming down from the col. Had they reached the summit?

We knew they had from the great whoop one of them – it had to be Dick – made before they were even in shouting distance. When they reached us, Dick told how he and Rick had gone for the top in a single push, while the other four had used the intermediate camp. They also had reached the top and would soon be on their way down. It was a tremendous relief to me that they had all realised their ambitions and that we could now celebrate our success without reservation.

A few hours later we were all back at the plane. Frank was tired and his nose raw, adorned with an unsightly black scab that he wore like a medal. This had been very much his expedition for without his drive and determination we would never even have reached Antarctica. I could sense a feeling of achievement that went very deep, but he had only just made it. He had slipped just below the summit and fallen eight metres or so, fortunately without hurting himself. On climbing back up, characteristically, he had asked Marts, 'Have you got it on film?' only to learn that Marts hadn't even seen the fall. But his arrival on top of Antarctica was recorded just a few minutes later. Miura had also reached the top and then skied most of the way back down.

It only took us a couple of hours to load the gear, take group photographs of the successful team and warm up the engines. Soon the plane was bumping over the sastrugi in search of a clear run. We were now more lightly laden and, in spite of the altitude, took off effortlessly, making a swing past our mountain and then following the line of the Sentinel Range on our way to Siple. We were going to pay a social call on the American base and, at the same time, try to buy some fuel to give us a better reserve for the return journey.

The atmosphere was celebratory as we skimmed close to the mountains. There was a lunar quality to the terrain in its empty sterility and the harshness of the contrast between light and shade. I longed to return here and was already talking to Rick of the possibility of trying that huge West Face of Mount Tyree.

We were coming to the end of the range; the peaks now beneath us were little more than scattered rocks jutting out of a frozen ocean of ice and then we were over the ice cap, smooth, monotonous, featureless for mile after mile.

'There it is. That's Siple.'

There were just a few dots in the snow and gradually, as we circled down, we could pick out a couple of huts and a cluster of aerials. Empty fuel drums marked the runway and we could see a little group of people gathered near its end. In the last fortnight our aircrew had built up a real relationship with the Siple radio operators, chatting to them daily and discovering mutual acquaintances from former polar trips.

Our welcoming committee crowded round the hatch as we climbed down to be greeted by their warm congratulations. I could now see that what had appeared to be huts were merely large tunnel tents, built on much the same principle as wartime nissen huts. But we were heading for a box-like structure, little larger than a workman's hut. There was no hint of what we would find inside. It was a little like Dr Who's Tardis. On swinging open a heavy door, we found a shaft plunging down through the snow. Twelve metres of steel ladder led into a cavernous chamber dimly lit by electric lights. You could hear the steady throb of an engine. A long single-storey windowless hut crouched in the cavern. Access was through large doors, like those in big commercial freezers.

As we pushed open the door, we went into another world – a cosy, centrally heated middle America. The living room had murals of forest and mountains on one wall, bookcases and cheerful posters on the others. A hi-fi was playing pop music. Easy chairs and coffee tables rested on a deep pile carpet. We were offered beer and then a magnificent meal of succulent steaks, french fries and frozen vegetables, ending up with water melon and kiwi fruit that had been flown in from New Zealand a few days earlier. This wasn't even a special feast laid on for us but just their standard fare.

It was a very different atmosphere from the base at Rothera which was rather like an Outward Bound school.

In Siple there was more a feeling of people doing a job of work and of having transported, as far as possible, a little chunk of suburban America into the middle of the Antarctic ice cap. Although they were heavily out-numbered, women are employed on the American bases. There were two women to twenty-seven men at Siple. It's still a man's world with the British Antarctic Survey, however. They don't allow women into Antarctica.

The American summer field trips tend to be on a larger scale than the British ventures, with greater logistic support, so that the field camps become mini-bases with a fair number of home comforts and a rule against anyone straying more than a kilometre outside the base perimeter. We were told the story of a climber, working at the big base at McMurdo Sound which is the size of a small town. He had been unable to resist the temptation of attempting nearby Mount Erebus, the only known active volcano in Antarctica. He set out one morning without asking permission, since he knew he wouldn't get it. He was sighted from the base when he was about half-way up. The base commander ordered out a helicopter that hovered over him and he was told by loud-hailer to turn back immediately. He took no notice. They then dropped a net over him, he was bundled into the helicopter and put on the next C130 flight back to New Zealand.

The bad weather that had threatened but never quite arrived was now sweeping down the Graham Land peninsula. Rothera was already storm-bound, a few hours later it reached Siple. It was a strange contrast, between the air-conditioned womb of civilised comfort under the snows and the screaming, driving snow of an Antarctic blizzard on top. We were at Siple for four days and nights, though they were even more timeless than had been the climb. We watched successive videos for hours at a stretch – *Bridge on the River Kwai, Love Story, The War of the Worlds* – made ourselves TV snacks in the well-stocked kitchen, cat-napped on the sofa in the lounge and then watched more videos.

Giles was on the radio every few hours, checking the weather conditions at Rothera. 'Time to go, folks. We're off in an hour.'

Outside, it was as wild as ever. You could only see to the next marker flag which were set at intervals of about ten metres. The plane was lost in a white murk, and it took an hour to dig it out of the snow. We were all tensed and silent as Giles taxied out into an almost total white-out but if we waited for the weather to clear at Siple, the next front would have already reached Rothera. The plane surged forward; it was barely possible to tell when and if it had become airborne, except from the tone of the engine, until we had climbed out above the cloud bank into the sun.

The hours went by. Giles was in radio contact with Rothera. It was still clear there, but clouds were beginning to form. The next front was rolling in faster than they had anticipated. We were now over the Graham Land peninsula and caught glimpses of peaks, dark water and the jigsaw of ice floes below us. Then Alexander Island came into view, its higher peaks jutting into cloud. A low mist was settled over the airstrip. We couldn't land. We were now totally committed. We didn't have enough fuel to get back to Siple or to fly on to the Chilean base on the far tip of Graham Land.

'Don't worry,' Giles told us over the intercom. 'I know a few spots which might be clear where we can go and sit it out.'

He swung the plane round and followed the coast where big ice cliffs spawned bergs and dark slopes of rock and snow swept up into the lowering clouds. We flew over a deserted base, a little collection of brightly painted toy houses, and coasted in to a flat stretch of snow, a uniform grey white that merged with the grey sky. The engine whined and we were thrust back in our seats as he accelerated quickly.

'No good, not enough contrast.'

I began to imagine the consequences if we had to circle round and round until we ran out of fuel. I suspect the same thought was going through everyone's mind. Giles turned to look back into the passenger compartment, a wolfish grin on his face.

'Don't worry, Chris isn't the only one who knows about bolt-holes.'

We swung inland getting height, flew through a bank of cloud into the sun, and there, between two high snow peaks, was a flat glacier. He flew over it, examining it carefully for hidden crevasses, did another circuit, and brought the plane down gently in the deep soft snow.

'Just a matter of a little patience. I picked this place out a few years ago when I was based on Rothera.'

We waited there for a couple of hours with the radio open. We received the call that the airstrip was clear. We were in the air within five minutes, plunged through the low cloud and then, seeming almost to brush the waves, roared back down the coast. Cloud was still hugging the low hills round the airstrip but Giles didn't attempt a circuit. He slid the plane between cloud and col, dropped it the other side, and suddenly we were bumping along the snow, racing past the parked Otters of the British Antarctic Survey. There was barely time for more than a few hurried words, a quick cup of coffee in the Chileans' bunker mess while the plane was refuelled, and we were on our way once again, this time bound for Punta Arenas and civilisation, scheduled air lines, air beacons and traffic control.

Our adventure might have been nothing compared to what Shackleton attempted in 1914 when he sailed down into the Weddell Sea, hoping to cross the Antarctic continent, and then lost his boat and made one of the greatest retreats in history to get his expedition back to safety, but you have to live in, and make the most of, your own age and environment. Our adventure, in its compressed three weeks, had its own special quality. In many ways the star was Giles Kershaw. Without his skill, nerve and deep knowledge of flying in Antarctica we could never have reached Mount Vinson. Equally, without Frank Wells' at times abrasive drive the adventure would never have got off the ground. I was very conscious of just how much I owed them all as we flew back over the turbulent waters of the Drake Passage to a Christmas at home.

CHAPTER SIXTEEN

A Promise Broken

'My name is Arne Naess. I do hope you don't mind me ringing you. I wonder if I could come and see you. I'm organising an expedition to Nepal and would appreciate your advice.'

He had a slight foreign accent but his English was fluent. I often get enquiries about expeditioning.

'Of course. When do you want to come up?'

'How about next week? What day would suit you best?'

'What about Monday? Could you make it in the afternoon, say, just after lunch? I'm working flat out on a book at the moment and try to do my writing in the mornings.'

'That's fine. Have you got an airport near you?'

'Not really. Newcastle's the nearest, but that's sixty miles away on the other side of the Pennines; but the train service isn't bad. It takes just under four hours to Carlisle.'

'I'll check and get back to you.'

He phoned again, an hour later.

'You've an airfield just by Carlisle. I'm chartering a plane. I'll be with you at two o'clock on Monday.'

I was impressed.

It was early 1979 and I was working on my book, *Quest for Adventure*. He arrived by taxi promptly at two, presented Wendy with a side of smoked salmon, which he mentioned later he had caught in Iceland, and a couple of bottles of Burgundy of the very best vintage. Slightly built, with a mop of receding hair over irregular yet very mobile features, there was both an intensity and a boyish enthusiasm about him.

He told me that he was Norwegian and in shipping. He had climbed as a youngster but then had given it up to concentrate on his business. Having achieved success in this field, he was looking, in much the same way that Dick Bass and Frank Wells were to do a couple of years later, for fresh and different challenges. He was more of a mountaineer, however, having come from a family strongly associated with climbing and having shown talent in his youth. His uncle, a professor of philosophy, also called Arne Naess, was the father figure of Norwegian mountaineering who had made many new routes in Norway and led the first Norwegian expedition to the Himalaya. Arne junior had kept up his climbing in a spasmodic way over the years. He owned a pair of chalets in Switzerland at Verbier, climbed with guides from time to time and was a very bold and forceful skier. He now wanted to get back into climbing in a big way. He had booked Everest for 1985, so that he could lead the first Norwegian expedition to the mountain and, as a training climb, he was going to a peak called Numbur in the Rowaling Himal in Nepal. He wanted to ask my advice on equipment and the general planning of the expedition.

He spent a couple of hours with me and then returned to his waiting plane. As well as being impressed with his dynamism and success, I liked him as a person. I have met many successful businessmen and entrepreneurs over the years but none quite like Arne. He had a twinkle of humour, and the mind and attitude of a climber. I suppose even his work, which was a high-risk business, reflected this. We climbed together from time to time in the next few years. Funnily enough, most of our efforts were abortive. On a climbing weekend in the Lakes, it rained non-stop and we made a long wet walk to Scafell. During a skiing holiday in the Alps we set out to make a winter ascent of the Frendo Spur on the Aiguille du Midi as a single-day ascent. The route finishes near the top station of the Midi téléphérique and we planned to catch the last cable car down at the end of our climb. It was a typical piece of Bonington optimism and complete lack of research. After spending three hours on the snow-covered rocks at the bottom of the 700-metre spur, it was obvious we were not going to get more than a third of the way up in the day. We had an epic retreat in the dark through the steep forested slopes above Chamonix.

We also met up in Yosemite. It poured all weekend and we achieved nothing. But this didn't harm our friendship or, amazingly, seem to dent Arne's confidence in my ability as an organiser and planner, for he invited me to join his 1985 expedition to Everest. I had my own attempt in 1982 and so I temporised, asking him to let me make my decision in the light of what happened on the North-East Ridge.

Immediately after dropping out of the summit push in 1982, I consoled myself with the thought that I could return to Everest with Arne, but the death of Pete and Joe changed all that. In the aftermath of their loss I could not contemplate returning to the mountain and volunteered to Wendy the promise that I would never go back. I told Arne shortly after my return that I wouldn't be joining him on Everest, but promised to do everything I could to help him. In the following months he played me rather like a fly-fisherman would a salmon, teasing me with questions about equipment or

Sherpas and then mentioning that I could always change my mind. I remained firm into 1983, but my two trips that autumn to Shivling and Vinson had rekindled all my old enthusiasm. I thought about it whilst in Antarctica. Here was a chance of reaching the highest point on earth being handed to me on a silver platter – Sherpas, oxygen, the easiest route to the summit, the chance of indulging my penchant for organisation and planning, without the ultimate responsibility of leadership. I just couldn't resist it.

I phoned Arne shortly after getting back from Antarctica to ask if the invitation was still open. He wasn't surprised. But how to tell Wendy? As I had done frequently in the past, I put it off and it was by chance that she heard, when she came into my study while I was talking on the phone to Arne about the detailed planning of the expedition. Inevitably she was deeply upset and yet I suspect she always half-knew that I'd go back. It is the wives of climbers that are the courageous ones, who have to cope with real stress, who have to sit back and wait, and all too often break the news to wives of the ones who don't come back. I had no excuse except the strength of my need to return to Everest. There were no recriminations, except from my two sons who were indignant.

'But you promised. You can't go back. What about Mum?'

Wendy, having accepted it, gave me total support and concentrated on getting me fit for the climb. She has always been interested in diet, and has been a vegetarian for some years. We don't have meat at home, although I do eat it when away. I am sure that a well balanced vegetarian diet helped build up both my stamina and resistance to ailments whilst on the climb.

In the following year (1984) I enjoyed helping with the expedition planning very much on a consultancy basis. I advised on choice of equipment and the composition of the Sherpa team and played out the expedition logistics on my Apple computer, while Wendy used it to analyse the expedition diet. Yet I did not have that ultimate responsibility of leadership or the sheer hard work of implementing the plans I proposed. This fell to Stein Aasheim, a young journalist and climber to whom Arne was paying a salary as full-time organiser.

I only met the entire team once before flying out to join them in Oslo in February 1985. However, that one meeting had been enough to reassure me that I should not find it too difficult to be accepted as part of a Norwegian expedition. For a start they all spoke excellent English and struck me as being relaxed and easy-going, and I knew that once we reached Kathmandu I would be seeing plenty of old friends, since quite a few of our Sherpas had been with me in 1975.

Originally there had been twelve on the expedition but in the summer of 1984 the two who were undoubtedly the most talented climbers in the team and, in fact, in Norway, were killed whilst descending from the summit of the Great Trango Tower in the Karakoram. They had died, presumably, in an abseiling accident after completing a very difficult new Alpine-style route on its huge East Face. Stein Aasheim had been with them but had turned back earlier because of lack of food. It was a serious blow to the team, both emotionally and because of their considerable ability as climbers. It was also a severe shock to the general public in Norway, since there had been comparatively few Norwegian expeditions to the Himalaya and none of them had suffered fatalities.

I hadn't been back to Nepal since our 1975 expedition and, as we walked from the plane to the terminal building in Kathmandu, the smell of wood smoke in the evening air brought rich memories of former times. The baggage collection and Customs were as chaotic yet friendly as ever. After an hour's shouting we had managed to clear a huge pile of boxes and kitbags containing oxygen equipment, film and camera gear, my portable computers and a dozen other items that had arrived at the last minute, without paying anything in customs duty. Pertemba, looking hardly a day older than when he had been with us ten years earlier, was waiting on the other side of the barrier. I had recommended him as Sirdar to Arne, who had written asking him to join us. Pertemba had replied that he would be happy to take on the job but that he had promised his wife Dawa that he would not go through the Everest Icefall again. I felt this did not matter too much, since the main job of the Sirdar is one of administration and this could be carried out from Base Camp. Arne agreed that Pertemba should be Chief Sirdar and that we would get a Climbing Sirdar to take charge of the Sherpas above Base Camp.

We spent three days in Kathmandu. I noticed that there were many more hotels, traffic and tourists, but the essential character of the city had not changed. The old bazaar was as colourful, noisy and dirty as ever, its narrow streets crowded with little shops selling everything from vegetables to transistors and tourist handcrafts.

I was sharing a room with Bjørn Myrer-Lund, a male nurse in an intensive care unit, and probably the most talented all-round mountaineer of the team. A first-class rock climber, he had made the only Norwegian ascent of the North Wall of the Eiger in winter and had also climbed the Cassin route on Mount McKinley. This was, however, his first Himalayan expedition. Tall and thin, and initially taciturn, with features that seemed drawn with an inner tension, it took a little time to break through his reticence to discover a wry but very rich sense of humour.

We were due to fly to Luglha, the airstrip twenty-four miles to the south of Everest, but the weather had been unsettled and no planes had been able to land there for some days. As a result there was a backlog of passengers which was going to take several days to clear. Arne, who was not accustomed to waiting, decided to fly us in by helicopter. On my three previous expeditions to the Everest massif I had walked in. We hadn't had any choice for on my first trip, to Nuptse in 1961, there had been no airstrips and no roads beyond Kathmandu. In 1972 and 1975 we had been approaching Sola Khumbu at the height of the monsoon, when Luglha was almost permanently clouded in. We had walked from Lamosangu, about fifty miles from Kathmandu on the road to the frontier with Tibet.

It had taken us eight days from Lamosangu to reach the Dudh Kosi. It was a very important part of a trip, allowing one to sink gently into the rhythm of an expedition, giving a relaxed interval between the inevitable last-minute panic that precedes departure and the physical stress of the climb ahead. It was also a time to settle down together.

We were missing all this in the busy whine of the helicopter's turbine as we chased over the familiar hills and valleys of Nepal. They were a dusty brown, still in the grip of the Nepalese dry season and winter. Paths I had walked in the past snaked round the contours of valleys and zig-zagged up narrow arêtes in a ribbon of red or brown. We raced over houses clinging improbably to the crests of ridges, and there were tell-tale scars of brown and yellow, the signs of earth slides caused by the erosion from defor-estation. The rivers in the beds of the valleys were little more than trickles, glinting blue, grey and silver in the sun. In the monsoon they would be a turbulent brown, carrying the precious topsoil of Nepal down to the Bay of Bengal.

We skipped between clouds, slid over a high pass and were above the Dudh Kosi, the river whose source is the Khumbu Glacier on Everest. The airstrip at Luglha was little more than a brown stripe. There was a crowd to greet us as we hovered in, most of them trekkers and tourists who had been waiting several days to get out. They clamoured around the helicopter even before the doors had opened, anxious to get a seat and be on their way back to the bustle of cities and everyday life.

Our Sherpas were also waiting for us. I was constantly being greeted by old friends who had been with me in 1972 or 1975. After a day in Luglha, issuing the Sherpas with the gear and organising loads, we were ready to set out for Namche Bazaar. We were going to make a leisurely progress to Base Camp to enable the team to acclimatise and make up for the shortness of our approach.

Luglha had certainly changed since 1975. There were many more buildings, most of them so-called hotels, though they were really just hostels with dormitory accommodation. You could even get hot showers, though these were no more than an empty tin with holes punched in the bottom, set in the roof of a hut, through which a Sherpa lad would pour buckets of hot water. The men wore western clothes, but the Sherpanis still wore their traditional dress and apron. There was certainly more money around. This was reflected in the difficulty we had getting porters to carry our gear to Base Camp. We were using more yaks than we had done in the past and Pertemba was having a hard job finding enough of these. Our gear was going up the valley in a trickle. Gone were the big porter trains of the seventies.

I could remember Namche Bazaar as it had been in 1961, a collection of houses clinging in a little crescent to a basin-like valley above the Dudh Kosi. We had been given a meal at the police post and had had to eat traditionally without knives or forks, shovelling the rice and dahl into our mouths with our fingers. It was very different now, packed with new hotels, some of which really merited the title. The most lavish belonged to Pasang Kami, my Sirdar on the 1970 Annapurna South Face Expedition. Fine-boned and now wearing horn-rimmed glasses, he had always been more an organiser than a climber. He was one of the most successful Sherpa businessmen and, besides part-owning a trekking company with Pertemba, had built a three-storey hotel with a penthouse restaurant. It even had electric light, an innovation that had come with a small hydro-electric scheme for Namche Bazaar.

I walked up the hill behind, through the woods to Khumde and Khumjung, the two Sherpa villages from which many of our porters came. These had changed little since I had last been there – the same two-storey houses with the byres on the ground floor and living room up a steep ladder, on the first. True, the windows were bigger now and glazed, a partition divided the living room from the kitchen, and there was usually a cowl over the cooking fire to channel out the smoke which on my previous visits had filled the single big living room before finding its way out through chinks in the roof.

I dropped down to the bridge over the Dudh Kosi and sought out the tea-house of Ang Phurba, the Sherpa with whom I had climbed on those memorable final days of our 1972 expedition. He was sitting on the porch, nursing his youngest child, a rosy-cheeked baby. We exchanged news of the expeditions we had been on in the intervening years. His wife offered me some chang, the Sherpa equivalent of beer, a thin milk-coloured drink made from fermented rice or wheat. It hardly tastes alcoholic but its effects are insidious and I felt slightly tipsy as I strode up the path leading to

Tengpoche gompa, the monastery that is the spiritual centre of the Sherpa community.

We had our puja the following day. In return for a contribution to monastery funds the monks bless the expedition. The team trooped into the big dark temple and sat on low benches with the Sherpas while five monks with horns and cymbals played and chanted. To our western ears it was discordant and yet I found it emotionally moving and reassuring. At the end of the ceremony we lined up and were each given a thin red thread, blessed by the head lama, which we were told to tie round our necks. I kept mine on throughout the expedition, as did all the others. Mine finally disintegrated some months after returning to Britain.

We were to have another puja at the gompa at Pangpoche, the last village of Khumbu, but I was walking with an English girl I'd met on the trail, overshot the turning, and by the time we had turned back the ceremony was over. However, we met Pertemba and a group of Sherpas who urged us to go along anyway to receive our blessing.

The gompa was above the village, shielded by pine trees. Much smaller than the Tengpoche gompa, it was in the same style with a big dark chamber on the ground floor and a smaller room upstairs. We were ushered up a narrow winding staircase by an elderly Sherpani. An old monk and two Sherpas in lay dress were crouched behind a low table, the monk chanting from an open book, the Sherpas playing a horn and banging a drum. We were beckoned to a Tibetan carpet in front of the table and invited to sit down. A big jar of chang was produced and we were each poured a cup which, whenever we sipped, was immediately filled up. It was a cheerful affair, its very informality making it mean even more than the grander ceremony at Tengpoche.

We then moved on to Pheriche, the little collection of what had once been yak-herders' huts and were now Sherpa lodges, lying at the foot of a steep little scarp beside a flat-bottomed valley among some of the loveliest mountains of the Himalaya. Everest was hidden by the great wall of Nuptse but the eye was drawn to the dramatic spires of Ama Dablam and Taboche and, looking back down the valley up which we had just come, Kang Taiga and Tramserku.

It was here that we were going to spend the next week acclimatising. It was a pleasant interlude, for there were no pressures and no schedule to follow. The sun was bright but the air still had a chill bite. Winter was barely over. I made a pilgrimage to a small peak immediately opposite the South Face of Nuptse. Gazing up at its huge wall I found it difficult to conceive that I had been there twenty-five years before. Ang Pema, cook to the trekking party accompanying our present expedition, had been with me to the top of Nuptse all those years ago. It had been his first expedition as a high-altitude porter. The previous year, on Annapurna II, he had been a kitchen boy. He hadn't changed much, with his round almost moon-like face, open easy grin and a simple kindness that had perhaps stopped him from becoming as prosperous as some of his fellow Sherpas, but he had a few fields and yaks, and seemed well content with his life.

Our most ambitious acclimatisation foray was at the end of the week. We split into two groups and four of us, Odd Eliassen, Ola Einang, Christian Larson and I set off up the Tshola valley to the north of Pheriche, hoping to reach the high col at its end and perhaps even climb one of the peaks that flanked it. We brought with us neither tents nor stoves, so that night gathered bits of scrub and dried yak dung to make a cooking fire.

Over six foot and blond, in his early forties, Odd Eliassen was the archetypal Norwegian and also one of the most experienced members of the team. He had pioneered several new routes on the huge granite walls of his native Romsdal in the sixties and had been a member of that ill-fated International Expedition to Everest in 1971. He was one of the best expedition men I have ever been with. His practical skills, he was a carpenter by profession, were invaluable in making the many repairs that are always necessary on any trip but, much more than that, if there was any work to do, Odd would just quietly get on with it. He was a wonderfully kind, generous person.

Ola Einang was similar. He ran a climbing school in the west of Norway. At first glance he looked like a Viking. Thick-set with a great bushy beard, I could just see him standing helmeted in the prow of a long ship, a double-headed axe in his hands. But here the resemblance ended. With a twinkle in his eye, a broad smile and ready laugh, he also was one of the quiet workers of the expedition.

Odd bent over our smouldering yak-dung fire, trying to blow some life into it, whilst the rest of us ranged over the alp, covered in clumps of brown frost-nipped grass, looking for fuel. Across the valley, the tip of Ama Dablam was still catching the soft yellow light of the dying sun, while closer at hand the dark silhouettes of Taboche and Jobo Lhaptshan cleaved the sky. The Everest massif was hidden by Lobuche Peak which guarded the northern flank of our high valley. I savoured every detail, in the simple enjoyment of the moment and the anticipation of the following day with a walk up an easy, but unknown, glacier to a col which would bring fresh views of mountains, some of them familiar, others new.

We slept under the stars that night and lit the fire two hours before dawn, drank cups of tea and gulped down muesli before starting out up a long scree slope that led to a higher alp. Picking our way over rocky spines and a frozen pond, we reached the crest of the moraine just after dawn. Loose boulder slopes and little scrambles followed. It was an adventure and, as so often, I wondered why this didn't content me. It was such fun, and yet I could only savour it to the full because I knew that Everest was just round the corner.

We reached the col at nine after a scramble up steep loose shale. It yielded an exciting view of the back of Pumo Ri, with steep snow leading to the summit, as shapely as the more familiar aspect from the other side. Beyond it was the great wall of Gyachung Kang, a peak of just under 8000 metres and only climbed once, by a Japanese expedition in 1964. The view was dominated by the mass of Cho Oyu, at 8153 metres one of the fourteen peaks over the magic 8000-metre mark, but it was big and lumpish, and I quickly glanced past it to the west, where three distant peaks formed a perfect trinity. They were shapely pyramids of ice and rock, and I calculated that the one on the right had to be Menlungtse, a peak that has intrigued me ever since my first visit to the Everest region in 1961. Tantalisingly, it stands just over the border in Tibet and has consequently remained inviolate, even though it must be one of the shapeliest, and perhaps technically most difficult, 7000-metre peaks in the main Himalayan chain. I had applied to the Chinese for permission to attempt it in 1987 and had learnt only a few days earlier that my request had been granted. I gazed at its tapering ridges through my binoculars before tearing myself away – back to the immediate challenge of Everest.

They were already packing loads by the time we got back. It was planned to have two nights in Lobuche, at a height of 4930 metres, to enable everyone to acclimatise, but I was impatient to reach Base Camp, wanted to look quietly at the Icefall to assess its dangers and try to pick a route through it. I therefore asked Arne if he minded my walking straight through to Base the following day.

The Sherpas had been there for the past week and had already constructed the kitchen shelter, a dry stone wall structure with a tarpaulin roof. A few hundred metres away was another camp, that of an American expedition attempting the West Ridge of Everest. The following morning, 14 March, I left early with Pema Dorje, our Climbing Sirdar, to find a vantage point from which to view the Icefall. We scrambled up the broken rocks at the foot of Khumbutse, the peak immediately above Base Camp, to the crest of a small spur, until we were looking down on to the lower part of the Icefall and could see across to its centre. It was completely lacking in snow, very different from the two previous occasions on which I had been there, when many of the crevasses had been hidden by the monsoon snows and even the sérac walls and towers had been softened by the depth of their cover. Now it was bare, gleaming in the early morning sun, seamed with the black lines of crevasses and pebbled with a chaos of icy talus slopes, the debris of collapsed walls and towers.

'Have you ever seen it as bare as this?' I asked Pema Dorje.

'Never. It looks very dangerous,' was the reply.

Pema Dorje was tall for a Sherpa, clean-cut and cheerfully eager. He had been to the top of Everest with the Canadian expedition in the autumn of 1982 and had done a lot of climbing with Adrian and Alan Burgess, the talented British mountaineering twins who now live in America. He spoke excellent English and I could see by the way he had scrambled up to our vantage point that he was a good natural climber.

On the way back down we called in at the American camp. They were a larger team than ours, numbering twenty in all, but they had fewer Sherpas and a much more difficult route. They had already made the section of their climb up to the Lho La, the col at the foot of the ridge, reached by a series of tottering spurs of loose rock and dangerous gullies. Some of the Americans were gathered around a petrol-operated winch when I arrived. They had just persuaded it to come to life. This was to be carried up to the foot of the final head-wall of ice to winch up their supplies to their first camp.

The climbing leader, Jim Bridwell, was an old friend. I had last seen him on our search for Pete and Joe on the eastern side of Everest back in 1982. He was looking as cheerfully debauched as ever, smoking a Camel cigarette and coughing between puffs. Over cups of coffee and biscuits spread thickly with peanut butter, I listened to their plans. Their team were very different from my fellow Norwegians. Long-haired, bearded and macho, they were more extravagant in their claims and certainly much more individualistic. There was none of the self-disciplined restraint that marked the Scandinavians. But they were a warm-hearted, likeable group and I was to get to know them much better in the coming weeks.

By the time I got back to our camp, the others were beginning to arrive, seeking out sites for their tents in the rocky rubble. By dusk the camp was fully established, the mess tent with its tables and chairs placed near the kitchen, and our own personal tents scattered amongst the boulders. But we couldn't venture into the Icefall until the next day when the Sherpas would hold their puja to bless the Base Camp altar.

It was the first time the entire expedition of ten climbers and twenty-eight Sherpas had been together. Up to now they had been scattered between Luglha and Base Camp, supervising the trickle of supplies up through the Khumbu valley. The bulk of the expedition gear had still not arrived.

Arne got us all together and gave a welcoming speech aimed particularly at the Sherpas, expressing his appreciation of their quality and the work they were going to do for us. He was certainly right in telling them that they were the strongest team that had ever been assembled. Quite apart from Pertemba, who had now been twice to the summit, and Pema Dorje who had been once, Sundhare had the record, having reached the top on three previous occasions. In his late twenties, his first expedition had been with us to the South-West Face in 1975 when he had reached Camp 5. He appeared to be very westernised, loved pop music and disco dancing and cultivated the fashions of a smart young man about Kathmandu, with a trendy shoulder-length hair-style and tight jeans. Ang Rita had perhaps achieved even more, having reached the summit twice without oxygen. He was very different from Sundhare. Stolid and very much a farmer, one felt he had a firmer hold on his own heritage and background. Three other members of the Sherpa team had been to the summit of Everest once before and over half the team had reached the South Col.

After Arne's speech the Sherpas conducted their puja, lighting a fire of juniper wood on the chorten of piled stones they had built in front of the camp. One of their number, a lay lama, chanted prayers whilst the rest stood around, drinking chang, chatting and laughing. The climax to the ceremony came when a big flag pole was manœuvred into position on top of the chorten, with much cheering and shouting. It was an unsanctimonious jolly ceremony and yet, at the same time, it was very moving. They had built two other chortens at either end of the camp and the three flag poles were linked by cords carrying gaily coloured flags, fluttering in the wind above our tents to give us protection from misfortune.

It was 15 March and on the following day we planned to venture into the Icefall.

CHAPTER SEVENTEEN

The Build-Up

There are many rituals associated with climbing Everest, and their very familiarity was a reassurance, a series of signposts towards the summit. I enjoyed waking in the dark of the pre-dawn in my own little tent, then going across to the cook's shelter which was so much warmer and cosier than the mess tent. The cooking stoves, which had been lit by one of the cook boys, were standing on a table of piled stones in the middle of the shelter, roaring away under the big detchies. Ang Tendi, our chief cook, was still in his sleeping-bag, curled up on a mattress on top of some boxes at the end of the shelter. Ang Nima, one of the cook boys, poured me a mug of tea and I sat on a box.

'What are the Sherpas having?'

'Dahl bhatt, you want some?'

'Yes, please.'

Ang Nima ladled out a plateful of rice covered with dahl in which swam big red chillies. I nursed the hot plate as other Sherpas trooped in one by one. Soon the shelter was packed with Sherpas and the three other climbers going into the Icefall that day.

There were no commands. The Sherpas drifted out, picked up the loads which had been allocated to them the previous evening, and then, pausing at the chorten on which a fire was smouldering, muttered a prayer, tossed on it a handful of rice or tsampa, and plodded off in the dim light towards the Icefall. I, too, always uttered the prayer that everyone would return safely from the Icefall that day.

The way started gently over rocky debris past the American camp, then wound through shallow valleys between fins of ice and piled boulders, onto the lower slopes of the Icefall. It was a steady crescendo of drama; the first little ice towers, the first crevasse, and then a complete network of them, which we laddered one by one. The first hint of danger came as the towers became bigger and we reached the debris of collapsed séracs, a slope of ice boulders, one piled on top of the other, smooth, hard, slippery and insecure. I disturbed one the size of a kitchen table and Bjørn lunged out of the way only just in time as it bounced down the slope, dislodging others in a domino effect.

We nibbled away at the route through the Icefall, the climbers divided into two teams taking alternate days. As is always the case, what seemed frighteningly dangerous on first acquaintance quickly became familiar with the introduction of ladders and fixed ropes. The higher we climbed, the more insecure it became, so that what had seemed appalling one day became comparatively safe in contrast to the next barrier.

It was nerve-racking yet invigorating, trying to pick out a safe route through this maze of ice. We were also starting to work as a team, not just the climbers, but also with the Sherpas, who took their full share in route finding. Each day we pushed the route out a little further but it was taking too long. A week had gone by and we still hadn't broken through into the Western Cwm. It was the morning of 22 March and I was having breakfast in the Sherpa kitchen when Pertemba came in, dressed for the hill.

'I think I'll have a look at the Icefall today,' he said.

I certainly didn't mind. Apart from anything else it meant that I was not the only one to have broken a promise to his wife! Pertemba wanted to get things moving and to see for himself why we hadn't pushed the route through to Camp 1. But I don't think that was the only reason. I had sensed his growing frustration with his administrative role on the expedition, grappling with the problems of getting all our loads ferried to Base Camp in the face of a porter and yak shortage. Whilst relations between Sherpas and climbers had been getting steadily stronger as we worked together in the Icefall, back at Base Camp, as so often happens, petty mis-understandings were causing tension. It was all about money and food – it nearly always is.

Arne and Christian Larsson, our Base Camp manager, were used to doing business in the world of shipping with firm contracts which were honoured to the letter, every dollar accounted for. Business in Sherpa country is different. Pertemba had had to pay over the odds for both porters and yaks. In sending back some of our high-altitude porters to bring up a consignment of ladders which had got no further than Pheriche, there had been a dispute over their ration allowance. But the greatest irritant of all was over food. The Sherpas had opted to be paid a ration allowance so that all their food could be bought locally but then, almost inevitably, they had yearned for the chocolates, sweets and biscuits that the climbers were eating.

It all came to a head over a load of fresh oranges. The trekkers who had come in with us to Base Camp had chartered a helicopter to take them back to Kathmandu from Pheriche and Arne had used it to bring in the oranges.

Ang Tendi asked if the Sherpas could have some but was told they were reserved for the climbers. It was the only time I had anything approaching a row with Arne.

'It's inevitable they're going to want to share in the goodies,' I pointed out. 'You always want something all the more if you're not allowed to have it. It's human nature.'

'It cost me a great deal of money getting those oranges in,' he replied. 'The Sherpas said they wanted to buy their own food and we've already paid out a hell of a lot for it. They should stick by their agreements. Anyway, if we shared out the oranges amongst everyone at Base Camp, there'd hardly be enough to go round.'

'But can't you see? We're going to depend on the Sherpas' enthusiasm to get us up this mountain. What on earth are a few oranges compared to keeping them happy? It's worth making concessions at this stage when it could make all the difference between success and failure later on.'

In the end Arne agreed to share out the oranges and, once the concession had been made, very few Sherpas bothered with them. We ended up throwing most of the oranges away after they had become rotten. As the expedition progressed Arne and Christian became much more relaxed in their dealings with the Sherpas and consequently their relationship with them got better and better.

That morning Pertemba wanted to escape from all these niggles and grapple with the much more tangible problems of the Icefall. The worst section was near the top. A tottering cliff of ice about seventy metres high barred our route. The only way to bypass it was through a canyon filled with ice blocks spawned from the sérac walls. About half-way along a huge fin of ice protruded. Instinctively I chose the narrow passage behind it. It seemed to give what could have been little more than psychological protection from the threatening wall above.

The passage was shoulder-width and about five metres long. I had walked a dozen paces or so beyond when I heard a sharp crack, followed by a dull heavy crunch. Glancing behind me I saw that the fin, for no apparent reason, had broken off at its base and, like a vice, had closed the passage I had just walked through. It needed little imagination to visualise what would have happened had this occurred just ten seconds earlier. I was badly shaken. There was none of the adrenalin rush, in itself a stimulant, that you get from a fall or near-miss from an avalanche, just a dull, nagging fear with the knowledge that I was going to be exposed to this kind of risk every time I went through the Icefall. I made a weak joke about it to Arne, who had been behind me, and pressed on into the sunlight that had just reached the slope beyond. In its dazzling brightness the piled ice blocks seemed less threatening.

But the danger was still there, though at least now we were on top of the huge peeling flakes of ice. It was like a gigantic toy box into which had been tossed a pile of multi-shaped building bricks; shift one, and the whole lot would collapse. We had reached a stable island of ice near the head of the cataract. A good place to pause. Odd was already there.

'Pertemba and Pemba Tsering have gone ahead,' he told me. 'I couldn't keep up with them. There's just one more big crevasse system between us and the cwm. They've climbed down into it.'

We sat in the sun and ate our lunch, constantly glancing across the waves of broken ice to the smooth haven of the Western Cwm, but there was no sign of Pertemba. An hour went by and then someone shouted.

'There they are, you can see them, they've made it.'

They were two tiny dots dwarfed by the plunging walls of Nuptse but very definitely on the other side of the crevasse system and in the Western Cwm.

On his return Pertemba told us they had gone beyond the site of Camp I and that the Western Cwm looked straightforward. He was full of bounce and seemed happier than I had seen him so far on the expedition. I suspect that the sight of his fellow Sherpas going into the Ice-fall had begun to irk him. He was a good administrator but he was still a climber. His lightning foray had been important for his own self-respect and perhaps even his standing with his fellow Sherpas, though on getting back to Base Camp he settled into his administrative role once again and showed no signs of wanting to go back to the mountain.

We were now ready to establish our first camp and Arne discussed the plan over lunch the following day. In deference to my lack of Norwegian, conversation when I was around was nearly always in English. He didn't go in for formal meetings but used mealtimes as a forum for discussion and planning. He proposed ideas, listened to counter-suggestions, but it was always Arne that made the eventual decision and, through this, maintained an effective control. With the exception of Christian Larsson he was the least experienced mountaineer in the team but, nonetheless, he was a good leader with a combination of charisma, a good sense of humour and a quick analytical mind that enabled him to absorb a series of conflicting ideas and come up with a sound conclusion.

Odd, Bjørn and Stein were to move up to Camp 1 the following day and push the route on up the Western Cwm to Camp 2, which would be Advance Base – all good familiar stuff, for this was identical to the build up for the South-West Face. I enjoyed my position within the expedition. Arne had agreed that I should look after the logistics, which meant supervising the flow of supplies up the mountain. Although at times I found it frustrating, not being able immediately to implement my own ideas, I could be very much more relaxed than I had been on previous trips.

During the next two days, however, a difference in approach emerged. Arne announced at dinner that, in view of the danger and instability of the Ice-fall, he proposed keeping all the Sherpa force at Base Camp until we had ferried everything we should need for the climb beyond up to Camp 1. There was a sound logic in the idea, since it would reduce the number of days we would have big Sherpa teams moving through the Icefall. In addition, once everything we needed was in the Western Cwm, a major collapse in the Ice-fall need not delay the build-up of supplies.

Even so, I was not happy with his plan. I preferred dividing the Sherpa team between the camps from the beginning to maintain the forward momentum of the climb, trying to keep a stream of supplies behind the climbers out in front. I felt that this was psychologically important, so that the entire team would have a sense of urgency and drive. It would also mean we were making maximum use of the good weather we were experiencing. I didn't say anything at the time but slept very little that night, exploring the implications of Arne's plan. He was not at all well at this stage with a severe throat infection that he just couldn't throw off. If you are feeling ill, this inevitably influences your judgement, and I was worried that Arne subconsciously was favouring a slower build-up on the mountain because of his throat condition.

I had brought with me an Apple Mac computer that was powered by batteries and a solar panel. I was using it both for writing my reports and letters and also for calculating logistic problems. First thing next morning, as soon as the sun hit the tent, I switched it on and, using the spreadsheet, calculated the implications for the next ten days of Arne's plan and of my own idea of distributing the Sherpas more evenly. I then went over to his tent before breakfast to show him my calculations, demonstrating that with the build-up we already had, we should be able to station a Sherpa team at Camp 1 the moment we had the route to Camp 2 opened. I suggested that I should also move up to Camp 1 to supervise the flow of supplies through to Camp 2. Arne saw the point and we agreed to a compromise. Six Sherpas would join me at Camp 1 the following day when we moved up.

I was going up with Ola Einang, Ralph Hoøibakk and Håvard Nesheim. The latter two were the strongest climbers in the expedition, one of the oldest and the youngest. Ralph was managing director of a big computer company yet, in spite of being forty-six and having a sedentary job, he was the only member of the team who was as fast if not faster than the Sherpas.

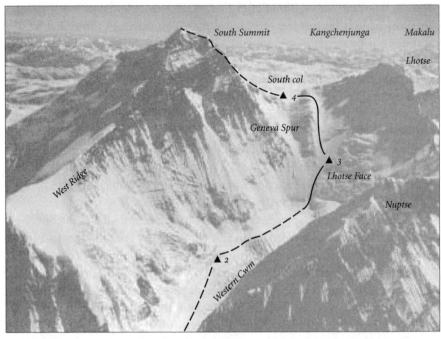

South Summit   Kangchenjunga   Makalu

Lhotse

South col
▲ 4

Geneva Spur

▲ 3
Lhotse Face

West Ridge

Nuptse

▲ 2

Western Cwm

▲ *Tented camp* ————— *Route using fixed ropes* _ _ _ _ *Route not using fixed ropes*
Everest and the Western Cwm

When making the route through the Icefall, he had always been far ahead, often soloing steep ice in his search for the best route. He was not remotely interested in my computerised logistics.

'I'm managing and planning all the year round. This is my escape,' he told me. 'I'm happy just climbing.'

Håvard, at the other end of the age spectrum, had the same attitude. He had just qualified as a doctor but was on the expedition as a climber. He held the Norwegian height record, having joined a Polish expedition to Lhotse, and reached their top camp on the Lhotse Face just below the South Col. Håvard came from Tromso in the far north of Norway, beyond the Arctic Circle, where the sun never sets in the summer and it never rises in winter. His personality perhaps mirrored his home environment. He was the expedition joker, flamboyant and full of laughter, yet beneath it there was steel. The jokiness was a thin protective layer over a strong ambition. He very much wanted to reach the top of Everest.

They moved up to Camp 2, sited on a bare rocky moraine just below the South-West Face, while I stayed at Camp 1, checking through the supplies as they came up from Base Camp. I learnt over the radio that Kjell Torgeir, our doctor, had recommended that Arne, Christian and Stein should drop back down to Pheriche to help get rid of their sore throats. Arne hadn't delegated the command in any way, but at this stage it didn't really matter since the expedition was now running in the natural pattern of a siege ascent. Ralph, Håvard and Ola were out in front making the route up the Lhotse Face and behind them the Sherpas were relaying supplies to Camp 2. Liaising with Pertemba at Base Camp and Pema Dorje at Camp 1, I was able to control the flow of loads and the distribution of Sherpas on the mountain.

My Apple IIc had stood up amazingly well to the dust and glacier grit, to temperatures ranging between −10°C at night and the mid-eighties inside the tent during the day, all of which computers tend to hate. It had been bumped on the back of a yak as far as Base Camp and then carried by a porter up through the Icefall. I could only operate it during the day when the temperature rose above freezing and the power of the sun could charge the battery through the solar panel. It was to achieve a record of its own when I took it up to Camp 2 at 6400 metres, as I suspect this is the highest on the earth's surface that a computer has ever been used.

Once the three out in front had reached the middle of the Lhotse Face where we planned to establish Camp 3, the only people available to replace them were Odd, Bjørn and myself. I was beginning to look forward to being in the lead. It would be our job to make the route to the South Col which would put the other three into position for the first summit bid. I didn't mind that. It seemed appropriate that it should be an all-Norwegian effort for the first push, but I was worried about my own stamina and was frightened of burning myself out while pushing the route up to nearly 8000 metres. From my experience in 1982 I knew that my recovery rate had slowed down, an unwelcome product of my years.

Odd, Bjørn and I moved up to Camp 2 on 3 April. It was already a little village of tents perched amongst rocky mounds and, sadly, littered with the debris of former expeditions. With several large expeditions a year visiting the mountain this has become a serious problem on Everest. It's not just the rubbish that has been left behind but also the pollution of water supplies. We had all suffered from Giardia, a form of dysentry, at Camp 1, almost certainly because the snow from which our water was melted was polluted from the latrines of earlier expeditions.

The previous autumn Dick Bass had financed a Nepalese police exped- ition whose main function was to clean up the mountain, though at the same time they were hoping to make a bid for the summit and for Dick to complete his Seven Summits odyssey. Unfortunately, through a series of misunderstandings with the authorities, Dick was forced to withdraw before they had even reached the foot of the Lhotse Face. The police pressed

on, however, making a bid for the summit which ended with two of them
falling to their deaths. They also cleared a large quantity of rubbish from
the lower part of the mountain though, perhaps because of the sheer
volume of it, there was still a great deal in the immediate environs of Camp
2.

The others that day had reached a point just below the proposed site of
our next camp. They had had three hard days out in front and were keen
to get back down for a rest. They told us that they had found the shattered
body of a Sherpa at the foot of the Lhotse Face, a grim relic of the previous
autumn's expedition.

We spent the following day sorting out the camp, checking gear and
getting ready for our move on to the Lhotse Face, deciding to make a carry
in the first instance, and actually get the camp established before moving
up. I was feeling fit and well acclimatised, largely due to my steady progress
up the mountain, ferrying light loads and working on the logistics.

But it was good to be moving up into the lead, as we zig-zagged through
the crevasses that guard the upper part of the Cwm. The Lhotse Face, a
thousand metres of bare ice leading up to the South Col, looked formidably
steep. An avalanche cone dropped down from the bergschrund that guarded
its base. The bergschrund itself was filled with snow but the wall beyond
was sheer for about twenty metres. It had been a fine lead by Håvard
Nesheim who made the first ascent. The previous day Sundhare and Ang
Rita had carried up some ladders and put them in position.

Walking below the South-West Face, and now looking across towards it,
brought many memories. Most amazing of all, though, was the site of our
old Camp 4. The super-Boxes, specially designed by Hamish MacInnes,
were still there, faded into a brown yellow, no doubt stuffed with ice, but
clinging to the snow slope below the little rock spur we had feared would
give all too little protection from the avalanches coming down from the
walls above. The site had been better than we had thought, and the boxes
themselves had more than justified their weight.

The Sherpas were pulling far ahead. Odd was with them. Bjørn and I
went more slowly, pulling up the fixed ropes over endless slopes of ice,
broken only by steeper bulges. The average angle was little more than forty
degrees but the ice was so hard that it must have been intimidating to lead.
I glanced up to see Odd and the Sherpas now on their way down. They had
pushed beyond the high point of the others and had found a site for Camp
3. It was on a wide shelf, sheltered by a sérac wall. A small blue tent left by
the Korean winter expedition that had attempted the mountain just a few
weeks before hid from the winds in a little depression. We were at a height
of around 7400 metres.

By the time we reached Camp 2, Kjell Torgeir had arrived. He wasn't a climber but was a keen cross-country skier, marathon runner and an excellent expedition doctor, conscientious, kindly and very capable. He had brought with him a small battery-operated centrifuge and was using this to check the haematocrit levels of the team. At sea level about forty-eight per cent of the blood is made up from the red cells that absorb oxygen from the lungs but, to help compensate for the lack of oxygen at altitude, the body manufactures more red cells. The problem occurs if there are too many, for then the blood becomes as thick as treacle and there is a danger of it clotting, causing heart attacks or strokes.

Kjell had just checked Odd's blood to find that the haematocrit level was dangerously high, at about seventy per cent, and he had just advised him to return to Base in the hope that a loss in altitude would thin down the blood. Odd, who had been going so much more strongly than either Bjørn or I, was both shocked and depressed by the discovery.

And so the following morning it was just Bjørn and I who set out with Ang Rita and Sundhare for Camp 3. We were quickly left behind by the two Sherpas as we slogged up the ropes, weighed down with our personal gear, much heavier loads than the previous day. One advantage of this was that by the time we reached the camp the Sherpas had erected both tents. All we had to do was crawl inside and light the stove for our first brew.

That night we slept on oxygen. On the South-West Face in 1975, we had only started using oxygen at Camp 5, at about 7700 metres, but since we had plenty of oxygen bottles and the Sherpa-power to carry it, it seemed to make sense to start using it at Camp 3 as Bjørn and I wanted to avoid burning ourselves out in this push to the South Col. Snuggled in my sleeping-bag, the hiss of oxygen was reassuring as I woke from time to time through the long night.

The following morning I started cooking just after dawn, but we were slow in getting away and had extra brews as we waited for the sun to creep over the shoulder of Everest and give us the benefit of its warmth. I poked my head out of our tent and saw the Sherpas just emerging from theirs. Time to move. Bjørn and I were using oxygen that day, but the Sherpas weren't. Consequently they were ready first, shouldering rucksacks filled with rope and climbing hardwear. I was still struggling with my oxygen system. The straps of the mask were the wrong length. I couldn't fasten one of the buckles, lost my temper and hurled the mask into the snow. Bjørn seemed quietly amused. By the time I had got myself organised the others had vanished round the corner of the sérac. I plodded behind them, feeling flustered and tired before I had even started. The oxygen didn't seem to be doing anything at all for me.

I soon arrived at a steep little step. They hadn't bothered to put a fixed rope on it. I climbed it clumsily, goggles misting up, and the snout of the oxygen mask making it impossible to glance down and see where I was kicking my cramponed boots. Why the hell hadn't they put a rope here? I cursed them, cursed the mountain, cursed the whole expedition. Sundhare and Ang Rita were no more than little dots on the other side of a sweep of ice leading to the distinctive broken limestone rocks known as the Yellow Band and Bjørn was already half-way across the ice slope on his way to join them.

'Come on Bonington; get a grip. You're behaving like a small child,' I told myself.

I was going so badly there seemed little point in trying to catch up with the others. Sundhare and Ang Rita were obviously capable of fixing the route and Bjørn would soon be with them. They had run the rope out almost horizontally across the slope towards the lowest point of the barrier formed by the Yellow Band. It looked as if it could do with a few intermediate anchor points, and that the approach to the traverse needed some fixed rope. I decided I might just as well spend the rest of the day doing this. I'd be conserving my energy yet doing something useful. I immediately felt better, dropped back down to the camp and collected some more ice pitons and rope, dumped the oxygen gear that had been so cumbersome, and returned to the fray in a much better humour.

I have always enjoyed putting in fixed ropes; there's an element of craft to it, getting the rope to just the right tension and placing the anchors so that it is easy to transfer from one rope-length to the next. I was enjoying myself. Meanwhile I could see that the others were making good progress, slowly climbing up alongside the Geneva Spur.

After a couple of hours I returned to the tents to prepare tea for Bjørn and the Sherpas when they came back. They had fixed about 300 metres of rope, most of it salvaged from the many old ropes left embedded in the snow and ice. Sundhare had done most of the leading and it is in this that one major change since 1975 can be seen. Then most of the Sherpas had still been essentially load-carriers, but today an increasing number of them are becoming first-rate mountaineers, accustomed on some expeditions to guiding their clients up the mountain. The Lhotse Face was familiar territory to Sundhare and Ang Rita. Not only were they much faster than we were, they knew the way from previous experience.

Next day both Bjørn and I felt terrible. We hadn't slept well and had dysentry. Could the snow of Camp 3 be polluted too? On the morning radio call Bjørn spoke to Arne, who had now recovered from his sore throat and had moved up to Camp 2.

'Chris and I are feeling lousy. We've both got the shits. I don't think we'll go up, but don't worry, Sundhare and Ang Rita should make it to the South Col today.'

There was a long pause.

'Hello, Bjørn, this is Arne at 2. I'm very concerned with what you say. You can't leave it all to the Sherpas. What do you think the Norwegian press are going to say if it's the Sherpas who reach the South Col while you're lying in your pits?'

'Yeh Arne, I see what you mean. I'll have a word with Chris, over. What do you think?' he asked me.

'Hell, put like that I suppose we've got to go.'

'Hello, Arne, we agree with you. We'll go with the Sherpas.'

I was determined to get away early this time, got my mask sorted out and was away first, but I didn't stay in front for long. Sundhare and Ang Rita stormed past before I had got half-way across the ice slope and Bjørn caught up with me above the Yellow Band when I sat down in the snow for a prolonged rest. I felt profoundly discouraged and couldn't help wondering whether I was going to have the strength to make it to the top. In theory the oxygen flow should have reduced the altitude to 5000 metres or so but, in effect, it didn't seem to be helping at all.

'I don't see the point in going on any further,' I told Bjørn. 'There's no way I'm going to catch them up. I'm not going to burn myself out just for a bit of public relations.'

'Oh well, I think I'll go on a bit further. I'd like to see the view from the South Col,' he explained diplomatically.

So Bjørn went on up the ropes, and I returned to the tents. I could at least have some tea ready when they got back. Bjørn never caught them up, but met them on their way back down. They had reached the South Col and fixed rope all the way. Bjørn went on to the crest of the Geneva Spur so that he could at least look across to the Col. The route was now complete to the site of our top camp. All we had to do was stock it and we would be able to put in our first summit bid.

We dropped back down to Camp 2 that same afternoon. Christian Larsson and Arne, looking better although he still had a bad cough, had arrived there the day before. That night over supper we discussed the summit bids. Arne had already decided the obvious choice for the first summit bid would be Ralph, Håvard and Ola. He told us that he wanted Bjørn, Odd, if his haematocrit level allowed it, and me to make the second attempt, while he and Stein would make up a third party.

'I don't want to hold you guys up, and I could do with a bit more time anyway to get rid of my cold,' he concluded.

The following morning Arne called a meeting in the cook tent. We now had sixteen Sherpas at Camp 2 and most of them crowded in. There was an atmosphere of relaxed, yet excited, anticipation. The gas stove was purring away and mugs of tea or coffee were being served by Ang Rinzay. The meeting mostly involved a discussion between Arne and Pema Dorje on the composition of the Sherpa part of the summit teams.

'On that first attempt the Sherpas will not be asked to help the climbers at all,' Arne told Pema. 'The climbers must carry their own oxygen and get to the top without any kind of help, but on the second and third attempts the climbers will want some help. Their Sherpas can carry the spare oxygen.

'We've got enough oxygen and equipment for any number of attempts. You Sherpas can make a fourth attempt of your own if you want. There's no reason why anyone wanting to go to the top shouldn't have a try.'

We spent an hour discussing the composition of the summit teams, the Sherpas listening and occasionally adding their comments. The important thing was that they felt fully involved and, even though the majority had no ambition to reach the summit, I'm sure they appreciated being given the opportunity.

The excitement was infectious. I was already suffering from an acute attack of summititis, was impatient of logistics and wanted to get back down to Base Camp or even lower to recuperate for my own bid for the top of Everest. But there was work to do. I had to check through the gear we were going to send up to the South Col in the next few days. The Sherpas did not want to stay at Camp 3 and preferred to make their carry straight through to the South Col from Advance Base, a distance of three miles and a height gain of 800 metres, carrying fifteen kilos without using oxygen.

Christian was going to be in charge of this vital phase of the expedition. He has a methodical thorough mind and questions the logic behind every proposal. It's certainly an ideal quality for a Base manager, but that afternoon I was at my most impatient, like a small boy at the end of term time, unable to wait for the holidays to start. I found it impossible to concentrate, muttered bad-temperedly about needing all the rest I could get after staying so long at altitude and added aggressively that whatever happened I was getting back to Base that evening.

'I'm sure you'll manage,' I told Christian, as I quickly packed a rucksack and set out down the Western Cwm. Bjørn and I met Stein in solitary residence in Camp 1. He had worked so hard in organising the expedition back in Norway but had acclimatised slowly and was now gradually making his way back up the mountain, hoping to get sufficiently fit to make a summit bid.

Back down through the Icefall, the upper section had collapsed yet again.

The route wound through narrow corridors, across ladder bridges, warped by the shifting pressure of the ice, and over ice boulders jumbled from a recent fall. Odd had found a better line to avoid the death alley of the way up, but it went beneath a huge blade of ice that was going to collapse sooner rather than later. I ran beneath it, balancing over the slippery ice boulders. At last we were down but paused at the American camp to chat about their progress. They were now established high on the West Ridge, but still short of their top camp. Those at base looked tired and drawn.

Back at our camp, great platefuls of boiled potatoes spiced with chilli awaited us. It was positively hot in the late afternoon sun. Bjørn Resse, the photographer from *VG*, the newspaper that was sponsoring us, lay stripped to his shorts, soaking up the warmth.

Kjell Torgeir had come down with us and the following morning carried out a transfusion on Odd, removing a litre of blood and replacing it with saline solution, in an effort to bring down the red blood cell count. Ralph and Håvard were on their way back from Pheriche. They had been there for four days. On my previous expeditions I had stayed at Camp 2 throughout the expedition and no one had gone below Base, but it certainly seemed good sense. Base at 5400 metres is too high for fast recovery. In fact, at that altitude the body is still slowly deteriorating. Bjørn, Odd and I therefore decided to go down as well, but just before we set out Pertemba came over.

'You know, Chris, I'd really like to go to the top with you,' he said.

It was something that I had thought of, particularly after his little foray into the Icefall, but I had never liked to say anything to influence him. It meant a great deal to me, because of our friendship over the years, the link that he formed with my previous visits to the mountain and all the experiences, rich and good, as well as tragic, that those had involved.

We set off for Pheriche just after lunch. It was so easy, lightly laden, going down hill with halts at the tea-houses at Gorak Shep and Lobuche. Night fell as we came off the terminal moraines of the Khumbu Glacier on to the flat valley floor. The kitchen-living room of Ang Nima's lodge was crammed with trekkers and Sherpas sitting on the benches at the two tables and on stools round the open range. A cacophony of languages, English, French, Japanese, Italian, Dutch and Sherpa made the place a colourful Tower of Babel.

Ang Nima greeted me warmly. He had been with me on the Annapurna South Face Expedition in 1970 and on Everest in 1972, but his climbing days were over. He had a good head for business, had started his hotel in a tiny yak shelter in 1975, and had built it up over the years with a big bunk room and a well-stocked shop. That night we gorged ourselves on Sherpa stew, fried potatoes and fried eggs, washed down with copious draughts of chang.

It was a different world from Base Camp with new people to talk to and fresh food to eat. It was difficult to believe that I had been only 300 metres below the South Col just three days earlier, and even harder to imagine going back again.

I spent most of the next three days sleeping but during my waking time I became increasingly tensed at the prospect of the summit bid. For the first time I felt isolated from my fellow climbers. Several Norwegians, friends of team members, had trekked into Sola Khumbu. Inevitably they talked amongst themselves in Norwegian. Experiences and friendships that I hadn't shared, as much as the difference in language, heightened my own sense of isolation and, through this, my homesickness, a longing for Wendy, a longing for the expedition to end so that I could get back to my Cumbrian hills.

But then the brief holiday was over. It was time to return to the mountain. In just five days' time, with a bit of luck I could have climbed 5000 metres to stand, at last, on the highest point on earth.

CHAPTER EIGHTEEN

Fulfilment

All the doubts of the last three days dropped away. I felt energetic and refreshed as I strode out over the well-worn trail, past sleepy browsing yaks and the herders' huts, with smoke seeping through their stone roofs. I was careful to skirt the small untidy mani walls on the left in the prescribed way. The high peaks, Ama Dablam, Kang Taiga and Tramserku, were lit by the first rays of the sun, whilst down here in the valley we were still in the chill shadows. The path began to climb the moraines of the Khumbu Glacier and the line of sunlight dropped slowly towards us, picking out the ochre brown of the trampled earth and the dusty grey-green of juniper shrubs. I climbed up on to the crest of a moraine ridge that overlooked the tumbling stream of the Dudh Kosi to feel the life-giving warmth of the sun's early rays and revelled in anticipation of the climb ahead.

The path dropped down towards the river. I crossed it by a small bridge, passed some yak herders' huts, now turned tea-houses, and waited on the other side. Time for a second breakfast in the morning sun. Odd and Bjørn were just behind. We sat and talked, sipped black tea and nibbled biscuits. We were just ready to leave when a bizarre figure arrived. He was clad in navy-blue shorts, matching Lifa long-johns and vest, with a little white sun hat on his head and a furled umbrella clutched in his hand. It was Dick Bass, with his broad Cheshire Cat grin and unquenchable enthusiasm. He had arrived at Pheriche the previous afternoon and he, also, was on his way to Everest.

Dick had bought his way into Arne's expedition on the agreement that he would be allowed to make an attempt on the summit, employing his own Sherpa team, but using our camps and fixed ropes, once the Norwegians had completed their summit bids. He had with him just one other American climber, David Breashears, who had made the first ever video transmission from the summit of Everest on his 1983 expedition. David had the job both of filming Dick and also guiding him to the top. They had arrived at Base Camp whilst I had been up at Camp 2, but since Dick's agreement with Arne dictated that he could not venture on the mountain until we had finished our climb, he had turned tail and returned to Namche

Bazar, just to keep himself in trim and to start getting acclimatised.

'Hell, my feet are killing me,' he told us.

He took off his boot to show some of the worst blisters I have ever seen. He had carried a heavy pack back down to Namche and with typical guts, but also lack of experience, had ignored the tell-tale stabs of pain on the heels and soles of his feet with the result that he was not only blistered but badly bruised as well. But this did not affect his irrepressible spirit. He was planning to make his bid for the summit immediately behind our third attempt, even though this would mean he had barely time to become acclimatised. He admitted that he wasn't fit. Snowbird, as usual, was full of problems and he had been working flat out trying to sell apartments in a huge new block he had built, right up to the day he flew out to Nepal.

We walked the rest of the way up to Base Camp with Dick. In spite of his obvious pain he kept up a good pace and his usual flood of talk. It was also a royal progress. He had become a favourite of the Sherpanis running the tea-houses and lodges all the way to Base. He loved flirting with them and treated them with a gallantry they enjoyed. At Gorak Shep we met up with Pertemba who had come down to order some local rations. We all crowded into the tiny kitchen of the single-storeyed shack to eat potatoes, washed down by chang and hot rakshi. Then on to the glacier over stony moraines and past little groups of trekkers returning from their pilgrimage to Base Camp.

The following morning Kjell Torgeir checked Odd's haematocrit level. It was still on the high side but much better than it had been before the transfusion.

'It is up to you,' Kjell told him. 'You must decide for yourself.'

Odd decided to go for the summit, but it was a decision that didn't come easily. He has a strong sense of responsibility in everything he does, particularly in relation to his family, but he felt the risk was acceptable with the highest point on earth seeming so very accessible.

There are many parallels between climbing a mountain and fighting a war. This is perhaps why the vocabulary is very similar – assault, siege, logistics. The dangers of climbing the higher Himalayan peaks are probably greater than those encountered in most wartime battles, yet the essence and spirit of climbing is very different. The climber doesn't fight anyone or, for that matter, any thing. He is working with, and through, the natural forces. He doesn't fight the storm; he works his way through it, perhaps shelters from it. But a climb, particularly one using set camps and a support team, needs planning that is very similar to a successful military assault. It doesn't matter how talented the lead climbers are. If their supplies don't reach them, they are going to be forced to retreat, just as a brilliant military advance can be halted through lack of fuel or ammunition.

We were now like troops at the start line for a big offensive, programmed to move from one holding area to the next. It was 18 April. Ralph, Håvard and Ola were at Camp 3 and would move up to the South Col, while Ang Rita and Pema Dorje would go straight through from Camp 2 to join them at the top camp. Odd, Bjørn, Pertemba and I were moving up to Camp 2 that same day to come in behind them for the second summit bid.

We set out before dawn. Just short of the top of the Icefall there had been yet another collapse. There was a deep valley where the previous day it had been a precarious walk over chaotically piled blocks. Now our ladders were down amongst the rubble, twisted and broken in the collapse. The Sherpas were already trying to rebuild a route, digging out the ladders and looking for a way through new formed walls of ice.

I clambered up a ridge on to what had appeared to be a ledge, only to find that it was a sharp honeycombed fin with deep crevasses on the other side. I edged across it. An ice block broke away underneath me and went bouncing and clattering into the depths beneath. I froze, heart pounding, then slowly and carefully balanced across the fragile arête to reach solider ground. 'This must be the last time I ever go up through the Icefall!' I promised myself.

But soon we emerged into the sun and the Western Cwm. The danger was over. A serpentine track was formed by the scratch marks of crampons and a trail of marker poles, most of them flying bright red bunting, the occasional one with a prayer flag to bless us on our way.

Christian greeted us at Camp 1. He had come of age in the course of the expedition. He had started as a gauche bright young man of the town, finding it difficult to relate to the Sherpas, and was abrupt and terse in giving orders in an environment that was strange, perhaps even hostile to him. But he had learnt a great deal in those weeks and had formed a warm friendship and sound working partnership with Pema Dorje in masterminding the stocking of the South Col. The fact that our move was being made with this military precision was largely due to Christian.

19th April was to be summit day for Ralph, Håvard and Ola. We made a leisurely start from Advance Base, just having to reach Camp 3, half-way up the Lhotse Face. I walked steadily but slowly, soon dropping behind the others, but I didn't mind, feeling that I was maintaining a steady rhythm, of pushing up the jumar clamp, kicking crampon points into the hard ice and of measuring the slow, slow progress upwards against landmarks that had become all too familiar – a rock sticking out of the ice, the foot of the Geneva Spur. A great plume of cloud was flying from the summit pyramid;

gusts like whirlwinds picked up flurries of spindrift and chased them across the face.

I was just short of the camp and noticed a figure coming down the fixed ropes from above. It could only be one of the summit team. Had they made it? As the figure came closer, moving slowly, ponderously even though it was downhill, the face hidden by oxygen mask and goggles, I somehow didn't think he had. It wouldn't have mattered how tired he was, he'd have waved, there would be more spring in his step. I reached the tents first. The approaching figure staggered those last few metres, sank into the snow and pulled off his mask. It was Ralph Høibakk.

'How did it go?' asked Odd.

'We didn't make it.'

They had set out at four that morning and made steady progress with Ralph breaking trail for most of the way. He had reached the South Summit forty minutes in front of the others.

'The wind wasn't too bad when I got there and I was tempted to go for the top, but we'd agreed we'd all go together. So I waited. But the wind got worse and worse. By the time the others arrived it was hurricane force. The Sherpas wanted to turn back and so we did too.'

They had been so close. Now we were in line to make the first ascent of the expedition. That didn't mean very much to me – I'd be the seventh Briton to reach the top of Everest – but Bjørn and Odd had the chance of being the first Scandinavians to get there.

The following morning we climbed the fixed rope to the South Col. It was less windy than the previous day and there wasn't a cloud in the sky. I handled the ropes with care. Sundhare and Ang Rita had done a good job, but some of the old ropes we were using were frayed and knotted in great clusters at the anchor points.

It was a surprisingly long walk from the top of the Geneva Spur to the South Col, over slaty rocks that resembled tiles on a roof. Looking back down the Western Cwm, I was level with the summit of Nuptse. The col itself was more extensive than I had ever imagined, a wild flattish expanse the size of a football field, covered with the same slaty rock I had just crossed, and littered with the debris of previous expeditions; the skeletons of tents, oxygen bottles, old food boxes in little clusters – ugly memorials to the ambitions of our predecessors. The final slopes of Everest rose on the other side, in not so much a ridge as a face of snow and broken rocks that looked steep and inhospitable. Three tents, moored down by cradles of climbing ropes, were pitched near the centre of the col. The Sherpas, Dawa Nuru and Ang Lhakpa, had come up from Camp 2 that same day long straggly hair, the wire-rimmed glasses and could sense his reassurance and encouragement. It was as if he was pushing me on. Les, my father-in-law, was there as well. He has a quiet wisdom and great compassion. He had thrown the I Ching just before I left home and had predicted my success. This was something that had given me renewed confidence whenever I doubted my ability to make it.

Doug and Les got me to the top of the Hillary Step. The others had now vanished round the corner and I seemed to have the mountain to myself. The angle eased and all I had to do was put one foot in front of the other for that last stretch to the highest point on earth. And suddenly I was there, everything on all sides dropping away below me. I hugged Pertemba who crouched beside me. The summit is the size of a pool table. We could all move around on it without fear of being pushed over the edge. Odd and Bjørn, who were raising and photographing the Norwegian flag, came over and embraced me.

Then there was time to look around us. From west through north to east lay the Tibetan plateau, a rolling ocean of brown hills with the occasional white cap. To the east rose Kangchenjunga, a huge snowy mass, first climbed by George Band and Joe Brown in 1955, and to the west the great chain of the Himalaya, with Shisha Pangma, China's 8000-metre peak dominating the horizon. Doug, Alex McIntyre and Roger Baxter-Jones had climbed its huge South Face in 1982. Immediately below us, just the other side of the Western Cwm, was Nuptse, looking stunted, the very reverse of that view I had enjoyed twenty-four years earlier, when Everest had seemed so unattainable. To the south was a white carpet of cloud covering the foothills and plains of India. We were indeed on top of the world.

At that moment another figure appeared, moving slowly and painfully. It was Dawa Nuru. He hadn't turned back; he was coming to the summit without oxygen. I still felt numbed, took pictures automatically, without really being aware of what I was taking or how well they were framed. There was no longer any sign of the Chinese maypole that Doug and Dougal had found in 1975. It had finally been blown away some years earlier. There were, however, some paper prayer flags embedded in the snow which must have been left there the previous autumn.

Pertemba had brought with him the tee-shirt that Pete Boardman had worn to the summit of Everest in 1975. It was a hand-painted one that Pete's local club, the Mynedd, had presented to him. Hilary, Pete's widow, had given it to Pertemba when he had visited her in Switzerland, and now he had brought it to the top of Everest once more in honour of his friend.

We lingered for another twenty minutes or so before starting the descent. I was first away, pausing just below the summit to collect a few pebbles of

and were going for the summit with us. Neither of them had been to the top before.

Pertemba was already ensconced in our tent, with the gas stove going. Inside, with the stove and the heat from the afternoon sun, it was quite warm. I lay on my sleeping-bag, sipping tea and savouring the knowledge that I was on the threshold of fulfilment. It was good to be sharing a tent with Pertemba.

Just before dusk I forced myself out to check the oxygen sets of Dawa Nuru and Ang Lhakpa. This would be the first time they had used oxygen. They were going to carry two bottles the following day, one of which would have to last to the summit, and the other was for one of us to change on the crest of the South-East Ridge. Pertemba was also going to take two bottles, but both of these would be for him, for Ralph had told us that there was a spare bottle left by Ang Rita at the dump on the ridge. This would mean that Odd, Bjørn and I would only have to carry one bottle for our summit attempt but, because we had the use of two, we would be able to use a higher flow rate of between three and four litres a minute. Ang Lhakpa and Dawa Nuru, on the other hand, would have to complete the climb on two litres a minute.

I wondered whether it was unfair? Were we being carried to the top by the Sherpas? Perhaps, but their stamina and acclimatisation was so much better than ours that I certainly didn't feel guilty. We were giving them the chance to reach the summit and I knew that I was going to need all the help I could get. The sun was now dropping below the peaks to the west, a chill wind blew across the col and it was bitterly cold. I had a quick word with Odd and Bjørn, agreeing that we would set our alarms for eleven that night to try to get away by 2 a.m. We had noticed that there was less wind first thing in the morning and wanted to reach the South Summit as early as possible.

I was glad to crawl back into our tent. We had a supper of tsampa stew and dried yak meat. I half-heartedly offered to cook but Pertemba wouldn't hear of it, and so I curled up in the back of the tent and read the paperback I had carried up with me. It was hardly the most intellectual of reads, if appropriate for the altitude – Tom Sharpe's *The Wilt Alternative*. It had me giggling happily and irreverently.

I didn't sleep much – I doubt whether any of us did – although I was excited rather than apprehensive. There was none of the stabbing fear that had preceded climbs like the North Wall of the Eiger or the Central Tower of Paine in Patagonia so many years before. I drifted into sleep, to wake to the purr of the gas stove. Pertemba had started to heat the water he had melted that evening and had stored in a thermos.

Two hours later we were ready to start; boots, kept warm in our sleeping-bags, forced on to our feet, outer windproofs and down jackets turning us into Michelin men as we wriggled out into the bitter cold of the night. It was −30°C and the wind gusted around the tents. A struggle with oxygen equipment, last minute fitting of the Sherpas' face masks and we were ready.

It was one thirty when we set out across the flatness of the col, crampons slipping and catching on the stones underfoot, and then on to a bulge of hard smooth ice that slowly increased in angle as we approached the ridge. Each of us followed the pool of light cast by our head-torch. Pertemba was out in front. He had been here before. I was bringing up the rear and it wasn't long before the gap between me and the person in front increased. We were now on a snow slope, a tongue reaching up into the broken rocks that guarded the base of the ridge. At the top of the snow was rock, crumbling steps, easy scrambling but unnerving in the dark with all the impedimenta of high-altitude gear.

I was tired already; not out of breath but just listless, finding it progressively harder to force one foot in front of the other. Three hundred metres, an hour and a half went by. I was so tired. I had dropped behind, the lights of the others becoming ever distant weakening glimmers. They had stopped for a rest but, as I caught up, they started once again. I slumped into the snow and involuntarily muttered, almost cried, 'I'll never make it.'

Odd heard me. 'You'll do it, Chris. Just get on your feet. I'll stay behind you.'

And on it went, broken rock, hard snow, then deep soft snow, which Pertemba ploughed through, allowing me to keep up as I could plod up the well-formed steps made so laboriously by the people in front. The stars were beginning to vanish in the grey of the dawn and the mountains, most of them below us, assumed dark silhouettes. The crest of the ridge, still above us, lightened and then the soaring peak of the South Summit was touched with gold as the sun crept over the horizon far to the east.

By the time we reached the crest, the site of Hillary and Tenzing's top camp in 1953, all the peaks around us were lit by the sun's low-flung rays. The Kangshung Glacier, still in shadow, stretched far beneath us. The Kangshung (East) Face itself was a great sweep of snow set at what seemed an easy angle. Just beneath us some fixed rope protruded, a relic of the American expedition that climbed the East Face in the autumn of 1983. Across the face was the serrated crest of the North-East Ridge. I could pick out the shoulder where we had had our third snow cave and the snow-plastered teeth of the Pinnacles where we had last seen Pete and Joe in 1982. I wondered whether the climbers of Mal Duff's expedition were somewhere

there, in their turn looking across towards our ridge, wonderi[ng] whereabouts. We knew from news reports that they had st[arted] North-East Ridge at the beginning of April.

We were at 8300 metres and it was five in the morning. Tim[e to change] our cylinders. There was still some oxygen in the old bottle bu[t it could] be used as a reserve on our return. We set out again, the Eur[opeans and] Pertemba with full cylinders, but Dawa Nuru and Ang Lhakp[a had the] same ones which they had used from the South Col. They wou[ld have to] nurse their flow rate very carefully.

We plodded up the crest of the ridge, our shadows cast far in[to] Ever steepening, sometimes rock, mostly snow, it was much har[der than I] had imagined. It seemed to go on for ever. Glancing behind me, [the] rocky summit of Lhotse still seemed higher than us. A last swell[of snow] with the wind gusting hard, threatening to blow us from our perch[and we] were on the South Summit. We gathered on the corniced col just [below] it. This was where Doug and Dougal had bivouacked on their w[ay] down from the top in 1975. The gully they had climbed dropped [away] into the South-West Face.

There was a pause. Pertemba had broken trail all the way so far [and the] ridge between the South Summit and the Hillary Step looked form[idable,] a fragile drop on either side. Odd was worried about our oxygen sup[ply. It] had been three hours since we had changed bottles and he quest[ioned] whether we had enough to get back. The others had been climbing [on a] flow rate of three litres per minute, but I had found that this had not [been] enough. I had frequently turned mine on to four and so would have [even] less than they. But I knew I wanted to go on and at this stage was prep[ared] to risk anything to get to the top.

Pertemba said decisively, 'We go on.'

Ang Lhakpa got out the rope, twenty metres between six of us. Bj[orn] took the initiative. He tied one end round his waist and pushed out [in] front, trailing the rope behind him, more of a token than anything else[as] we followed. The going to the foot of the step was more spectacular th[an] difficult, but the step itself was steep.

Odd took a belay and Bjorn started up, wallowing in the deep so[ft] snow, getting an occasional foothold on the rock wall to the left. Pertemb[a] followed, digging out an old fixed rope left by a previous expedition. Th[e] step was about twenty metres high and Bjørn anchored the rope round [a] rock bollard near its top. The others followed using the rope as a handrail.

I was last, but Dawa Nuru waved me past. I gathered he had run out o[f] oxygen. I struggled up the step, panting, breathless, apprehensive and then [I felt what was almost the physical presence of Doug Scott. I could see his shattered rock. The limestone had been formed many millions of years ago at the bottom of the ocean from living organisms and had then been thrust up here, to the highest point of earth, by the drift together of the two tectonic plates of India and the Asian land-mass. It was a thrust that is continuous. The Himalaya, the youngest of the earth's great mountain ranges, is still being pushed upwards. Each year Everest is a few centimetres higher.

CHAPTER NINETEEN

Back to Earth

There was no room for elation; the steepness of the drop ensured that. I concentrated on every step down, now full of apprehension. My oxygen lasted out to our dump of bottles on the South-East Ridge. I changed my cylinder and continued down. The others had caught me up and passed me. I was feeling progressively more tired, experiencing a heavy languor that made even my downhill effort increasingly difficult. I sat down every few paces, beyond thought, and just absorbed the mountains around me. Lhotse was now above me but everything else was still dwarfed and far below.

Someone, probably Pertemba, had reached the tents, tiny little blobs on the South Col. I got up slowly, walked a few more paces and sank on to the rocks once again. But almost imperceptibly I was losing height. I reached the top of the snow slope that stretched down to the col, cramponed down it cautiously, zig-zagging from side to side, then noticed what looked like another tent in the middle of the slope. I veered towards it without thinking and, as I came closer, realised that it was a woman sitting very upright in the snow, fair hair blowing in the wind, teeth bared in a fixed grimace. I didn't go any closer but looked away and hurried past. I guessed that it was the body of Hannelore Schmatz, the wife of the leader of the 1979 German expedition. She had reached the summit but had died from exhaustion on the South-East Ridge on the way down. Sundhare had been with her. She had died higher on the mountain but her body must have been carried down to its present exposed position by an avalanche.

Once I was past her, my pace slowed down. I had used the last of my oxygen, paused to discard the cylinder, and continued down even more slowly. There was a short climb at the end. It took me a quarter of an hour to walk about fifty metres gently up hill. Odd and Bjørn had decided to drop down to Camp 3 that afternoon. We had forgotten to bring a radio up to 4, and they were anxious to let Arne and the others know of our success, but Pertemba and I decided to stay the night on the South Col. We dozed through the afternoon, were too tired to eat, but drank endless brews of tea.

Next morning we descended the fixed ropes to Camp 3, collected Bjørn and Odd and continued on towards the Western Cwm. Running down the fixed ropes I was beginning to relax; the worst danger was over and after a night's sleep I felt refreshed. We met Arne and Stein who were on their way up for their attempt. We hugged and laughed, received their congratulations and wished them the best of fortune. At the foot of the Lhotse Face another reception awaited, this time from the Sherpas at Camp 2 who had come out to greet us with a bottle of rum. Dick Bass and David Breashears, who were also there ready for their summit bid, joined in the congratulations. At last we set off for Base Camp with what I vowed would be my final trip through the Everest Icefall. I ran most of it, just to get out of the danger area quickly. There were more greetings, bottles of beer and rejoicing, but I couldn't relax completely, because the others were still on the mountain. For me the final stages of so many expeditions had ended in tragedy.

The next day was windy. Arne and Stein stayed at Camp 3. On 24 April a banner of snow was flying from the summit of Everest. They reported over the radio that the wind, even at Camp 3, was fierce, so they dropped back down to Advance Base. Ralph and Håvard were now also on their way back up the mountain to have another try. Ola agonised over making a second attempt. He was experiencing stomach cramps and was worried also about the safety and chances of success for a second bid. The Sherpas, who were making the vital carries of supplies to the South Col, were becoming tired and the reserves of food and oxygen were less than they had been for either the first bid or our own ascent. Ola finally decided to stay behind. It was characteristic of Ola, though, that having made this decision, in part based on considerations of safety, he went up into the Icefall on several occasions to help repair the route after sérac collapses. He felt that it was unfair to expect the Sherpas to do this without the presence of one of the climbers. The time now began to drag, as the weather closed in. Bjørn and I, restless in our waiting, even dropped down to Pheriche to spend three days bouldering and carousing before returning to Base.

The perseverance of the others paid off. On 29 April Arne, Stein, Ralph and Håvard, with their four Sherpas, reached the summit of Everest on a day that was so warm and still they stripped off their down gear. The following day Dick Bass, with Dave Breashears and the Sherpa Ang Phurba, also reached the top.

These days an ascent by the South Col route is almost routine, but nonetheless our expedition achieved a large number of records of varying merit; we had put seventeen on the summit, the largest number of any single expedition; it was also the earliest pre-monsoon ascent; the first Scandinavian ascent; Sundhare now had the personal record for the number of ascents of the mountain, having climbed it four times; and Ang Rita had climbed it three times without oxygen; I had had the dubious honour of being the oldest person, by ten days, to climb Everest, a record I held for all of nine days, when Dick Bass took it from me. Being fifty-five, I suspect he might hold the record for a long time. He also achieved his ambition of being the first man to climb the highest point of every continent.

Looked upon purely as records, I don't think they mean very much. The speed with which we climbed the mountain and the number who reached the top are an indication of the efficiency and teamwork on the expedition. But perhaps most important was the level of personal satisfaction, in that all but one person who had aspired to reach the summit actually did so, and could consequently return home with a sense of total fulfilment. Ola, the one who didn't go to the top, was probably the best equipped to cope with that disappointment. He has such a generous spirit, was happy just to be amongst the mountains and had given as much, if not more than any of us, to the success of the expedition.

As I walked back towards Luglha, I had a sense of profound contentment. I hadn't achieved any records. I was the seventh Briton and the 173rd person to reach the summit of Everest. I had had a great deal of help from the Sherpas, as we all had. But standing on that highest point of earth had meant a great deal. Gratification of ego? Without a doubt. But it was so much more than that, though I still find it difficult to define exactly what that drive was. It is as difficult as finding a precise definition of why one climbs.

There was certainly very little physical pleasure at the time – none of the elation of rock-climbing on a sunny day near to sea level where the air is rich in oxygen, there is strength in one's limbs, and a joy in being poised on tiny holds over the abyss, moving with precision from one hold to the next. There is none of that on Everest. There had been little questing into the unknown or even the challenge of picking out a route. I had been content, indeed only capable, of following the others to the top. But there had been the awareness of the mountains, slowly dropping away around me, the summit of Everest caught in the first golden glow of the rising sun, the North-East Ridge, with all its memories, glimpsed through a gap in the cornice, winding, convoluted, threatening in its steep flutings and jagged towers, now far below me. It was a focal point in a climbing life, a gathering of so many ambitions and memories, that had climaxed in that burst of grief and yet relief, when I reached the summit.

I cannot regard Himalayan climbing lightly – the catalogue of death doesn't allow it. Since our Annapurna South Face Expedition, four of the eight lead climbers (Ian Clough, Mick Burke, Nick Estcourt and Dougal

Haston) have died in the mountains. From Everest in 1975, out of ten with summit aspirations, four also are dead. Two of our Kongur team of four who reached the summit are dead. Looking across to Kangchenjunga, of the four who went to the mountain with Doug Scott in 1979, three (Pete Boardman, Joe Tasker and Georges Bettembourg) are dead; and to the west, to Shisha Pangma, of the three who went to the summit in 1982, Alex McIntyre and Roger Baxter-Jones are dead.

I don't get inured to tragedy. If anything it gets harder and harder to take. I dread another accident, the personal sadness, the void created by the death of another friend but, even more, the bearing of bad news to the parents and the woman who loved that man. Their grief has an intensity that goes so much further than the sorrow of a friend. It is something that I can understand from my own grief at the loss of Conrad, our first child, in an accident in 1966. Now, twenty years later, I still find it difficult to talk about, still wonder what he would be doing now, had he not wandered down that friend's garden and had the stream in spate not taken him.

Wendy knew that I was safe and could relax again until the next expedition. But how strong was my love for her? How could I claim to love her and yet threaten her with the cruel, catastrophic loss that I had seen cause such havoc so many times in the past? She had spent her birthday on her own, stricken with 'flu. She has both a vulnerability and yet an extraordinary inner strength that has enabled her to come through these twenty-four years of marriage, to bear the constant threat of danger, that is so much harder to cope with when it is to someone far away, and about which there is nothing she can do, but sit and wait.

All these thoughts were crowding through my head as we made our way from the mountains that are such an integral part of my life. I was half-way between Pheriche and Pangpoche; dwarf irises, their deep purple petals like pouted lips round the delicate yellow tongues of the stamen, clustered amongst the rocks at the side of the path. A prayer flag, like an upheld sword, reached up towards the cloud banners far above. I was careful to pass a mani wall on the left. This time the fates had been kind to us. We were all alive, able to enjoy success without restraint.

I was impatient to reach Kathmandu so that I could at least talk to Wendy on the telephone. I longed even more to be back in England, to be able to hold her close once again. But I no longer deluded myself that I'd be happy to give up serious climbing and knew that I'd be planning my next expedition within days of getting home. Indeed, I was already making the initial preparations for my trip to Menlungtse. I had invited Arne, if he was likely to be free, and Bjørn to join Jim Fotheringham and me on the mountain. (When Arne couldn't make it, I was delighted Odd could accept

the invitation instead.) Our expedition to Everest had been such a happy experience that it seemed both appropriate and propitious to make this small, very different, expedition to one of the most beautiful and technically challenging unclimbed peaks in the Himalaya a joint British/Norwegian one, linking two of my best climbing experiences together.

Beyond Menlungtse, I know that there will be other climbs stretching into the future. I also accept the fact that the ageing process is beginning to bite. I no longer have the recovery rate of a younger man and take a week or more to recoup from a hard push at altitude, when a few years earlier it would have only taken a day or so. I had certainly struggled on our summit bid and had been much slower than Odd or Bjørn, but I reckon I have a good few years more in me of climbing on peaks in the 7000-metre range. Then there are Antarctic fjords to explore and perhaps those wild mountain areas in Tibet that we had flown over in 1982 on our way from Chengdu to Lhasa.

The fresh-flowered rhododendron forests around Tengpoche seemed the more lush and fragrant for what had happened in the preceding weeks. I joined Pertemba at the little nunnery just below the monastery where we were entertained by his three aunts, all of them nuns. We drank chang and ate potato pancakes spiced with hot chillies. I just sat back and allowed the flow of Sherpa speech to sweep over me, basked in the warmth of their friendship and the richness of their way of life. We said farewell to most of our Sherpas in Namche Bazar with a party in Pasang Kami's hotel that lasted most of the night. The Sherpas danced, with the solemn chant and beat that they enjoy so much and can sustain for so many hours, there was the wilder more raucous Norwegian dancing and singing, bawdy recitations from Dick Bass, and gallons of beer and chang.

Then it was on to Kathmandu and civilisation; the first hot bath, a phone call home, more celebratory meals, press conferences, a red carpet and brass band to greet us in Oslo. Then, most important of all, Wendy, on the other side of the barrier at Heathrow, clinging, crying, kissing me. My two lads, Daniel and Rupert, Daniel very nearly as tall as me, both slightly embarrassed by their demonstrative parents, nonetheless hugged me.

I was home at last.

Climbing Record

1951   Ash Tree Gully *Dinas Bach* (Tom Blackburn) – first climb; Hope *Idwal Slabs* (Charles Verender) – first lead.

1952   Chimney Route *Clogwyn Du'r Arddu* (Dave Pullin); Rana Temporia *Quinag* * (Tony) – first new route, a VS.

1953   Agag's Groove *Buachaille Etive Mor* *w (Hamish MacInnes, Kerr McPhaill, John Hammond, G. McIntosh) – first winter climb; Crowberry Ridge Direct *w and Raven's Gully *Buachaille Etive Mor* *w (Hamish MacInnes); Hangover *Clogwyn y Grochan* (Geoff Francis) – first 'Brown' route.

1954   Surplomb *Clogwyn y Grochan* (Steve Lane) – second ascent.

1955   Macavity *Avon Gorge* * (Geoff Francis) – first new route on Avon's Main Wall.

1957   First alpine season: South-East Face of Aig. du Tacul * (Hamish MacInnes). Steger Route *Cattinacio* and Yellow Edge and Demuth Route *Tre Cime* (Jim Swallow); North Wall Direct of Cima Una † (German climber). Malbogies *Avon Gorge* * (Geoff Francis, Henry Rogers).

1958   Bonatti Pillar of Petit Dru † (Hamish MacInnes, Don Whillans and Paul Ross, with Walter Phillip and Richard Blach); West Face of Petites Jorasses † (Ronnie Wathen).

1959   Comici/Dimai, Brandler/Hasse † and Cassin/Ratti routes *Tre Cime* (Gunn Clark); Woubits (Jim O'Neill) and Mostest (Jim Swallow) *Clogwyn Du'r Arddu* – second ascents.

1960   Annapurna 2 * by West Ridge Nepal (Dick Grant and Ang Nyima) – expedition led by Col. James Roberts; King Cobra *Skye* * (Tom Patey).

1961   Nuptse * by South Face *Nepal* (part of second summit team with Jim Swallow, Ang Pemba and Les Brown – first pair: Dennis Davis and Tashi) – expedition led by Joe Walmsley; Central Pillar of Frêney, Mt Blanc * (Don Whillans, Ian Clough and Jan Djuglosz).

1962   Trango *Castell Cidwm* * (Joe Brown); Ichabod *Scafell* (Mike Thompson) – second ascent; Schmid/Krebs Route *Karwendal* † (Don Whillans); Walker Spur of Grandes Jorasses (Ian Clough); North Wall of the Eiger † (Ian Clough).

1963   Central Tower of Paine * by West Face *Chile* (Don Whillans) – expedition led by Barrie Page.

1964   North Face of Pointe Migot * and West Ridge of Aig. de Lepiney * (Tom Patey, Joe Brown and Robin Ford); Andrich/Fae Route on Civetta (Jim McCarthy); Medlar * (Martin Boysen) and Totalitarian * (Mike Thompson) *Raven Crag, Thirlmere*.

1965   Coronation Street *Cheddar* * (Tony Greenbank); The Holy Ghost *Scafell* * (Mike Thompson); West Face of the Cardinal * (Tom Patey and another); West Face Direct of Aig. du Plan * (Lito Tejada Flores); North-East Ridge of Dent du Midi * (Rusty Baillie and John Harlin); Right-Hand Pillar of Brouillard, Mt Blanc * (Rusty Baillie, John Harlin and Brian Robertson).

1966   North Face Direct of the Eiger * – in supporting role; Old Man of Hoy *Orkneys* * (Tom Patey and Rusty Baillie).

1968   North Face of Aig. d'Argentière (Dougal Haston) – in winter.

1969   March Hare's Gully *Applecross* *w (Tom Patey); Great Gully of Garbh Bheinn *w (Tom Patey and Don Whillans).

1970   South Face of Annapurna *Nepal* * – leader of expedition -summit reached by Dougal Haston and Don Whillans.

1971   East Face of Moose's Tooth *Alaska* – attempt with Jim McCarthy, Tom Frost and Sandy Bill curtailed by bad weather; White Wizard *Scafell* * (Nick Estcourt).

1972   South-West Face of Everest *Nepal* – leader of expedition curtailed by cold and high wind; Great Gully of Grandes Jorasses (Dougal Haston with Mick Burke and Bev Clarke in support) – attempt in winter.

1973   Brammah * by the South Ridge *India* (Nick Escourt) – joint leader of expedition with Balwant Sandhu.

1974   Changabang * by East Ridge *India* (Martin Boysen, Doug Scott, Dougal Haston, Tashi and Balwant Sandhu) – joint leader of expedition with Sandhu.

1975   North Face Direct of Aig. du Triolet *w (Dougal Haston); South-West Face of Everest *Nepal* * – leader of expedition – summit reached by Dougal Haston and Doug Scott, Pete Boardman, Pertemba and Mick Burke(?).

1976   North Face of Pt.20,309 *Kishtwar, India* (Ronnie Richards) – attempt gaining two-thirds height; East Ridge of Mt Cook and Symes Ridge of Mt Tasman *New Zealand* (Nick Banks, Keith Woodford and Bob Cunningham).

1977   The Ogre * by the South Face *Pakistan* (Nick Escourt) and the West Ridge (Doug Scott) – the South Face climb ended at the West Summit. Clive Rowland and Mo Anthoine took part in the West Ridge ascent to the foot of the summit tower.

1978	West Ridge of K2 *Pakistan* – leader of expedition curtailed after death of Nick Escourt in an avalanche below Camp 2.
1980	Pts 6200m * and 5400 * *Kongur Group, China* (Al Rouse and Mike Ward) – climbed during a reconnaissance expedition.
1981	Kongur * by the West Ridge *China* (Al Rouse, Pete Boardman and Joe Tasker) – expedition led by Mike Ward.
1982	North-East Ridge of Everest *Tibet* – leader of expedition curtailed after disappearance of Pete Boardman and Joe Tasker.
1983	Orion Face of Ben Nevis (Stuart Fife); South-West Summit of Shivling * by the South-East Ridge *India* (Jim Fotheringham); Mt Vinson *Antarctica* † (Dick Bass, Tae Maeda, Yuichior Miura, Steve Marts, Rick Ridgeway and Frank Wells) – soloed final section prior to ascent by the others. Expedition led jointly by Bass and Wells.
1984	West Ridge of Karun Koh *Pakistan* (Ikram Khan, Maqsood Ahmed and Al Rouse) – leader of expedition curtailed by bad weather; Cruel Sister *Pavey Ark* (Jim Loxham) – first E3 lead.
1985	South-East Ridge of Everest *Nepal* (Odd Eliassen, Bjørn Myrer-Lund, Pertemba, Ang Lhakpa and Dawa Nuru) – expedition led by Arne Naess.
1986	North-East Pillar of Norliga Skagastozstind *Norway* (Odd Eliassen); Athanor *Goat Crag* (Dave Absalom) – first 6a lead. Yellow Edge *Avon Gorge* (Steve Berry); South Pillar of Grosse Drusenturm *Rätikon* and North-East Diedre of Brenta Alta (Jim Fotheringham).
1987	South-West Buttress of Menlungtse West *Tibet* – leader of expedition curtailed by bad weather.
1988	Menlungste West * by the West Ridge and Face *Tibet* – leader of expedition – summit reached by Andy Fanshawe and Alan Hinkes.
1991	Lemon Mountains *Greenland* – as climbing leader with Robin Knox-Johnston.
1992	Panch Chuli II * *Kumaon, India* West Ridge, with Graham Little on Indian/British Kumaon expedition – joint leader with Harish Kapadia.
1993	Chisel *, Ivory Tower *, Needle * *Lemon Mountains, Greenland* (Lowther, Little, Ferguson).
1993	Elbrus and North-East Ridge of Ushba *Caucasus*.
1994	Rangrik Rang * *Kinnaur, India* – Indian/British expedition with Harish Kapadia.
1995	Drangnag-Ri * *Rolwaling, India* (Hoibakk, Myrer-Lund, Pema Dorge, Lhakpu Gyalu).
1996	Sepu Kangri *Tibet* – reconnaissance with Charles Clarke.
1997	Sepu Kangri *Tibet* – expedition defeated by heavy snowfall.
1998	Sepu Kangri *Tibet* – Muir and Saunders reach West Shoulder; Seamo Uylmitok * Little.

Index